Getting Money for Graduate School

2003

THOMSON
TM
PETERSON'S

Australia • Canada • Mexico • Singapore • Spain • United Kingdom • United States

About The Thomson Corporation and Peterson's

With revenues of US$7.2 billion, The Thomson Corporation (www.thomson.com) is a leading global provider of integrated information solutions for business, education, and professional customers. Its Learning businesses and brands (www.thomsonlearning.com) serve the needs of individuals, learning institutions, and corporations with products and services for both traditional and distributed learning.

Peterson's, part of The Thomson Corporation, is one of the nation's most respected providers of lifelong learning online resources, software, reference guides, and books. The Education Supersite[SM] at www.petersons.com—the Internet's most heavily traveled education resource—has searchable databases and interactive tools for contacting U.S.-accredited institutions and programs. In addition, Peterson's serves more than 105 million education consumers annually.

For more information, contact Peterson's, 2000 Lenox Drive, Lawrenceville, NJ 08648; 800-338-3282; or find us on the World Wide Web at www.petersons.com/about.

ISBN 0-7689-1294-6

Printed in Canada

10 9 8 7 6 5 4 3 2 1   04 03 02

CONTENTS

PAYING FOR YOUR GRADUATE SCHOOL EDUCATION

WHAT IS FINANCIAL AID?

Financial aid is the monetary assistance available to help students pay for the costs of attending an educational institution. Such aid is provided by federal, state, institutional, or private sources and may consist of grants, loans, work, or scholarships. Qualified students may be offered combinations of the various types of aid or aid from a single source. Each year, billions of dollars are given or lent to students, and about half of all students receive some sort of financial aid.

Most financial aid is awarded based on an individual's financial need, education costs, and the availability of funds. This aid is provided to students because neither they nor their families have all of the necessary resources needed to pay for an education. This kind of aid is referred to as need-based aid.

Merit-based aid is awarded to students who may or may not have financial need. Students are given assistance because they have a special skill or ability, display a particular talent, have a certain grade point average, or are enrolled in a specific program.

TYPES AND SOURCES OF FINANCIAL AID

There are several types of financial aid offered to help pay for educational expenses: grants, loans, student employment (work), and scholarships. Grants and scholarships are "gifts" and do not have to be repaid. Loans are borrowed money that the borrower must pay back over a period of time, usually after the student leaves school. Student employment is normally part-time work arranged for a student during the school year. Wages received by the student are used for specific college expenses. In addition, many companies offer tuition reimbursement to their employees and/or their employees' dependents. The personnel department at either your or your parent's place of employment can tell you whether or not the company offers this benefit and who may be eligible. Lastly, there are some colleges that offer awards from their own funds or from money received from various organizations. This type of aid is often referred to as "institutional aid."

FEDERAL FINANCIAL AID PROGRAMS

The federal government is the single largest source of financial aid for students.

REPAYMENT OPTIONS

A number of repayment options are available to borrowers of federally guaranteed student loans.

- **The Standard Repayment Plan**—requires fixed monthly payments (at least $50) over a fixed period of time (up to ten years). The length of the repayment period depends on the loan amount. This plan usually results in the lowest total interest paid because the repayment period is shorter than under the other plans.

- **The Extended Repayment Plan**—allows loan repayment to be extended over a period generally from twelve to thirty years, depending on the total amount borrowed. Borrowers still pay a fixed amount each month (at least $50), but usually monthly payments will be less than under the Standard Repayment Plan. This plan may make repayment more manageable; however, borrowers usually will pay more interest because the repayment period is longer.

- **The Graduated Repayment Plan**—allows payments to start out low and increase every two years. This plan may be helpful to borrowers whose incomes are low initially but will increase steadily. A borrower's monthly payments must be either equal to the interest that accumulates on the loan or at least half, but may not be more than one-and-a-half times, of what he or she would pay under Standard Repayment. As in the Extended Repayment Plan, the repayment period will usually vary from twelve to thirty years, depending on the total amount borrowed. Again, monthly payments may be more manageable at first because they are lower, but borrowers will pay more interest because the repayment period is longer.

- **The Income Contingent Repayment Plan**—bases monthly payments on adjusted gross income (AGI) and the total amount borrowed. This is currently only available to students who participate in Direct Loans; however, some lenders and guaranty agencies provide income-sensitive repayment plans. As income rises or falls each year, monthly payments will be adjusted accordingly. The required monthly payment will not exceed 20 percent of the borrower's discretionary income as calculated under a published formula. Borrowers have up to twenty-five years to repay; after twenty-five years, any unpaid amount will be discharged, and borrowers must pay taxes on the amount discharged. In other words, if the federal government forgives the balance of a loan, the amount is considered to be part of the borrower's income for that year.

In the 2001–2002 academic year, the U.S. Department of Education's student financial aid programs provided approximately $61 billion in aid to an estimated 8.1 million people. At the present time, there are two federal grant programs—the Federal Pell Grant and the Federal Supplemental Educational Opportunity Grant (FSEOG). There are three federal loan programs: the Federal Perkins Loan, the Direct Loan, and the Stafford Loan. The federal government also has a job program, Federal Work-Study, or FWS, that helps colleges provide employment for students. In addition to the student aid programs, there are also tuition tax credits. They are the HOPE Scholarship for freshmen and sophomores and the Lifetime Learning Tax Credit for undergraduate students after their second year and for graduate students. Both programs work the same way. The federal tax bill is reduced by the amount of tuition paid up to specified limits.

More than ninety percent of federal higher education loans are either Direct or Stafford. The difference between these loans is the lending source, but for the borrower, the difference is virtually invisible. Both Direct and Stafford programs make available two kinds of loans: Stafford Loans to students and PLUS Loans to parents. Stafford Loans are either subsidized or unsubsidized. Subsidized Stafford Loans are made on the basis of demonstrated student need and have their interest paid by the government during the time you are in school. For the non-need-based loans, the unsubsidized Stafford Loans and PLUS Loans, interest begins to accrue as soon as the money is received.

To qualify for the Pell and FSEOG programs, Federal Work-Study, the Perkins Loan, and the subsidized Stafford Loan, you must demonstrate financial need.

FEDERAL PELL GRANT

The Federal Pell Grant is the largest grant program; almost 4 million students received Pell Grants last year. This grant is intended to be the starting point of assistance for lower-income families. Eligibility for a Federal Pell Grant depends on the Expected Family Contribution (EFC). The amount you receive will depend on your EFC and the cost of education at the college you will attend. The highest award depends on how much the program is funded. The maximum for 2002–2003 is $4000, but this amount is expected to increase in 2003.

FEDERAL SUPPLEMENTAL EDUCATIONAL OPPORTUNITY GRANT (FSEOG)

As its name implies, the Federal Supplemental Educational Opportunity Grant provides additional need-based federal grant money to supplement the Federal Pell Grant. Each participating college is given funds to award to especially needy students. The maximum award is $4000 per year, but the amount you receive depends on the college's policy, the availability of FSEOG funds, the total cost of education, and the amount of other aid awarded.

FEDERAL WORK-STUDY (FWS)

This program provides jobs for students who demonstrate need. Salaries are paid by funds from the federal government as well as the college. You work on an hourly basis

FEDERAL FINANCIAL AID PROGRAMS

Name of Program	Type of Program	Maximum Award Per Year
Federal Pell Grant	Need-based grant	$4000
Federal Supplemental Educational Opportunity Grant (FSEOG)	Need-based grant	$4000
Federal Work-Study	Need-based part-time job	no maximum
Federal Perkins Loan	Need-based loan	$4000
Subsidized Stafford/Direct Loan	Need-based student loan	$2625 (first year)
Unsubsidized Stafford/ Direct Loan	Non-need-based student loan	$2625 (first year, dependent student)
PLUS Loans	Non-need-based parent loan	Up to the cost of education

Note: Both Direct and Stafford Loans have higher maximums after the freshman year. Students who meet the federal qualifications for independent status are eligible for increased loan limits in the loan programs.

on or off campus and must be paid at least the federal minimum wage. You may earn only up to the amount awarded in the financial aid package.

FEDERAL PERKINS LOAN

This loan is a low-interest (5 percent) loan for students with exceptional financial need. Federal Perkins Loans are made through the college's financial aid office with the college as the lender. You can borrow a maximum of $4000 per year for up to five years of undergraduate study. Borrowers may take up to ten years to repay the loan, beginning nine months after they graduate, leave school, or drop below half-time status. No interest accrues while they are in school, and, under certain conditions (e.g., they teach in low-income areas, work in law enforcement, are full-time nurses or medical technicians, serve as Peace Corps or VISTA volunteers, etc.), some or all of the loan can be canceled. In addition, payments can be deferred under certain conditions such as unemployment.

STAFFORD AND DIRECT LOANS

Stafford and Direct Loans have the same interest rates, loan maximums, deferments, and cancellation benefits. A Stafford Loan may be borrowed from a commercial lender, such as a bank or credit union. A Direct Loan is borrowed directly from the U.S. Department of Education.

The interest rate varies annually (there is a maximum of 8.25 percent), and the rate for 2002–2003 is 5.99 percent during repayment and 5.39 percent while you are in college. If you qualify for a need-based subsidized Stafford Loan, the interest is paid by the federal government while you are enrolled in college. There is also an unsubsidized Stafford Loan that is not based on need for which you are eligible regardless of your family income.

The maximum amount dependent students may borrow in any one year is $2625 for freshmen, $3500 for sophomores, and $5500 for juniors and seniors, with a maximum of $23,000 for the total undergraduate program. The maximum amount independent students can borrow is $6625 for freshmen (of which no more than $2625 can be subsidized), $7500 for sophomores (of which no more than $3500 can be subsidized), and $10,500 for juniors and seniors (of which no more than $5500 can be subsidized). Borrowers must pay a 3 percent fee, which is deducted from the loan proceeds.

To apply for a Stafford Loan, you must first complete a FAFSA to determine eligibility for a subsidized loan and then complete a separate loan application that is submitted to a lender. The financial aid office can help in selecting a lender. The lender will send a promissory note where you agree to repay the loan. The proceeds of the loan, less the origination fee, will be sent to the college to be either credited to your account or released to you directly.

Once the repayment period starts, borrowers of both subsidized and unsubsidized Stafford or Direct Loans will have to pay a combination of interest and principal monthly for up to a ten-year period.

PLUS LOANS

PLUS is for parents of dependent students to help families who may not have cash readily available to pay their share of the charges. There is no needs test to qualify. The loan has a variable interest rate that cannot exceed 9 percent (for loans disbursed between July 1, 2002 and June 30, 2003, the interest rate is 4.86 percent). There is no yearly limit; you can borrow up to the cost of your education, less other financial aid received. Repayment begins sixty days after the money is advanced. A 3 or 4 percent fee is subtracted from the proceeds. Parent borrowers must generally have a good credit record to qualify. PLUS Loans may be processed under either the Direct or Stafford Loan system, depending on the type of loan program for which the college has contracted.

TUITION TAX CREDITS

Tuition tax credits allow families to reduce their tax bill by the amount of out-of-pocket college tuition expense. Unlike a tax deduction, which is modified according to your tax bracket, a tax credit is a dollar-for-dollar reduction in taxes paid.

There are two programs: the HOPE Scholarship and the Lifetime Learning Tax Credit. As is true of many federal programs, there are numerous rules and restrictions that apply. You should check with your tax preparer or financial adviser for information about your own particular situation.

HOPE Scholarship

The HOPE Scholarship offsets some of the expense for the first two years of college or vocational school. Students or the parents of dependent students can claim an annual income tax credit of up to $1500–100 percent of the first $1000 of tuition and required fees and 50 percent credit of the second $1000. Grants, scholarships, and other tax-free educational assistance must be deducted from the total tuition and fee payments.

This credit can be claimed for students who are in their first two years of college and who are enrolled on at least a half-time basis in a degree or certificate program for any portion of the year. This credit phases out for joint filers who have an income between $80,000 and $100,000 and for single filers who have between $40,000 and $50,000 of income. Parents may claim credits for more than one qualifying student. (After the 2001 tax year, the income limits will be adjusted for inflation. See the 2002 IRS form 8863 for the revised AGI limits.)

Lifetime Learning Tax Credit

The Lifetime Learning Tax Credit is the counterpart of the HOPE Scholarship for college juniors, seniors, graduate students, and part-time students pursuing lifelong learning to improve or upgrade their job skills. The qualifying taxpayer can claim an annual tax credit of up to $1000—20 percent of the first $5000 of tuition. The credit is available for net tuition and fees, less grant aid. The total credit available is limited to $1000 per year per taxpayer (or joint-filing couple), and is phased out at the same income levels as the HOPE Scholarship. (The income figures are subject to change.)

AMERICORPS

AmeriCorps is a national umbrella group of service programs for students. Participants work in a public or private nonprofit agency and provide service to the community in one of four priority areas: education, human services, the environment, and public safety. In exchange, you earn a stipend (for living expenses) of between $7400 and $14,800 a year, health insurance coverage, and $4725 per year for up to two years to apply toward college expenses. Many student-loan lenders will postpone the repayment of student loans during service in AmeriCorps, and AmeriCorps will pay the interest that is accrued on qualified student loans for members who complete the service program. You can work before, during, or after you go to college and can use the funds to either pay current educational expenses or repay federal student loans. The AmeriCorps Web site is http://www.americorps.org. Speak to a college financial aid officer for more details about this program.

DETERMINING FINANCIAL AID ELIGIBILITY AND FINANCIAL NEED

Eligibility for financial aid is determined by subtracting the amount you and/or your parents can contribute from the cost of attendance. An assessment of your family's ability to contribute toward educational expenses is made based on the information you provide when applying for financial aid. Income, assets, size of family, and number of family members in college are some of the factors considered in this calculation. This assessment, referred to as need analysis, determines your financial need, which is defined as the difference between the total cost of attendance and what you are expected to pay.

ESTIMATED COST OF EDUCATION
Use this table to compare costs for the schools to which you're interested in applying.

		School 1	School 2
1.	TUITION AND FEES multiplied by number of years in school	$	$
2. add	FOREGONE WAGES multiplied by number of years in school	$	$
3. total	TOTAL COST OF SCHOOL add Line 1 and Line 2	$	$
4.	PART-TIME INCOME multiplied by number of years in school	$	$
5. add	GRANTS AND TAX CREDITS	$	$
6. total	TOTAL AMOUNT OF EARNINGS AND FINANCIAL ASSISTANCE add Line 4 and Line 5	$	$
7. total	TOTAL COST subtract Line 6 from Line 3	$	$

The need analysis uses a formula mandated by legislation. It determines the ability, not the willingness, of the student and parents to finance the cost of attendance. Everyone who applies is treated equally under this analysis. The end result of the need analysis is your expected family contribution (EFC) and represents the amount your family should be able to contribute toward the cost of attendance. The cost of attendance will vary at each college, but the amount your family is expected to contribute should stay the same. Financial need will vary between colleges because of each school's different costs of attendance.

DETERMINING THE STUDENT'S STATUS: INDEPENDENT OR DEPENDENT?

If you are considered dependent by federal definition, then your parents' income and assets, as well as yours, will be counted toward the family contribution. If you are considered independent of your parents, only your income (and that of your spouse, if you are married) will count in the need analysis formula.

In order to be considered independent for financial aid, you must meet one of the following criteria:

- Be at least 24 years old;

- Be a veteran of the U.S. armed forces;

- Be married;

- Be an orphan or ward of the court;

- Have legal dependents other than a spouse; or

- Be a graduate professional student.

If you can document extraordinary circumstances that might indicate independent status, you will need to show this information to the financial aid administrator at the college you will be attending. Only the financial aid administrator has the authority to make exceptions to those requirements listed above.

APPLYING FOR FINANCIAL AID

To apply for financial aid, it is essential that you properly complete the necessary forms so that your individual financial need can be evaluated. It is important to read all application materials and instructions very carefully. The application process can be a bit long and confusing, so remember to take it one step at a time. If you run into any problems or have specific questions, contact the financial aid office at the college you will be attending. The financial aid office will be happy to provide you with guidance and assistance.

Most colleges use just one financial aid application called the Free Application for Federal Student Aid (FAFSA). This form is a four-page application available at your college's financial aid office and state education department offices. Students can apply for federal student aid via the Internet by using FAFSA on the Web (http://fafsa.ed.gov). The process is self-paced and interactive, with step-by-step guidance. Depending on the availability of information about your income and financial situation, the process can take as little as 20 minutes to complete. The FAFSA that students will use to apply for aid for each school year becomes available in the

December prior to the year in which aid is needed. However, do not fill the form out until after January 1. (Note: You should complete the FAFSA as soon as possible after January 1. Although you may apply for aid at any time during the year, many state agencies have early cut-off dates for state aid funding.)

To complete this application, you will need to gather specific information and financial records, such as tax forms, if they are available. If they are not, use estimates and you can make corrections later. Be sure to answer all questions. Omitted information may delay processing of your application. Be sure that you and your parents (if needed) have signed the form and that you keep a copy of the form for your records.

The FAFSA processing center will calculate your expected family contribution and will distribute the information back to the college.

About two to four weeks after you submit your completed FAFSA, you will receive a Student Aid Report (SAR) that shows the information you reported and your calculated EFC. If you need to make any corrections, you may do so at this time. The college may also have this same information in an Institutional Student Information Record (ISIR) or Electronic Student Aid Report (ESAR).

If you are chosen for verification by the school, you may be asked to submit documentation that will verify the information you reported on the FAFSA. Once the financial aid office is satisfied that all of the information is correct, the college can then determine your financial need and provide you with a financial aid offer for funding your education. If you are eligible to receive aid, most schools will either mail you an award letter or ask you to come into the financial aid office to discuss your financial aid eligibility. (Note: Financial aid is not renewed automatically; you must apply each year. Often, if you are in a program that lasts for more than one year, a renewal application will automatically be mailed to you by the federal processor.)

STUDENT LOANS AND DEBT MANAGEMENT

More than ever before, loans have become an important part of financial assistance. The majority of students find that they must borrow money to finance their education. If you accept a loan, you are incurring a financial obligation. You will have to repay the loan in full, along with all of the interest and any additional fees (collection, legal, etc.). Since you will be making loan payments to satisfy the loan obligation, carefully consider the burden your loan amount will impose on you after you leave college. Defaulting on a student loan can jeopardize your financial future. Borrow intelligently.

Article adapted from *Peterson's Vocational and Technical Schools,* by Heidi Granger, © 2001 Peterson's. Sidebars supplied by Career Training Foundation, © 2000.

SCHOLARSHIP SCAMS: WHAT THEY ARE AND WHAT TO WATCH OUT FOR

Several hundred thousand students seek and find scholarships every year. Most require some outside help to pay for tuition costs. Although most of this outside help, in the form of grants, scholarships, low-interest loans, and work-study programs, comes from either the federal government or the colleges themselves, scholarships from private sources are an extremely important component of this network. An award from a private source can tilt the scales with respect to a student's ability to attend a specific college during a particular year. Unfortunately for prospective scholarship seekers, the private aid sector is virtually without patterns or rules. It has, over many years, developed as a haphazard conglomeration of individual programs, each with its own award criteria, timetables, application procedures, and decision-making processes. Considerable effort is required to understand and effectively benefit from private scholarships. Regrettably, the combination of a sharp urgency to locate money, limited time, and this complex and bewildering system has created opportunities for fraud. For every 10 students who receive a legitimate scholarship, 1 is victimized by a fraudulent scheme or scam that poses as a legitimate foundation, scholarship sponsor, or scholarship search service.

These fraudulent businesses advertise in campus newspapers, distribute flyers, mail letters and postcards, provide toll-free phone numbers, and even have sites on the World Wide Web. The most obvious frauds operate as scholarship search services or scholarship clearinghouses. Another quieter segment sets up as a scholarship sponsor, pockets the money from the fees and charges that are paid by thousands of hopeful scholarship seekers, and returns little, if anything, in proportion to the amounts it collects. A few of these frauds inflict great harm by gaining access to individuals' credit or checking accounts with the intent to extort funds.

A typical mode of operation is for a fraudulent firm to send out a huge mailing (more than a million postcards each year for some outfits) to college and high school students, claiming that the company has either a scholarship or a scholarship list for the students. These companies often provide toll-free numbers. When recipients call, they are told by high-pressure telemarketers that the company has unclaimed scholarships and that for fees ranging from $10 to $400 the callers get back at least $1000 in scholarship money or the fee will be refunded. Customers who pay, if they receive anything at all, are mailed a list of sources of financial aid that are no better than, and are in many cases inferior to, what can be found in any major scholarship guide available in bookstores or libraries. The "lucky" recipients have to apply on their own for the scholarships. Many of the programs are contests, loans, or work-study programs rather than gift aid. Some are no longer in existence, have expired deadlines, or demand eligibility requirements that the students cannot meet. Customers who seek refunds have to demonstrate that they have applied in writing to each source on the list and received a rejection letter from each of them. Frequently, even when customers can provide this almost-impossible-to-obtain proof, refunds are not made. In the worst cases, the companies ask for consumers' checking account or credit card numbers and take funds without authorization.

The Federal Trade Commission (FTC) warns students to be wary of fraudulent search services that promise to do all the work for you. "Bogus scholarship search services are just a variation on the 'you have won' prize-promotion scam, targeted to a particular audience—students and their parents who are anxious about paying for college," said Jodie Bernstein, former director of the FTC's Bureau of Consumer Protection. "They guarantee students free scholarship money . . . all they have to do to claim it is pay an up-front fee."

There are legitimate scholarship search services. However, a scholarship search service cannot truthfully guarantee that a student will receive a scholarship, and students almost always will fare as well or better by doing their own homework using a reliable scholarship information source than by wasting money, and sometimes more importantly, time, with a search service that promises a scholarship.

The FTC warns scholarship seekers to be alert for these six warning signs of a scam:

- "This scholarship is guaranteed or your money back."

   No service can guarantee that it will get you a grant or scholarship. Refund guarantees often have impossible conditions attached. Review a service's refund policies in writing before you pay a fee. Typically, fraudulent scholarship search services require that applicants show rejection letters from each of the sponsors on the list they provide. If a sponsor no longer exists, if it really does not provide scholarships, or if it has a rolling application deadline, letters of rejection are almost impossible to obtain.

- "The scholarship service will do all the work."

   Unfortunately, nobody else can fill out the personal information forms, write the essays, and supply the references that many scholarships may require.

- "The scholarship will cost some money."

  Be wary of any charges related to scholarship information services or individual scholarship applications, especially in significant amounts. Some legitimate scholarship sponsors charge fees to defray their processing expenses. True scholarship sponsors, however, should give out money, not make it from application fees. Before you send money to apply for a scholarship, investigate the sponsor.

- "You can't get this information anywhere else."

  In addition to Peterson's, scholarship directories from other publishers are available in any large bookstore, public library, or high school guidance office. Additional information on private scholarship programs, including scams, can be found at www.finaid.org.

- "You are a finalist—in a contest you never entered," or "You have been selected by a national foundation to receive a scholarship."

  Most legitimate scholarship programs almost never seek particular applicants. Most scholarship sponsors will only contact you in response to an inquiry. Most lack the budget and mandate to do anything more than this. Should you think that there is any real possibility that you may have been selected to receive a scholarship, before you send any money investigate first to be sure that the sponsor or program is legitimate.

- "The scholarship service needs your credit card or checking account number in advance."

  Never provide your credit card or bank account number on the telephone to the representative of an organization that you do not know. A legitimate need-based scholarship program will not ask for your checking account number. Get information in writing first. An unscrupulous operation does not need your signature on a check. It schemes to set up situations that allow it to drain a victim's account with unauthorized withdrawals.

- "You are invited to a free seminar (or interview) with a trained financial aid consultant who will unlock the secrets on how to make yourself eligible for more financial aid."

  Sometimes these consultants offer some good tips on preparing for college, but often they are trying to get you to sign up for a long-term contract for services you don't need. Often these "consultants" are trying to sell you other financial products, such as annuities, life insurance, or other financial services that have little to do with financial aid. By doing your own research, using the Web, working with your high school guidance office and the college financial aid office, you will get all the help you need to ensure you have done a thorough job in preparing for the financing of your college education.

In addition to the FTC's six signs, here are some other points to keep in mind when considering a scholarship program:

- Fraudulent scholarship operations often use official-sounding names containing words such as *federal, national, administration, division, federation,* and *foundation.* Their names often are a slight variant of the name of a legitimate government or private organization. Do not be fooled by a name that seems reputable or official, looks like an official-looking seal, or has a Washington, D.C. address.

- If you win a scholarship, you will receive written official notification by mail not by telephone. If the sponsor calls to inform you, it will follow up with a letter in the mail. If a request for money is made by phone, the operation is very probably fraudulent.

- Be wary if an organization's address is a box number or a residential address. If a bona fide scholarship program uses a post office box number, it usually will include a street address and telephone number on its stationery.

- Beware of telephone numbers with a 900 area code. These may charge you a fee of several dollars a minute for a call that could be a long recording that provides only a list of addresses or names.

- A dishonest operation may put pressure on an applicant by saying that awards are on a first-come, first-served basis. Some scholarship programs give preference to the earlier qualified applications. However, if you are told, especially on the telephone, that you must respond quickly, but you will not hear about the results for several months, there may be a problem.

- Be wary of endorsements. Fraudulent operations claim endorsements by groups with names similar to well-known private or government organizations. The Better Business Bureau (BBB) and government agencies do not endorse businesses.

If an organization requires you to pay money for a scholarship and you have never heard of it before and cannot verify that it is a legitimate operation, the best advice is not to pay anything. If you have already paid money to such an organization and find reason to doubt its legitimacy, call your bank to stop payment on your check, if possible, or call your credit card company and tell it that you think you were the victim of a consumer fraud.

To find out how to recognize, report, and stop a scholarship scam, contact the Federal Trade Commission at 600 Pennsylvania Avenue, N.W., Washington, D.C. 20580. On the Web go to http://www.ftc.gov or the National Fraud Information Center at http://www.fraud.org. The National Fraud Information Center also can be contacted by calling 800-876-7060 (toll-free). The Better Business Bureau maintains files of businesses about which it has received complaints. You should call both your local BBB office and the BBB office in the area of the organization in question; each local BBB has different records. Call 703-276-0100 to get the telephone number of your local BBB or look at http://www.bbb.org for a directory of local BBBs and downloadable BBB complaint forms. The national address is The Council of Better Business Bureaus, 4200 Wilson Boulevard, Suite 800, Arlington, Virginia 22203-1838.

There are many wonderful scholarships available to qualified students who spend the time and effort to locate and apply for them. We advise you to exercise caution in using scholarship search services and, when you must pay money, to practice careful judgment in considering a scholarship program's sponsor. We hope that you take full advantage of the many real opportunities that have been opened to college students and their families by the many organizations, foundations, and businesses that have organized to help you with the burden of college expenses.

HOW MILITARY SERVICE CAN HELP YOU PAY

EDUCATIONAL OPPORTUNITIES IN THE MILITARY

The military offers several avenues by which you can reach your educational goals. Military educational programs benefit men and women who serve in the country's defense forces.

Participants can receive an education while serving in the military or serve in the military first and then concentrate on a college education. Some programs offer only one of these options while others combine them.

FINANCIAL ASSISTANCE FROM THE ARMY AND ARMY RESERVE

The Army and Army Reserve offer students a variety of educational opportunities as they serve in the military. By enlisting in the Army or Army Reserve, you can either earn money to pay for your education or choose to have the Army repay student loans that you incurred while in college. The following is a summary of the programs sponsored by the Army.

Army College Fund

If you score at least 50 on the Armed Forces Qualification Test, you may choose an Army job specialty that provides benefits from the Army College Fund, up to $50,000 for college, when combined with Montgomery G.I. Bill benefits.

If you enlist for two years in one of the jobs that offers the Army College Fund, you receive financial assistance for attending college after your active-duty term. A three-year enlistment provides you with a larger benefit and a choice of job specialties. By enlisting for four years in one of the jobs that qualifies for this option, you receive the largest possible financial benefit. In each case, you contribute $100 each month for the first year of enlistment to the Montgomery G.I. Bill fund, for a total contribution of $1200.

The Army College Fund benefits are paid directly to you on a monthly basis, with the number of months and the amount received per month based on your enrollment status. Army benefits are not affected by other scholarships, grants, or assistance. You have up to ten years from the date of discharge to use your benefits.

Specialized Training for Army Reserve Readiness (STARR)

Under this program, the Army Reserve pays you a maximum of $6000 for tuition, books, fees, and equipment for up to two years to train in selected medical specialties at your local college. You are responsible for paying your living expenses. If you have prior military service, you may also be eligible for a bonus.

Because of the shortage of training seats, the Army Reserve pays you to study for the following positions:

- Dental Laboratory Specialist
- Medical Noncommissioned Officer
- Licensed Practical Nurse
- Operating Room Specialist
- X-Ray Specialist
- Pharmacy Specialist
- Respiratory Therapy Specialist

Before enlisting, the local Army Reserve recruiter helps you select and apply to a state-approved college or other educational institution in the chosen medical specialty.

If you do not have prior military experience, you must attend basic training during the summer prior to beginning your enrollment. You must also participate in drills, with pay, one weekend each month during the school year.

After applying for and receiving the appropriate license for the chosen medical specialty, you must complete four weeks at an Army medical treatment facility. As a fully trained medical specialist, you then pursue a civilian medical career, while fulfilling your obligation in the U.S. Army Reserve. You may also participate in the Montgomery G.I. Bill or loan repayment programs.

Army Loan Repayment Program

If you are a qualified student who has attended college on federal student loans

made after October 1, 1975, you may choose the Loan Repayment Program when you enlist in the Army for a minimum three-year term in any job specialty. However, if you choose the repayment option, you may not receive benefits under the Montgomery G.I. Bill. For each year served on active duty, you reduce your indebtedness by one third or $1500, whichever is greater, up to a maximum of $65,000. To be eligible for this program, your loan may not be in default.

In addition to repaying loans borrowed before entry into the service, this program repays student loans incurred while in the service. Loans that qualify for repayment are:

- Auxiliary Loan Assistance for Students (ALAS)
- Stafford Student Loan or Guaranteed Student Loan (GSL)
- Parents Loans for Undergraduate Students (PLUS Loans)
- Federally Insured Student Loans (FISL)
- Perkins Loan or National Direct Student Loan (NDSL)
- Supplemental Loans for Students (SLS)

To qualify for the Army's Loan Repayment Program, you must be a high school graduate, have no prior military service, and score at least 50 on the Armed Forces Qualification Test.

Army Reserve Student Loan Repayment Program

The same federally funded student loans that qualify for complete repayment with an active duty enlistment also qualify for partial repayment when you enlist in the Army Reserve. For each year of satisfactory service, the Army Reserve pays 15 percent or $1,500 of the loan. Up to $10,000 total (or $20,000 in some critical job specialties) may be repaid through this program.

Although you must choose the loan repayment option at the time of enlistment, the Army Reserve repays loans taken out after enlistment. Repayment begins when you have served one year after securing the loan and when you become skill-qualified.

For more information, check out the Army's Web site at www.goarmy.com or contact your nearest Army recruiter.

EDUCATIONAL BENEFITS FOR VETERANS

The current version of veterans' benefits is applicable to individuals entering the military on or after July 1, 1985. Authorized under the Montgomery G.I. Bill (also called the New G.I. Bill), the program differs based on whether you are on active duty (referred to as Chapter 30 benefits) or are in the Reserves (Chapter 1606 benefits).

Chapter 30 Benefits for Active Duty

Chapter 30 benefits may be used for the purpose of obtaining a college education while on active duty, after serving at least two years, or may be redeemed after separation from the service. In order to be eligible, you must have a high school diploma or its equivalent before completing the required period of active duty.

You contribute $100 per month in the form of pay reduction for the first twelve months of active duty. If you have separated from the service, you must have received an honorable discharge and must have served either continuously on active duty for three years or for two years followed by four years in the Selected Reserves.

After serving a minimum of two years, you are entitled to a monthly educational benefit of up to $900 per month for thirty-six months for full-time study. Supplementary benefits are also available in the following forms:

- Tutorial assistance for those who need it
- Work-study for the Department of Veterans Affairs for those who need extra assistance (with preference given to individuals with service-connected disabilities)

Chapter 1606 Benefits for Selected Reserve Duty

While in the Selected Reserves, you may take advantage of educational benefits authorized under the Montgomery G.I. Bill (Chapter 1606, formerly Chapter 106). The service commitment must be for at least six years, and you must meet certain eligibility requirements, including having a high school diploma or its equivalent. You are not eligible if you already have a bachelor's degree. These benefits are available only during the period of your participation in the Selected Reserves. Benefits are payable for up to thirty-six months. Depending upon a your enrollment status, you may receive benefits of up to $276 per month for full-time attendance.

For more information on veterans' educational benefits, check out www.gibill.va.gov/

Servicemember Opportunity College/ Community College of the Air Force

Enlisted personnel can also receive degrees through the Community College of the Air Force or the Servicemembers Opportunity College of the Army, Navy, Marines, or Coast Guard. These networks enable enlisted men and women to pursue a traditional degree through arrangements with a number of colleges. Participating schools offer flexible academic programs that take into account the unique lifestyle of a servicemember, with its time constraints and pattern of frequent reassignments.

To take advantage of one of these opportunities, you must be stationed at a base near a college campus that has provided the necessary scheduling for off-duty military personnel. Each base has an education officer who can assist you if you want to enroll in a local college or advance in your education by taking correspondence courses.

Tuition assistance is available in the form of tuition discounts for servicemembers pursuing their education through this network. The military covers 75 to 90 percent of the tuition cost. You can take advantage of this program while still in the service and still receive benefits under the G.I. Bill when you get out.

HOW TO USE THIS BOOK

Despite the importance of financial aid in the lives of most college students, only a handful develop more than a limited knowledge of the financial aid system that frequently provides a tremendous amount of help. Graduate students, to whom this publication is addressed, frequently assume that they are too old to qualify for financial aid. This is not so! Most federal programs are without age restrictions. Almost all, however, are need-based, and an average adult's income level might adversely affect chances for need-based aid. Still, it is definitely worth becoming familiar with the options. For example, many adults have prior military experience, which forms the basis for a great many awards. There are many programs to meet many needs and there may be one or more that fits your circumstances.

The profile section of this guide provides complete profiles of more than 1,000 award programs, scholarships, fellowships, grants, prizes, and other gift aid, worth in aggregate more than $266 million, that are specifically available to graduate students.

Eleven indexes include an Award Name Index, a Sponsor Index, an Index to Academic Field/Career Goals, a Civic, Professional, Social, or Union Affiliation Index, an Employment/Volunteer Experience Index, an Impairment Index, a Military Service Index, a Nationalality or Ethnic Heritage Index, a Religious Affiliation Index, a State/Province of Residence Index, and a Talent/Areas of Interest Index.

The awards described in this book are organized into broad categories that represent the major factors used to determine eligibility for scholarship awards and prizes. To find a basic list of awards available to you, look under the broad category or categories that fit your particular academic goals, skills, personal characteristics, or background. The categories are:

- Academic/Career Areas

- Civic, Professional, Social, or Union Affiliation

- Employment/Volunteer Experience

- Impairment

- Military Service

- Nationality or Ethnic Heritage

- Religious Affiliation

- State/Province of Residence

- Talent/Areas of Interest

- Miscellaneous Criteria

The Academic/Career Areas category is subdivided into individual subject areas that are organized alphabetically.

Full descriptive profiles of awards are sequentially numbered. The profile number appears with a bullet in front of it in the upper right-hand corner of the profile. You will find that most awards have more than one criterion that needs to be met before a student can be eligible. Cross-references by name and sequential number within each section are made to the main description from locations under the other relevant categories where the award might also be listed. The full description appears in the first relevant location, cross-references in the later ones.

Because your major academic field of study and/or career goal has central importance in college planning, we give this factor precedence over others. This means that the Academic/Career Areas category appears first. If an academic major or career goal is a criterion for an award, the description of this award will appear within this category rather than in the later sections under other criteria. Within the appropriate categories, descriptive profiles are organized alphabetically by the name of the sponsoring organization. If more than one award from the same organization appears in a particular section, the awards are then listed alphabetically by the name of the award under the name of the sponsor.

HOW THE DESCRIPTIVE PROFILES ARE ORGANIZED

Here are the elements of a full descriptive profile:

I. Name of Sponsoring Organization and Web Addresses

This appears alphabetically under the appropriate category. In most instances, acronyms are given as full names. Occasionally, a sponsor will refer to itself throughout the material that it publishes by acronym, and in deference to this seeming preference, we present its name as an acronym.

II. Award Name and Sequence Number

III. Brief Textual Description of the Award

IV. Academic/Career Areas (only in the Academic/Career Areas categories of the book)

This is a list of all academic or career subject terms that are assigned to this award.

V. Award Descriptors

Is it a scholarship? A prize for winning a competition? A fellowship? What years of college can it be used for? Is it renewable or is it for only one year?

VI. Eligibility Requirements

VII. Application Requirements

What do you need to supply in order to be considered? What are the deadlines?

VIII. Contact

Information provided here includes contact name, address, phone number, fax number, and e-mail address.

Some sponsors prefer that the first contact with applicants be by mail and have requested that their telephone numbers not be published. Peterson's honors this request. Most scholarship sponsors are willing to provide their telephone numbers to serious applicants after an initial screening.

WHERE OUR INFORMATION COMES FROM

The award data were collected in winter 2001 and spring 2002 through Peterson's Annual Survey of Non-institutional Financial Awards. We sent detailed surveys to more than 1,600 organizations offering scholarships, grants, prizes, fellowships, and/or forgiveable loans. Officials com-

pleted and returned the surveys. We entered the information we received into our database, verifying anything that seemed unusual and gathering any missing information via telephone updates and Web research. Because of the comprehensive editorial review that takes place in our offices, we have every reason to believe that the data presented in this book are accurate. However, students should always confirm eligibility requirements and application fees with a specific organization at the time of application, since organizations can and do change policies whenever necessary.

ACADEMIC/CAREER AREAS

AGRIBUSINESS

AMERICAN AGRICULTURAL ECONOMICS ASSOCIATION FOUNDATION
http://www.aaea.org

FARM CREDIT GRADUATE SCHOLARSHIP FOR THE STUDY OF YOUNG, BEGINNING OR SMALL FARMERS AND RANCHERS • 1

The Farm Credit Scholarships are provided to support graduate student work or a thesis, dissertation, or similar project addressing an applied problem or issue facing young, beginning, or small farmers and ranchers in the United States and its possessions. One Ph.D. scholarship of $5,000 and one master's degree scholarship of $3,000. Deadline is May 1.

Academic/Career Areas Agribusiness; Agriculture; Economics; Natural Resources; Science, Technology and Society.

Award Scholarship for use in graduate years; not renewable. *Number:* 2. *Amount:* $3000–$5000.

Eligibility Requirements Applicant must be enrolled or expecting to enroll full-time at a four-year institution or university. Available to U.S. and non-U.S. citizens.

Application Requirements Application, essay, resume. *Deadline:* May 1.

Contact Ms. Donna Dunn, Executive Director
American Agricultural Economics
Association Foundation
415 South Duff Avenue, Suite C
Ames, IA 50010-6600
Phone: 515-233-3202
Fax: 515-233-3101
E-mail: donna@aaea.org

OUTSTANDING DOCTORAL AND MASTER'S THESIS AWARDS • 2

One-time award for graduate students of agriculture, natural resources, or rural economics who have written outstanding master's or doctoral theses. Must be nominated by department of participating institution. Write for further details. Deadline is February 1.

Academic/Career Areas Agribusiness; Agriculture; Economics; Natural Resources; Science, Technology and Society; Social Sciences.

Award Prize for use in graduate, or postgraduate years; not renewable. *Number:* 3–6. *Amount:* $500–$1000.

Eligibility Requirements Applicant must be enrolled or expecting to enroll full-time at a four-year institution or university. Available to U.S. and non-U.S. citizens.

Application Requirements Application, references, thesis. *Deadline:* February 1.

Contact Ms. Donna Dunn, Executive Director
American Agricultural Economics
Association Foundation
415 South Duff, Suite C
Ames, IA 50010-6600
Phone: 515-233-3202
Fax: 515-233-3101
E-mail: donna@aaea.org

SYLVIA LANE MENTOR RESEARCH FELLOWSHIP FUND • 3

Award for female graduate and post-graduate students in agricultural economics. Submit curriculum vitae, budget, research statement, and letter of intent from mentor with application. Write for more information. One-time award of $2000-$4000.

Academic/Career Areas Agribusiness; Agriculture; Economics; Natural Resources; Science, Technology and Society; Social Sciences.

Award Fellowship for use in graduate, or postgraduate years; not renewable. *Number:* 1–3. *Amount:* $2000–$4000.

Eligibility Requirements Applicant must be enrolled or expecting to enroll full-time at a four-year institution or university and female. Available to U.S. and non-U.S. citizens.

Application Requirements Application, references. *Deadline:* Continuous.

Contact Ms. Donna Dunn, Executive Director
American Agricultural Economics
Association Foundation
415 South Duff, Suite C
Ames, IA 50010-6600
Phone: 515-233-3202
Fax: 515-233-3101
E-mail: donna@aaea.org

AMERICAN SHEEP INDUSTRY ASSOCIATION
http://www.sheepusa.org

NATIONAL WOOL GROWERS MEMORIAL FELLOWSHIP • 4

Must be a graduate student involved in sheep-related research studies. Must outline (minimum 250 words)

American Sheep Industry Association (continued)

specific research project and give reasons for pursuing that area. Also submit proof of acceptance into graduate school.

Academic/Career Areas Agribusiness; Agriculture; Animal/Veterinary Sciences.

Award Fellowship for use in graduate years; not renewable. *Number:* 1. *Amount:* $2500.

Eligibility Requirements Applicant must be enrolled or expecting to enroll at an institution or university. Available to U.S. citizens.

Application Requirements Application, references. *Deadline:* June 1.

Contact Judy Brown, Executive Assistant
American Sheep Industry Association
6911 South Yosemite Street, Suite 200
Englewood, CO 80112-1414
Phone: 303-771-3500 Ext. 46
Fax: 303-771-8200
E-mail: judy@sheepusa.org

NATIONAL MILK PRODUCERS FEDERATION
http://www.nmpf.org

NATIONAL MILK PRODUCERS FEDERATION NATIONAL DAIRY LEADERSHIP SCHOLARSHIP PROGRAM • 5

Assists graduate and post-graduate students who have chosen to conduct their research in the field of dairy science, agricultural economics, animal health, food safety, environmental, or any field of study which may benefit the dairy industry and its dairy producers.

Academic/Career Areas Agribusiness; Agriculture; Animal/Veterinary Sciences; Applied Sciences; Chemical Engineering; Economics; Food Science/ Nutrition; Health and Medical Sciences; Horticulture/Floriculture; Natural Resources; Trade/Technical Specialties.

Award Scholarship for use in graduate, or postgraduate years; not renewable. *Number:* 3–4. *Amount:* $2000–$3000.

Eligibility Requirements Applicant must be enrolled or expecting to enroll full-time at a four-year institution or university. Available to U.S. and non-U.S. citizens.

Application Requirements Application, essay, financial need analysis, references, research proposal and curriculum vitae. *Deadline:* May 26.

Contact Robert Burn
National Milk Producers Federation
2101 Wilson Boulevard, Suite 400
Arlington, VA 22201
Phone: 703-243-6111

POTASH AND PHOSPHATE INSTITUTE
http://www.ppi-far.org

J. FIELDING REED FELLOWSHIPS • 6

One time award for graduate students in soil and plant science attending a U.S. or Canadian degree-granting institution. Priority for students of agronomy and horticulture majoring in soil fertility or other areas related to plant nutrition.

Academic/Career Areas Agribusiness; Agriculture; Earth Science; Horticulture/Floriculture.

Award Fellowship for use in graduate years; not renewable. *Number:* 3–5. *Amount:* $2000.

Eligibility Requirements Applicant must be enrolled or expecting to enroll full-time at an institution or university. Available to U.S. and non-U.S. citizens.

Application Requirements Application, references, transcript. *Deadline:* January 15.

Contact Sheryl Danner, Executive Assistant
Potash and Phosphate Institute
655 Engineering Drive, Suite 110
Norcross, GA 30092-2843
Phone: 770-825-8062
Fax: 770-448-0439

AGRICULTURE

AMERICAN AGRICULTURAL ECONOMICS ASSOCIATION FOUNDATION
http://www.aaea.org

FARM CREDIT GRADUATE SCHOLARSHIP FOR THE STUDY OF YOUNG, BEGINNING OR SMALL FARMERS AND RANCHERS
• *See number 1*

OUTSTANDING DOCTORAL AND MASTER'S THESIS AWARDS
• *See number 2*

SYLVIA LANE MENTOR RESEARCH FELLOWSHIP FUND
• *See number 3*

AMERICAN SHEEP INDUSTRY ASSOCIATION
http://www.sheepusa.org

NATIONAL WOOL GROWERS MEMORIAL FELLOWSHIP
• *See number 4*

AMERICAN WINE SOCIETY EDUCATIONAL FOUNDATION
http://www.americanwinesociety.com

AMERICAN WINE SOCIETY EDUCATIONAL FOUNDATION SCHOLARSHIP PROGRAM • 7

The AWSEF provides scholarships to graduate students who are citizens of a North American country (U.S., Canada, Mexico, Bahamas, West Indie Islands) who are studying any aspect of enology (wine making), viticulture (grape growing), or health aspects of wine. Application deadline is March 31. Four scholarships of $2500 each will be awarded, two students will be invited to the AWS meeting. Applicants must have B.S. and be currently enrolled in graduate school.

Academic/Career Areas Agriculture; Food Science/Nutrition.

Award Scholarship for use in graduate years; not renewable. *Number:* 4. *Amount:* $2500.

Eligibility Requirements Applicant must be enrolled or expecting to enroll full-time at an institution or university. Available to U.S. and non-U.S. citizens.

Application Requirements Application, essay, references, transcript. *Deadline:* March 31.

Contact Les Sperling, President
American Wine Society Educational
Foundation
1134 Prospect Avenue
Bethlehem, PA 18018-4914
Phone: 610-865-2401
Fax: 610-758-3526
E-mail: lhs0@lehigh.edu

FIRST - FLORICULTURE INDUSTRY RESEARCH AND SCHOLARSHIP TRUST
http://www.firstinfloriculture.org

JOHN CAREW MEMORIAL SCHOLARSHIP • 8

One scholarship available to graduate students at four-year institutions with specific interest in greenhouse crops. Must be majoring in horticulture or a related field. One-time award of $1500. Application available at website from January 1 to May 1. Visit http://www.firstinfloriculture.org to download application.

Academic/Career Areas Agriculture; Horticulture/Floriculture.

Award Scholarship for use in graduate years; not renewable. *Number:* 1. *Amount:* $1500.

Eligibility Requirements Applicant must be enrolled or expecting to enroll at an institution or university. Applicant must have 3.0 GPA or higher. Available to U.S. and Canadian citizens.

Application Requirements Application, essay, financial need analysis, references, self-addressed stamped envelope, transcript. *Deadline:* May 1.

Contact Scholarship Information
FIRST - Floriculture Industry Research
and Scholarship Trust
PO Box 280
East Lansing, MI 48826-0280
E-mail: scholarship@firstinfloriculture.org

GEM CONSORTIUM
http://www.nd.edu/~gem

GEM PH.D. ENGINEERING FELLOWSHIP • 9

Renewable award for U.S. citizen who has attained or is in process of attaining master's degree in engineering. Minimum 3.0 GPA required. Must be American Indian, Black American, or Hispanic American. Must attend GEM Ph.D. fellowship program member university. May major in any discipline within engineering. Includes summer internship.

Academic/Career Areas Agriculture; Architecture; Biology; Civil Engineering; Computer Science/Data Processing; Earth Science; Electrical Engineering/Electronics; Engineering/Technology; Materials Science, Engineering and Metallurgy; Mechanical Engineering; Nuclear Science.

Award Fellowship for use in graduate years; renewable. *Number:* 20–30. *Amount:* $60,000.

Eligibility Requirements Applicant must be American Indian/Alaska Native, Black (non-Hispanic), or Hispanic and enrolled or expecting to enroll full-time at an institution or university. Applicant must have 3.0 GPA or higher. Available to U.S. citizens.

Application Requirements Application, resume, references, transcript, statement of purpose. *Deadline:* December 1.

Contact Saundra D. Johnson, Executive Director
GEM Consortium
PO Box 537
Notre Dame, IN 46556-0537
Phone: 219-631-7771
Fax: 219-287-1486
E-mail: gem.1@nd.edu

INTERNATIONAL DEVELOPMENT RESEARCH CENTER
http://www.idrc.ca/awards

AGROPOLIS • 10

Up to 14 annual awards to support master's or doctoral thesis research in any of the following disciplines: agricultural extension and financing, agronomy, animal health and production, architecture, communications and information sciences, economics, environmental studies and environmental impact assessment, fisheries, food marketing, forestry,

International Development Research Center (continued)

gender analysis, geography, health and nutrition, horticulture, sociology, urban planning, and waste/water engineering. Award will cover justifiable field research expenses up to $20,000 Canadian. Research must be related to urban or peri-urban agriculture. Contact for application procedures and further information. Must submit research budget and proof of citizenship.

Academic/Career Areas Agriculture; Animal/Veterinary Sciences; Architecture; Business/Consumer Services; Communications; Economics; Engineering/Technology; Health and Medical Sciences; Horticulture/Floriculture; Natural Resources; Social Sciences.

Award Grant for use in graduate years; not renewable. *Number:* up to 14. *Amount:* up to $20,000.

Eligibility Requirements Applicant must be enrolled or expecting to enroll full or part-time at an institution or university. Available to Canadian and non-U.S. citizens.

Application Requirements Application, essay, resume, references, transcript, copy of passport or birth certificate; curriculum vitae. *Deadline:* December 31.

Contact Wendy Storey, AGROPOLIS Awards
Administrator
International Development Research
Center
250 Albert Street, PO Box 8500
Ottawa, ON K1G 3H9
Canada
Phone: 613-236-6163 Ext. 2040
Fax: 613-567-7749
E-mail: agropolis@idrc.ca

FORAGE CROPS IN SUSTAINABLY MANAGED AGROECOSYSTEMS: THE BENTLEY FELLOWSHIP
• 11

Award of Can$20,000 providing assistance to Canadian graduate students undertaking applied research on how increased use of forage crops in cropping systems can improve the sustainability and profitability of agricultural production by farmers in developing countries. Must be Canadian citizen or permanent resident and be registered in a Canadian university at the master's or doctoral level. Must have an academic background in agriculture or biology. Contact for application procedures.

Academic/Career Areas Agriculture; Biology.

Award Fellowship for use in graduate years; not renewable. *Number:* 1. *Amount:* up to $20,000.

Eligibility Requirements Applicant must be Canadian citizenship and enrolled or expecting to enroll full-time at an institution or university.

Application Requirements Application, financial need analysis, resume, references, transcript, letter from institution, proof of citizenship. *Deadline:* October 2.

Contact Danielle Reinhardt, Program Assistant
International Development Research
Center
PO Box 8500
Ottawa, ON K1G 3H9
Canada
Phone: 613-236-6163
Fax: 613-563-0815
E-mail: cta@idrc.ca

IDRC DOCTORAL RESEARCH AWARD   • 12

One-time awards for Canadian graduate students to undertake thesis research in international development. Research usually takes place in Latin America, Africa, Asia, and the Middle East. Submit curriculum vitae and proof of Canadian citizenship. Application deadlines: May 14 and November 30. Write for details. Award is up to Can$20,000.

Academic/Career Areas Agriculture; Applied Sciences; Area/Ethnic Studies; Computer Science/Data Processing; Food Science/Nutrition; Natural Resources; Political Science; Science, Technology and Society; Social Sciences.

Award Scholarship for use in graduate, or postgraduate years; not renewable. *Number:* 8–20. *Amount:* up to $20,000.

Eligibility Requirements Applicant must be Canadian citizenship and enrolled or expecting to enroll full-time at an institution or university.

Application Requirements Application, essay, financial need analysis, resume, references, transcript, letter from institution, thesis proposal.

Contact Danielle Reinhardt, Program Assistant
International Development Research
Center
PO Box 8500
Ottawa, ON K1G 3H9
Canada
Phone: 613-236-6163
Fax: 613-563-0815
E-mail: cta@idrc.ca

JAPANESE GOVERNMENT/THE MONBUSHO SCHOLARSHIP PROGRAM
http://embjapan.org/la

RESEARCH STUDENT SCHOLARSHIP   • 13

Award open to those who want to pursue graduate studies in any major at a Japanese university. Must be less than 35 years of age. Ability to speak Japanese is not required; however, must be willing to study and receive instruction in the language. Scholarship comprises transportation, accommodations, medical expenses and monthly and arrival allowances. Contact for more information.

Academic/Career Areas Agriculture; Area/Ethnic Studies; Dental Health/Services; Economics; Engineering/Technology; Health and Medical Sciences; History; Home Economics; Humanities; Law/Legal Services; Literature/English/Writing; Social Sciences.

Award Scholarship for use in graduate, or postgraduate years; renewable.

Eligibility Requirements Applicant must be age 34 or under; enrolled or expecting to enroll full-time at an institution or university and must have an interest in Japanese language. Available to U.S. and non-U.S. citizens.

Application Requirements Application, autobiography, essay, interview, photo, references, test scores, transcript.

Contact Japanese Government/The Monbusho
Scholarship Program
350 South Grand Avenue, Suite 1700
Los Angeles, CA 90071

NATIONAL MILK PRODUCERS FEDERATION
http://www.nmpf.org

NATIONAL MILK PRODUCERS FEDERATION NATIONAL DAIRY LEADERSHIP SCHOLARSHIP PROGRAM
• *See number 5*

POTASH AND PHOSPHATE INSTITUTE
http://www.ppi-far.org

J. FIELDING REED FELLOWSHIPS
• *See number 6*

ANIMAL/VETERINARY SCIENCES

AFRICAN NETWORK OF SCIENTIFIC AND TECHNOLOGICAL INSTITUTIONS - ANSTI
http://www.ansti.org

AFRICAN NETWORK OF SCIENTIFIC AND TECHNOLOGICAL INSTITUTIONS POSTGRADUATE FELLOWSHIPS • 14

Each year a limited number of postgraduate fellowships are available for the staff members of ANSTI member institutions. The fellowships are tenable only in ANSTI institutions outside applicant's home country. To qualify for fellowship, the applicant must be below 36 years of age and possess a good bachelor's degree (at least 2nd class upper division).

Academic/Career Areas Animal/Veterinary Sciences; Applied Sciences; Chemical Engineering; Civil Engineering; Computer Science/Data Processing; Earth Science; Electrical Engineering/Electronics; Engineering/Technology; Engineering-Related Technologies; Food Science/Nutrition; Materials Science, Engineering and Metallurgy.

Award Fellowship for use in postgraduate years; not renewable. *Number:* 5. *Amount:* $15,000.

Eligibility Requirements Applicant must be of African heritage and African citizenship; age 36 or under and enrolled or expecting to enroll full-time at an institution or university. Available to citizens of countries other than the U.S. or Canada.

Application Requirements Application, photo, resume, transcript. *Deadline:* May 31.

Contact Prof. J.G.M. Massaquoi, ANSTI
Coordinator
African Network of Scientific and
Technological Institutions - ANSTI
PO Box 30592
Nairobi
Kenya
Phone: 254-2-622620
Fax: 254-2-622750
E-mail: info@ansti.org

ALBERT SCHWEITZER FELLOWSHIP
http://www.schweitzerfellowship.org

NEW HAMPSHIRE/VERMONT SCHWEITZER FELLOWS PROGRAM • 15

The New Hampshire/Vermont Schweitzer Fellows Program is a yearlong fellowship for students enrolled in a degree-granting program in health, law, and other disciplines related to health care. Each Fellow carries out a health-related service project of at least 200 hours which addresses unmet health needs of an underserved community.

Academic/Career Areas Animal/Veterinary Sciences; Dental Health/Services; Food Science/Nutrition; Health Administration; Health and Medical Sciences; Health Information Management/Technology; Law/Legal Services; Nursing.

Award Fellowship for use in graduate years; not renewable. *Number:* 16–20. *Amount:* $2000.

Eligibility Requirements Applicant must be enrolled or expecting to enroll full-time at an institution or university; resident of New Hampshire or Vermont and studying in New Hampshire or Vermont. Available to U.S. and non-U.S. citizens.

Application Requirements Essay, interview, resume, references. *Deadline:* February 15.

Contact Becky Torrey, Program Coordinator
Albert Schweitzer Fellowship
c/o 10 Sausville Road
Etna, NH 03750
Phone: 603-643-1479
Fax: 603-643-6069
E-mail: rebecca.b.torrey@dartmouth.edu

AMERICAN SHEEP INDUSTRY ASSOCIATION
http://www.sheepusa.org

NATIONAL WOOL GROWERS MEMORIAL FELLOWSHIP
• *See number 4*

ATLANTIC SALMON FEDERATION
http://www.asf.ca

ATLANTIC SALMON FEDERATION OLIN FELLOWSHIP
• **16**

Nonrenewable annual fellowship to improve and advance skills and knowledge that may help to solve current problems in Atlantic salmon biology, management, and conservation. Must be legal resident of U.S. or Canada and enrolled in accredited management program.

Academic/Career Areas Animal/Veterinary Sciences; Biology; Natural Resources.

Award Fellowship for use in graduate years; not renewable. *Number:* 1–7. *Amount:* $1000–$3000.

Eligibility Requirements Applicant must be enrolled or expecting to enroll full or part-time at an institution or university. Available to U.S. and Canadian citizens.

Application Requirements Application, essay, references, transcript. *Deadline:* March 15.

Contact Mrs. Ellen Merrill, Executive Assistant
Atlantic Salmon Federation
PO Box 5200
St. Andrews, NB E5B 3S8
Canada
Phone: 506-529-1021
Fax: 506-529-4985
E-mail: emerrill@nbnet.nb.ca

DELTA SOCIETY
http://www.deltasociety.org

HARRIS SWEATT TRAVEL GRANT
• **17**

A grant will be awarded to pay the travel costs for students to attend the Delta Society's conference. Students must be enrolled in a full-time veterinary or human health professional training program pursuing a master's or doctoral degree. Applicants must submit a detailed plan on how information learned at the conference will be shared. For more information go to http://www.deltasociety.org.

Academic/Career Areas Animal/Veterinary Sciences; Education; Health and Medical Sciences; Nursing; Social Services; Special Education; Therapy/Rehabilitation.

Award Grant for use in graduate years; not renewable. *Number:* 1–5. *Amount:* $200–$600.

Eligibility Requirements Applicant must be enrolled or expecting to enroll full-time at an institution or university. Available to U.S. and non-U.S. citizens.

Application Requirements Application. *Deadline:* March 11.

Contact Michelle Cobey
Delta Society
289 Perimeter Road East
Renton, WA 98055-1329
Phone: 425-430-2355
Fax: 425-235-1076
E-mail: info@deltasociety.org

EDMUND NILES HUYCK PRESERVE AND BIOLOGICAL RESEARCH STATION
http://www.huyckpreserve.org

HUYCK STATION RESEARCH GRANTS
• **18**

Renewable grant for graduate students and professionals with a Ph.D. to pursue research on the ecology, evolution, natural history, and conservation biology of the flora and fauna at the Huyck Preserve and its vicinity. Write for more information.

Academic/Career Areas Animal/Veterinary Sciences; Biology; Natural Resources.

Award Grant for use in graduate, or postgraduate years; renewable. *Number:* 8–12. *Amount:* $1200–$2500.

Eligibility Requirements Applicant must be enrolled or expecting to enroll full or part-time at a four-year institution or university and studying in New York. Available to U.S. and non-U.S. citizens.

Application Requirements Application, references. *Deadline:* February 1.

Contact Richard Wyman, Executive Director
Edmund Niles Huyck Preserve and
Biological Research Station
PO Box 189
Rennselaerville, NY 12147
Phone: 518-797-3440
Fax: 518-797-3440
E-mail: rlwyman@capital.net

INTERNATIONAL DEVELOPMENT RESEARCH CENTER
http://www.idrc.ca/awards

AGROPOLIS
• *See number 10*

INTERNATIONAL WOMEN'S FISHING ASSOCIATION SCHOLARSHIP TRUST
http://www.iwfa.org

INTERNATIONAL WOMEN'S FISHING ASSOCIATION GRADUATE SCHOLARSHIPS IN THE MARINE SCIENCES • 19

Renewable award for matriculated graduate students pursuing master's or Ph.D. in a marine science. Must be studying at a U.S. institution. Award based upon ability and financial need. Write for more information.

Academic/Career Areas Animal/Veterinary Sciences; Biology; Natural Resources.

Award Scholarship for use in graduate, or postgraduate years; renewable. *Number:* 1–20. *Amount:* $500–$2000.

Eligibility Requirements Applicant must be enrolled or expecting to enroll full or part-time at a four-year institution or university. Available to U.S. and non-U.S. citizens.

Application Requirements Application, autobiography, essay, financial need analysis, photo, references, transcript. *Deadline:* March 1.

Contact Chairman, Scholarship Trust
International Women's Fishing
Association Scholarship Trust
PO Drawer 3125
Palm Beach, FL 33480

NATIONAL MILK PRODUCERS FEDERATION
http://www.nmpf.org

NATIONAL MILK PRODUCERS FEDERATION NATIONAL DAIRY LEADERSHIP SCHOLARSHIP PROGRAM
• *See number 5*

NOVARTIS FOUNDATION
http://wwwl.novartisfound.org.uk/bursary.htm

NOVARTIS FOUNDATION BURSARY SCHEME • 20

Enables a young scientist to attend a Novartis Foundation Symposium to spend 4.12 weeks in the laboratory of one of the participants. Covers all travel plus board and lodging during symposium week and bursary period. Applicants must be actively engaged in relevant research. Age range 23-35 years.

Academic/Career Areas Animal/Veterinary Sciences; Applied Sciences; Biology; Natural Sciences.

Award Prize for use in postgraduate years; not renewable. *Number:* up to 8. *Amount:* up to $6000.

Eligibility Requirements Applicant must be age 23-35 and enrolled or expecting to enroll full-time at an institution or university. Available to U.S. and non-U.S. citizens.

Application Requirements Application, resume. *Deadline:* Continuous.

Contact Novartis Foundation
41 Portland Place
London W1B 1BN
United Kingdom
E-mail: bursary@novartisfound.org.uk

PARALYZED VETERANS OF AMERICA - SPINAL CORD RESEARCH FOUNDATION
http://www.pva.org/scrf

FELLOWSHIPS IN SPINAL CORD INJURY RESEARCH • 21

Award for research done in U.S. or Canadian laboratory and dedicated to improving quality of life for individuals with spinal cord injury and spinal cord dysfunction and to finding an eventual cure for paralysis. Must submit curriculum vitae, ten copies of grant application. Deadline is June 1.

Academic/Career Areas Animal/Veterinary Sciences; Biology; Engineering/Technology; Engineering-Related Technologies; Health and Medical Sciences; Therapy/Rehabilitation.

Award Fellowship for use in postgraduate years; not renewable. *Number:* 20. *Amount:* $25,000–$75,000.

Eligibility Requirements Applicant must be enrolled or expecting to enroll at an institution or university. Available to U.S. and non-U.S. citizens.

Application Requirements Application, references. *Deadline:* June 1.

Contact Associate Director
Paralyzed Veterans of America - Spinal
Cord Research Foundation
801 18th Street, NW
Washington, DC 20006
Phone: 800-424-8200
E-mail: scrfw@pva.org

ROB & BESSIE WELDER WILDLIFE FOUNDATION

WILDLIFE RESEARCH SCHOLARSHIP • 22

Award for graduate students who are approved candidates for MS or Ph.D. degrees after project proposals have been submitted to and approved by the Foundation. Minimum GRE score of 1100 and B average in last two years of undergraduate or graduate work required. $1000 per month for full-time M.S. candidates and $1100 per month for Ph.D. candidates.

Academic/Career Areas Animal/Veterinary Sciences; Biology; Natural Resources.

Award Scholarship for use in graduate years; renewable. *Number:* 1. *Amount:* $5000–$15,000.

Eligibility Requirements Applicant must be enrolled or expecting to enroll full-time at an

Rob & Bessie Welder Wildlife Foundation (continued)

institution or university. Applicant must have 3.0 GPA or higher. Available to U.S. and non-U.S. citizens.

Application Requirements Application, autobiography, resume, references, test scores, transcript. *Deadline:* October 1.

Contact Lynn Drawe, Director
Rob & Bessie Welder Wildlife Foundation
PO Box 1400
Sinton, TX 78387
Phone: 361-364-2643
Fax: 361-364-2650

UNITED STATES ARMY RECRUITING COMMAND
http://www.goarmy.com

ARMED FORCES HEALTH PROFESSIONS SCHOLARSHIP PROGRAM-ARMY • 23

Award provides up to four years of tuition, books, fees, associated expenses, and monthly stipend of over $1000. Must attend accredited school of medicine, optometry, dentistry, veterinary medicine, clinical psychology, osteopathy, or nursing. Must undergo physical examination. Application must include statement of motivation. Military service required upon graduation.

Academic/Career Areas Animal/Veterinary Sciences; Dental Health/Services; Health and Medical Sciences; Nursing.

Award Scholarship for use in graduate years; renewable. *Number:* 200–400.

Eligibility Requirements Applicant must be age 19-43 and enrolled or expecting to enroll full-time at an institution or university. Available to U.S. citizens. Applicant must have served in the Army.

Application Requirements Application, interview, references, test scores, transcript. *Deadline:* Continuous.

Contact United States Army Recruiting Command
Health Services Directorate
1307 Third Avenue
Fort Knox, KY 40121-2726

APPLIED SCIENCES

AFRICAN NETWORK OF SCIENTIFIC AND TECHNOLOGICAL INSTITUTIONS - ANSTI
http://www.ansti.org

AFRICAN NETWORK OF SCIENTIFIC AND TECHNOLOGICAL INSTITUTIONS POSTGRADUATE FELLOWSHIPS
• *See number 14*

AIR AND WASTE MANAGEMENT ASSOCIATION
http://www.awma.org

AIR AND WASTE MANAGEMENT ASSOCIATION SCHOLARSHIP ENDOWMENT TRUST FUND • 24

One-time award to a full-time graduate student pursuing coursework and research leading to careers in air pollution and/or waste management.

Academic/Career Areas Applied Sciences; Biology; Chemical Engineering; Earth Science; Engineering/ Technology; Engineering-Related Technologies; Health Information Management/Technology; Meteorology/Atmospheric Science; Natural Sciences; Physical Sciences and Math; Science, Technology and Society.

Award Scholarship for use in graduate years; not renewable. *Number:* 5. *Amount:* $2000–$7000.

Eligibility Requirements Applicant must be enrolled or expecting to enroll full-time at an institution or university. Available to U.S. and non-U.S. citizens.

Application Requirements Application, autobiography, essay, portfolio, resume, references, transcript. *Deadline:* December 1.

Contact Carrie Hartz, Education Programs
Coordinator
Air and Waste Management Association
International Headquarters
One Gateway Center, Third Floor, 420
Fort Duquesne Boulevard
Pittsburgh, PA 15222
Phone: 412-232-3444
Fax: 412-232-3450
E-mail: chartz@awma.org

AMERICAN GEOPHYSICAL UNION
http://www.agu.org

AMERICAN GEOPHYSICAL UNION HORTON RESEARCH GRANT • 25

Grant for research in hydrology and/or water resources by Ph.D. candidate. Proposals may be in hydrology (physics, chemistry, or biology aspects) or water resource policy sciences (economics, systems analysis, sociology, or law). Must submit executive summary. Two one-time awards of $10,000 each.

Academic/Career Areas Applied Sciences; Biology; Civil Engineering; Earth Science; Economics; Engineering/Technology; Law/Legal Services; Natural Resources; Social Sciences.

Award Grant for use in postgraduate years; not renewable. *Number:* 2. *Amount:* $10,000.

Eligibility Requirements Applicant must be enrolled or expecting to enroll full-time at an institution or university. Applicant must have 3.5 GPA or higher. Available to U.S. and non-U.S. citizens.

Application Requirements Application, references, statement of purpose, detailed budget. *Deadline:* March 1.

Contact Wynetta Singhateh, O&RS Grants and
        Awards
        American Geophysical Union
        2000 Florida Avenue, NW
        Washington, DC 20009-9202
        Phone: 202-462-6900
        Fax: 202-328-0566
        E-mail: wsinghateh@agu.org

AMERICAN INSTITUTE OF AERONAUTICS AND ASTRONAUTICS
http://www.aiaa.org

AIAA FOUNDATION GRADUATE AWARDS • 26

One-time award to graduate students who have completed at least one year of full-time graduate college work. Must have a department approved thesis or research project. Must be an AIAA student member. Study program must be in a specialized area of science and engineering.

Academic/Career Areas Applied Sciences; Aviation/Aerospace; Biology; Electrical Engineering/Electronics; Engineering/Technology; Materials Science, Engineering and Metallurgy; Mechanical Engineering; Physical Sciences and Math; Science, Technology and Society.

Award Prize for use in graduate years; not renewable. *Number:* up to 10. *Amount:* $5000.

Eligibility Requirements Applicant must be enrolled or expecting to enroll full-time at an institution or university. Applicant must have 3.0 GPA or higher. Available to U.S. and non-U.S. citizens.

Application Requirements Application, essay, references, transcript, research program. *Deadline:* January 31.

Contact Stephen Brock, Student Programs Director
        American Institute of Aeronautics and
        Astronautics
        1801 Alexander Bell Drive, Suite 500
        Reston, VA 20191
        Phone: 703-264-7536
        Fax: 703-264-7551
        E-mail: stephenb@aiaa.org

AIAA FOUNDATION ORVILLE AND WILBUR WRIGHT AWARDS • 27

One-time award to graduate students who have completed at least one year of full-time graduate college work. Must have a department approved thesis or research project. Must be an AIAA student member. Study program must be in a specialized area of science and engineering. Minimum 3.0 GPA required.

Academic/Career Areas Applied Sciences; Aviation/Aerospace; Biology; Electrical Engineering/Electronics; Engineering/Technology; Materials Science, Engineering and Metallurgy; Mechanical Engineering; Physical Sciences and Math; Science, Technology and Society.

Award Prize for use in graduate years; not renewable. *Number:* 4. *Amount:* $10,000.

Eligibility Requirements Applicant must be enrolled or expecting to enroll full-time at an institution or university. Applicant must have 3.0 GPA or higher. Available to U.S. and non-U.S. citizens.

Application Requirements Application, essay, references, transcript, research program. *Deadline:* January 31.

Contact Stephen Brock, Student Programs Director
        American Institute of Aeronautics and
        Astronautics
        1801 Alexander Bell Drive, Suite 500
        Reston, VA 20191
        Phone: 703-264-7536
        Fax: 703-264-7551
        E-mail: stephenb@aiaa.org

AMERICAN METEOROLOGICAL SOCIETY
http://www.ametsoc.org/AMS

AMERICAN METEOROLOGICAL SOCIETY/INDUSTRY/GOVERNMENT GRADUATE FELLOWSHIPS • 28

Award for full-time-students entering their first year of graduate study who wish to pursue advanced degrees in the atmospheric and related oceanic and hydrologic sciences. Must be a citizen of the U.S. to apply. One-time award of $15,000.

Academic/Career Areas Applied Sciences; Engineering/Technology; Meteorology/Atmospheric Science; Physical Sciences and Math.

Award Fellowship for use in graduate years; not renewable. *Amount:* $15,000.

Eligibility Requirements Applicant must be enrolled or expecting to enroll full-time at an institution or university. Applicant must have 3.0 GPA or higher. Available to U.S. citizens.

Application Requirements Application, essay, references, test scores, transcript. *Deadline:* February 15.

Contact Donna Fernandez, Fellowship/Scholarship
        Coordinator
        American Meteorological Society
        45 Beacon Street
        Boston, MA 02108-3693
        Phone: 617-227-2426 Ext. 246
        Fax: 617-742-8718
        E-mail: dfernand@ametsoc.org

AMERICAN NUCLEAR SOCIETY
http://www.ans.org

ALAN F. HENRY/PAUL A. GREEBLER
SCHOLARSHIP • 29

One-time award for students pursuing graduate studies in the field of reactor physics. Must be sponsored by the ANS and be a U.S. citizen or permanent resident. Application available at website.

Academic/Career Areas Applied Sciences; Engineering/Technology; Nuclear Science.

Award Scholarship for use in graduate years; not renewable. *Number:* 1. *Amount:* $3500.

Eligibility Requirements Applicant must be enrolled or expecting to enroll full-time at a four-year institution or university. Available to U.S. citizens.

Application Requirements Application, references, transcript. *Deadline:* February 1.

Contact Scholarship Coordinator
American Nuclear Society
555 North Kensington Avenue
La Grange Park, IL 60526
Phone: 708-352-6611
Fax: 708-352-0499
E-mail: outreach@ans.org

AMERICAN NUCLEAR SOCIETY GRADUATE
SCHOLARSHIPS • 30

One-time scholarships available for full-time graduate students pursuing a degree in nuclear science or nuclear engineering, material science or technology with nuclear application. Must have ANS member sponsor and be U.S. citizen or permanent resident

Academic/Career Areas Applied Sciences; Engineering/Technology; Materials Science, Engineering and Metallurgy; Nuclear Science; Physical Sciences and Math.

Award Scholarship for use in graduate years; not renewable. *Number:* 1–29. *Amount:* $3000.

Eligibility Requirements Applicant must be enrolled or expecting to enroll full-time at a four-year institution. Available to U.S. citizens.

Application Requirements Application, references, transcript. *Deadline:* February 1.

Contact Scholarship Coordinator
American Nuclear Society
555 North Kensington Avenue
La Grange Park, IL 60526
Phone: 708-352-6611
Fax: 708-352-0499
E-mail: outreach@ans.org

AMERICAN OPTOMETRIC
FOUNDATION
http://www.ezell.org

WILLIAM C. EZELL FELLOWSHIP • 31

For students pursuing a graduate or post-graduate degree in physiological optics, vision science, and related fields with goal of full-time career in optometric education and research. Will acknowledge AOF support where appropriate. Reapply to renew. Must rank in upper third of class and have a minimum GPA of 3.0.

Academic/Career Areas Applied Sciences; Biology; Health and Medical Sciences; Physical Sciences and Math.

Award Fellowship for use in graduate, or postgraduate years; not renewable. *Number:* 5–9. *Amount:* up to $8000.

Eligibility Requirements Applicant must be enrolled or expecting to enroll full-time at an institution or university. Applicant must have 3.0 GPA or higher. Available to U.S. and non-U.S. citizens.

Application Requirements Application, financial need analysis, references, transcript. *Deadline:* March 15.

Contact Christine Armstrong, Foundation Director
American Optometric Foundation
6110 Executive Boulevard, Suite 506
Rockville, MD 20852
Phone: 301-984-4734
Fax: 301-984-4737
E-mail: christine@aaoptom.org

AMERICAN RESPIRATORY CARE
FOUNDATION
http://www.aarc.org

RESPIRONICS FELLOWSHIP IN MECHANICAL
VENTILATION • 32

Fellowship to foster projects dealing with mechanical ventilation, especially outside the intensive care unit. Detailed proposal of no more than twenty pages. Project can be device development or evaluation, cost effectiveness analysis, or education program.

Academic/Career Areas Applied Sciences; Health and Medical Sciences; Therapy/Rehabilitation.

Award Fellowship for use in graduate years; not renewable. *Number:* 1. *Amount:* $1000.

Eligibility Requirements Applicant must be enrolled or expecting to enroll at an institution or university. Available to U.S. and non-U.S. citizens.

Application Requirements Application, references, project proposal. *Deadline:* May 31.

Contact Diane Shearer, Administrative Coordinator
American Respiratory Care Foundation
11030 Ables Lane
Dallas, TX 75229-4593
Phone: 972-243-2272
Fax: 972-484-2720
E-mail: info@aarc.org

AMERICAN SOCIETY FOR PHOTOGRAMMETRY AND REMOTE SENSING
http://www.asprs.org

AMERICAN SOCIETY FOR PHOTOGRAMMETRY AND REMOTE SENSING OUTSTANDING PAPERS AWARDS • 33

Several awards to authors of papers published in the ASPRS journal Photogrammetric Engineering and Remote Sensing (PE & RS). Papers published during the calendar year are reviewed by judges, with awards given to the authors of the best papers. Please note: These awards cannot be applied for.

Academic/Career Areas Applied Sciences; Engineering/Technology; Physical Sciences and Math.

Award Prize for use in graduate years; not renewable. *Number:* 5.

Eligibility Requirements Applicant must be enrolled or expecting to enroll full-time at a four-year institution or university. Available to U.S. and non-U.S. citizens.

Application Requirements Application, references, transcript, paper.

Contact Jesse Winch, Program Manager
American Society for Photogrammetry
and Remote Sensing
5410 Grosvenor Lane, Suite 210
Bethesda, MD 20814-2160
Phone: 301-493-0290 Ext. 101
Fax: 301-493-0208
E-mail: scholarships@asprs.org

TA LIANG MEMORIAL AWARD • 34

Award facilitates research-related travel by outstanding graduate students in remote sensing. Must be a member of ASPRS. One award of $500.

Academic/Career Areas Applied Sciences; Engineering/Technology; Physical Sciences and Math.

Award Scholarship for use in graduate years; renewable. *Number:* 1. *Amount:* $500.

Eligibility Requirements Applicant must be enrolled or expecting to enroll full-time at an institution or university and must have an interest in photography/photogrammetry/filmmaking.

Applicant or parent of applicant must be member of American Society for Photogrammetry and Remote Sensing.

Application Requirements Application, references, test scores, transcript. *Deadline:* December 3.

Contact Jesse Winch, Program Manager
American Society for Photogrammetry
and Remote Sensing
5410 Grosvenor Lane, Suite 210
Bethesda, MD 20814-2160
Phone: 301-493-0290 Ext. 101
Fax: 301-493-0208
E-mail: scholarships@asprs.org

WILLIAM A. FISCHER MEMORIAL SCHOLARSHIP • 35

Award facilitates graduate-level studies and career goals deemed to address new and innovative uses of remote sensing data/techniques that relate to the resources of the earth. Must be ASPRS member. Must submit statement of plans and goals. One scholarship of $2000.

Academic/Career Areas Applied Sciences; Engineering/Technology; Physical Sciences and Math.

Award Scholarship for use in graduate years; renewable. *Number:* 1. *Amount:* $2000.

Eligibility Requirements Applicant must be enrolled or expecting to enroll full-time at an institution or university and must have an interest in photography/photogrammetry/filmmaking. Applicant or parent of applicant must be member of American Society for Photogrammetry and Remote Sensing.

Application Requirements Application, references, transcript. *Deadline:* December 3.

Contact Jesse Winch, Program Manager
American Society for Photogrammetry
and Remote Sensing
5410 Grosvenor Lane, Suite 210
Bethesda, MD 20814-2160
Phone: 301-493-0290 Ext. 101
Fax: 301-493-0208
E-mail: scholarships@asprs.org

AMERICAN VACUUM SOCIETY
http://www.avs.org

ALBERT NERKEN AWARD • 36

One-time award for scientists and engineers to recognize outstanding contributions to the solution of technical problems. Must be a recognized worker in his or her field with an outstanding record of five or more years of contributions.

Academic/Career Areas Applied Sciences; Engineering/Technology; Physical Sciences and Math.

American Vacuum Society (continued)

Award Scholarship for use in graduate, or postgraduate years; not renewable. *Amount:* $5000.
Eligibility Requirements Applicant must be enrolled or expecting to enroll at an institution or university. Applicant or parent of applicant must have employment or volunteer experience in designated career field. Available to U.S. citizens.
Application Requirements Application, references, transcript. *Deadline:* March 31.
Contact Ms. Angela Mulligan, Member Services
  Coordinator
  American Vacuum Society
  120 Wall Street, 32nd Floor
  New York, NY 10005-3993
  Phone: 212-248-0200
  Fax: 212-248-0245
  E-mail: avsnyc@avs.org

AMERICAN VACUUM SOCIETY GRADUATE RESEARCH AWARD • 37

One-time award for registered graduate student at an accredited academic institution in North America in field of interest of AVS. Must submit a two-page summary of the research planned or in progress.
Academic/Career Areas Applied Sciences; Engineering/Technology; Physical Sciences and Math.
Award Scholarship for use in graduate years; not renewable. *Number:* 10. *Amount:* $1000–$1750.
Eligibility Requirements Applicant must be enrolled or expecting to enroll full-time at a four-year institution or university. Available to U.S. citizens.
Application Requirements Application, essay, references, transcript. *Deadline:* March 31.
Contact Ms. Angela Mulligan, Member Services
  Coordinator
  American Vacuum Society
  120 Wall Street, 32nd Floor
  New York, NY 10005-3993
  Phone: 212-248-0200
  Fax: 212-248-0245
  E-mail: angela@avs.org

GAEDE-LANGMUIR AWARD • 38

One-time award for scientists and engineers to encourage outstanding discoveries and inventions in the sciences and technology. Offered biannually. Must submit nomination letter, research highlights, biographical materials, and support letters.
Academic/Career Areas Applied Sciences; Engineering/Technology; Physical Sciences and Math.

Award Scholarship for use in graduate, or postgraduate years; not renewable. *Amount:* $10,000.
Eligibility Requirements Applicant must be enrolled or expecting to enroll at an institution or university. Available to U.S. citizens.
Application Requirements Application, references, transcript. *Deadline:* March 31.
Contact Ms. Angela Mulligan, Member Services
  Coordinator
  American Vacuum Society
  120 Wall Street, 32nd Floor
  New York, NY 10005-3993
  Phone: 212-248-0200
  Fax: 212-248-0245

JOHN A. THORNTON MEMORIAL AWARD AND LECTURE • 39

One-time award for scientists and engineers to recognize outstanding research or technological innovation in the fields of thin films, plasma processing, and related topics. Must have made a pioneering contribution in science or technology.
Academic/Career Areas Applied Sciences; Engineering/Technology; Physical Sciences and Math.
Award Scholarship for use in graduate, or postgraduate years; not renewable. *Amount:* $10,000.
Eligibility Requirements Applicant must be enrolled or expecting to enroll at an institution or university. Available to U.S. citizens.
Application Requirements Application, references, transcript. *Deadline:* March 31.
Contact Ms. Angela Mulligan, Member Services
  Coordinator
  American Vacuum Society
  120 Wall Street, 32nd Floor
  New York, NY 10005-3993
  Phone: 212-248-0200
  Fax: 212-248-0245

MEDARD W. WELCH AWARD • 40

One-time award for scientists and engineers who have accomplished outstanding theoretical experimental research within past 10 years. Must submit nomination letter, research highlights, biographical materials, and supporting letters.
Academic/Career Areas Applied Sciences; Engineering/Technology; Physical Sciences and Math.
Award Scholarship for use in graduate, or postgraduate years; not renewable. *Amount:* $10,000.
Eligibility Requirements Applicant must be enrolled or expecting to enroll at an institution or university. Applicant or parent of applicant must have employment or volunteer experience in designated career field. Available to U.S. citizens.

Application Requirements Application. *Deadline:* March 31.

Contact Ms. Angela Mulligan, Member Services Coordinator
American Vacuum Society
120 Wall Street, 32nd Floor
New York, NY 10005-3993
Phone: 212-248-0200
Fax: 212-248-0245

NELLIE YEOH WHETTEN AWARD • 41

One-time award for outstanding female graduate student in sciences and technologies of interest to the AVS. Nominee must be registered graduate student in an accredited academic institution in North America.

Academic/Career Areas Applied Sciences; Engineering/Technology; Physical Sciences and Math.

Award Scholarship for use in graduate years; not renewable. *Number:* 1. *Amount:* $1500.

Eligibility Requirements Applicant must be enrolled or expecting to enroll at a four-year institution or university and female. Available to U.S. citizens.

Application Requirements Application, references, transcript. *Deadline:* March 31.

Contact Ms. Angela Mulligan, Member Services Coordinator
American Vacuum Society
120 Wall Street, 32nd Floor
New York, NY 10005-3993
Phone: 212-248-0200
Fax: 212-248-0245

PETER MARK MEMORIAL AWARD • 42

One-time award for young scientist or engineer who has contributed outstanding theoretical or experimental work, at least part of which was published in the Journal of Vacuum Science and Technology. Must be under the age of thirty-six.

Academic/Career Areas Applied Sciences; Engineering/Technology; Physical Sciences and Math.

Award Scholarship for use in graduate, or postgraduate years; not renewable. *Number:* 1. *Amount:* $6500.

Eligibility Requirements Applicant must be age 35 or under and enrolled or expecting to enroll at an institution or university. Available to U.S. citizens.

Application Requirements Application. *Deadline:* March 31.

Contact Ms. Angela Mulligan, Member Services Coordinator
American Vacuum Society
120 Wall Street, 32nd Floor
New York, NY 10005-3993
Phone: 212-248-0200
Fax: 212-248-0245

RUSSELL AND SIGURD VARIAN FELLOWSHIP • 43

One-time award to recognize and encourage excellence in graduate studies in vacuum science. Must be full-time graduate student in North America. Must include two-page summary of research plan and two letters of recommendation.

Academic/Career Areas Applied Sciences; Engineering/Technology; Physical Sciences and Math.

Award Scholarship for use in graduate years; not renewable. *Amount:* $1500.

Eligibility Requirements Applicant must be enrolled or expecting to enroll full-time at an institution or university. Available to U.S. citizens.

Application Requirements Application, essay, references, transcript. *Deadline:* March 31.

Contact Ms. Angela Mulligan, Member Services Coordinator
American Vacuum Society
120 Wall Street, 32nd Floor
New York, NY 10005-3993
Phone: 212-248-0200
Fax: 212-248-0245

AMERICAN WATER WORKS ASSOCIATION
http://www.awwa.org

AMERICAN WATER WORKS ASSOCIATION/ABEL WOLMAN FELLOWSHIP • 44

One fellowship for graduate students pursuing advanced training and research in field related to water supply and treatment. Application must include curriculum and research plans. One $20,000 fellowship renewable for second year.

Academic/Career Areas Applied Sciences; Biology; Engineering/Technology; Natural Resources.

Award Fellowship for use in graduate years; renewable. *Number:* 1. *Amount:* $20,000–$40,000.

Eligibility Requirements Applicant must be enrolled or expecting to enroll at an institution or university. Available to U.S. and non-U.S. citizens.

American Water Works Association (continued)

Application Requirements Application, references, test scores, transcript, dissertation plans, proposed curriculum of study. *Deadline:* January 15.

Contact Annette Carabetta, Scholarship
Coordinator
American Water Works Association
6666 Quincy Avenue
Denver, CO 80235
Phone: 303-347-6206
Fax: 303-794-6303
E-mail: acarabetta@awwa.org

AMERICAN WATER WORKS ASSOCIATION/ HOLLY A. CORNELL SCHOLARSHIP • 45

One scholarship for female and/or minority students researching water supply and treatment. Applicant must submit GRE scores, proposed curriculum of studies, and career objectives. One-time award of $5000 for master's degree study.

Academic/Career Areas Applied Sciences; Biology; Engineering/Technology; Natural Resources.

Award Scholarship for use in graduate years; not renewable. *Number:* 1. *Amount:* $5000.

Eligibility Requirements Applicant must be enrolled or expecting to enroll at an institution or university. Available to U.S. and non-U.S. citizens.

Application Requirements Application, references, test scores, transcript, proposed curriculum of study, career objectives. *Deadline:* January 15.

Contact Annette Carabetta, Scholarship
Coordinator
American Water Works Association
6666 Quincy Avenue
Denver, CO 80235
Phone: 303-347-6206
Fax: 303-794-6303
E-mail: acarabetta@awwa.org

AMERICAN WATER WORKS ASSOCIATION/ LARSON AQUATIC RESEARCH SUPPORT SCHOLARSHIP • 46

Two scholarships for applicants pursuing an advanced degree relating to public drinking water. For study at institution in Canada, Guam, Mexico, Puerto Rico, or U.S. Must include educational plans. Must submit resume, GRE scores, and plan of study. One-time awards of $5000 for Masters student recipient and $7000 for Ph.D. student recipient.

Academic/Career Areas Applied Sciences; Biology; Health and Medical Sciences; Natural Resources.

Award Scholarship for use in graduate years; not renewable. *Number:* 2. *Amount:* $5000–$7000.

Eligibility Requirements Applicant must be enrolled or expecting to enroll at an institution or university. Available to U.S. and non-U.S. citizens.

Application Requirements Application, resume, references, test scores, transcript, proposed curriculum of study, statement of educational plans. *Deadline:* January 15.

Contact Annette Carabetta, Scholarship
Coordinator
American Water Works Association
6666 Quincy Avenue
Denver, CO 80235
Phone: 303-347-6206
Fax: 303-794-6303
E-mail: acarabetta@awwa.org

AMERICAN WATER WORKS ASSOCIATION/ THOMAS R. CAMP MEMORIAL SCHOLARSHIP • 47

One scholarship for graduate research related to drinking water. Applicant must include a one-page statement of educational plans, career objectives, a two-page research proposal, GRE scores, and resume. One-time award of $5000.

Academic/Career Areas Applied Sciences; Biology; Health and Medical Sciences; Natural Resources.

Award Scholarship for use in graduate years; not renewable. *Number:* 1. *Amount:* $5000.

Eligibility Requirements Applicant must be enrolled or expecting to enroll at an institution or university. Available to U.S. and non-U.S. citizens.

Application Requirements Application, resume, references, test scores, transcript, educational plans, research plan. *Deadline:* January 15.

Contact Annette Carabetta, Scholarship
Coordinator
American Water Works Association
6666 Quincy Avenue
Denver, CO 80235
Phone: 303-347-6206
Fax: 303-794-6303
E-mail: acarabetta@awwa.org

ASSOCIATED WESTERN UNIVERSITIES, INC.
http://www.awu.org

ASSOCIATED WESTERN UNIVERSITIES FACULTY FELLOWSHIPS • 48

One-time award for faculty members of universities to contribute to research and development at a participating university. Submit application and references by February 1. Write for further information. Amount of award depends on recipient's salary.

Academic/Career Areas Applied Sciences; Chemical Engineering; Civil Engineering; Computer Science/ Data Processing; Earth Science; Engineering/ Technology; Mechanical Engineering; Meteorology/ Atmospheric Science; Nuclear Science; Physical Sciences and Math.

Award Fellowship for use in graduate years; not renewable. *Number:* 100–200.

Eligibility Requirements Applicant must be enrolled or expecting to enroll at a four-year institution or university. Applicant or parent of applicant must have employment or volunteer experience in teaching.

Application Requirements Application, references. *Deadline:* February 1.

Contact Programs Specialist
  Associated Western Universities, Inc.
  4190 South Highland Drive, Suite 211
  Salt Lake City, UT 84124-4234
  Phone: 801-273-8900
  Fax: 801-277-5632
  E-mail: info@awu.org

ASSOCIATED WESTERN UNIVERSITIES GRADUATE RESEARCH FELLOWSHIPS • 49

One-time award for graduate students to conduct thesis or dissertation research at a participating university. Submit application, transcript, and references by February 1. Write for further information.

Academic/Career Areas Applied Sciences; Chemical Engineering; Civil Engineering; Computer Science/Data Processing; Earth Science; Engineering/Technology; Mechanical Engineering; Meteorology/Atmospheric Science; Nuclear Science; Physical Sciences and Math.

Award Fellowship for use in graduate years; not renewable. *Number:* 200–300. *Amount:* $5000–$20,000.

Eligibility Requirements Applicant must be enrolled or expecting to enroll at an institution or university.

Application Requirements Application, references, transcript. *Deadline:* February 1.

Contact Programs Specialist
  Associated Western Universities, Inc.
  4190 South Highland Drive, Suite 211
  Salt Lake City, UT 84124-4234
  Phone: 801-273-8900
  Fax: 801-277-5632
  E-mail: info@awu.org

ASSOCIATED WESTERN UNIVERSITIES POSTGRADUATE FELLOWSHIP • 50

One-time award for postgraduates to participate in and contribute to research and technology at cooperating facilities. Designed to encourage the selection of a professional career in science or engineering. Submit transcript and references with application.

Academic/Career Areas Applied Sciences; Chemical Engineering; Civil Engineering; Computer Science/Data Processing; Earth Science; Electrical Engineering/Electronics; Engineering/Technology;

Mechanical Engineering; Meteorology/Atmospheric Science; Nuclear Science; Physical Sciences and Math.

Award Fellowship for use in postgraduate years; not renewable. *Number:* 200–300. *Amount:* $5000–$30,000.

Eligibility Requirements Applicant must be enrolled or expecting to enroll at an institution or university.

Application Requirements Application, references, transcript. *Deadline:* Continuous.

Contact Programs Specialist
  Associated Western Universities, Inc.
  4190 South Highland Drive, Suite 211
  Salt Lake City, UT 84124-4234
  Phone: 801-273-8900
  Fax: 801-277-5632
  E-mail: info@awu.org

CHEMICAL HERITAGE FOUNDATION
http://www.chemheritage.org

BECKMAN CENTER FOR THE HISTORY OF CHEMISTRY RESEARCH TRAVEL GRANTS AT THE CHEMICAL HERITAGE FOUNDATION • 51

Travel grants to interested individuals to make use of research resources of Beckman Center for History of Chemistry, Othmer Library of Chemical History, and associated facilities. Deadlines: February 1, May 1, August 1, and November 1. Submit proposal, curriculum vitae, and one letter of recommendation

Academic/Career Areas Applied Sciences; Business/Consumer Services; Chemical Engineering; History; Physical Sciences and Math.

Award Grant for use in graduate, or postgraduate years; not renewable. *Number:* 20–25. *Amount:* $500–$1000.

Eligibility Requirements Applicant must be enrolled or expecting to enroll at an institution or university. Available to U.S. and non-U.S. citizens.

Application Requirements Resume, references, research proposal, SP curriculum vitae.

Contact Tom Lassman, Historian
  Chemical Heritage Foundation
  315 Chestnut Street
  Philadelphia, PA 19106
  Phone: 215-925-2222
  Fax: 215-925-1954
  E-mail: travelgrants@chemheritage.org

DELAWARE VALLEY SPACE GRANT CONSORTIUM
http://www.delspace.org

NASA/DELAWARE VALLEY SPACE GRANT FELLOWSHIP • 52

DVSGC Graduate Student Fellowships are stipends for graduate students embarking on or involved in

Delaware Valley Space Grant Consortium (continued)

aerospace-related research, technology, or design. Students must be enrolled in a DVSGC affiliate member college or university. Must be a U.S. citizen.

Academic/Career Areas Applied Sciences; Aviation/ Aerospace; Chemical Engineering; Civil Engineering; Earth Science; Electrical Engineering/Electronics; Engineering/Technology; Engineering-Related Technologies; Mechanical Engineering; Meteorology/ Atmospheric Science; Physical Sciences and Math; Science, Technology and Society.

Award Fellowship for use in graduate years; not renewable. *Number:* 1–3. *Amount:* $15,000–$30,000.

Eligibility Requirements Applicant must be enrolled or expecting to enroll full-time at a four-year institution or university and studying in Delaware or Pennsylvania. Available to U.S. citizens.

Application Requirements Application, essay, references, transcript. *Deadline:* March 1.

Contact Sherry Rowland-Perry, Administrative
　　　　　Assistant, Bartol Research Institute
　　　　　Delaware Valley Space Grant Consortium
　　　　　104 Center Mall, Room 217, University of
　　　　　Delaware
　　　　　Newark, DE 19716-4793
　　　　　Phone: 302-831-1094
　　　　　Fax: 302-831-1843
　　　　　E-mail: desgc@bartol.udel.edu

FANNIE AND JOHN HERTZ FOUNDATION
http://www.hertzfoundation.org

FANNIE AND JOHN HERTZ FOUNDATION FELLOWSHIP
• 53

Award for graduate students of outstanding potential in the applied physical sciences. Stipend is $25,000 with up to $15,000 expenses at specified schools. Must have 3.75 GPA in last two undergraduate years. Renewable up to five years.

Academic/Career Areas Applied Sciences; Chemical Engineering; Civil Engineering; Computer Science/ Data Processing; Earth Science; Electrical Engineering/Electronics; Engineering/Technology; Mechanical Engineering; Meteorology/Atmospheric Science; Nuclear Science; Physical Sciences and Math.

Award Fellowship for use in graduate years; renewable. *Number:* 20–30. *Amount:* $25,000.

Eligibility Requirements Applicant must be enrolled or expecting to enroll full-time at an institution or university. Available to U.S. citizens.

Application Requirements Application, essay, interview, references, test scores, transcript. *Deadline:* November 2.

Contact Fannie and John Hertz Foundation
　　　　　2456 Research Drive
　　　　　Livermore, CA 94550
　　　　　Phone: 925-373-1642

FOUNDATION FOR SCIENCE AND DISABILITY
http://www.as.wvu.edu/~scidis/organize/fsd.html

GRANTS FOR DISABLED STUDENTS IN THE SCIENCES
• 54

Available to graduate students who are disabled. Awards are given for an assistive device or as financial support for scientific research. Undergraduate seniors may apply. One time award. Electronic application is available.

Academic/Career Areas Applied Sciences; Biology; Chemical Engineering; Civil Engineering; Computer Science/Data Processing; Electrical Engineering/ Electronics; Engineering/Technology; Health and Medical Sciences; Mechanical Engineering; Physical Sciences and Math.

Award Grant for use in graduate years; not renewable. *Number:* 1–3. *Amount:* $1000.

Eligibility Requirements Applicant must be enrolled or expecting to enroll at an institution or university. Applicant must be hearing impaired, learning disabled, physically disabled, or visually impaired. Available to U.S. and non-U.S. citizens.

Application Requirements Application, essay, references, transcript. *Deadline:* December 1.

Contact Richard Mankin, Grants Committee Chair
　　　　　Foundation for Science and Disability
　　　　　503 NW 89th Street
　　　　　Gainesville, FL 32607
　　　　　Phone: 352-374-5774
　　　　　Fax: 352-374-5781
　　　　　E-mail: rmankin@gainesville.usda.ufl.edu

HUDSON RIVER NATIONAL ESTUARINE RESEARCH RESERVE
http://www.ocm.nos.noaa/nerr/fellow.html

NATIONAL ESTUARINE RESEARCH RESERVE GRADUATE FELLOWSHIP PROGRAM
• 55

Program supports graduate student research in Hudson River tidal wetlands. Work must be part of student's thesis or dissertation work. May be funded for up to three years.

Academic/Career Areas Applied Sciences; Biology; Earth Science; Natural Resources; Natural Sciences; Social Sciences.

Award Fellowship for use in graduate years; not renewable. *Number:* up to 18. *Amount:* $17,500.

Eligibility Requirements Applicant must be enrolled or expecting to enroll full-time at a four-year institution or university. Available to U.S. and non-U.S. citizens.

Application Requirements References, transcript, research proposal. *Deadline:* November 1.

Contact Chuck Nieder, Research Coordinator
Hudson River National Estuarine
Research Reserve
c/o Bard College Field Station
Annandale, NY 12504
Phone: 845-758-7010
Fax: 845-758-7033
E-mail: wcnieder@gw.dec.state.ny.us

HUNTINGTON LIBRARY, ART COLLECTIONS, AND BOTANICAL GARDENS
http://www.huntington.org

HUNTINGTON RESEARCH AWARDS • 56

Award in the amount of $2000 per month. For tenured scholars, doctoral candidates, and non-tenured faculty members to help carry out significant research pertinent to the Huntington's collections. For work in the fields of American and British history, literature, art history, and history of science. Research must be conducted at the Huntington Library.

Academic/Career Areas Applied Sciences; Art History; History; Literature/English/Writing; Physical Sciences and Math.

Award Fellowship for use in graduate, or postgraduate years; not renewable. *Number:* up to 100. *Amount:* $2000–$10,000.

Eligibility Requirements Applicant must be enrolled or expecting to enroll at a four-year institution or university and studying in California. Available to U.S. and non-U.S. citizens.

Application Requirements Application, references. *Deadline:* December 15.

Contact Chair, Committee of Fellowships
Huntington Library, Art Collections, and
Botanical Gardens
1151 Oxford Road
San Marino, CA 91108

INTERNATIONAL DESALINATION ASSOCIATION
http://www.ida.bm

INTERNATIONAL DESALINATION ASSOCIATION SCHOLARSHIP • 57

Award to assist young engineers and scientists to further their education in subjects related to desalination. Provides assistance for graduate students with a minimum 3.0 GPA. One to three renewable awards of $3000 to $6000.

Academic/Career Areas Applied Sciences; Biology; Chemical Engineering; Civil Engineering; Electrical Engineering/Electronics; Engineering/Technology; Engineering-Related Technologies; Mechanical Engineering; Natural Sciences.

Award Scholarship for use in graduate years; renewable. *Number:* 1–3. *Amount:* $3000–$6000.

Eligibility Requirements Applicant must be enrolled or expecting to enroll full or part-time at an institution or university. Applicant must have 3.0 GPA or higher.

Application Requirements Application, photo, references, transcript. *Deadline:* Continuous.

Contact David Furukawa, Scholarship Chairman
International Desalination Association
13511 Willow Run Road
Poway, CA 92064
E-mail: davfuruk@aol.com

INTERNATIONAL DEVELOPMENT RESEARCH CENTER
http://www.idrc.ca/awards

IDRC DOCTORAL RESEARCH AWARD
• *See number 12*

INTERNATIONAL UNION FOR VACUUM SCIENCE, TECHNIQUE AND APPLICATIONS
http://www.iuvsta.org/welch.html

WELCH FOUNDATION SCHOLARSHIP • 58

One scholarship available to a promising scholar who wishes to contribute to the study of vacuum science techniques or their application in any field. Candidates should hold at least a bachelor's degree and plan to spend a year in a research lab in another country. Must submit curriculum vitae, two recommendations, and a research proposal. One-time award of $15,000. Information and application forms are available at the website.

Academic/Career Areas Applied Sciences; Chemical Engineering; Electrical Engineering/Electronics; Engineering/Technology.

Award Scholarship for use in graduate, or postgraduate years; not renewable. *Number:* 1. *Amount:* $15,000.

Eligibility Requirements Applicant must be enrolled or expecting to enroll full-time at an institution or university. Available to U.S. and non-U.S. citizens.

International Union for Vacuum Science, Technique and Applications (continued)

Application Requirements Application, autobiography, references, transcript. *Deadline:* April 15.

Contact Administrator
International Union for Vacuum Science, Technique and Applications
Nortel Networks, 3500 Carling Avenue
Nepean, ON K2H 8E9
Canada
Phone: 613-763-3285

METROPOLITAN MUSEUM OF ART
http://www.metmuseum.org

L.W. FROHLICH CHARITABLE TRUST FELLOWSHIP • 59

Two-year fellowship for conservators, art historians, or scientist who are at an advanced level in their training. Must have demonstrated a commitment to the examination and treatment of art objects. Submit resume, statement or purpose, proposed work schedule and letters of recommendation with application.

Academic/Career Areas Applied Sciences; Art History; Museum Studies.

Award Fellowship for use in graduate, or postgraduate years; renewable. *Amount:* $25,000.

Eligibility Requirements Applicant must be enrolled or expecting to enroll full-time at an institution or university and studying in New York. Available to U.S. and non-U.S. citizens.

Application Requirements Application, essay, resume, references, transcript. *Deadline:* January 3.

Contact Marcie Karp, Coordinator of Fellowships
Metropolitan Museum of Art
1000 Fifth Avenue
New York, NY 10028-0198
Phone: 212-650-2763
Fax: 212-396-5168
E-mail: marcie.karp@metmuseum.org

NASA IDAHO SPACE GRANT CONSORTIUM
http://www.uidaho.edu/nasa_isgc

NASA ID SPACE GRANT CONSORTIUM FELLOWSHIP PROGRAM • 60

NASA ISGC awards $6000 fellowships renewable for two years based upon GPA (above a 3.0), area of study (science/math/engineering or math/science education), full-time status, attending an Idaho institution, and graduate student proposal (relevant to NASA mission/goals). $6000 per academic year ($3000 each semester).

Academic/Career Areas Applied Sciences; Aviation/Aerospace; Biology; Chemical Engineering;

Computer Science/Data Processing; Earth Science; Education; Electrical Engineering/Electronics; Engineering/Technology; Health and Medical Sciences; Physical Sciences and Math; Science, Technology and Society.

Award Fellowship for use in graduate years; renewable. *Number:* 1–7. *Amount:* $6000.

Eligibility Requirements Applicant must be enrolled or expecting to enroll full-time at an institution or university and studying in Idaho. Applicant must have 3.0 GPA or higher. Available to U.S. citizens.

Application Requirements Application, essay, resume, references, test scores, transcript. *Deadline:* March 1.

Contact Dr. Jean Teasdale, Director
NASA Idaho Space Grant Consortium
NASA ISGC, University of Idaho, PO Box 441011
Moscow, ID 83844-1011
Phone: 208-885-6438
Fax: 208-885-6645
E-mail: isgc@uidaho.edu

NASA WYOMING SPACE GRANT CONSORTIUM
http://www.wyomingspacegrant.uwyo.edu

WYOMING NASA SPACE GRANT CONSORTIUM RESEARCH FELLOWSHIP • 61

Fellowship for graduate students. Principal objective of fellowship is to provide students with positive rewarding research experience. Awards can be used for summer or academic year research in Wyoming. Awards are to provide student salary for research done with a faculty supervisor. Award also provides tuition waiver of $3,000 a year. Quality of proposal and scientific merit of project are part of the selection criteria. Applicant must submit verification of U.S. citizenship. Minimum 3.0 GPA required.

Academic/Career Areas Applied Sciences; Aviation/Aerospace; Biology; Chemical Engineering; Civil Engineering; Earth Science; Electrical Engineering/Electronics; Engineering-Related Technologies; Materials Science, Engineering and Metallurgy; Mechanical Engineering; Natural Sciences; Physical Sciences and Math.

Award Fellowship for use in graduate years; renewable. *Number:* 1–4. *Amount:* $10,500–$11,500.

Eligibility Requirements Applicant must be enrolled or expecting to enroll full-time at an institution or university and studying in Wyoming. Applicant must have 3.0 GPA or higher. Available to U.S. citizens.

Application Requirements Application, essay, references, transcript, verification of citizenship. *Deadline:* February 1.

Contact Kathleen Harper, Project Coordinator
NASA Wyoming Space Grant Consortium
PO Box 3905, University of Wyoming
Laramie, WY 82071-3905
Phone: 307-766-2862
Fax: 307-766-2852
E-mail: wy.spacegrant@uwyo.edu

NATIONAL MILK PRODUCERS FEDERATION
http://www.nmpf.org

NATIONAL MILK PRODUCERS FEDERATION NATIONAL DAIRY LEADERSHIP SCHOLARSHIP PROGRAM
• See number 5

NATIONAL SCIENCE FOUNDATION
http://www.nsf.gov/grfp

NATIONAL SCIENCE FOUNDATION GRADUATE RESEARCH FELLOWSHIPS • 62

Awarded for graduate study leading to research-based master's, or doctoral degrees in the fields of science, mathematics, and engineering. Awards are also made for work toward a research-based Ph.D. in science education that requires a science competence comparable to that for Ph.D. candidates in those disciplines. Award is renewable. Deadline early November.

Academic/Career Areas Applied Sciences; Biology; Earth Science; Education; Engineering/Technology; Meteorology/Atmospheric Science; Physical Sciences and Math.

Award Fellowship for use in graduate years; renewable. *Number:* up to 900. *Amount:* up to $25,500.

Eligibility Requirements Applicant must be enrolled or expecting to enroll full-time at an institution or university. Available to U.S. citizens.

Application Requirements Application, essay, references, test scores, transcript. *Deadline:* November 1.

Contact Oak Ridge Associated Universities
National Science Foundation
PO Box 3010
Oak Ridge, TN 37831-3010
Phone: 865-241-4300
Fax: 865-241-4513
E-mail: nsfgrfp@orau.gov

NOVARTIS FOUNDATION
http://wwwl.novartisfound.org.uk/bursary.htm

NOVARTIS FOUNDATION BURSARY SCHEME
• See number 20

ARCHAEOLOGY

AMERICAN CENTER OF ORIENTAL RESEARCH
http://www.bu.edu/acor

HARRELL FAMILY FELLOWSHIP • 63

Award to support graduate student for participation in ACOR-supported archaeological project which has passed an academic review process, or ACOR-funded archaeological research project.

Academic/Career Areas Archaeology.

Award Fellowship for use in graduate years; not renewable. *Number:* 1. *Amount:* $1500.

Eligibility Requirements Applicant must be enrolled or expecting to enroll at an institution or university. Available to U.S. and non-U.S. citizens.

Application Requirements Application, references, transcript. *Deadline:* February 1.

Contact Dr. Donald Keller, Assistant Director
American Center of Oriental Research
656 Beacon Street, 5th Floor
Boston, MA 02215-2010
Phone: 617-353-6571
Fax: 617-353-6575
E-mail: acor@bu.edu

KRESS FELLOWSHIP IN THE ART AND ARCHAEOLOGY OF JORDAN • 64

Three- to six-month fellowships for pre-doctoral students completing dissertation research in an art historical topic. Includes art history, archaeology, architectural history, and in some cases classical studies. Must be U.S. citizen or foreign national who has matriculated at U.S. institution. Subject to funding.

Academic/Career Areas Archaeology; Architecture; Art History.

Award Fellowship for use in graduate years; not renewable. *Number:* 1. *Amount:* $14,000.

Eligibility Requirements Applicant must be enrolled or expecting to enroll at an institution or university. Available to U.S. and non-U.S. citizens.

Application Requirements Application, references, transcript. *Deadline:* February 1.

Contact Dr. Donald Keller, Assistant Director
American Center of Oriental Research
656 Beacon Street, 5th Floor
Boston, MA 02215-2010
Phone: 617-353-6571
Fax: 617-353-6575
E-mail: acor@bu.edu

NATIONAL ENDOWMENT FOR THE HUMANITIES POST-DOCTORAL RESEARCH FELLOWSHIPS • 65

Four to six month fellowships for post-doctoral scholars. Must be U.S. citizen or foreign national

Archaeology

American Center of Oriental Research (continued)

living in U.S. for three years preceding application. Fields of research include modern and classical languages, linguistics, literature, history, jurisprudence, philosophy, archeology, religion, ethics and the arts.

Academic/Career Areas Archaeology; Art History; Arts; Foreign Language; History; Law/Legal Services; Literature/English/Writing; Religion/Theology.

Award Fellowship for use in postgraduate years; not renewable. *Number:* 1. *Amount:* $20,000.

Eligibility Requirements Applicant must be enrolled or expecting to enroll at an institution or university. Available to U.S. and non-U.S. citizens.

Application Requirements Application, references. *Deadline:* February 1.

Contact Dr. Donald Keller, Assistant Director
American Center of Oriental Research
656 Beacon Street, 5th Floor
Boston, MA 02215-2010
Phone: 617-353-6571
Fax: 617-353-6575
E-mail: acor@bu.edu

AMERICAN RESEARCH INSTITUTE IN TURKEY (ARIT)
http://www.mec.sas.upenn.edu/ARIT

ILSE AND GEORGE HANFMANN FELLOWSHIP • 66

For Nationals of Republic of Turkey who are advanced graduate students or PhD's to study/research broad (US or elsewhere) in archaeology and related fields for three months up to one year.

Academic/Career Areas Archaeology.

Award Fellowship for use in graduate, or postgraduate years; not renewable. *Number:* up to 3. *Amount:* $5000–$15,000.

Eligibility Requirements Applicant must be enrolled or expecting to enroll full-time at an institution or university. Available to citizens of countries other than the U.S. or Canada.

Application Requirements Application, essay, financial need analysis, references, transcript. *Deadline:* March 29.

Contact Antony Greenwood, Director, American
Research Institute in Turkey
American Research Institute in Turkey
(ARIT)
Uvez Sokak, No. 5, Arnavutkoy, 80820
Istanbul
Turkey
Phone: 90-212-257-8111
Fax: 90-212-257-8369
E-mail: gwood@boun.edu.tr

KRESS/ARIT PREDOCTORAL FELLOWSHIP IN THE HISTORY OF ART AND ARCHAEOLOGY • 67

Award to support advanced dissertation research necessitating a period of study in Turkey. Eligible fields include history of art and architecture from antiquity to present, and archaeology. Open to U.S. citizens and students matriculating at a U.S. or Canadian college or university. One-time award of $15,000 for one academic year; shorter periods of time also possible. Must submit three letters of recommendation. Application deadline: November 15.

Academic/Career Areas Archaeology; Architecture; Art History.

Award Fellowship for use in graduate years; not renewable. *Number:* 1–4. *Amount:* $4000–$15,000.

Eligibility Requirements Applicant must be enrolled or expecting to enroll full-time at an institution or university. Available to U.S. and non-U.S. citizens.

Application Requirements Application, essay, references, transcript, research permit. *Deadline:* November 15.

Contact Nancy Leinwand, Administrator
American Research Institute in Turkey
(ARIT)
University of Pennsylvania Museum
Philadelphia, PA 19104-6324
Phone: 215-898-3474
Fax: 215-898-0657
E-mail: leinwand@sas.upenn.edu

AMERICAN SCHOOLS OF ORIENTAL RESEARCH (ASOR)
http://www.asor.org

MESOPOTAMIAN FELLOWSHIP • 68

Award for one three- to six-month period of research. Primarily for field research in ancient Mesopotamian civilization carried out in Middle East, but other research projects such as museum or archival research related to Mesopotamian studies may also be considered. One-time award of $7000. Deadline: February 1. Must be a member of ASOR.

Academic/Career Areas Archaeology; History; Social Sciences.

Award Fellowship for use in graduate, or postgraduate years; not renewable. *Number:* 1. *Amount:* $7000.

Eligibility Requirements Applicant must be enrolled or expecting to enroll at an institution or university. Applicant or parent of applicant must be member of American Schools of Oriental Research. Available to U.S. and non-U.S. citizens.

Application Requirements Application, references, transcript. *Deadline:* February 1.

Contact Program Coordinator
American Schools of Oriental Research
(ASOR)
656 Beacon Street, 5th Floor
Boston, MA 02215
Phone: 617-353-6570
Fax: 617-353-6675
E-mail: asor@bu.edu

W.F. ALBRIGHT INSTITUTE OF ARCHAEOLOGICAL RESEARCH - JAMES A. MONTGOMERY FELLOW AND RESEARCH COORDINATOR • 69

One-time award for pre-doctoral students and post-doctoral scholars specializing in Near East archaeology, geography, history, and biblical studies. Research period is for 10 months. Recipient is expected to assist the Albright Director in planning and implementing the Ernest S. Frerichs Program for Albright Fellows. Application deadline: October 12.

Academic/Career Areas Archaeology; Geography; History; Religion/Theology.

Award Fellowship for use in postgraduate years; not renewable. *Amount:* $14,000.

Eligibility Requirements Applicant must be enrolled or expecting to enroll at an institution or university and studying in Ohio. Available to U.S. citizens.

Application Requirements Application. *Deadline:* October 12.

Contact Dr. John R. Spencer, AIAR, Department of Religious Studies
American Schools of Oriental Research
(ASOR)
20700 North Park Boulevard
University Heights, OH 44118
Phone: 216-397-4705
Fax: 216-397-4478
E-mail: spencer@jcu.edu

W.F. ALBRIGHT INSTITUTE OF ARCHAEOLOGICAL RESEARCH GEORGE A. BARTON FELLOWSHIP • 70

Five month fellowship open to seminarians, predoctoral students and recent Ph.D. recipients specializing in Near Eastern archaeology, geography, history and Biblical Studies. $7000 award includes stipend, room and half board at the Institute in Jerusalem. Application deadline: October 12.

Academic/Career Areas Archaeology; Geography; History; Religion/Theology.

Award Fellowship for use in postgraduate years; not renewable. *Number:* 1. *Amount:* $7000.

Eligibility Requirements Applicant must be enrolled or expecting to enroll at an institution or university.

Application Requirements Application. *Deadline:* October 12.

Contact Dr. John R. Spencer, W. F. Albright
Institute of Archaeological Research
American Schools of Oriental Research
(ASOR)
20700 North Park Boulevard
University Heights, OH 44118
Phone: 216-397-4705
Fax: 216-397-4478
E-mail: spencer@jcu.edu

W.F. ALBRIGHT INSTITUTE OF ARCHAEOLOGICAL RESEARCH/NATIONAL ENDOWMENT OF THE HUMANITIES FELLOWSHIPS • 71

Two awards for scholars holding a Ph.D. or equivalent as of January 1, 2002 who are U.S. citizens or alien residents residing in the U.S. for the last three years. Research project must have a clear humanities focus. Residence at the Institute in Jerusalem is preferred. Research period is for 4 to 12 months; stipend varies with the duration of the fellowship. Application deadline: October 12.

Academic/Career Areas Archaeology; Art History; History; Literature/English/Writing; Religion/Theology; Social Sciences.

Award Fellowship for use in postgraduate years; not renewable. *Number:* 2. *Amount:* up to $30,000.

Eligibility Requirements Applicant must be enrolled or expecting to enroll at an institution or university. Available to U.S. and non-U.S. citizens.

Application Requirements Application. *Deadline:* October 12.

Contact Dr. John R. Spencer, W. F. Albright
Institute of Archaeological Research
American Schools of Oriental Research
(ASOR)
20700 North Park Boulevard
University Heights, OH 44118
Phone: 216-397-4705
Fax: 216-397-4478
E-mail: spencer@jcu.edu

W.F. ALRBIGHT INSTITUTE OF ARCHAEOLOGICAL RESEARCH SAMUEL H. KRESS JOINT ATHENS-JERUSALEM FELLOWSHIP • 72

Predoctoral research fellowship for students who are U.S. citizens or North American citizens studying at U.S. universities and specializing in art history, architecture, archaeology or classical studies. Research is to be conducted at the American School of Classical Studies in Athens and at the W. F. Albright Institute of Archaeological Research in Jerusalem. Stipend is $7,600; remainder is for room and board at the two institutions. Research period is for 10 months—5 months in Athens and 5 months in Jerusalem. Application deadline: October 26.

Archaeology

American Schools of Oriental Research (ASOR) (continued)

Academic/Career Areas Archaeology; Architecture; Art History; Social Sciences.

Award Fellowship for use in postgraduate years; not renewable. *Number:* 1. *Amount:* $14,300.

Eligibility Requirements Applicant must be enrolled or expecting to enroll at an institution or university. Available to U.S. and Canadian citizens.

Application Requirements Application. *Deadline:* October 26.

Contact Dr. John R. Spencer, W. F. Albright
Institute of Archaeological Research
American Schools of Oriental Research
(ASOR)
20700 North Park Boulevard
University Heights, OH 44118
Phone: 216-397-4705
Fax: 216-397-4478
E-mail: spencer@jcu.edu

ARCHAEOLOGICAL INSTITUTE OF AMERICA
http://www.archaeological.org

ARCHAEOLOGICAL INSTITUTE OF AMERICA/ OLIVIA JAMES TRAVELING FELLOWSHIP • 73

Fellowship for Ph.D. candidates or recent recipients of the Ph.D. Must be U.S. citizen or permanent resident. May be used to study classics, sculpture, architecture, archaeology, or history. Merit-based award. Award is $22,000 for one year of research relating to archaeology in the Mediterranean area.

Academic/Career Areas Archaeology; Architecture; Art History; Historic Preservation and Conservation; History; Humanities.

Award Fellowship for use in graduate, or postgraduate years; not renewable. *Number:* 1. *Amount:* $22,000.

Eligibility Requirements Applicant must be enrolled or expecting to enroll at an institution or university. Available to U.S. citizens.

Application Requirements Application, essay, references, transcript. *Deadline:* November 1.

Contact Executive Assistant
Archaeological Institute of America
656 Beacon Street
Boston, MA 02215-2006
Phone: 617-353-9361
Fax: 617-353-6550
E-mail: aiaexa@bu.edu

HARRIET AND LEON POMERANCE FELLOWSHIP • 74

Fellowship available to a U.S. or Canadian citizen for scholarly project related to Aegean Bronze Age archaeology. Applicant must be a doctoral student or recent Ph.D. Preference given to projects requiring travel to the Mediterranean. Deadline: November 1.

Academic/Career Areas Archaeology; Architecture; Art History; Historic Preservation and Conservation; History; Humanities.

Award Fellowship for use in graduate, or postgraduate years; not renewable. *Number:* 1. *Amount:* $4000.

Eligibility Requirements Applicant must be enrolled or expecting to enroll full-time at an institution or university. Applicant must have 3.5 GPA or higher. Available to U.S. and Canadian citizens.

Application Requirements Application, essay, references, transcript. *Deadline:* November 1.

Contact Executive Assistant
Archaeological Institute of America
656 Beacon Street
Boston, MA 02215-2006
Phone: 617-353-9361
Fax: 617-353-6550
E-mail: aiaexa@bu.edu

HELEN M. WOODRUFF FELLOWSHIP • 75

One award to conduct archaeological research at the American Academy in Rome. Award for advanced graduate students and holders of the Ph.D. Must be U.S. citizen or permanent resident. Applications should be made directly to the American Academy in Rome.

Academic/Career Areas Archaeology; Architecture; Art History; Historic Preservation and Conservation; History; Humanities.

Award Fellowship for use in graduate, or postgraduate years; not renewable. *Number:* 1.

Eligibility Requirements Applicant must be enrolled or expecting to enroll full-time at an institution or university. Applicant must have 3.5 GPA or higher. Available to U.S. citizens.

Application Requirements Application, essay, references, transcript. *Deadline:* November 1.

Contact Executive Assistant
Archaeological Institute of America
656 Beacon Street
Boston, MA 02215-2006
Phone: 617-353-9361
Fax: 617-353-6550
E-mail: aiaexa@bu.edu

WOODRUFF TRAVELING FELLOWSHIP • 76

Fellowship for the support of dissertation archeological research in Italy (outside of Sicily and Magna Graecia) and the western Mediterranean. Applicants must have completed all requirements for the Ph.D. except the dissertation. Preference will be given to field-oriented projects. Ph.D. students working on any time period are eligible.

Academic/Career Areas Archaeology; Art History; Historic Preservation and Conservation; History; Humanities.

Award Fellowship for use in graduate years; not renewable. *Amount:* $6000.

Eligibility Requirements Applicant must be enrolled or expecting to enroll full-time at an institution or university.

Application Requirements Application, essay, references, transcript. *Deadline:* November 1.

Contact Executive Assistant
Archaeological Institute of America
656 Beacon Street
Boston, MA 02215-2006
Phone: 617-353-9361
Fax: 617-353-6550
E-mail: aiaexa@bu.edu

ASSOCIATION FOR WOMEN IN SCIENCE EDUCATIONAL FOUNDATION
http://www.awis.org

ASSOCIATION FOR WOMEN IN SCIENCE PREDOCTORAL FELLOWSHIP • 77

The Predoctoral Fellowship is for women completing a Ph.D. in the natural or social sciences or engineering. Applicants must have passed their qualifying exam and be within two years of completion of the Ph.D. U.S. citizens may study anywhere; others only in the U.S. The success rate is about 10%.

Academic/Career Areas Archaeology; Biology; Computer Science/Data Processing; Earth Science; Engineering/Technology; Materials Science, Engineering and Metallurgy; Meteorology/Atmospheric Science; Natural Sciences; Physical Sciences and Math; Social Sciences.

Award Fellowship for use in graduate years; not renewable. *Number:* 5–15. *Amount:* $100–$1000.

Eligibility Requirements Applicant must be enrolled or expecting to enroll full-time at an institution or university and female. Available to U.S. and non-U.S. citizens.

Application Requirements Application, essay, resume, references, transcript. *Deadline:* January 25.

Contact Barbara Filner, President
Association for Women in Science
Educational Foundation
7008 Richard Drive
West Bethesda, MD 20817-4838
E-mail: awisedfd@awis.org

GEOLOGICAL SOCIETY OF AMERICA
http://www.geosociety.org

CLAUDE C. ALBRITTON JR. SCHOLARSHIPS • 78

Awards for graduate students in the earth sciences and archaeology. Contact for application procedures and requirements. Must be a member of the Geological Society of America in order to apply.

Academic/Career Areas Archaeology; Earth Science.

Award Scholarship for use in graduate years; not renewable. *Number:* 1–2. *Amount:* $500–$1000.

Eligibility Requirements Applicant must be enrolled or expecting to enroll at an institution or university. Applicant or parent of applicant must be member of Geological Society of America. Available to U.S. and non-U.S. citizens.

Application Requirements Application, references. *Deadline:* February 1.

Contact Ms. Leah Carter, Program Officer, Grants, Awards and Medals
Geological Society of America
3300 Penrose Place, PO Box 9140
Boulder, CO 80301-9140
Phone: 303-357-1037
Fax: 303-357-1070
E-mail: lcarter@geosociety.org

L.S.B. LEAKEY FOUNDATION
http://www.leakeyfoundation.org

RESEARCH GRANTS • 79

Leakey Foundation was formed to further research into human origins. Recent priorities include research into archaeology, and human paleontology, behavior of the now human primates, especially the great apes; and into the behavioral ecology of contemporary hunters gatherers. Other areas in geology, molecular biology and human genetics have been funded occasionally. Application deadlines: January 5 and August 15.

Academic/Career Areas Archaeology; Natural Sciences; Science, Technology and Society.

Award Grant for use in graduate, or postgraduate years; not renewable. *Number:* 50–70. *Amount:* $5000–$20,000.

Eligibility Requirements Applicant must be enrolled or expecting to enroll full or part-time at an institution or university. Available to U.S. and non-U.S. citizens.

Application Requirements Application, references.

Contact Alan Almquist, Program and Grants Officer
L.S.B. Leakey Foundation
PO Box 29346, 1002A O'Reilly Avenue
San Francisco, CA 94129
Phone: 415-561-4646
Fax: 415-561-4647
E-mail: alan@leakeyfoundation.org

LAMBDA ALPHA NATIONAL COLLEGIATE HONORS SOCIETY FOR ANTHROPOLOGY
http://www.lambdaalpha.com

LAMBDA ALPHA NATIONAL COLLEGIATE HONOR SOCIETY FOR ANTHROPOLOGY SCHOLARSHIP AWARD • 80

Award to give academic recognition to graduate students and to encourage them to pursue a career in anthropology. Must submit statement of future plans. Deadline: March 1. Must include six copies of essay. Minimum GPA 2.5. For further information applicant should contact the Lambda Alpha Faculty sponsor at their own department.

Academic/Career Areas Archaeology.

Award Scholarship for use in graduate years; not renewable. *Number:* 1. *Amount:* $5000.

Eligibility Requirements Applicant must be enrolled or expecting to enroll full or part-time at an institution or university. Applicant must have 2.5 GPA or higher. Available to U.S. and non-U.S. citizens.

Application Requirements Application, autobiography, essay, references, transcript. *Deadline:* March 1.

Contact Lambda Alpha Faculty Sponsor
Lambda Alpha National Collegiate
Honors Society for Anthropology
Department of Anthropology, Ball State
University
Muncie, IN 47306-1099
Phone: 765-285-1575
E-mail: 01bkswartz@bsuvc.bsu.edu

LAMBDA ALPHA NATIONAL COLLEGIATE HONOR SOCIETY OF ANTHROPOLOGY GRADUATE RESEARCH GRANT • 81

Applicant must be a member of Lambda Alpha and be enrolled in the graduate program in their department for at least one-year. They must have selected their thesis advisor and have formally formed their thesis and dissertation committee. There must be an agreement with the advisor to be responsible for the dispersal of the grant funds to the student (possibly in conjunction with the school's research office). A statement to this effect from the advisor would be required with the application. For further information the applicant should contact the Lambda Alpha faculty sponsor at their own department.

Academic/Career Areas Archaeology.

Award Grant for use in graduate years; not renewable. *Number:* 1. *Amount:* $2000–$6000.

Eligibility Requirements Applicant must be enrolled or expecting to enroll full or part-time at an institution or university. Available to U.S. and non-U.S. citizens.

Application Requirements Application, autobiography, references, transcript, proposal approved by chairperson of thesis committee. *Deadline:* March 1.

Contact Lambda Alpha Faculty Sponsor
Lambda Alpha National Collegiate
Honors Society for Anthropology
Department of Anthropology, Ball State
University
Muncie, IN 47306-1099
Phone: 765-285-1575
E-mail: 01bkswartz@bsuvc.bsu.edu

METROPOLITAN MUSEUM OF ART
http://www.metmuseum.org

ANDREW W. MELLON FELLOWSHIPS • 82

One-time fellowship for graduate and postgraduate students. Open to citizens from all countries. Deadline: November 1. Available for promising young scholars with commendable research projects related to the Museum's collections.

Academic/Career Areas Archaeology; Architecture; Art History; Arts.

Award Fellowship for use in graduate, or postgraduate years; not renewable. *Amount:* $25,000–$30,000.

Eligibility Requirements Applicant must be enrolled or expecting to enroll at an institution or university and studying in New York. Available to U.S. and non-U.S. citizens.

Application Requirements Essay, resume, references, transcript. *Deadline:* November 1.

Contact Marcie Karp, Coordinator of Fellowships
Metropolitan Museum of Art
1000 Fifth Avenue
New York, NY 10028
Phone: 212-650-2763
Fax: 212-396-5168
E-mail: marcie.karp@metmuseum.org

CHESTER DALE FELLOWSHIPS • 83

Fellowships available to individuals whose fields of study are related to the fine arts of the Western World. Awards are for research at the Metropolitan Museum of Art and last from three months to one year. Prefer American citizens under age 40.

Academic/Career Areas Archaeology; Architecture; Art History; Arts.

Award Fellowship for use in graduate, or postgraduate years; not renewable. *Amount:* $25,000–$30,000.

Eligibility Requirements Applicant must be enrolled or expecting to enroll at an institution or university and studying in New York. Available to U.S. citizens.

Application Requirements Essay, resume, references, transcript. *Deadline:* November 1.

Contact Marcie Karp, Coordinator of Fellowships
Metropolitan Museum of Art
1000 Fifth Avenue
New York, NY 10028
Phone: 212-650-2763
Fax: 212-396-5168
E-mail: marcie.karp@metmuseum.org

PITT RIVERS MUSEUM

JAMES A. SWAN FUND • 84

Grants are given to students and established researchers, regardless of nationality. Research must pertain to archaeological and anthropological related fields. Preference will be given to proposals concentrating on the Later Stone Age prehistory of southern Africa and the study of the contemporary Bushman and Pygmy peoples of Africa.

Academic/Career Areas Archaeology.

Award Grant for use in graduate, or postgraduate years; not renewable.

Eligibility Requirements Applicant must be enrolled or expecting to enroll at an institution or university. Available to U.S. and non-U.S. citizens.

Application Requirements Application, references, budget, curriculum vitae. *Deadline:* March 1.

Contact Secretary of the Swan Fund
Pitt Rivers Museum
University of Oxford South Parks Road
Oxford OX1 3PP
United Kingdom

WINTERTHUR MUSEUM, GARDEN, AND LIBRARY
http://www.winterthur.org

LOIS F. MCNEIL DISSERTATION RESEARCH FELLOWSHIPS • 85

Fellowship for doctoral candidates in departments of history, art history, American studies, African-American history, anthropology, folklore, historic preservation, and related fields. Applicants must have completed course work, passed qualifying exams, fulfilled language requirements, and have an approved prospectus. Two nine-month or four semester-length fellowships will be awarded. Recipients expected to be in residence at Winterthur and to use the term of fellowship researching in Winterthur library and museum collections. For more information: www.winterthur.org.

Academic/Career Areas Archaeology; Architecture; Art History; Arts; History.

Award Fellowship for use in graduate years; not renewable. *Number:* 2–4. *Amount:* $6500–$13,000.

Eligibility Requirements Applicant must be enrolled or expecting to enroll full-time at an

institution or university and studying in Delaware. Available to U.S. and non-U.S. citizens.

Application Requirements Application, references. *Deadline:* January 15.

Contact Pat Elliott, Advanced Studies Coordinator
Winterthur Museum, Garden, and Library
Advanced Studies Office
Winterthur, DE 19735
Phone: 302-888-4649
Fax: 302-888-4870
E-mail: pelliott@winterthur.org

ARCHITECTURE

AMERICAN ARCHITECTURAL FOUNDATION
http://www.archfoundation.org

AMERICAN INSTITUTE OF ARCHITECTS/ AMERICAN HOSPITAL ASSOCIATION FELLOWSHIP IN HEALTH FACILITIES DESIGN • 86

Award for graduate study or independent graduate-level study or research in health facilities design. Must be citizen of the U.S., Canada, or Mexico. Write for further requirements. Deadline: January 30. Co-sponsored by AIA and AHA.

Academic/Career Areas Architecture.

Award Fellowship for use in graduate years; not renewable.

Eligibility Requirements Applicant must be enrolled or expecting to enroll full-time at a four-year institution or university. Available to U.S. and non-U.S. citizens.

Application Requirements Application, essay, references, transcript. *Deadline:* January 30.

Contact Mary Felber, Director of Scholarship Programs
American Architectural Foundation
1735 New York Avenue, NW
Washington, DC 20006-5292
Phone: 202-626-7511
Fax: 202-626-7420
E-mail: mfelber@archfoundation.org

AMERICAN ASSOCIATION OF UNIVERSITY WOMEN (AAUW) EDUCATIONAL FOUNDATION
http://www.aauw.org

AAUW EDUCATIONAL FOUNDATION SELECTED PROFESSIONS FELLOWSHIPS • 87

One-time award for women pursuing full-time graduate degrees in one of the designated degree programs where women's participation traditionally has been low. Must be U.S. citizens or permanent residents. Application fee: $25-$30.

American Association of University Women (AAUW) Educational Foundation (continued)

Academic/Career Areas Architecture; Business/ Consumer Services; Computer Science/Data Processing; Electrical Engineering/Electronics; Engineering/Technology; Engineering-Related Technologies; Health and Medical Sciences; Law/Legal Services; Physical Sciences and Math.

Award Scholarship for use in graduate years; not renewable. *Number:* 35–45. *Amount:* $5000–$20,000.

Eligibility Requirements Applicant must be enrolled or expecting to enroll full-time at an institution or university and female. Available to U.S. citizens.

Application Requirements Application, autobiography, essay, resume, references, test scores, transcript. *Deadline:* January 10.

Contact Customer Service
American Association of University
Women (AAUW) Educational
Foundation
2201 North Dodge Street
Iowa City, IA 52243-4030
Phone: 319-337-1716
E-mail: aauw@act.org

AMERICAN CENTER OF ORIENTAL RESEARCH
http://www.bu.edu/acor

KRESS FELLOWSHIP IN THE ART AND ARCHAEOLOGY OF JORDAN
• See number 64

AMERICAN INSTITUTE OF ARCHITECTS, NEW YORK CHAPTER
http://www.aiany.org

AIA, NEW YORK CHAPTER, STEWARDSON KEEFE LEBRAUN TRAVEL GRANT • 88

Three to five grants will be awarded to encourage travel within North America and overseas in furtherance of the architectural education and professional development of the recipients. Applicants must be a U.S. citizen with a degree in architecture, a full time practitioner, either licensed or unlicensed. For more information go to the web site (http://www.aiany.org).

Academic/Career Areas Architecture.

Award Grant for use in graduate, or postgraduate years; not renewable. *Number:* 3–5. *Amount:* up to $6000.

Eligibility Requirements Applicant must be enrolled or expecting to enroll at an institution or university. Available to U.S. citizens.

Application Requirements Application, resume, outline of travel plans. *Deadline:* April 19.

Contact Manager of Special Programs and
Communications
American Institute of Architects, New
York Chapter
200 Lexington Avenue, 6th Floor
New York, NY 10016
Phone: 212-683-0023
Fax: 212-696-5022

AIA, NEW YORK CHPATER, ARNOLD W. BRUNNER GRANT • 89

A $15,000 grant will be awarded for an advanced study in area of architectural investigation, which will effectively contribute to the knowledge, teaching, or practice of the art and science of architecture. The proposed investigation is to result in a final written work, design project, research paper or other form of presentation. Applicants must be U.S. citizen engaged in the profession of architecture or a related field and has a professional background more advanced than five years of architectural training or its equivalent. For more information go to the web site (http://www.aiany.org).

Academic/Career Areas Architecture.

Award Grant for use in postgraduate years; not renewable. *Number:* 1. *Amount:* $15,000.

Eligibility Requirements Applicant must be enrolled or expecting to enroll at an institution or university. Available to U.S. citizens.

Application Requirements Application, references, proposal. *Fee:* $25. *Deadline:* November 1.

Contact Manager of Special Programs and
Communications
American Institute of Architects, New
York Chapter
200 Lexington Avenue, 6th Floor
New York, NY 10016
Phone: 212-683-0023
Fax: 212-696-5022

AMERICAN RESEARCH INSTITUTE IN TURKEY (ARIT)
http://www.mec.sas.upenn.edu/ARIT

KRESS/ARIT PREDOCTORAL FELLOWSHIP IN THE HISTORY OF ART AND ARCHAEOLOGY
• See number 67

AMERICAN SCHOOLS OF ORIENTAL RESEARCH (ASOR)
http://www.asor.org

W.F. ALRBIGHT INSTITUTE OF ARCHAEOLOGICAL RESEARCH SAMUEL H. KRESS JOINT ATHENS-JERUSALEM FELLOWSHIP
• See number 72

ARCHAEOLOGICAL INSTITUTE OF AMERICA
http://www.archaeological.org

ARCHAEOLOGICAL INSTITUTE OF AMERICA/ OLIVIA JAMES TRAVELING FELLOWSHIP
• See number 73

HARRIET AND LEON POMERANCE FELLOWSHIP
• See number 74

HELEN M. WOODRUFF FELLOWSHIP
• See number 75

ASIAN CULTURAL COUNCIL
http://www.asianculturalcouncil.org

ASIAN ART AND RELIGION FELLOWSHIPS • 90

One-time award for American scholars, specialists, and artists to conduct research and projects in Asia involving the analysis of religion and the arts. Graduate scholars are eligible to apply. Write for details.

Academic/Career Areas Architecture; Art History; Arts; Historic Preservation and Conservation; Museum Studies; Performing Arts; Religion/Theology.

Award Fellowship for use in graduate years; not renewable. *Number:* 1–2.

Eligibility Requirements Applicant must be enrolled or expecting to enroll at an institution or university. Available to U.S. citizens.

Application Requirements Application. *Deadline:* February 1.

Contact Ralph Samuelson, Director
Asian Cultural Council
437 Madison Avenue
New York, NY 10022-7001
Phone: 212-812-4300
Fax: 212-812-4299
E-mail: acc@accny.org

ASIAN CULTURAL COUNCIL FELLOWSHIPS • 91

One-time fellowships of less than one year duration for American artists or scholars to pursue projects in designated fields of the arts, humanities, and religion. Contact the Asian Cultural Council for specific guidelines.

Academic/Career Areas Architecture; Area/Ethnic Studies; Art History; Arts; Foreign Language; Humanities; Museum Studies; Performing Arts; Religion/Theology.

Award Fellowship for use in graduate years; not renewable.

Eligibility Requirements Applicant must be enrolled or expecting to enroll at an institution or university and must have an interest in art or music/singing. Available to U.S. citizens.

Application Requirements Application. *Deadline:* February 1.

Contact Ralph Samuelson, Director
Asian Cultural Council
437 Madison Avenue
New York, NY 10022-7001
Phone: 212-812-4300
Fax: 212-812-4299
E-mail: acc@accny.org

ASIAN CULTURAL COUNCIL HUMANITIES FELLOWSHIPS • 92

One-time awards for American graduate scholars to pursue projects concerning the visual and performing arts of Asia. Projects should emphasize designated fields of the arts, humanities, and religion. Write for more information.

Academic/Career Areas Architecture; Area/Ethnic Studies; Art History; Arts; Foreign Language; Humanities; Museum Studies; Performing Arts; Religion/Theology.

Award Fellowship for use in graduate years; not renewable. *Amount:* $5000–$10,000.

Eligibility Requirements Applicant must be enrolled or expecting to enroll at an institution or university. Available to U.S. citizens.

Application Requirements Application. *Deadline:* February 1.

Contact Ralph Samuelson, Director
Asian Cultural Council
437 Madison Avenue
New York, NY 10022-7001
Phone: 212-812-4300
Fax: 212-812-4299
E-mail: acc@accny.org

ATHENAEUM OF PHILADELPHIA
http://www.philaathenaeum.org

CHARLES E. PETERSON FELLOWSHIP • 93

Research in early American architecture and building technology prior to 1860. Application deadline is March 30.

Academic/Career Areas Architecture; Historic Preservation and Conservation; Landscape Architecture.

Award Fellowship for use in postgraduate years; not renewable. *Number:* 5–10. *Amount:* $1250–$5000.

Eligibility Requirements Applicant must be enrolled or expecting to enroll full or part-time at an institution or university. Available to U.S. and non-U.S. citizens.

Athenaeum of Philadelphia (continued)

Application Requirements Application, references. *Deadline:* March 30.

Contact Roger W. Moss, Executive Director
Athenaeum of Philadelphia
219 South 6th Street
Philadelphia, PA 19106
Phone: 215-925-2688
Fax: 215-925-3755
E-mail: rwmoss@philaathenaeum.org

DUMBARTON OAKS
http://www.doaks.org

DUMBARTON OAKS PROJECT GRANTS • 94

Grants assist with scholarly projects in Byzantine studies, Pre-Columbian studies, and landscape architecture. Support is generally for archaeological research, recovery, recording, and analysis of materials that would otherwise be lost. Must submit application letter, curriculum vitae, proposal, budget, and timetable. One-time award of $3000-$10,000. Contact for further details.

Academic/Career Areas Architecture; Area/Ethnic Studies; Art History; History; Humanities; Landscape Architecture.

Award Grant for use in graduate, or postgraduate years; not renewable. *Amount:* $3000–$10,000.

Eligibility Requirements Applicant must be enrolled or expecting to enroll at an institution or university. Available to U.S. and non-U.S. citizens.

Application Requirements Application, essay, resume, references. *Deadline:* November 1.

Contact Office of the Director
Dumbarton Oaks
1703 32nd Street, NW
Washington, DC 20007-2961
Phone: 202-339-6410

RESIDENTIAL FELLOWSHIP IN BYZANTINE, PRE-COLUMBIAN, AND LANDSCAPE ARCHITECTURE STUDIES • 95

Residential fellowships to pursue Byzantine studies, Pre-Columbian studies, and studies in landscape architecture. Junior fellows must have fulfilled preliminary requirements for Ph.D. and be working on dissertation. Other fellows must have conferred degrees or have established themselves in their field and wish to pursue their own research. One-time award. Must submit application letter, proposal, and personal and professional data, transcripts, and letters of recommendation. Contact for details.

Academic/Career Areas Architecture; Area/Ethnic Studies; Art History; Arts; History; Humanities; Landscape Architecture; Religion/Theology.

Award Fellowship for use in graduate, or postgraduate years; not renewable. *Amount:* $18,550–$39,300.

Eligibility Requirements Applicant must be enrolled or expecting to enroll full-time at an institution or university. Available to U.S. and non-U.S. citizens.

Application Requirements Application, essay, resume, references, transcript. *Deadline:* November 1.

Contact Office of the Director
Dumbarton Oaks
1703 32nd Street, NW
Washington, DC 20007-2961
Phone: 202-339-6410

DURRANT FOUNDATION
http://www.durrant.com/foundation.html

DURRANT FOUNDATION SCHOLARSHIP/INTERNSHIP • 96

The Durrant Foundation scholarship/internship program offers young professionals financial assistance during academic study and an internship, in one of Durrant's offices, in which to learn while working in the disciplines of architecture, engineering, construction management, and interior design. Minimum 3.0 GPA required.

Academic/Career Areas Architecture; Civil Engineering; Criminal Justice/Criminology; Electrical Engineering/Electronics; Interior Design; Landscape Architecture; Mechanical Engineering.

Award Scholarship for use in graduate years; renewable. *Number:* 10–12. *Amount:* $1500–$25,000.

Eligibility Requirements Applicant must be enrolled or expecting to enroll full-time at an institution or university. Applicant must have 3.0 GPA or higher. Available to U.S. and non-U.S. citizens.

Application Requirements Application, interview, portfolio, resume, references.

Contact Marilyn Eisenberg, National Public
Relations Director
Durrant Foundation
426 North 44th Street, #300
Phoenix, AZ 85008
Phone: 602-275-6830
Fax: 602-244-2915
E-mail: meisenberg@durrant.com

GEM CONSORTIUM
http://www.nd.edu/~gem

GEM PH.D. ENGINEERING FELLOWSHIP
• *See number 9*

HAGLEY MUSEUM AND LIBRARY
http://www.hagley.org

HAGLEY MUSEUM AND LIBRARY
GRANTS-IN-AID • 97

Award for graduate research using the Hagley Library and Museum. Research must be relevant to the Library's collections. Submit curriculum vitae and five-page proposal of research project. Maximum amount of award $2400, minimum $350 per week. Deadlines: March 29, June 28, and October 31.

Academic/Career Areas Architecture; Art History; Arts; Humanities; Landscape Architecture; Museum Studies.

Award Fellowship for use in graduate, or postgraduate years; renewable. *Number:* 15–20. *Amount:* up to $2400.

Eligibility Requirements Applicant must be enrolled or expecting to enroll at an institution or university. Available to U.S. and non-U.S. citizens.

Application Requirements Application.

Contact Carol Ressler Lockman, Hagley Center
Coordinator
Hagley Museum and Library
PO Box 3630
Wilmington, DE 19807-0630
Phone: 302-658-2400
Fax: 302-655-3188
E-mail: crl@udel.edu

HAGLEY/WINTERTHUR FELLOWSHIPS IN ARTS
AND INDUSTRIES • 98

Residential fellowship to use both the collections of the Hagley Museum and Library and the Winterthur Library. Must submit five-page proposal description. Write for more information. Maximum award of $3000. Deadline: December 1.

Academic/Career Areas Architecture; Art History; Arts; Humanities; Landscape Architecture; Museum Studies.

Award Fellowship for use in graduate, or postgraduate years; renewable. *Amount:* up to $3000.

Eligibility Requirements Applicant must be enrolled or expecting to enroll at an institution or university and must have an interest in art. Available to U.S. and non-U.S. citizens.

Application Requirements Application, essay, references. *Deadline:* December 1.

Contact Carol Ressler Lockman, Hagley Center
Coordinator
Hagley Museum and Library
PO Box 3630
Wilmington, DE 19807-0630
Phone: 302-658-2400
Fax: 302-655-3188
E-mail: crl@udel.edu

HENRY BELIN DU PONT DISSERTATION
FELLOWSHIP • 99

One-time award for graduate students to conduct research at the Hagley Museum and Library. Research must be relevant to the Library's collections. Submit curriculum vitae, dissertation prospectus, transcript, and two letters of recommendation. Deadline: November 15.

Academic/Career Areas Architecture; Art History; Arts; Humanities; Landscape Architecture; Museum Studies.

Award Fellowship for use in graduate years; not renewable. *Amount:* up to $6000.

Eligibility Requirements Applicant must be enrolled or expecting to enroll at an institution or university and studying in Delaware. Available to U.S. and non-U.S. citizens.

Application Requirements Application, essay, references, transcript. *Deadline:* November 15.

Contact Carol Ressler Lockman, Hagley Center
Coordinator
Hagley Museum and Library
PO Box 3630
Wilmington, DE 19807-0630
Phone: 302-658-2400 Ext. 243
Fax: 302-655-3188
E-mail: crl@udel.edu

INTERNATIONAL DEVELOPMENT
RESEARCH CENTER
http://www.idrc.ca/awards

AGROPOLIS
• *See number 10*

JOHN F. KENNEDY LIBRARY
FOUNDATION
http://www.jfklibrary.org

KENNEDY RESEARCH GRANTS • 100

One-time grants for students and scholars doing research on any topic relating to the Kennedy period. Must include ten-page writing sample, project budget and a vita. See application for further details. Preference given to Ph.D. dissertation research, research in recently opened or unused collections, and recent dissertations being prepared for publication. Deadlines for spring grants, March 15; for fall grants, August 15.

Academic/Career Areas Architecture; Criminal Justice/Criminology; Economics; Education; History; Humanities; Library Sciences; Literature/English/Writing; Political Science; Social Sciences.

Award Grant for use in graduate years; not renewable. *Number:* 15–20. *Amount:* $500–$2500.

John F. Kennedy Library Foundation (continued)

Eligibility Requirements Applicant must be enrolled or expecting to enroll at an institution or university and studying in Massachusetts. Available to U.S. citizens.

Application Requirements Application, driver's license, essay, financial need analysis, references, transcript.

Contact Grant and Fellowship Coordinator
John F. Kennedy Library Foundation
Columbia Point
Boston, MA 02125
Phone: 617-929-1200

METROPOLITAN MUSEUM OF ART
http://www.metmuseum.org

ANDREW W. MELLON FELLOWSHIPS
• *See number 82*

CHESTER DALE FELLOWSHIPS
• *See number 83*

SENSE OF SMELL INSTITUTE
http://www.senseofsmell.org

TOVA FELLOWSHIP • 101

Annual $10,000 award. Purpose of award is to encourage students at the thesis stage of a masters or doctoral program to pursue the study of the sense of smell and the positive psychological effects of aroma on human behavior.

Academic/Career Areas Architecture; Arts; Biology; Education; Food Science/Nutrition; Health and Medical Sciences; Heating, Air-Conditioning, and Refrigeration Mechanics; Interior Design; Science, Technology and Society; Social Sciences; Sports-related; Therapy/Rehabilitation.

Award Fellowship for use in graduate years; not renewable. *Number:* 1. *Amount:* $10,000.

Eligibility Requirements Applicant must be enrolled or expecting to enroll full or part-time at an institution or university. Available to U.S. and non-U.S. citizens.

Application Requirements Application, resume, references, transcript. *Deadline:* May 25.

Contact Theresa Molnar, Executive Director
Sense of Smell Institute
145 East 32nd Street
New York, NY 10016-6002
Phone: 212-725-2755 Ext. 228
Fax: 212-779-9072
E-mail: info@senseofsmell.org

SKIDMORE, OWINGS, AND MERRILL FOUNDATION
http://www.som.com

CHICAGO INSTITUTE OF ARCHITECTURE AND URBANISM AWARD • 102

Award for the best unpublished essay or research paper addressing the physical development of American cities. Papers are nominated by accredited U.S. graduate programs in architecture, urban design, or physical planning. Faculty and students in these fields may apply. One-time award of $5000. Submit curriculum vitae. Contact for deadlines.

Academic/Career Areas Architecture.

Award Prize for use in graduate, or postgraduate years; not renewable. *Number:* 1. *Amount:* up to $5000.

Eligibility Requirements Applicant must be enrolled or expecting to enroll full or part-time at an institution or university. Available to U.S. and non-U.S. citizens.

Application Requirements Essay, curriculum vitae.

Contact Lisa Westerfield, Administrative Director
Skidmore, Owings, and Merrill
Foundation
224 South Michigan Avenue, Suite 1000
Chicago, IL 60604
Phone: 312-427-4202
Fax: 312-360-4545
E-mail: somfoundation@som.com

URBAN DESIGN TRAVELING FELLOWSHIP PROGRAM • 103

Award for architect with a bachelor's in architecture, landscape architecture, or urban design, and a master's concentrating in urban design to be used to broaden recipient's knowledge of the design of modern, high-density cities. Must be a student or recent graduate and must be nominated by faculty of U.S. degree-granting institution. Submit curriculum vitae, proposed travel itinerary, portfolio, and signed copyright release. Contact for further information.

Academic/Career Areas Architecture; Landscape Architecture.

Award Fellowship for use in graduate years; not renewable. *Number:* 1. *Amount:* $7500.

Eligibility Requirements Applicant must be enrolled or expecting to enroll full-time at an institution or university. Available to U.S. and non-U.S. citizens.

Application Requirements Interview, portfolio, references, travel plan.

Contact Lisa Westerfield, Administrative Director
Skidmore, Owings, and Merrill Foundation
224 South Michigan Avenue, Suite 1000
Chicago, IL 60604
Phone: 312-427-4202
Fax: 312-360-4545
E-mail: somfoundation@som.com

SOCIETY OF ARCHITECTURAL HISTORIANS
http://www.sah.org

CARROLL L.V. MEEKS FELLOWSHIP • 104

One-time award for one graduate student of art history, architecture, or historic preservation to participate in the Society of Architectural Historians annual domestic tour. Submit essay, references, and resume with application. Applicants must be student members of the Society.

Academic/Career Areas Architecture; Art History; Historic Preservation and Conservation.

Award Fellowship for use in graduate years; not renewable. *Number:* 1. *Amount:* $1000–$2000.

Eligibility Requirements Applicant must be enrolled or expecting to enroll full-time at an institution or university. Applicant or parent of applicant must be member of Society of Architectural Historians. Available to U.S. and non-U.S. citizens.

Application Requirements Application, essay, resume, references. *Deadline:* July 15.

Contact Angela FitzSimmons, Director of Programs
Society of Architectural Historians
1385 North Astor Street
Chicago, IL 60610-2144
Phone: 312-573-1365
Fax: 312-573-1141
E-mail: afitzsimmons@sah.org

EDILIA AND FRANCOIS-AUGUSTE DE MONTEQUIN FELLOWSHIP IN IBERIAN AND LATIN AMERICAN ARCHITECTURE • 105

Award to be used for research at the graduate level. Research must focus on Spanish, Portuguese, or Ibero-American architecture. Submit curriculum vitae with application. One-time $2,000 award to junior scholar. Bi-annual $6,000 award to senior scholar.

Academic/Career Areas Architecture; Art History.

Award Fellowship for use in graduate, or postgraduate years; not renewable. *Number:* 2. *Amount:* $2000–$6000.

Eligibility Requirements Applicant must be enrolled or expecting to enroll at an institution or university. Available to U.S. and non-U.S. citizens.

Application Requirements Application, essay, references, curriculum vitae. *Deadline:* November 15.

Contact Angela FitzSimmons, Director of Programs
Society of Architectural Historians
1385 North Astor Street
Chicago, IL 60610-2144
Phone: 312-573-1365
Fax: 312-573-1141
E-mail: afitzsimmons@sah.org

ROSANN S. BERRY ANNUAL MEETING FELLOWSHIP • 106

Award for an advanced graduate student of architecture or art history to attend the annual meeting of the Society of Architectural Historians. Submit essay, references, and resume with application. One-time award of $500. Applicants must be student members of the Society.

Academic/Career Areas Architecture; Art History.

Award Fellowship for use in graduate years; not renewable. *Number:* 1. *Amount:* $500.

Eligibility Requirements Applicant must be enrolled or expecting to enroll at an institution or university. Applicant or parent of applicant must be member of Society of Architectural Historians. Available to U.S. and non-U.S. citizens.

Application Requirements Application, essay, resume, references. *Deadline:* November 15.

Contact Angela FitzSimmons, Director of Programs
Society of Architectural Historians
1385 North Astor Street
Chicago, IL 60610-2144
Phone: 312-573-1365
Fax: 312-573-1141
E-mail: afitzsimmons@sah.org

SPIRO KOSTOF ANNUAL MEETING FELLOWSHIP • 107

Award for an advanced graduate student of architecture or architectural history to attend the annual meeting of the Society of Architectural Historians. Submit essay, references, and resume with application. One-time award of $500. Applicants must be student members of the Society.

Academic/Career Areas Architecture.

Award Fellowship for use in graduate years; not renewable. *Number:* 1. *Amount:* $500.

Eligibility Requirements Applicant must be enrolled or expecting to enroll full-time at an institution or university. Applicant or parent of applicant must be member of Society of Architectural Historians. Available to U.S. and non-U.S. citizens.

Society of Architectural Historians (continued)

Application Requirements Application, essay, references. *Deadline:* November 15.

Contact Angela FitzSimmons, Director of Programs
Society of Architectural Historians
1365 North Astor Street
Chicago, IL 60610-2144
Phone: 312-573-1365
Fax: 312-573-1141
E-mail: afitzsimmons@sah.org

STEEDMAN GOVERNING COMMITTEE
http://www.arch.wustl.edu

STEEDMAN TRAVELING FELLOWSHIP IN ARCHITECTURE • 108

Award of $30,000 to graduates of accredited professional architecture programs for architectural study for nine months in foreign countries. Must be employed in, or have completed one year's experience in an architectural office. Candidates may apply up to eight years after receiving their professional degrees, regardless of age. Submit competition entry, research proposal, curriculum vitae, and photocopies of work along with application and $75 application fee by January 2. Contact for more information.

Academic/Career Areas Architecture.

Award Fellowship for use in postgraduate years; not renewable. *Number:* 1. *Amount:* $30,000.

Eligibility Requirements Applicant must be enrolled or expecting to enroll full-time at an institution or university. Applicant or parent of applicant must have employment or volunteer experience in designated career field. Available to U.S. and non-U.S. citizens.

Application Requirements Application. *Fee:* $75. *Deadline:* January 2.

Contact Shannon Platt, Coordinator, Steedman
Competition
Steedman Governing Committee
Washington University in St. Louis,
School of Architecture
St. Louis, MO 63130-4899
Phone: 314-935-6293
Fax: 314-935-8520
E-mail: steedman@arch.wustl.edu

SWANN FOUNDATION FUND
http://www.lcweb.loc.gov/rr/print/swann/swann_foundation.html

SWANN FOUNDATION FUND FELLOWSHIP • 109

Fellowship to assist ongoing scholarly research and writing projects in the field of caricature and cartoon. Applicant must be a candidate for MA or Ph.D. degree in a North American university, working toward the completion of a dissertation or thesis, or must be engaged in postgraduate research within three years of receiving an MA or Ph.D. Must make use of the collections at the Library of Congress and be in residence there for at least two weeks of the award period. Submit proposal with application materials by February 15. Fellow must also deliver a public lecture on his/her work during the award period.

Academic/Career Areas Architecture; Area/Ethnic Studies; Art History; Arts; Education; Graphics/Graphic Arts/Printing; History; Humanities; Journalism; Literature/English/Writing; Museum Studies; Performing Arts.

Award Fellowship for use in graduate, or postgraduate years; not renewable. *Number:* 1. *Amount:* $15,000.

Eligibility Requirements Applicant must be enrolled or expecting to enroll full or part-time at an institution or university. Available to U.S. and non-U.S. citizens.

Application Requirements Application, essay, resume, references, transcript, visual materials, statement with budget. *Deadline:* February 15.

Contact Harry Katz, Head Curator
Swann Foundation Fund
Prints and Photographs Division, Library of Congress, 101 Independence Avenue, S.E.
Washington, DC 20540-4730
Phone: 202-707-8696
Fax: 202-707-1486
E-mail: swann@loc.gov

WINTERTHUR MUSEUM, GARDEN, AND LIBRARY
http://www.winterthur.org

LOIS F. MCNEIL DISSERTATION RESEARCH FELLOWSHIPS
• See number 85

NEH FELLOWSHIPS • 110

Fellowships for postgraduate students to conduct advanced residential research at Winterthur Library. Research must coincide with the Library's resources. Must be a U.S. resident or a non-resident living in the U.S. for at least three years prior to application. Visit website for details, www.winterthur.org.

Academic/Career Areas Architecture; Art History; Arts; Historic Preservation and Conservation; History; Home Economics; Interior Design; Landscape Architecture; Literature/English/Writing; Museum Studies; Travel/Tourism.

Award Fellowship for use in postgraduate years; not renewable. *Number:* 1–3. *Amount:* up to $30,000.

Eligibility Requirements Applicant must be enrolled or expecting to enroll full-time at an institution or university and studying in Delaware. Available to U.S. and non-U.S. citizens.

Application Requirements Application, essay, references. *Deadline:* January 15.

Contact Pat Elliott, Advanced Studies Coordinator
Winterthur Museum, Garden, and Library
Advanced Studies Office
Winterthur, DE 19735
Phone: 302-888-4649
Fax: 302-888-4870
E-mail: pelliott@winterthur.org

WINTERTHUR RESEARCH FELLOWSHIPS • 111

One-time fellowships of $1500 per month for academic, museum, and independent scholars to use library archival materials for dissertation research and other study. Research must coincide with Winterthur's available resources. Submit application, essay, and references. Visit website for more details, www.winterthur.org. Research must take place at the Winterthur Library.

Academic/Career Areas Architecture; Art History; Arts; Historic Preservation and Conservation; History; Home Economics; Interior Design; Landscape Architecture; Literature/English/Writing; Museum Studies; Travel/Tourism.

Award Fellowship for use in graduate, or postgraduate years; not renewable. *Number:* 15–20. *Amount:* $1500.

Eligibility Requirements Applicant must be enrolled or expecting to enroll full-time at an institution or university and studying in Delaware. Available to U.S. and non-U.S. citizens.

Application Requirements Application, essay, references. *Deadline:* January 15.

Contact Pat Elliott, Advanced Studies Coordinator
Winterthur Museum, Garden, and Library
Advanced Studies Office
Winterthur, DE 19735
Phone: 302-888-4649
Fax: 302-888-4870
E-mail: pelliott@winterthur.org

AREA/ETHNIC STUDIES

AFRICAN AMERICAN SUCCESS FOUNDATION, INC.
http://www.blacksuccessfoundation.org

LYDIA DONALDSON TUTT-JONES MEMORIAL AWARD • 112

Grant to support research that identifies attitudinal and behavioral contributors to African- American academic success. Purpose is to increase the body of knowledge about African- American students who are excelling in school to help replicate that success for others. Focus may be upon student or parental variables, or both. This award is not restricted to school settings. Other organizations are eligible. Faculty/professionals from all institutions are eligible.

Academic/Career Areas Area/Ethnic Studies; Education; Social Sciences.

Award Grant for use in graduate, or postgraduate years; not renewable. *Number:* 1. *Amount:* $1000.

Eligibility Requirements Applicant must be enrolled or expecting to enroll full or part-time at a four-year institution or university. Available to U.S. citizens.

Application Requirements Application, references, self-addressed stamped envelope, letter of interest, curriculum vitae, description of research project including timeline. *Deadline:* June 28.

Contact Dr. E. Carol Webster, President/CEO
African American Success Foundation, Inc.
4330 West Broward Boulevard, Suite H
Fort Lauderdale, FL 33317-3753
Phone: 954-792-1117
Fax: 954-792-9191
E-mail: drcarolwebster@
blacksuccessfoundation.org

AMERICAN COUNCIL OF LEARNED SOCIETIES (ACLS)
http://www.acls.org

AMERICAN COUNCIL OF LEARNED SOCIETIES GRANTS FOR EAST EUROPEAN STUDIES-DISSERTATION FELLOWSHIPS • 113

One-time award for doctoral candidates to support dissertation writing or research. Research must be in the fields of humanities or social science, and focused on Eastern Europe. Fellowships are to be used for work outside Eastern Europe. Must be U.S. citizen or permanent legal resident. Application deadline: November 1.

Academic/Career Areas Area/Ethnic Studies; Humanities; Social Sciences.

Award Fellowship for use in graduate years; not renewable. *Number:* up to 10. *Amount:* up to $15,000.

Eligibility Requirements Applicant must be enrolled or expecting to enroll at an institution or university. Available to U.S. citizens.

Application Requirements Application. *Deadline:* November 1.

Contact Office of Fellowships and Grants
American Council of Learned Societies (ACLS)
228 East 45th Street
New York, NY 10017-3398
Fax: 212-949-8058
E-mail: grants@acls.org

AMERICAN COUNCIL OF TEACHERS OF RUSSIAN
http://www.actr.org

TITLE VIII RESEARCH SCHOLAR AND COMBINED RESEARCH AND LANGUAGE STUDY PROGRAM • 114

Scholarships and grants for U.S. students (graduate and post-graduate) seeking to study languages or conduct research in the former Soviet Union and Eastern Europe. Applicants must be permanent residents of US. Deadlines: January 15 and October 1.

Academic/Career Areas Area/Ethnic Studies; Economics; Foreign Language; History; Humanities; International Studies; Law/Legal Services; Peace and Conflict Studies; Physical Sciences and Math; Social Services.

Award Fellowship for use in graduate, or postgraduate years; not renewable. *Number:* 20. *Amount:* $2500–$12,000.

Eligibility Requirements Applicant must be enrolled or expecting to enroll full-time at a four-year institution or university. Available to U.S. citizens.

Application Requirements Application, essay, financial need analysis, resume, references, transcript.

Contact Graham Hettlinger, Program Manager
American Council of Teachers of Russian
1776 Massachusetts Avenue NW, Suite 700
Washington, DC 20036
Phone: 202-833-7522
Fax: 202-833-7523
E-mail: hettlinger@actr.org

AMERICAN HISTORICAL ASSOCIATION
http://www.theaha.org

ALBERT J. BEVERIDGE GRANT FOR RESEARCH IN THE HISTORY OF THE WESTERN HEMISPHERE • 115

Supports research in the history of the Western hemisphere. Applicants must be members of the association; preference to junior scholars and Ph.D. candidates. The grants are intended to further research in progress and may not be used for tuition or partial salary replacement. Submit curriculum vitae, 750-word project statement, and one-page bibliography with application. Contact for deadline information.

Academic/Career Areas Area/Ethnic Studies; History; Humanities.

Award Grant for use in postgraduate years; not renewable. *Number:* 10–25. *Amount:* $100–$1000.

Eligibility Requirements Applicant must be enrolled or expecting to enroll at an institution or university. Applicant or parent of applicant must be member of American Historical Association.

Application Requirements Application, essay, curriculum vitae. *Deadline:* February 1.

Contact Administrative Assistant
American Historical Association
400 A Street, SE
Washington, DC 20003
Phone: 202-544-2422 Ext. 104
Fax: 202-544-8307
E-mail: aha@theaha.org

BERNADETTE E. SCHMITT GRANTS FOR RESEARCH IN EUROPEAN, AFRICAN, OR ASIAN HISTORY • 116

Supports research in the history of Europe, Africa, and Asia. Applicants must be members of the association; preference to junior scholars and Ph.D. candidates. The grants are intended to further research in progress and may not be used for tuition or partial salary replacement. Submit curriculum vitae, 750-word project statement, and one-page bibliography with application.

Academic/Career Areas Area/Ethnic Studies; History.

Award Grant for use in postgraduate years; not renewable.

Eligibility Requirements Applicant must be enrolled or expecting to enroll at an institution or university. Applicant or parent of applicant must be member of American Historical Association.

Application Requirements Application, essay, curriculum vitae. *Deadline:* September 15.

Contact Administrative Assistant
American Historical Association
400 A Street, SE
Washington, DC 20003
Phone: 202-544-2422 Ext. 104
Fax: 202-544-8307
E-mail: aha@theaha.org

AMERICAN INSTITUTE OF INDIAN STUDIES
http://www.indiastudies.org

AMERICAN INSTITUTE OF INDIAN STUDIES RESEARCH FELLOWSHIPS • 117

For U.S. citizen or foreign national enrolled or teaching full-time at a U.S. institution. For postdoctoral study in India by specialist in Indian studies. Application fee: $25. Deadline: July 1.

Academic/Career Areas Area/Ethnic Studies; Foreign Language.

Award Fellowship for use in postgraduate years; not renewable.

Eligibility Requirements Applicant must be enrolled or expecting to enroll at an institution or university. Available to U.S. and non-U.S. citizens.

Application Requirements Application. *Fee:* $25. *Deadline:* July 1.

Contact Administrator
American Institute of Indian Studies
1130 East 59th Street
Chicago, IL 60637
Phone: 773-702-8638
Fax: 773-702-6636
E-mail: aiis@uchicago.edu

ARCTIC INSTITUTE OF NORTH AMERICA
http://www.ucalgary.ca/aina

LORRAINE ALLISON SCHOLARSHIP • 118

One scholarship for any student enrolled at a Canadian university in a program of graduate study related to northern issues. Based on academic excellence and commitment to northern research. Submit two-page proposal, a complete curriculum vitae, and current funding sources. One-time award of $2000.

Academic/Career Areas Area/Ethnic Studies; Biology; Humanities; Social Sciences.

Award Scholarship for use in graduate years; not renewable. *Number:* 1. *Amount:* $2000.

Eligibility Requirements Applicant must be enrolled or expecting to enroll full-time at an institution or university.

Application Requirements References, transcript. *Deadline:* January 7.

Contact Executive Director
Arctic Institute of North America
University of Calgary, 2500 University
Drive NW
Calgary, AB T2N IN4
Canada
Phone: 403-220-7515
Fax: 403-282-4609
E-mail: wkjessen@ucalgary.ca

ASIAN CULTURAL COUNCIL
http://www.asianculturalcouncil.org

ASIAN CULTURAL COUNCIL FELLOWSHIPS
• *See number 91*

ASIAN CULTURAL COUNCIL HUMANITIES FELLOWSHIPS
• *See number 92*

CANADIAN NORTHERN STUDIES TRUST - ASSOCIATION OF CANADIAN UNIVERSITIES FOR NORTHERN STUDIES
http://www.cyberus.ca/~acuns

CANADIAN NORTHERN STUDIES TRUST STUDENTSHIPS IN NORTHERN STUDIES • 119

One-time award for Canadian citizens or permanent residents enrolled in a doctoral program at a Canadian university to cover one year of study. Candidate's educational program should include Canada's northern territories and adjacent regions. Preference given to those researching thesis or similar document. Supervisor's assessment of suitability should be forwarded under separate cover. Research must be done in northern Canada. Current application forms may be obtained from the ACUNS website.

Academic/Career Areas Area/Ethnic Studies.

Award Scholarship for use in graduate years; not renewable. *Number:* 1–3. *Amount:* $10,000.

Eligibility Requirements Applicant must be Canadian citizenship and enrolled or expecting to enroll full-time at an institution or university.

Application Requirements Application, references, transcript. *Deadline:* January 31.

Contact Sandra Malcolm, Executive Officer
Canadian Northern Studies Trust -
Association of Canadian Universities
for Northern Studies
405-17 York Street
Ottawa, ON K1N 9J6
Canada
Phone: 613-562-0515
Fax: 613-562-0533
E-mail: acuns@cyberus.ca

RESEARCH SUPPORT OPPORTUNITIES IN ARCTIC ENVIRONMENTAL STUDIES • 120

One-time award for Canadian citizens or permanent residents enrolled in graduate studies at a Canadian university in any physical and/or biological sciences. Preference will be given to Master's and doctoral students at an early stage in their programs, and to proposals for which a High Arctic Weather Station location is advantageous. Current applications can be obtained from the ACUNS website. Supervisor's assessment of suitability should be forwarded under separate cover.

Academic/Career Areas Area/Ethnic Studies; Biology; Physical Sciences and Math.

Award Scholarship for use in graduate years; not renewable. *Number:* 1–2.

Eligibility Requirements Applicant must be Canadian citizenship and enrolled or expecting to enroll full-time at an institution or university.

Canadian Northern Studies Trust - Association of Canadian Universities for Northern Studies (continued)

Application Requirements Application, references, transcript. *Deadline:* January 31.

Contact Sandra Malcolm, Executive Officer
Canadian Northern Studies Trust - Association of Canadian Universities for Northern Studies
405-17 York Street
Ottawa, ON K1N 9J6
Canada
Phone: 613-562-0515
Fax: 613-562-0533
E-mail: acuns@cyberus.ca

CENTER FOR HELLENIC STUDIES
http://www.chs.harvard.edu

CENTER FOR HELLENIC STUDIES FELLOWSHIPS • 121

One-time fellowships for postdoctoral scholars of ancient Greek studies. Contact the Center for Hellenic Studies for more information and deadline. Twelve awards of $21,000 to $24,000. Must submit detailed research proposal.

Academic/Career Areas Area/Ethnic Studies; Humanities; Social Sciences.

Award Fellowship for use in postgraduate years; not renewable. *Number:* 12. *Amount:* $21,000–$24,000.

Eligibility Requirements Applicant must be enrolled or expecting to enroll full-time at an institution or university. Available to U.S. and non-U.S. citizens.

Application Requirements Application, references, research proposal. *Deadline:* October 15.

Contact Fellowship Director
Center for Hellenic Studies
3100 Whitehaven Street, NW
Washington, DC 20008
Phone: 202-234-3738
Fax: 202-797-3745
E-mail: chs@fas.harvard.du

CHINA TIMES CULTURAL FOUNDATION

CHINA TIMES CULTURAL FOUNDATION DOCTORAL DISSERTATION RESEARCH IN CHINESE STUDIES SCHOLARSHIPS • 122

Award for doctoral candidates in Chinese Studies who are enrolled in a university in the U.S. or Canada. Include transcript, autobiography, essay, a project description in English and Chinese, and photo with application. Award primarily based on scholarly merit. One-time award of $10,000.

Academic/Career Areas Area/Ethnic Studies; Communications; Economics; Education; Foreign Language; History; Humanities; International Studies; Journalism; Peace and Conflict Studies; Political Science; Social Sciences.

Award Scholarship for use in graduate years; not renewable. *Number:* 8–10. *Amount:* $10,000.

Eligibility Requirements Applicant must be enrolled or expecting to enroll at an institution or university. Available to U.S. and non-U.S. citizens.

Application Requirements Application, autobiography, essay, photo, references, transcript. *Deadline:* June 30.

Contact China Times Cultural Foundation
136-39 41st Avenue, #1A
Flushing, NY 11355
Phone: 718-460-4900
Fax: 718-460-4900

DUMBARTON OAKS
http://www.doaks.org

BLISS PRIZE FELLOWSHIP IN BYZANTINE STUDIES • 123

Renewable award for college graduate or graduating senior from a U.S. or Canadian college or university or to American or Canadian citizens enrolled at non-north American universities or colleges, to pursue graduate studies in Byzantine civilization and culture. Must be graduate school applicant. Must have completed one year of ancient or medieval Greek and be nominated by scholastic adviser by October 15. Fellowship covers graduate school tuition and living expenses for two years. Additional $5000 available for summer travel. Submit writing sample, application letter, and personal and scholarly data. Contact for further details.

Academic/Career Areas Area/Ethnic Studies; Art History; Arts; History; Humanities; Religion/Theology.

Award Fellowship for use in graduate years; renewable. *Number:* 1.

Eligibility Requirements Applicant must be enrolled or expecting to enroll full-time at an institution or university. Available to U.S. and non-U.S. citizens.

Application Requirements Application, resume, references, transcript, writing sample. *Deadline:* November 1.

Contact Office of the Director
Dumbarton Oaks
1703 32nd Street, NW
Washington, DC 20007-2961
Phone: 202-339-6410

DUMBARTON OAKS PROJECT GRANTS
• *See number 94*

RESIDENTIAL FELLOWSHIP IN BYZANTINE,
PRE-COLUMBIAN, AND LANDSCAPE
ARCHITECTURE STUDIES
• *See number 95*

FREDERICK DOUGLASS INSTITUTE FOR AFRICAN AND AFRICAN-AMERICAN STUDIES
http://www.rochester.edu/college/aas

FREDERICK DOUGLAS POSTDOCTORAL
FELLOWSHIP • **124**

The Postdoctoral Fellowship is awarded to scholars who hold a Ph.D. degree in a field related to the African and African-American experience. It carries an annual stipend of $35,000 and supports the completion of a research project for one academic year. The Fellow will teach two courses (one per semester) in his or her area of specialization.

Academic/Career Areas Area/Ethnic Studies.

Award Fellowship for use in graduate years; renewable. *Amount:* $35,000.

Eligibility Requirements Applicant must be enrolled or expecting to enroll full-time at an institution or university. Available to U.S. and non-U.S. citizens.

Application Requirements Application, essay, resume, references, transcript, sample of published or unpublished writing on topic related to the proposal. *Deadline:* January 31.

Contact Associate Director for Research Fellowships
Frederick Douglass Institute for African
and African-American Studies
c/o University of Rochester
302 Morey Hall
Rochester, NY 14627
Phone: 585-275-7235
Fax: 585-256-2594
E-mail: fdi@troi.cc.rochester.edu

FREDERICK DOUGLASS INSTITUTE FOR AFRICAN
AND AFRICAN-AMERICAN STUDIES
PREDOCTORAL DISSERTATION FELLOWSHIP
• **125**

The Predoctoral Fellowship is awarded annually to a graduate student of any university who studies aspects of the African and African-American experience. This fellowship, which carries an annual stipend of $15,000, does not come with any teaching obligation, but will require the Fellow to work with the Institute's Director in organizing colloquium, lectures, and other events. The principal aim of this award is to expedite the complete of the Fellow's dissertation.

Academic/Career Areas Area/Ethnic Studies.

Award Fellowship for use in graduate years; renewable. *Number:* 1. *Amount:* $15,000.

Eligibility Requirements Applicant must be enrolled or expecting to enroll full-time at an institution or university. Available to U.S. and non-U.S. citizens.

Application Requirements Application, autobiography, essay, resume, references, transcript, sample chapter from the dissertation. *Deadline:* January 31.

Contact Associate Director for Research Fellowships
Frederick Douglass Institute for African
and African-American Studies
c/o University of Rochester
302 Morey Hall
Rochester, NY 14627
Phone: 585-275-7235
Fax: 585-256-2594
E-mail: fdi@troi.cc.rochester.edu

GERMAN ACADEMIC EXCHANGE SERVICE (DAAD)
http://www.daad.org

LEO BAECK INSTITUTE - DAAD GRANTS • **126**

One-time award to assist doctoral students and recent PhD's in research on history of German-speaking Jewry. Research may be conducted at Leo Baeck Institute in New York City or in Germany. Deadline: November 1.

Academic/Career Areas Area/Ethnic Studies; History; Humanities; Social Sciences.

Award Grant for use in graduate, or postgraduate years; not renewable.

Eligibility Requirements Applicant must be enrolled or expecting to enroll at an institution or university. Available to U.S. citizens.

Application Requirements Application, financial need analysis, references, transcript. *Deadline:* November 1.

Contact Leo Baeck Institute
German Academic Exchange Service
(DAAD)
15 West 16th Street
New York, NY 10011
Phone: 212-744-6400
Fax: 212-988-1305
E-mail: lbi1@lbi.com

INTERNATIONAL DEVELOPMENT RESEARCH CENTER
http://www.idrc.ca/awards

IDRC DOCTORAL RESEARCH AWARD
• *See number 12*

JAPANESE GOVERNMENT/THE MONBUSHO SCHOLARSHIP PROGRAM
http://embjapan.org/la

RESEARCH STUDENT SCHOLARSHIP
• *See number 13*

MEMORIAL FOUNDATION FOR JEWISH CULTURE
http://www.mfjc.org

INTERNATIONAL DOCTORAL SCHOLARSHIPS FOR STUDIES SPECIALIZING IN JEWISH FIELDS • 127

Renewable scholarship for postgraduate work specializing in Jewish fields. Must include completed application, transcript, and references when applying.

Academic/Career Areas Area/Ethnic Studies.

Award Scholarship for use in postgraduate years; renewable. *Amount:* $3000–$7500.

Eligibility Requirements Applicant must be enrolled or expecting to enroll at an institution or university.

Application Requirements Application, references, transcript.

Contact Dr. Jerry Hochbaum, Executive Vice
President
Memorial Foundation for Jewish Culture
15 East 26th Street, Room 1703
New York, NY 10010
Phone: 212-679-4074

INTERNATIONAL FELLOWSHIPS IN JEWISH CULTURE PROGRAM • 128

One-time fellowship awarded to individuals pursuing independent work in Jewish literature, Jewish scholarship, or Jewish art. Number of fellowships awarded varies by year. Request application in writing with a short description of the proposed project. Application deadline is January 31.

Academic/Career Areas Area/Ethnic Studies; Arts; Literature/English/Writing; Religion/Theology.

Award Fellowship for use in graduate, or postgraduate years; not renewable. *Amount:* $2000–$6000.

Eligibility Requirements Applicant must be enrolled or expecting to enroll full or part-time at an institution or university.

Application Requirements Application, photo, references. *Deadline:* January 31.

Contact Dr. Jerry Hochbaum, Executive Vice
President
Memorial Foundation for Jewish Culture
15 East 26th Street, Room 1703
New York, NY 10010
Phone: 212-679-4074

INTERNATIONAL FELLOWSHIPS IN JEWISH STUDIES • 129

One-time fellowship award for postgraduate work in Jewish studies. Applicant must show committed interest. Award can range up to $7500.

Academic/Career Areas Area/Ethnic Studies.

Award Fellowship for use in postgraduate years; not renewable. *Amount:* $3000–$7500.

Eligibility Requirements Applicant must be enrolled or expecting to enroll at an institution or university.

Contact Dr. Jerry Hochbaum, Executive Vice
President
Memorial Foundation for Jewish Culture
15 East 26th Street, Room 1703
New York, NY 10010
Phone: 212-679-4074

MEMORIAL FOUNDATION FOR JEWISH CULTURE INTERNATIONAL DOCTORAL SCHOLARSHIP • 130

Purpose of scholarship is to train qualified individuals for careers in Jewish scholarship and research and to help Jewish educational, religious, and communal workers train for leadership positions. Award for graduate study only.

Academic/Career Areas Area/Ethnic Studies; Religion/Theology.

Award Scholarship for use in graduate years; not renewable. *Amount:* $2000–$7500.

Eligibility Requirements Applicant must be enrolled or expecting to enroll at an institution or university.

Application Requirements Application, references, transcript. *Deadline:* October 31.

Contact Dr. Jerry Hochbaum, Executive Vice
President
Memorial Foundation for Jewish Culture
15 East 26th Street, Room 1703
New York, NY 10010
Phone: 212-679-4074

NORWEGIAN-AMERICAN HISTORICAL ASSOCIATION
http://www.naha.stolaf.edu

EINAR AND EVA LUND HAUGEN MEMORIAL SCHOLARSHIP • 131

Award for Ph.D. candidates doing a dissertation on a topic falling under the heading "Scandinavian or Scandinavian-American Studies." Submit academic record, three references, thesis proposal, applicant work plan, and future professional goals.

Academic/Career Areas Area/Ethnic Studies.

Award Scholarship for use in graduate years; not renewable. *Number:* 1. *Amount:* $3000.

Eligibility Requirements Applicant must be enrolled or expecting to enroll full or part-time at an institution or university. Available to U.S. and non-U.S. citizens.

Application Requirements Application, references, transcript. *Deadline:* March 1.

Contact Todd Nichol, Chairman, Awards Committee
Norwegian-American Historical Association
Haugen Scholarship Committee, 1510 St. Olaf Avenue
Northfield, MN 55057-1097
Phone: 507-646-3235
E-mail: naha@stolaf.edu

PHI BETA KAPPA SOCIETY
http://www.pbk.org

MARY ISABEL SIBLEY FELLOWSHIP FOR GREEK AND FRENCH STUDIES • 132

Awarded alternately in the fields of Greek and French. Must be used for the study of Greek language, literature, history, or archaeology; or of French language and literature. Must be single female ages 25-35 in doctoral or postdoctoral study program. Submit project description and plans for work.

Academic/Career Areas Area/Ethnic Studies; Art History; Arts; Foreign Language; History; Humanities; Literature/English/Writing; Religion/Theology; Social Sciences.

Award Fellowship for use in postgraduate years; not renewable. *Number:* 1. *Amount:* $20,000.

Eligibility Requirements Applicant must be age 25-35; enrolled or expecting to enroll full-time at a four-year institution or university; single female and must have an interest in French language or Greek language. Available to U.S. and non-U.S. citizens.

Application Requirements Application, references, transcript, project statement and plans for future work. *Deadline:* January 15.

Contact Ms. Cameron Curtis, Program Officer
Phi Beta Kappa Society
1785 Massachusetts Avenue, NW, 4th Floor
Washington, DC 20036
Phone: 202-265-3808
Fax: 202-986-1601
E-mail: ccurtis@pbk.org

SWANN FOUNDATION FUND
http://www.lcweb.loc.gov/rr/print/swann/swann_foundation.html

SWANN FOUNDATION FUND FELLOWSHIP
• *See number 109*

SWEDISH INFORMATION SERVICE
http://www.swedeninfo.com

BICENTENNIAL SWEDISH-AMERICAN EXCHANGE FUND TRAVEL GRANTS • 133

One-time travel grant for faculty, researchers and professionals to spend two to four weeks studying in Sweden. Must be U.S. citizen or permanent resident. Submit two letters of recommendation and a detailed project plan by Friday of the first week in February. Application forms available on line.

Academic/Career Areas Area/Ethnic Studies; Business/Consumer Services; Education; Foreign Language; Humanities; Social Sciences.

Award Grant for use in postgraduate years; not renewable. *Number:* 2–6. *Amount:* $2500.

Eligibility Requirements Applicant must be enrolled or expecting to enroll full or part-time at an institution or university. Available to U.S. citizens.

Application Requirements Application, essay, references.

Contact Linnea Kralik, Information Assistant
Swedish Information Service
885 2nd Avenue, 45th Floor
New York, NY 10017
Phone: 212-583-2550
Fax: 212-752-4789
E-mail: requests@swedeninfo.com

WOODROW WILSON NATIONAL FELLOWSHIP FOUNDATION
http://www.woodrow.org

ANDREW W. MELLON FELLOWSHIPS IN HUMANISTIC STUDIES • 134

One-time fellowships to help exceptionally promising students prepare for careers of teaching and scholarship in humanistic studies. Must be a U. S. citizen or permanent resident entering into a graduate program leading to a Ph.D. Application must be requested at website http://www.woodrow.org/mellon by December 4. All materials must be received by December 18.

Academic/Career Areas Area/Ethnic Studies; Art History; Foreign Language; History; Humanities; Literature/English/Writing; Political Science; Religion/Theology.

Award Fellowship for use in graduate years; not renewable. *Number:* 80–85. *Amount:* $20,000–$45,000.

Eligibility Requirements Applicant must be enrolled or expecting to enroll full-time at an institution or university. Available to U.S. citizens.

Application Requirements Application, essay, interview, references, test scores, transcript, writing sample. *Deadline:* December 18.

Contact Ms. Teresa Stevens, Program Coordinator
Woodrow Wilson National Fellowship Foundation
CN 5329
Princeton, NJ 08543-5329
Phone: 800-899-9963 Ext. 149
Fax: 609-452-0066
E-mail: mellon@woodrow.org

WOODROW WILSON NATIONAL FELLOWSHIP FOUNDATION DISSERTATION GRANTS IN WOMEN'S STUDIES • 135

Women's studies research grants for Ph.D. candidates writing their dissertation on topics concerning women. Must submit research prospectus, bibliography, and timetable. One-time award of $2000. To encourage original and significant research about women on such topics as the evolution of women's role in society, women in history, women's health, psychology of women, and women as seen in literature and art.

Academic/Career Areas Area/Ethnic Studies; Art History; History; Humanities; Literature/English/ Writing; Political Science; Religion/Theology; Social Sciences.

Award Grant for use in graduate years; not renewable. *Number:* 15. *Amount:* up to $3000.

Eligibility Requirements Applicant must be enrolled or expecting to enroll full-time at an institution or university. Available to U.S. citizens.

Application Requirements Application, references, transcript, dissertation proposal. *Deadline:* October 15.

Contact Judith L. Pinch, Secretary/Director
Woodrow Wilson National Fellowship
Foundation
CN 5281
Princeton, NJ 08543-5281
Phone: 609-452-7007
Fax: 609-452-0066
E-mail: charlotte@woodrow.org

WOODROW WILSON POSTDOCTORAL FELLOWSHIPS IN THE HUMANITIES • 136

The Woodrow Wilson Postdoctoral Fellowships in the Humanities are designed to provide top new PhD's opportunities to expand their skills, while allowing time and resources for preparing the dissertation for publication and broadening teaching experience.

Academic/Career Areas Area/Ethnic Studies; Art History; Foreign Language; History; Humanities; Literature/English/Writing; Political Science; Religion/Theology.

Award Fellowship for use in postgraduate years; renewable. *Number:* 15–25. *Amount:* $30,000–$40,000.

Eligibility Requirements Applicant must be enrolled or expecting to enroll full-time at a four-year institution or university. Available to U.S. citizens.

Application Requirements Application, essay, resume, transcript, dissertation summary. *Deadline:* November 1.

Contact Teresa Stevens, Program Coordinator
Woodrow Wilson National Fellowship
Foundation
CN 5281
Princeton, NJ 08543-5281
Phone: 609-452-7007 Ext. 149
Fax: 609-452-0066
E-mail: stevens@woodrow.org

ART HISTORY

AMERICAN CENTER OF ORIENTAL RESEARCH
http://www.bu.edu/acor

KRESS FELLOWSHIP IN THE ART AND ARCHAEOLOGY OF JORDAN
• *See number 64*

NATIONAL ENDOWMENT FOR THE HUMANITIES POST-DOCTORAL RESEARCH FELLOWSHIPS
• *See number 65*

AMERICAN COUNCIL OF LEARNED SOCIETIES (ACLS)
http://www.acls.org

HENRY LUCE FOUNDATION/AMERICAN COUNCIL OF LEARNED SOCIETIES DISSERTATION FELLOWSHIP IN AMERICAN ART HISTORY • 137

Award for art history graduate students to assist in any stage of Ph.D. dissertation writing or research. Must be U.S. citizen or permanent legal resident. Students preparing theses for the Master of Fine Arts degree are not eligible. One-time award of $20,000. Application deadline: November 15.

Academic/Career Areas Art History.

Award Fellowship for use in graduate years; not renewable. *Number:* 10. *Amount:* $20,000.

Eligibility Requirements Applicant must be enrolled or expecting to enroll at an institution or university. Available to U.S. citizens.

Application Requirements Application. *Deadline:* November 15.

Contact Office of Fellowships and Grants
American Council of Learned Societies
(ACLS)
228 East 45th Street
New York, NY 10017-3398
Fax: 212-949-8058
E-mail: grants@acls.org

AMERICAN RESEARCH INSTITUTE IN TURKEY (ARIT)
http://www.mec.sas.upenn.edu/ARIT

KRESS/ARIT PREDOCTORAL FELLOWSHIP IN THE HISTORY OF ART AND ARCHAEOLOGY
• See number 67

AMERICAN SCHOOLS OF ORIENTAL RESEARCH (ASOR)
http://www.asor.org

W.F. ALBRIGHT INSTITUTE OF ARCHAEOLOGICAL RESEARCH/NATIONAL ENDOWMENT OF THE HUMANITIES FELLOWSHIPS
• See number 71

W.F. ALRBIGHT INSTITUTE OF ARCHAEOLOGICAL RESEARCH SAMUEL H. KRESS JOINT ATHENS-JERUSALEM FELLOWSHIP
• See number 72

AMERICAN SOCIETY OF ARMS COLLECTORS

AMERICAN SOCIETY OF ARMS COLLECTORS SCHOLARSHIP • 138

Annual stipend of $5,000 granted to a student working toward a master's or doctoral degree in an area consistent with the Society's aims and purposes. Student's research must eventually result in a scholarly report that can be published in the Society's Bulletin. Serious scholars in areas of Arms and Armor may also apply.

Academic/Career Areas Art History; History; Museum Studies; Science, Technology and Society.

Award Grant for use in graduate, or postgraduate years; not renewable. *Number:* 1. *Amount:* $5000.

Eligibility Requirements Applicant must be enrolled or expecting to enroll full or part-time at a four-year institution or university and must have an interest in designated field specified by sponsor. Available to U.S. and non-U.S. citizens.

Application Requirements Application. *Deadline:* March 15.

Contact Robert Palmer, Scholarship Committee
Chairman
American Society of Arms Collectors
551 Spradley Drive
Troy, AL 36079
Phone: 334-566-4526
E-mail: palmerhaus@mindspring.com

AMON CARTER MUSEUM
http://www.cartermuseum.org

DAVIDSON FAMILY FELLOWSHIP PROGRAM • 139

Candidate either initiates new research or continues work on an existing topic in American art that draws on the museum's outstanding collections of painting, sculpture, works on paper, and photographs. Designed for object-oriented research; it is not intended to directly support thesis or dissertation preparation. Independent study program that reflects the candidate's major interest.

Academic/Career Areas Art History.

Award Fellowship for use in graduate, or postgraduate years; not renewable. *Number:* 1. *Amount:* $3500.

Eligibility Requirements Applicant must be enrolled or expecting to enroll full or part-time at a four-year institution or university; studying in Texas and must have an interest in art or museum/ preservation work. Available to U.S. and non-U.S. citizens.

Application Requirements Application, resume, references, transcript, visa if foreign student, work plan, synopsis of masters thesis, synopsis of doctoral thesis. *Deadline:* March 1.

Contact Miriam Hermann, Education
Administrative Assistant
Amon Carter Museum
3501 Camp Bowie Boulevard
Fort Worth, TX 76107
Phone: 817-738-1933 Ext. 235
Fax: 817-246-3422
E-mail:
miriam.hermann@cartermuseum.org

ARCHAEOLOGICAL INSTITUTE OF AMERICA
http://www.archaeological.org

ARCHAEOLOGICAL INSTITUTE OF AMERICA/ OLIVIA JAMES TRAVELING FELLOWSHIP
• See number 73

HARRIET AND LEON POMERANCE FELLOWSHIP
• See number 74

HELEN M. WOODRUFF FELLOWSHIP
• See number 75

WOODRUFF TRAVELING FELLOWSHIP
• See number 76

ASIAN CULTURAL COUNCIL
http://www.asianculturalcouncil.org

ASIAN ART AND RELIGION FELLOWSHIPS
• See number 90

ASIAN CULTURAL COUNCIL FELLOWSHIPS
• See number 91

Asian Cultural Council (continued)

ASIAN CULTURAL COUNCIL HUMANITIES FELLOWSHIPS
• *See number 92*

ASIAN CULTURAL COUNCIL RESIDENCY PROGRAM IN ASIA • 140

Award for research, teaching, or creative residency at a cultural and educational institution in Asia. Deadlines: February 1 and August 1. Results must be tangible and show a benefit to U.S.-Asian relations.

Academic/Career Areas Art History; Arts; Humanities; Museum Studies; Performing Arts; Trade/Technical Specialties.

Award Fellowship for use in graduate years; not renewable.

Eligibility Requirements Applicant must be enrolled or expecting to enroll at an institution or university and must have an interest in art, music/singing, or photography/photogrammetry/filmmaking. Available to U.S. citizens.

Application Requirements Application.

Contact Ralph Samuelson, Director
Asian Cultural Council
437 Madison Avenue
New York, NY 10022-7001
Phone: 212-812-4300
Fax: 212-812-4299
E-mail: acc@accny.org

FORD FOUNDATION FELLOWSHIPS • 141

One-time award for graduate support to Asian individuals for training, travel, and research in the U.S. Individuals must be engaged in the documentation and preservation of Asian traditional arts. Write for more information.

Academic/Career Areas Art History; Arts; Filmmaking; Historic Preservation and Conservation; Museum Studies; Performing Arts.

Award Fellowship for use in graduate years; not renewable.

Eligibility Requirements Applicant must be Asian/Pacific Islander and enrolled or expecting to enroll at an institution or university. Available to citizens of countries other than the U.S. or Canada.

Application Requirements Application. *Deadline:* February 1.

Contact Ralph Samuelson, Director
Asian Cultural Council
437 Madison Avenue
New York, NY 10022-7001
Phone: 212-812-4300
Fax: 212-812-4299
E-mail: acc@accny.org

COLLEGE ART ASSOCIATION
http://www.collegeart.org

PROFESSIONAL DEVELOPMENT FELLOWSHIP PROGRAM • 142

Fellowships awarded to artists and art historians from socially, economically diverse backgrounds. Must receive M.F.A., terminal M.A. or Ph.D. in year following application; be U.S. citizen or permanent resident; demonstrate financial need. Program designed to bridge gap between graduate study and career. Fellows receive support over two years.

Academic/Career Areas Art History; Arts.

Award Fellowship for use in graduate years; not renewable. *Number:* 3–5. *Amount:* $5000–$10,000.

Eligibility Requirements Applicant must be enrolled or expecting to enroll full-time at an institution or university. Available to U.S. citizens.

Application Requirements Application, autobiography, essay, financial need analysis, portfolio, references, transcript. *Deadline:* January 31.

Contact Fellowship Coordinator
College Art Association
275 Seventh Avenue
New York, NY 10001
Phone: 212-691-1051 Ext. 242
Fax: 212-627-2381
E-mail: fellowship@collegeart.org

DUMBARTON OAKS
http://www.doaks.org

BLISS PRIZE FELLOWSHIP IN BYZANTINE STUDIES
• *See number 123*

DUMBARTON OAKS PROJECT GRANTS
• *See number 94*

RESIDENTIAL FELLOWSHIP IN BYZANTINE, PRE-COLUMBIAN, AND LANDSCAPE ARCHITECTURE STUDIES
• *See number 95*

GETTY GRANT PROGRAM
http://www.getty.edu/grants

COLLABORATIVE RESEARCH GRANTS • 143

Provides opportunities for teams of scholars (one or more art historians, or art historians and scholars from other disciplines) to collaborate on interpretive research projects that offer new explanations of art and its history. Also funds research and planning of scholarly exhibitions (these teams should include scholars from both museums and universities). Must submit writing sample and curriculum vitae.

Academic/Career Areas Art History.

Award Grant for use in postgraduate years; not renewable. *Amount:* $10,000–$200,000.

Eligibility Requirements Applicant must be enrolled or expecting to enroll full or part-time at a four-year institution or university. Available to U.S. and non-U.S. citizens.

Application Requirements Application, financial need analysis. *Deadline:* November 1.

Contact Nancy Micklewright, Program Officer
Getty Grant Program
1200 Getty Center Drive, Suite 800
Los Angeles, CA 90049-1685
Phone: 310-440-7320
Fax: 310-440-7703
E-mail: researchgrants@getty.edu

CURATORIAL RESEARCH FELLOWSHIPS • 144

Curatorial Research Fellowships support the professional scholarly development of curators by providing them with time off from regular museum duties to undertake short-term research or study projects. Fellowships are reserved for full-time curators who have a minimum of three years professional experience and are employed at museums with art collections. Must submit writing sample and curriculum vitae.

Academic/Career Areas Art History.

Award Fellowship for use in postgraduate years; not renewable. *Amount:* $3500–$13,500.

Eligibility Requirements Applicant must be enrolled or expecting to enroll full-time at a four-year institution or university. Applicant or parent of applicant must have employment or volunteer experience in designated career field. Available to U.S. and non-U.S. citizens.

Application Requirements Application. *Deadline:* November 1.

Contact Nancy Micklewright, Senior Program Officer
Getty Grant Program
1200 Getty Center Drive, Suite 800
Los Angeles, CA 90049-1685
Phone: 310-440-7320
Fax: 310-440-7703
E-mail: researchgrants@getty.edu

GETTY SCHOLAR AND VISITING SCHOLAR GRANTS • 145

Grants for established scholars, artists, or writers who have attained distinction in their fields. Researchers working in the arts, humanities or social sciences are eligible. Scholars are in residence at Getty Research Institute. Getty scholars receive salary replacement, up to maximum of $75,000. Visiting scholars, receive monthly stipend of $3500, up to a maximum of $10,500. See website for details.

Academic/Career Areas Art History; Arts; Humanities; Social Sciences.

Award Grant for use in postgraduate years; not renewable. *Amount:* $3500–$75,000.

Eligibility Requirements Applicant must be enrolled or expecting to enroll at an institution or university. Available to U.S. and non-U.S. citizens.

Application Requirements *Deadline:* November 1.

Contact Nancy Micklewright, Program Officer
Getty Grant Program
1200 Getty Center Drive, Suite 800
Los Angeles, CA 90049-1685
Phone: 310-440-7320
Fax: 310-440-7703
E-mail: researchgrants@getty.edu

J. PAUL GETTY POSTDOCTORAL FELLOWSHIPS IN THE HISTORY OF ART • 146

One-time award for outstanding scholars who have earned a doctoral degree (or the equivalent in countries outside the U.S.) within the past six years and who are undertaking interpretive research projects that promise to make a substantial and original contribution to the understanding of art and its history. Fellowships are awarded once a year and generally support a research period of twelve months. Award may be used wherever necessary to complete project. Must submit writing sample, a list of publications and dissertation abstract.

Academic/Career Areas Art History.

Award Fellowship for use in postgraduate years; not renewable. *Number:* 15. *Amount:* $40,000.

Eligibility Requirements Applicant must be enrolled or expecting to enroll full-time at a four-year institution or university. Available to U.S. and non-U.S. citizens.

Application Requirements Application, references. *Deadline:* November 1.

Contact Nancy Micklewright, Program Officer
Getty Grant Program
1200 Getty Center Drive, Suite 800
Los Angeles, CA 90049-1685
Phone: 310-440-7320
Fax: 310-440-7703
E-mail: researchgrants@getty.edu

PREDOCTORAL AND POSTDOCTORAL FELLOWSHIPS • 147

Fellowships provided to scholars working in the arts, humanities, or social sciences. Program provides support for emerging scholars to complete their dissertations or expand them for publication. Projects must address the Institute's scholar theme for the particular year. Predoctoral fellows receive stipend of $36,000. Postdoctoral fellows receive $44,000. See website for details. Recipients are in residence at the Getty Research Institute.

Academic/Career Areas Art History; Arts; Humanities; Social Sciences.

Getty Grant Program (continued)

Award Fellowship for use in graduate, or postgraduate years; not renewable. *Amount:* $36,000–$44,000.

Eligibility Requirements Applicant must be enrolled or expecting to enroll at an institution or university and studying in California. Available to U.S. and non-U.S. citizens.

Application Requirements *Deadline:* November 1.

Contact Nancy Micklewright, Program Officer
Getty Grant Program
1200 Getty Center Drive, Suite 800
Los Angeles, CA 90049-1685
Phone: 310-440-7320
Fax: 310-440-7703
E-mail: researchgrants@getty.edu

HAGLEY MUSEUM AND LIBRARY
http://www.hagley.org

HAGLEY MUSEUM AND LIBRARY GRANTS-IN-AID
• *See number 97*

HAGLEY/WINTERTHUR FELLOWSHIPS IN ARTS AND INDUSTRIES
• *See number 98*

HENRY BELIN DU PONT DISSERTATION FELLOWSHIP
• *See number 99*

HUNTINGTON LIBRARY, ART COLLECTIONS, AND BOTANICAL GARDENS
http://www.huntington.org

HUNTINGTON RESEARCH AWARDS
• *See number 56*

METROPOLITAN MUSEUM OF ART
http://www.metmuseum.org

ANDREW W. MELLON FELLOWSHIPS
• *See number 82*

ANNETTE KADE FELLOWSHIP • **148**

Awarded to French and German pre-doctoral art history students for study or research at the Metropolitan Museum. For French and German students who would not otherwise have the opportunity to study in the U.S.

Academic/Career Areas Art History.

Award Fellowship for use in graduate years; not renewable. *Amount:* $25,000–$30,000.

Eligibility Requirements Applicant must be French or German citizenship; enrolled or expecting to enroll full-time at an institution or university and studying in New York.

Application Requirements Essay, resume, references, transcript. *Deadline:* November 1.

Contact Marcie Karp, Coordinator of Fellowships
Metropolitan Museum of Art
1000 Fifth Avenue
New York, NY 10028
Phone: 212-650-2763
Fax: 212-396-5168
E-mail: marcie.karp@metmuseum.org

CHESTER DALE FELLOWSHIPS
• *See number 83*

DOUGLAS FOUNDATION FELLOWSHIP IN AMERICAN ART • **149**

One-time award to promising young scholar for study or research in the American Wing of MMA. Must have been enrolled for at least one year in an advanced degree program in the field of American art or culture.

Academic/Career Areas Art History.

Award Fellowship for use in graduate years; not renewable. *Amount:* $25,000–$30,000.

Eligibility Requirements Applicant must be enrolled or expecting to enroll full-time at an institution or university and studying in New York.

Application Requirements Resume, references, transcript. *Deadline:* November 1.

Contact Marcie Karp, Coordinator of Fellowships
Metropolitan Museum of Art
1000 Fifth Avenue
New York, NY 10028
Phone: 212-650-2763
Fax: 212-396-5168
E-mail: marcie.karp@metmuseum.org

JANE AND MORGAN WHITNEY FELLOWSHIPS • **150**

Awarded for study, work, or research to students of the fine arts whose fields are related to the museum's collections. Preference given to those in decorative arts who are under 40 years old.

Academic/Career Areas Art History; Arts.

Award Fellowship for use in graduate, or postgraduate years; not renewable. *Amount:* $25,000–$30,000.

Eligibility Requirements Applicant must be enrolled or expecting to enroll at an institution or university and studying in New York. Available to U.S. and non-U.S. citizens.

Application Requirements Essay, resume, references, transcript. *Deadline:* November 1.

Contact Marcie Karp, Coordinator of Fellowships
Metropolitan Museum of Art
1000 Fifth Avenue
New York, NY 10028
Phone: 212-650-2763
Fax: 212-396-5168
E-mail: marcie.karp@metmuseum.org

L.W. FROHLICH CHARITABLE TRUST FELLOWSHIP
• *See number 59*

METROPOLITAN MUSEUM OF ART BOTHMER FELLOWSHIP • 151

Awarded to an outstanding graduate student who has been admitted to the doctoral program at a U.S. university. Thesis must deal with Greek or Roman art. One-time award for fellowship at the Metropolitan Museum of Art. No application forms.

Academic/Career Areas Art History.

Award Fellowship for use in graduate years; not renewable. *Amount:* $25,000–$30,000.

Eligibility Requirements Applicant must be enrolled or expecting to enroll at an institution or university and studying in New York. Available to U.S. and non-U.S. citizens.

Application Requirements Essay, resume, references, transcript. *Deadline:* November 1.

Contact Marcie Karp, Coordinator of Fellowships
Metropolitan Museum of Art
1000 Fifth Avenue
New York, NY 10028
Phone: 212-650-2763
Fax: 212-396-5168
E-mail: marcie.karp@metmusuem.org

POLAIRE WEISSMAN FUND • 152

For qualified graduate students who preferably will have completed graduate studies in the fine arts, or studies in costume. Should be interested in pursuing costume history in a museum, teaching career, or other career (including conservation) related to the field of costume.

Academic/Career Areas Art History; Arts.

Award Fellowship for use in graduate years; not renewable. *Amount:* $25,000.

Eligibility Requirements Applicant must be enrolled or expecting to enroll at an institution or university and studying in New York. Available to U.S. and non-U.S. citizens.

Application Requirements Essay, resume, references, transcript. *Deadline:* November 1.

Contact Marcie Karp, Coordinator of Fellowships
Metropolitan Museum of Art
1000 Fifth Avenue
New York, NY 10028
Phone: 212-650-2763
Fax: 212-396-5168
E-mail: marcie.karp@metmuseum.org

THEODORE ROUSSEAU FELLOWSHIP • 153

This award is for graduate students who have completed one year of advanced study in the field of art history. The award is to be used to study paintings in Europe. Submit proposal and resume. No application forms.

Academic/Career Areas Art History.

Award Fellowship for use in graduate years; not renewable. *Amount:* $25,000.

Eligibility Requirements Applicant must be enrolled or expecting to enroll at an institution or university. Available to U.S. and non-U.S. citizens.

Application Requirements Autobiography, essay, resume, references, proposal. *Deadline:* November 1.

Contact Marcie Karp, Coordinator of Fellowships
Metropolitan Museum of Art
1000 Fifth Avenue
New York, NY 10028
Phone: 212-650-2763
Fax: 212-396-5168
E-mail: marcie.karp@metmuseum.org

NATIONAL GALLERY OF ART
http://www.nga.gov/resources/casva.htm

FELLOWSHIP PROGRAMS • 154

Candidates may apply for a Senior Fellowship, a Visiting Senior Fellowship or a Predoctoral Fellowship. Fellowships are for full-time research. Scholars are expected to reside in Washington, D.C. and participate in activities of the Center. Areas of study vary. Visit website for additional information and deadlines.

Academic/Career Areas Art History; Humanities.

Award Fellowship for use in graduate, or postgraduate years; not renewable. *Number:* up to 29. *Amount:* $2500–$40,000.

Eligibility Requirements Applicant must be enrolled or expecting to enroll full-time at a four-year institution or university and studying in District of Columbia. Available to U.S. and non-U.S. citizens.

National Gallery of Art (continued)

Application Requirements Application, autobiography, essay, references, transcript. *Deadline:* Continuous.

Contact National Gallery of Art
Center for Advanced Study in the Visual Arts
Sixth Street and Constitution Avenue, NW
Washington, DC 20565-0002

PHI BETA KAPPA SOCIETY
http://www.pbk.org

MARY ISABEL SIBLEY FELLOWSHIP FOR GREEK AND FRENCH STUDIES
• *See number 132*

SAMUEL H. KRESS FOUNDATION
http://www.kressfoundation.org

KRESS TRAVEL FELLOWSHIPS • 155

One-time award for pre-doctoral candidates to travel to view materials essential for the completion of dissertation research in European Art. Must be nominated by art history department. Several fellowships of up to $10,000. Applicant should speak with art history chair at his or her university for current forms. Applicant must be U.S. citizen or matriculated at U.S. institution.

Academic/Career Areas Art History.

Award Fellowship for use in graduate years; not renewable. *Number:* 15–20. *Amount:* $1000–$10,000.

Eligibility Requirements Applicant must be enrolled or expecting to enroll full-time at an institution or university. Available to U.S. and non-U.S. citizens.

Application Requirements Application, references, transcript, proposal. *Deadline:* November 30.

Contact Mr. Wyman Meers, Program Associate
Samuel H. Kress Foundation
174 East 80th Street
New York, NY 10021
Phone: 212-861-4993 Ext. 23

TWO-YEAR KRESS RESEARCH FELLOWSHIPS AT FOREIGN INSTITUTIONS • 156

Award for advanced dissertation research in association with a selected foreign art historical institute. Must be nominated by art history department. Four fellowships of $18,000 each. Applicant should contact the art history chair at his or her university. Applicant must be U.S. citizen or matriculated at U.S. institution.

Academic/Career Areas Art History.

Award Fellowship for use in postgraduate years; not renewable. *Number:* 4. *Amount:* $18,000.

Eligibility Requirements Applicant must be enrolled or expecting to enroll full-time at an institution or university. Available to U.S. and non-U.S. citizens.

Application Requirements Application, references, transcript, proposal. *Deadline:* November 30.

Contact Mr. Wyman Meers, Program Assistant
Samuel H. Kress Foundation
174 East 80th Street
New York, NY 10021
Phone: 212-861-4993 Ext. 23

SHASTRI INDO-CANADIAN INSTITUTE
http://www.ucalgary.ca/~sici

SHASTRI INDIA STUDIES SENIOR ARTS FELLOWSHIPS • 157

Senior fellowships available to accomplished artists to travel to India to enrich their experience, obtain additional training, and expand their repertoire. One-time grants of varying amounts. Must be Canadian citizen or permanent resident.

Academic/Career Areas Art History; Arts; Filmmaking; Performing Arts.

Award Fellowship for use in graduate years; not renewable. *Number:* 1–2.

Eligibility Requirements Applicant must be of Canadian heritage and enrolled or expecting to enroll at an institution or university. Available to Canadian citizens.

Application Requirements Application, photo, portfolio. *Deadline:* June 30.

Contact Programme Officer
Shastri Indo-Canadian Institute
2500 University Drive, NW
Calgary, AB T2N 1N4
Canada
Phone: 403-220-7467
Fax: 403-289-0100
E-mail: sici@ucalgary.ca

SOCIETY OF ARCHITECTURAL HISTORIANS
http://www.sah.org

CARROLL L.V. MEEKS FELLOWSHIP
• *See number 104*

EDILIA AND FRANCOIS-AUGUSTE DE MONTEQUIN FELLOWSHIP IN IBERIAN AND LATIN AMERICAN ARCHITECTURE
• *See number 105*

ROSANN S. BERRY ANNUAL MEETING FELLOWSHIP
• *See number 106*

SWANN FOUNDATION FUND
http://www.lcweb.loc.gov/rr/print/swann/
swann_foundation.html

SWANN FOUNDATION FUND FELLOWSHIP
• See number 109

VIRGINIA MUSEUM OF FINE ARTS
http://www.vmfa.state.va.us

VIRGINIA MUSEUM OF FINE ARTS GRADUATE
FELLOWSHIP PROGRAM • 158

Must be able to prove residence in Virginia for one year prior to deadline. Nonrenewable award for graduate students planning to be enrolled full-time for full academic year at accepted institution. Must submit 10 slides of recent work. Art history applicants must submit three research papers or published articles.

Academic/Career Areas Art History; Arts; Filmmaking.

Award Fellowship for use in graduate years; not renewable. *Amount:* $6000.

Eligibility Requirements Applicant must be enrolled or expecting to enroll full-time at an institution or university; resident of Virginia and studying in Virginia. Available to U.S. citizens.

Application Requirements Application, references, self-addressed stamped envelope, transcript. *Deadline:* March 1.

Contact Fellowship Director
Virginia Museum of Fine Arts
2800 Grove Avenue
Richmond, VA 23221-2466

WELLESLEY COLLEGE
http://www.wellesley.edu/CWS/

HARRIET A. SHAW FELLOWSHIP • 159

One-time award for graduates of Wellesley College to study or research music, art, or allied subjects, in the U.S. or abroad. Preference given to music candidates; undergraduate work in art history is required of other candidates. Submit resume. Award based on merit and need.

Academic/Career Areas Art History; Arts; Museum Studies.

Award Fellowship for use in graduate years; not renewable. *Amount:* up to $10,000.

Eligibility Requirements Applicant must be enrolled or expecting to enroll at an institution or university and female. Available to U.S. citizens.

Application Requirements Application, financial need analysis, resume, references, test scores, transcript. *Deadline:* January 3.

Contact Rose Crawford, Secretary to the
Committee on Graduate Fellowships
Wellesley College
106 Central Avenue, Green Hall 441
Wellesley, MA 02481-8200
Phone: 781-283-3525
Fax: 781-283-3674
E-mail: cws-fellowships@wellesley.edu

WINTERTHUR MUSEUM, GARDEN, AND LIBRARY
http://www.winterthur.org

LOIS F. MCNEIL DISSERTATION RESEARCH
FELLOWSHIPS
• See number 85

NEH FELLOWSHIPS
• See number 110

WINTERTHUR RESEARCH FELLOWSHIPS
• See number 111

WOODROW WILSON NATIONAL FELLOWSHIP FOUNDATION
http://www.woodrow.org

ANDREW W. MELLON FELLOWSHIPS IN
HUMANISTIC STUDIES
• See number 134

WOODROW WILSON NATIONAL FELLOWSHIP
FOUNDATION DISSERTATION GRANTS IN
WOMEN'S STUDIES
• See number 135

WOODROW WILSON POSTDOCTORAL
FELLOWSHIPS IN THE HUMANITIES
• See number 136

ARTS

ALBERTA HERITAGE SCHOLARSHIP FUND
http://www.alis.gov.ab.ca/scholarships

ALBERTA FOUNDATION FOR THE ARTS
GRADUATE LEVEL SCHOLARSHIPS • 160

Awards for Albertans for master's level or equivalent study in music, drama, dance, literary arts, and the visual arts. Five awards of Can$10,000. Deadline: February 1. Must be ranked in upper quarter of class or have a minimum 3.5 GPA.

Academic/Career Areas Arts; Literature/English/ Writing; Performing Arts.

Award Scholarship for use in graduate years; not renewable. *Number:* 5. *Amount:* $10,000.

Alberta Heritage Scholarship Fund (continued)

Eligibility Requirements Applicant must be Canadian citizenship; enrolled or expecting to enroll full-time at an institution or university and resident of Alberta. Applicant must have 3.5 GPA or higher.

Application Requirements Application, essay, references, transcript. *Deadline:* February 1.

Contact Alberta Heritage Scholarship Fund
9940 106th Street, 9th Floor, Box 28000
Station Main
Edmonton, AB T5J 4R4
Canada
Phone: 780-427-8640
Fax: 780-422-4516
E-mail: heritage@gov.ab.ca

ALPHA DELTA KAPPA FOUNDATION
http://www.alphadeltakappa.org

APHA DELTA KAPPA FOUNDATION FINE ARTS GRANTS • 161

Awarded biennially in two categories, Performing Arts and Visual Arts. Next Performing Arts awards will be given in Instrumental Music (strings only) and the next Visual Arts awards will be given in Painting (all media). Applications available after September 1. Deadline for application is April 1.

Academic/Career Areas Arts; Performing Arts.

Award Grant for use in graduate, or postgraduate years; not renewable. *Number:* up to 6. *Amount:* $1000–$5000.

Eligibility Requirements Applicant must be enrolled or expecting to enroll full or part-time at an institution or university and must have an interest in art or music. Available to U.S. and non-U.S. citizens.

Application Requirements Application, applicant must enter a contest, references, supportive materials. *Fee:* $50. *Deadline:* April 1.

Contact Dee Frost, Scholarships and Grants Coordinator
Alpha Delta Kappa Foundation
1615 West 92nd Street
Kansas City, MO 64114-3296
Phone: 816-363-5525
Fax: 816-363-4010
E-mail: dfrost@www.alphadeltakappa.org

AMERICAN CENTER OF ORIENTAL RESEARCH
http://www.bu.edu/acor

NATIONAL ENDOWMENT FOR THE HUMANITIES POST-DOCTORAL RESEARCH FELLOWSHIPS
• See number 65

AMERICAN COUNCIL OF LEARNED SOCIETIES (ACLS)
http://www.acls.org

CONTEMPLATIVE PRACTICE FELLOWSHIPS • 162

Up to 10 fellowships offered to support individual or collaborative research leading to the development of courses and teaching materials that integrate an awareness of contemplative practice. Submit proposals from the full range of disciplinary and interdisciplinary perspectives in the arts, humanities, humanities-related sciences and social sciences. Application deadline: November 1.

Academic/Career Areas Arts; Humanities; Social Sciences.

Award Fellowship for use in postgraduate years; not renewable. *Number:* up to 10. *Amount:* up to $20,000.

Eligibility Requirements Applicant must be enrolled or expecting to enroll at an institution or university.

Application Requirements Application. *Deadline:* November 1.

Contact Office of Fellowships and Grants
American Council of Learned Societies (ACLS)
228 East 45th Street
New York, NY 10017-3398
Fax: 212-949-8058
E-mail: grants@acls.org

ASIAN CULTURAL COUNCIL
http://www.asianculturalcouncil.org

ASIAN ART AND RELIGION FELLOWSHIPS
• See number 90

ASIAN CULTURAL COUNCIL FELLOWSHIPS
• See number 91

ASIAN CULTURAL COUNCIL HUMANITIES FELLOWSHIPS
• See number 92

ASIAN CULTURAL COUNCIL RESIDENCY PROGRAM IN ASIA
• See number 140

FORD FOUNDATION FELLOWSHIPS
• See number 141

ASSOCIATION ON AMERICAN INDIAN AFFAIRS, INC.
http://www.indian-affairs.org

ASSOCIATION ON AMERICAN INDIAN AFFAIRS, INC. • 163

One-time award for Native American graduate student. Preference given to those majoring in art, particularly Native American Art. Deadline is September 15.

Academic/Career Areas Arts.

Award Scholarship for use in graduate years; not renewable. *Number:* 1. *Amount:* $5000.

Eligibility Requirements Applicant must be American Indian/Alaska Native and enrolled or expecting to enroll full-time at a four-year institution or university. Available to U.S. citizens.

Application Requirements Application, essay, financial need analysis, transcript. *Deadline:* September 15.

Contact Association on American Indian Affairs, Inc.
PO Box 268
Sisseton, SD 57262
Phone: 605-698-3998
Fax: 605-698-3316

COLLEGE ART ASSOCIATION
http://www.collegeart.org

PROFESSIONAL DEVELOPMENT FELLOWSHIP PROGRAM
• See number 142

CULTURAL SERVICES OF THE FRENCH EMBASSY
http://www.frenchculture.org

CHATEAUBRIAND SCHOLARSHIP PROGRAM • 164

The French government awards scholarships to conduct research in France. Must be a U.S. citizen enrolled in a graduate or post-graduate program at an American University. Visit website to download application.

Academic/Career Areas Arts; Filmmaking; History; Humanities; Political Science; Social Sciences.

Award Fellowship for use in graduate, or postgraduate years; not renewable. *Number:* 20–25. *Amount:* $20,000.

Eligibility Requirements Applicant must be enrolled or expecting to enroll full-time at an institution or university and must have an interest in French language. Available to U.S. citizens.

Application Requirements Application, references, transcript, research proposal, copy of diplomas. *Deadline:* January 15.

Contact Alessandra Benedicty
Cultural Services of the French Embassy
4101 Reservoir Road NW
Washington, DC 20007
Phone: 202-944-6294
Fax: 202-944-6268
E-mail: alessandra.benedicty@diplomate.fr

DUMBARTON OAKS
http://www.doaks.org

BLISS PRIZE FELLOWSHIP IN BYZANTINE STUDIES
• See number 123

RESIDENTIAL FELLOWSHIP IN BYZANTINE, PRE-COLUMBIAN, AND LANDSCAPE ARCHITECTURE STUDIES
• See number 95

FRENCH INSTITUTE OF WASHINGTON (INSTITUT FRANÇAIS DE WASHINGTON)
http://www.unc.edu/depts/institut

EDOUARD MOROT-SIR FELLOWSHIP IN LITERATURE • 165

One award for research in France in the areas of art, economics, history, history of science, linguistics, literature, and social sciences. Must have held Ph.D. for no longer than six years or be in the final stage of Ph.D. dissertation writing. Submit description of research project (two pages maximum), curriculum vitae, and recommendations (Ph.D. candidates only). Deadline: January 14.

Academic/Career Areas Arts; Economics; History; Literature/English/Writing; Social Sciences.

Award Fellowship for use in graduate, or postgraduate years; not renewable. *Number:* 1. *Amount:* $1500.

Eligibility Requirements Applicant must be enrolled or expecting to enroll full or part-time at an institution or university. Available to U.S. and Canadian citizens.

Application Requirements Essay, references, curriculum vitae. *Deadline:* January 14.

Contact Dr. Catherine Maley, President
French Institute of Washington (Institut Français de Washington)
CB 3170, 234 Dey Hall
Chapel Hill, NC 27599-3170
Phone: 919-962-0154
Fax: 919-962-5457
E-mail: cmaley@email.unc.edu

GILBERT CHINARD FELLOWSHIPS AND EDOUARD MOROT-SIR FELLOWSHIP IN LITERATURE • 166

Two awards for research in France in the areas of art, economics, history, history of science, linguistics, literature, and social sciences. Must have held Ph.D. for no longer than six years or be in the final stage of Ph.D. dissertation writing. Submit description of research project (two pages maximum), curriculum vitae, and recommendation (Ph.D. candidates only). Deadline: January 14.

Academic/Career Areas Arts; Economics; History; Literature/English/Writing; Social Sciences.

Award Fellowship for use in graduate, or postgraduate years; not renewable. *Number:* 2. *Amount:* $1500.

French Institute of Washington (Institut Français de Washington) (continued)

Eligibility Requirements Applicant must be enrolled or expecting to enroll full or part-time at an institution or university. Available to U.S. and Canadian citizens.

Application Requirements Essay, references, curriculum vitae. *Deadline:* January 14.

Contact Dr. Catherine A. Maley, President
French Institute of Washington (Institut Français de Washington)
CB 3170, 234 Dey Hall
Chapel Hill, NC 27599-3170
Phone: 919-962-0154
Fax: 919-962-5457
E-mail: cmaley@email.unc.edu

HARMON CHADBOURN RORISON FELLOWSHIP
• 167

Award is for research in France in the areas of art, economics, history, history of science, linguistics, literature, and social sciences. Must have held Ph.D. for no longer than six years or be in the final stage of Ph.D. dissertation writing. Submit description of research project (two-pages maximum), curriculum vitae, and recommendations (Ph.D. candidates only). Deadline: January 14.

Academic/Career Areas Arts; Economics; History; Literature/English/Writing; Social Sciences.

Award Fellowship for use in graduate, or postgraduate years; not renewable. *Number:* 1. *Amount:* $1500.

Eligibility Requirements Applicant must be enrolled or expecting to enroll full or part-time at an institution or university. Available to U.S. and Canadian citizens.

Application Requirements Essay, references, curriculum vitae. *Deadline:* January 14.

Contact Dr. Catherine Maley, President
French Institute of Washington (Institut Français de Washington)
CB 3170, 234 Dey Hall
Chapel Hill, NC 27599-3170
Phone: 919-962-0154
Fax: 919-962-5457
E-mail: cmaley@email.unc.edu

GETTY GRANT PROGRAM
http://www.getty.edu/grants

GETTY SCHOLAR AND VISITING SCHOLAR GRANTS
• *See number 145*

PREDOCTORAL AND POSTDOCTORAL FELLOWSHIPS
• *See number 147*

HAGLEY MUSEUM AND LIBRARY
http://www.hagley.org

HAGLEY MUSEUM AND LIBRARY GRANTS-IN-AID
• *See number 97*

HAGLEY/WINTERTHUR FELLOWSHIPS IN ARTS AND INDUSTRIES
• *See number 98*

HENRY BELIN DU PONT DISSERTATION FELLOWSHIP
• *See number 99*

MEMORIAL FOUNDATION FOR JEWISH CULTURE
http://www.mfjc.org

INTERNATIONAL FELLOWSHIPS IN JEWISH CULTURE PROGRAM
• *See number 128*

METROPOLITAN MUSEUM OF ART
http://www.metmuseum.org

ANDREW W. MELLON FELLOWSHIPS
• *See number 82*

CHESTER DALE FELLOWSHIPS
• *See number 83*

J. CLAWSON MILLS SCHOLARSHIP   • 168

Award for one year's study or research at the Metropolitan Museum of Art in any branch of fine arts relating to the museum's collections. Possibility of renewal for second year. Reserved for mature scholars of demonstrated ability.

Academic/Career Areas Arts.

Award Fellowship for use in graduate, or postgraduate years; not renewable. *Amount:* $25,000–$30,000.

Eligibility Requirements Applicant must be enrolled or expecting to enroll full-time at an institution or university and studying in New York. Available to U.S. and non-U.S. citizens.

Application Requirements Resume, references, transcript. *Deadline:* November 1.

Contact Marcie Karp, Coordinator of Fellowships
Metropolitan Museum of Art
1000 Fifth Avenue
New York, NY 10028-0198
Phone: 212-650-2763
Fax: 212-396-5168
E-mail: marcie.karp@metmuseum.org

JANE AND MORGAN WHITNEY FELLOWSHIPS
• *See number 150*

LEO AND JULIA FORCHHEIMER FELLOWSHIP
• 169

Awarded for three to six months study and research at the Antonio Ratti Textile Center on an aspect of the museums textile collection. Intended for graduate students or mature scholars of demonstrated ability. No application forms.

Academic/Career Areas Arts.

Award Fellowship for use in graduate, or postgraduate years; not renewable. *Amount:* $25,000–$30,000.

Eligibility Requirements Applicant must be enrolled or expecting to enroll full-time at an institution or university and resident of New York. Available to U.S. and non-U.S. citizens.

Application Requirements Essay, resume, references, transcript. *Deadline:* November 1.

Contact Marcie Karp, Coordinator of Fellowships
Metropolitan Museum of Art
1000 Fifth Avenue
New York, NY 10028
Phone: 212-650-2763
Fax: 212-396-5168
E-mail: marcie.karp@metmuseum.org

POLAIRE WEISSMAN FUND
• *See number 152*

PHI BETA KAPPA SOCIETY
http://www.pbk.org

MARY ISABEL SIBLEY FELLOWSHIP FOR GREEK AND FRENCH STUDIES
• *See number 132*

POLLOCK-KRASNER FOUNDATION, INC.
http://www.pkf.org

POLLOCK-KRASNER GRANTS • 170

One-time award for professional artists for personal and art-related expenses. Specifically available to visual artists. Selection is based upon artistic merit, professional record, and financial need. Submit resume and slides of work with application.

Academic/Career Areas Arts.

Award Grant for use in postgraduate years; not renewable. *Amount:* $5000–$30,000.

Eligibility Requirements Applicant must be enrolled or expecting to enroll at an institution or university. Applicant or parent of applicant must have employment or volunteer experience in designated career field. Available to U.S. and non-U.S. citizens.

Application Requirements Application, financial need analysis, slides. *Deadline:* Continuous.

Contact Caroline Black, Program Officer
Pollock-Krasner Foundation, Inc.
863 Park Avenue
New York, NY 10021
Phone: 212-517-5400
Fax: 212-288-2836
E-mail: grants@pkf.org

POSEY FOUNDATION
http://www.selbyfdn.org

GRADUATE ARTS SCHOLARSHIP • 171

Up to 5 one-time awards for full-time graduate student. Study in sculpture preferred. Minimum 3.0 GPA required. Application deadline is March 1. Must send in slides of work.

Academic/Career Areas Arts.

Award Scholarship for use in graduate years; not renewable. *Number:* up to 5. *Amount:* $3000–$4000.

Eligibility Requirements Applicant must be enrolled or expecting to enroll full-time at a four-year institution or university and must have an interest in art. Applicant must have 3.0 GPA or higher. Available to U.S. and non-U.S. citizens.

Application Requirements Application, essay, financial need analysis, photo, references, test scores, transcript, slides of work. *Deadline:* March 1.

Contact Jan Noah, Grants Manager
Posey Foundation
1800 Second Street, Suite 750
Sarasota, FL 34286
Phone: 941-957-0442
Fax: 941-957-3135
E-mail: jnoah@selbyfdn.org

RHODE ISLAND FOUNDATION
http://www.rifoundation.org

ANTONIO CIRINO MEMORIAL ART EDUCATION FELLOWSHIP • 172

Provides support to Rhode Island artists wishing to become educators. For writers, composers, and actors, with preference to visual artists. Rhode Island School of Design students or graduates excluded. Financial need a must. Must be a Rhode Island resident of at least 5 years and include proof of residency.

Academic/Career Areas Arts; Education; Filmmaking; Performing Arts.

Award Fellowship for use in graduate, or postgraduate years; renewable. *Number:* 8–10. *Amount:* $2000–$10,000.

Eligibility Requirements Applicant must be enrolled or expecting to enroll full or part-time at an institution or university and resident of Rhode Island.

Rhode Island Foundation (continued)

Application Requirements Application, driver's license, financial need analysis, portfolio, references, self-addressed stamped envelope, transcript, proof of residency. *Deadline:* June 7.

Contact Libby Monahan, Scholarship Coordinator
      Rhode Island Foundation
      1 Union Station
      Providence, RI 02903
      Phone: 401-274-4564
      Fax: 401-272-1359

SAN FRANCISCO FOUNDATION
http://www.sff.org

CADOGAN FELLOWSHIP • 173

Award for graduate students at one of seven Bay Area colleges or universities. Must be nominated and have completed one semester of graduate study in fine arts. Must submit portfolio slides. Artwork submitted must have been completed within the past two years. One-time award of $2500. Must have at least two semesters remaining before graduation. Application deadline is March 15.

Academic/Career Areas Arts.

Award Scholarship for use in graduate years; not renewable. *Number:* 5–10. *Amount:* $2500.

Eligibility Requirements Applicant must be enrolled or expecting to enroll full-time at an institution or university and studying in California. Available to U.S. and non-U.S. citizens.

Application Requirements Application, portfolio, self-addressed stamped envelope, artwork. *Deadline:* March 15.

Contact Awards Coordinator
      San Francisco Foundation
      225 Bush Street, Suite 500
      San Francisco, CA 94104-4224
      Phone: 415-733-8500
      E-mail: rec@sff.org

MURPHY FINE ARTS FELLOWSHIP • 174

Award for graduate student at one of seven Bay Area colleges or universities. Must be nominated and have completed one semester of graduate study in fine arts. Must submit portfolio slides. Artwork submitted must have been completed within the past two years. Must have at least two semesters before graduation. Application deadline is March 15.

Academic/Career Areas Arts.

Award Fellowship for use in graduate years; not renewable. *Number:* 5–10. *Amount:* $2500.

Eligibility Requirements Applicant must be enrolled or expecting to enroll full-time at an institution or university and studying in California. Available to U.S. and non-U.S. citizens.

Application Requirements Application, portfolio, artwork. *Deadline:* March 15.

Contact Awards Coordinator
      San Francisco Foundation
      225 Bush Street, Suite 500
      San Francisco, CA 94104-4224
      Phone: 415-733-8560
      E-mail: rec@sff.org

SENSE OF SMELL INSTITUTE
http://www.senseofsmell.org

TOVA FELLOWSHIP
• *See number 101*

SHASTRI INDO-CANADIAN INSTITUTE
http://www.ucalgary.ca/~sici

SHASTRI INDIA STUDIES SENIOR ARTS FELLOWSHIPS
• *See number 157*

SWANN FOUNDATION FUND
http://www.lcweb.loc.gov/rr/print/swann/swann_foundation.html

SWANN FOUNDATION FUND FELLOWSHIP
• *See number 109*

VIRGINIA MUSEUM OF FINE ARTS
http://www.vmfa.state.va.us

VIRGINIA MUSEUM OF FINE ARTS GRADUATE FELLOWSHIP PROGRAM
• *See number 158*

WELLESLEY COLLEGE
http://www.wellesley.edu/CWS/

HARRIET A. SHAW FELLOWSHIP
• *See number 159*

WINTERTHUR MUSEUM, GARDEN, AND LIBRARY
http://www.winterthur.org

LOIS F. MCNEIL DISSERTATION RESEARCH FELLOWSHIPS
• *See number 85*

NEH FELLOWSHIPS
• *See number 110*

WINTERTHUR RESEARCH FELLOWSHIPS
• *See number 111*

AVIATION/AEROSPACE

AMERICAN HISTORICAL ASSOCIATION
http://www.theaha.org

NASA FELLOWSHIP IN AEROSPACE HISTORY • 175

Provides a Fellow with an opportunity to engage in significant and sustained advanced research in all aspects of the history of aerospace from the earliest human interest in flight to the present, including cultural and intellectual history, economic history, history of law and public policy, and the history of science, engineering, and management.

Academic/Career Areas Aviation/Aerospace; Economics; Engineering/Technology; History.

Award Fellowship for use in postgraduate years; not renewable. *Number:* 1–2. *Amount:* $20,000.

Eligibility Requirements Applicant must be enrolled or expecting to enroll full-time at an institution or university. Available to U.S. and non-U.S. citizens.

Application Requirements Application, references. *Deadline:* March 1.

Contact Fellowship Administrator
American Historical Association
400 A Street, SE
Washington, DC 20003
Phone: 202-544-2422
Fax: 202-544-8307
E-mail: aha@theaha.org

AMERICAN INSTITUTE OF AERONAUTICS AND ASTRONAUTICS
http://www.aiaa.org

AIAA FOUNDATION GRADUATE AWARDS
• *See number 26*

AIAA FOUNDATION ORVILLE AND WILBUR WRIGHT AWARDS
• *See number 27*

DELAWARE VALLEY SPACE GRANT CONSORTIUM
http://www.delspace.org

NASA/DELAWARE VALLEY SPACE GRANT FELLOWSHIP
• *See number 52*

GENERAL AVIATION MANUFACTURERS ASSOCIATION
http://www.generalaviation.org

EXCELLENCE IN AVIATION EDUCATION AWARD • 176

One-time award given to educators whose activities bring a better understanding of general aviation to students in the classroom. Winners will be chosen from four grade groups, (K-3, 4-6, 7-9, 10-12). Each award recipient will receive a $500 cash award. See website for additional details.

Academic/Career Areas Aviation/Aerospace.

Award Prize for use in postgraduate years; not renewable. *Number:* 8. *Amount:* $500.

Eligibility Requirements Applicant must be enrolled or expecting to enroll at an institution or university. Applicant or parent of applicant must have employment or volunteer experience in teaching. Available to U.S. citizens.

Application Requirements Application, applicant must enter a contest, sample lesson. *Deadline:* March 1.

Contact General Aviation Manufacturers Association
1400 K Street, NW, Suite 801
Washington, DC 20005-2485

MONTANA SPACE GRANT CONSORTIUM
http://www.montana.edu/msgc

MONTANA SPACE GRANT FELLLOWSHIP PROGRAM • 177

Awards are made on a competitive basis to students enrolled in fields of study relevant to the aerospace sciences and engineering. Must be U.S. citizen enrolled as full-time student at a Montana Consortium campus.

Academic/Career Areas Aviation/Aerospace; Engineering/Technology.

Award Fellowship for use in graduate years; not renewable. *Number:* 5–7. *Amount:* $15,000.

Eligibility Requirements Applicant must be enrolled or expecting to enroll full-time at a four-year institution or university and studying in Montana. Available to U.S. citizens.

Application Requirements Application, essay, references, transcript. *Deadline:* April 2.

Contact Laurie Howell, Program Assistant
Montana Space Grant Consortium
261 EPS Building, Montana State University
Bozeman, MT 59717-3835
Phone: 406-994-4223
Fax: 406-994-4452
E-mail: howell@physics.montana.edu

NASA IDAHO SPACE GRANT CONSORTIUM
http://www.uidaho.edu/nasa_isgc

NASA ID SPACE GRANT CONSORTIUM FELLOWSHIP PROGRAM
• *See number 60*

NASA WYOMING SPACE GRANT CONSORTIUM
http://www.wyomingspacegrant.uwyo.edu

WYOMING NASA SPACE GRANT CONSORTIUM RESEARCH FELLOWSHIP
• See number 61

SOCIETY OF AUTOMOTIVE ENGINEERS
http://www.sae.org/students/stuschol.htm

SOCIETY OF AUTOMOTIVE ENGINEERS DOCTORAL SCHOLARS PROGRAM • **178**

For North American citizens with engineering degree from an accredited program and accepted for doctoral studies. Based on interest in teaching at college level, merit, and interest in mobility technology. Renewable. Loan forgiven if recipient agrees to teach. Application should be retrieved from the SAE website at www.sae.org/students/stuschol.htm.

Academic/Career Areas Aviation/Aerospace; Chemical Engineering; Electrical Engineering/Electronics; Engineering/Technology; Engineering-Related Technologies; Materials Science, Engineering and Metallurgy; Mechanical Engineering.

Award Forgivable loan for use in graduate years; renewable. *Number:* 1–2. *Amount:* $5000–$15,000.

Eligibility Requirements Applicant must be enrolled or expecting to enroll full-time at an institution or university. Available to U.S. and Canadian citizens.

Application Requirements Application, essay, references, test scores, transcript. *Deadline:* April 1.

Contact Connie Harnish, Scholarship and Loan Coordinator
Society of Automotive Engineers
400 Commonwealth Drive
Warrendale, PA 15096-0001
Phone: 724-772-4047
Fax: 724-776-0890
E-mail: connie@sae.org

UNITED NEGRO COLLEGE FUND
http://www.uncf.org

FEDEX EXPRESS FLIGHT SCHOLARSHIPS • **179**

Three scholarships for mid-level to advanced flight ratings. Applicants must be graduate of or currently enrolled in accredited college or university with minimum 3.0 GPA and must currently hold a private or commercial pilot certificate. Scholarship may be used for fixed wing, commercial, instructor, multi-engine/and, or multi-engine instructor certificate.

Academic/Career Areas Aviation/Aerospace.

Award Scholarship for use in graduate years; not renewable.

Eligibility Requirements Applicant must be Black (non-Hispanic) and enrolled or expecting to enroll at a four-year institution or university. Applicant must have 3.0 GPA or higher.

Application Requirements Application, essay.

Contact Program Services Department
United Negro College Fund
8260 Willow Oaks Corporate Drive
Fairfax, VA 22031

ZONTA INTERNATIONAL FOUNDATION
http://www.zonta.org

AMELIA EARHART FELLOWSHIP AWARDS • **180**

Awards for female graduate students with a BS in science or engineering in an aerospace-related field. Must have completed one year of graduate study, senior research project or publication, and be pursuing an advanced degree in aerospace-related studies. One-time award of $6000.

Academic/Career Areas Aviation/Aerospace.

Award Fellowship for use in graduate years; not renewable. *Number:* 35. *Amount:* $6000.

Eligibility Requirements Applicant must be enrolled or expecting to enroll at an institution or university and female.

Application Requirements Application, essay, photo, references, transcript, proof of acceptance or enrollment in graduate program. *Deadline:* November 15.

Contact Ms. Ana Ubides, Foundation Assistant
Zonta International Foundation
557 West Randolph Street
Chicago, IL 60661-2206
Phone: 312-930-5848 Ext. 629
Fax: 312-930-0951
E-mail: zontafdtn@zonta.org

BIOLOGY

AGA FOUNDATION FOR DIGESTIVE HEALTH AND NUTRITION
http://www.fdhn.org

AMERICAN GASTROENTEROLOGICAL ASSOCIATION ASTRAZENECA FELLOWSHIP/FACULTY TRANSITION AWARDS • **181**

Award to provide support for current trainees in gastroenterology-related fields so they may gain additional research training in an area of gastrointestinal, liver function, or related disease. Award of $36,000 per year for two years. Applicants must be M.D.'s currently in gastroenterology-related fellowships in accredited U.S. or Canadian institutions. Applicant must be a member or be sponsored by a member of AGA. Application deadline: September 2.

Academic/Career Areas Biology; Health and Medical Sciences.

Award Fellowship for use in postgraduate years; not renewable. *Number:* up to 4. *Amount:* $36,000.

Eligibility Requirements Applicant must be enrolled or expecting to enroll at an institution or university. Available to U.S. and Canadian citizens.

Application Requirements Application, essay, references. *Deadline:* September 2.

Contact Desta Wallace, Research Awards
Coordinator
AGA Foundation for Digestive Health
and Nutrition
7910 Woodmont Avenue, 7th Floor
Bethesda, MD 20814
Phone: 301-222-4005
Fax: 301-222-4010
E-mail: desta@gastro.org

AIR AND WASTE MANAGEMENT ASSOCIATION
http://www.awma.org

AIR AND WASTE MANAGEMENT ASSOCIATION SCHOLARSHIP ENDOWMENT TRUST FUND
• *See number 24*

AMERICAN FISHERIES SOCIETY
http://www.fisheries.org

J. FRANCES ALLEN SCHOLARSHIP AWARD • 182

The qualified applicant must be a female Ph.D. student who was an AFS member as of December of the preceding year. The applicant must be conducting aquatic research in line with AFS objectives, which include all branches of fisheries science, including but not limited to aquatic biology, engineering, fish culture, limnology, oceanography, and sociology.

Academic/Career Areas Biology; Natural Resources; Natural Sciences.

Award Scholarship for use in postgraduate years; not renewable. *Number:* 1. *Amount:* $2500.

Eligibility Requirements Applicant must be enrolled or expecting to enroll full-time at a four-year institution or university and female. Available to U.S. and non-U.S. citizens.

Application Requirements Application, references, transcript, publications, presentations, professional experience history, AFS participating history, dissertation proposal. *Deadline:* March 1.

Contact Laura Bird, Unit Services Coordinator
American Fisheries Society
5410 Grosvenor Lane
Bethesda, MD 20814-8096
Phone: 301-897-8616 Ext. 201
Fax: 301-897-8096
E-mail: lbird@fisheries.org

AMERICAN GEOPHYSICAL UNION
http://www.agu.org

AMERICAN GEOPHYSICAL UNION HORTON RESEARCH GRANT
• *See number 25*

AMERICAN INSTITUTE OF AERONAUTICS AND ASTRONAUTICS
http://www.aiaa.org

AIAA FOUNDATION GRADUATE AWARDS
• *See number 26*

AIAA FOUNDATION ORVILLE AND WILBUR WRIGHT AWARDS
• *See number 27*

AMERICAN LIVER FOUNDATION
http://www.liverfoundation.org

AMERICAN LIVER FOUNDATION POSTDOCTORAL RESEARCH FELLOWSHIPS • 183

To encourage the development of individuals with research potential who require additional research training and experience, specifically in investigational work relating to liver physiology and disease in preparation for a career of independent research in this field.

Academic/Career Areas Biology; Health and Medical Sciences; Physical Sciences and Math.

Award Fellowship for use in postgraduate years; not renewable. *Number:* 1–15. *Amount:* $10,000.

Eligibility Requirements Applicant must be enrolled or expecting to enroll full-time at an institution or university. Available to U.S. and non-U.S. citizens.

Application Requirements Application, references. *Deadline:* January 5.

Contact Arlene Fraraccio, Research Grants
Coordinator
American Liver Foundation
1425 Pompton
Cedar Grove, NJ 07009
Phone: 973-256-2550 Ext. 225
Fax: 973-256-3214
E-mail: afraraccio@liverfoundation.org

LIVER SCHOLAR AWARDS • 184

Designed to permit scientists with liver research training to bridge the gap between completion of research training and attainment of status as an independent research scientist.

Academic/Career Areas Biology; Health and Medical Sciences; Physical Sciences and Math.

Award Grant for use in postgraduate years; not renewable. *Number:* 1–6. *Amount:* $150,000.

American Liver Foundation (continued)

Eligibility Requirements Applicant must be enrolled or expecting to enroll full-time at an institution or university. Available to U.S. and non-U.S. citizens.

Application Requirements Application, references, description of project, curriculum vitae, and bibliography. *Deadline:* January 1.

Contact Arlene Fraraccio, Research Grants
Coordinator
American Liver Foundation
1425 Pompton
Cedar Grove, NJ 07009
Phone: 973-256-2550 Ext. 225
Fax: 973-256-3214
E-mail: afraiaccio@liverfoundation.org

AMERICAN OPTOMETRIC FOUNDATION
http://www.ezell.org

WILLIAM C. EZELL FELLOWSHIP
• See number 31

AMERICAN ORCHID SOCIETY
http://www.orchidweb.org

AMERICAN ORCHID SOCIETY/ORCHID RESEARCH GRANT • 185

Grant for graduate study in orchid research. Must submit research proposal with application. Deadlines are January 1 and July 1. Must be qualified research personnel at accredited institution or graduate student.

Academic/Career Areas Biology; Horticulture/Floriculture.

Award Grant for use in graduate years; renewable. *Amount:* $500–$12,000.

Eligibility Requirements Applicant must be enrolled or expecting to enroll at an institution or university. Applicant or parent of applicant must have employment or volunteer experience in designated career field. Available to U.S. and non-U.S. citizens.

Application Requirements Application, financial need analysis, references.

Contact Lee S. Cooke, Executive Director
American Orchid Society
16700 AOS Lane
Delray Beach, FL 33446-4351
Phone: 561-404-2000
Fax: 561-404-2100
E-mail: theaos@aos.org

AMERICAN PHYSIOLOGICAL SOCIETY
http://www.faseb.org/aps

CAROLINE TUM SUDEN/FRANCES A. HELLEBRANDT PROFESSIONAL OPPORTUNITY AWARD • 186

Award for junior physiologists to attend and fully participate in Experimental Biology meeting. Award for graduate or postdoctoral students who are the first author of an abstract submitted to American Physiological Society. Candidate or sponsor must be American Physiological Society member. Contact for deadline information.

Academic/Career Areas Biology; Health and Medical Sciences; Physical Sciences and Math.

Award Scholarship for use in graduate, or postgraduate years; not renewable. *Number:* up to 36. *Amount:* $500.

Eligibility Requirements Applicant must be enrolled or expecting to enroll at a four-year institution or university. Applicant or parent of applicant must be member of American Physiological Society. Available to U.S. and non-U.S. citizens.

Application Requirements Application, essay, references, abstract.

Contact Dr. Marsha Matyas, Education Officer
American Physiological Society
9650 Rockville Pike
Bethesda, MD 20814-3991
Phone: 301-530-7132
Fax: 301-571-8305
E-mail: mmatyas@the-aps.org

PORTER PHYSIOLOGY FELLOWSHIPS • 187

Award for students pursuing careers in physiology. Must be Hispanic, Native American, African-American, Pacific Islander, or Native Alaskan. Submit application, transcript, and references. Application deadlines are January 15 and June 15.

Academic/Career Areas Biology; Health and Medical Sciences; Physical Sciences and Math.

Award Fellowship for use in graduate years; not renewable. *Amount:* $15,000.

Eligibility Requirements Applicant must be American Indian/Alaska Native, Black (non-Hispanic), or Hispanic and enrolled or expecting to enroll full-time at a four-year institution or university. Available to U.S. citizens.

Application Requirements Application, references, transcript.

Contact Dr. Marsha Matyas, Education Officer
American Physiological Society
9650 Rockville Pike
Bethesda, MD 20814-3991
Phone: 301-530-7132
Fax: 301-571-8305
E-mail: mmatyas@the-aps.org

PROCTER AND GAMBLE PROFESSIONAL
OPPORTUNITY AWARD • 188

Award allows students within twelve to eighteen months of Ph.D. to participate in Experimental Biology meeting. Must be U.S. citizen or permanent resident and first author of abstract submitted to American Physiological Society. Student, adviser, or sponsor must be American Physiological Society member. Contact for deadline information.

Academic/Career Areas Biology; Health and Medical Sciences; Physical Sciences and Math.

Award Scholarship for use in graduate years; not renewable. *Number:* 17. *Amount:* $500.

Eligibility Requirements Applicant must be enrolled or expecting to enroll at a four-year institution. Applicant or parent of applicant must be member of American Physiological Society. Available to U.S. citizens.

Application Requirements Application, abstract.

Contact Dr. Marsha Matyas, Education Officer
American Physiological Society
9650 Rockville Pike
Bethesda, MD 20814-3991
Phone: 301-530-7132
Fax: 301-571-8306
E-mail: mmatyas@the-aps.org

AMERICAN PSYCHOLOGICAL
ASSOCIATION
http://www.apa.org/mfp

MINORITY FELLOWSHIP FOR NEUROSCIENCE
TRAINING • 189

Renewable award for U.S. citizen or permanent resident enrolled in a full-time doctoral program in the area of neuroscience. An important goal of the program is to increase the representation of under-represented students within neuroscience. Based on academic research ability. Students from all disciplines related to neuroscience may apply. Application available at website.

Academic/Career Areas Biology; Health and Medical Sciences.

Award Fellowship for use in graduate, or postgraduate years; renewable.

Eligibility Requirements Applicant must be enrolled or expecting to enroll full-time at an institution or university. Available to U.S. citizens.

Application Requirements Application, essay, financial need analysis, references, transcript. *Deadline:* January 15.

Contact Dr. Kim Nickerson, Program Assistant
Director
American Psychological Association
750 First Street, NE
Washington, DC 20002-4242
Phone: 202-336-6027
Fax: 202-336-6012
E-mail: mfp@apa.org

AMERICAN SOCIETY FOR
MICROBIOLOGY
http://www.asmusa.org/

AMERICAN SOCIETY FOR MICROBIOLOGY/NCID
POSTDOCTORAL RESEARCH PROGRAM • 190

Award for persons who earned doctorate degrees within three years of proposed start date. For full-time research on infectious diseases which cause public health programs. Associate receives annual stipend, health benefits and funds for professional development.

Academic/Career Areas Biology; Health and Medical Sciences.

Award Fellowship for use in postgraduate years; not renewable. *Number:* up to 10. *Amount:* $30,800–$32,300.

Eligibility Requirements Applicant must be enrolled or expecting to enroll at an institution or university and studying in Georgia.

Application Requirements Application, essay, references, transcript. *Deadline:* November 15.

Contact Irene Hulede, Manager, Student Programs
American Society for Microbiology
1752 N Street, NW
Washington, DC 20036
Phone: 202-942-9295
Fax: 202-942-9329

ROBERT D. WATKINS MINORITY GRADUATE
RESEARCH FELLOWSHIP • 191

Award for formally admitted doctoral student who has successfully completed first year as doctoral candidate in the microbiology sciences at an accredited U.S. institution. Must be an ASM member and have an approved research project, and be a member of an under-represented minority group. Program lasts three years. Must be U.S. citizen.

Academic/Career Areas Biology.

Award Fellowship for use in graduate years; not renewable. *Number:* 1. *Amount:* $15,000.

Eligibility Requirements Applicant must be American Indian/Alaska Native, Black (non-Hispanic), or Hispanic and enrolled or expecting to enroll at an institution or university. Applicant or

American Society for Microbiology (continued)

parent of applicant must be member of American Society for Microbiology. Available to U.S. citizens.

Application Requirements Application, essay, references, transcript. *Deadline:* May 1.

Contact Irene Hulede, Manager, Student Programs
American Society for Microbiology
1752 N Street, NW
Washington, DC 20036
Phone: 202-942-9295
Fax: 202-942-9329

AMERICAN WATER WORKS ASSOCIATION
http://www.awwa.org

AMERICAN WATER WORKS ASSOCIATION/ABEL WOLMAN FELLOWSHIP
• *See number 44*

AMERICAN WATER WORKS ASSOCIATION/ HOLLY A. CORNELL SCHOLARSHIP
• *See number 45*

AMERICAN WATER WORKS ASSOCIATION/ LARSON AQUATIC RESEARCH SUPPORT SCHOLARSHIP
• *See number 46*

AMERICAN WATER WORKS ASSOCIATION/ THOMAS R. CAMP MEMORIAL SCHOLARSHIP
• *See number 47*

ARCTIC INSTITUTE OF NORTH AMERICA
http://www.ucalgary.ca/aina

JENNIFER ROBINSON SCHOLARSHIP • **192**

One award for graduate student majoring in biology with concentration on North American issues. Must submit statement of research objectives, curriculum vitae, references, and current funding information. One-time award of $5000.

Academic/Career Areas Biology.

Award Scholarship for use in graduate years; not renewable. *Number:* 1. *Amount:* $5000.

Eligibility Requirements Applicant must be enrolled or expecting to enroll full-time at an institution or university.

Application Requirements References, transcript. *Deadline:* January 7.

Contact Executive Director
Arctic Institute of North America
University of Calgary, 2500 University
Drive NW
Calgary, AB T2N IN4
Canada
Phone: 403-220-7515
Fax: 403-282-4609
E-mail: wkjessen@ucalgary.ca

LORRAINE ALLISON SCHOLARSHIP
• *See number 118*

ASSOCIATION FOR WOMEN IN SCIENCE EDUCATIONAL FOUNDATION
http://www.awis.org

ASSOCIATION FOR WOMEN IN SCIENCE PREDOCTORAL FELLOWSHIP
• *See number 77*

ATLANTIC SALMON FEDERATION
http://www.asf.ca

ATLANTIC SALMON FEDERATION OLIN FELLOWSHIP
• *See number 16*

CANADIAN NORTHERN STUDIES TRUST - ASSOCIATION OF CANADIAN UNIVERSITIES FOR NORTHERN STUDIES
http://www.cyberus.ca/~acuns

RESEARCH SUPPORT OPPORTUNITIES IN ARCTIC ENVIRONMENTAL STUDIES
• *See number 120*

EDMUND NILES HUYCK PRESERVE AND BIOLOGICAL RESEARCH STATION
http://www.huyckpreserve.org

HUYCK STATION RESEARCH GRANTS
• *See number 18*

ENTOMOLOGICAL SOCIETY OF AMERICA
http://www.entsoc.org

ENTOMOLOGICAL SOCIETY OF AMERICA FELLOWSHIPS • **193**

Up to 10 fellows selected on the basis of outstanding contributions made in one or more of the following areas of entomology: research, teaching, extension, or administration. Each regular Entomological Society of America member may nominate one candidate each year. Contact website for application procedures and further information. All nominations must be submitted electronically.

Academic/Career Areas Biology.

Award Fellowship for use in graduate, or postgraduate years; not renewable. *Number:* up to 10.

Eligibility Requirements Applicant must be enrolled or expecting to enroll at an institution or university. Available to U.S. citizens.

Application Requirements Application. *Deadline:* March 15.

Contact Education Committee
Entomological Society of America
9301 Annapolis Road
Suite 300
Lanham, MD 20706-3115
Phone: 301-731-4535 Ext. 3029
Fax: 301-731-4538
E-mail: awards@entsoc.org

HENRY AND SYLVIA RICHARDSON RESEARCH GRANT • 194

One-time award to provide research funds to postdoctoral members of Entomological Society of America with minimum one year of promising work experience. For work in insect control by attractants, repellents, biological, thermo, or chemical controls. Minimum GPA 3.0. Merit-based award of $1000. Must be nominated.

Academic/Career Areas Biology.

Award Grant for use in postgraduate years; not renewable. *Amount:* $1000.

Eligibility Requirements Applicant must be enrolled or expecting to enroll at an institution or university. Applicant or parent of applicant must be member of Entomological Society of America. Applicant or parent of applicant must have employment or volunteer experience in designated career field. Applicant must have 3.0 GPA or higher.

Application Requirements Application, references, transcript, description of research. *Deadline:* July 1.

Contact Education Committee
Entomological Society of America
9301 Annapolis Road
Suite 300
Lanham, MD 20706-3115
Phone: 301-731-4535 Ext. 3029
Fax: 301-731-4538
E-mail: awards@entsoc.org

JEFFERY P. LAFAGE GRADUATE STUDENT RESEARCH AWARD • 195

Renewable award for graduate student who proposes innovative research in biology or control of pests in urban environment. Must submit two letters of recommendation; materials and budget; and title, duration, and background information concerning the significance of the proposed research to the field. Must be nominated. Must be a candidate for a master's or doctoral degree at an accredited university.

Academic/Career Areas Biology.

Award Grant for use in graduate years; renewable. *Number:* 1. *Amount:* up to $2000.

Eligibility Requirements Applicant must be enrolled or expecting to enroll at an institution or university.

Application Requirements Application, references, research proposal; materials and budget. *Deadline:* July 1.

Contact Education Committee
Entomological Society of America
9301 Annapolis Road
Suite 300
Lanham, MD 20706-3115
Phone: 301-731-4535 Ext. 3029
Fax: 301-731-4538
E-mail: awards@entsoc.org

JOHN HENRY COMSTOCK GRADUATE STUDENT AWARD • 196

Each award consists of an all-expense-paid trip to the ESA Annual Meeting, plus $100 and a certificate. Must be pursuing graduate degree with a concentration in entomology or have acquired a degree within twelve months of application. Must have applied for society membership prior to January 1. Submit photo and documentation. Must be nominated. All award nominations must be submitted electronically.

Academic/Career Areas Biology.

Award Prize for use in graduate years; not renewable. *Number:* 5. *Amount:* $100.

Eligibility Requirements Applicant must be enrolled or expecting to enroll at an institution or university. Applicant or parent of applicant must be member of Entomological Society of America.

Application Requirements Application, photo. *Deadline:* September 1.

Contact Education Committee
Entomological Society of America
9301 Annapolis Road
Suite 300
Lanham, MD 20706-3115
Phone: 301-731-4535 Ext. 3029
Fax: 301-731-4538
E-mail: awards@entsoc.org

NORMAND R. DUBOIS MEMORIAL SCHOLARSHIP • 197

Scholarship to encourage research by graduate students directed toward the use of biologically based technologies to protect and preserve forests in an environmentally acceptable manner. Nominations must be electronically submitted by July 1.

Academic/Career Areas Biology; Natural Resources.

Award Scholarship for use in graduate years; not renewable. *Amount:* $1500.

Biology

Entomological Society of America (continued)

Eligibility Requirements Applicant must be enrolled or expecting to enroll at an institution or university.

Application Requirements Application, references, research proposal. *Deadline:* July 1.

Contact Education Committee
Entomological Society of America
9301 Annapolis Road
Suite 300
Lanham, MD 20706-3115
Phone: 301-731-4535 Ext. 3029
Fax: 301-731-4538
E-mail: awards@entsoc.org

PLANT RESISTANCE TO INSECTS GRADUATE STUDENT RESEARCH AWARD • 198

Awarded to a graduate student in entomology or plant breeding/genetics for innovative research that contributes significantly to knowledge of plant resistance to insects. Renewable grant for a U.S. citizen who is a candidate for a master's or doctoral degree at an accredited university. Submit research background information, materials and budget, and two letters of recommendation.

Academic/Career Areas Biology.

Award Prize for use in graduate years; renewable.

Eligibility Requirements Applicant must be enrolled or expecting to enroll at an institution or university. Available to U.S. citizens.

Application Requirements References, research background, materials, budget. *Deadline:* July 1.

Contact Education Committee
Entomological Society of America
9301 Annapolis Road
Suite 300
Lanham, MD 20706-3115
Phone: 301-731-4535 Ext. 3029
Fax: 301-731-4538
E-mail: awards@entsoc.org

SNODGRASS MEMORIAL RESEARCH AWARD • 199

One-time award for graduate student researching arthropod morphology, systematics, taxonomy or evolution at a recognized college or university within two calendar years previous to the application due date. Submit application, three copies of research thesis/dissertation (including date approval page), and two letters of recommendation. Must be a member of ESA. Deadline is July 1. Must be nominated.

Academic/Career Areas Biology.

Award Prize for use in graduate years; not renewable.

Eligibility Requirements Applicant must be enrolled or expecting to enroll at a four-year institution or university. Applicant or parent of applicant must be member of Entomological Society of America.

Application Requirements Application, references, description of research, 3 copies of research thesis/dissertation.. *Deadline:* July 1.

Contact Education Committee
Entomological Society of America
9301 Annapolis Road
Suite 300
Lanham, MD 20706-3115
Phone: 301-731-4535 Ext. 3029
Fax: 301-731-4538
E-mail: awards@entsoc.org

EPILEPSY FOUNDATION
http://www.epilepsyfoundation.org

PREDOCTORAL RESEARCH TRAINING FELLOWSHIP • 200

Award to pre-doctoral students with dissertation research related to epilepsy. Number of awards depends on funds available. Students must be pursuing a Ph.D. in neuroscience, physiology, pharmacology, psychology, biochemistry, genetics, nursing, or pharmacy. Research must be done in the U.S. or its territories. Submit all application materials by September 5.

Academic/Career Areas Biology; Nursing; Physical Sciences and Math; Social Sciences.

Award Fellowship for use in graduate years; not renewable. *Amount:* up to $16,000.

Eligibility Requirements Applicant must be enrolled or expecting to enroll at an institution or university.

Application Requirements Application, autobiography, financial need analysis, references. *Deadline:* September 5.

Contact Cathy Morris, Administrative Coordinator,
Programs and Research
Epilepsy Foundation
4351 Garden City Drive
Landover, MD 20785
Phone: 301-459-3700
Fax: 301-577-4941
E-mail: grants@efa.org

FOUNDATION FOR CHIROPRACTIC EDUCATION AND RESEARCH
http://www.fcer.org

FOUNDATION FOR CHIROPRACTIC EDUCATION AND RESEARCH FELLOWSHIPS, SCHOLARSHIPS, AND RESIDENCY STIPENDS • 201

Fellowship and residency awards are made primarily to graduate chiropractors pursuing research training in programs leading to a doctorate or MPH in scientific and non-clinical health-related areas. Must submit curriculum vitae of academic supervisor. Several renewable awards of varying amounts available. Must rank in upper half of class or have a 2.75 GPA.

Academic/Career Areas Biology; Health and Medical Sciences.

Award Fellowship for use in graduate, or postgraduate years; renewable. *Number:* 4–7. *Amount:* $2000–$20,000.

Eligibility Requirements Applicant must be enrolled or expecting to enroll full or part-time at an institution or university. Available to U.S. and non-U.S. citizens.

Application Requirements Application, essay, financial need analysis, references, transcript, curriculum vitae of advisor (mentor). *Deadline:* March 1.

Contact Dr. Anthony Rosner, Director of Research
and Education
Foundation for Chiropractic Education
and Research
1330 Beacon Street, Suite 315
Brookline, MA 02446-3202
Phone: 617-734-3397
Fax: 617-734-0989
E-mail: rosnerfcer@aol.com

FOUNDATION FOR SCIENCE AND DISABILITY
http://www.as.wvu.edu/~scidis/organize/fsd.html

GRANTS FOR DISABLED STUDENTS IN THE SCIENCES
• *See number 54*

GEM CONSORTIUM
http://www.nd.edu/~gem

GEM PH.D. ENGINEERING FELLOWSHIP
• *See number 9*

GREAT LAKES COMMISSION
http://www.glc.org

GREAT LAKES COMMISSION - SEA GRANT FELLOWSHIP • 202

The Fellow is a full-time employee of the Great Lakes Commission, based in Ann Arbor, Michigan. Working with members of the Great Lakes science, policy and information/education communities, the Fellow will contribute to and benefit from research coordination and policy analysis activities.

Academic/Career Areas Biology; Natural Resources; Natural Sciences.

Award Fellowship for use in graduate, or postgraduate years; not renewable. *Number:* 1. *Amount:* $38,000.

Eligibility Requirements Applicant must be enrolled or expecting to enroll full or part-time at a four-year institution or university and studying in Illinois, Indiana, Michigan, Minnesota, New York, Ohio, Pennsylvania, or Wisconsin. Available to U.S. and non-U.S. citizens.

Application Requirements Application, resume, references, transcript, education/career goal statement. *Deadline:* February 22.

Contact Michael Donahue, President/CEO
Great Lakes Commission
400 Fourth Street
Argus II Building
Ann Arbor, MI 48103-4816
Phone: 734-665-9135
Fax: 734-665-4370
E-mail: mdonahue@glc.org

HOWARD HUGHES MEDICAL INSTITUTE, OFFICE OF GRANTS AND SPECIAL PROGRAMS
http://www.hhmi.org

HOWARD HUGHES MEDICAL INSTITUTE PREDOCTORAL FELLOWSHIPS IN BIOLOGICAL SCIENCES • 203

The purpose of the predoctoral fellowship program is to promote excellence in biomedical research by helping prospective researchers with exceptional promise to obtain high-quality graduate education. These are five-year awards for graduate students pursuing full-time study toward a Ph.D. or Sc.D. degree in selected biological sciences. Students must be at or near the beginning of graduate study.

Academic/Career Areas Biology; Health and Medical Sciences.

Award Fellowship for use in graduate years; not renewable. *Number:* 80. *Amount:* $37,000.

Eligibility Requirements Applicant must be enrolled or expecting to enroll full-time at an institution or university. Available to U.S. and non-U.S. citizens.

Application Requirements Application, essay, references, test scores, transcript. *Deadline:* November 12.

Contact Dr. Maryrose Franko, Senior Program
Officer
Howard Hughes Medical Institute, Office
of Grants and Special Programs
4000 Jones Bridge Road
Chevy Chase, MD 20815-6789
Phone: 301-215-8883
Fax: 301-215-8888
E-mail: fellows@hhmi.org

HOWARD HUGHES MEDICAL INSTITUTE RESEARCH TRAINING FELLOWSHIPS FOR MEDICAL STUDENTS • 204

The HHMI program provides medical student fellows the opportunity to perform a year of intensive laboratory research studying fundamental biological processes or disease mechanisms. Applicants must be full-time students enrolled in U.S. medical schools, and the research must be performed at medical schools, universities, or non-profit institutions within the U.S.

Academic/Career Areas Biology; Health and Medical Sciences.

Award Fellowship for use in graduate years; not renewable. *Number:* 60. *Amount:* $37,000.

Eligibility Requirements Applicant must be enrolled or expecting to enroll full-time at an institution or university. Available to U.S. and non-U.S. citizens.

Application Requirements Application, essay, references, test scores, transcript. *Deadline:* November 14.

Contact Dr. Andrea Stith, Program Officer
Howard Hughes Medical Institute, Office
of Grants and Special Programs
4000 Jones Bridge Road
Chevy Chase, MD 20815-6789
Phone: 301-215-8883
Fax: 301-215-8888
E-mail: fellows@hhmi.org

HUDSON RIVER FOUNDATION
http://www.hudsonriver.org

HUDSON RIVER FOUNDATION GRADUATE FELLOWSHIPS • 205

One year of support for graduate research on Hudson River-specific study. Also includes support for research expenses. Up to six one-time awards: $11,000 master's level award and $15,000 Ph.D. award. Application deadline is March 4.

Academic/Career Areas Biology; Earth Science; Engineering/Technology; Natural Sciences; Science, Technology and Society.

Award Fellowship for use in graduate years; not renewable. *Number:* up to 6. *Amount:* $11,000–$15,000.

Eligibility Requirements Applicant must be enrolled or expecting to enroll at an institution or university. Available to U.S. and non-U.S. citizens.

Application Requirements Application, resume, references, proposal. *Deadline:* March 4.

Contact Science Director
Hudson River Foundation
40 West 20th Street, 9th Floor
New York, NY 10011
Phone: 212-924-8290
E-mail: info@hudsonriver.org

HUDSON RIVER RESEARCH GRANTS • 206

Grants available to researchers with institutional affiliation. Proposed study must be appropriate to mission of the Hudson River Foundation.

Academic/Career Areas Biology; Natural Resources; Natural Sciences.

Award Grant for use in postgraduate years; not renewable.

Eligibility Requirements Applicant must be enrolled or expecting to enroll at a four-year institution or university.

Application Requirements Resume, proposal. *Deadline:* September 24.

Contact Science Director
Hudson River Foundation
40 West 20th Street, 9th Floor
New York, NY 10011
Phone: 212-924-8290
E-mail: info@hudsonriver.org

HUDSON RIVER NATIONAL ESTUARINE RESEARCH RESERVE
http://www.ocm.nos.noaa/nerr/fellow.html

NATIONAL ESTUARINE RESEARCH RESERVE GRADUATE FELLOWSHIP PROGRAM
• See number 55

INTERNATIONAL DESALINATION ASSOCIATION
http://www.ida.bm

INTERNATIONAL DESALINATION ASSOCIATION SCHOLARSHIP
• See number 57

INTERNATIONAL DEVELOPMENT RESEARCH CENTER
http://www.idrc.ca/awards

FORAGE CROPS IN SUSTAINABLY MANAGED AGROECOSYSTEMS: THE BENTLEY FELLOWSHIP
• See number 11

INTERNATIONAL FOUNDATION FOR ETHICAL RESEARCH
http://www.ifer.org

FELLOWSHIPS IN ALTERNATIVES IN ETHICAL RESEARCH • 207

IFER's fellowships are awarded to graduate students and other scientists whose projects enhance involvement in the study of or use of alternatives to animals in scientific research and how the projects' outcome will replace, reduce or refine the use of animals in research, product testing or education.

Academic/Career Areas Biology; Humanities; Journalism; Social Sciences.

Award Fellowship for use in graduate, or postgraduate years; renewable. *Number: 7. Amount:* $16,000.

Eligibility Requirements Applicant must be enrolled or expecting to enroll full or part-time at an institution or university. Available to U.S. and non-U.S. citizens.

Application Requirements Application. *Deadline:* March 15.

Contact Peter O'Donovan, Executive Director
International Foundation for Ethical Research
55 West Jackson Boulevard, Suite 1552
Chicago, IL 60604
Phone: 312-427-6025
Fax: 312-427-6524
E-mail: ifer@navs.org

INTERNATIONAL WOMEN'S FISHING ASSOCIATION SCHOLARSHIP TRUST
http://www.iwfa.org

INTERNATIONAL WOMEN'S FISHING ASSOCIATION GRADUATE SCHOLARSHIPS IN THE MARINE SCIENCES
• *See number 19*

LIFE SCIENCES RESEARCH FOUNDATION
http://www.lsrf.org

POSTDOCTORAL FELLOWSHIPS • 208

LSEF awards fellowships in the life sciences; biochemistry; cell development, molecular, plant, structural, organismic population and evolutionary biology; endocrinology; immunology; microbiology; neurology; physiology; and virology. 3-year fellowships will be awarded on a competitive basis to graduates of medical and graduate schools in the biological sciences holding M.D., Ph.D., D.V.M. or D.D.S. degrees. Awards based solely on quality of applicants previous accomplishments, and on the merit of the proposal for postdoctoral research. Fellowship can not be used to support research that has patent commitment or agreement with commercial profit-making company.

Academic/Career Areas Biology; Earth Science; Health and Medical Sciences; Natural Sciences.

Award Fellowship for use in graduate, or postgraduate years; not renewable. *Number:* 16–20. *Amount:* $150,000.

Eligibility Requirements Applicant must be enrolled or expecting to enroll full-time at an institution or university. Available to U.S. and non-U.S. citizens.

Application Requirements Application, resume, references, self-addressed stamped envelope. *Deadline:* October 1.

Contact Susan Di Renzo, Assistant Director
Life Sciences Research Foundation
Lewis Thomas Lab, Princeton University
Washington Road
Princeton, NJ 08544
Fax: 609-258-2957

MOUNTAIN LAKE BIOLOGICAL STATION
http://www.virginia.edu/~mtlake

MOUNTAIN LAKE BIOLOGICAL STATION RESEARCH FELLOWSHIP • 209

One-time award for graduate and post-doctoral students conducting research in field biology at Mountain Lake Biological Station.

Academic/Career Areas Biology.

Award Fellowship for use in graduate, or postgraduate years; not renewable. *Number:* 4–6. *Amount:* $300–$2000.

Eligibility Requirements Applicant must be enrolled or expecting to enroll full-time at an institution or university. Available to U.S. and non-U.S. citizens.

Application Requirements Application. *Deadline:* March 16.

Contact Eric Nagy, Associate Director
Mountain Lake Biological Station
238 Gilmer Hall, University of Virginia,
PO Box 400327
Charlottesville, VA 22904-4327
Phone: 434-982-5486
Fax: 434-982-5626
E-mail: mtlake@virginia.edu

MYASTHENIA GRAVIS FOUNDATION OF AMERICA, INC.
http://www.myasthenia.org

DR. HENRY R. VIETS MEDICAL STUDENT RESEARCH FELLOWSHIP • 210

Fellowship for medical student or recent graduate for research in myasthenia gravis or related field. Must be U.S. or Canadian citizen or be in the U.S. on valid visa. Submit abstract of proposed study. Inquire for guidelines. One-time award of $3000.

Academic/Career Areas Biology; Health and Medical Sciences; Physical Sciences and Math.

Award Fellowship for use in graduate, or postgraduate years; not renewable. *Number:* 1–4. *Amount:* $3000.

Eligibility Requirements Applicant must be enrolled or expecting to enroll full or part-time at an institution or university. Available to U.S. and non-U.S. citizens.

Myasthenia Gravis Foundation of America, Inc. (continued)

Application Requirements Autobiography, references, transcript, abstract of proposed study. *Deadline:* March 15.

Contact Debora Boelz, Chief Executive
Myasthenia Gravis Foundation of
America, Inc.
5841 Cedar Lake Road
Suite 204
Minneapolis, MN 55416
Phone: 800-541-5454
Fax: 952-646-2028
E-mail: myastheniagravis@msn.com

OSSERMAN/SOSIN/MCCLURE POSTDOCTORAL FELLOWSHIP • 211

One-time postdoctoral award for investigators to pursue the treatment, etiology, and/or cure of myasthenia gravis. Submit autobiography and references. Write for further details.

Academic/Career Areas Biology; Health and Medical Sciences; Physical Sciences and Math.

Award Fellowship for use in postgraduate years; not renewable. *Number:* 1–4. *Amount:* $50,000.

Eligibility Requirements Applicant must be enrolled or expecting to enroll full or part-time at an institution or university. Available to U.S. and non-U.S. citizens.

Application Requirements Autobiography, references. *Deadline:* October 15.

Contact Debora Boelz, Chief Executive
Myasthenia Gravis Foundation of
America, Inc.
5841 Cedar Lake Road
Suite 204
Minneapolis, MN 55416
Phone: 800-541-5454
Fax: 952-646-2028
E-mail: myastheniagravis@msn.com

NASA IDAHO SPACE GRANT CONSORTIUM
http://www.uidaho.edu/nasa_isgc

NASA ID SPACE GRANT CONSORTIUM FELLOWSHIP PROGRAM
• *See number 60*

NASA WYOMING SPACE GRANT CONSORTIUM
http://www.wyomingspacegrant.uwyo.edu

WYOMING NASA SPACE GRANT CONSORTIUM RESEARCH FELLOWSHIP
• *See number 61*

NATIONAL RESEARCH COUNCIL
http://www.nationalacademies.org/fellowships/

HOWARD HUGHES MEDICAL INSTITUTE PREDOCTORAL FELLOWSHIP IN BIOLOGICAL SCIENCES • 212

Eighty renewable fellowships to assist beginning graduate students to complete a Ph.D. or Sc.D. degree in biological sciences. In addition to $21,000 stipend, an allowance of $16,000 allotted to fellowship institution in lieu of tuition and fees. Deadline is November 13.

Academic/Career Areas Biology.

Award Fellowship for use in graduate years; renewable. *Number:* 80. *Amount:* $21,000.

Eligibility Requirements Applicant must be enrolled or expecting to enroll full-time at an institution or university. Available to U.S. and non-U.S. citizens.

Application Requirements Application, essay, references, test scores, transcript. *Deadline:* November 13.

Contact Program Specialist
National Research Council
Fellowships, TJ 2041, 2101 Constitution
Avenue
Washington, DC 20418
Phone: 202-334-2872
Fax: 202-334-3419
E-mail: infofell@nas.edu

NATIONAL SCIENCE FOUNDATION
http://www.nsf.gov/grfp

NATIONAL SCIENCE FOUNDATION GRADUATE RESEARCH FELLOWSHIPS
• *See number 62*

NATIONAL SLEEP FOUNDATION
http://www.sleepfoundation.org

NATIONAL SLEEP FOUNDATION POSTDOCTORAL FELLOWSHIP PROGRAM • 213

Awards support researchers in training to pursue basic, applied, or clinical research in the study of sleep and sleep disorders. Must have received an MD, DVM, Ph.D., or DO degree within the past five years and demonstrate aptitude for research. Awards for two-year period contingent upon satisfactory progress in the first year. Must be U.S. citizens or resident aliens in recognized American or Canadian programs of study or laboratories.

Academic/Career Areas Biology; Health and Medical Sciences; Social Sciences.

Award Fellowship for use in postgraduate years; renewable. *Number:* 2. *Amount:* $40,000.

Eligibility Requirements Applicant must be enrolled or expecting to enroll full or part-time at an institution or university. Available to U.S. and non-U.S. citizens.

Application Requirements Application, references. *Deadline:* December 15.

Contact Pat Britz, Education and Research Manager
National Sleep Foundation
1522 K Street, NW, Suite 500
Washington, DC 20005
Phone: 202-347-3471 Ext. 203
Fax: 202-347-3472

NOVARTIS FOUNDATION
http://wwwl.novartisfound.org.uk/bursary.htm

NOVARTIS FOUNDATION BURSARY SCHEME
• *See number 20*

PARALYZED VETERANS OF AMERICA - SPINAL CORD RESEARCH FOUNDATION
http://www.pva.org/scrf

FELLOWSHIPS IN SPINAL CORD INJURY RESEARCH
• *See number 21*

ROB & BESSIE WELDER WILDLIFE FOUNDATION

WILDLIFE RESEARCH SCHOLARSHIP
• *See number 22*

SENSE OF SMELL INSTITUTE
http://www.senseofsmell.org

SENSE OF SMELL INSTITUTE RESEARCH GRANTS • **214**

Research award for the advanced study of olfaction. Applicants must hold a doctorate degree and submit a research proposal including abstract, budget, and curriculum vitae of applicant and collaborators. Priority given to specific topics that change each year. Applicants should call organization or check website for current topic.

Academic/Career Areas Biology; Education; Health and Medical Sciences; Science, Technology and Society; Social Sciences; Sports-related; Therapy/Rehabilitation.

Award Grant for use in postgraduate years; not renewable. *Number:* 1–6. *Amount:* $30,000–$45,000.

Eligibility Requirements Applicant must be enrolled or expecting to enroll full or part-time at an institution or university. Available to U.S. and non-U.S. citizens.

Application Requirements Application, autobiography, curriculum vitae, budget. *Deadline:* January 15.

Contact Theresa Molnar, Executive Director
Sense of Smell Institute
145 East 32nd Street
New York, NY 10016-6002
Phone: 212-725-2755 Ext. 228
Fax: 212-779-9072
E-mail: info@senseofsmell.org

TOVA FELLOWSHIP
• *See number 101*

SOCIETY OF TOXICOLOGY
http://www.toxicology.org

COLGATE-PALMOLIVE AWARD FOR STUDENT RESEARCH • **215**

Awards to enhance student research training using in vitro or alternative techniques to traditional animal models in toxicology research, either for graduate students or to institutions for research internships.

Academic/Career Areas Biology; Health and Medical Sciences.

Award Grant for use in graduate years; not renewable. *Number:* up to 6. *Amount:* up to $2500.

Eligibility Requirements Applicant must be enrolled or expecting to enroll full-time at an institution or university. Available to U.S. and non-U.S. citizens.

Application Requirements Application, references, proposal. *Deadline:* October 9.

Contact Society of Toxicology
1767 Business Center Drive, Suite 302
Reston, VA 20190

COLGATE-PALMOLIVE POSTDOCTORAL FELLOWSHIP • **216**

Awarded in alternate years to advance the development of alternatives to animal testing in toxicology research; includes stipend and research-related costs for post-doctoral study.

Academic/Career Areas Biology; Health and Medical Sciences.

Award Fellowship for use in postgraduate years; not renewable. *Number:* up to 1. *Amount:* up to $33,000.

Eligibility Requirements Applicant must be enrolled or expecting to enroll full-time at an institution or university. Available to U.S. and non-U.S. citizens.

Application Requirements Application, interview, references, proposal. *Deadline:* October 9.

Contact Society of Toxicology
1767 Business Center Drive, Suite 302
Reston, VA 20190

Biology

GRADUATE STUDENT FELLOWSHIP • 217

Graduate Fellowship Awards are based on originality of dissertation research, productivity, relevance to toxicology, scholastic achievement, and references. Fellowship award includes stipend and/or research-related expenses.

Academic/Career Areas Biology; Health and Medical Sciences.

Award Fellowship for use in graduate years; not renewable. *Number:* up to 2. *Amount:* up to $16,000.

Eligibility Requirements Applicant must be enrolled or expecting to enroll full-time at an institution or university. Available to U.S. and Canadian citizens.

Application Requirements Application, interview, references, transcript, proposal. *Deadline:* October 9.

Contact Society of Toxicology
1767 Business Center Drive, Suite 302
Reston, VA 20190

GRADUATE STUDENT TRAVEL AWARDS • 218

Graduate Travel Awards defray travel costs for SOT member students presenting talks or posters at the annual meeting. The deadline is October 9.

Academic/Career Areas Biology; Health and Medical Sciences.

Award Grant for use in graduate years; not renewable. *Number:* 50–70. *Amount:* $500–$800.

Eligibility Requirements Applicant must be enrolled or expecting to enroll full-time at an institution or university. Available to U.S. and non-U.S. citizens.

Application Requirements Application, references, abstract. *Deadline:* October 9.

Contact Society of Toxicology
1767 Business Center Drive, Suite 302
Reston, VA 20190

ROBERT L. DIXON INTERNATIONAL TRAVEL AWARD • 219

Award for students in the area of reproductive toxicology to attend International Congress of Toxicology meeting, which is held every 3 years.

Academic/Career Areas Biology; Health and Medical Sciences.

Award Grant for use in graduate years; not renewable. *Number:* up to 1. *Amount:* up to $2000.

Eligibility Requirements Applicant must be enrolled or expecting to enroll full-time at an institution or university. Available to U.S. and non-U.S. citizens.

Application Requirements Application, references, transcript, statement.

Contact Society of Toxicology
1767 Business Center Drive, Suite 302
Reston, VA 20190

SOT/ACC EARLY AWARD IN INHALATION TOXICOLOGY • 220

Award designed to encourage early career scientists to conduct research that will improve the scientific basis for risk assessment and decision making. The deadline is October 9.

Academic/Career Areas Biology; Health and Medical Sciences.

Award Fellowship for use in postgraduate years; not renewable. *Number:* up to 1. *Amount:* up to $100,000.

Eligibility Requirements Applicant must be enrolled or expecting to enroll full-time at an institution or university. Available to U.S. and non-U.S. citizens.

Application Requirements Application, resume, references, proposal. *Deadline:* October 9.

Contact Society of Toxicology
1767 Business Center Drive, Suite 302
Reston, VA 20190

UNITED NEGRO COLLEGE FUND
http://www.uncf.org

UNCF/PFIZER POSTDOCTORAL FELLOWSHIPS • 221

Scholarship established to support the career development of underrepresented minority post-graduate in biomedical research fields.

Academic/Career Areas Biology; Health and Medical Sciences.

Award Fellowship for use in postgraduate years; not renewable. *Number:* up to 4. *Amount:* up to $53,500.

Eligibility Requirements Applicant must be American Indian/Alaska Native, Asian/Pacific Islander, Black (non-Hispanic), or Hispanic and enrolled or expecting to enroll at a four-year institution or university.

Application Requirements Application, references, transcript, curriculum vitae. *Deadline:* April 15.

Contact Dr. Jerry L. Bryant, Director, Pfizer
Biomedical Research Initiative
United Negro College Fund
8260 Willow Oaks Corporate Drive
Fairfax, VA 22031-4511
Phone: 703-205-3503
Fax: 703-205-3574
E-mail: uncfpfizer@uncf.org

BUSINESS/CONSUMER SERVICES

ACADEMY OF MARKETING SCIENCE FOUNDATION
http://www.ams-web.org

MARY KAY DOCTORAL DISSERTATION AWARD • 222

One-time award for the best dissertation abstract in marketing science submitted. Must be no more than 30 double-spaced pages, including tables and figures. Must be AMS member.

Academic/Career Areas Business/Consumer Services.

Award Prize for use in graduate years; not renewable. *Amount:* $500.

Eligibility Requirements Applicant must be enrolled or expecting to enroll at an institution or university. Available to U.S. citizens.

Application Requirements *Deadline:* December 11.

Contact Central Office
Academy of Marketing Science Foundation
University of Miami, PO Box 248012
Coral Gables, FL 33124-6536

STANLEY C. HOLLANDER BEST RETAILING PAPER COMPETITION • 223

Competition for best retailing paper. Submit four copies of manuscript, which is no longer than fifteen pages total. One-time award for college graduates. Write for deadline and further information. Must be AMS member.

Academic/Career Areas Business/Consumer Services.

Award Prize for use in graduate years; not renewable. *Amount:* $100.

Eligibility Requirements Applicant must be enrolled or expecting to enroll at an institution or university and must have an interest in writing.

Application Requirements Application, applicant must enter a contest.

Contact Central Office
Academy of Marketing Science Foundation
University of Miami, PO Box 248012
Coral Gables, FL 33124-6536

AMERICAN ASSOCIATION OF UNIVERSITY WOMEN (AAUW) EDUCATIONAL FOUNDATION
http://www.aauw.org

AAUW EDUCATIONAL FOUNDATION SELECTED PROFESSIONS FELLOWSHIPS
• *See number 87*

ARMENIAN RELIEF SOCIETY OF NORTH AMERICA INC.-REGIONAL OFFICE

ARMENIAN RELIEF SOCIETY GRADUATE SCHOLARSHIP PROGRAM • 224

One-time award to a student with Armenian heritage. Must be a citizen of the U.S. or Canada. Deadline: April 1. This program has been made possible through the George and Beatrice Lazarian Scholarship Fund.

Academic/Career Areas Business/Consumer Services; Economics; Health and Medical Sciences; History; International Studies; Journalism; Law/Legal Services; Political Science.

Award Scholarship for use in graduate years; not renewable. *Amount:* $13,000–$15,000.

Eligibility Requirements Applicant must be of Armenian heritage and enrolled or expecting to enroll full-time at a four-year institution or university. Available to U.S. and Canadian citizens.

Application Requirements Application, financial need analysis, references, self-addressed stamped envelope, transcript. *Deadline:* April 1.

Contact Lazarian Scholarship Committee
Armenian Relief Society of North America Inc.-Regional Office
80 Bigelow Avenue, Suite 200
Watertown, MA 02472
Phone: 617-926-3801
Fax: 617-924-7238
E-mail: arseastus@aol.com

ATTORNEY - CPA FOUNDATION
http://www.attorney-cpa.com/foundation.html

ATTORNEY-CPA FOUNDATION SCHOLARSHIPS • 225

Ten scholarships available to second year students in law school who are Certified Public Accountants. Must exhibit leadership in school and community, as well as outstanding academic performance.

Academic/Career Areas Business/Consumer Services; Law/Legal Services.

Award Scholarship for use in graduate years; not renewable. *Number:* 10. *Amount:* $250–$1000.

Eligibility Requirements Applicant must be enrolled or expecting to enroll full or part-time at an institution or university. Available to U.S. citizens.

Application Requirements Application, resume. *Deadline:* April 30.

Contact Attorney - CPA Foundation
24196 Alicia Parkway, Suite K
Mission Viejo, CA 92691-3926

CHEMICAL HERITAGE FOUNDATION
http://www.chemheritage.org

BECKMAN CENTER FOR THE HISTORY OF CHEMISTRY RESEARCH TRAVEL GRANTS AT THE CHEMICAL HERITAGE FOUNDATION
• *See number 51*

CONSORTIUM FOR GRADUATE STUDY IN MANAGEMENT
http://www.cgsm.org

CONSORTIUM FELLOWSHIP • 226

Fellowship pays full tuition for minority applicant at one of 14 consortium member schools. Must be a U.S. citizen. Application fee of $120 and up. Early apply deadline: December 1. Regular apply deadline: January 15.

Academic/Career Areas Business/Consumer Services.

Award Fellowship for use in graduate years; renewable. *Number:* 250–300.

Eligibility Requirements Applicant must be American Indian/Alaska Native, Black (non-Hispanic), or Hispanic and enrolled or expecting to enroll full-time at an institution or university. Available to U.S. citizens.

Application Requirements Application, essay, interview, photo, resume, references, test scores, transcript. *Fee:* $120. *Deadline:* January 15.

Contact Receptionist
Consortium for Graduate Study in
Management
5585 Pershing Avenue #240
St. Louis, MO 63112
Phone: 314-877-5500
Fax: 314-877-5505
E-mail: frontdesk@cgsm.org

DELOITTE FOUNDATION
http://www.deloitte.com

DELOITTE AND TOUCHE DOCTORAL FELLOWSHIP • 227

One-time award program for graduate student enrolled and successfully pursuing a doctorate program in accounting at an accredited U.S. university. Citizens of other countries may apply only if they are studying at a U.S. institution. Applicant must be completing two or more semesters and have two or more years left in the program. Applications are mailed to the Accounting Department Chair at each institution.

Academic/Career Areas Business/Consumer Services.

Award Fellowship for use in postgraduate years; not renewable. *Number:* up to 10. *Amount:* $25,000.

Eligibility Requirements Applicant must be enrolled or expecting to enroll full-time at a four-year institution or university. Available to U.S. and non-U.S. citizens.

Application Requirements Application, references, test scores, transcript. *Deadline:* October 15.

Contact Janet Butchko
Deloitte Foundation
Ten Westport Road
Wilton, CT 06897
E-mail: jbutchko@deloittle.com

EDUCATIONAL FOUNDATION FOR WOMEN IN ACCOUNTING (EFWA)
http://www.efwa.org

LAURELS FUND • 228

One-year academic scholarship for women pursuing advanced degrees in accounting. Applicants must have completed at least one full year of a doctoral program. Must be a U.S. citizen.

Academic/Career Areas Business/Consumer Services.

Award Scholarship for use in postgraduate years; not renewable. *Amount:* $1500–$5000.

Eligibility Requirements Applicant must be enrolled or expecting to enroll at an institution or university and female. Available to U.S. citizens.

Application Requirements Application, autobiography, essay, financial need analysis, references, test scores, transcript. *Deadline:* March 15.

Contact Cynthia Hires, Administrator
Educational Foundation for Women in
Accounting (EFWA)
PO Box 1925
Southeastern, PA 19399-1925
Phone: 610-407-9229
Fax: 610-644-3713
E-mail: info@efwa.org

GOVERNMENT FINANCE OFFICERS ASSOCIATION
http://www.GFOA.org

DANIEL B. GOLDBERG SCHOLARSHIP • 229

One-time award to a full-time student in a graduate program that prepares students for careers in state and local government finance. Must have baccalaureate degree. Must be citizen or permanent resident of U.S. or Canada.

Academic/Career Areas Business/Consumer Services.

Award Scholarship for use in graduate years; not renewable. *Number:* 1. *Amount:* $5000.

Eligibility Requirements Applicant must be enrolled or expecting to enroll full-time at an institution or university. Available to U.S. and Canadian citizens.

Application Requirements Application, essay, resume, references, transcript. *Deadline:* February 8.

Contact Carole Colin, Manager
Government Finance Officers Association
Scholarship Committee
180 North Michigan Avenue, Suite 800
Chicago, IL 60601-7476
Phone: 312-977-9700
Fax: 312-977-4806
E-mail: ccolin@gfoa.org

PUBLIC EMPLOYEE RETIREMENT RESEARCH AND ADMINISTRATION SCHOLARSHIP • 230

One-time award for graduate study in public administration, finance, business administration, or social sciences. Application deadline is February 8th.

Academic/Career Areas Business/Consumer Services; Social Sciences.

Award Scholarship for use in graduate years; not renewable. *Number:* 1. *Amount:* $3500.

Eligibility Requirements Applicant must be enrolled or expecting to enroll full or part-time at an institution or university. Available to U.S. and Canadian citizens.

Application Requirements Application, essay, resume, references, transcript. *Deadline:* February 8.

Contact Carole Colin, Manager
Government Finance Officers Association
Scholarship Committee
180 North Michigan Avenue, Suite 800
Chicago, IL 60601-7476
Phone: 312-977-9700
Fax: 312-977-4806
E-mail: ccolin@gfoa.org

HOLSTEIN ASSOCIATION USA, INC.
http://www.holsteinusa.com

ROBERT H. RUMLER SCHOLARSHIP • 231

To encourage deserving and qualified persons with an established interest in dairy and who have demonstrated leadership qualities and managerial abilities to pursue a Master's Degree in Business at a certified school issuing a Master's Degree in Business Administration.

Academic/Career Areas Business/Consumer Services.

Award Scholarship for use in graduate years; not renewable. *Number:* 1. *Amount:* $3000.

Eligibility Requirements Applicant must be enrolled or expecting to enroll full or part-time at an institution or university. Applicant must have 3.0 GPA or higher. Available to U.S. and non-U.S. citizens.

Application Requirements Application, essay, photo, references, transcript. *Deadline:* April 15.

Contact Mr. John Meyer, CEO
Holstein Association USA, Inc.
PO Box 808
Brattleboro, VT 05302
Phone: 802-254-4551
Fax: 802-254-8251
E-mail: jmeyer@holstein.com

INSTITUTE FOR SUPPLY MANAGEMENT
http://www.ism.ws

INSTITUTE FOR SUPPLY MANAGEMENT DISSERTATION GRANT PROGRAM • 232

Four awards of $10,000 for support of doctoral research. Applicants must be doctoral candidates who are pursuing a Ph.D. or DBA in purchasing, business, logistics, management, economics, industrial engineering, or related fields. Must be enrolled in accredited U.S. university. Submit application letter, transcripts, proposal abstract, three letters of recommendation, and curriculum vitae. Contact for research sample topics.

Academic/Career Areas Business/Consumer Services; Economics; Engineering/Technology.

Award Grant for use in graduate years; not renewable. *Number:* 4. *Amount:* $10,000.

Eligibility Requirements Applicant must be enrolled or expecting to enroll full or part-time at a four-year institution or university. Available to U.S. citizens.

Application Requirements Application, references, transcript. *Deadline:* January 31.

Contact Dr. Joseph Cavinato, Senior Vice President
Institute for Supply Management
2055 East Centennial Circle
Tempe, AZ 85284
Phone: 480-752-6276 Ext. 3029
Fax: 480-752-7890
E-mail: jcavinato@ism.ws

INSTITUTE FOR SUPPLY MANAGEMENT SENIOR RESEARCH FELLOWSHIP PROGRAM • 233

Two fellowship awards. Applicants must be pursuing a post-graduate degree in business, consumer services, or economics.

Academic/Career Areas Business/Consumer Services; Economics.

Award Fellowship for use in postgraduate years; not renewable. *Number:* 2. *Amount:* up to $5000.

Institute for Supply Management (continued)

Eligibility Requirements Applicant must be enrolled or expecting to enroll full-time at an institution or university. Available to U.S. and non-U.S. citizens.

Application Requirements Application. *Deadline:* April 1.

Contact Joseph Cavinato, Senior Vice President
Institute for Supply Management
2055 East Centennial Circle
Tempe, AZ 85284
Phone: 480-752-6276 Ext. 3029
Fax: 480-752-7890
E-mail: jcavinato@ism.ws

INTERNATIONAL DEVELOPMENT RESEARCH CENTER
http://www.idrc.ca/awards

AGROPOLIS
• *See number 10*

JACKI TUCKFIELD MEMORIAL GRADUATE BUSINESS SCHOLARSHIP FUND
http://www.jackituckfield.org

JACKI TUCKFIELD MEMORIAL SCHOLARSHIP • 234

The goal of the Jacki Tuckfield Memorial Graduate Business Scholarship Fund is to improve the diversity of career professionals employed in the executive, administrative and managerial levels of the South Florida workforce. The Fund helps the brightest and most motivated U.S. citizens of African-American heritage attain their master's and doctoral degrees in business programs at Florida universities. Applicants must be between the ages of 21-40.

Academic/Career Areas Business/Consumer Services.

Award Scholarship for use in graduate, or postgraduate years; renewable. *Number:* 22. *Amount:* $1000–$2000.

Eligibility Requirements Applicant must be Black (non-Hispanic); age 21-40; enrolled or expecting to enroll full-time at an institution or university; resident of Florida and studying in Florida. Applicant must have 3.5 GPA or higher. Available to U.S. citizens.

Application Requirements Application, essay, interview, resume, references, transcript. *Deadline:* May 11.

Contact Gloria Tuckfield, Vice President
Jacki Tuckfield Memorial Graduate
Business Scholarship Fund
1160 NW 87th Street
Miami, FL 33150-2544
Phone: 305-693-4144 Ext. 32
Fax: 305-696-2069
E-mail: gtuckfield@aol.com

KPMG FOUNDATION
http://www.kpmgfoundation.org

KPMG MINORITY ACCOUNTING AND INFORMATION SYSTEMS DOCTORAL SCHOLARSHIP • 235

Renewable award for African American, Hispanic American, and Native Americans who will be in full-time accounting or information systems doctoral program in September of the year application is made. It is recommended that the University will waive tuition and fees, and provide stipend and teaching assistantship opportunities. Applications are available at website (http://www.kpmgfoundation.org).

Academic/Career Areas Business/Consumer Services.

Award Scholarship for use in graduate years; renewable. *Number:* 20. *Amount:* $10,000.

Eligibility Requirements Applicant must be American Indian/Alaska Native, Black (non-Hispanic), or Hispanic and enrolled or expecting to enroll full-time at an institution or university. Available to U.S. citizens.

Application Requirements Application, transcript. *Deadline:* May 1.

Contact Fiona Rose, KPMG Foundation Program
Manager
KPMG Foundation
3 Chestnut Ridge Road
Montvale, NJ 07645-0435
Phone: 201-307-7628
Fax: 201-307-7093
E-mail: fionarose@kpmg.com

MACKENZIE KING SCHOLARSHIPS BOARD

MACKENZIE KING TRAVELLING SCHOLARSHIPS • 236

Award for graduates of Canadian universities who are pursuing postgraduate study in international relations in the U.S. or the U.K. Include transcripts and references with application. One-time award of Can$10,000-Can$12,000. Must rank in upper quarter of class or have minimum GPA of 3.5.

Academic/Career Areas Business/Consumer Services; Economics; History; Law/Legal Services; Political Science; Social Sciences.

Award Scholarship for use in postgraduate years; not renewable. *Number:* 3–4. *Amount:* $10,000–$12,000.

Eligibility Requirements Applicant must be enrolled or expecting to enroll full-time at an institution or university. Applicant must have 3.5 GPA or higher.

Application Requirements Application, references, transcript. *Deadline:* February 1.

Contact J. Blom, Professor of Law and Chair of
Selection Committee
MacKenzie King Scholarships Board
1822 East Mall
Vancouver, BC V6T 1Z1
Canada
Phone: 604-822-4564
Fax: 604-822-8108
E-mail: blom@law.ubc.ca

PENNSYLVANIA INSTITUTE OF CERTIFIED PUBLIC ACCOUNTANTS
http://www.picpa.org

CHARLES V. CLEGHORN GRADUATE ACCOUNTING SCHOOL SCHOLARSHIP • 237

To promote the accounting profession, the PICPA awards $5,000 annually in the name of the Charles V. Cleghorn Graduate Accounting School Scholarship to a full-time graduate student enrolled at a Pennsylvania college or university. Minimum 3.0 GPA required.

Academic/Career Areas Business/Consumer Services.

Award Scholarship for use in graduate years; renewable. *Number:* 1. *Amount:* $5000.

Eligibility Requirements Applicant must be enrolled or expecting to enroll full-time at a four-year institution or university and studying in Pennsylvania. Applicant must have 3.0 GPA or higher. Available to U.S. and non-U.S. citizens.

Application Requirements References. *Deadline:* March 2.

Contact Craig Brodbeck, Marketing Administrator
Pennsylvania Institute of Certified Public
Accountants
1650 Arch Street
17th Floor
Philadelphia, PA 19103-2099
Phone: 215-496-9272

ELIZABETH C. AND JOHN L. RICKETTS GRADUATE ACCOUNTING SCHOLARSHIP • 238

To promote the accounting profession, the PICPA awards $5,000 annually in the name of the Elizabeth C. and John L. Ricketts Scholarship to a full-time graduate student enrolled at a Pennsylvania college or university. Minimum 3.0 GPA required.

Academic/Career Areas Business/Consumer Services.

Award Scholarship for use in graduate years; renewable. *Number:* 1. *Amount:* $5000.

Eligibility Requirements Applicant must be enrolled or expecting to enroll full-time at a four-year institution or university and studying in Pennsylvania. Applicant must have 3.0 GPA or higher. Available to U.S. citizens.

Application Requirements References. *Deadline:* March 2.

Contact Craig Brodbeck, Marketing Administrator
Pennsylvania Institute of Certified Public
Accountants
1650 Arch Street
17th Floor
Philadelphia, PA 19103-2099
Phone: 215-496-9272

STATE FARM COMPANIES FOUNDATION
http://www.statefarm.com

DOCTORAL DISSERTATION AWARD IN INSURANCE/BUSINESS • 239

Must be a US citizen. Must be enrolled in a graduate program and have completed a major portion of coursework. Must have an approved proposal. Must have started writing but not completed a dissertation. Must be seeking a career in insurance and business/consumer services. Request application from the dean or director of doctoral programs at your university or see website for additional information: www.statefarm.com.

Academic/Career Areas Business/Consumer Services.

Award Scholarship for use in graduate years; not renewable. *Number:* 6. *Amount:* $10,000.

Eligibility Requirements Applicant must be enrolled or expecting to enroll full-time at a four-year institution or university. Available to U.S. citizens.

Application Requirements Application, references, proposed dissertation. *Deadline:* March 31.

Contact State Farm Companies Foundation
One State Farm Plaza, SC-3
Bloomington, IL 61710
Phone: 309-766-2161

SWEDISH INFORMATION SERVICE
http://www.swedeninfo.com

BICENTENNIAL SWEDISH-AMERICAN EXCHANGE FUND TRAVEL GRANTS
• *See number 133*

VIRGINIA SOCIETY OF CERTIFIED PUBLIC ACCOUNTANTS EDUCATION FOUNDATION
http://www.vscpa.com

VIRGINIA SOCIETY OF CPAS EDUCATIONAL FOUNDATION GRADUATE SCHOLARSHIP • 240

One-time award of $1,200 for student enrolled in a graduate accounting program. Applicant must be accepted or currently enrolled at a Virginia college or university.

Academic/Career Areas Business/Consumer Services.

Award Scholarship for use in graduate years; not renewable. *Number:* 3. *Amount:* $1200.

Eligibility Requirements Applicant must be enrolled or expecting to enroll at a four-year institution or university and studying in Virginia. Available to U.S. citizens.

Application Requirements Application, essay, resume, references, transcript. *Deadline:* July 15.

Contact Tracey Zink, Public Affairs Coordinator
Virginia Society of Certified Public
Accountants Education Foundation
PO Box 4620
Glen Allen, VA 23058-4620
Phone: 800-733-8272
Fax: 804-273-1741
E-mail: tzink@vscpa.com

WOODROW WILSON NATIONAL FELLOWSHIP FOUNDATION
http://www.woodrow.org

THOMAS R. PICKERING GRADUATE FOREIGN AFFAIRS FELLOWSHIP PROGRAM • 241

Prepares individuals to become Foreign Service Officers in U.S. Dept. of State. At time of application, candidates must be seeking admission to graduate school for the following academic year. Must enroll in two-year master's degree programs (such as public policy, international affairs, public administration, or business, economics, political science, sociology or foreign languages). Must be U.S. citizens and have undergraduate GPA of 3.2 or above.

Academic/Career Areas Business/Consumer Services; Economics; Foreign Language; International Studies; Political Science; Social Sciences.

Award Fellowship for use in graduate years; renewable.

Eligibility Requirements Applicant must be enrolled or expecting to enroll full-time at an institution or university and must have an interest in leadership. Available to U.S. citizens.

Application Requirements Application, autobiography, essay, financial need analysis, interview, references, test scores, transcript. *Deadline:* March 1.

Contact Dr. Richard Hope, Vice President
Woodrow Wilson National Fellowship
Foundation
PO Box 2437
Princeton, NJ 08543-2437
E-mail: pickeringfaf@woodrow.org

CHEMICAL ENGINEERING

AFRICAN NETWORK OF SCIENTIFIC AND TECHNOLOGICAL INSTITUTIONS - ANSTI
http://www.ansti.org

AFRICAN NETWORK OF SCIENTIFIC AND TECHNOLOGICAL INSTITUTIONS POSTGRADUATE FELLOWSHIPS
• *See number 14*

AIR AND WASTE MANAGEMENT ASSOCIATION
http://www.awma.org

AIR AND WASTE MANAGEMENT ASSOCIATION SCHOLARSHIP ENDOWMENT TRUST FUND
• *See number 24*

AMERICAN INSTITUTE OF CHEMICAL ENGINEERS
http://www.aiche.org

ENVIRONMENTAL DIVISION GRADUATE STUDENT PAPER AWARD • 242

Three cash prizes recognizing the best graduate student papers on environmental protection through chemical engineering. Graduate student must be primary author and be a member of the American Institute of Chemical Engineers at the time paper is submitted. Paper must describe original research and be suitable for publication in a refereed journal. Must be nominated.

Academic/Career Areas Chemical Engineering.

Award Prize for use in graduate years; not renewable. *Number:* 3. *Amount:* $150–$450.

Eligibility Requirements Applicant must be enrolled or expecting to enroll at an institution or university.

Application Requirements Applicant must enter a contest, student paper. *Deadline:* September 2.

Contact Awards Administrator
American Institute of Chemical Engineers
Three Park Avenue
New York, NY 10016-5991
Phone: 212-591-7478
Fax: 212-591-8882
E-mail: awards@aiche.org

ASSOCIATED WESTERN UNIVERSITIES, INC.
http://www.awu.org

ASSOCIATED WESTERN UNIVERSITIES FACULTY FELLOWSHIPS
• *See number 48*

ASSOCIATED WESTERN UNIVERSITIES GRADUATE RESEARCH FELLOWSHIPS
• *See number 49*

ASSOCIATED WESTERN UNIVERSITIES POSTGRADUATE FELLOWSHIP
• *See number 50*

CHEMICAL HERITAGE FOUNDATION
http://www.chemheritage.org

BECKMAN CENTER FOR THE HISTORY OF CHEMISTRY RESEARCH TRAVEL GRANTS AT THE CHEMICAL HERITAGE FOUNDATION
• *See number 51*

DELAWARE VALLEY SPACE GRANT CONSORTIUM
http://www.delspace.org

NASA/DELAWARE VALLEY SPACE GRANT FELLOWSHIP
• *See number 52*

FANNIE AND JOHN HERTZ FOUNDATION
http://www.hertzfoundation.org

FANNIE AND JOHN HERTZ FOUNDATION FELLOWSHIP
• *See number 53*

FOUNDATION FOR SCIENCE AND DISABILITY
http://www.as.wvu.edu/~scidis/organize/fsd.html

GRANTS FOR DISABLED STUDENTS IN THE SCIENCES
• *See number 54*

INTERNATIONAL DESALINATION ASSOCIATION
http://www.ida.bm

INTERNATIONAL DESALINATION ASSOCIATION SCHOLARSHIP
• *See number 57*

INTERNATIONAL UNION FOR VACUUM SCIENCE, TECHNIQUE AND APPLICATIONS
http://www.iuvsta.org/welch.html

WELCH FOUNDATION SCHOLARSHIP
• *See number 58*

NASA IDAHO SPACE GRANT CONSORTIUM
http://www.uidaho.edu/nasa_isgc

NASA ID SPACE GRANT CONSORTIUM FELLOWSHIP PROGRAM
• *See number 60*

NASA WYOMING SPACE GRANT CONSORTIUM
http://www.wyomingspacegrant.uwyo.edu

WYOMING NASA SPACE GRANT CONSORTIUM RESEARCH FELLOWSHIP
• *See number 61*

NATIONAL ACTION COUNCIL FOR MINORITIES IN ENGINEERING-NACME, INC.
http://www.nacme.org

SLOAN PH.D PROGRAM • **243**

Award available to minority scholars pursuing Ph.D. in mathematical, scientific, or engineering doctoral program. Applicant must apply and be accepted to one of the 30 institutions supported by the Sloan Foundation. For additional information and to see a list of institutions, visit website: http://www.nacme.org

Academic/Career Areas Chemical Engineering; Civil Engineering; Computer Science/Data Processing; Economics; Electrical Engineering/Electronics; Engineering/Technology; Engineering-Related Technologies; Materials Science, Engineering and Metallurgy; Meteorology/Atmospheric Science; Nuclear Science; Physical Sciences and Math; Science, Technology and Society.

Award Grant for use in graduate years; renewable.

Eligibility Requirements Applicant must be American Indian/Alaska Native, Asian/Pacific Islander, Black (non-Hispanic), or Hispanic and enrolled or expecting to enroll at an institution or university. Available to U.S. citizens.

National Action Council for Minorities in Engineering-NACME, Inc. (continued)

Application Requirements Application, financial need analysis, references. *Deadline:* Continuous.

Contact National Action Council for Minorities in Engineering-NACME, Inc.
The Empire State Building, 350 Fifth Avenue, Suite 2212
New York, NY 10118-2299

NATIONAL MILK PRODUCERS FEDERATION
http://www.nmpf.org

NATIONAL MILK PRODUCERS FEDERATION NATIONAL DAIRY LEADERSHIP SCHOLARSHIP PROGRAM
• *See number 5*

NATIONAL PHYSICAL SCIENCE CONSORTIUM
http://www.npsc.org

NATIONAL PHYSICAL SCIENCE CONSORTIUM GRADUATE FELLOWSHIPS IN THE PHYSICAL SCIENCES • **244**

Fellowship renewable for duration of six-year doctoral program. Emphasis on recruitment of underrepresented minorities and females. Must be college senior with at least a 3.0 GPA or in first year of a doctoral program, who has the ability to pursue graduate work at a National Physical Science Consortium member institution. Award ranges from $156,000 to $200,000 total.

Academic/Career Areas Chemical Engineering; Computer Science/Data Processing; Earth Science; Electrical Engineering/Electronics; Materials Science, Engineering and Metallurgy; Mechanical Engineering; Meteorology/Atmospheric Science; Physical Sciences and Math.

Award Fellowship for use in graduate years; renewable. *Number:* 20–25. *Amount:* $156,000–$200,000.

Eligibility Requirements Applicant must be enrolled or expecting to enroll full-time at an institution or university. Applicant must have 3.0 GPA or higher. Available to U.S. citizens.

Application Requirements Application, references, test scores, transcript. *Deadline:* November 5.

Contact Mr. Gene Bailey, Administrator
National Physical Science Consortium
MSC-3NPS, Box 30001
Las Cruces, NM 88003-8001
Phone: 800-952-4118
Fax: 505-646-6097
E-mail: npsc@npsc.org

SOCIETY OF AUTOMOTIVE ENGINEERS
http://www.sae.org/students/stuschol.htm

SOCIETY OF AUTOMOTIVE ENGINEERS DOCTORAL SCHOLARS PROGRAM
• *See number 178*

SOCIETY OF WOMEN ENGINEERS
http://www.swe.org

GENERAL MOTORS FOUNDATION GRADUATE SCHOLARSHIP • **245**

One award for a first-year female graduate student who has demonstrated previous leadership role and career interest in engineering technology or mechanical, chemical, industrial, automotive, materials science, or manufacturing engineering. Send self-addressed stamped envelope for application. One-time award of $1000. Includes $500 travel grant for SWE National Conference. Deadline: February 1.

Academic/Career Areas Chemical Engineering; Engineering/Technology; Mechanical Engineering; Trade/Technical Specialties.

Award Scholarship for use in graduate years; not renewable. *Number:* 1. *Amount:* $1000.

Eligibility Requirements Applicant must be enrolled or expecting to enroll full-time at a four-year institution or university; female and must have an interest in leadership. Applicant must have 3.5 GPA or higher.

Application Requirements Application, essay, references, self-addressed stamped envelope, test scores, transcript. *Deadline:* February 1.

Contact Program Coordinator
Society of Women Engineers
230 East Ohio Street, Suite 400
Chicago, IL 60611-3265
Phone: 312-596-5223
Fax: 312-644-8557
E-mail: hq@swe.org

CIVIL ENGINEERING

AFRICAN NETWORK OF SCIENTIFIC AND TECHNOLOGICAL INSTITUTIONS - ANSTI
http://www.ansti.org

AFRICAN NETWORK OF SCIENTIFIC AND TECHNOLOGICAL INSTITUTIONS POSTGRADUATE FELLOWSHIPS
• *See number 14*

AMERICAN GEOPHYSICAL UNION
http://www.agu.org

AMERICAN GEOPHYSICAL UNION HORTON RESEARCH GRANT
• *See number 25*

AMERICAN WATER WORKS ASSOCIATION
http://www.awwa.org

AMERICAN WATER WORKS ASSOCIATION/ ACADEMIC ACHIEVEMENT AWARDS • 246

Award to encourage academic excellence by recognizing contributions to field of public water supply. Submit completed doctoral dissertation or master's thesis. One-time award.

Academic/Career Areas Civil Engineering.

Award Prize for use in graduate, or postgraduate years; not renewable. *Number:* 4. *Amount:* $1500–$3000.

Eligibility Requirements Applicant must be enrolled or expecting to enroll at an institution or university. Available to U.S. and non-U.S. citizens.

Application Requirements Application. *Deadline:* October 1.

Contact Annette Carabetta, Scholarship
Coordinator
American Water Works Association
6666 Quincy Avenue
Denver, CO 80235
Phone: 303-347-6206
Fax: 303-794-6303
E-mail: acarabetta@awwa.org

ASSOCIATED GENERAL CONTRACTORS EDUCATION AND RESEARCH FOUNDATION
http://www.agcfoundation.org

AGC EDUCATION AND RESEARCH FOUNDATION GRADUATE SCHOLARSHIPS • 247

Applicants for the Saul Horowitz, Jr. Memorial Graduate Award and Heffner Scholarships for Graduate Students must be college seniors enrolled in an undergraduate construction or civil engineering degree program with plans to pursue a graduate program full-time; or graduate or doctoral students pursuing a construction or civil engineering degree program with at least one academic year remaining. Must maintain a 2.0 GPA. Award is $7,500 in two payments of $3,750. Application and guidelines are available on the web. Deadline: November 1.

Academic/Career Areas Civil Engineering.

Award Scholarship for use in graduate, or postgraduate years; not renewable. *Number:* 2. *Amount:* $3750.

Eligibility Requirements Applicant must be enrolled or expecting to enroll full-time at an institution or university. Available to U.S. citizens.

Application Requirements Application, essay, financial need analysis, transcript. *Deadline:* November 1.

Contact Floretta Slade, Director of Programs
Associated General Contractors Education
and Research Foundation
333 John Carlyle Street, Suite 200
Alexandria, VA 22314
Phone: 703-837-5342
Fax: 703-837-5402
E-mail: sladef@agc.org

ASSOCIATED WESTERN UNIVERSITIES, INC.
http://www.awu.org

ASSOCIATED WESTERN UNIVERSITIES FACULTY FELLOWSHIPS
• *See number 48*

ASSOCIATED WESTERN UNIVERSITIES GRADUATE RESEARCH FELLOWSHIPS
• *See number 49*

ASSOCIATED WESTERN UNIVERSITIES POSTGRADUATE FELLOWSHIP
• *See number 50*

DELAWARE VALLEY SPACE GRANT CONSORTIUM
http://www.delspace.org

NASA/DELAWARE VALLEY SPACE GRANT FELLOWSHIP
• *See number 52*

DURRANT FOUNDATION
http://www.durant.com/foundation.html

DURRANT FOUNDATION SCHOLARSHIP/ INTERNSHIP
• *See number 96*

FANNIE AND JOHN HERTZ FOUNDATION
http://www.hertzfoundation.org

FANNIE AND JOHN HERTZ FOUNDATION FELLOWSHIP
• *See number 53*

FOUNDATION FOR SCIENCE AND DISABILITY
http://www.as.wvu.edu/~scidis/organize/fsd.html

GRANTS FOR DISABLED STUDENTS IN THE SCIENCES
• *See number 54*

GEM CONSORTIUM
http://www.nd.edu/~gem

GEM PH.D. ENGINEERING FELLOWSHIP
• See number 9

INTERNATIONAL DESALINATION ASSOCIATION
http://www.ida.bm

INTERNATIONAL DESALINATION ASSOCIATION SCHOLARSHIP
• See number 57

NASA WYOMING SPACE GRANT CONSORTIUM
http://www.wyomingspacegrant.uwyo.edu

WYOMING NASA SPACE GRANT CONSORTIUM RESEARCH FELLOWSHIP
• See number 61

NATIONAL ACTION COUNCIL FOR MINORITIES IN ENGINEERING-NACME, INC.
http://www.nacme.org

SLOAN PH.D PROGRAM
• See number 243

SKIDMORE, OWINGS, AND MERRILL FOUNDATION
http://www.som.com

STRUCTURAL ENGINEERING TRAVELING FELLOWSHIP PROGRAM • 248

Award for a recent graduate with a master's or Ph.D. in civil or architectural engineering and a specialization in structural engineering to allow recipient to experience buildings, bridges, and other structures firsthand. Must have attended a U.S. school and must be nominated by faculty of degree-granting institution. Submit curriculum vitae, proposed travel itinerary, and signed copyright release. Contact for further information.

Academic/Career Areas Civil Engineering.

Award Fellowship for use in graduate, or postgraduate years; not renewable. *Number:* 1. *Amount:* $7500.

Eligibility Requirements Applicant must be enrolled or expecting to enroll full-time at an institution or university. Available to U.S. and non-U.S. citizens.

Application Requirements Essay, interview, references, transcript, school nomination, travel plan. *Deadline:* November 16.

Contact Lisa Westerfield, Administrative Director
Skidmore, Owings, and Merrill Foundation
224 South Michigan Avenue, Suite 1000
Chicago, IL 60604
Phone: 312-427-4202
Fax: 312-360-4545
E-mail: somfoundation@som.con

TRANSPORTATION ASSOCIATION OF CANADA
http://www.tac-atc.ca

TRANSPORTATION ASSOCIATION OF CANADA SCHOLARSHIPS • 249

Five scholarships available to postgraduate university students. Must be a promising student or professional in a transportation-related field and a Canadian citizen or a landed immigrant in Canada. Must rank in upper quarter of class and have a minimum GPA of "B". Nonrenewable award ranging from Can$3000-Can$6000. Deadline: March 1.

Academic/Career Areas Civil Engineering; Earth Science; Economics; Engineering/Technology; Engineering-Related Technologies; Transportation.

Award Scholarship for use in postgraduate years; not renewable. *Number:* 5. *Amount:* $3000–$6000.

Eligibility Requirements Applicant must be Canadian citizenship and enrolled or expecting to enroll full-time at an institution or university. Applicant must have 3.5 GPA or higher.

Application Requirements Application, references, transcript. *Deadline:* March 1.

Contact Gilbert Morier, Manager, Member Services and Public Affairs
Transportation Association of Canada
2323 St. Laurent Boulevard
Ottawa, ON K1G 4J8
Canada
Phone: 613-736-1350
Fax: 613-736-1395
E-mail: gmorier@tac-atc.ca

COMMUNICATIONS

AMERICAN POLITICAL SCIENCE ASSOCIATION
http://www.apsanet.org

CONGRESSIONAL FELLOWSHIP FOR JOURNALISTS • 250

One-time award for graduate students with BA from U.S. institutions who have two to ten years of full-time professional experience in newspaper, magazine, radio, or television reporting. Must be U.S. citizen and have a minimum 3.0 GPA. Submit resume.

Academic/Career Areas Communications; Political Science.

Award Fellowship for use in graduate, or postgraduate years; not renewable. *Number:* 3–5. *Amount:* $35,000.

Eligibility Requirements Applicant must be enrolled or expecting to enroll at an institution or university. Applicant or parent of applicant must have employment or volunteer experience in journalism. Applicant must have 3.0 GPA or higher. Available to U.S. citizens.

Application Requirements Application, essay, references. *Deadline:* December 1.

Contact Dr. Jeffrey Biggs, Director
American Political Science Association
1527 New Hampshire Avenue, NW
Washington, DC 20036-1206
Phone: 202-483-2512
Fax: 202-483-2657

ARMED FORCES COMMUNICATIONS AND ELECTRONICS ASSOCIATION, EDUCATIONAL FOUNDATION
http://www.afcea.org

MILTON E. COOPER/YOUNG AFCEAN GRADUATE SCHOOL SCHOLARSHIP • 251

Applicant must be a young professional (age 35 or under) already employed in a field related to communications, computer science or electronics. Applicant must be a current student in an accredited college or university in the United States and demonstrate a strong commitment to the pursuit of an advanced college degree (MS or Ph.D.) relating to communications, computer science, electronics/electrical engineering in preparation for a career in science or engineering and maintain a GPA of 3.2 or higher. Application available at website.

Academic/Career Areas Communications; Computer Science/Data Processing; Electrical Engineering/Electronics.

Award Scholarship for use in graduate years; not renewable. *Amount:* $3000.

Eligibility Requirements Applicant must be age 35 or under and enrolled or expecting to enroll full-time at an institution or university. Applicant or parent of applicant must have employment or volunteer experience in designated career field. Available to U.S. citizens.

Application Requirements Application, references, transcript. *Deadline:* April 12.

Contact Luanne Balestrucci
E-mail: lbalestrucci@madentechnj.com

ASSOCIATION FOR EDUCATION IN JOURNALISM AND MASS COMMUNICATIONS
http://www.aejmc.org

ASSOCIATION FOR EDUCATION IN JOURNALISM AND MASS COMMUNICATIONS COMM.THEORY & METHODOLOGY DIVISION MINORITY DOCTORAL SCHOLARSHIPS • 252

Award for minority student pursuing a doctoral degree in journalism or communications. Focus is on communication, theory, and methodology. Must be a U.S. citizen. One-time award of $1,200.

Academic/Career Areas Communications; Journalism.

Award Scholarship for use in graduate years; not renewable. *Number:* 1. *Amount:* $1200.

Eligibility Requirements Applicant must be American Indian/Alaska Native, Asian/Pacific Islander, Black (non-Hispanic), or Hispanic and enrolled or expecting to enroll full-time at a four-year institution or university. Applicant must have 3.0 GPA or higher. Available to U.S. citizens.

Application Requirements Application. *Deadline:* June 5.

Contact Jennifer McGill, Executive Director
Association for Education in Journalism
and Mass Communications
234 Outlet Pointe Boulevard, Suite A
Columbia, SC 29210
Phone: 803-798-0271
Fax: 803-772-3509
E-mail: aejmchq@aol.com

CHINA TIMES CULTURAL FOUNDATION

CHINA TIMES CULTURAL FOUNDATION DOCTORAL DISSERTATION RESEARCH IN CHINESE STUDIES SCHOLARSHIPS
• *See number 122*

CONSORTIUM OF COLLEGE AND UNIVERSITY MEDIA CENTERS
http://www.ccumc.org

CONSORTIUM OF COLLEGE AND UNIVERSITY MEDIA CENTERS RESEARCH AWARDS • 253

One-time research award for faculty, staff, and students at member institutions of the Consortium of College and University Media Centers. Submit a one- to two-page description of proposed study, budget, and resume. Research must be in progress.

Academic/Career Areas Communications; Education; Filmmaking; Library Sciences; Photojournalism; TV/Radio Broadcasting.

Award Grant for use in graduate, or postgraduate years; not renewable. *Number:* 1–5. *Amount:* $2000.

Consortium of College and University Media Centers (continued)

Eligibility Requirements Applicant must be enrolled or expecting to enroll full or part-time at a four-year institution or university. Available to U.S. and non-U.S. citizens.

Application Requirements Application, resume, description of proposed study, budget. *Deadline:* May 1.

Contact Dr. Don Rieck, Director, ITC
Consortium of College and University Media Centers
1200 Communications Building, Iowa State University
Ames, IA 50011-3243
Phone: 515-294-1811
Fax: 515-294-8089
E-mail: ccumc@ccumc.org

INTERNATIONAL DEVELOPMENT RESEARCH CENTER
http://www.idrc.ca/awards

AGROPOLIS
• *See number 10*

NATIONAL ASSOCIATION OF BROADCASTERS
http://www.nab.org/Research/Grants/grants.asp

NATIONAL ASSOCIATION OF BROADCASTERS GRANTS FOR RESEARCH IN BROADCASTING • 254

Grants awarded to graduate students and academic personnel for pursuit of research on important issues in the U.S. commercial broadcast industry. Must submit a proposal. One-time awards average $5000. If applicant is graduate student, they must have a recommendation from academic advisor.

Academic/Career Areas Communications; Journalism; TV/Radio Broadcasting.

Award Grant for use in graduate, or postgraduate years; not renewable. *Number:* 4–6. *Amount:* $5000–$25,000.

Eligibility Requirements Applicant must be enrolled or expecting to enroll full-time at a four-year institution or university. Available to U.S. and non-U.S. citizens.

Application Requirements Application, references. *Deadline:* January 28.

Contact David Gunzerath, Vice President, Research and Planning
National Association of Broadcasters
1771 N Street, NW
Washington, DC 20036-2891

NATIONAL ASSOCIATION OF THE DEAF
http://www.nad.org

WILLIAM C. STOKOE SCHOLARSHIPS • 255

Scholarship limited to deaf graduate students pursuing full- or part-time studies in a field related to sign language or the deaf community. Deaf graduate students developing a special project in one of these topics are also eligible. Project proposal is required. Send a self-addressed, stamped, #10 business envelope to request an application. 301-587-1789 TTY.

Academic/Career Areas Communications; Education; Social Sciences.

Award Scholarship for use in graduate years; not renewable. *Number:* 1. *Amount:* $2000.

Eligibility Requirements Applicant must be enrolled or expecting to enroll full or part-time at an institution or university. Applicant must be hearing impaired.

Application Requirements Application, essay, references, self-addressed stamped envelope, transcript, project description. *Deadline:* March 15.

Contact Stokoe Scholarship Secretary
National Association of the Deaf
814 Thayer Avenue, #250
Silver Spring, MD 20910-4500
Phone: 301-587-1788
Fax: 301-587-1791
E-mail: nadinfo@nad.org

NATIONAL RESEARCH COUNCIL
http://www.nationalacademies.org/fellowships/

FORD FOUNDATION DISSERTATION FELLOWSHIPS FOR MINORITIES • 256

Forty dissertation completion fellowships for the final year of dissertation writing. Intended for underrepresented minorities in research-based fields of study. Must be U.S. citizen of the following: Native American, Alaskan Native, Native Pacific Islander, African American, Mexican American or Puerto Rican.

Academic/Career Areas Communications; Engineering-Related Technologies; Foreign Language; History; Literature/English/Writing; Physical Sciences and Math; Political Science; Religion/Theology; Social Sciences.

Award Fellowship for use in graduate years; not renewable. *Number:* 40. *Amount:* $24,000.

Eligibility Requirements Applicant must be American Indian/Alaska Native, Black (non-Hispanic), or Hispanic and enrolled or expecting to enroll full-time at an institution or university. Available to U.S. citizens.

Application Requirements Application, essay, resume, references, transcript. *Deadline:* December 3.

Contact Program Specialist
National Research Council
Fellowships, TJ 2041, 2101 Constitution Avenue
Washington, DC 20418
Phone: 202-334-2872
Fax: 202-334-3419
E-mail: infofell@nas.edu

FORD FOUNDATION POSTDOCTORAL FELLOWSHIP FOR MINORITIES • 257

One year fellowship for Ph.D./Sc.D. recipients to help their academic career. Intended for under represented minorities in research-based fields of study. Stipend of $35,000 plus $7500 in travel and research allowances. Must be U.S. citizen and one of the following: Native American, Alaskan Native, African American, Native Pacific Islander, Mexican American or Puerto Rican.

Academic/Career Areas Communications; Engineering-Related Technologies; Foreign Language; History; Literature/English/Writing; Physical Sciences and Math; Political Science; Religion/Theology; Social Sciences.

Award Fellowship for use in postgraduate years; not renewable. *Number:* 30. *Amount:* $35,000.

Eligibility Requirements Applicant must be American Indian/Alaska Native, Black (non-Hispanic), or Hispanic and enrolled or expecting to enroll full-time at an institution or university. Available to U.S. citizens.

Application Requirements Application, essay, resume, references, transcript. *Deadline:* January 7.

Contact Program Specialist
National Research Council
Fellowships, TJ 2041, 2101 Constitution Avenue
Washington, DC 20418
Phone: 202-334-2872
Fax: 202-334-3419
E-mail: infofell@nas.edu

FORD FOUNDATION PREDOCTORAL FELLOWSHIPS FOR MINORITIES • 258

Sixty renewable awards to individuals near the beginning of graduate work toward a Ph.D. or Sc.D. in research-based fields of study. Intended for underrepresented minority groups. Must be U.S. citizen and one of the following: Native American, Native Alaskan, Native Pacific Islander, African American, Mexican American or Puerto Rican. Deadline is November 19.

Academic/Career Areas Communications; Computer Science/Data Processing; Engineering-Related Technologies; Foreign Language; History; Literature/English/Writing; Physical Sciences and Math; Political Science; Religion/Theology; Social Sciences.

Award Fellowship for use in graduate years; renewable. *Number:* 60. *Amount:* $16,000.

Eligibility Requirements Applicant must be American Indian/Alaska Native, Black (non-Hispanic), or Hispanic and enrolled or expecting to enroll full-time at an institution or university. Available to U.S. citizens.

Application Requirements Application, essay, resume, references, test scores, transcript. *Deadline:* November 19.

Contact Program Specialist
National Research Council
Fellowships, TJ 2041, 2101 Constitution Avenue
Washington, DC 20418
Phone: 202-334-2872
Fax: 202-334-3419
E-mail: infofell@nas.edu

PACIFIC TELECOMMUNICATIONS COUNCIL
http://www.ptc.org

PACIFIC TELECOMMUNICATIONS COUNCIL ESSAY PRIZE COMPETITION • 259

Prizes awarded for original, unpublished essays on the communications needs and concerns of the Pacific region: Asia, Oceania, and the Americas. Winning entrants will be invited to present their papers at the Pacific Telecommunications Conference in Honolulu, Hawaii. Applicants must certify that they are currently in graduate school or are recent graduates of a masters or doctorate program.

Academic/Career Areas Communications; Engineering/Technology; Engineering-Related Technologies.

Award Prize for use in graduate years; not renewable. *Number:* 1–3. *Amount:* $500–$2000.

Eligibility Requirements Applicant must be enrolled or expecting to enroll full-time at a four-year institution or university. Available to U.S. and non-U.S. citizens.

Application Requirements Application, essay, self-addressed stamped envelope. *Deadline:* May 30.

Contact Mr. Richard Nickelson, Senior Advisor
Pacific Telecommunications Council
2454 South Beretania Street, 3rd Floor
Honolulu, HI 96826-1596
Phone: 808-256-5637
Fax: 808-944-4874
E-mail: richard@ptc.org

QUILL AND SCROLL FOUNDATION
http://www.uiowa.edu/~quill-sc

LESTER BENZ MEMORIAL SCHOLARSHIP • 260

One-time award to upgrade journalism, teaching, and advising skills. Open to all high school journalism teachers and publication advisers with at least six semester hours of journalism courses and minimum four years teaching and advising experience.

Academic/Career Areas Communications; Education; Journalism.

Award Scholarship for use in graduate years; not renewable. *Number:* 1. *Amount:* $500.

Eligibility Requirements Applicant must be enrolled or expecting to enroll at an institution or university. Applicant or parent of applicant must have employment or volunteer experience in journalism or teaching. Available to U.S. citizens.

Application Requirements Application. *Deadline:* April 15.

Contact Richard Johns, Executive Director
Quill and Scroll Foundation
312 WSSH, School of Journalism
Iowa City, IA 52242
Phone: 319-335-3321
Fax: 319-335-5210
E-mail: quill-scroll@uiowa.edu

UNITED METHODIST COMMUNICATIONS
http://www.umcom.org/scholarships

STOODY-WEST FELLOWSHIP FOR GRADUATE STUDY IN RELIGIOUS JOURNALISM • 261

One time award to assist Christians in post-graduate study in the field of religious journalism. Deadline is March 15.

Academic/Career Areas Communications; Journalism; Photojournalism; Religion/Theology; TV/Radio Broadcasting.

Award Fellowship for use in graduate, or postgraduate years; not renewable. *Number:* 2. *Amount:* $6000.

Eligibility Requirements Applicant must be enrolled or expecting to enroll full-time at an institution or university. Available to U.S. and non-U.S. citizens.

Application Requirements Application, essay, photo, references, transcript, graduate school acceptance. *Deadline:* March 15.

Contact Ms. Mickey Slayden, Administrator
United Methodist Communications
810 12th Avenue, S
Nashville, TN 37203
Phone: 615-742-5407
Fax: 615-742-5404
E-mail: scholarships@umcom.umc.org

COMPUTER SCIENCE/DATA PROCESSING

AFRICAN NETWORK OF SCIENTIFIC AND TECHNOLOGICAL INSTITUTIONS - ANSTI
http://www.ansti.org

AFRICAN NETWORK OF SCIENTIFIC AND TECHNOLOGICAL INSTITUTIONS POSTGRADUATE FELLOWSHIPS

• See number 14

AMERICAN ASSOCIATION OF UNIVERSITY WOMEN (AAUW) EDUCATIONAL FOUNDATION
http://www.aauw.org

AAUW EDUCATIONAL FOUNDATION SELECTED PROFESSIONS FELLOWSHIPS

• See number 87

AMERICAN SOCIETY FOR INFORMATION SCIENCE AND TECHNOLOGY
http://www.asis.org

INSTITUTE FOR SCIENTIFIC INFORMATION DOCTORAL DISSERTATION PROPOSAL SCHOLARSHIP • 262

Nonrenewable scholarship for active doctoral student in information science who has completed all course work and has dissertation approval. Purpose of scholarship is to foster research in information science by encouraging and assisting doctoral students with dissertation research. Must submit curriculum vitae, detailed research proposal, budget, and other supporting data.

Academic/Career Areas Computer Science/Data Processing; Library Sciences.

Award Scholarship for use in graduate, or postgraduate years; not renewable. *Number:* 1. *Amount:* $1500.

Eligibility Requirements Applicant must be enrolled or expecting to enroll at an institution or university. Available to U.S. citizens.

Application Requirements Application, references. *Deadline:* July 1.

Contact Vanessa Foss, Awards Coordinator
American Society for Information Science and Technology
1320 Fenwick Lane, Suite 510
Silver Spring, MD 20910
Phone: 301-495-0900
Fax: 301-495-0810
E-mail: vfoss@asis.org

ISI OUTSTANDING INFORMATION SCIENCE TEACHER AWARD • 263

Award for a teacher of information science who has demonstrated excellence and unique contributions to the information science field. Must be nominated by a member of American Society for Information Science and Technology. Submit resume and statement of nominee's contributions. One-time award of $1000 with $500 travel expenses to ASIST meeting.

Academic/Career Areas Computer Science/Data Processing; Library Sciences.

Award Prize for use in graduate years; not renewable. *Number:* 1. *Amount:* $1000.

Eligibility Requirements Applicant must be enrolled or expecting to enroll at an institution or university. Applicant or parent of applicant must have employment or volunteer experience in teaching. Available to U.S. citizens.

Application Requirements Application, references. *Deadline:* July 1.

Contact Vanessa Foss, Awards Coordinator
American Society for Information Science
and Technology
1320 Fenwick Lane, Suite 510
Silver Spring, MD 20910
Phone: 301-495-0900
Fax: 301-495-0810
E-mail: vfoss@asis.org

UMI DOCTORAL DISSERTATION AWARD • 264

One-time award for information scientists honoring outstanding achievements in the completion of dissertation projects. Must have completed dissertation within the past year. Recognizes outstanding recent doctoral candidates whose research contributes significantly to an understanding of some aspect of information science. Submit letter of endorsement and manuscript or full dissertation.

Academic/Career Areas Computer Science/Data Processing; Library Sciences.

Award Prize for use in graduate, or postgraduate years; not renewable. *Number:* 1. *Amount:* $1000.

Eligibility Requirements Applicant must be enrolled or expecting to enroll at an institution or university. Available to U.S. citizens.

Application Requirements Application, references. *Deadline:* June 1.

Contact Vanessa Foss, Awards Coordinator
American Society for Information Science
and Technology
1320 Fenwick Lane, Suite 510
Silver Spring, MD 20910
Phone: 301-495-0900
Fax: 301-495-0810
E-mail: vfoss@asis.org

ARMED FORCES COMMUNICATIONS AND ELECTRONICS ASSOCIATION, EDUCATIONAL FOUNDATION
http://www.afcea.org

ARMED FORCES COMMUNICATIONS & ELECTRONICS ASSOCIATION EDUCATIONAL FOUNDATION FELLOWSHIP • 265

Award for students pursuing doctoral degrees or postdoctoral studies in electrical engineering, electronic or communications engineering, physics, mathematics, computer science or technology, or information management. The dean of the college of engineering at an accredited university in the U.S. may nominate one candidate. Only one candidate per university will be considered. Must be a U.S. citizen. Submit abstract or prospectus.

Academic/Career Areas Computer Science/Data Processing; Electrical Engineering/Electronics; Engineering/Technology; Physical Sciences and Math.

Award Fellowship for use in graduate, or postgraduate years; not renewable. *Amount:* $15,000.

Eligibility Requirements Applicant must be enrolled or expecting to enroll full-time at an institution or university. Available to U.S. citizens.

Application Requirements Application, references, transcript, prospectus. *Deadline:* February 1.

Contact Armed Forces Communications and
Electronics Association, Educational
Foundation
4400 Fair Lakes Court
Fairfax, VA 22033-3899
E-mail: scholarship@afcea.org

ARMED FORCES COMMUNICATIONS AND ELECTRONICS ASSOCIATION RALPH W. SHRADER SCHOLARSHIPS • 266

One-time awards for students working towards master's degrees in electrical, electronic, or communications engineering; physics; math; computer science; or information management at an accredited college or university in the United States. Provided eligibility criteria is met, at least one scholarship will be awarded to a woman or minority student. Must be U.S. citizen.

Academic/Career Areas Computer Science/Data Processing; Electrical Engineering/Electronics; Engineering/Technology; Physical Sciences and Math.

Award Scholarship for use in graduate years; not renewable. *Amount:* $3000.

Eligibility Requirements Applicant must be enrolled or expecting to enroll full-time at an institution or university. Available to U.S. citizens.

Armed Forces Communications and Electronics Association, Educational Foundation (continued)

Application Requirements Application, references, transcript. *Deadline:* February 1.

Contact Armed Forces Communications and
Electronics Association, Educational
Foundation
4400 Fair Lakes Court
Fairfax, VA 22033-3899
E-mail: scholarship@afcea.org

MILTON E. COOPER/YOUNG AFCEAN GRADUATE SCHOOL SCHOLARSHIP
• *See number 251*

ASSOCIATED WESTERN UNIVERSITIES, INC.
http://www.awu.org

ASSOCIATED WESTERN UNIVERSITIES FACULTY FELLOWSHIPS
• *See number 48*

ASSOCIATED WESTERN UNIVERSITIES GRADUATE RESEARCH FELLOWSHIPS
• *See number 49*

ASSOCIATED WESTERN UNIVERSITIES POSTGRADUATE FELLOWSHIP
• *See number 50*

ASSOCIATION FOR WOMEN IN SCIENCE EDUCATIONAL FOUNDATION
http://www.awis.org

ASSOCIATION FOR WOMEN IN SCIENCE PREDOCTORAL FELLOWSHIP
• *See number 77*

CHARLES BABBAGE INSTITUTE
http://www.cbi.umn.edu

ADELLE AND ERWIN TOMASH FELLOWSHIP IN THE HISTORY OF INFORMATION PROCESSING • 267

One-time award for graduate students addressing a topic in the history of computer and information processing. Submit research proposal and biographical information. Priority given to students who have completed all requirements for doctoral degree except the research and writing of the dissertation. Contact CBI for details.

Academic/Career Areas Computer Science/Data Processing; Electrical Engineering/Electronics; Engineering/Technology; History; Humanities; Science, Technology and Society.

Award Fellowship for use in graduate years; not renewable. *Number:* 1. *Amount:* $10,000.

Eligibility Requirements Applicant must be enrolled or expecting to enroll full-time at an institution or university.

Application Requirements References, transcript, research proposal, curriculum vitae. *Deadline:* January 15.

Contact Director
Charles Babbage Institute
University of Minnesota, 211 Elmer
Anderson Library, 222 21st. Avenue
South
Minneapolis, MN 55455
Phone: 612-624-5050
Fax: 612-625-8054
E-mail: cbi@tc.umn.edu

COUNCIL ON LIBRARY AND INFORMATION RESOURCES
http://www.clir.org

A.R. ZIPF FELLOWSHIP • 268

One-time award for a graduate student showing great promise for leadership and technical achievement in information management. Applications are available in January. Write for more information. Deadline: April 1.

Academic/Career Areas Computer Science/Data Processing; Library Sciences.

Award Fellowship for use in graduate years; not renewable. *Number:* 1. *Amount:* $5000–$8000.

Eligibility Requirements Applicant must be enrolled or expecting to enroll at an institution or university. Available to U.S. citizens.

Application Requirements Application, essay, references, transcript. *Deadline:* April 1.

Contact Council on Library and Information
Resources
1755 Massachusetts Avenue, NW, Suite
500
Washington, DC 20036-2124
Phone: 202-939-4750
Fax: 202-939-4765
E-mail: info@clir.org

FANNIE AND JOHN HERTZ FOUNDATION
http://www.hertzfoundation.org

FANNIE AND JOHN HERTZ FOUNDATION FELLOWSHIP
• *See number 53*

FOUNDATION FOR SCIENCE AND DISABILITY
http://www.as.wvu.edu/~scidis/organize/fsd.html

GRANTS FOR DISABLED STUDENTS IN THE SCIENCES
• *See number 54*

GEM CONSORTIUM
http://www.nd.edu/~gem

GEM PH.D. ENGINEERING FELLOWSHIP
• *See number 9*

ILLINOIS STUDENT ASSISTANCE COMMISSION (ISAC)
http://www.isac-online.org

ARTHUR F. QUERN INFORMATION TECHNOLOGY GRANT • **269**

One-time grants to Illinois residents who have previously received a baccalaureate degree and are seeking additional training and additional certification in a field of information technology. Deadline is May 1. Must study in Illinois.

Academic/Career Areas Computer Science/Data Processing.

Award Grant for use in graduate years; not renewable. *Number:* 1000–2000. *Amount:* $2300–$2500.

Eligibility Requirements Applicant must be enrolled or expecting to enroll full or part-time at a four-year institution or university; resident of Illinois and studying in Illinois. Available to U.S. and non-U.S. citizens.

Application Requirements Application, FAFSA. *Deadline:* May 1.

Contact David Barinholtz, Client Information
Illinois Student Assistance Commission (ISAC)
1755 Lake Cook Road
Deerfield, IL 60015-5209
Phone: 847-948-8500 Ext. 2385

INTERNATIONAL DEVELOPMENT RESEARCH CENTER
http://www.idrc.ca/awards

IDRC DOCTORAL RESEARCH AWARD
• *See number 12*

KRELL INSTITUTE
http://www.krellinst.org

HIGH-PERFORMANCE COMPUTER SCIENCE GRADUATE FELLOWSHIP • **270**

The DOE High-Performance Computer Science Graduate Fellowship was formed by Los Alamos National Laboratory, Lawrence Livermore National Library, and Sandia National Laboratory to foster long-range computer science research efforts in support of the distinctive challenges of high-performance computing. Renewable award of up to $49,000 for full-time graduate students only. Must be U.S. citizen.

Academic/Career Areas Computer Science/Data Processing.

Award Fellowship for use in graduate years; renewable. *Number:* 1–4. *Amount:* $39,000–$49,000.

Eligibility Requirements Applicant must be enrolled or expecting to enroll full-time at a four-year institution or university. Available to U.S. citizens.

Application Requirements Application, references, test scores, transcript. *Deadline:* February 11.

Contact Deanne Eggers
Krell Institute
1609 Golden Aspen Drive, Suite 101
Ames, IA 50010
Phone: 515-956-3696
Fax: 515-956-3699
E-mail: eggers@krellinst.org

NASA IDAHO SPACE GRANT CONSORTIUM
http://www.uidaho.edu/nasa_isgc

NASA ID SPACE GRANT CONSORTIUM FELLOWSHIP PROGRAM
• *See number 60*

NATIONAL ACTION COUNCIL FOR MINORITIES IN ENGINEERING-NACME, INC.
http://www.nacme.org

SLOAN PH.D PROGRAM
• *See number 243*

NATIONAL PHYSICAL SCIENCE CONSORTIUM
http://www.npsc.org

NATIONAL PHYSICAL SCIENCE CONSORTIUM GRADUATE FELLOWSHIPS IN THE PHYSICAL SCIENCES
• *See number 244*

NATIONAL RESEARCH COUNCIL
http://www.nationalacademies.org/fellowships/

FORD FOUNDATION PREDOCTORAL FELLOWSHIPS FOR MINORITIES
• *See number 258*

SOCIETY OF WOMEN ENGINEERS
http://www.swe.org

LYDIA I. PICKUP MEMORIAL SCHOLARSHIP • **271**

Available to female student entering the first year of a master's degree program. For graduate education to advance applicant's career in engineering or computer science. Minimum 3.0 GPA required. Deadline: February 1.

Society of Women Engineers (continued)

Academic/Career Areas Computer Science/Data Processing; Engineering/Technology.

Award Scholarship for use in graduate years; not renewable. *Number:* 1. *Amount:* $2000.

Eligibility Requirements Applicant must be enrolled or expecting to enroll at an institution or university and female. Applicant must have 3.0 GPA or higher. Available to U.S. citizens.

Application Requirements Application, references, self-addressed stamped envelope, transcript. *Deadline:* February 1.

Contact Program Coordinator
Society of Women Engineers
230 East Ohio Street, Suite 400
Chicago, IL 60611-3265
Phone: 312-596-5223
Fax: 312-644-8557
E-mail: hq@swe.org

MICROSOFT CORPORATION GRADUATE SCHOLARSHIPS • 272

Scholarships for entering female graduate students. Recipients must be pursuing a degree in computer science or computer engineering and exhibit career interest in the field of computer software. Minimum 3.5 GPA required. Deadline: February 1.

Academic/Career Areas Computer Science/Data Processing.

Award Scholarship for use in graduate years; not renewable. *Number:* 2. *Amount:* $2500.

Eligibility Requirements Applicant must be enrolled or expecting to enroll at an institution or university and female. Applicant must have 3.5 GPA or higher.

Application Requirements Application, essay, references, self-addressed stamped envelope, test scores, transcript. *Deadline:* February 1.

Contact Program Coordinator
Society of Women Engineers
230 East Ohio Street, Suite 400
Chicago, IL 60611-3265
Phone: 312-596-5223
Fax: 312-644-8557
E-mail: hq@swe.org

CRIMINAL JUSTICE/ CRIMINOLOGY

DURRANT FOUNDATION
http://www.durant.com/foundation.html

DURRANT FOUNDATION SCHOLARSHIP/ INTERNSHIP
• *See number 96*

JOHN F. KENNEDY LIBRARY FOUNDATION
http://www.jfklibrary.org

KENNEDY RESEARCH GRANTS
• *See number 100*

PI GAMMA MU INTERNATIONAL HONOR SOCIETY IN SOCIETY SCIENCE
http://www.sckans.edu/~pgm

PI GAMMA MU SCHOLARSHIP • 273

Ten scholarships available to graduate students in social sciences, criminal justice, economics, sociology, anthropology, law, international relations, social work, social psychology, social philosophy, cultural geography, history, and political science. Must have a minimum 3.0 GPA. One-time award of $1000-$2000. Must be a member of Pi Gamma Mu.

Academic/Career Areas Criminal Justice/ Criminology; Economics; History; Law/Legal Services; Political Science; Social Sciences; Social Services.

Award Scholarship for use in graduate years; not renewable. *Number:* 10. *Amount:* $1000–$2000.

Eligibility Requirements Applicant must be enrolled or expecting to enroll full or part-time at an institution or university. Applicant must have 3.0 GPA or higher. Available to U.S. and non-U.S. citizens.

Application Requirements Application, essay, resume, references, transcript. *Deadline:* January 30.

Contact Mrs. Sue Watters, Executive Director
Pi Gamma Mu International Honor
Society in Society Science
1001 Millington, Suite B
Winfield, KS 67156-3629
Phone: 316-221-3128
Fax: 316-221-7124
E-mail: pgm@sckans.edu

DENTAL HEALTH/SERVICES

ALBERT SCHWEITZER FELLOWSHIP
http://www.schweitzerfellowship.org

NEW HAMPSHIRE/VERMONT SCHWEITZER FELLOWS PROGRAM
• *See number 15*

AMERICAN ACADEMY OF ORAL AND MAXILLOFACIAL RADIOLOGY
http://www.aaomr.org

ALBERT G. RICHARDS GRADUATE STUDENT RESEARCH GRANT • 274

One-time award to assist graduate students doing applied research in oral and maxillofacial radiology. It provides funds for supplies, equipment and other costs such as computer time or shop work.

Academic/Career Areas Dental Health/Services.

Award Grant for use in graduate, or postgraduate years; not renewable. *Number:* 1. *Amount:* $1000.

Eligibility Requirements Applicant must be enrolled or expecting to enroll full-time at an institution or university. Available to U.S. and non-U.S. citizens.

Application Requirements Application, curriculum vitae. *Deadline:* April 15.

Contact Dr. M. K. Nair
American Academy of Oral and
Maxillofacial Radiology
G120 Salk Hall, 3501 Terrace Street
Pittsburgh, PA 15261-1923
Phone: 412-648-8633
Fax: 412-383-7796
E-mail: mkn2@pitt.edu

HOWARD RILEY PAPER GRADUATE STUDENT ORAL AND MAXILLOFACIAL RADIOLOGY AWARD • 275

One-time award to recognize a graduate student in oral and maxillofacial radiology with promise for an academic career. Must be nominated by program director.

Academic/Career Areas Dental Health/Services.

Award Grant for use in graduate years; not renewable. *Number:* 1. *Amount:* $500.

Eligibility Requirements Applicant must be enrolled or expecting to enroll full-time at an institution or university. Available to U.S. and non-U.S. citizens.

Application Requirements Nomination. *Deadline:* August 15.

Contact Dr. Margot L. Van Dis
American Academy of Oral and
Maxillofacial Radiology
Indiana University School of Dentistry,
1121 West Michigan Street
Indianapolis, IN 46202
Phone: 317-274-5117
Fax: 317-274-2419
E-mail: mvandis@iupui.edu

RADIOLOGY CENTENNIAL SCHOLARSHIP • 276

Renewable scholarship for a graduate student in the second year of a two or more year program in oral and maxillofacial radiology. Submit confirmation of matriculation in program.

Academic/Career Areas Dental Health/Services.

Award Scholarship for use in graduate years; renewable. *Number:* 1. *Amount:* $5000.

Eligibility Requirements Applicant must be enrolled or expecting to enroll full-time at an institution or university. Available to U.S. and non-U.S. citizens.

Application Requirements Application, essay, references, transcript. *Deadline:* March 30.

Contact Dr. M. K. Nair
American Academy of Oral and
Maxillofacial Radiology
G120 Salk Hall, 3501 Terrace Street
Pittsburgh, PA 15261-1923
Phone: 412-648-8633
Fax: 412-383-7796
E-mail: mkn2@pitt.edu

WILLIAM H. ROLLINS AWARD • 277

One-time award to a graduate student currently enrolled in an American Dental Association-accredited graduate program with an oral and maxillofacial radiology track. The award is for completed research, the results of which are expected to be published as a master's thesis or manuscript in the Academy's Journal and presented at the Academy's forthcoming annual session.

Academic/Career Areas Dental Health/Services.

Award Prize for use in graduate, or postgraduate years; not renewable. *Number:* 1. *Amount:* $1500.

Eligibility Requirements Applicant must be enrolled or expecting to enroll full-time at an institution or university. Available to U.S. and non-U.S. citizens.

Application Requirements Application. *Deadline:* March 30.

Contact Dr. M. K. Nair
American Academy of Oral and
Maxillofacial Radiology
G 120 Salk Hall, 3501 Terrace Street
Pittsburgh, PA 15261-1923
Phone: 412-648-8633
Fax: 412-383-7796
E-mail: mkn2@pitt.edu

AMERICAN ASSOCIATION FOR DENTAL RESEARCH
http://www.iadr.com

AADR STUDENT RESEARCH FELLOWSHIPS • 278

Applicant must be enrolled in an accredited DDA/DMD or hygiene program in a dental institution in the USA. Must be sponsored by a faculty member. Proposals are sought in basic and clinical research related to oral health.

Academic/Career Areas Dental Health/Services.

Award Fellowship for use in graduate years; not renewable. *Number:* 23–25. *Amount:* up to $3000.

American Association for Dental Research (continued)

Eligibility Requirements Applicant must be enrolled or expecting to enroll at an institution or university.

Application Requirements References, curriculum vitae, proposal. *Deadline:* January 15.

Contact American Association for Dental Research
1619 Duke Street
Alexandria, VA 22314-3406

AMERICAN DENTAL ASSOCIATION (ADA) ENDOWMENT AND ASSISTANCE FUND, INC.

AMERICAN DENTAL ASSOCIATION ENDOWMENT AND ASSISTANCE FUND DENTAL STUDENT SCHOLARSHIP PROGRAM • 279

One-time award for second-year students at an accredited dental school. Must have 3.0 GPA based on a 4.0 scale, and be enrolled full-time (minimum of twelve hours). Must show financial need and be a U.S. citizen.

Academic/Career Areas Dental Health/Services.

Award Scholarship for use in graduate years; not renewable. *Number:* 25. *Amount:* $2500.

Eligibility Requirements Applicant must be enrolled or expecting to enroll full-time at an institution or university. Applicant must have 3.0 GPA or higher. Available to U.S. citizens.

Application Requirements Application, autobiography, essay, financial need analysis, references, transcript. *Deadline:* July 31.

Contact Marsha L. Mountz
American Dental Association (ADA)
Endowment and Assistance Fund, Inc.
211 East Chicago Avenue, Suite 820
Chicago, IL 60611

AMERICAN DENTAL ASSOCIATION ENDOWMENT AND ASSISTANCE FUND MINORITY DENTAL STUDENT SCHOLARSHIP PROGRAM • 280

For member of underrepresented minority group for second year of study. Based on financial need and academic achievement. Must be U.S. citizen and full-time-student, minimum twelve hours. Must have minimum 3.0 GPA on a 4.0 scale. Applicant must be enrolled in a dental school accredited by the Commission on Dental Accreditation.

Academic/Career Areas Dental Health/Services.

Award Scholarship for use in graduate years; not renewable. *Number:* 25. *Amount:* $2500.

Eligibility Requirements Applicant must be American Indian/Alaska Native, Black (non-Hispanic), or Hispanic and enrolled or expecting to enroll full-time at a four-year institution or university. Applicant must have 3.0 GPA or higher. Available to U.S. citizens.

Application Requirements Application, autobiography, essay, financial need analysis, references. *Deadline:* July 31.

Contact Marsha L. Mountz
American Dental Association (ADA)
Endowment and Assistance Fund, Inc.
211 East Chicago Avenue, Suite 820
Chicago, IL 60611

AMERICAN DENTAL HYGIENISTS' ASSOCIATION (ADHA) INSTITUTE
http://www.adha.org

ALFRED C. FONES SCHOLARSHIP • 281

One-time award to an applicant in the baccalaureate or graduate degree categories who intends to become a dental hygiene teacher/educator. ADHA membership required. Must be a U.S. citizen and have a minimum 3.5 GPA.

Academic/Career Areas Dental Health/Services.

Award Scholarship for use in graduate years; not renewable. *Number:* 1. *Amount:* $1500.

Eligibility Requirements Applicant must be enrolled or expecting to enroll full-time at a four-year institution. Applicant or parent of applicant must be member of American Dental Hygienist's Association. Applicant must have 3.5 GPA or higher. Available to U.S. citizens.

Application Requirements Application, financial need analysis, references. *Deadline:* June 1.

Contact Robert Han, Assistant
American Dental Hygienists' Association (ADHA) Institute
444 North Michigan Avenue, Suite 3400
Chicago, IL 60611
Phone: 312-440-8900

AMERICAN DENTAL HYGIENISTS' ASSOCIATION INSTITUTE GRADUATE SCHOLARSHIP PROGRAM • 282

One-time award for licensed dental hygienists who are accepted at a graduate program in dental hygiene. Must provide proof of acceptance and provide statement on research interests. Must have a minimum GPA of 3.0. ADHA membership required. Must be a U.S. citizen.

Academic/Career Areas Dental Health/Services.

Award Scholarship for use in graduate years; not renewable. *Amount:* $1000–$2000.

Eligibility Requirements Applicant must be enrolled or expecting to enroll at an institution or university. Applicant or parent of applicant must be member of American Dental Hygienist's

Association. Applicant must have 3.0 GPA or higher. Available to U.S. citizens.

Application Requirements Application, references, transcript. *Deadline:* June 1.

Contact Robert Han, Assistant
American Dental Hygienists' Association
(ADHA) Institute
444 North Michigan Avenue, Suite 3400
Chicago, IL 60611

AMERICAN DENTAL HYGIENISTS' ASSOCIATION INSTITUTE RESEARCH GRANT • 283

One-time award for a licensed dental hygienist or a student pursuing a dental hygiene degree to promote the oral health of the public by improving dental hygiene education and practice. Must submit research proposal. ADHA membership required. Must be a U.S. citizen.

Academic/Career Areas Dental Health/Services.

Award Grant for use in graduate years; not renewable. *Amount:* $1000–$5000.

Eligibility Requirements Applicant must be enrolled or expecting to enroll at an institution or university. Applicant or parent of applicant must be member of American Dental Hygienist's Association. Available to U.S. citizens.

Application Requirements Application, references. *Deadline:* January 15.

Contact Robert Han, Administrative Assistant
American Dental Hygienists' Association
(ADHA) Institute
444 North Michigan Avenue, Suite 3400
Chicago, IL 60611

SIGMA PHI ALPHA GRADUATE SCHOLARSHIP • 284

One-time award for students pursuing a graduate degree in dental hygiene or related field. Must include a statement of professional activities related to dental hygiene. Minimum 3.0 GPA required. ADHA membership required. Must be a U.S. citizen.

Academic/Career Areas Dental Health/Services.

Award Scholarship for use in graduate years; not renewable. *Number:* 1. *Amount:* up to $2000.

Eligibility Requirements Applicant must be enrolled or expecting to enroll full-time at an institution or university. Applicant or parent of applicant must be member of American Dental Hygienist's Association. Applicant must have 3.0 GPA or higher. Available to U.S. citizens.

Application Requirements Application, financial need analysis, references. *Deadline:* June 1.

Contact Ms. Mary Carroll, Administrator
American Dental Hygienists' Association
(ADHA) Institute
444 North Michigan Avenue, Suite 3400
Chicago, IL 60611
Phone: 312-440-8900

CHINESE AMERICAN MEDICAL SOCIETY (CAMS)
http://www.camsociety.org

CHINESE AMERICAN MEDICAL SOCIETY SCHOLARSHIP • 285

One-time award for full-time medical or dental students. Preference given to students of Chinese descent. Must be enrolled in a medical or dental school in the U.S.

Academic/Career Areas Dental Health/Services; Health and Medical Sciences.

Award Scholarship for use in graduate years; not renewable. *Number:* 4–6. *Amount:* $1000–$1500.

Eligibility Requirements Applicant must be enrolled or expecting to enroll full-time at an institution or university. Available to U.S. and non-U.S. citizens.

Application Requirements Application, autobiography, financial need analysis, references, test scores, transcript. *Deadline:* March 31.

Contact Dr. Hsuen-Hwa Wang, Executive Director
Chinese American Medical Society
(CAMS)
281 Edgewood Avenue
Teaneck, NJ 07666
Phone: 201-833-1506
Fax: 201-833-8252
E-mail: hw5@columbia.edu

FINANCE AUTHORITY OF MAINE
http://www.famemaine.com

MAINE DENTAL EDUCATION LOAN PROGRAM • 286

Program is intended to increase access to dental care to underserved populations in Maine by providing need-based dental education loans to Maine residents. Forgivable loans available up to $20,000 per year for 4 years. Loan forgiveness rate is 25 percent per year of service. Recipients must provide dental services regardless of patient's ability to pay. See website for details (http://www.famemaine.com)

Academic/Career Areas Dental Health/Services.

Award Forgivable loan for use in graduate years; not renewable. *Amount:* up to $20,000.

Eligibility Requirements Applicant must be enrolled or expecting to enroll at an institution or university and resident of Maine. Available to U.S. citizens.

Dental Health/Services

Finance Authority of Maine (continued)

Application Requirements Application.

Contact Thomas Patenaude, Program Officer
Finance Authority of Maine
5 Community Drive
Augusta, ME 04332-0949
Phone: 800-228-3734
Fax: 207-623-3263
E-mail: tom@famemaine.com

HEALTH PROFESSIONS EDUCATION FOUNDATION
http://www.healthprofessions.ca.gov

HEALTH PROFESSIONS EDUCATION LOAN REPAYMENT PROGRAM • 287

The loan repayment program awards up to $20,000 over a two year period for the repayment of educational debt. Eligible applicants must agree to practice in a medically under-served area of California for a minimum of two years. Deadline: March 27. Must be resident of CA and a U.S. citizen.

Academic/Career Areas Dental Health/Services; Health and Medical Sciences; Nursing.

Award Grant for use in graduate, or postgraduate years; not renewable. *Number:* 10–15. *Amount:* $10,000–$20,000.

Eligibility Requirements Applicant must be enrolled or expecting to enroll at an institution or university; resident of California and studying in California. Available to U.S. citizens.

Application Requirements Application, driver's license, financial need analysis, references, transcript, 2 copies of application; and transcript with degree posted. *Deadline:* March 27.

Contact Lisa Montgomery, Program Director
Health Professions Education Foundation
1600 Ninth Street, Suite 436
Sacramento, CA 95814
Phone: 800-773-1669
Fax: 916-653-1438
E-mail: lmontgom@oshpd.state.ca.us

JAPANESE GOVERNMENT/THE MONBUSHO SCHOLARSHIP PROGRAM
http://embjapan.org/la

RESEARCH STUDENT SCHOLARSHIP
• *See number 13*

MARYLAND STATE HIGHER EDUCATION COMMISSION
http://www.mhec.state.md.us

MARYLAND DENT-CARE LOAN ASSISTANCE REPAYMENT PROGRAM • 288

Provides assistance for repayment of loan debt to Maryland dentists working with under-served populations.

Academic/Career Areas Dental Health/Services.

Award Forgivable loan for use in postgraduate years; renewable. *Number:* up to 20. *Amount:* up to $23,000.

Eligibility Requirements Applicant must be enrolled or expecting to enroll at an institution or university; resident of Maryland and studying in Maryland. Available to U.S. citizens.

Application Requirements Application. *Deadline:* Continuous.

Contact Carla Rich, Scholarship Administration
Maryland State Higher Education Commission
16 Francis Street
Annapolis, MD 21401-1781
Phone: 410-260-4513
Fax: 410-974-5994
E-mail: ssamail@mhec.state.md.us

MINNESOTA DEPARTMENT OF HEALTH
http://www.health.state.mn.us

MINNESOTA DENTAL LOAN FORGIVENESS PROGRAM • 289

Program funded to offer loan repayment to dental students attending dental program to become a licensed dentist. Individuals must plan to serve public program enrollees. Applications must be submitted while applicants are in residency. Up to 14 selections per year contingent upon state funding.

Academic/Career Areas Dental Health/Services.

Award Grant for use in graduate, or postgraduate years; not renewable. *Number:* up to 14. *Amount:* up to $10,000.

Eligibility Requirements Applicant must be enrolled or expecting to enroll full or part-time at an institution or university. Available to U.S. citizens.

Application Requirements Application, essay. *Deadline:* December 1.

Contact Karen Welter
Minnesota Department of Health
121 East Seventh Place, Suite 460, PO Box 64975
St. Paul, MN 55164-0975
Phone: 651-282-6302
E-mail: karen.welter@health.state.mn.us

NATIONAL ARAB AMERICAN MEDICAL ASSOCIATION
http://www.naama.com

FOUNDATION SCHOLARSHIP • 290

The NAAMA Foundation offers annual scholarship grants of $1,000 each to qualified students of Arabic extraction enrolled in a U.S. or Canadian medical, osteopathic, or dental school.

Academic/Career Areas Dental Health/Services; Health and Medical Sciences.

Award Grant for use in graduate years; not renewable. *Number:* 1–5. *Amount:* $1000.

Eligibility Requirements Applicant must be of Arab heritage and enrolled or expecting to enroll full-time at an institution or university. Applicant must have 3.0 GPA or higher. Available to U.S. and Canadian citizens.

Application Requirements Application, essay, financial need analysis, transcript. *Deadline:* June 1.

Contact Ellen R. Potter, Executive Director
National Arab American Medical
Association
801 South Adams Road, Suite 208
Birmingham, MI 48009
Phone: 248-646-3661
Fax: 248-646-0617
E-mail: naamausa@aol.com

NATIONAL HEMOPHILIA FOUNDATION
http://www.hemophilia.org

NATIONAL HEMOPHILIA FOUNDATION JUDITH GRAHAM POOL POSTDOCTORAL FELLOWSHIP • 291

Up to four fellowships of $42,000 for candidates having completed doctoral training in a doctoral, postdoctoral, internship or residency training program. Fellow must spend at least 90% of the time on research project; remaining 10% may be devoted to teaching or clinical work that is relevant to the research.

Academic/Career Areas Dental Health/Services; Health and Medical Sciences.

Award Fellowship for use in postgraduate years; not renewable. *Number:* up to 4. *Amount:* $42,000.

Eligibility Requirements Applicant must be enrolled or expecting to enroll at an institution or university. Available to U.S. and non-U.S. citizens.

Application Requirements Application, references, description of proposed research project. *Deadline:* December 1.

Contact Rita Barsky, Assistant Director
National Hemophilia Foundation
116 West 32nd Street, 11th Floor
New York, NY 10001
Phone: 212-328-3730
Fax: 212-328-3788
E-mail: rbarsky@hemophilia.org

NEBRASKA HEALTH AND HUMAN SERVICES SYSTEM, OFFICE OF RURAL HEALTH

RURAL HEALTH SCHOLARSHIP PROGRAM • 292

Must be enrolled or accepted for enrollment in medical or dental school at Creighton University or University of Nebraska Medical Center, or in Physician Assistant Program at a Nebraska college. Students must agree to practice one year in shortage area for each year a scholarship is awarded, and to specialize in family practice, general surgery, internal medicine, pediatrics, obstetrics/gynecology, or psychiatry. Applications accepted April 1 to June 1. Must be a Nebraska resident.

Academic/Career Areas Dental Health/Services; Health and Medical Sciences.

Award Forgivable loan for use in graduate years; not renewable. *Amount:* $5000–$20,000.

Eligibility Requirements Applicant must be enrolled or expecting to enroll at an institution or university; resident of Nebraska and studying in Nebraska. Applicant or parent of applicant must have employment or volunteer experience in designated career field.

Application Requirements Application, interview.

Contact Nebraska Health and Human Services
System, Office of Rural Health
301 Centennial Mall South PO Box 95044
Lincoln, NE 68509
Phone: 402-471-2337

NEW MEXICO COMMISSION ON HIGHER EDUCATION
http://www.nmche.org

NEW MEXICO HEALTH PROFESSIONAL LOAN REPAYMENT PROGRAM • 293

Program to provide for repayment of outstanding student loans of practicing health professionals in return for two-year service commitment with optional one-year renewals in a designated medical shortage area in New Mexico. Deadline: May 15. To apply call the Commission at the CHE Student Helpline: 1-800-279-9777.

Academic/Career Areas Dental Health/Services; Health and Medical Sciences; Nursing.

Award Forgivable loan for use in postgraduate years; renewable. *Amount:* up to $12,500.

Eligibility Requirements Applicant must be enrolled or expecting to enroll at an institution or university and studying in New Mexico. Applicant or parent of applicant must have employment or volunteer experience in designated career field. Available to U.S. citizens.

Application Requirements Application. *Deadline:* May 15.

Contact Barbara Serna, Clerk Specialist
New Mexico Commission on Higher
Education
PO Box 15910
Santa Fe, NM 87506-5910
Phone: 505-827-4026
Fax: 505-827-7392

NEW YORK STATE EDUCATION DEPARTMENT

REGENTS HEALTH CARE SCHOLARSHIPS FOR MEDICINE AND DENTISTRY-NEW YORK • 294

Renewable award for New York residents enrolled in medical or dental schools in New York. Priority for minorities or disadvantaged students. Must agree to practice in an area of New York with a shortage of physicians or dentists for a minimum of two years and a maximum of four.

Academic/Career Areas Dental Health/Services; Health and Medical Sciences.

Award Forgivable loan for use in graduate years; renewable. *Number:* 100. *Amount:* up to $10,000.

Eligibility Requirements Applicant must be American Indian/Alaska Native, Black (non-Hispanic), or Hispanic; enrolled or expecting to enroll full-time at an institution or university; resident of New York and studying in New York. Available to U.S. citizens.

Application Requirements Application, autobiography, driver's license, financial need analysis, references, transcript. *Deadline:* May 1.

Contact Lewis J. Hall, Coordinator
New York State Education Department
Room 1078 EBA
Albany, NY 12234
Phone: 518-486-1319
Fax: 518-486-5346

OREGON STUDENT ASSISTANCE COMMISSION
http://www.osac.state.or.us

JEANNETTE MOWERY SCHOLARSHIP • 295

One-time award for Oregon graduate students pursuing a course of study in law, medicine or dentistry. Must attend Oregon law schools or Oregon Health Sciences University.

Academic/Career Areas Dental Health/Services; Health and Medical Sciences; Law/Legal Services.

Award Scholarship for use in graduate years; not renewable.

Eligibility Requirements Applicant must be enrolled or expecting to enroll at an institution or university; resident of Oregon and studying in Oregon. Available to U.S. citizens.

Application Requirements Application, essay, financial need analysis, references, transcript, activity chart. *Deadline:* March 1.

Contact Director of Grant Programs
Oregon Student Assistance Commission
1500 Valley River Drive, Suite 100
Eugene, OR 97401-7020
Phone: 800-452-8807 Ext. 7395
E-mail:
awardinfo@mercury.osac.state.or.us

UNITED STATES ARMY RECRUITING COMMAND
http://www.goarmy.com

ARMED FORCES HEALTH PROFESSIONS SCHOLARSHIP PROGRAM-ARMY
• See number 23

F.E. HEBERT FINANCIAL ASSISTANCE PROGRAM • 296

Award provides annual grant plus monthly stipend. For graduates of dental school who intend to do residencies in oral surgery, endodontics, pedodontics, or periodontics; and for graduates of medical school who intend to do residencies in various specialties. Contact Army healthcare recruiter for current applicable specialties. Military service required upon completion of residency.

Academic/Career Areas Dental Health/Services; Health and Medical Sciences.

Award Fellowship for use in postgraduate years; renewable. *Number:* 300–400. *Amount:* $12,696.

Eligibility Requirements Applicant must be age 21-47 and enrolled or expecting to enroll full-time at an institution or university. Available to U.S. citizens. Applicant must have served in the Army.

Application Requirements Application, interview, references, test scores, transcript.

Contact United States Army Recruiting Command
Health Services Directorate
1307 Third Avenue
Fort Knox, KY 40121-2726

HEALTH PROFESSIONS LOAN REPAYMENT • 297

Provides over $100,000 in payment of student loan for students pursuing a doctoral degree in Pharmacy and certain dental specialists. Must be in the U.S. Army.

Academic/Career Areas Dental Health/Services.

Award Forgivable loan for use in graduate years; renewable. *Number:* 5–15. *Amount:* $25,000–$100,000.

Eligibility Requirements Applicant must be age 21-47 and enrolled or expecting to enroll full-time at an institution or university. Available to U.S. citizens. Applicant must have served in the Army.

Application Requirements Application, interview, references, test scores, transcript. *Deadline:* Continuous.

Contact United States Army Recruiting Command
Health Services Directorate
1307 Third Avenue
Fort Knox, KY 40121-2726

UNIVERSITY OF MEDICINE AND DENTISTRY OF NJ SCHOOL OF OSTEOPATHIC MEDICINE
http://www.3.umdnj.edu/faidweb

M.L. KING PHYSICIAN/DENTIST SCHOLARSHIPS • 298

Renewable award available to New Jersey residents enrolled full-time in a medical or dental program. Several scholarships are available. Dollar amount varies. Must be a former or current EOF recipient, a minority or from a disadvantaged background. Applicant must attend a New Jersey institution and apply for financial aid.

Academic/Career Areas Dental Health/Services; Health and Medical Sciences.

Award Scholarship for use in graduate years; renewable.

Eligibility Requirements Applicant must be enrolled or expecting to enroll full-time at an institution or university; resident of New Jersey and studying in New Jersey. Available to U.S. citizens.

Application Requirements Application, financial need analysis. *Deadline:* Continuous.

Contact Sandra Rollins, Associate Director of Financial Aid
University of Medicine and Dentistry of NJ School of Osteopathic Medicine
40 East Laurel Road,
Primary Care Center 119
Stratford, NJ 08084
Phone: 856-566-6008
Fax: 856-566-6015
E-mail: rollins@umdnj.edu

EARTH SCIENCE

AFRICAN NETWORK OF SCIENTIFIC AND TECHNOLOGICAL INSTITUTIONS - ANSTI
http://www.ansti.org

AFRICAN NETWORK OF SCIENTIFIC AND TECHNOLOGICAL INSTITUTIONS POSTGRADUATE FELLOWSHIPS
• See number 14

AIR AND WASTE MANAGEMENT ASSOCIATION
http://www.awma.org

AIR AND WASTE MANAGEMENT ASSOCIATION SCHOLARSHIP ENDOWMENT TRUST FUND
• See number 24

AMERICAN GEOPHYSICAL UNION
http://www.agu.org

AMERICAN GEOPHYSICAL UNION HORTON RESEARCH GRANT
• See number 25

CONGRESSIONAL SCIENCE FELLOWSHIP PROGRAM • 299

One-time award to fund postgraduate work in the fields of earth science, meterology and atmospheric science, and physical sciences and mathematics, as a staff member in Congress. Minimum 3.5 GPA required. Deadline: February 2.

Academic/Career Areas Earth Science; Meteorology/Atmospheric Science; Physical Sciences and Math.

Award Fellowship for use in postgraduate years; not renewable. *Number:* 1. *Amount:* $40,000–$50,000.

Eligibility Requirements Applicant must be enrolled or expecting to enroll at an institution or university. Applicant must have 3.5 GPA or higher. Available to U.S. citizens.

Application Requirements Application, essay, interview, references, transcript. *Deadline:* February 2.

Contact Emily Crum, Administrative Secretary of Public Affairs
American Geophysical Union
2000 Florida Avenue, NW
Washington, DC 20009-9202
Phone: 202-462-6900
Fax: 202-328-0566
E-mail: ecrum@agu.org

ASSOCIATED WESTERN UNIVERSITIES, INC.
http://www.awu.org

ASSOCIATED WESTERN UNIVERSITIES FACULTY FELLOWSHIPS
• See number 48

ASSOCIATED WESTERN UNIVERSITIES GRADUATE RESEARCH FELLOWSHIPS
• See number 49

ASSOCIATED WESTERN UNIVERSITIES POSTGRADUATE FELLOWSHIP
• See number 50

ASSOCIATION FOR WOMEN IN SCIENCE EDUCATIONAL FOUNDATION
http://www.awis.org

ASSOCIATION FOR WOMEN IN SCIENCE PREDOCTORAL FELLOWSHIP
• See number 77

ASSOCIATION OF ENGINEERING GEOLOGISTS
http://www.aegweb.org

GARDNER FUND • 300

Grants awarded to individuals and organizations conducting research in engineering geology or geotechnical engineering. Write for information. One-time award.

Academic/Career Areas Earth Science; Engineering/Technology.

Award Scholarship for use in graduate years; not renewable.

Eligibility Requirements Applicant must be enrolled or expecting to enroll at an institution or university. Available to U.S. citizens.

Application Requirements Application.

Contact Kim Samford, Executive Secretary
Association of Engineering Geologists
Texas A&M University, Department of
Geology and Geophysics
College Station, TX 77843-3115
Phone: 979-845-0142
Fax: 979-862-7959

DELAWARE VALLEY SPACE GRANT CONSORTIUM
http://www.delspace.org

NASA/DELAWARE VALLEY SPACE GRANT FELLOWSHIP
• *See number 52*

FANNIE AND JOHN HERTZ FOUNDATION
http://www.hertzfoundation.org

FANNIE AND JOHN HERTZ FOUNDATION FELLOWSHIP
• *See number 53*

GEM CONSORTIUM
http://www.nd.edu/~gem

GEM PH.D. ENGINEERING FELLOWSHIP
• *See number 9*

GEOLOGICAL SOCIETY OF AMERICA
http://www.geosociety.org

A.L. MEDLIN SCHOLARSHIP • 301

Awards for students who submit the best proposals for research projects in the field of coal geology. Contact for application procedures and further information. Must be a member of the Geological Society of America in order to apply.

Academic/Career Areas Earth Science.

Award Scholarship for use in graduate years; not renewable. *Number:* 2. *Amount:* $500–$2000.

Eligibility Requirements Applicant must be enrolled or expecting to enroll at an institution or university. Applicant or parent of applicant must be member of Geological Society of America. Available to U.S. and non-U.S. citizens.

Application Requirements Application, references. *Deadline:* February 15.

Contact Ms. Leah Carter, Program Officer, Grants, Awards and Medals
Geological Society of America
3300 Penrose Place, PO Box 9140
Boulder, CO 80301-9140
Phone: 303-357-1037
Fax: 303-357-1070
E-mail: lcarter@geosociety.org

ALEXANDER SISSON AWARD • 302

One-time award for graduate students pursuing research in Alaska and the Caribbean. Only members of the Geological Society are eligible. Write for more information.

Academic/Career Areas Earth Science.

Award Grant for use in graduate years; not renewable. *Number:* 1. *Amount:* $1550.

Eligibility Requirements Applicant must be enrolled or expecting to enroll at an institution or university. Applicant or parent of applicant must be member of Geological Society of America. Available to U.S. and non-U.S. citizens.

Application Requirements Application, references. *Deadline:* February 1.

Contact Ms. Leah Carter, Program Officer, Grants, Awards and Medals
Geological Society of America
3300 Penrose Place, PO Box 9140
Boulder, CO 80301-9140
Phone: 303-357-1037
Fax: 303-357-1070
E-mail: lcarter@geosociety.org

ARTHUR D. HOWARD RESEARCH GRANTS • 303

One-time award to support graduate student research in the field of Quaternary geology or geomorphology. Submit references and proposal. Must be a member of the Geological Society of America in order to apply.

Academic/Career Areas Earth Science; Natural Resources; Physical Sciences and Math.

Award Grant for use in graduate years; not renewable. *Number:* 1–2. *Amount:* $500.

Eligibility Requirements Applicant must be enrolled or expecting to enroll at an institution or university. Applicant or parent of applicant must be member of Geological Society of America.

Application Requirements Application, references, transcript. *Deadline:* February 15.

Contact Ms. Leah Carter, Program Officer, Grants, Awards and Medals
Geological Society of America
3300 Penrose Place, PO Box 9140
Boulder, CO 80301-9140
Phone: 303-357-1037
Fax: 303-357-1070
E-mail: lcarter@geosociety.org

BRUCE L. "BIFF" REED AWARD • 304

One-time award for graduate students pursuing studies in the tectonic and magmatic evolution of Alaska and its mineral deposits. Only members of the Geological Society of America are eligible. Write for more information.

Academic/Career Areas Earth Science.

Award Scholarship for use in graduate years; not renewable. *Number:* 1. *Amount:* $1500.

Eligibility Requirements Applicant must be enrolled or expecting to enroll full-time at an institution or university and studying in Alaska. Applicant or parent of applicant must be member of Geological Society of America. Available to U.S. and non-U.S. citizens.

Application Requirements Application, references. *Deadline:* February 1.

Contact Ms. Leah Carter, Program Officer, Grants, Awards and Medals
Geological Society of America
3300 Penrose Place, PO Box 9140
Boulder, CO 80301-9140
Phone: 303-357-1037
Fax: 303-357-1070
E-mail: lcarter@geosociety.org

CLAUDE C. ALBRITTON JR. SCHOLARSHIPS
• *See number 78*

GEOLOGICAL SOCIETY OF AMERICA STUDENT RESEARCH GRANTS • 305

Research grants in geology provide support for master's and doctoral research at universities in the U.S., Canada, Mexico, and Central America. Applications available through GSA campus representatives and geology department chairpersons and at website (http://www.geosociety.org). Must be a member of GSA in order to apply.

Academic/Career Areas Earth Science.

Award Grant for use in graduate years; not renewable. *Number:* 200–250. *Amount:* $500–$5000.

Eligibility Requirements Applicant must be enrolled or expecting to enroll full-time at an institution or university. Applicant or parent of applicant must be member of Geological Society of America. Available to U.S. and non-U.S. citizens.

Application Requirements Application, references. *Deadline:* February 1.

Contact Ms. Leah Carter, Program Officer, Grants, Awards and Medals
Geological Society of America
3300 Penrose Place, PO Box 9140
Boulder, CO 80301-9140
Phone: 303-357-1037
Fax: 303-357-1070
E-mail: lcarter@geosociety.org

GRETCHEN L. BLECHSCHMIDT AWARD • 306

One-time awards for women interested in achieving a Ph.D. in the geological sciences and a career in academic research. Only members of the Geological Society of America are eligible. Please visit website (http://www.geosociety.org) for more information.

Academic/Career Areas Earth Science.

Award Grant for use in graduate years; not renewable. *Number:* 1. *Amount:* $1200.

Eligibility Requirements Applicant must be enrolled or expecting to enroll full-time at an institution or university and female. Applicant or parent of applicant must be member of Geological Society of America. Available to U.S. and non-U.S. citizens.

Application Requirements Application, references. *Deadline:* February 1.

Contact Ms. Leah Carter, Program Officer, Grants, Awards and Medals
Geological Society of America
3300 Penrose Place, PO Box 9140
Boulder, CO 80301-9140
Phone: 303-357-1037
Fax: 303-357-1070
E-mail: lcarter@geosociety.org

HAROLD T. STEARNS FELLOWSHIP AWARD • 307

One-time award to graduate students for research on one or more aspects of the geology of the Pacific Islands and of the circum-Pacific region. Only members of the Geological Society of America are eligible. Please visit website for more information (http://www.geosociety.org).

Academic/Career Areas Earth Science.

Award Scholarship for use in graduate years; not renewable. *Number:* 1–4. *Amount:* $500–$3000.

Eligibility Requirements Applicant must be enrolled or expecting to enroll at an institution or university. Applicant or parent of applicant must be member of Geological Society of America. Available to U.S. and non-U.S. citizens.

Earth Science

Geological Society of America (continued)

Application Requirements Application, references.
Deadline: February 1.

Contact Ms. Leah Carter, Program Officer, Grants,
      Awards and Medals
      Geological Society of America
      3300 Penrose Place, PO Box 9140
      Boulder, CO 80301-9140
      Phone: 303-357-1037
      Fax: 303-357-1070
      E-mail: lcarter@geosociety.org

Application Requirements Application, references.
Deadline: February 1.

Contact Ms. Leah Carter, Program Officer, Grants,
      Awards and Medals
      Geological Society of America
      3300 Penrose Place, PO Box 9140
      Boulder, CO 80301-9140
      Phone: 303-357-1037
      Fax: 303-357-1070
      E-mail: lcarter@geosociety.org

J. HOOVER MACKIN RESEARCH GRANTS • 308

One-time award to support graduate student research
in the field of Quaternary geology or geomorphology.
Submit references and proposal to division secretary.
Must be a member of the Geological Society of
America in order to apply.

Academic/Career Areas Earth Science; Natural
Resources; Physical Sciences and Math.

Award Grant for use in graduate years; not
renewable. *Number:* 1–2. *Amount:* $500–$1000.

Eligibility Requirements Applicant must be
enrolled or expecting to enroll at an institution or
university. Applicant or parent of applicant must be
member of Geological Society of America. Available
to U.S. and non-U.S. citizens.

Application Requirements Application, references,
transcript. *Deadline:* February 1.

Contact Ms. Leah Carter, Program Officer, Grants,
      Awards and Medals
      Geological Society of America
      3300 Penrose Place, PO Box 9140
      Boulder, CO 80301-9140
      Phone: 303-357-1037
      Fax: 303-357-1070
      E-mail: lcarter@geosociety.org

LIPMAN RESEARCH AWARD • 310

One-time award to promote and support graduate
research in volcanology and petrology. Only members
of the Geological Society of America are eligible.
Please visit website (http://www.geosociety.org) for
more information.

Academic/Career Areas Earth Science.

Award Scholarship for use in graduate years; not
renewable. *Number:* 1. *Amount:* $1000.

Eligibility Requirements Applicant must be
enrolled or expecting to enroll full-time at an
institution or university. Applicant or parent of
applicant must be member of Geological Society of
America. Available to U.S. and non-U.S. citizens.

Application Requirements Application, references.
Deadline: February 1.

Contact Ms. Leah Carter, Program Officer, Grants,
      Awards and Medals
      Geological Society of America
      3300 Penrose Place, PO Box 9140
      Boulder, CO 80301-9140
      Phone: 303-357-1037
      Fax: 303-357-1070
      E-mail: lcarter@geosociety.org

JOHN T. DILLON ALASKA RESEARCH AWARD • 309

One-time awards to support research which addresses
earth science problems particular to Alaska. Graduate
students may be studying at universities in the U.S.,
Canada, Mexico, and Central America. Only members of the Geological Society of America are eligible.

Academic/Career Areas Earth Science.

Award Scholarship for use in graduate years; not
renewable. *Number:* 1. *Amount:* $1900.

Eligibility Requirements Applicant must be
enrolled or expecting to enroll full-time at an
institution or university. Applicant or parent of
applicant must be member of Geological Society of
America. Available to U.S. and non-U.S. citizens.

ROBERT K. FAHNESTOCK MEMORIAL AWARD • 311

One-time award for graduate research in the field of
sediment transport or related aspects of fluvial
geomorphology. Applicants must be a member of the
Geological Society of America. Please visit website
(http://www.geosociety.org) for more information.

Academic/Career Areas Earth Science.

Award Scholarship for use in graduate years; not
renewable. *Number:* 1. *Amount:* $500–$2000.

Eligibility Requirements Applicant must be
enrolled or expecting to enroll at an institution or
university. Applicant or parent of applicant must be
member of Geological Society of America. Available
to U.S. and non-U.S. citizens.

Application Requirements Application, references. *Deadline:* February 1.

Contact Ms. Leah Carter, Program Officer, Grants, Awards and Medals
Geological Society of America
3300 Penrose Place, PO Box 9140
Boulder, CO 80301-9140
Phone: 303-357-1037
Fax: 303-357-1070
E-mail: lcarter@geosociety.org

S.E. DWORNIK STUDENT PAPER AWARDS • 312

Two awards for graduate students studying planetary geology. Must be a member of the Geological Society of America. Contact for application procedures and further information.

Academic/Career Areas Earth Science.

Award Prize for use in graduate years; not renewable. *Number:* 2. *Amount:* $500.

Eligibility Requirements Applicant must be enrolled or expecting to enroll full-time at an institution or university. Applicant or parent of applicant must be member of Geological Society of America. Available to U.S. and non-U.S. citizens.

Application Requirements *Deadline:* February 1.

Contact Ms. Leah Carter, Program Officer, Grants, Awards and Medals
Geological Society of America
3300 Penrose Place, PO Box 9140
Boulder, CO 80301-9140
Phone: 303-357-1037
Fax: 303-357-1070
E-mail: lcarter@geosociety.org

HUDSON RIVER FOUNDATION
http://www.hudsonriver.org

HUDSON RIVER FOUNDATION GRADUATE FELLOWSHIPS
• *See number 205*

HUDSON RIVER NATIONAL ESTUARINE RESEARCH RESERVE
http://www.ocm.nos.noaa/nerr/fellow.html

NATIONAL ESTUARINE RESEARCH RESERVE GRADUATE FELLOWSHIP PROGRAM
• *See number 55*

LIFE SCIENCES RESEARCH FOUNDATION
http://www.lsrf.org

POSTDOCTORAL FELLOWSHIPS
• *See number 208*

NASA IDAHO SPACE GRANT CONSORTIUM
http://www.uidaho.edu/nasa_isgc

NASA ID SPACE GRANT CONSORTIUM FELLOWSHIP PROGRAM
• *See number 60*

NASA WYOMING SPACE GRANT CONSORTIUM
http://www.wyomingspacegrant.uwyo.edu

WYOMING NASA SPACE GRANT CONSORTIUM RESEARCH FELLOWSHIP
• *See number 61*

NATIONAL PHYSICAL SCIENCE CONSORTIUM
http://www.npsc.org

NATIONAL PHYSICAL SCIENCE CONSORTIUM GRADUATE FELLOWSHIPS IN THE PHYSICAL SCIENCES
• *See number 244*

NATIONAL SCIENCE FOUNDATION
http://www.nsf.gov/grfp

NATIONAL SCIENCE FOUNDATION GRADUATE RESEARCH FELLOWSHIPS
• *See number 62*

POTASH AND PHOSPHATE INSTITUTE
http://www.ppi-far.org

J. FIELDING REED FELLOWSHIPS
• *See number 6*

SOIL AND WATER CONSERVATION SOCIETY
http://www.swcs.org

SWCS KENNETH E. GRANT SCHOLARSHIP • 313

Research scholarships will be given to members of SWCS for graduate-level research on a specific urban conservation topic that will extend the SWCS mission of fostering the science and the art of soil, water, and related natural resource management to achieve sustainability. Must show financial need. Download the application form from the SWCS homepage at http://www.swcs.org.

Academic/Career Areas Earth Science; Natural Resources; Natural Sciences.

Award Scholarship for use in graduate, or postgraduate years; not renewable. *Number:* 1. *Amount:* $1300.

Eligibility Requirements Applicant must be enrolled or expecting to enroll at an institution or university. Applicant or parent of applicant must be

Soil and Water Conservation Society (continued)

member of Soil and Water Conservation Society. Available to U.S. and non-U.S. citizens.

Application Requirements Application, financial need analysis. *Deadline:* February 12.

Contact Judy Hansen, Administrative Assistant
Soil and Water Conservation Society
7515 NE Ankeny Road
Ankeny, IA 50021-9764
Phone: 515-289-2331 Ext. 19
Fax: 515-289-1227
E-mail: judyh@swcs.org

TRANSPORTATION ASSOCIATION OF CANADA
http://www.tac-atc.ca

TRANSPORTATION ASSOCIATION OF CANADA SCHOLARSHIPS
• *See number 249*

WELLESLEY COLLEGE
http://www.wellesley.edu/CWS/

PROFESSOR ELIZABETH F. FISHER
FELLOWSHIP   • **314**

One or more fellowships available for research or further study in geology or geography, including urban, environment or ecological studies. Preference given to geology and geography. Must be graduate of Wellesley College. Based on merit and need. E-mail inquiries to cws-fellowships@wellesley.edu

Academic/Career Areas Earth Science.

Award Fellowship for use in graduate years; not renewable. *Amount:* up to $2000.

Eligibility Requirements Applicant must be enrolled or expecting to enroll full-time at an institution or university. Available to U.S. citizens.

Application Requirements Application, essay, financial need analysis, resume, transcript. *Deadline:* January 3.

Contact Rose Crawford, Secretary to the
Committee on Graduate Fellowships
Wellesley College
106 Central Avenue, Green Hall 441
Wellesley, MA 02481-8200
Phone: 781-283-3525
Fax: 781-283-3674
E-mail: cws-fellowships@wellesley.edu

ECONOMICS

ALEXANDER VON HUMBOLDT FOUNDATION
http://www.humboldt-foundation.de

TRANSCOOP PROGRAM   • **315**

Award to support joint research projects among German, U.S., and/or Canadian scholars in the fields of humanities, social sciences, economics, and law. Maximum duration of award is three years. Award must be matched by funds from U.S. and/or Canadian sources. Applicants must hold at least a Ph.D. Must submit detailed research plan, curriculum vitae, and selected list of publications. Contact Humboldt Foundation for details. Application deadlines: July, October 30.

Academic/Career Areas Economics; Humanities; Law/Legal Services; Social Sciences.

Award Grant for use in postgraduate years; renewable. *Amount:* up to $43,000.

Eligibility Requirements Applicant must be enrolled or expecting to enroll at an institution or university. Available to U.S. and non-U.S. citizens.

Application Requirements Application, references.

Contact Dr. Robert Grathwol, Director, US Liaison
Office
Alexander von Humboldt Foundation
1012 14th Street, NW, Suite 301
Washington, DC 20005
Phone: 202-783-1907
Fax: 202-783-1908
E-mail: avh@bellatlantic.net

AMERICAN AGRICULTURAL ECONOMICS ASSOCIATION FOUNDATION
http://www.aaea.org

FARM CREDIT GRADUATE SCHOLARSHIP FOR THE STUDY OF YOUNG, BEGINNING OR SMALL FARMERS AND RANCHERS
• *See number 1*

OUTSTANDING DOCTORAL AND MASTER'S THESIS AWARDS
• *See number 2*

SYLVIA LANE MENTOR RESEARCH FELLOWSHIP FUND
• *See number 3*

AMERICAN COUNCIL OF TEACHERS OF RUSSIAN
http://www.actr.org

TITLE VIII RESEARCH SCHOLAR AND COMBINED RESEARCH AND LANGUAGE STUDY PROGRAM
• *See number 114*

AMERICAN GEOPHYSICAL UNION
http://www.agu.org

AMERICAN GEOPHYSICAL UNION HORTON RESEARCH GRANT
• *See number 25*

AMERICAN HISTORICAL ASSOCIATION
http://www.theaha.org

NASA FELLOWSHIP IN AEROSPACE HISTORY
• See number 175

AMERICAN INSTITUTE FOR ECONOMIC RESEARCH
http://www.aier.org

AMERICAN INSTITUTE FOR ECONOMIC RESEARCH SUMMER FELLOWSHIP PROGRAM • 316

One-time, eight-week fellowship for graduating college or university seniors applying to doctoral programs in economics, or those already enrolled for no more than one year. Must speak and write English with native fluency. Must submit recent paper or thesis, if available, as a writing sample.

Academic/Career Areas Economics.

Award Fellowship for use in graduate years; not renewable. *Number:* 10–12. *Amount:* $2000–$9000.

Eligibility Requirements Applicant must be enrolled or expecting to enroll full-time at an institution or university. Available to U.S. and non-U.S. citizens.

Application Requirements Application, autobiography, essay, references, transcript. *Deadline:* March 31.

Contact Susan Gillette, Assistant to the President
American Institute for Economic Research
PO Box 1000
Great Barrington, MA 01230-1000
Phone: 413-528-1216
Fax: 413-528-0103
E-mail: info@aier.org

ARMENIAN RELIEF SOCIETY OF NORTH AMERICA INC.-REGIONAL OFFICE

ARMENIAN RELIEF SOCIETY GRADUATE SCHOLARSHIP PROGRAM
• See number 224

CHINA TIMES CULTURAL FOUNDATION

CHINA TIMES CULTURAL FOUNDATION DOCTORAL DISSERTATION RESEARCH IN CHINESE STUDIES SCHOLARSHIPS
• See number 122

COMMUNITY ASSOCIATIONS INSTITUTE RESEARCH FOUNDATION
http://www.cairf.org

BYRON HANKE FELLOWSHIP FOR GRADUATE RESEARCH • 317

Graduate fellowship for research dealing with community associations in fields including law, economics, sociology, and urban planning. Projects may address management, institutions, organization and administration, public policy, architecture, as well as political, economic, social, and intellectual trends in community association housing. Projects may focus on either applied or theoretical research. Must submit 5-20 page writing sample and research proposal.

Academic/Career Areas Economics; Law/Legal Services; Social Sciences.

Award Fellowship for use in graduate, or postgraduate years; not renewable. *Amount:* up to $2000.

Eligibility Requirements Applicant must be enrolled or expecting to enroll full-time at an institution or university.

Application Requirements Application, references, writing sample (5-20 pages) and research proposal. *Deadline:* Continuous.

Contact Ms. Amanda Perl, Research Foundation
Coordinator and Special Projects
Manager
Community Associations Institute
Research Foundation
225 Reinekers Lane, Suite 300
Alexandria, VA 22314
Phone: 703-548-8600
Fax: 703-684-1581
E-mail: aperl@caionline.org

EPILEPSY FOUNDATION
http://www.epilepsyfoundation.org

EPILEPSY FOUNDATION BEHAVIORAL SCIENCES RESEARCH TRAINING FELLOWSHIP • 318

Award for students who have received their doctoral degree in behavioral sciences. Fellowship carries stipend of up to $30,000 for one-year training experience in epilepsy research related to behavioral sciences. Deadline: March 1.

Academic/Career Areas Economics; Health and Medical Sciences; Political Science; Social Sciences; Social Services.

Award Fellowship for use in postgraduate years; not renewable. *Amount:* up to $30,000.

Eligibility Requirements Applicant must be enrolled or expecting to enroll full-time at a four-year institution or university.

Epilepsy Foundation (continued)

Application Requirements Application, autobiography, financial need analysis, references. *Deadline:* March 1.

Contact Cathy Morris, Administrative Coordinator,
Programs and Research
Epilepsy Foundation
4351 Garden City Drive
Landover, MD 20785
Phone: 301-459-3700
Fax: 301-577-4941
E-mail: grants@efa.org

FRENCH INSTITUTE OF WASHINGTON (INSTITUT FRANÇAIS DE WASHINGTON)
http://www.unc.edu/depts/institut

EDOUARD MOROT-SIR FELLOWSHIP IN LITERATURE
• *See number 165*

GILBERT CHINARD FELLOWSHIPS AND EDOUARD MOROT-SIR FELLOWSHIP IN LITERATURE
• *See number 166*

HARMON CHADBOURN RORISON FELLOWSHIP
• *See number 167*

FRIEDRICH EBERT FOUNDATION

EBERT FOUNDATION ADVANCED GRADUATE FELLOWSHIPS   • 319

One-time award for highly qualified graduate students intending to pursue a doctoral degree that requires research or study in Germany. Must have completed two years of study. Submit proposal of study and/or research objective and recommendation from graduate advisor. Must also have sufficient knowledge of German and a German counterpart who would be available for cooperation and assistance during stay. Must be U.S. citizen.

Academic/Career Areas Economics; History; Political Science; Social Sciences.

Award Fellowship for use in graduate years; not renewable.

Eligibility Requirements Applicant must be enrolled or expecting to enroll at an institution or university and must have an interest in German language. Available to U.S. citizens.

Application Requirements Application, references, transcript, study/research proposal. *Deadline:* February 28.

Contact Barbara Kess
Friedrich Ebert Foundation
Godesberger Alee 149
53170 Bonn
Germany
Phone: 49-228-8364 Ext. 9
E-mail: barbara.kess@fes.de

EBERT FOUNDATION DOCTORAL RESEARCH FELLOWSHIP   • 320

Fellowship for qualified Ph.D. candidates in social science, economics, history, and political science at American university who need to undertake dissertation research in German archives, libraries and other institutions. Submit proposal. Must provide evidence that knowledge of German is adequate and indicate a German counterpart who would be available for cooperation and assistance during stay. Must be U.S. citizen.

Academic/Career Areas Economics; History; Political Science; Social Sciences.

Award Fellowship for use in graduate years; not renewable.

Eligibility Requirements Applicant must be enrolled or expecting to enroll at an institution or university and must have an interest in German language. Available to U.S. citizens.

Application Requirements Application, references. *Deadline:* February 28.

Contact Barbara Kess
Friedrich Ebert Foundation
Godesberger Allee 149
53170 Bonn
Germany
Phone: 49-228-8836 Ext. 49
E-mail: barbara.kess@fes.de

EBERT FOUNDATION POSTDOCTORAL FELLOWSHIPS   • 321

Supports postdoctoral research for young American scholars in the social sciences, history, political science, and economics. Submit research proposal and copies of relevant academic publications. Must have appropriate knowledge of German and a German counterpart who would be available for cooperation and assistance during stay in Germany. Must have at least two years of subsequent experience in research and/or teaching.

Academic/Career Areas Economics; History; Political Science; Social Sciences.

Award Fellowship for use in postgraduate years; not renewable.

Eligibility Requirements Applicant must be enrolled or expecting to enroll at an institution or university and must have an interest in German language. Applicant or parent of applicant must have employment or volunteer experience in designated career field or teaching. Available to U.S. citizens.

Application Requirements Application, references. *Deadline:* February 28.

Contact Barbara Kess
　　　　Friedrich Ebert Foundation
　　　　Godesberger Allee 149
　　　　53170 Bonn
　　　　Germany
　　　　Phone: 49-228-8836 Ext. 49
　　　　E-mail: barbara.kess@fes.de

GENEVA ASSOCIATION
http://www.genevaassociation.org

ERNST MEYER PRIZE • **322**

The Geneva Association awards every year the prestigious Ernst Meyer Prize for university research work, usually in the form of a doctoral thesis, which makes a significant and original contribution to the study of risk and insurance economics. Applicants for the Ernst Meyer Prize must be accompanied by a curriculum vitae, a description of the research undertaken and letter of recommendation from two professors of economics. Applicants must also submit three copies of their work and a summary of 1000 to 1500 words in English as hardcopy and as Win Word file on diskette or per email. Visit http://www.genevaassociation.org for more details.

Academic/Career Areas Economics.

Award Prize for use in graduate, or postgraduate years; renewable. *Number:* 1. *Amount:* $3100.

Eligibility Requirements Applicant must be enrolled or expecting to enroll full or part-time at an institution or university. Available to U.S. and non-U.S. citizens.

Application Requirements Application, autobiography, resume, references, transcript. *Deadline:* September 30.

Contact Martina Balet, Assistant to the Secretary
　　　　　　General
　　　　Geneva Association
　　　　53 Route de Malagnou
　　　　Geneva CH-12
　　　　Switzerland
　　　　Phone: 41-2-2707660 Ext. 0
　　　　Fax: 41-2-2736753 Ext. 6
　　　　E-mail: info@genevaassociation.org

RESEARCH GRANTS FOR RESEARCH INTO RISK AND INSURANCE ECONOMICS • **323**

Annually, the Geneva Association offers two grants for research into risk and insurance economics: one on economic theory and one on economic practice. The grants are primarily intended for research for a thesis leading to a doctoral degree in economics. For more information on the grants and more specifically suggested topics visit http://www.genevaassociation.org.

Academic/Career Areas Economics.

Award Grant for use in postgraduate years; renewable. *Number:* 2. *Amount:* $6000.

Eligibility Requirements Applicant must be enrolled or expecting to enroll full or part-time at an institution or university. Available to U.S. and non-U.S. citizens.

Application Requirements Application, autobiography, resume, references. *Deadline:* September 30.

Contact Martina Balet, Assistant to the Secretary
　　　　　　General
　　　　Geneva Association
　　　　53 Route de Malagnou
　　　　Geneva CH-12
　　　　Switzerland
　　　　Phone: 41-2-2707660 Ext. 0
　　　　Fax: 41-2-2736753 Ext. 6
　　　　E-mail: info@genevaassociation.org

HARRY S TRUMAN LIBRARY INSTITUTE
http://www.trumanlibrary.org

HARRY S. TRUMAN BOOK AWARD • **324**

Biennial competition for the best book on Harry S. Truman or the period of his presidency, published between January 1, 2002 and December 31, 2003. Five copies of each book entered must be received by January 20, 2004. Award given in even-numbered years. Winner announced in May of even-numbered years.

Academic/Career Areas Economics; Historic Preservation and Conservation; History; Political Science.

Award Prize for use in postgraduate years; not renewable. *Number:* 1. *Amount:* $1000.

Eligibility Requirements Applicant must be enrolled or expecting to enroll at an institution or university and must have an interest in writing. Available to U.S. and non-U.S. citizens.

Application Requirements Applicant must enter a contest, five copies of submitted book.

Contact Lisa Sullivan, Office Manager
　　　　Harry S Truman Library Institute
　　　　500 West U.S. Highway 24
　　　　Independence, MO 64050-1798
　　　　Phone: 816-833-0425 Ext. 234
　　　　Fax: 816-833-2715
　　　　E-mail: lisa.sullivan@nara.gov

HARRY S. TRUMAN LIBRARY INSTITUTE DISSERTATION YEAR FELLOWSHIPS • **325**

One-time award for graduate students who have completed their dissertation research and are ready to begin writing. Research should be related to the history of the Truman administration and the public career of Harry S Truman. Preference given to projects based on extensive research at the Truman

Harry S Truman Library Institute (continued)

Library, but since research is presumed to be complete, there is no requirement of residence at the Library during the fellowship year. Must submit curriculum vitae, prospectus or introduction, and tentative time schedule for completion.

Academic/Career Areas Economics; Historic Preservation and Conservation; History; Political Science.

Award Fellowship for use in graduate years; not renewable. *Number:* 1. *Amount:* $16,000.

Eligibility Requirements Applicant must be enrolled or expecting to enroll at an institution or university. Available to U.S. and non-U.S. citizens.

Application Requirements Application, references, curriculum vitae, prospectus, time schedule. *Deadline:* February 1.

Contact Lisa Sullivan, Office Manager
Harry S Truman Library Institute
500 West U.S. Highway 24
Independence, MO 64050-1798
Phone: 816-833-0425 Ext. 234
Fax: 816-833-2715
E-mail: lisa.sullivan@nara.gov

HARRY S. TRUMAN LIBRARY INSTITUTE RESEARCH GRANTS   • 326

Bi-annual, one-time award for graduate students and postdoctoral scholars to use the Library archival facilities on Truman-related topics for one to three weeks. May only be used for travel and expenses. Application deadlines are April 1 and October 1 and results are announced six weeks later. Submit curriculum vitae and description and justification for project, not to exceed five pages.

Academic/Career Areas Economics; Historic Preservation and Conservation; History; Political Science.

Award Grant for use in graduate, or postgraduate years; not renewable. *Amount:* up to $2500.

Eligibility Requirements Applicant must be enrolled or expecting to enroll at a four-year institution or university and studying in Missouri. Available to U.S. and non-U.S. citizens.

Application Requirements Application, references, curriculum vitae, project description and justification.

Contact Lisa Sullivan, Office Manager
Harry S Truman Library Institute
500 West U.S. Highway 25
Independence, MO 64050
Phone: 816-833-0425 Ext. 234
Fax: 816-833-2715
E-mail: lisa.sullivan@nara.gov

HARRY S. TRUMAN LIBRARY INSTITUTE SCHOLAR'S AWARD   • 327

One-time award offered in even-numbered years to a scholar who is engaged in a study of the public career of Harry Truman or some aspect of the Truman administration or of the U.S. during that administration. Scholar's work must be based on extensive research at the Truman Library. The award is intended to free the applicant from teaching or other employment, but will not exceed $30,000. Submit informal proposal by December 15 of year preceding the one in which award is available. If selected, submit budget, time-line, and other forms by February 15.

Academic/Career Areas Economics; Historic Preservation and Conservation; History; Physical Sciences and Math.

Award Grant for use in postgraduate years; not renewable. *Number:* 1. *Amount:* up to $30,000.

Eligibility Requirements Applicant must be enrolled or expecting to enroll at an institution or university. Available to U.S. and non-U.S. citizens.

Application Requirements Application, references, proposal.

Contact Lisa Sullivan, Office Manager
Harry S Truman Library Institute
500 West U.S. Highway 24
Independence, MO 64050-1798
Phone: 816-833-0425 Ext. 234
Fax: 816-833-2715
E-mail: lisa.sullivan@nara.gov

INSTITUTE FOR SUPPLY MANAGEMENT
http://www.ism.ws

INSTITUTE FOR SUPPLY MANAGEMENT DISSERTATION GRANT PROGRAM
• *See number 232*

INSTITUTE FOR SUPPLY MANAGEMENT SENIOR RESEARCH FELLOWSHIP PROGRAM
• *See number 233*

INTERNATIONAL DEVELOPMENT RESEARCH CENTER
http://www.idrc.ca/awards

AGROPOLIS
• *See number 10*

JAPANESE GOVERNMENT/THE MONBUSHO SCHOLARSHIP PROGRAM
http://embjapan.org/la

RESEARCH STUDENT SCHOLARSHIP
• *See number 13*

JOHN F. KENNEDY LIBRARY FOUNDATION
http://www.jfklibrary.org

KENNEDY RESEARCH GRANTS
• *See number 100*

MACKENZIE KING SCHOLARSHIPS BOARD

MACKENZIE KING TRAVELLING SCHOLARSHIPS
• *See number 236*

NATIONAL ACTION COUNCIL FOR MINORITIES IN ENGINEERING-NACME, INC.
http://www.nacme.org

SLOAN PH.D PROGRAM
• *See number 243*

NATIONAL MILK PRODUCERS FEDERATION
http://www.nmpf.org

NATIONAL MILK PRODUCERS FEDERATION NATIONAL DAIRY LEADERSHIP SCHOLARSHIP PROGRAM
• *See number 5*

PI GAMMA MU INTERNATIONAL HONOR SOCIETY IN SOCIETY SCIENCE
http://www.sckans.edu/~pgm

PI GAMMA MU SCHOLARSHIP
• *See number 273*

POPULATION COUNCIL
http://www.popcouncil.org

POPULATION COUNCIL FELLOWSHIPS IN THE SOCIAL SCIENCES, MID-CAREER LEVEL • **328**

Awards open to scholars with minimum five years of professional experience in the population field. Must hold a Ph.D. or equivalent and wish to undertake specific study with a research institute. Strong preference given to applicants from developing countries who have a firm commitment to return home upon completion of training programs. Minimum 3.5 GPA required. For application forms and additional information, see http://www.popcouncil. org. Submit letter, proposal, and application by December 15. Applicant's research topic must deal with population issues in order to be considered.

Academic/Career Areas Economics; Health and Medical Sciences; International Migration; Social Sciences.

Award Fellowship for use in postgraduate years; not renewable. *Amount:* $45,000–$64,500.

Eligibility Requirements Applicant must be enrolled or expecting to enroll full-time at an institution or university. Applicant must have 3.5 GPA or higher. Available to U.S. and non-U.S. citizens.

Application Requirements Application, references, transcript, 3-page proposal. *Deadline:* December 15.

Contact Jude Lam-Garrison, Fellowship
        Coordinator
      Population Council
      Policy Research Division, 1 Dag
        Hammarskjold Plaza
      New York, NY 10017
      Phone: 212-339-0671
      Fax: 212-755-6052
      E-mail: jlam-garrison@popcouncil.org

POPULATION COUNCIL FELLOWSHIPS IN THE SOCIAL SCIENCES, POSTDOCTORAL LEVEL • **329**

Awards for persons with Ph.D. or equivalent who wish to continue postdoctoral training or research at an institution other than where Ph.D. was received. Minimum 3.5 GPA required. Include a letter from adviser at proposed institution. For application forms and additional information, see http://www.popcouncil. org. Submit letter, proposal, and application by December 15. Research must be population related dealing with the developing world in order for application to be considered.

Academic/Career Areas Economics; Health and Medical Sciences; International Migration; Social Sciences.

Award Fellowship for use in postgraduate years; not renewable. *Amount:* $30,000–$52,000.

Eligibility Requirements Applicant must be enrolled or expecting to enroll full-time at an institution or university. Applicant must have 3.5 GPA or higher. Available to U.S. and non-U.S. citizens.

Application Requirements Application, references, transcript, 3-page proposal. *Deadline:* December 15.

Contact Jude Lam-Garrison, Fellowship
        Coordinator
      Population Council
      Policy Research Division, 1 Dag
        Hammarskjold Plaza
      New York, NY 10017
      Phone: 212-339-0671
      Fax: 212-755-6052
      E-mail: jlam-garrison@popcouncil.org

POPULATION COUNCIL FELLOWSHIPS IN THE SOCIAL SCIENCES, PREDOCTORAL LEVEL • **330**

One-time award for advanced training in population studies. Must have completed all course work for

Population Council (continued)

Ph.D., or an equivalent degree in an area of population studies in combination with a social science discipline. Provides support for dissertation fieldwork or dissertation writing period. Minimum 3.5 GPA required. For application forms and additional information, see http://www.popcouncil. org. Submit letter, proposal, and application by December 15. Applicant's research topic must deal with population study in order to apply.

Academic/Career Areas Economics; Health and Medical Sciences; International Migration; Social Sciences.

Award Fellowship for use in graduate years; not renewable. *Amount:* $15,000–$35,000.

Eligibility Requirements Applicant must be enrolled or expecting to enroll full-time at an institution or university. Applicant must have 3.5 GPA or higher. Available to U.S. and non-U.S. citizens.

Application Requirements Application, references, transcript, 3-page proposal. *Deadline:* December 15.

Contact Jude Lam-Garrison, Fellowship
Coordinator
Population Council
Policy Research Division, 1 Dag
Hammarskjold Plaza
New York, NY 10017
Phone: 212-339-0671
Fax: 212-755-6052
E-mail: jlam-garrison@popcouncil.org

RESOURCES FOR THE FUTURE
http://www.rff.org

GILBERT F. WHITE POSTDOCTORAL FELLOWSHIPS • 331

Two postdoctoral fellowship for social or natural scientists with Ph.D. who wish to devote a year to scholarly work in areas related to natural resources, energy, or the environment. Teaching and/or research experience at postdoctoral level preferred though not essential. May hold position in government as well as at academic institution. Must submit resume, budget, and proposal. Deadline: February 28.

Academic/Career Areas Economics; Engineering-Related Technologies; Natural Resources; Political Science; Social Sciences.

Award Fellowship for use in postgraduate years; not renewable. *Number:* 2. *Amount:* $35,000–$50,000.

Eligibility Requirements Applicant must be enrolled or expecting to enroll full-time at an institution or university.

Application Requirements Autobiography, resume, references, project description and budget. *Deadline:* February 28.

Contact Coordinator for Academic Programs
Resources for the Future
1616 P Street, NW
Washington, DC 20036-1400
Phone: 202-328-5060
Fax: 202-939-3460

JOSEPH L. FISHER DISSERTATION AWARDS • 332

Award intended for doctoral candidates in final year of dissertation research on issues related to the environment, natural resources, or energy. Students whose research emphasizes policy aspects of environmental issues are encouraged to apply. Proof of Ph.D. status, curriculum vita, proposal, and technical summary are required.

Academic/Career Areas Economics; Engineering-Related Technologies; Natural Resources; Political Science; Social Sciences.

Award Fellowship for use in graduate years; not renewable. *Number:* 4–6. *Amount:* $12,000.

Eligibility Requirements Applicant must be enrolled or expecting to enroll full-time at an institution or university.

Application Requirements Autobiography, essay, references, transcript. *Deadline:* February 28.

Contact Coordinator for Academic Programs
Resources for the Future
1616 P Street, NW
Washington, DC 20036
Phone: 202-328-5060
Fax: 202-939-3460

TRANSPORTATION ASSOCIATION OF CANADA
http://www.tac-atc.ca

TRANSPORTATION ASSOCIATION OF CANADA SCHOLARSHIPS
• *See number 249*

UNITED STATES INSTITUTE OF PEACE
http://www.usip.org

JENNINGS RANDOLPH SENIOR FELLOW AWARD • 333

Awards to scholars and practitioners from a variety of professions, including college and university faculty, journalists, diplomats, writers, educators, military officers, international negotiators, lawyers. Funds projects related to preventive diplomacy, ethnic and regional conflicts, peacekeeping and peace operations, peace settlements, post-conflict reconstruction and reconciliation, democratization and the rule of law, cross-cultural negotiations, U.S. foreign policy in the

21st century, and related topics. Projects which demonstrate relevance to current policy debates will be highly competitive. Open to citizens of all nations. Women and members of minorities are especially encouraged to apply. Deadline: September 17.

Academic/Career Areas Economics; History; Humanities; International Migration; International Studies; Journalism; Law/Legal Services; Peace and Conflict Studies; Political Science; Social Sciences; TV/Radio Broadcasting.

Award Fellowship for use in graduate, or postgraduate years; not renewable. *Number:* 10–12.

Eligibility Requirements Applicant must be enrolled or expecting to enroll full-time at an institution or university. Available to U.S. and non-U.S. citizens.

Application Requirements Application, references. *Deadline:* September 17.

Contact United States Institute of Peace
1200 17th Street, NW, Suite 200
Washington, DC 20036-3011
Phone: 202-429-3886
Fax: 202-429-6063
E-mail: jrprogram@usip.org

PEACE SCHOLAR DISSERTATION FELLOWSHIP
• 334

Award supports doctoral dissertations that explore the sources and nature of international conflict, and strategies to prevent or end conflict and to sustain peace. Dissertations from a broad range of disciplines and interdisciplinary fields are eligible. Priority given to projects that contribute knowledge relevant to the formulation of policy on international peace and conflict issues. Citizens of all countries are eligible, but must be enrolled in an accredited U.S. university. Must have completed all degree requirements except the dissertation by the commencement of the award. Deadline: November 15.

Academic/Career Areas Economics; History; Humanities; International Migration; International Studies; Journalism; Law/Legal Services; Peace and Conflict Studies; Political Science; Social Sciences; TV/Radio Broadcasting.

Award Fellowship for use in graduate years; not renewable. *Number:* 5–10. *Amount:* $17,000.

Eligibility Requirements Applicant must be enrolled or expecting to enroll full-time at an institution or university. Available to U.S. and non-U.S. citizens.

Application Requirements Application, references, transcript. *Deadline:* November 15.

Contact Jennings Randolph Program
United States Institute of Peace
1200 17th Street, NW, Suite 200
Washington, DC 20036-3011
Phone: 202-429-3886
E-mail: jrprogram@usip.org

W. E. UPJOHN INSTITUTE FOR EMPLOYMENT RESEARCH
http://www.upjohninst.org

UPJOHN INSTITUTE DISSERTATION AWARD
• 335

Honors best Ph.D. dissertation on an employment related issue. Two honorable mention awards available at $750 each. Requires letter of recommendation from adviser and 10-page summary of dissertation. Deadline: July 5.

Academic/Career Areas Economics; Social Sciences.

Award Prize for use in graduate years; not renewable. *Number:* 1–3. *Amount:* $750–$2000.

Eligibility Requirements Applicant must be enrolled or expecting to enroll at an institution or university. Available to U.S. and non-U.S. citizens.

Application Requirements References, 10 page summary of dissertation. *Deadline:* July 5.

Contact Richard Wyrwa, Marketing Manager
W. E. Upjohn Institute for Employment Research
300 South Westnedge Avenue
Kalamazoo, MI 49007-4686
E-mail: webmaster@we.upjohninst.org

UPJOHN INSTITUTE GRANT PROGRAM
• 336

Award for professional researchers to conduct policy-relevant research on employment issues. Funds both original research and authoritative surveys that provide a synthesis or critique of existing research, but not dissertation research. Must submit proposal by February 1.

Academic/Career Areas Economics; Social Sciences.

Award Grant for use in postgraduate years; not renewable. *Number:* 3–5. *Amount:* $30,000–$50,000.

Eligibility Requirements Applicant must be enrolled or expecting to enroll full or part-time at a four-year institution or university. Available to U.S. and non-U.S. citizens.

Application Requirements Proposal/curriculum vitae. *Deadline:* February 1.

Contact Richard Wyrwa, Marketing Manager
W. E. Upjohn Institute for Employment Research
300 South Westnedge Avenue
Kalamazoo, MI 49007-4686
E-mail: webmaster@we.upjohninst.org

UPJOHN INSTITUTE MINI-GRANT PROGRAM
• 337

Award for professional researchers to conduct policy-relevant research on employment issues. Targeting untenured junior faculty, this grant program provides flexibility to meet special funding needs that,

W. E. Upjohn Institute for Employment Research (continued)

without support, would prevent researchers from pursuing the project. Must submit proposal by February 1.

Academic/Career Areas Economics; Social Sciences.

Award Grant for use in postgraduate years; not renewable. *Number:* 10. *Amount:* up to $5000.

Eligibility Requirements Applicant must be enrolled or expecting to enroll full or part-time at a four-year institution or university. Available to U.S. and non-U.S. citizens.

Application Requirements 3 page proposal. *Deadline:* February 1.

Contact W. E. Upjohn Institute for Employment Research
300 South Westnedge Avenue
Kalamazoo, MI 49007-4686
Phone: 616-343-5541
E-mail: webmaster@we.upjohninst.org

WELLESLEY COLLEGE
http://www.wellesley.edu/CWS/

PEGGY HOWARD FELLOWSHIP IN ECONOMICS • 338

One or more fellowships in economics to provide financial aid for Wellesley students or alumnae continuing their study of economics. The application and supporting material should be returned in early April. Based on merit and need.

Academic/Career Areas Economics.

Award Fellowship for use in graduate years; not renewable.

Eligibility Requirements Applicant must be enrolled or expecting to enroll full-time at an institution or university and female. Available to U.S. citizens.

Application Requirements Application, essay, financial need analysis, resume, references, transcript.

Contact Economics Department
Wellesley College
106 Central Street
Wellesley, MA 02481-8260

WOODROW WILSON NATIONAL FELLOWSHIP FOUNDATION
http://www.woodrow.org

THOMAS R. PICKERING GRADUATE FOREIGN AFFAIRS FELLOWSHIP PROGRAM
• *See number 241*

WORLD BANK
http://www.worldbank.org/wbi/scholarships

ROBERT S. MCNAMARA FELLOWSHIP • 339

One-time award for nationals of a World Bank member country. Groups may apply. Must hold at least a master's degree in public policy. Promotes the study of economic development. Contact organization for deadline. Award not available to U.S. or Canadian citizens.

Academic/Career Areas Economics; Social Sciences.

Award Fellowship for use in graduate years; not renewable. *Number:* up to 15.

Eligibility Requirements Applicant must be enrolled or expecting to enroll full-time at an institution or university. Available to citizens of countries other than the U.S. or Canada.

Application Requirements Application, resume, references.

Contact Abdul Al-Mashat, Administrator
World Bank
1818 H Street, NW
Washington, DC 20433
Phone: 202-473-6414
Fax: 202-522-4036
E-mail: aalmashat@worldbank.org

EDUCATION

AFRICAN AMERICAN SUCCESS FOUNDATION, INC.
http://www.blacksuccessfoundation.org

LYDIA DONALDSON TUTT-JONES MEMORIAL AWARD
• *See number 112*

AMERICAN ASSOCIATION FOR HEALTH EDUCATION
http://www.aahperd.org/aahe

AMERICAN ASSOCIATION FOR HEALTH EDUCATION BARBARA A. COOLEY SCHOLARSHIP • 340

Award for masters-level student enrolled in health education program. Must submit resume, essay, and three letters of recommendation. One-time award of $1000. Deadline: December 1.

Academic/Career Areas Education; Health and Medical Sciences.

Award Scholarship for use in graduate years; not renewable. *Amount:* $1000.

Eligibility Requirements Applicant must be enrolled or expecting to enroll full or part-time at a four-year institution or university. Applicant must have 3.0 GPA or higher. Available to U.S. and non-U.S. citizens.

Application Requirements Application, essay, references, transcript. *Deadline:* December 1.

Contact Linda Moore, Program Administrator
American Association for Health Education
1900 Association Drive
Reston, VA 20191-1599
Phone: 703-476-3437
Fax: 703-476-6638
E-mail: aahe@aahperd.org

AMERICAN ASSOCIATION FOR HEALTH EDUCATION DELBERT OBERTEUFFER SCHOLARSHIP • 341

Award for doctoral level student enrolled in health education program. Must submit resume, three letters of recommendations, and essay. One time award $1500. Deadline: December 1st.

Academic/Career Areas Education; Health and Medical Sciences.

Award Scholarship for use in graduate years; not renewable. *Amount:* $1500.

Eligibility Requirements Applicant must be enrolled or expecting to enroll full or part-time at a four-year institution or university. Applicant must have 3.5 GPA or higher. Available to U.S. and non-U.S. citizens.

Application Requirements Application, essay, references, transcript. *Deadline:* December 1.

Contact Linda Moore, Program Administrator
American Association for Health Education
1900 Association Drive
Reston, VA 20191-1599
Phone: 703-476-3437
Fax: 703-476-6638
E-mail: ahe@aahperd.org

AMERICAN ASSOCIATION FOR HEALTH EDUCATION MARION B. POLLOCK FELLOWSHIP • 342

Award for master's level student enrolled in health education program with three years teaching experience in health education. Must submit resume, sample work, essay, and three letters of recommendation. One-time award of $5000. Deadline: December 1.

Academic/Career Areas Education; Health and Medical Sciences.

Award Fellowship for use in graduate years; not renewable. *Amount:* $5000.

Eligibility Requirements Applicant must be enrolled or expecting to enroll full or part-time at a four-year institution or university. Applicant must have 3.5 GPA or higher. Available to U.S. and non-U.S. citizens.

Application Requirements Application, essay, references, transcript, sample of work. *Deadline:* December 1.

Contact Linda Moore, Program Administrator
American Association for Health Education
1900 Association Drive
Reston, VA 20191-1599
Phone: 703-476-3437
Fax: 703-476-6638
E-mail: aahe@aahperd.org

AMERICAN ASSOCIATION OF UNIVERSITY WOMEN (AAUW) EDUCATIONAL FOUNDATION
http://www.aauw.org

ELEANOR ROOSEVELT TEACHER FELLOWSHIPS • 343

Fellowships are open to all public school K-12 women teachers who are U.S. citizens or permanent residents, and who have taught for at least three year. Supports professional development.

Academic/Career Areas Education; Physical Sciences and Math; Science, Technology and Society.

Award Fellowship for use in graduate years; not renewable. *Number:* 25. *Amount:* $5000.

Eligibility Requirements Applicant must be enrolled or expecting to enroll at an institution or university and female. Applicant or parent of applicant must have employment or volunteer experience in teaching. Available to U.S. citizens.

Application Requirements Application, references. *Deadline:* January 10.

Contact Customer Service Center
American Association of University Women (AAUW) Educational Foundation
2201 North Dodge Street
Iowa City, IA 52245-4030
Phone: 319-337-1716
E-mail: aauw@act.org

AMERICAN COUNCIL OF TEACHERS OF RUSSIAN
http://www.actr.org

ACTR SUMMER RUSSIAN LANGUAGE TEACHER PROGRAM • 344

Award for full-time teachers, professors or teachers in training of Russian with a minimum 3.5 GPA. Fellowship money awarded is automatically credited to the cost of participating in the Summer Language Teacher Exchange Program. Must submit photocopy of passport, current curriculum vitae or resume, and completed application form. Deadline: March 1.

Academic/Career Areas Education; Foreign Language.

American Council of Teachers of Russian (continued)

Award Fellowship for use in graduate, or postgraduate years; not renewable. *Number:* 12–15. *Amount:* $3500–$5000.

Eligibility Requirements Applicant must be enrolled or expecting to enroll full-time at an institution or university. Applicant must have 3.5 GPA or higher. Available to U.S. citizens.

Application Requirements Application, essay, financial need analysis, resume, references, transcript, photocopy of passport or date for receipt of new passport. *Deadline:* March 1.

Contact Gabriel Coleman, Program Officer
American Council of Teachers of Russian
1776 Massachusetts Avenue, NW, Suite 700
Washington, DC 20036
Phone: 202-833-7522
Fax: 202-833-7523
E-mail: outbound@actr.org

AMERICAN LEGION AUXILIARY, DEPARTMENT OF NEBRASKA

AMERICAN LEGION AUXILIARY DEPARTMENT OF NEBRASKA GRADUATE SCHOLARSHIPS • 345

One-time award for Nebraska resident who is a veteran or a child of a veteran during dates of eligibility for American Legion membership. For use at a Nebraska institution for training as a teacher of special education for the handicapped. Must rank in upper third of class or have a minimum 3.0 GPA.

Academic/Career Areas Education; Special Education.

Award Scholarship for use in graduate years; not renewable. *Amount:* $200.

Eligibility Requirements Applicant must be enrolled or expecting to enroll full-time at an institution or university; resident of Nebraska and studying in Nebraska. Applicant must have 3.0 GPA or higher. Available to U.S. citizens. Applicant or parent must meet one or more of the following requirements: general military experience; retired from active duty; disabled or killed as a result of military service; prisoner of war; or missing in action.

Application Requirements Application, test scores, transcript. *Deadline:* April 5.

Contact Terry Walker, Department Secretary
American Legion Auxiliary, Department of Nebraska
PO Box 5227
Lincoln, NE 68505
Phone: 402-466-1808
Fax: 402-466-0182
E-mail: neaux@alltel.net

AMERICAN LEGION AUXILIARY, DEPARTMENT OF WISCONSIN
http://www.amlegionauxwi.org

CHILD WELFARE SCHOLARSHIPS • 346

One-time award of $1000. Applicant must be a graduate student in some facet of Special Education. If there is no applicant in special education, the scholarship will be in the field of education. Applicant must be a daughter, son, wife, or widow of a veteran. Granddaughters and great-granddaughters of veterans who are auxiliary members may also apply. Must send with completed application: certification of an American Legion Auxiliary Unit President, copy of proof that veteran was in service (i.e. discharge papers), letters of recommendation, transcripts and essay. Must have minimum 3.2 GPA, show financial need, and be a resident of Wisconsin. Refer questions to Department Secretary, (608) 745-0214. Applications available on website: www.legion-aux.org.

Academic/Career Areas Education; Special Education.

Award Scholarship for use in graduate years; not renewable. *Number:* 1. *Amount:* $1000.

Eligibility Requirements Applicant must be enrolled or expecting to enroll at an institution or university and resident of Wisconsin. Applicant or parent of applicant must be member of American Legion or Auxiliary. Available to U.S. citizens.

Application Requirements Application, essay, financial need analysis, references, transcript. *Deadline:* March 15.

Contact Scholarship Information
American Legion Auxiliary, Department of Wisconsin
PO Box 140
Portage, WI 53901-0140
Phone: 608-745-0124

AMERICAN ORFF-SCHULWERK ASSOCIATION
http://www.aosa.org

AMERICAN ORFF-SCHULWERK ASSOCIATION RESEARCH GRANT • 347

Nonrenewable award to graduate students with work experience in music, who are also members of AOSA, for projects that promote the philosophy and the Orff-Schulwerk processes developed by Carl Orff and Gunild Keetman. Must be U.S. citizen or U.S. resident for past five years. The deadlines are January 15 and July 15.

Academic/Career Areas Education; Performing Arts; Therapy/Rehabilitation.

Award Grant for use in graduate, or postgraduate years; not renewable. *Number:* 1–2. *Amount:* $500–$2500.

Eligibility Requirements Applicant must be enrolled or expecting to enroll full or part-time at an institution or university and must have an interest in music/singing. Applicant or parent of applicant must be member of American Orff-Schulwerk Association. Applicant or parent of applicant must have employment or volunteer experience in designated career field. Available to U.S. citizens.

Application Requirements Application, financial need analysis, references, self-addressed stamped envelope.

Contact Cindi Wobig, Executive Director
American Orff-Schulwerk Association
PO Box 391089
Cleveland, OH 44139-8089
Phone: 440-543-5366
Fax: 440-543-2687
E-mail: aosahdq@msn.com

AOSA-TRAINING AND PROJECTS FUND • 348

Provides financial aid to teachers of elementary or junior high school students from low-income populations. Must be a citizen of the United States of America or have resided in the United States for the past five years.

Academic/Career Areas Education; Performing Arts; Therapy/Rehabilitation.

Award Scholarship for use in graduate, or postgraduate years; not renewable. *Number:* 1–3. *Amount:* $200–$1000.

Eligibility Requirements Applicant must be enrolled or expecting to enroll full or part-time at a four-year institution or university and must have an interest in music/singing. Applicant or parent of applicant must be member of American Orff-Schulwerk Association. Applicant or parent of applicant must have employment or volunteer experience in designated career field. Available to U.S. citizens.

Application Requirements Application, financial need analysis, references. *Deadline:* January 15.

Contact Cindi Wobig, Executive Director
American Orff-Schulwerk Association
PO Box 391089
Cleveland, OH 44139-8089
Phone: 440-543-5366
Fax: 440-543-2687
E-mail: aosahdq@msn.com

GUNILD KEETMAN ASSISTANCE FUND • 349

Scholarship for graduate students interested in furthering their growth in Orff-Schulwerk teacher training courses. Must be a U.S. citizen or U.S. resident for past five years, a member of AOSA for last two years, and have financial need.

Academic/Career Areas Education; Performing Arts; Therapy/Rehabilitation.

Award Scholarship for use in graduate, or postgraduate years; not renewable. *Number:* 1–15. *Amount:* $500–$2000.

Eligibility Requirements Applicant must be enrolled or expecting to enroll full or part-time at an institution or university and must have an interest in music/singing. Applicant or parent of applicant must be member of American Orff-Schulwerk Association. Applicant or parent of applicant must have employment or volunteer experience in designated career field. Available to U.S. citizens.

Application Requirements Application, financial need analysis, references. *Deadline:* January 15.

Contact Cindi Wobig, Executive Director
American Orff-Schulwerk Association
PO Box 391089
Cleveland, OH 44139-8089
Phone: 440-543-5366
Fax: 440-543-2687
E-mail: aosahdq@msn.com

SHIELDS-GILLESPIE SCHOLARSHIP • 350

Applicant must be member of AOSA for a minimum of two years, U.S. citizen or have resided in U.S. for last five years, and a college graduate who teaches preschool or kindergarten minority or low-income students. Nonrenewable award to be used for O-S teacher training.

Academic/Career Areas Education; Performing Arts; Therapy/Rehabilitation.

Award Scholarship for use in graduate, or postgraduate years; not renewable. *Number:* 2–5. *Amount:* $200–$2000.

Eligibility Requirements Applicant must be enrolled or expecting to enroll full or part-time at an institution or university and must have an interest in music/singing. Applicant or parent of applicant must be member of American Orff-Schulwerk Association. Applicant or parent of applicant must have employment or volunteer experience in designated career field. Available to U.S. citizens.

Application Requirements Application, financial need analysis, references. *Deadline:* January 15.

Contact Cindi Wobig, Executive Director
American Orff-Schulwerk Association
PO Box 391089
Cleveland, OH 44139-8089
Phone: 440-543-5366
Fax: 440-543-2687
E-mail: aosahdq@msn.com

ARKANSAS DEPARTMENT OF HIGHER EDUCATION
http://www.arscholarships.com

MINORITY MASTER'S FELLOWS PROGRAM • 351

Renewable award for graduate students who are African-Americans, Hispanics, or Asian-Americans, enrolled in full-time teacher certification program in math, science, or foreign language. Must be Arkansas resident and have 2.75 minimum GPA. Must teach two years following certification or repay scholarship. Recipients must have received Arkansas Minority Teachers' Scholarship as an undergraduate. Must attend Arkansas graduate school.

Academic/Career Areas Education; Foreign Language; Physical Sciences and Math; Science, Technology and Society.

Award Forgivable loan for use in graduate years; renewable. *Amount:* up to $7500.

Eligibility Requirements Applicant must be Asian/Pacific Islander, Black (non-Hispanic), or Hispanic; enrolled or expecting to enroll full-time at an institution or university; resident of Arkansas and studying in Arkansas. Available to U.S. citizens.

Application Requirements Application, transcript. *Deadline:* June 1.

Contact Lillian Williams, Assistant Coordinator
Arkansas Department of Higher Education
114 East Capitol
Little Rock, AR 72201
Phone: 501-371-2050
Fax: 501-371-2001
E-mail: lillianw@adhe.arknet.edu

ASSOCIATION FOR INSTITUTIONAL RESEARCH
http://www.airweb.org

AIR RESEARCH GRANTS-IMPROVING INSTITUTIONAL RESEARCH IN POSTSECONDARY EDUCATION INSTITUTIONS • 352

The program provides grants to principal investigators to: conduct research on institutional research in post-secondary education using the NCES and NSF national databases; conduct other institutional research that promises a significant contribution to the national knowledge of the nature and operation of post-secondary education; conduct other institutional research activities that will make a contribution to our knowledge of post-secondary education; or conduct institutional research activities that will contribute to the professional development of professional personnel working in post-secondary education.

Academic/Career Areas Education; Social Sciences.

Award Grant for use in postgraduate years; not renewable. *Number:* up to 10. *Amount:* up to $30,000.

Eligibility Requirements Applicant must be enrolled or expecting to enroll at a four-year institution or university. Available to U.S. and non-U.S. citizens.

Application Requirements Proposal. *Deadline:* January 15.

Contact Grants Administrator and Professional Development
Association for Institutional Research
114 Stone Building, Florida State University
Tallahassee, FL 32306-4462
Phone: 850-644-6387
Fax: 850-644-8824
E-mail: air@mailer.fsu.edu

DISSERTATION SUPPORT GRANT- IMPROVING INSTITUTIONAL RESEARCH IN POSTSECONDARY EDUCATIONAL INSTITUTIONS • 353

Dissertation Grant proposals are solicited from doctoral students beginning their dissertation work. Grant support is available for one year to assist the student in the acquisition, analysis, and reporting of data from the NCES and NSF datasets. The program provides grants to conduct research on post-secondary education using the NCES and NSF national databases that promises a significant contribution to the national knowledge of the nature and operation of post-secondary education.

Academic/Career Areas Education; Social Sciences.

Award Grant for use in graduate years; not renewable. *Amount:* $15,000.

Eligibility Requirements Applicant must be enrolled or expecting to enroll at an institution or university. Available to U.S. and non-U.S. citizens.

Application Requirements Proposal. *Deadline:* January 15.

Contact Grants Administrator and Professional Development
Association for Institutional Research
114 Stone Building, Florida State University
Tallahassee, FL 32306-4462
Phone: 850-644-6387
Fax: 850-544-8824
E-mail: air@mailer.fsu.edu

SUMMER DATA POLICY INSTITUTE • 354

This two-week intensive Institute will be offered in the Washington, D.C. area to train fellows in the uses of national data on human resources and post-secondary education in science, engineering, and technology. Fellows should have at least a basic knowledge of statistical methods and be experienced in the use of software packages (i.e., SPSS, SAS), and should have an interest in using national databases in institutional research. Fellowships to cover transportation, hotel accommodations, meals, and incidental expenses (M&IE), for the duration of the Institute will be awarded to fellows accepted on the basis of a brief (five-page maximum) proposal.

Academic/Career Areas Education; Social Sciences.

Award Grant for use in graduate, or postgraduate years; not renewable. *Number:* 40.

Eligibility Requirements Applicant must be enrolled or expecting to enroll at a four-year institution or university. Available to U.S. and non-U.S. citizens.

Application Requirements Proposal. *Deadline:* January 15.

Contact Grants Administrator and Professional
Development
Association for Institutional Research
114 Stone Building, Florida State
University
Tallahassee, FL 32306-4462
Phone: 850-644-6387
Fax: 850-644-8824
E-mail: air@mailer.fsu.edu

CHINA TIMES CULTURAL FOUNDATION

CHINA TIMES CULTURAL FOUNDATION DOCTORAL DISSERTATION RESEARCH IN CHINESE STUDIES SCHOLARSHIPS
• *See number 122*

CONSORTIUM OF COLLEGE AND UNIVERSITY MEDIA CENTERS
http://www.ccumc.org

CONSORTIUM OF COLLEGE AND UNIVERSITY MEDIA CENTERS RESEARCH AWARDS
• *See number 253*

DELTA SOCIETY
http://www.deltasociety.org

HARRIS SWEATT TRAVEL GRANT
• *See number 17*

FLORIDA STATE DEPARTMENT OF EDUCATION
http://www.firn.edu/doe/osfa

EXCEPTIONAL STUDENT EDUCATION TRAINING GRANT FOR TEACHERS • **355**

Provides reimbursement to those persons who are under full-time contract to teach in Pre K-12 exceptional student education programs and do not have certification or endorsement in the specific subject area for the current teaching assignment. Areas include foreign languages, teaching the physically handicapped, chemistry, etc. See website for details. (http://www.firn.edu/doe/ofsa)

Academic/Career Areas Education.

Award Grant for use in graduate years; not renewable. *Amount:* up to $702.

Eligibility Requirements Applicant must be enrolled or expecting to enroll part-time at an institution or university and studying in Florida. Applicant or parent of applicant must have employment or volunteer experience in teaching. Applicant must have 3.0 GPA or higher. Available to U.S. citizens.

Application Requirements Application, financial need analysis. *Deadline:* September 15.

Contact Bureau of Student Financial Assistance
Florida State Department of Education
1940 North Monroe
Suite 70
Tallahassee, FL 32303-4759
Phone: 888-827-2004
E-mail: osfa@mail.doe.state.fl.us

GEORGIA STUDENT FINANCE COMMISSION
http://www.gsfc.org

GEORGIA HOPE TEACHER SCHOLARSHIP PROGRAM • **356**

Forgivable loan program for Georgia residents who have been admitted into an advanced degree teacher education program leading to certification in a critical shortage field. Recipients are obligated to teach/serve in their area of study at a Georgia public school for one year for each $2500 awarded, with a maximum of four years. Write for deadlines.

Academic/Career Areas Education; Special Education.

Award Forgivable loan for use in graduate years; renewable. *Number:* 1500–2500. *Amount:* $1000–$10,000.

Eligibility Requirements Applicant must be enrolled or expecting to enroll full or part-time at an institution or university; resident of Georgia and studying in Georgia. Available to U.S. citizens.

Application Requirements Application, transcript. *Deadline:* Continuous.

Contact William Flook, Director of Scholarships
and Grants Division
Georgia Student Finance Commission
2082 East Exchange Place, Suite 100
Tucker, GA 30084

JAPAN-AMERICA SOCIETY OF WASHINGTON, DC
http://www.us-japan.org/dc

WASHINGTON-TOKYO PUBLIC SERVICE FELLOWSHIP PROGRAM • **357**

The fellowship concentrates on professionals in the early stages of their public service career. Fellows will

Japan-America Society of Washington, DC (continued)

be placed in Japanese agencies and organizations related to their fields of professional interest for a period of two months. Minimum 3.5 GPA required.

Academic/Career Areas Education.

Award Fellowship for use in postgraduate years; not renewable. *Number:* 1. *Amount:* $10,000.

Eligibility Requirements Applicant must be enrolled or expecting to enroll at an institution or university. Applicant or parent of applicant must have employment or volunteer experience in designated career field. Applicant must have 3.5 GPA or higher. Available to U.S. citizens.

Application Requirements Application, interview, resume, references, project statement/goal.

Contact Ms. JoAnna Phillips, Executive Director
Japan-America Society of Washington, DC
1020 19th Street, NW, LL Suite 40
Washington, DC 20036-6117
Phone: 202-833-2210
Fax: 202-833-2456
E-mail: jaswdc@intr.net

JEWISH FOUNDATION FOR EDUCATION OF WOMEN
http://www.jfew.org

FELLOWSHIP PROGRAM FOR EMIGRES PURSUING CAREERS IN JEWISH EDUCATION • 358

Awards for female émigrés from the former Soviet Union who intend to enter the field of Jewish education. Must be enrolled in rabbinical/cantorial programs or graduate-level programs in Jewish studies/Jewish education. Must meet monthly to share learning and teaching experiences. Applicants are required to live within 50 miles of New York City and must demonstrate financial need and a good academic record.

Academic/Career Areas Education; Religion/Theology.

Award Scholarship for use in graduate years; renewable. *Number:* up to 8. *Amount:* $10,000–$20,000.

Eligibility Requirements Applicant must be of the former Soviet Union heritage; enrolled or expecting to enroll full-time at an institution or university; female and resident of Connecticut, New Jersey, or New York. Available to U.S. and non-Canadian citizens.

Application Requirements Application, financial need analysis, interview, transcript. *Deadline:* Continuous.

Contact Marge Goldwater, Executive Director
Jewish Foundation for Education of Women
135 East 64th Street
New York, NY 10021
Phone: 212-288-3931
Fax: 212-288-5798
E-mail: fdnscholar@aol.com

JOHN F. KENNEDY LIBRARY FOUNDATION
http://www.jfklibrary.org

KENNEDY RESEARCH GRANTS
• *See number 100*

KNIGHTS OF COLUMBUS

BISHOP CHARLES P. GRECO GRADUATE FELLOWSHIP PROGRAM • 359

Renewable award for full-time study leading to master's in teaching persons with mental retardation. Must be member, wife, or child of a member of the Knights of Columbus and show an interest or aptitude for working with persons with mental retardation.

Academic/Career Areas Education; Special Education.

Award Fellowship for use in graduate years; renewable. *Number:* 1–4. *Amount:* $1000.

Eligibility Requirements Applicant must be Roman Catholic and enrolled or expecting to enroll full-time at an institution or university. Applicant or parent of applicant must be member of Knights of Columbus. Applicant or parent of applicant must have employment or volunteer experience in helping handicapped. Applicant must have 2.5 GPA or higher. Available to U.S. citizens.

Application Requirements Application, transcript. *Deadline:* May 1.

Contact Rev. Donald Barry, Director of Scholarship Aid
Knights of Columbus
PO Box 1670
New Haven, CT 06507-0901
Phone: 203-772-2130 Ext. 332

NASA IDAHO SPACE GRANT CONSORTIUM
http://www.uidaho.edu/nasa_isgc

NASA ID SPACE GRANT CONSORTIUM FELLOWSHIP PROGRAM
• *See number 60*

NATIONAL ACADEMY OF EDUCATION
http://www.nae.nyu.edu

NATIONAL ACADEMY OF EDUCATION/SPENCER POSTDOCTORAL FELLOWSHIP PROGRAM • 360

One-time research award for Ph.D. holders who had Ph.D. conferred within the last five years in education, social or behavioral science, or the humanities. Must submit three recommendations. Must describe research relevant to education. Write for details.

Academic/Career Areas Education; Humanities; Social Sciences.

Award Fellowship for use in postgraduate years; not renewable. *Number:* up to 30. *Amount:* up to $50,000.

Eligibility Requirements Applicant must be enrolled or expecting to enroll full or part-time at an institution or university. Available to U.S. and non-U.S. citizens.

Application Requirements Application, references. *Deadline:* December 1.

Contact Executive Director
National Academy of Education
726 Broadway, Room 509
New York, NY 10003-9580
Phone: 212-998-9035
Fax: 212-995-4435
E-mail: nae.info@nyu.edu

NATIONAL ASSOCIATION OF JUNIOR AUXILIARIES, INC.
http://www.najanet.org

NATIONAL ASSOCIATION OF JUNIOR AUXILIARIES GRADUATE SCHOLARSHIP PROGRAM • 361

Graduate level scholarships only. Must reside in AL, AR, LA, MS, TN, TX, MO. Must have at least a 3.0 GPA. For graduate level studies in fields that address the needs of children and youth. Must plan to work directly with children. Include one photo. Renewal by reapplication. Application available only at web site (9/1 to 2/1).

Academic/Career Areas Education; Social Services; Special Education.

Award Scholarship for use in graduate, or postgraduate years; not renewable. *Number:* 10–15. *Amount:* $500–$7000.

Eligibility Requirements Applicant must be enrolled or expecting to enroll full or part-time at an institution or university and resident of Alabama, Arkansas, Louisiana, Mississippi, Missouri, Tennessee, or Texas. Applicant must have 3.0 GPA or higher.

Application Requirements Application, autobiography, photo, references, self-addressed stamped envelope, transcript. *Deadline:* February 1.

Contact Merrill Greenlee, Executive Director
National Association of Junior Auxiliaries, Inc.
PO Box 1873
Greenville, MS 38702-1873
Phone: 662-332-3000
Fax: 662-332-3076
E-mail: najanet@bellsouth.net

NATIONAL ASSOCIATION OF THE DEAF
http://www.nad.org

WILLIAM C. STOKOE SCHOLARSHIPS
• *See number 255*

NATIONAL SCIENCE FOUNDATION
http://www.nsf.gov/grfp

NATIONAL SCIENCE FOUNDATION GRADUATE RESEARCH FELLOWSHIPS
• *See number 62*

OREGON STUDENT ASSISTANCE COMMISSION
http://www.osac.state.or.us

OREGON SCHOLARSHIP FUND GRADUATE STUDENT AWARD • 362

Scholarship open to Oregon residents enrolled in graduate programs for education, social work or environmental or public service. Must attend a school in Oregon. May apply for 1 additional year.

Academic/Career Areas Education; Social Services.

Award Scholarship for use in graduate years; not renewable.

Eligibility Requirements Applicant must be enrolled or expecting to enroll at an institution or university; resident of Oregon and studying in Oregon. Available to U.S. citizens.

Application Requirements Application, essay, financial need analysis, transcript, activity chart. *Deadline:* March 1.

Contact Director of Grant Programs
Oregon Student Assistance Commission
1500 Valley River Drive, Suite 100
Eugene, OR 97401-7020
Phone: 800-452-8807 Ext. 7395
E-mail:
awardinfo@mercury.osac.state.or.us

Education

PHI DELTA KAPPA INTERNATIONAL
http://www.pdkintl.org

PHI DELTA KAPPA INTERNATIONAL GRADUATE FELLOWSHIPS IN EDUCATIONAL LEADERSHIP • 363

One-time graduate fellowship for members of Phi Delta Kappa pursuing a degree in educational leadership. Must have minimum 3.0 GPA. Submit all graduate transcripts, synopsis of PDK activities, position paper describing role as educational leader.

Academic/Career Areas Education.

Award Fellowship for use in graduate years; not renewable. *Number:* 6. *Amount:* $500–$1500.

Eligibility Requirements Applicant must be enrolled or expecting to enroll at an institution or university. Applicant must have 3.0 GPA or higher. Available to U.S. and non-U.S. citizens.

Application Requirements Application, essay, portfolio, transcript. *Deadline:* May 1.

Contact Dr. James Fogarty, Associate Executive Director
Phi Delta Kappa International
408 North Union Avenue, PO Box 789
Bloomington, IN 47402-0789
Phone: 812-339-1156
Fax: 812-339-0018
E-mail: headquarters@pdkintl.org

PI LAMBDA THETA, INC.
http://www.pilambda.org

GRADUATE STUDENT SCHOLAR AWARD • 364

The Graduate Student Scholar Award is presented in recognition of an outstanding graduate student who is an education major. Award given out in even years. Minimum 3.5 GPA required.

Academic/Career Areas Education.

Award Prize for use in graduate years; not renewable. *Number:* 1. *Amount:* $1000.

Eligibility Requirements Applicant must be enrolled or expecting to enroll full or part-time at a four-year institution or university and must have an interest in leadership. Applicant or parent of applicant must have employment or volunteer experience in community service. Applicant must have 3.5 GPA or higher. Available to U.S. and non-U.S. citizens.

Application Requirements Application, essay, resume, references, transcript. *Deadline:* November 1.

Contact Pam Todd, Manager, Member Services
Pi Lambda Theta, Inc.
4101 East 3rd Street, PO Box 6626
Bloomington, IN 47407-6626
Phone: 812-339-3411
Fax: 812-339-3462
E-mail: pam@pilambda.org

RESEARCH GRANTS • 365

Pi Lambda Theta Research Grants are awarded in amounts up to $2500 for clearly conceptualized research proposals concerning education. Semiannual application deadlines are January 1 and June 1. Minimum 3.5 GPA required. Grants restricted to Pi Lambda Theta members.

Academic/Career Areas Education.

Award Grant for use in graduate, or postgraduate years; not renewable. *Number:* 1–10. *Amount:* $500–$2500.

Eligibility Requirements Applicant must be enrolled or expecting to enroll full or part-time at a four-year institution or university. Applicant must have 3.5 GPA or higher. Available to U.S. and non-U.S. citizens.

Application Requirements Application, resume.

Contact Pam Todd, Manager, Member Services
Pi Lambda Theta, Inc.
4101 East 3rd Street, PO Box 6626
Bloomington, IN 47407-6626
Phone: 812-339-3411
Fax: 812-339-3462
E-mail: endowment@pilambda.org

QUILL AND SCROLL FOUNDATION
http://www.uiowa.edu/~quill-sc

LESTER BENZ MEMORIAL SCHOLARSHIP
• *See number 260*

RHODE ISLAND FOUNDATION
http://www.rifoundation.org

ANTONIO CIRINO MEMORIAL ART EDUCATION FELLOWSHIP
• *See number 172*

SCHOOL FOR INTERNATIONAL TRAINING/ENGLISH TEACHING FELLOWS PROGRAM
http://www.sit.edu/elf

ENGLISH LANGUAGE FELLOW PROGRAM • 366

Program funded by the U.S. Department of State's English Language Program Office of the "Educational and Cultural Affairs" Bureau. Teachers and teacher trainers are sent to host country universities to teach English. Award for post-graduate students only. One-time award given in the form of individual grants. 10 to 25 grants are available for Junior award. 20 to 30 grants are available for Senior award.

Academic/Career Areas Education.

Award Grant for use in postgraduate years; not renewable. *Amount:* $13,750–$21,000.

Eligibility Requirements Applicant must be enrolled or expecting to enroll full or part-time at a four-year institution or university. Applicant or parent of applicant must have employment or volunteer experience in teaching. Available to U.S. citizens.

Application Requirements Application, essay, interview, references, transcript. *Deadline:* April 30.

Contact School for International Training/English
Teaching Fellows Program
PO Box 676
Brattleboro, VT 05302-0676

SENSE OF SMELL INSTITUTE
http://www.senseofsmell.org

SENSE OF SMELL INSTITUTE RESEARCH GRANTS
• *See number 214*

TOVA FELLOWSHIP
• *See number 101*

SIGMA ALPHA IOTA PHILANTHROPIES, INC.
http://www.sai-national.org

GRADUATE SCHOLARSHIP IN MUSIC EDUCATION • **367**

One-time award offered yearly to members of SAI who are accepted into a graduate program leading to master's or doctoral degree in music education. Submit videotape of work. Contact local chapter for further information. Application fee: $25.

Academic/Career Areas Education; Performing Arts.

Award Scholarship for use in graduate years; not renewable. *Number:* 1. *Amount:* $1500.

Eligibility Requirements Applicant must be enrolled or expecting to enroll full or part-time at an institution or university; female and must have an interest in music/singing. Available to U.S. and non-U.S. citizens.

Application Requirements Application, essay, references, transcript, videotape of work. *Fee:* $25. *Deadline:* April 15.

Contact Ms. Ruth Sieber Johnson, Secretary
Sigma Alpha Iota Philanthropies, Inc.
7 Hickey Drive
Framingham, MA 01701-8812
Phone: 828-251-0606
Fax: 828-251-0644
E-mail: nh@sai-national.org

SIGMA ALPHA IOTA DOCTORAL GRANT • **368**

One-time award offered triennially to SAI member who is enrolled in a doctoral program in music education, music therapy, musicology, ethnomusicology, theory, psychology of music, or applied music degree programs. Submit dissertation

or other required written materials outline. Contact local chapter for further information. Application fee: $25.

Academic/Career Areas Education; Performing Arts; Therapy/Rehabilitation.

Award Grant for use in graduate years; not renewable. *Number:* 1. *Amount:* $1000.

Eligibility Requirements Applicant must be enrolled or expecting to enroll at an institution or university; female and must have an interest in music/singing. Available to U.S. and non-U.S. citizens.

Application Requirements Application, essay, references, transcript, dissertation outline. *Fee:* $25. *Deadline:* April 15.

Contact Ms. Ruth Sieber Johnson, Secretary
Sigma Alpha Iota Philanthropies, Inc.
7 Hickey Drive
Framingham, MA 01701-8812
Phone: 828-251-0606
Fax: 828-251-0644
E-mail: nh@sai-national.org

SWANN FOUNDATION FUND
http://www.lcweb.loc.gov/rr/print/swann/swann_foundation.html

SWANN FOUNDATION FUND FELLOWSHIP
• *See number 109*

SWEDISH INFORMATION SERVICE
http://www.swedeninfo.com

BICENTENNIAL SWEDISH-AMERICAN EXCHANGE FUND TRAVEL GRANTS
• *See number 133*

TEACHERS OF ENGLISH TO SPEAKERS OF OTHER LANGUAGES (TESOL)
http://www.tesol.org

ALBERT H. MARCKWARDT TRAVEL GRANTS • **369**

Award for Teachers of English to Speakers of Other Languages members to travel to a TESOL convention. Applicant must be a graduate student of education. Write for more information. One-time award of $500, plus waiver of convention registration fee. Deadline: October of each year.

Academic/Career Areas Education.

Award Grant for use in graduate years; not renewable. *Number:* up to 5. *Amount:* $600.

Eligibility Requirements Applicant must be enrolled or expecting to enroll at an institution or university. Applicant or parent of applicant must be member of Teachers of English to Speakers of Other Languages. Available to U.S. and non-U.S. citizens.

*Teachers of English to Speakers of Other Languages
(TESOL) (continued)*

Application Requirements Application,
autobiography, references.

Contact Betsey Backman, Awards Coordinator
Teachers of English to Speakers of Other
Languages (TESOL)
700 South Washington Street, Suite 200
Alexandria, VA 22314-4287
Phone: 703-836-0774
Fax: 703-836-6447
E-mail: awards@tesol.org

RUTH CRYMES FELLOWSHIP FOR GRADUATE STUDY • 370

Award for TESOL members who are or have been
enrolled within the past year in a TESOL or TEFL
graduate program that prepares teachers to teach
ESOL. Supports graduate studies in the teaching of
ESOL and supports the development of projects with
direct application to second language classroom
instruction. Must submit three-page description of
graduate studies project. Contact for details. Deadline: October each year.

Academic/Career Areas Education.

Award Fellowship for use in graduate years; not
renewable. *Amount:* $1500.

Eligibility Requirements Applicant must be
enrolled or expecting to enroll at an institution or
university. Applicant or parent of applicant must be
member of Teachers of English to Speakers of Other
Languages. Available to U.S. and non-U.S. citizens.

Application Requirements Application,
autobiography, references, description of graduate
studies project.

Contact Betsey Backman, Awards Coordinator
Teachers of English to Speakers of Other
Languages (TESOL)
700 South Washington Street, Suite 200
Alexandria, VA 22314-4287
Phone: 703-836-0774
Fax: 703-836-6447
E-mail: awards@tesol.org

TEACHERS OF ENGLISH TO SPEAKERS OF OTHER LANGUAGES RESEARCH INTEREST SECTION/ HEINLE & HEINLE DISTINGUISHED RESEARCH AWARD • 371

Award for Teachers of English to Speakers of Other
Languages member who has completed a scholarly
paper and has not submitted a report on it for
publication before October. Write for more information. One-time award of $1000.

Academic/Career Areas Education.

Award Prize for use in graduate years; not
renewable. *Number:* 1. *Amount:* $1000.

Eligibility Requirements Applicant must be
enrolled or expecting to enroll at an institution or
university. Applicant or parent of applicant must be
member of Teachers of English to Speakers of Other
Languages. Available to U.S. citizens.

Application Requirements Transcript.

Contact Betsey Backman, Awards Coordinator
Teachers of English to Speakers of Other
Languages (TESOL)
700 South Washington Street, Suite 200
Alexandria, VA 22314-4287
Phone: 703-836-0774
Fax: 703-836-6447
E-mail: awards@tesol.org

ELECTRICAL ENGINEERING/ ELECTRONICS

AFRICAN NETWORK OF SCIENTIFIC AND TECHNOLOGICAL INSTITUTIONS - ANSTI
http://www.ansti.org

AFRICAN NETWORK OF SCIENTIFIC AND TECHNOLOGICAL INSTITUTIONS POSTGRADUATE FELLOWSHIPS
• *See number 14*

AMERICAN ASSOCIATION OF UNIVERSITY WOMEN (AAUW) EDUCATIONAL FOUNDATION
http://www.aauw.org

AAUW EDUCATIONAL FOUNDATION SELECTED PROFESSIONS FELLOWSHIPS
• *See number 87*

AMERICAN INSTITUTE OF AERONAUTICS AND ASTRONAUTICS
http://www.aiaa.org

AIAA FOUNDATION GRADUATE AWARDS
• *See number 26*

AIAA FOUNDATION ORVILLE AND WILBUR WRIGHT AWARDS
• *See number 27*

ARMED FORCES COMMUNICATIONS AND ELECTRONICS ASSOCIATION, EDUCATIONAL FOUNDATION
http://www.afcea.org

ARMED FORCES COMMUNICATIONS & ELECTRONICS ASSOCIATION EDUCATIONAL FOUNDATION FELLOWSHIP
• *See number 265*

ARMED FORCES COMMUNICATIONS AND ELECTRONICS ASSOCIATION RALPH W. SHRADER SCHOLARSHIPS
• *See number 266*

MILTON E. COOPER/YOUNG AFCEAN GRADUATE SCHOOL SCHOLARSHIP
• *See number 251*

ASSOCIATED WESTERN UNIVERSITIES, INC.
http://www.awu.org

ASSOCIATED WESTERN UNIVERSITIES POSTGRADUATE FELLOWSHIP
• *See number 50*

CHARLES BABBAGE INSTITUTE
http://www.cbi.umn.edu

ADELLE AND ERWIN TOMASH FELLOWSHIP IN THE HISTORY OF INFORMATION PROCESSING
• *See number 267*

DELAWARE VALLEY SPACE GRANT CONSORTIUM
http://www.delspace.org

NASA/DELAWARE VALLEY SPACE GRANT FELLOWSHIP
• *See number 52*

DURRANT FOUNDATION
http://www.durant.com/foundation.html

DURRANT FOUNDATION SCHOLARSHIP/ INTERNSHIP
• *See number 96*

FANNIE AND JOHN HERTZ FOUNDATION
http://www.hertzfoundation.org

FANNIE AND JOHN HERTZ FOUNDATION FELLOWSHIP
• *See number 53*

FOUNDATION FOR SCIENCE AND DISABILITY
http://www.as.wvu.edu/~scidis/organize/fsd.html

GRANTS FOR DISABLED STUDENTS IN THE SCIENCES
• *See number 54*

GEM CONSORTIUM
http://www.nd.edu/~gem

GEM PH.D. ENGINEERING FELLOWSHIP
• *See number 9*

IMGIP/ICEOP
http://www.imgip.siu.edu

ILLINOIS MINORITY GRADUATE INCENTIVE PROGRAM FELLOWSHIP • **372**

Purpose is to increase the number of minority members of the faculties and professional staffs at Illinois institutions of higher education where there is severe under-representation of minorities. Minimum GPA of 2.75 in the last sixty hours of undergraduate work or over a 3.2 in at least 9 hours of graduate study. Award restricted to applicants studying one or more of the following: electrical engineering/ electronics, engineering/technology, engineering-related technologies, physical sciences and math, or science, technology and society..

Academic/Career Areas Electrical Engineering/ Electronics; Engineering/Technology; Engineering-Related Technologies; Physical Sciences and Math; Science, Technology and Society.

Award Grant for use in graduate years; renewable. *Number:* 30. *Amount:* $16,000.

Eligibility Requirements Applicant must be American Indian/Alaska Native, Black (non-Hispanic), or Hispanic; enrolled or expecting to enroll full-time at an institution or university and studying in Illinois. Available to U.S. citizens.

Application Requirements Application, essay, references, test scores, transcript. *Deadline:* February 15.

Contact Ms. Jane Meuth, IMGIP/ICEOP
        Administrator
        IMGIP/ICEOP
        Woody Hall C-224, Southern Illinois
          University
        Carbondale, IL 62901-4723
        Phone: 618-453-4558
        Fax: 618-453-1800
        E-mail: fellows@siu.edu

INTERNATIONAL DESALINATION ASSOCIATION
http://www.ida.bm

INTERNATIONAL DESALINATION ASSOCIATION SCHOLARSHIP
• *See number 57*

INTERNATIONAL UNION FOR VACUUM SCIENCE, TECHNIQUE AND APPLICATIONS
http://www.iuvsta.org/welch.html

WELCH FOUNDATION SCHOLARSHIP
• *See number 58*

NASA IDAHO SPACE GRANT CONSORTIUM
http://www.uidaho.edu/nasa_isgc

NASA ID SPACE GRANT CONSORTIUM FELLOWSHIP PROGRAM
• See number 60

NASA WYOMING SPACE GRANT CONSORTIUM
http://www.wyomingspacegrant.uwyo.edu

WYOMING NASA SPACE GRANT CONSORTIUM RESEARCH FELLOWSHIP
• See number 61

NATIONAL ACTION COUNCIL FOR MINORITIES IN ENGINEERING-NACME, INC.
http://www.nacme.org

SLOAN PH.D PROGRAM
• See number 243

NATIONAL PHYSICAL SCIENCE CONSORTIUM
http://www.npsc.org

NATIONAL PHYSICAL SCIENCE CONSORTIUM GRADUATE FELLOWSHIPS IN THE PHYSICAL SCIENCES
• See number 244

SOCIETY OF AUTOMOTIVE ENGINEERS
http://www.sae.org/students/stuschol.htm

SOCIETY OF AUTOMOTIVE ENGINEERS DOCTORAL SCHOLARS PROGRAM
• See number 178

ENGINEERING-RELATED TECHNOLOGIES

AFRICAN NETWORK OF SCIENTIFIC AND TECHNOLOGICAL INSTITUTIONS - ANSTI
http://www.ansti.org

AFRICAN NETWORK OF SCIENTIFIC AND TECHNOLOGICAL INSTITUTIONS POSTGRADUATE FELLOWSHIPS
• See number 14

AIR AND WASTE MANAGEMENT ASSOCIATION
http://www.awma.org

AIR AND WASTE MANAGEMENT ASSOCIATION SCHOLARSHIP ENDOWMENT TRUST FUND
• See number 24

AMERICAN ASSOCIATION OF UNIVERSITY WOMEN (AAUW) EDUCATIONAL FOUNDATION
http://www.aauw.org

AAUW EDUCATIONAL FOUNDATION SELECTED PROFESSIONS FELLOWSHIPS
• See number 87

AMERICAN SOCIETY OF SAFETY ENGINEERS (ASSE) FOUNDATION
http://www.asse.org/foundat.htm

RESEARCH FELLOWSHIP PROGRAM   • **373**

Two safety research fellowships available at the Liberty Mutual Research Center. Following four to six weeks of research, each recipient must write an 800-word article for publication in Professional Safety magazine or ASSE Foundation's Advocate. Preference given to ASSE members with a Ph.D. Must be a U.S. citizen.

Academic/Career Areas Engineering/Technology; Engineering-Related Technologies.

Award Fellowship for use in graduate, or postgraduate years; not renewable. *Number:* up to 2. *Amount:* up to $8000.

Eligibility Requirements Applicant must be enrolled or expecting to enroll at an institution or university and studying in Massachusetts. Available to U.S. citizens.

Application Requirements Application, essay, resume, references. *Deadline:* April 15.

Contact Customer Service Department
American Society of Safety Engineers (ASSE) Foundation
1800 East Oakton Street
Des Plaines, IL 60018
Phone: 847-699-2929
Fax: 847-296-9220

DELAWARE VALLEY SPACE GRANT CONSORTIUM
http://www.delspace.org

NASA/DELAWARE VALLEY SPACE GRANT FELLOWSHIP
• See number 52

IMGIP/ICEOP
http://www.imgip.siu.edu

ILLINOIS MINORITY GRADUATE INCENTIVE PROGRAM FELLOWSHIP
• See number 372

INTERNATIONAL DESALINATION ASSOCIATION
http://www.ida.bm

INTERNATIONAL DESALINATION ASSOCIATION SCHOLARSHIP
• See number 57

MINERALS, METALS, AND MATERIALS SOCIETY (TMS)
http://www.tms.org

TMS OUTSTANDING STUDENT PAPER CONTEST—GRADUATE • 374

Two prizes for graduate student papers of a technical/research nature that deal with any of the following disciplines: physical and mechanical metallurgy, extractive and process metallurgy, or materials science. May be written from material in applicant's master's or Ph.D. thesis. Only one entry per student. Applicants must be TMS student members or include completed membership application with dues payment and essay to become eligible.

Academic/Career Areas Engineering/Technology; Engineering-Related Technologies; Materials Science, Engineering and Metallurgy.

Award Prize for use in graduate years; not renewable. *Number:* 2. *Amount:* $500–$1000.

Eligibility Requirements Applicant must be enrolled or expecting to enroll full-time at an institution or university. Available to U.S. and non-U.S. citizens.

Application Requirements Essay. *Deadline:* May 1.

Contact Minerals, Metals, and Materials Society
(TMS)
184 Thorn Hill Road
Warrendale, PA 15086
Phone: 724-776-9000
Fax: 724-776-3770

NASA WYOMING SPACE GRANT CONSORTIUM
http://www.wyomingspacegrant.uwyo.edu

WYOMING NASA SPACE GRANT CONSORTIUM RESEARCH FELLOWSHIP
• See number 61

NATIONAL ACTION COUNCIL FOR MINORITIES IN ENGINEERING-NACME, INC.
http://www.nacme.org

SLOAN PH.D PROGRAM
• See number 243

NATIONAL RESEARCH COUNCIL
http://www.nationalacademies.org/fellowships/

FORD FOUNDATION DISSERTATION FELLOWSHIPS FOR MINORITIES
• See number 256

FORD FOUNDATION POSTDOCTORAL FELLOWSHIP FOR MINORITIES
• See number 257

FORD FOUNDATION PREDOCTORAL FELLOWSHIPS FOR MINORITIES
• See number 258

PACIFIC TELECOMMUNICATIONS COUNCIL
http://www.ptc.org

PACIFIC TELECOMMUNICATIONS COUNCIL ESSAY PRIZE COMPETITION
• See number 259

PARALYZED VETERANS OF AMERICA - SPINAL CORD RESEARCH FOUNDATION
http://www.pva.org/scrf

FELLOWSHIPS IN SPINAL CORD INJURY RESEARCH
• See number 21

RESOURCES FOR THE FUTURE
http://www.rff.org

GILBERT F. WHITE POSTDOCTORAL FELLOWSHIPS
• See number 331

JOSEPH L. FISHER DISSERTATION AWARDS
• See number 332

SOCIETY OF AUTOMOTIVE ENGINEERS
http://www.sae.org/students/stuschol.htm

SOCIETY OF AUTOMOTIVE ENGINEERS DOCTORAL SCHOLARS PROGRAM
• See number 178

TRANSPORTATION ASSOCIATION OF CANADA
http://www.tac-atc.ca

TRANSPORTATION ASSOCIATION OF CANADA SCHOLARSHIPS
• See number 249

ENGINEERING/ TECHNOLOGY

AFRICAN NETWORK OF SCIENTIFIC AND TECHNOLOGICAL INSTITUTIONS - ANSTI
http://www.ansti.org

AFRICAN NETWORK OF SCIENTIFIC AND TECHNOLOGICAL INSTITUTIONS POSTGRADUATE FELLOWSHIPS
• See number 14

AIR AND WASTE MANAGEMENT ASSOCIATION
http://www.awma.org

AIR AND WASTE MANAGEMENT ASSOCIATION SCHOLARSHIP ENDOWMENT TRUST FUND
• See number 24

AMERICAN ASSOCIATION OF CEREAL CHEMISTS
http://www.aaccnet.org

GRADUATE FELLOWSHIP AWARD • 375

One-time award to encourage graduate research in grain-based food science and technology. Research in such disciplines like genetics, horticulture, nutrition, microbiology, biochemistry, engineering, or chemistry are not eligible, unless it is directly related to primary research program dealing with grain-based food science and technology-related areas. Minimum 3.0 GPA required. Application must be submitted to department head by 3/15; it must reach AACC by 4/1.

Academic/Career Areas Engineering/Technology; Food Science/Nutrition.

Award Fellowship for use in graduate, or postgraduate years; not renewable. *Number:* up to 15. *Amount:* $2000–$3000.

Eligibility Requirements Applicant must be enrolled or expecting to enroll full-time at a four-year institution or university. Applicant must have 3.0 GPA or higher. Available to U.S. and non-U.S. citizens.

Application Requirements Application, essay, references, transcript. *Deadline:* March 15.

Contact Linda Schmitt, Scholarship Coordinator
American Association of Cereal Chemists
3340 Pilot Knob Road
St. Paul, MN 55121-2097
Phone: 651-994-3828
Fax: 651-454-0766
E-mail: lschmitt@scisoc.org

AMERICAN ASSOCIATION OF UNIVERSITY WOMEN (AAUW) EDUCATIONAL FOUNDATION
http://www.aauw.org

AAUW EDUCATIONAL FOUNDATION SELECTED PROFESSIONS FELLOWSHIPS
• See number 87

AMERICAN GEOPHYSICAL UNION
http://www.agu.org

AMERICAN GEOPHYSICAL UNION HORTON RESEARCH GRANT
• See number 25

AMERICAN HISTORICAL ASSOCIATION
http://www.theaha.org

NASA FELLOWSHIP IN AEROSPACE HISTORY
• See number 175

AMERICAN INSTITUTE OF AERONAUTICS AND ASTRONAUTICS
http://www.aiaa.org

AIAA FOUNDATION GRADUATE AWARDS
• See number 26

AIAA FOUNDATION ORVILLE AND WILBUR WRIGHT AWARDS
• See number 27

AMERICAN METEOROLOGICAL SOCIETY
http://www.ametsoc.org/AMS

AMERICAN METEOROLOGICAL SOCIETY/ INDUSTRY/GOVERNMENT GRADUATE FELLOWSHIPS
• See number 28

AMERICAN NUCLEAR SOCIETY
http://www.ans.org

ALAN F. HENRY/PAUL A. GREEBLER SCHOLARSHIP
• See number 29

AMERICAN NUCLEAR SOCIETY GRADUATE SCHOLARSHIPS
• See number 30

AMERICAN RESPIRATORY CARE FOUNDATION
http://www.aarc.org

MONAGHAN/TRUDELL FELLOWSHIP FOR AEROSOL TECHNIQUE DEVELOPMENT • 376

One-time postgraduate fellowship to support projects dealing with aerosol delivery and cost effectiveness issues. Must detail project, budget, and resources in no more than twenty pages. Can include modeling, in-vitro, or clinical studies.

Academic/Career Areas Engineering/Technology; Health and Medical Sciences; Therapy/Rehabilitation.

Award Fellowship for use in postgraduate years; not renewable. *Number:* 1. *Amount:* $1000.

Eligibility Requirements Applicant must be enrolled or expecting to enroll at an institution or university. Available to U.S. and non-U.S. citizens.

Application Requirements Application, references, proposal.

Contact Diane Shearer, Administrative Coordinator
American Respiratory Care Foundation
11030 Ables Lane
Dallas, TX 75229-4593
Phone: 972-243-2272
Fax: 972-484-2720
E-mail: info@aarc.org

AMERICAN SOCIETY FOR PHOTOGRAMMETRY AND REMOTE SENSING
http://www.asprs.org

AMERICAN SOCIETY FOR PHOTOGRAMMETRY AND REMOTE SENSING OUTSTANDING PAPERS AWARDS
• See number 33

TA LIANG MEMORIAL AWARD
• See number 34

WILLIAM A. FISCHER MEMORIAL SCHOLARSHIP
• See number 35

AMERICAN SOCIETY OF MECHANICAL ENGINEERS (ASME INTERNATIONAL)
http://www.asme.org/educate/aid

AMERICAN SOCIETY OF MECHANICAL ENGINEERS SOLID WASTE PROCESSING DIVISION GRADUATE STUDY SCHOLARSHIP • 377

Two scholarships available to graduate students at North American universities with established programs in solid waste management. All awards are divided equally between the student and the school. Must be members of the American Society of Mechanical Engineers.

Academic/Career Areas Engineering/Technology; Mechanical Engineering.

Award Scholarship for use in graduate years; not renewable. *Number:* 2. *Amount:* $2000–$4000.

Eligibility Requirements Applicant must be enrolled or expecting to enroll full-time at an institution or university. Available to U.S. and non-U.S. citizens.

Application Requirements Application, essay, references, transcript. *Deadline:* March 1.

Contact Ms. Theresa Oluwanifise, Administrative Assistant
American Society of Mechanical Engineers (ASME International)
3 Park Avenue
New York, NY 10016-5990
Phone: 212-591-8131
Fax: 212-591-7143
E-mail: oluwanifiset@asme.org

RICE-CULLIMORE SCHOLARSHIP • 378

Grant of $2000 to an international ASME student member doing graduate work in mechanical engineering or engineering technology in the U.S. Students should contact the U.S. Information Service or the American Embassy to find out if their country has a sponsor with a contract with the Institute of International Education. Only those applications received from the IIE will be considered.

Academic/Career Areas Engineering/Technology; Mechanical Engineering.

Award Scholarship for use in graduate years; not renewable. *Number:* 1. *Amount:* $2000.

Eligibility Requirements Applicant must be enrolled or expecting to enroll full-time at an institution or university. Available to Canadian and non-U.S. citizens.

Contact Ms. Theresa Oluwanifise, Administrative Assistant
American Society of Mechanical Engineers (ASME International)
3 Park Avenue
New York, NY 10016-5990
Phone: 212-591-8131
Fax: 212-591-7143
E-mail: oluwanifiset@asme.org

AMERICAN SOCIETY OF SAFETY ENGINEERS (ASSE) FOUNDATION
http://www.asse.org/foundat.htm

RESEARCH FELLOWSHIP PROGRAM
• See number 373

AMERICAN VACUUM SOCIETY
http://www.avs.org

ALBERT NERKEN AWARD
• See number 36

American Vacuum Society (continued)

AMERICAN VACUUM SOCIETY GRADUATE RESEARCH AWARD
• *See number 37*

GAEDE-LANGMUIR AWARD
• *See number 38*

JOHN A. THORNTON MEMORIAL AWARD AND LECTURE
• *See number 39*

MEDARD W. WELCH AWARD
• *See number 40*

NELLIE YEOH WHETTEN AWARD
• *See number 41*

PETER MARK MEMORIAL AWARD
• *See number 42*

RUSSELL AND SIGURD VARIAN FELLOWSHIP
• *See number 43*

AMERICAN WATER WORKS ASSOCIATION
http://www.awwa.org

AMERICAN WATER WORKS ASSOCIATION/ABEL WOLMAN FELLOWSHIP
• *See number 44*

AMERICAN WATER WORKS ASSOCIATION/ HOLLY A. CORNELL SCHOLARSHIP
• *See number 45*

ARMED FORCES COMMUNICATIONS AND ELECTRONICS ASSOCIATION, EDUCATIONAL FOUNDATION
http://www.afcea.org

ARMED FORCES COMMUNICATIONS & ELECTRONICS ASSOCIATION EDUCATIONAL FOUNDATION FELLOWSHIP
• *See number 265*

ARMED FORCES COMMUNICATIONS AND ELECTRONICS ASSOCIATION RALPH W. SHRADER SCHOLARSHIPS
• *See number 266*

ASSOCIATED WESTERN UNIVERSITIES, INC.
http://www.awu.org

ASSOCIATED WESTERN UNIVERSITIES FACULTY FELLOWSHIPS
• *See number 48*

ASSOCIATED WESTERN UNIVERSITIES GRADUATE RESEARCH FELLOWSHIPS
• *See number 49*

ASSOCIATED WESTERN UNIVERSITIES POSTGRADUATE FELLOWSHIP
• *See number 50*

ASSOCIATION FOR WOMEN IN SCIENCE EDUCATIONAL FOUNDATION
http://www.awis.org

ASSOCIATION FOR WOMEN IN SCIENCE PREDOCTORAL FELLOWSHIP
• *See number 77*

ASSOCIATION OF ENGINEERING GEOLOGISTS
http://www.aegweb.org

GARDNER FUND
• *See number 300*

CHARLES BABBAGE INSTITUTE
http://www.cbi.umn.edu

ADELLE AND ERWIN TOMASH FELLOWSHIP IN THE HISTORY OF INFORMATION PROCESSING
• *See number 267*

DELAWARE VALLEY SPACE GRANT CONSORTIUM
http://www.delspace.org

NASA/DELAWARE VALLEY SPACE GRANT FELLOWSHIP
• *See number 52*

FANNIE AND JOHN HERTZ FOUNDATION
http://www.hertzfoundation.org

FANNIE AND JOHN HERTZ FOUNDATION FELLOWSHIP
• *See number 53*

FOUNDATION FOR SCIENCE AND DISABILITY
http://www.as.wvu.edu/~scidis/organize/fsd.html

GRANTS FOR DISABLED STUDENTS IN THE SCIENCES
• *See number 54*

GEM CONSORTIUM
http://www.nd.edu/~gem

GEM PH.D. ENGINEERING FELLOWSHIP
• *See number 9*

GERMAN ACADEMIC EXCHANGE SERVICE (DAAD)
http://www.daad.org

NSF-DAAD GRANTS FOR THE NATURAL, ENGINEERING, AND SOCIAL SCIENCES • 379

Grant provides support for travel and living expenses for scholars and scientists at U.S. universities and affiliated research institutes who wish to carry out joint research projects in natural, engineering, and social sciences with German colleagues. Deadline: June 15. Please visit website at http://www.nsf.gov/sbe/int.

Academic/Career Areas Engineering/Technology; Natural Sciences; Social Sciences.

Award Grant for use in postgraduate years; not renewable.

Eligibility Requirements Applicant must be enrolled or expecting to enroll at an institution or university. Available to U.S. citizens.

Application Requirements Application. *Deadline:* June 15.

Contact Dr. Mark A. Suskin, National Science Foundation
German Academic Exchange Service (DAAD)
4201 Wilson Boulevard
Arlington, VA 22230
Phone: 703-292-8702
Fax: 703-292-9177
E-mail: msuskin@nsf.gov

HUDSON RIVER FOUNDATION
http://www.hudsonriver.org

HUDSON RIVER FOUNDATION GRADUATE FELLOWSHIPS
• *See number 205*

IMGIP/ICEOP
http://www.imgip.siu.edu

ILLINOIS MINORITY GRADUATE INCENTIVE PROGRAM FELLOWSHIP
• *See number 372*

INSTITUTE FOR SUPPLY MANAGEMENT
http://www.ism.ws

INSTITUTE FOR SUPPLY MANAGEMENT DISSERTATION GRANT PROGRAM
• *See number 232*

INSTITUTE OF INDUSTRIAL ENGINEERS
http://www.iieet.org

GILBERTH MEMORIAL FELLOWSHIP • 380

One-time award to graduate students enrolled in any school in the U.S. and its territories. Must pursue an advanced degree in industrial engineering or its equivalent. Minimum 3.4 GPA required. Must be nominated.

Academic/Career Areas Engineering/Technology.

Award Fellowship for use in graduate years; not renewable.

Eligibility Requirements Applicant must be enrolled or expecting to enroll full-time at an institution or university. Applicant or parent of applicant must be member of Institute of Industrial Engineers.

Application Requirements References, nomination. *Deadline:* November 30.

Contact Sherry Richards, Chapter Operations Assistant
Institute of Industrial Engineers
25 Technology Park
Norcross, GA 30092-2988
Phone: 770-449-0461 Ext. 140
Fax: 770-263-8532
E-mail: srichards@iienet.org

INTERNATIONAL DESALINATION ASSOCIATION
http://www.ida.bm

INTERNATIONAL DESALINATION ASSOCIATION SCHOLARSHIP
• *See number 57*

INTERNATIONAL DEVELOPMENT RESEARCH CENTER
http://www.idrc.ca/awards

AGROPOLIS
• *See number 10*

INTERNATIONAL UNION FOR VACUUM SCIENCE, TECHNIQUE AND APPLICATIONS
http://www.iuvsta.org/welch.html

WELCH FOUNDATION SCHOLARSHIP
• *See number 58*

JAPANESE GOVERNMENT/THE MONBUSHO SCHOLARSHIP PROGRAM
http://embjapan.org/la

RESEARCH STUDENT SCHOLARSHIP
• *See number 13*

MINERALS, METALS, AND MATERIALS SOCIETY (TMS)
http://www.tms.org

TMS OUTSTANDING STUDENT PAPER CONTEST— GRADUATE
• *See number 374*

MONTANA SPACE GRANT CONSORTIUM
http://www.montana.edu/msgc

MONTANA SPACE GRANT FELLLOWSHIP PROGRAM
• See number 177

NASA IDAHO SPACE GRANT CONSORTIUM
http://www.uidaho.edu/nasa_isgc

NASA ID SPACE GRANT CONSORTIUM FELLOWSHIP PROGRAM
• See number 60

NATIONAL ACTION COUNCIL FOR MINORITIES IN ENGINEERING-NACME, INC.
http://www.nacme.org

SLOAN PH.D PROGRAM
• See number 243

NATIONAL SCIENCE FOUNDATION
http://www.nsf.gov/grfp

NATIONAL SCIENCE FOUNDATION GRADUATE RESEARCH FELLOWSHIPS
• See number 62

NATIONAL SCIENCE FOUNDATION MINORITY CAREER ADVANCEMENT AWARDS • 381

One-time award expands the research opportunity of minority scientists, and engineers. Open to minority scientists and engineers with Ph.D. or equivalent experience in National Science Foundation-supported fields who hold faculty positions at U.S. universities. May be used for salary, travel, consultant fees, or research assistant.

Academic/Career Areas Engineering/Technology; Physical Sciences and Math.

Award Scholarship for use in postgraduate years; not renewable. *Amount:* up to $50,000.

Eligibility Requirements Applicant must be American Indian/Alaska Native, Black (non-Hispanic), or Hispanic and enrolled or expecting to enroll at an institution or university. Applicant or parent of applicant must have employment or volunteer experience in teaching. Available to U.S. citizens.

Application Requirements Application, references.

Contact Program Director
National Science Foundation
4201 Wilson Boulevard, Room 907N
Arlington, VA 22230
E-mail: grfp@nsf.gov

NATIONAL SCIENCE FOUNDATION MINORITY RESEARCH PLANNING GRANTS • 382

Nonrenewable grants to support preliminary studies and other activities related to the development of research projects and proposals. Open to minority scientists and engineers with a doctoral degree or equivalent experience in National Science Foundation fields who hold faculty positions at a U.S. university.

Academic/Career Areas Engineering/Technology; Physical Sciences and Math.

Award Grant for use in postgraduate years; not renewable. *Amount:* up to $18,000.

Eligibility Requirements Applicant must be American Indian/Alaska Native, Black (non-Hispanic), or Hispanic and enrolled or expecting to enroll at an institution or university. Applicant or parent of applicant must have employment or volunteer experience in teaching. Available to U.S. citizens.

Application Requirements Application, references.

Contact Program Director
National Science Foundation
4201 Wilson Boulevard, Room 907N
Arlington, va 22230
E-mail: grfp@nsf.gov

PACIFIC TELECOMMUNICATIONS COUNCIL
http://www.ptc.org

PACIFIC TELECOMMUNICATIONS COUNCIL ESSAY PRIZE COMPETITION
• See number 259

PARALYZED VETERANS OF AMERICA - SPINAL CORD RESEARCH FOUNDATION
http://www.pva.org/scrf

FELLOWSHIPS IN SPINAL CORD INJURY RESEARCH
• See number 21

SOCIETY OF AUTOMOTIVE ENGINEERS
http://www.sae.org/students/stuschol.htm

SOCIETY OF AUTOMOTIVE ENGINEERS DOCTORAL SCHOLARS PROGRAM
• See number 178

SOCIETY OF MANUFACTURING ENGINEERS EDUCATION FOUNDATION
http://www.sme.org/foundation

WAYNE KAY GRADUATE FELLOWSHIP • 383

One-time award for full-time graduate students pursuing manufacturing or industrial engineering degrees. Must have 3.5 minimum GPA. Submit application cover sheet, resume, transcript, essay, references, and statement of career goals. Must demonstrate potential for future leadership in the profession.

Academic/Career Areas Engineering/Technology.

Award Fellowship for use in graduate years; not renewable. *Number:* 10. *Amount:* $4000–$12,000.

Eligibility Requirements Applicant must be enrolled or expecting to enroll full-time at an institution or university. Applicant must have 3.5 GPA or higher. Available to U.S. and Canadian citizens.

Application Requirements Application, essay, resume, references, transcript. *Deadline:* February 1.

Contact Cindy Monzon, Program Coordinator
Society of Manufacturing Engineers
Education Foundation
One SME Drive
PO Box 930
Dearborn, MI 48121-0930
Phone: 313-271-1500 Ext. 1707
Fax: 313-240-6095
E-mail: monzcyn@sme.org

SOCIETY OF WOMEN ENGINEERS
http://www.swe.org

GENERAL MOTORS FOUNDATION GRADUATE SCHOLARSHIP
• *See number 245*

LYDIA I. PICKUP MEMORIAL SCHOLARSHIP
• *See number 271*

TAU BETA PI ASSOCIATION
http://www.tbp.org/

TAU BETA PI FELLOWSHIPS FOR GRADUATE STUDY IN ENGINEERING • **384**

Award for graduate scholars pursuing engineering studies. Must be member of Tau Beta Pi or be initiated by March 1. Preference given to first-time graduate students. Must submit typewritten application and two letters of reference by January 15. One-time award of $10,000.

Academic/Career Areas Engineering/Technology.

Award Fellowship for use in graduate years; not renewable. *Number:* 17–22. *Amount:* $10,000.

Eligibility Requirements Applicant must be enrolled or expecting to enroll full-time at an institution or university. Applicant must have 3.5 GPA or higher. Available to U.S. and non-U.S. citizens.

Application Requirements Application, essay, references. *Deadline:* January 15.

Contact D. Stephen Pierre Jr., Director of
Fellowships
Tau Beta Pi Association
PO Box 2697
Knoxville, TN 37901-2697
Fax: 334-694-2310
E-mail: dspierre@southernco.com

TRANSPORTATION ASSOCIATION OF CANADA
http://www.tac-atc.ca

TRANSPORTATION ASSOCIATION OF CANADA SCHOLARSHIPS
• *See number 249*

FASHION DESIGN

AMERICAN SCHOOL FOOD SERVICE ASSOCIATION
http://www.asfsa.org

LINCOLN FOOD SERVICE GRANT FOR INNOVATIONS IN SCHOOL FOOD SERVICE • **385**

One-time grant for ASFSA members to conduct or supervise research in child nutrition or school foodservice management. Must be U.S. citizen. Submit proposal by April 30.

Academic/Career Areas Fashion Design; Food Science/Nutrition.

Award Grant for use in graduate years; not renewable. *Number:* up to 1. *Amount:* up to $2500.

Eligibility Requirements Applicant must be enrolled or expecting to enroll full or part-time at an institution or university. Applicant or parent of applicant must be member of American School Food Service Association. Applicant or parent of applicant must have employment or volunteer experience in food service. Available to U.S. citizens.

Application Requirements Proposal. *Deadline:* April 30.

Contact Ruth O'Brien, Scholarship Coordinator
American School Food Service
Association
700 South Washington Street
3rd Floor, Suite 300
Alexandria, VA 22314
Phone: 703-739-3900 Ext. 150
Fax: 703-739-3915
E-mail: robrien@asfsa.org

KAPPA OMICRON NU HONOR SOCIETY
http://www.kon.org

EILEEN C. MADDEX FELLOWSHIP • 386

One award for members of Kappa Omicron Nu who have demonstrated scholarship, research, and leadership potential. One-time award of $2000. Deadline is April 1.

Academic/Career Areas Fashion Design; Food Science/Nutrition; Food Service/Hospitality; Home Economics; Hospitality Management; Interior Design.

Award Fellowship for use in graduate years; not renewable. *Number: 1. Amount: $2000.*

Eligibility Requirements Applicant must be enrolled or expecting to enroll full-time at an institution or university and must have an interest in leadership. Available to U.S. and non-U.S. citizens.

Application Requirements Application, references. *Deadline:* April 1.

Contact Dorothy Mitstifer, Executive Director
Kappa Omicron Nu Honor Society
4990 Northwind Drive, Suite 140
East Lansing, MI 48823-5031
Phone: 517-351-8335
Fax: 517-351-8336
E-mail: dmitstifer@kon.org

HETTIE M. ANTHONY FELLOWSHIP • 387

Award for doctoral research in home economics. Must be member of Kappa Omicron Nu who has demonstrated scholarship, research, and leadership potential. One-time award of $2000. Deadline is January 15.

Academic/Career Areas Fashion Design; Food Science/Nutrition; Food Service/Hospitality; Home Economics; Hospitality Management; Interior Design.

Award Fellowship for use in graduate years; not renewable. *Number: 1. Amount: $2000.*

Eligibility Requirements Applicant must be enrolled or expecting to enroll full or part-time at an institution or university and must have an interest in leadership. Available to U.S. and non-U.S. citizens.

Application Requirements Application, references. *Deadline:* January 15.

Contact Dorothy Mitstifer, Executive Director
Kappa Omicron Nu Honor Society
4990 Northwind Drive, Suite 140
East Lansing, MI 48823-5031
Phone: 517-351-8335
Fax: 517-351-8336
E-mail: dmitstifer@kon.org

KAPPA OMICRON NU NATIONAL ALUMNI CHAPTER GRANT • 388

Award given to graduate home economics students who are members of Kappa Omicron Nu. Candidate must demonstrate scholarship, research, and leadership potential. Cross-specialization and integrative research should be the research priority. Multiyear proposals are considered. Recipient must submit annual progress report. One-time award of $1000. Deadline is February 15.

Academic/Career Areas Fashion Design; Food Science/Nutrition; Food Service/Hospitality; Home Economics; Hospitality Management; Interior Design.

Award Grant for use in graduate years; not renewable. *Number: 1. Amount: $1000.*

Eligibility Requirements Applicant must be enrolled or expecting to enroll at an institution or university and must have an interest in leadership. Available to U.S. and non-U.S. citizens.

Application Requirements Application, references. *Deadline:* February 15.

Contact Dorothy Mitstifer, Executive Director
Kappa Omicron Nu Honor Society
4990 Northwind Drive, Suite 140
East Lansing, MI 48823-5031
Phone: 517-351-8335
Fax: 517-351-8336
E-mail: dmitstifer@kon.org

KAPPA OMICRON NU NATIONAL ALUMNI FELLOWSHIP • 389

One award given to graduate home economics student who is a member of Kappa Omicron Nu. Candidates must demonstrate scholarship, research, and leadership potential. Applicants may pursue part-time study. Recipient of award must submit annual progress report. One-time award of $2000 every other year. Deadline is April 1.

Academic/Career Areas Fashion Design; Food Science/Nutrition; Food Service/Hospitality; Home Economics; Hospitality Management; Interior Design.

Award Fellowship for use in graduate years; not renewable. *Number: 1. Amount: $2000.*

Eligibility Requirements Applicant must be enrolled or expecting to enroll full or part-time at an institution or university and must have an interest in leadership. Available to U.S. and non-U.S. citizens.

Application Requirements Application, references. *Deadline:* April 1.

Contact Dorothy Mitstifer, Executive Director
Kappa Omicron Nu Honor Society
4990 Northwind Drive, Suite 140
East Lansing, MI 48823-5031
Phone: 517-351-8335
Fax: 517-351-8336
E-mail: dmitstifer@kon.org

FILMMAKING

ASIAN CULTURAL COUNCIL
http://www.asianculturalcouncil.org

FORD FOUNDATION FELLOWSHIPS
• *See number 141*

CONSORTIUM OF COLLEGE AND UNIVERSITY MEDIA CENTERS
http://www.ccumc.org

CONSORTIUM OF COLLEGE AND UNIVERSITY MEDIA CENTERS RESEARCH AWARDS
• *See number 253*

CULTURAL SERVICES OF THE FRENCH EMBASSY
http://www.frenchculture.org

CHATEAUBRIAND SCHOLARSHIP PROGRAM
• *See number 164*

RHODE ISLAND FOUNDATION
http://www.rifoundation.org

ANTONIO CIRINO MEMORIAL ART EDUCATION FELLOWSHIP
• *See number 172*

SHASTRI INDO-CANADIAN INSTITUTE
http://www.ucalgary.ca/~sici

SHASTRI INDIA STUDIES SENIOR ARTS FELLOWSHIPS
• *See number 157*

VIRGINIA MUSEUM OF FINE ARTS
http://www.vmfa.state.va.us

VIRGINIA MUSEUM OF FINE ARTS GRADUATE FELLOWSHIP PROGRAM
• *See number 158*

FOOD SCIENCE/NUTRITION

AFRICAN NETWORK OF SCIENTIFIC AND TECHNOLOGICAL INSTITUTIONS - ANSTI
http://www.ansti.org

AFRICAN NETWORK OF SCIENTIFIC AND TECHNOLOGICAL INSTITUTIONS POSTGRADUATE FELLOWSHIPS
• *See number 14*

ALBERT SCHWEITZER FELLOWSHIP
http://www.schweitzerfellowship.org

NEW HAMPSHIRE/VERMONT SCHWEITZER FELLOWS PROGRAM
• *See number 15*

AMERICAN ASSOCIATION OF CEREAL CHEMISTS
http://www.aaccnet.org

GRADUATE FELLOWSHIP AWARD
• *See number 375*

AMERICAN SCHOOL FOOD SERVICE ASSOCIATION
http://www.asfsa.org

CONAGRA FELLOWSHIP IN CHILD NUTRITION   • **390**

Fellowship to a doctoral or postdoctoral candidate for high-level research in an approved child nutrition priority area. Submit proposal by October 1.

Academic/Career Areas Food Science/Nutrition.

Award Fellowship for use in postgraduate years; not renewable. *Number:* up to 1. *Amount:* up to $45,000.

Eligibility Requirements Applicant must be enrolled or expecting to enroll full or part-time at an institution or university. Available to U.S. citizens.

Application Requirements Application, proposal. *Deadline:* October 1.

Contact Ruth O'Brien, Scholarship Coordinator
American School Food Service
Association
700 South Washington Street
3rd Floor, Suite 300
Alexandria, VA 22314
Phone: 703-739-3900 Ext. 150
Fax: 703-739-3915
E-mail: robrien@asfsa.org

HUBERT HUMPHREY RESEARCH GRANT   • **391**

One-time grant for ASFSA members to conduct research in child nutrition or school foodservice

American School Food Service Association (continued)

management. Must be currently enrolled in a graduate program with a major in foods, nutrition or a related field. Submit proposal by April 30.

Academic/Career Areas Food Science/Nutrition; Food Service/Hospitality.

Award Grant for use in graduate years; not renewable. *Number:* up to 1. *Amount:* up to $2500.

Eligibility Requirements Applicant must be enrolled or expecting to enroll full or part-time at an institution or university. Applicant or parent of applicant must be member of American School Food Service Association. Applicant or parent of applicant must have employment or volunteer experience in food service. Applicant must have 3.0 GPA or higher. Available to U.S. citizens.

Application Requirements Application, references, proposal. *Deadline:* April 30.

Contact Ruth O'Brien, Scholarship Coordinator
American School Food Service
Association
700 South Washington Street
3rd Floor, Suite 300
Alexandria, VA 22314
Phone: 703-739-3900 Ext. 150
Fax: 703-739-3915
E-mail: robrien@asfsa.org

LINCOLN FOOD SERVICE GRANT FOR INNOVATIONS IN SCHOOL FOOD SERVICE
• *See number 385*

PROFESSIONAL GROWTH SCHOLARSHIP • **392**

One-time award for child nutrition professionals pursuing graduate education in a food science management or nutrition-related field of study.

Academic/Career Areas Food Science/Nutrition; Food Service/Hospitality.

Award Scholarship for use in graduate years; not renewable. *Number:* up to 10. *Amount:* $1500–$2500.

Eligibility Requirements Applicant must be enrolled or expecting to enroll full or part-time at an institution or university. Applicant or parent of applicant must be member of American School Food Service Association. Applicant or parent of applicant must have employment or volunteer experience in food service. Applicant must have 3.0 GPA or higher. Available to U.S. citizens.

Application Requirements Application, essay, resume, references, transcript, proof of enrollment. *Deadline:* April 15.

Contact Ruth O'Brien, Scholarship Coordinator
American School Food Service
Association
700 South Washington Street, Suite 300
Alexandria, VA 22314
Phone: 703-739-3900 Ext. 150
Fax: 703-739-3915
E-mail: robrien@asfsa.org

AMERICAN WINE SOCIETY EDUCATIONAL FOUNDATION
http://www.americanwinesociety.com

AMERICAN WINE SOCIETY EDUCATIONAL FOUNDATION SCHOLARSHIP PROGRAM
• *See number 7*

BLUE CROSS BLUE SHIELD OF MICHIGAN FOUNDATION
http://www.bcbsm.com/foundation

BLUE CROSS BLUE SHIELD OF MICHIGAN FOUNDATION STUDENT AWARD PROGRAM • **393**

Awards available to students pursuing a Ph.D. or MD at a Michigan university. Projects can address a major public health or medical issue, quality of care, cost containment, or access to care. Projects can include research, pilot projects, intervention, feasibility studies, demonstration and evaluation projects, and must relate to improving health care in Michigan. One-time award of $3000. Submit letter from faculty adviser.

Academic/Career Areas Food Science/Nutrition; Health Administration; Health and Medical Sciences; Health Information Management/Technology; Natural Sciences; Nursing; Social Sciences; Therapy/Rehabilitation.

Award Grant for use in postgraduate years; not renewable. *Number:* 20–35. *Amount:* $3000.

Eligibility Requirements Applicant must be enrolled or expecting to enroll full-time at an institution or university and studying in Michigan.

Application Requirements Application, autobiography, references, transcript, research proposal. *Deadline:* April 30.

Contact Elizabeth Greaves-Hoxsie, Program Officer
Blue Cross Blue Shield of Michigan
Foundation
600 Lafayette East, X520
Detroit, MI 48226-2927
Phone: 313-225-9099
Fax: 313-225-7730
E-mail: ehoxsie@bcbsm.com

INSTITUTE OF FOOD TECHNOLOGISTS
http://www.ift.org

GERBER ENDOWMENT IN PEDIATRIC NUTRITION
• 394

One fellowship intended for graduate students conducting research in nutrition with an emphasis in pediatrics. Submit application to Head of the Department by February 1.

Academic/Career Areas Food Science/Nutrition.

Award Fellowship for use in graduate years; not renewable. *Number:* 1. *Amount:* $3000.

Eligibility Requirements Applicant must be enrolled or expecting to enroll at an institution or university. Available to U.S. citizens.

Application Requirements Application, references, test scores, transcript. *Deadline:* February 1.

Contact Administrator
Institute of Food Technologists
221 North LaSalle Street, Suite 300
Chicago, IL 60601
Phone: 312-782-8424
Fax: 312-782-8348

INSTITUTE OF FOOD TECHNOLOGISTS CARBOHYDRATE DIVISION GRADUATE FELLOWSHIP
• 395

Fellowships intended for students conducting research in the area of food carbohydrates.

Academic/Career Areas Food Science/Nutrition.

Award Fellowship for use in graduate years; not renewable. *Number:* 2. *Amount:* $1000.

Eligibility Requirements Applicant must be enrolled or expecting to enroll at an institution or university. Available to U.S. citizens.

Application Requirements Application, references. *Deadline:* February 1.

Contact Administrator
Institute of Food Technologists
221 North LaSalle Street, Suite 300
Chicago, IL 60601
Phone: 312-782-8424
Fax: 312-782-8348

INSTITUTE OF FOOD TECHNOLOGISTS FOOD PACKAGING DIVISION GRADUATE FELLOWSHIP
• 396

One-time award for graduate students conducting fundamental investigations for the advancement of food packaging. Submit three recommendations. Must be a member of the IFT Food Packaging Division.

Academic/Career Areas Food Science/Nutrition.

Award Fellowship for use in graduate years; not renewable. *Number:* 2. *Amount:* $1000.

Eligibility Requirements Applicant must be enrolled or expecting to enroll at an institution or university. Applicant or parent of applicant must be member of Institute of Food Technologists. Available to U.S. citizens.

Application Requirements Application, references, test scores, transcript. *Deadline:* February 1.

Contact Administrator
Institute of Food Technologists
221 North LaSalle Street, Suite 300
Chicago, IL 60601
Phone: 312-782-8424
Fax: 312-782-8348

INSTITUTE OF FOOD TECHNOLOGISTS GRADUATE FELLOWSHIPS
• 397

Fellowships available to outstanding graduate students with above-average interest in research. Must be enrolled in an accredited food science or technology program, working toward an M.S. or Ph.D. at the time the fellowship becomes effective. School of enrollment can be any educational institution that is conducting fundamental investigations for the advancement of food science or technology.

Academic/Career Areas Food Science/Nutrition.

Award Fellowship for use in graduate years; not renewable. *Number:* 18. *Amount:* $2000–$5000.

Eligibility Requirements Applicant must be enrolled or expecting to enroll full-time at an institution or university. Available to U.S. citizens.

Application Requirements Application, references, test scores, transcript. *Deadline:* February 1.

Contact Administrator
Institute of Food Technologists
221 North LaSalle Street, Suite 300
Chicago, IL 60601
Phone: 312-782-8424
Fax: 312-782-8348

INSTITUTE OF FOOD TECHNOLOGISTS REFRIGERATED & FROZEN FOODS DIVISION GRADUATE FELLOWSHIP
• 398

One-time award for graduate students conducting research in the area of refrigerated and frozen foods. Submit three recommendations. Previous recipients must be Institute of Food Technologists members to reapply.

Academic/Career Areas Food Science/Nutrition.

Award Fellowship for use in graduate years; not renewable. *Number:* 7. *Amount:* $2500.

Eligibility Requirements Applicant must be enrolled or expecting to enroll full-time at an institution or university. Available to U.S. citizens.

Institute of Food Technologists (continued)

Application Requirements Application, references, test scores, transcript. *Deadline:* February 1.

Contact Administrator
Institute of Food Technologists
221 North LaSalle Street, Suite 300
Chicago, IL 60601
Phone: 312-782-8424
Fax: 312-782-8348

INSTITUTE OF FOOD TECHNOLOGISTS SENSORY EVALUATION DIVISION SILVER CELEBRATION GRADUATE FELLOWSHIP • 399

One award intended for graduate students conducting research in the area of sensory science in relation to food science or technology.

Academic/Career Areas Food Science/Nutrition.

Award Fellowship for use in graduate years; not renewable. *Number:* 4. *Amount:* $5000.

Eligibility Requirements Applicant must be enrolled or expecting to enroll at an institution or university. Available to U.S. citizens.

Application Requirements Application, references, transcript. *Deadline:* February 1.

Contact Administrator
Institute of Food Technologists
221 North LaSalle Street, Suite 300
Chicago, IL 60601
Phone: 312-782-8424
Fax: 312-782-8348

SOCIETY OF FLAVOR CHEMISTS MEMORIAL GRADUATE FELLOWSHIP • 400

Fellowship intended for graduate students conducting research either in flavor chemistry or in a food technology area related to flavor chemistry. Write for program details. One-time award of $2000.

Academic/Career Areas Food Science/Nutrition.

Award Scholarship for use in graduate years; not renewable. *Number:* 1. *Amount:* $2000.

Eligibility Requirements Applicant must be enrolled or expecting to enroll full-time at an institution or university. Available to U.S. citizens.

Application Requirements Application, essay, references, test scores, transcript. *Deadline:* February 1.

Contact Administrator
Institute of Food Technologists
221 North LaSalle Street, suite 300
Chicago, IL 60601
Phone: 312-782-8424
Fax: 312-782-8348

INTERNATIONAL DEVELOPMENT RESEARCH CENTER
http://www.idrc.ca/awards

IDRC DOCTORAL RESEARCH AWARD
• *See number 12*

KAPPA OMICRON NU HONOR SOCIETY
http://www.kon.org

EILEEN C. MADDEX FELLOWSHIP
• *See number 386*

HETTIE M. ANTHONY FELLOWSHIP
• *See number 387*

KAPPA OMICRON NU NATIONAL ALUMNI CHAPTER GRANT
• *See number 388*

KAPPA OMICRON NU NATIONAL ALUMNI FELLOWSHIP
• *See number 389*

KAPPA OMICRON NU NEW INITIATIVES GRANT • 401

One award given to a graduate home economics student who is a member of Kappa Omicron Nu. Candidate must demonstrate scholarship, research, and leadership potential. Cross-specialization and integrative research should be the research priority. Multiyear proposals are considered. Recipient must submit annual progress report. Renewable award of $3000.

Academic/Career Areas Food Science/Nutrition; Home Economics.

Award Grant for use in graduate years; renewable. *Number:* 1–2. *Amount:* $1500–$3000.

Eligibility Requirements Applicant must be enrolled or expecting to enroll at an institution or university and must have an interest in leadership. Available to U.S. and non-U.S. citizens.

Application Requirements Application, references. *Deadline:* February 15.

Contact Dorothy Mistifer, Executive Director
Kappa Omicron Nu Honor Society
4990 Northwind Drive, Suite 140
East Lansing, MI 48823-5031
Phone: 517-351-8335
Fax: 517-351-8336
E-mail: dmitstifer@kon.org

NATIONAL MILK PRODUCERS FEDERATION
http://www.nmpf.org

NATIONAL MILK PRODUCERS FEDERATION NATIONAL DAIRY LEADERSHIP SCHOLARSHIP PROGRAM
• *See number 5*

SENSE OF SMELL INSTITUTE
http://www.senseofsmell.org

TOVA FELLOWSHIP
• *See number 101*

FOOD SERVICE/HOSPITALITY

AMERICAN SCHOOL FOOD SERVICE ASSOCIATION
http://www.asfsa.org

HUBERT HUMPHREY RESEARCH GRANT
• *See number 391*

PROFESSIONAL GROWTH SCHOLARSHIP
• *See number 392*

KAPPA OMICRON NU HONOR SOCIETY
http://www.kon.org

EILEEN C. MADDEX FELLOWSHIP
• *See number 386*

HETTIE M. ANTHONY FELLOWSHIP
• *See number 387*

KAPPA OMICRON NU NATIONAL ALUMNI CHAPTER GRANT
• *See number 388*

KAPPA OMICRON NU NATIONAL ALUMNI FELLOWSHIP
• *See number 389*

NATIONAL TOURISM FOUNDATION
http://www.ntfonline.org

LURAY CAVERNS GRADUATE RESEARCH GRANT • **402**

Available to graduate students conducting research on travel-related topics. Selection based on quality of research, creative approach, usefulness and application, level of research and quality of presentation. Deadline is April 15.

Academic/Career Areas Food Service/Hospitality; Hospitality Management; Travel/Tourism.

Award Grant for use in graduate years; not renewable. *Number:* 1. *Amount:* $2500.

Eligibility Requirements Applicant must be enrolled or expecting to enroll full-time at an institution or university. Available to U.S. citizens.

Application Requirements Application, references, transcript, proposal. *Deadline:* April 15.

Contact Assistant Executive Director
National Tourism Foundation
546 East Main Street
Lexington, KY 40508-3071
Phone: 800-682-8886 Ext. 4265
Fax: 859-226-4437

FOREIGN LANGUAGE

AMERICAN CENTER OF ORIENTAL RESEARCH
http://www.bu.edu/acor

NATIONAL ENDOWMENT FOR THE HUMANITIES POST-DOCTORAL RESEARCH FELLOWSHIPS
• *See number 65*

AMERICAN COUNCIL OF TEACHERS OF RUSSIAN
http://www.actr.org

ACTR SUMMER RUSSIAN LANGUAGE TEACHER PROGRAM
• *See number 344*

TITLE VIII RESEARCH SCHOLAR AND COMBINED RESEARCH AND LANGUAGE STUDY PROGRAM
• *See number 114*

AMERICAN INSTITUTE OF INDIAN STUDIES
http://www.indiastudies.org

AIIS 9-MONTH LANGUAGE PROGRAM • **403**

Award for graduate student to attend an intensive language program in India. Must have studied at least two years in relevant language and be a U.S. citizen. Application fee: $25. Deadline: January 31.

Academic/Career Areas Foreign Language.

Award Fellowship for use in graduate years; not renewable.

Eligibility Requirements Applicant must be enrolled or expecting to enroll full-time at an institution or university. Available to U.S. citizens.

Application Requirements Application, essay, references, transcript. *Fee:* $25. *Deadline:* January 31.

Contact Administrator
American Institute of Indian Studies
1130 East 59th Street
Chicago, IL 60637
Phone: 773-702-8638
Fax: 773-702-6636
E-mail: aiis@uchicago.edu

AMERICAN INSTITUTE OF INDIAN STUDIES RESEARCH FELLOWSHIPS
• *See number 117*

ARKANSAS DEPARTMENT OF HIGHER EDUCATION
http://www.arscholarships.com

MINORITY MASTER'S FELLOWS PROGRAM
• *See number 351*

ASIAN CULTURAL COUNCIL
http://www.asianculturalcouncil.org

ASIAN CULTURAL COUNCIL FELLOWSHIPS
• *See number 91*

ASIAN CULTURAL COUNCIL HUMANITIES FELLOWSHIPS
• *See number 92*

BLAKEMORE FOUNDATION
http://www.blakemorefoundation.org

BLAKEMORE FREEMAN FELLOWSHIPS FOR ADVANCED STUDY OF ASIAN LANGUAGES • **404**

Award for individuals pursuing professional, business, or academic careers involving Asia to undertake advanced study of modern Chinese, Japanese, Korean, and Southeast Asian languages at an institution in Asia. Deadline: January 15. See website for application material. (www.blakemorefoundation. org)

Academic/Career Areas Foreign Language.

Award Grant for use in graduate, or postgraduate years; not renewable. *Number:* 20–40. *Amount:* $15,000–$40,000.

Eligibility Requirements Applicant must be enrolled or expecting to enroll full-time at an institution or university and must have an interest in foreign language. Available to U.S. citizens.

Application Requirements Application, essay, references, transcript. *Deadline:* January 15.

Contact Griffith Way, Trustee
Blakemore Foundation
1201 Third Avenue, Suite 4800
Seattle, WA 98101-3266
Phone: 206-583-8778
Fax: 206-583-8500
E-mail: blakemore@perkinscoie.com

CHINA TIMES CULTURAL FOUNDATION

CHINA TIMES CULTURAL FOUNDATION DOCTORAL DISSERTATION RESEARCH IN CHINESE STUDIES SCHOLARSHIPS
• *See number 122*

NATIONAL RESEARCH COUNCIL
http://www.nationalacademies.org/fellowships/

FORD FOUNDATION DISSERTATION FELLOWSHIPS FOR MINORITIES
• *See number 256*

FORD FOUNDATION POSTDOCTORAL FELLOWSHIP FOR MINORITIES
• *See number 257*

FORD FOUNDATION PREDOCTORAL FELLOWSHIPS FOR MINORITIES
• *See number 258*

PHI BETA KAPPA SOCIETY
http://www.pbk.org

MARY ISABEL SIBLEY FELLOWSHIP FOR GREEK AND FRENCH STUDIES
• *See number 132*

SWEDISH INFORMATION SERVICE
http://www.swedeninfo.com

BICENTENNIAL SWEDISH-AMERICAN EXCHANGE FUND TRAVEL GRANTS
• *See number 133*

UNITED NEGRO COLLEGE FUND
http://www.uncf.org

GEORGE S. LURCY CHARITABLE AND EDUCATIONAL TRUST • **405**

Scholarship is for junior faculty applicants who have a doctorate from an accredited institution. Applicants must be teaching at a UNCF institution and have less than eight years experience teaching at the high school or college level. The program is designed to expose recipients to other cultures; therefore, the applicant's field of interest should be foreign language, history, philosophy, anthropology, or literature.

Academic/Career Areas Foreign Language; History; Literature/English/Writing.

Award Scholarship for use in graduate, or postgraduate years; not renewable. *Amount:* $11,000.

Eligibility Requirements Applicant must be Black (non-Hispanic) and enrolled or expecting to enroll at a four-year institution or university. Applicant or parent of applicant must have employment or volunteer experience in designated career field. Available to U.S. citizens.

Application Requirements Application.

Contact Program Services Department
United Negro College Fund
8260 Willow Oaks Corporate Drive
Fairfax, VA 22031

WOODROW WILSON NATIONAL FELLOWSHIP FOUNDATION
http://www.woodrow.org

ANDREW W. MELLON FELLOWSHIPS IN HUMANISTIC STUDIES
• See number 134

THOMAS R. PICKERING GRADUATE FOREIGN AFFAIRS FELLOWSHIP PROGRAM
• See number 241

WOODROW WILSON POSTDOCTORAL FELLOWSHIPS IN THE HUMANITIES
• See number 136

GEOGRAPHY

AMERICAN SCHOOLS OF ORIENTAL RESEARCH (ASOR)
http://www.asor.org

W.F. ALBRIGHT INSTITUTE OF ARCHAEOLOGICAL RESEARCH - JAMES A. MONTGOMERY FELLOW AND RESEARCH COORDINATOR
• See number 69

W.F. ALBRIGHT INSTITUTE OF ARCHAEOLOGICAL RESEARCH GEORGE A. BARTON FELLOWSHIP
• See number 70

CANADIAN NORTHERN STUDIES TRUST - ASSOCIATION OF CANADIAN UNIVERSITIES FOR NORTHERN STUDIES
http://www.cyberus.ca/~acuns

JAMES W. BOURQUE STUDENTSHIP IN NORTHERN GEOGRAPHY
• 406

Award for students enrolled in master's or doctoral program who are conducting research leading to a thesis on a subject relating to northern geography. Preference given to those who include direct northern experience as a part of their studies. Research must be done in Canada, north of the southern boundary of the sporadic discontinuous permafrost zone. Write or see website to obtain an application package.

Academic/Career Areas Geography.

Award Scholarship for use in graduate, or postgraduate years; not renewable. *Number:* 1. *Amount:* $5000.

Eligibility Requirements Applicant must be Canadian citizenship and enrolled or expecting to enroll at an institution or university.

Application Requirements Application. *Deadline:* January 31.

Contact Sandra Malcolm, Executive Officer
Canadian Northern Studies Trust - Association of Canadian Universities for Northern Studies
405 -17 York Street
Ottawa, ON K1N 9J6
Canada
Phone: 613-562-0515
Fax: 613-562-0533
E-mail: acuns@cyberus.ca

GRAPHICS/GRAPHIC ARTS/PRINTING

SWANN FOUNDATION FUND
http://www.lcweb.loc.gov/rr/print/swann/swann_foundation.html

SWANN FOUNDATION FUND FELLOWSHIP
• See number 109

HEALTH ADMINISTRATION

ALBERT SCHWEITZER FELLOWSHIP
http://www.schweitzerfellowship.org

NEW HAMPSHIRE/VERMONT SCHWEITZER FELLOWS PROGRAM
• See number 15

AMERICAN FOUNDATION FOR UROLOGIC DISEASE, INC.
http://www.afud.org

AFUD/AUA HEALTH POLICY RESEARCH PROGRAM
• 407

Available to trained urologist (MD/DO) within five years of residency who aspires to conduct research in healthcare services related to urology. Must be committed to career in academic urology and be able to demonstrate current interest/accomplishments in issues related to delivery of health services, health economics, and policy.

Academic/Career Areas Health Administration; Health and Medical Sciences; Health Information Management/Technology.

Award Scholarship for use in postgraduate years; not renewable. *Number:* 1–3. *Amount:* $44,000.

Eligibility Requirements Applicant must be enrolled or expecting to enroll at an institution or university. Available to U.S. and non-U.S. citizens.

American Foundation for Urologic Disease, Inc. (continued)

Application Requirements Application, references, research proposal, curriculum vitae. *Deadline:* September 1.

Contact Kym Liddick, Director of Research
Program
American Foundation for Urologic
Disease, Inc.
1128 North Charles Street
Baltimore, MD 21201
Phone: 410-468-1812
Fax: 410-468-1808
E-mail: kym@afud.org

BLUE CROSS BLUE SHIELD OF MICHIGAN FOUNDATION
http://www.bcbsm.com/foundation

BLUE CROSS BLUE SHIELD OF MICHIGAN FOUNDATION STUDENT AWARD PROGRAM
• *See number 393*

CANADIAN SOCIETY FOR MEDICAL LABORATORY SCIENCE
http://www.csmls.org

CANADIAN SOCIETY FOR MEDICAL LABORATORY SCIENCE FOUNDERS' FUND AWARDS • **408**

Award available for members of the Canadian Society for Medical Laboratory Science to pursue postgraduate professional development education. Must be a Canadian resident. One-time award of Can$100-Can$500.

Academic/Career Areas Health Administration; Health and Medical Sciences; Health Information Management/Technology.

Award Grant for use in graduate years; not renewable. *Number:* 7. *Amount:* $100–$500.

Eligibility Requirements Applicant must be Canadian citizenship and enrolled or expecting to enroll at an institution or university. Applicant or parent of applicant must be member of Canadian Society for Medical Laboratory Science.

Application Requirements Application. *Deadline:* Continuous.

Contact Lynn Zehr, Executive Assistant
Canadian Society for Medical Laboratory
Science
LCD 1, PO Box 2830
Hamilton, ON L8N 3N8
Canada
Phone: 905-528-8642 Ext. 12
Fax: 905-528-4968
E-mail: lzehr@csmls.org

NATIONAL MEDICAL FELLOWSHIPS, INC
http://www.nmf-online.org

W.K. KELLOGG FELLOWSHIP PROGRAM IN HEALTH POLICY RESEARCH • **409**

Student must be a U.S. citizen; African American, Hispanic, Native American, or Asian with a demonstrated commitment to medically underserved areas; committed to working with underserved populations upon completion of doctorate; and willing to complete relevant dissertation research. Student must also be accepted or enrolled in a doctoral program in one of the following participating schools: The Heller Graduate School at Brandeis University, the Joseph L. Mailman School of Public Health of Columbia University, the Harvard School of Public Health, the Johns Hopkins School of Hygiene and Public Health, the RAND Graduate School, the UCLA School of Public Health, and the University of Michigan School of Public Health. Award will provide a yearly stipend to cover tuition, fees, and living expenses for up to five years. The deadline for applying is in the spring.

Academic/Career Areas Health Administration; Health Information Management/Technology.

Award Fellowship for use in graduate years; not renewable. *Number:* 5.

Eligibility Requirements Applicant must be American Indian/Alaska Native, Asian/Pacific Islander, Black (non-Hispanic), or Hispanic; enrolled or expecting to enroll at an institution or university and studying in California, Maryland, Massachusetts, Michigan, or New York. Available to U.S. citizens.

Application Requirements Application, essay, resume, references, transcript, curriculum vitae.

Contact Fellowship Coordinator
National Medical Fellowships, Inc
5 Hanover Square, 15th Floor
New York, NY 10004

HEALTH AND MEDICAL SCIENCES

AGA FOUNDATION FOR DIGESTIVE HEALTH AND NUTRITION
http://www.fdhn.org

AGA R. ROBERT AND SALLY D. FUNDERBURG RESEARCH SCHOLAR AWARD IN GASTRIC BIOLOGY RELATED TO CANCER • **410**

This grant (award of $25,000 per year for two years) is offered to an established investigator working on novel approaches in gastric cancer or conducting clinical research in diagnosis or treatment of gastric carcinoma. Must hold a faculty position at an accredited U.S. or Canadian institution and be a member of AGA. Deadline: September 2.

Academic/Career Areas Health and Medical Sciences.

Award Grant for use in postgraduate years; not renewable. *Number:* 1. *Amount:* $25,000.

Eligibility Requirements Applicant must be enrolled or expecting to enroll at an institution or university. Applicant or parent of applicant must have employment or volunteer experience in teaching. Available to U.S. and Canadian citizens.

Application Requirements Application, autobiography, references, abstract, plan. *Deadline:* September 2.

Contact Desta Wallace, Research Awards
Coordinator
AGA Foundation for Digestive Health
and Nutrition
7910 Woodmont Avenue, 7th Floor
Bethesda, MD 20814
Phone: 301-222-4005
Fax: 301-222-4010
E-mail: desta@gastro.org

AMERICAN GASTEROENTEROLOGICAL ASSOCIATION ELSEVIER RESEARCH INITIATIVE AWARD • 411

$25,000, one year, research initiative grant offered to investigators to support pilot research projects in gastroenterology or hepatology related areas. Provides non-salary funds for new investigators and supports pilot projects that represent new research directions for established investigators. Must possess an MD or Ph.D. degree or equivalent and must hold faculty positions at accredited U.S. or Canadian institutions. Must be a member of AGA. Deadline: January 4.

Academic/Career Areas Health and Medical Sciences.

Award Grant for use in postgraduate years; not renewable. *Number:* 1. *Amount:* $25,000.

Eligibility Requirements Applicant must be enrolled or expecting to enroll at an institution or university. Applicant or parent of applicant must have employment or volunteer experience in teaching. Available to U.S. and Canadian citizens.

Application Requirements Application, autobiography, references, abstract, budget. *Deadline:* January 4.

Contact Desta Wallace, Research Awards
Coordinator
AGA Foundation for Digestive Health
and Nutrition
7910 Woodmont Avenue, 7th Floor
Bethesda, MD 20814
Phone: 301-222-4005
Fax: 301-222-4010
E-mail: desta@gastro.org

AMERICAN GASTEROENTEROLOGICAL ASSOCIATION JUNE AND DONALD O. CASTELL, MD. ESOPHAGEAL CLINICAL RESEARCH AWARD • 412

Award of $35,000 to provide research and/or salary support for junior faculty involved in clinical research in esophageal function or diseases and have demonstrated a high potential to develop an independent, productive research career. Applicants must hold full-time faculty positions at an U.S. or Canadian university or professional institute and may hold a MD and/or Ph.D. or equivalent. Must be a member of AGA. Deadline: January 4.

Academic/Career Areas Health and Medical Sciences.

Award Grant for use in postgraduate years; not renewable. *Number:* 1. *Amount:* $35,000.

Eligibility Requirements Applicant must be enrolled or expecting to enroll at an institution or university. Applicant or parent of applicant must have employment or volunteer experience in teaching. Available to U.S. and Canadian citizens.

Application Requirements Application, references, abstract and research plan. *Deadline:* January 4.

Contact Desta Wallace, Research Awards
Coordinator
AGA Foundation for Digestive Health
and Nutrition
7910 Woodmont Avenue, 7th Floor
Bethesda, MD 20814
Phone: 301-222-4005
Fax: 301-222-4010
E-mail: desta@gastro.org

AMERICAN GASTEROENTEROLOGICAL ASSOCIATION MILES AND SHIRLEY FITERMAN FOUNDATION BASIC RESEARCH AWARDS • 413

Two awards each year to provide research and/or salary support for junior faculty members involved in basic research in any area of gastrointestinal, liver function or related diseases. Applicant must hold full-time faculty position at a U.S. or Canadian university or professional institute and must hold an MD, Ph.D. or equivalent degree. Must be a member of AGA.

Academic/Career Areas Health and Medical Sciences.

Award Grant for use in postgraduate years; not renewable. *Number:* 2. *Amount:* $35,000.

Eligibility Requirements Applicant must be enrolled or expecting to enroll at an institution or university. Applicant or parent of applicant must have employment or volunteer experience in teaching. Available to U.S. and Canadian citizens.

AGA Foundation for Digestive Health and Nutrition (continued)

Application Requirements Application, autobiography, references, abstract, research plan. *Deadline:* January 4.

Contact Desta Wallace, Research Awards
Coordinator
AGA Foundation for Digestive Health and Nutrition
7910 Woodmont Avenue, 7th Floor
Bethesda, MD 20814
Phone: 301-222-4005
Fax: 301-222-4010
E-mail: desta@gastro.org

AMERICAN GASTEROENTEROLOGICAL ASSOCIATION RESEARCH SCHOLAR AWARDS • 414

Award provides support for young investigators working toward an independent research career in any area of gastroenterology, hepatology or related areas. Applicants must hold full-time faculty positions at U.S. or Canadian universities or professional institutes at the time of application. Must be a member of AGA. Award is $65,000 per year for three years. Deadline: September 2.

Academic/Career Areas Health and Medical Sciences.

Award Grant for use in postgraduate years; not renewable. *Number:* 5. *Amount:* $65,000.

Eligibility Requirements Applicant must be enrolled or expecting to enroll at an institution or university. Applicant or parent of applicant must have employment or volunteer experience in teaching. Available to U.S. and Canadian citizens.

Application Requirements Application, autobiography, interview, references, abstract. *Deadline:* September 2.

Contact Desta Wallace, Research Awards
Coordinator
AGA Foundation for Digestive Health and Nutrition
7910 Woodmont Avenue, 7th Floor
Bethesda, MD 20814
Phone: 301-222-4005
Fax: 301-222-4010
E-mail: desta@gastro.org

AMERICAN GASTEROENTEROLOGICAL ASSOCIATION RESEARCH SCHOLAR AWARDS FOR UNDERREPRESENTED MINORITIES • 415

Award provides support for young, underrepresented minority investigators (American Indian/Alaska-Hawaii native, Mexican American and Mainland Puerto Rican) working toward an independent research career in any area of gastroenterology,

hepatology or related areas. Applicants must hold full-time faculty positions at U.S. or Canadian universities or professional institutes at the time of application. Must be a member of AGA. Award is $65,000 per year for three years. Deadline: September 2.

Academic/Career Areas Health and Medical Sciences.

Award Grant for use in postgraduate years; not renewable. *Number:* 1. *Amount:* $65,000.

Eligibility Requirements Applicant must be enrolled or expecting to enroll at an institution or university. Applicant or parent of applicant must have employment or volunteer experience in teaching. Available to U.S. and Canadian citizens.

Application Requirements Application, autobiography, references, abstract. *Deadline:* September 2.

Contact Desta Wallace, Research Awards
Coordinator
AGA Foundation for Digestive Health and Nutrition
7910 Woodmont Avenue, 7th Floor
Bethesda, MD 20814
Phone: 301-222-4005
Fax: 301-222-4010
E-mail: desta@gastro.org

AMERICAN GASTEROENTEROLOGICAL MERCK CLINICAL RESEARCH CAREER DEVELOPMENT AWARD • 416

This award ($50,000 per year for two years) provides salary support to a junior faculty member or fully-trained investigator at the outset of their career performing clinical research in any area of gastroenterology or hepatology. Research must be based upon or include, direct patient contact or medical records analysis. Must hold full-time faculty position at U.S. or Canadian University or professional institute at time of application. Must be a member of AGA.

Academic/Career Areas Health and Medical Sciences.

Award Grant for use in postgraduate years; not renewable. *Number:* 1. *Amount:* $50,000.

Eligibility Requirements Applicant must be enrolled or expecting to enroll at an institution or university. Applicant or parent of applicant must have employment or volunteer experience in teaching. Available to U.S. and Canadian citizens.

Application Requirements Application, autobiography, references, abstract. *Deadline:* January 4.

Contact Desta Wallace, Research Awards
   Coordinator
   AGA Foundation for Digestive Health
   and Nutrition
   7910 Woodmont Avenue, 7th Floor
   Bethesda, MD 20814
   Phone: 301-222-4005
   Fax: 301-222-4010
   E-mail: desta@gastro.org

AMERICAN GASTROENTEROLOGICAL ASSOCIATION ASTRAZENECA FELLOWSHIP/ FACULTY TRANSITION AWARDS
• *See number 181*

ALBERT SCHWEITZER FELLOWSHIP
http://www.schweitzerfellowship.org
LAMBARÉNÉ SCHWEITZER FELLOWS PROGRAM   • 417

Each year, the Lambaréné Schweitzer Fellows Program selects four New England medical students who are fluent in French to spend three months working at the Albert Schweitzer Hospital in Lambaréné, Gabon as junior physicians in pediatrics, surgery, or internal medicine. Complete funding for students (airfare, room, board, immunizations) is provided.

Academic/Career Areas Health and Medical Sciences.

Award Fellowship for use in graduate years; not renewable. *Number:* 4. *Amount:* up to $6000.

Eligibility Requirements Applicant must be enrolled or expecting to enroll full-time at an institution or university; resident of Connecticut, Maine, Massachusetts, New Hampshire, Rhode Island, or Vermont and must have an interest in French language. Available to U.S. and non-U.S. citizens.

Application Requirements Essay, interview, resume, references. *Deadline:* December 24.

Contact Stellar Kim
   Albert Schweitzer Fellowship
   330 Brookline Avenue, Libby 315
   Boston, MA 02215
   Phone: 617-667-3115
   Fax: 617-667-7989
   E-mail: info@schweitzerfellowship.org

NEW HAMPSHIRE/VERMONT SCHWEITZER FELLOWS PROGRAM
• *See number 15*

ALPHA EPSILON IOTA SCHOLARSHIP FUND
ALPHA EPSILON IOTA SCHOLARSHIP   • 418

Scholarships are open to women pursuing an M.D. or Doctor of Osteopathy degree at an accredited U.S. school or college of medicine. Selection based on financial need and academic record. Maximum net income of $15,000 per year and maximum assets of $10,000. Priority given to first-year students. Contact the Fund by mail for additional information.

Academic/Career Areas Health and Medical Sciences.

Award Scholarship for use in graduate, or postgraduate years; renewable. *Number:* 2. *Amount:* $3000–$4000.

Eligibility Requirements Applicant must be enrolled or expecting to enroll at an institution or university and female.

Application Requirements Financial need analysis. *Deadline:* May 31.

Contact Scholarship Information
   Alpha Epsilon Iota Scholarship Fund
   PO Box 8612
   Ann Arbor, MI 48107-8612

AMERICAN ACADEMY OF CHILD AND ADOLESCENT PSYCHIATRY (AACAP)
http://www.aacap.org
AACAP GEORGE TARJAN AWARD   • 419

Award to child and adolescent psychiatrist who has made a significant contribution in a lifetime career or single seminal work to the understanding or care of those with mental retardation and developmental disabilities. Contributions must have national or international stature and clearly demonstrate lasting effects, and may be in the areas of teaching, research, program development, direct clinical service, advocacy, or administrative commitment. Award of up to $1000. Must be a member of the AACAP. Nominations due June 1.

Academic/Career Areas Health and Medical Sciences.

Award Fellowship for use in postgraduate years; not renewable. *Number:* 1. *Amount:* $1000.

Eligibility Requirements Applicant must be enrolled or expecting to enroll at an institution or university. Applicant or parent of applicant must be member of American Academy of Child and Adolescent Psychiatry. Available to U.S. and non-U.S. citizens.

Health and Medical Sciences

American Academy of Child and Adolescent Psychiatry (AACAP) (continued)

Application Requirements Nomination. *Deadline:* June 1.

Contact Trish Brown, Director of Research and Training
American Academy of Child and Adolescent Psychiatry (AACAP)
3615 Wisconsion Avenue, NW
Washington, DC 20016-3007
Phone: 202-966-7300 Ext. 113
Fax: 202-966-2891
E-mail: tbrown@aacap.org

AACAP IRVING PHILIPS AWARD • 420

Award to child and adolescent psychiatrist who has made a significant contribution in a lifetime career or single seminal work to the prevention of mental illness in children and adolescents. Contributions must have national or international stature and clearly demonstrate lasting effects, and may be in the areas of teaching, program development, research, direct clinical service, advocacy or administrative commitment. Award of $2500 to winner and $2500 donation to a prevention program or center of awardee's choice. Must be a member of the AACAP. Nominations due May 1.

Academic/Career Areas Health and Medical Sciences.

Award Fellowship for use in postgraduate years; not renewable. *Number:* 1. *Amount:* $2500.

Eligibility Requirements Applicant must be enrolled or expecting to enroll at an institution or university. Applicant or parent of applicant must be member of American Academy of Child and Adolescent Psychiatry. Available to U.S. and non-U.S. citizens.

Application Requirements Nomination. *Deadline:* May 1.

Contact Trish Brown, Director of Research and Training
American Academy of Child and Adolescent Psychiatry (AACAP)
3615 Wisconsion Avenue, NW
Washington, DC 20016-3007
Phone: 202-966-7300 Ext. 113
Fax: 202-966-2891
E-mail: tbrown@aacap.org

AACAP JEANNE SPURLOCK MINORITY MEDICAL STUDENT CLINICAL FELLOWSHIP IN CHILD AND ADOLESCENT PSYCHIATRY • 421

Awards to African American, Asian American, Native American, Alaskan Native, Mexican American, Hispanic, and Pacific Islander students in accredited U.S. medical schools. Nine $2500 awards for work during the summer with a child and adolescent psychiatrist mentor, plus five days at the AACAP Annual Meeting. Deadline: April 1.

Academic/Career Areas Health and Medical Sciences.

Award Fellowship for use in graduate years; not renewable. *Number:* 5–7. *Amount:* $2500.

Eligibility Requirements Applicant must be American Indian/Alaska Native, Asian/Pacific Islander, Black (non-Hispanic), or Hispanic and enrolled or expecting to enroll at an institution or university. Available to U.S. citizens.

Application Requirements Application. *Deadline:* April 1.

Contact Trish Brown, Director of Research and Training
American Academy of Child and Adolescent Psychiatry (AACAP)
3615 Wisconsion Avenue, NW
Washington, DC 20016-3007
Phone: 202-966-7300 Ext. 113
Fax: 202-966-2891
E-mail: tbrown@aacap.org

AACAP JEANNE SPURLOCK RESEARCH FELLOWSHIP IN DRUG ABUSE AND ADDICTION FOR MINORITY MEDICAL STUDENTS • 422

Awards to African American, Asian American, Native American, Alaskan Native, Mexican American, Hispanic, and Pacific Islander students in accredited U.S. medical schools. Five $2500 awards for substance abuse-related research during the summer with a child and adolescent psychiatrist researcher-mentor, plus five days at the AACAP Annual Meeting. Deadline April 1.

Academic/Career Areas Health and Medical Sciences.

Award Fellowship for use in graduate years; not renewable. *Number:* 5. *Amount:* $2500.

Eligibility Requirements Applicant must be American Indian/Alaska Native, Asian/Pacific Islander, Black (non-Hispanic), or Hispanic and enrolled or expecting to enroll full-time at an institution or university. Available to U.S. citizens.

Application Requirements Application. *Deadline:* April 1.

Contact Trish Brown, Director of Research and Training
American Academy of Child and Adolescent Psychiatry (AACAP)
3615 Wisconsion Avenue, NW
Washington, DC 20016-3007
Phone: 202-966-7300 Ext. 113
Fax: 202-966-2891
E-mail: tbrown@aacap.org

AACAP PILOT RESEARCH AWARD SUPPORTED BY ELI LILLY AND COMPANY • 423

Five awards of $9000 each for pilot research, plus five days at the AACAP Annual Meeting in Chicago, IL. Candidates must be board eligible, certified in child and adolescent psychiatry, or enrolled in a child psychiatry residency or fellowship program. Must have a full-time faculty appointment in an accredited medical school or be in a fully accredited child and adolescent psychiatry clinical or research training program. May not have more than two years experience following graduation from residency/ fellowship training. Must not have any previous significant, non-salary, individual research funding. Submit curriculum vitae, research protocol, and budget and justification by March 15. Must be an AACAP member.

Academic/Career Areas Health and Medical Sciences.

Award Fellowship for use in postgraduate years; not renewable. *Number:* 5. *Amount:* $9000.

Eligibility Requirements Applicant must be enrolled or expecting to enroll at an institution or university. Applicant or parent of applicant must be member of American Academy of Child and Adolescent Psychiatry. Available to U.S. and non-U.S. citizens.

Application Requirements Curriculum vitae, research protocol and budget. *Deadline:* March 15.

Contact Trish Brown, Director of Research and
> Training
> American Academy of Child and
> Adolescent Psychiatry (AACAP)
> 3615 Wisconsin Avenue, NW
> Washington, DC 20016-3007
> *Phone:* 202-966-7300 Ext. 113
> *Fax:* 202-966-2891
> *E-mail:* tbrown@aacap.org

AACAP PRESIDENTIAL SCHOLAR AWARDS • 424

Awards for child and adolescent psychiatry residents in research, public policy, and innovative service systems. Must be nominated by program director. Must submit current curriculum vitae as well as statement about specific area of interest, plans for tutorial and exchange, and plans for presentation to home program. Deadline: March 15. Must be an Academy member.

Academic/Career Areas Health and Medical Sciences.

Award Fellowship for use in postgraduate years; not renewable. *Number:* 5. *Amount:* $2500–$3500.

Eligibility Requirements Applicant must be enrolled or expecting to enroll part-time at an institution or university. Applicant or parent of applicant must be member of American Academy of Child and Adolescent Psychiatry. Available to U.S. and non-U.S. citizens.

Application Requirements Nomination. *Deadline:* March 15.

Contact Trish Brown, Director of Research and
> Training
> American Academy of Child and
> Adolescent Psychiatry (AACAP)
> 3615 Wisconsin Avenue, NW
> Washington, DC 20016-3007
> *Phone:* 202-966-7300 Ext. 113
> *Fax:* 202-966-2891
> *E-mail:* tbrown@aacap.org

AACAP RIEGER PSYCHODYNAMIC PSYCHOTHERAPY AWARD • 425

This award acknowledges the best unpublished paper by a member of AACAP that addresses the use of psychodynamic psychotherapy in clinical practice. This award provides $4500 to the author. Deadline: May 1.

Academic/Career Areas Health and Medical Sciences.

Award Fellowship for use in postgraduate years; not renewable. *Amount:* $4500.

Eligibility Requirements Applicant must be enrolled or expecting to enroll at an institution or university. Applicant or parent of applicant must be member of American Academy of Child and Adolescent Psychiatry. Available to U.S. and non-U.S. citizens.

Application Requirements *Deadline:* May 1.

Contact Trish Brown, Director of Research and
> Training
> American Academy of Child and
> Adolescent Psychiatry (AACAP)
> 3615 Wisconsin Avenue, NW
> Washington, DC 20016-3007
> *Phone:* 202-966-7300 Ext. 113
> *Fax:* 202-966-2891
> *E-mail:* tbrown@aacap.org

AACAP RIEGER SERVICE PROGRAM AWARD FOR EXCELLENCE • 426

Award recognizes innovative programs that address prevention, diagnosis, or treatment of mental illnesses in children and adolescents, and serve as model program to the community. Award of $1000 to the nominee, $3000 to the service program, and $1000 to cover expenses for attendance at the AACAP Annual Meeting. Nominations due June 1. Must be a U.S. citizen and an AACAP member.

Academic/Career Areas Health and Medical Sciences.

Award Fellowship for use in postgraduate years; not renewable. *Amount:* $5000.

Eligibility Requirements Applicant must be enrolled or expecting to enroll at an institution or university. Applicant or parent of applicant must be

American Academy of Child and Adolescent Psychiatry (AACAP) (continued)

member of American Academy of Child and Adolescent Psychiatry. Available to U.S. citizens.

Application Requirements Nomination. *Deadline:* June 1.

Contact Trish Brown, Director of Research and Training
American Academy of Child and Adolescent Psychiatry (AACAP)
3615 Wisconson Avenue, NW
Washington, DC 20016-3007
Phone: 202-966-7300 Ext. 113
Fax: 202-966-2891
E-mail: tbrown@aacap.org

AACAP ROBINSON/CUNNINGHAM AWARDS • 427

Award for best paper on some aspect of child and adolescent psychiatry. Paper must have been started during residency and completed within three years of graduation. Must submit manuscript by May 1. Must be an AACAP member.

Academic/Career Areas Health and Medical Sciences.

Award Fellowship for use in postgraduate years; not renewable. *Number:* 1. *Amount:* $100.

Eligibility Requirements Applicant must be enrolled or expecting to enroll at an institution or university. Applicant or parent of applicant must be member of American Academy of Child and Adolescent Psychiatry. Available to U.S. and non-U.S. citizens.

Application Requirements Manuscript. *Deadline:* May 1.

Contact Trish Brown, Director of Research and Training
American Academy of Child and Adolescent Psychiatry (AACAP)
3615 Wisconsin Avenue, NW
Washington, DC 20016-3007
Phone: 202-966-7300 Ext. 113
Fax: 202-966-2891
E-mail: tbrown@aacap.org

AACAP SIDNEY BERMAN AWARD • 428

Award to child and adolescent psychiatrist who has shown outstanding leadership in public education and about the treatment of learning disabilities. Nominations due May 1. Must be a U.S. citizen or an AACAP member.

Academic/Career Areas Health and Medical Sciences.

Award Fellowship for use in postgraduate years; not renewable. *Amount:* $5000.

Eligibility Requirements Applicant must be enrolled or expecting to enroll at an institution or university. Applicant or parent of applicant must be member of American Academy of Child and Adolescent Psychiatry. Available to U.S. citizens.

Application Requirements Nomination. *Deadline:* May 1.

Contact Trish Brown, Director of Research and Training
American Academy of Child and Adolescent Psychiatry (AACAP)
3615 Wisconsin Avenue, NW
Washington, DC 20016-3007
Phone: 202-966-7300 Ext. 113
Fax: 202-966-2891
E-mail: tbrown@aacap.org

AACAP SIMON WILE AWARD • 429

Award acknowledges outstanding leadership and continuous contributions in the field of liaison child and adolescent psychiatry. Must be a U.S. citizen or an AACAP member. AACAP members should nominate distinguished colleagues by May 1.

Academic/Career Areas Health and Medical Sciences.

Award Fellowship for use in postgraduate years; not renewable. *Number:* 1. *Amount:* $1000.

Eligibility Requirements Applicant must be enrolled or expecting to enroll at an institution or university. Applicant or parent of applicant must be member of American Academy of Child and Adolescent Psychiatry. Available to U.S. citizens.

Application Requirements Nomination. *Deadline:* May 1.

Contact Trish Brown, Director of Research and Training
American Academy of Child and Adolescent Psychiatry (AACAP)
3615 Wisconsin Avenue, NW
Washington, DC 20016-3007
Phone: 202-966-7300 Ext. 113
Fax: 202-966-2891
E-mail: tbrown@aacap.org

AMERICAN ACADEMY OF FAMILY PHYSICIANS FOUNDATION
http://www.aafp.org/aafpf/jgap.html

AMERICAN ACADEMY OF FAMILY PHYSICIANS FOUNDATION RESEARCH STIMULATION GRANT • 430

One-time grant to family practitioner for research in family medicine. Will support efforts leading to development of research project, accomplishment of specific pilot project or data accumulation leading to research project.

Academic/Career Areas Health and Medical Sciences.

Award Grant for use in graduate, or postgraduate years; not renewable. *Amount:* up to $5000.

Eligibility Requirements Applicant must be enrolled or expecting to enroll at an institution or university. Available to U.S. and Canadian citizens.

Application Requirements Application. *Deadline:* Continuous.

Contact Ms. Susie Morantz, Manager, Grants and
Awards
American Academy of Family Physicians
Foundation
11400 Tomahawk Creek Parkway, Suite
440
Leawood, KS 66211-2672
Phone: 800-274-2237 Ext. 4470
Fax: 816-906-6095
E-mail: smorantz@aafp.org

AMERICAN ACADEMY OF FAMILY PHYSICIANS FOUNDATION/AMERICAN ACADEMY OF FAMILY PHYSICIANS RESEARCH GRANT AWARDS • 431

Nonrenewable research grants in family medicine or practice. Not for educational projects. Must be individual family physicians or part of a family practice association or department. Deadlines: December 1 and June 1.

Academic/Career Areas Health and Medical Sciences.

Award Grant for use in postgraduate years; not renewable. *Amount:* up to $20,000.

Eligibility Requirements Applicant must be enrolled or expecting to enroll at an institution or university. Available to U.S. and Canadian citizens.

Application Requirements Application.

Contact Ms. Susie Morantz, Manager, Grants and
Awards
American Academy of Family Physicians
Foundation
11400 Tomahawk Creek Parkway, Suite
440
Leawood, KS 66211-2672
Phone: 800-274-2237 Ext. 4470
Fax: 816-906-6095
E-mail: smorantz@aafp.org

MEAD JOHNSON AWARDS FOR GRADUATE EDUCATION IN FAMILY PRACTICE • 432

One-time award available to second-year residency students of family practice. Must submit reference letters and forms from active members of AAFP and residency program director. Leadership and service considered. Contact for further information.

Academic/Career Areas Health and Medical Sciences.

Award Scholarship for use in graduate years; not renewable. *Number:* 20. *Amount:* $2000.

Eligibility Requirements Applicant must be enrolled or expecting to enroll at an institution or university and must have an interest in leadership. Applicant or parent of applicant must have employment or volunteer experience in community service. Available to U.S. and non-U.S. citizens.

Application Requirements Application, references. *Deadline:* March 1.

Contact Penny Pine, Program Coordinator,
Member Services Department
American Academy of Family Physicians
Foundation
11400 Tomahawk Creek Parkway
Leawood, KS 66211
Phone: 913-906-6000 Ext. 6812
Fax: 913-906-6088
E-mail: pfletche@aafp.org

PARKE-DAVIS TEACHER DEVELOPMENT AWARDS • 433

Fifteen one-time awards of $2000 for teacher development. Deadline: January 15. Contact for further information.

Academic/Career Areas Health and Medical Sciences.

Award Prize for use in postgraduate years; not renewable. *Number:* up to 15. *Amount:* $2000.

Eligibility Requirements Applicant must be enrolled or expecting to enroll at an institution or university.

Application Requirements Application, references. *Deadline:* January 15.

Contact Ms. Susie Morantz, Manager, Grants and
Awards
American Academy of Family Physicians
Foundation
11400 Tomahawk Creek Parkway, Suite
440
Leawood, KS 66211-2672
Phone: 800-274-2237 Ext. 4470
Fax: 913-906-6095
E-mail: smorantz@aafp.org

AMERICAN ASSOCIATION FOR HEALTH EDUCATION
http://www.aahperd.org/aahe

AMERICAN ASSOCIATION FOR HEALTH EDUCATION BARBARA A. COOLEY SCHOLARSHIP
• *See number 340*

AMERICAN ASSOCIATION FOR HEALTH EDUCATION DELBERT OBERTEUFFER SCHOLARSHIP
• *See number 341*

AMERICAN ASSOCIATION FOR HEALTH EDUCATION MARION B. POLLOCK FELLOWSHIP
• *See number 342*

AMERICAN ASSOCIATION OF NEUROLOGICAL SURGEONS
http://www.aans.org

AMERICAN ASSOCIATION OF NEUROLOGICAL SURGEONS WILLIAM P. VAN WAGENEN FELLOWSHIP
• **434**

The Van Wagenen Fellowship was established to provide senior neurosurgical residents in approved programs with further training in a foreign country. Awarded annually, the Fellowship provides a $40,000 stipend for study in a foreign country or countries for a period of six months.

Academic/Career Areas Health and Medical Sciences.

Award Fellowship for use in postgraduate years; not renewable. *Number:* 1. *Amount:* $40,000.

Eligibility Requirements Applicant must be enrolled or expecting to enroll at an institution or university. Available to U.S. and non-U.S. citizens.

Application Requirements Application, autobiography, resume, references. *Deadline:* October 31.

Contact Laurie Singer, Grants Coordinator
American Association of Neurological
Surgeons
5550 Meadowbrook Drive
Rolling Meadows, IL 60008-3852
Phone: 847-378-0500
Fax: 847-378-0600
E-mail: info@aans.org

NEUROSURGERY RESEARCH AND EDUCATION FOUNDATION RESEARCH FELLOWSHIP AWARD
• **435**

The Research Fellowship provides training for neurosurgeons who are preparing for academic careers as clinician investigators. Applicants must be MD's who have been accepted into, or who are in, approved residency training programs in neurological surgery in North America. The Fellowship is a two-year commitment totaling $70,000.

Academic/Career Areas Health and Medical Sciences.

Award Fellowship for use in postgraduate years; not renewable. *Number:* 1–4. *Amount:* $70,000.

Eligibility Requirements Applicant must be enrolled or expecting to enroll full or part-time at an institution or university. Available to U.S. and Canadian citizens.

Application Requirements Application, autobiography, resume, references. *Deadline:* November 30.

Contact Laurie Singer, Grants Coordinator
American Association of Neurological
Surgeons
5550 Meadowbrook Drive
Rolling Meadows, IL 60008-3852
Phone: 847-378-0500
Fax: 847-378-0600
E-mail: info@aans.org

NEUROSURGERY RESEARCH AND EDUCATION FOUNDATION YOUNG CLINICIAN INVESTIGATOR AWARD
• **436**

Applicants must be neurosurgeons who are full-time faculty in North American teaching institutions and in the early years of their careers. The purpose of the award is to fund pilot studies, providing preliminary data used to strengthen applications for permanent funding from other sources. The one-year fellowship provides $40,000.

Academic/Career Areas Health and Medical Sciences.

Award Fellowship for use in graduate years; not renewable. *Number:* 1–4. *Amount:* $40,000.

Eligibility Requirements Applicant must be enrolled or expecting to enroll full or part-time at an institution or university. Available to U.S. and Canadian citizens.

Application Requirements Application, autobiography, resume, references. *Deadline:* November 30.

Contact Laurie Singer, Grants Coordinator
American Association of Neurological
Surgeons
5550 Meadowbrook Drive
Rolling Meadows, IL 60008-3852
Phone: 847-378-0500
Fax: 847-378-0600
E-mail: info@aans.org

AMERICAN ASSOCIATION OF NEUROSCIENCE NURSES
http://www.aann.org

NEUROSCIENCE NURSING FOUNDATION RESEARCH GRANT
• **437**

Grant available to registered nurse researcher prepared at the master's or doctoral level with previous research experience. Project must be well defined and contribute knowledge to neuroscience nursing. Funds are based on quality of proposed research and NNF research fund budget.

Academic/Career Areas Health and Medical Sciences.

Award Grant for use in graduate, or postgraduate years; not renewable.

Eligibility Requirements Applicant must be enrolled or expecting to enroll at an institution or university. Applicant or parent of applicant must have employment or volunteer experience in designated career field. Available to U.S. citizens.

Application Requirements Application, proposal, loan institution proposal. *Deadline:* November 1.

Contact Grant Application Department
American Association of Neuroscience Nurses
4700 West Lake Avenue
Glenview, IL 60025-1485

NEUROSCIENCE NURSING FOUNDATION CLINICAL RESEARCH FELLOWSHIP PROGRAM
• 438

Fellowship available to begin a program of research or further develop an established program of neuroscience clinical research. Applicant must be a nurse with a doctoral degree. Previous neuroscience nursing research is required. Research is to be conducted over a two-year period.

Academic/Career Areas Health and Medical Sciences.

Award Fellowship for use in postgraduate years; not renewable.

Eligibility Requirements Applicant must be enrolled or expecting to enroll at an institution or university. Applicant or parent of applicant must have employment or volunteer experience in designated career field. Available to U.S. citizens.

Application Requirements Application, references, budget page, proposal, institutional approval. *Deadline:* February 1.

Contact Eden Essex, Manager
American Association of Neuroscience Nurses
Attn: Neuroscience Nursing Foundation
4700 West Lake Avenue
Glenview, IL 60025-1485
Phone: 888-557-2266 Ext. 4844
Fax: 847-375-6333
E-mail: info@aann.org

AMERICAN ASSOCIATION OF UNIVERSITY WOMEN (AAUW) EDUCATIONAL FOUNDATION
http://www.aauw.org

AAUW EDUCATIONAL FOUNDATION SELECTED PROFESSIONS FELLOWSHIPS
• *See number 87*

AMERICAN BRAIN TUMOR ASSOCIATION
http://www.abta.org

AMERICAN BRAIN TUMOR ASSOCIATION RESEARCH FELLOWSHIP AWARDS
• 439

Five to ten $70,000 awards (depending on funding levels), payable over a two-year period. Research must be done in the U.S. Goal is to encourage students early in their careers to enter, or remain in, the field of brain tumor research. Criteria include the quality of the applicant; the quality of the training program; and the research work undertaken. Deadline varies, always early January. Samples of previous awards are available at website. (http://www.abta.org/professionals/index.html)

Academic/Career Areas Health and Medical Sciences.

Award Fellowship for use in postgraduate years; not renewable. *Number:* 5–10. *Amount:* $70,000.

Eligibility Requirements Applicant must be enrolled or expecting to enroll full-time at an institution or university. Applicant or parent of applicant must have employment or volunteer experience in designated career field. Available to U.S. and non-U.S. citizens.

Application Requirements Application, references.

Contact Naomi Berkowitz, Executive Director
American Brain Tumor Association
2720 River Road, Suite 146
Des Plaines, IL 60018
Phone: 847-827-9910
Fax: 847-827-9918
E-mail: info@abta.org

TRANSLATIONAL RESEARCH GRANTS
• 440

One-time awards of $50,000 for post-doctorate who intends to pursue a career in brain tumor research. Must submit application. Deadline early January of each year. Samples of previous awards are available at website. (http://www.abta.org/professionals/index.html/)

Academic/Career Areas Health and Medical Sciences.

Award Grant for use in postgraduate years; not renewable. *Number:* 1–3. *Amount:* $50,000.

Eligibility Requirements Applicant must be enrolled or expecting to enroll full-time at an institution or university. Available to U.S. and non-U.S. citizens.

Application Requirements Application.

Contact Ms. Naomi Berkowitz, Executive Director
American Brain Tumor Association
2720 River Road
Des Plaines, IL 60018
Phone: 847-827-9910 Ext. 19
Fax: 847-827-9918
E-mail: info@abta.org

AMERICAN COLLEGE OF OBSTETRICIANS AND GYNECOLOGISTS
http://www.acog.org

AMERICAN COLLEGE OF OBSTETRICIANS AND GYNECOLOGISTS RESEARCH AWARD IN ADOLESCENT HEALTH • 441

One award intended to provide seed grant funds to junior investigators for clinical research in the area of adolescent health with a focus on intervention and prevention. The applicant must be an ACOG Junior Fellow or Fellow in an approved obstetrics-gynecology residency program or within 3 years postresidency.

Academic/Career Areas Health and Medical Sciences.

Award Fellowship for use in graduate, or postgraduate years; not renewable. *Number:* 1. *Amount:* $20,000.

Eligibility Requirements Applicant must be enrolled or expecting to enroll full-time at an institution or university. Available to U.S. and Canadian citizens.

Application Requirements Application, autobiography, references. *Deadline:* October 1.

Contact M. Lee Cassidy, Director of Development
American College of Obstetricians and Gynecologists
409 12th Street, SW
Washington, DC 20024-2188
Phone: 202-863-2577
Fax: 202-554-3490
E-mail: lcassidy@acog.org

AMERICAN COLLEGE OF OBSTETRICIANS AND GYNECOLOGISTS/3M PHARMACEUTICALS RESEARCH AWARD IN LOWER GENITAL INFECTIONS • 442

Two awards intended to provide seed grant funds to junior investigators for clinical research in the area of lower genital infections. Recipients will also receive funds for transportation to the ACOG Annual Clinical Meeting. Applicant must be an ACOG Junior Fellow or Fellow in an approved obstetrics-gynecology residency program or within three years post-residency. Six copies of the application prepared in NIH format should be submitted along with curriculum vitae. One-time awards of $15,000 each. One award for viral infections and one award in bacterial infections.

Academic/Career Areas Health and Medical Sciences.

Award Fellowship for use in graduate, or postgraduate years; not renewable. *Number:* 2. *Amount:* $15,000.

Eligibility Requirements Applicant must be enrolled or expecting to enroll full-time at an institution or university. Available to U.S. and Canadian citizens.

Application Requirements Application, references, curriculum vitae. *Deadline:* October 1.

Contact M. Lee Cassidy, Director of Development
American College of Obstetricians and Gynecologists
409 12th Street, SW
Washington, DC 20024-2188
Phone: 202-863-2577
Fax: 202-554-3490
E-mail: lcassidy@acog.org

AMERICAN COLLEGE OF OBSTETRICIANS AND GYNECOLOGISTS/CYTYC CORPORATION RESEARCH AWARD FOR THE PREVENTION OF CERVICAL CANCER • 443

One award intended to provide seed grant funds to junior investigators for clinical research in the area of cervical cancer prevention. The recipient will also receive funds for travel expenses to attend the ACOG Annual Clinical Meeting. The applicant must be an ACOG Junior Fellow or Fellow in an approved obstetrics-gynecology residency program or within three years post-residency. Six copies of the application in NIH format including a curriculum vitae should be submitted.

Academic/Career Areas Health and Medical Sciences.

Award Fellowship for use in graduate, or postgraduate years; not renewable. *Number:* 1. *Amount:* $15,000.

Eligibility Requirements Applicant must be enrolled or expecting to enroll full-time at an institution or university. Available to U.S. and Canadian citizens.

Application Requirements Application, references. *Deadline:* October 1.

Contact M. Lee Cassidy, Director of Development
American College of Obstetricians and Gynecologists
409 12th Street, SW
Washington, DC 20024-2188
Phone: 202-863-2577
Fax: 202-554-3490
E-mail: lcassidy@acog.org

AMERICAN COLLEGE OF OBSTETRICIANS AND GYNECOLOGISTS/ORGANON INC. RESEARCH AWARD IN CONTRACEPTION • 444

The award is intended to provide seed grant funds to junior investigators for clinical research in the area of contraception. The applicant must be an ACOG

Junior Fellow or Fellow in an approved obstetrics-gynecology residency program or within 3 years postresidency.

Academic/Career Areas Health and Medical Sciences.

Award Fellowship for use in graduate, or postgraduate years; not renewable. *Number:* 1. *Amount:* $25,000.

Eligibility Requirements Applicant must be enrolled or expecting to enroll full-time at an institution or university. Available to U.S. and Canadian citizens.

Application Requirements Application, autobiography, references. *Deadline:* October 1.

Contact M. Lee Cassidy, Director of Development
American College of Obstetricians and
Gynecologists
409 12th Street, SW
Washington, DC 20024-2188
Phone: 202-863-2577
Fax: 202-554-3490
E-mail: lcassidy@acog.org

AMERICAN COLLEGE OF OBSTETRICIANS AND GYNECOLOGISTS/ORTHO-MCNEIL ACADEMIC TRAINING FELLOWSHIPS IN OBSTETRICS AND GYNECOLOGY • 445

Two fellowships will be awarded for one year. Reapplication for an extension of funding is possible. The applicant must be a Fellow or Junior Fellow of ACOG who has completed at least one year of training and is considered by the residency program director to be especially fitted for a career in medical education or academic obstetrics and gynecology. Five copies of the application letter in NIH format should be submitted. Two one-time awards of $30,000 each.

Academic/Career Areas Health and Medical Sciences.

Award Fellowship for use in graduate, or postgraduate years; not renewable. *Number:* 2. *Amount:* $30,000.

Eligibility Requirements Applicant must be enrolled or expecting to enroll full or part-time at an institution or university. Available to U.S. and Canadian citizens.

Application Requirements Application, essay, references, curriculum vitae. *Deadline:* October 1.

Contact M. Lee Cassidy, Director of Development
American College of Obstetricians and
Gynecologists
409 12th Street, SW
Washington, DC 20024-2188
Phone: 202-863-2577
Fax: 202-554-3490
E-mail: lcassidy@acog.org

AMERICAN COLLEGE OF OBSTETRICIANS AND GYNECOLOGISTS/PHARMACIA CORPORATION RESEARCH AWARD ON OVERACTIVE BLADDER • 446

One-time award for a Fellow or Junior Fellow of the American College of Obstetricians and Gynecologists for clinical research in the area of urogynecology of the post-reproductive woman. Must be in an obstetrics-gynecology residency program or within three years of post-residency. Submit letter of support, curriculum vitae, one-page budget, and written application.

Academic/Career Areas Health and Medical Sciences.

Award Fellowship for use in graduate, or postgraduate years; not renewable. *Number:* 1. *Amount:* $15,000.

Eligibility Requirements Applicant must be enrolled or expecting to enroll full-time at an institution or university. Available to U.S. and Canadian citizens.

Application Requirements Application, references, curriculum vitae, budget, letter of support. *Deadline:* October 1.

Contact M. Lee Cassidy, Director of Development
American College of Obstetricians and
Gynecologists
409 12th Street, SW
Washington, DC 20024-2188
Phone: 202-863-2577
Fax: 202-554-3490
E-mail: lcassidy@acog.org

AMERICAN COLLEGE OF OBSTETRICIANS AND GYNECOLOGISTS/SOLVAY PHARMACEUTICALS RESEARCH AWARD IN MENOPAUSE • 447

Award for a Fellow or Junior Fellow of the American College of Obstetricians and Gynecologists to re-search menopause. Must be in an obstetrics-gynecology residency program or within three years of post-residency. Submit written application, curriculum vitae, one-page budget, letter of support, and personal data by October 1. One-time award of $25,000.

Academic/Career Areas Health and Medical Sciences.

Award Fellowship for use in graduate, or postgraduate years; not renewable. *Number:* 1. *Amount:* $25,000.

Eligibility Requirements Applicant must be enrolled or expecting to enroll full-time at an institution or university. Available to U.S. and Canadian citizens.

American College of Obstetricians and Gynecologists (continued)

Application Requirements Application, autobiography, references, curriculum vitae, budget, letter of support. *Deadline:* October 1.

Contact M. Lee Cassidy, Director of Development
American College of Obstetricians and
Gynecologists
409 12th Street, SW
Washington, DC 20024-2188
Phone: 202-863-2577
Fax: 202-554-3490
E-mail: lcassidy@acog.org

WARREN H. PEARSE/WYETH-AYERST WOMEN'S HEALTH POLICY RESEARCH AWARD • 448

Award for a Fellow or Junior Fellow of the American College of Obstetricians and Gynecologists to support research in health care policy. The research should be about an aspect of policy that either defines, assists, or restricts the ability of the physician to deliver health care to women in general or in a specific area. Covers travel expenses to attend the ACOG Annual Clinical Meeting. One-time award of $15,000. Submit curriculum vitae.

Academic/Career Areas Health and Medical Sciences.

Award Fellowship for use in graduate, or postgraduate years; not renewable. *Number:* 1. *Amount:* $15,000.

Eligibility Requirements Applicant must be enrolled or expecting to enroll full-time at an institution or university. Available to U.S. and Canadian citizens.

Application Requirements Application, references, curriculum vitae. *Deadline:* October 1.

Contact M. Lee Cassidy, Director of Development
American College of Obstetricians and
Gynecologists
409 12th Street, SW
Washington, DC 20024-2188
Phone: 202-863-2577
Fax: 202-554-3490
E-mail: lcassidy@acog.org

AMERICAN FEDERATION FOR AGING RESEARCH
http://www.afar.org

GLENN/AFAR SCHOLARSHIPS FOR RESEARCH IN THE BIOLOGY OF AGING • 449

One-time $5000 award for pre-doctoral, Ph.D., and MD students to conduct biomedical research in aging for three months. Research must be conducted under the supervision of a faculty mentor in any not-for-profit setting. Contact for application.

Academic/Career Areas Health and Medical Sciences.

Award Scholarship for use in graduate years; not renewable. *Number:* 30. *Amount:* $5000.

Eligibility Requirements Applicant must be enrolled or expecting to enroll full-time at an institution or university. Available to U.S. and Canadian citizens.

Application Requirements Application, references, test scores, transcript. *Deadline:* February 26.

Contact Odette van der Willik, Director, Grants
Program
American Federation for Aging Research
1414 Avenue of the Americas, 18th Floor
New York, NY 10019
Phone: 212-752-2327
Fax: 212-832-2298
E-mail: amfedaging@aol.com

HARTFORD /AFAR MEDICAL STUDENT GERIATRIC SCHOLARS • 450

Award to encourage medical students-particularly budding researchers-to consider geriatrics as a career. Short-term scholarships granted through a national competition. Program provides an opportunity for these students to train at an acclaimed center of excellence in geriatrics. Each scholar receives a $3,000 stipend. The deadline for receipt of application is February 7.

Academic/Career Areas Health and Medical Sciences.

Award Scholarship for use in graduate years; not renewable. *Number:* 60. *Amount:* $3000.

Eligibility Requirements Applicant must be enrolled or expecting to enroll full-time at an institution or university. Available to U.S. citizens.

Application Requirements Application, references. *Deadline:* February 7.

Contact Odette van der Willik, Director, Grant
Programs
American Federation for Aging Research
1414 Avenue of the Americas, 18th Floor
New York, NY 10019
Phone: 212-752-2327
Fax: 212-832-2298
E-mail: amfedaging@aol.com

MERCK/AMERICAN FEDERATION FOR AGING RESEARCH RESEARCH SCHOLARSHIP IN GERIATRIC PHARMACOLOGY FOR MEDICAL AND PHARMACY STUDENTS • 451

One-time award for medical and Pharm.D. students to conduct full-time research projects in geriatric pharmacology for two to three months. Must be U.S. citizen or permanent resident. Include references with application.

Academic/Career Areas Health and Medical Sciences.

Award Scholarship for use in graduate years; not renewable. *Number:* 9. *Amount:* $4000.

Eligibility Requirements Applicant must be enrolled or expecting to enroll full-time at an institution or university. Available to U.S. citizens.

Application Requirements Application, references. *Deadline:* January 22.

Contact Odette van der Willik, Director, Grant
Programs and Program Officer
American Federation for Aging Research
1414 Avenue of the Americas, 18th Floor
New York, NY 10019
Phone: 212-752-2327
Fax: 212-832-2298
E-mail: amfedaging@aol.com

AMERICAN FOUNDATION FOR UROLOGIC DISEASE, INC.
http://www.afud.org

AFUD/AUA HEALTH POLICY RESEARCH PROGRAM
• *See number 407*

AFUD/AUA MD POST RESIDENT RESEARCH PROGRAM • 452

Award for urologist within five years of finishing residency. Must be committed to research career and submit evidence of research accomplishments. Two years in program required. Must spend 80% of time on research project to continue funding. Application must state how time will be allocated. Experience should prepare scholar to obtain independent research grant support.

Academic/Career Areas Health and Medical Sciences.

Award Scholarship for use in postgraduate years; not renewable. *Number:* 1–10. *Amount:* $30,000.

Eligibility Requirements Applicant must be enrolled or expecting to enroll at an institution or university. Available to U.S. and non-U.S. citizens.

Application Requirements Application, resume, references. *Deadline:* September 1.

Contact Kym Liddick, Director of Research
Program
American Foundation for Urologic
Disease, Inc.
1128 North Charles Street
Baltimore, MD 21201
Phone: 410-468-1812
Fax: 410-468-1808
E-mail: kym@afud.org

AFUD/AUA PH.D. POST DOCTORAL RESEARCH PROGRAM • 453

Available to postdoctoral basic scientists with research interests in urologic or related diseases and dysfunc-

tions. A commitment to dedicate two years in the AFUD/Ph.D. program as a full-time researcher is required.

Academic/Career Areas Health and Medical Sciences.

Award Scholarship for use in postgraduate years; not renewable. *Number:* 5–20. *Amount:* $30,000.

Eligibility Requirements Applicant must be enrolled or expecting to enroll full-time at an institution or university. Available to U.S. and non-U.S. citizens.

Application Requirements Application, resume, references. *Deadline:* September 1.

Contact Kym Liddick, Director of Research
Program
American Foundation for Urologic
Disease, Inc.
1128 North Charles Street
Baltimore, MD 21201
Phone: 410-468-1812
Fax: 410-468-1808
E-mail: kym@afud.org

AFUD/AUA PRACTICING UROLOGIST RESEARCH AWARD • 454

Available to practicing urologists with research ideas suitable for collaborative investigations at an established urology research laboratory. This award is designed to fund urologists practicing in a clinical practice that are not affiliated with a university.

Academic/Career Areas Health and Medical Sciences.

Award Fellowship for use in postgraduate years; not renewable. *Number:* 1–5. *Amount:* $10,000.

Eligibility Requirements Applicant must be enrolled or expecting to enroll at an institution or university. Available to U.S. and non-U.S. citizens.

Application Requirements Application, resume, references, research proposal, curriculum vitae. *Deadline:* September 1.

Contact Kym Liddick, Director of Research
Program
American Foundation for Urologic
Disease, Inc.
1128 North Charles Street
Baltimore, MD 21201
Phone: 410-468-1812
Fax: 410-468-1808
E-mail: kym@afud.org

MD/PH.D. ONE YEAR RESEARCH PROGRAM • 455

Fellowship program for urologists who have completed their residency within five years of date of application. Program provides for one year of full-time investigation in laboratory research of

American Foundation for Urologic Disease, Inc. (continued)

urologic diseases. It is not intended to fund a urology resident for a year of laboratory research either before or during residency training.

Academic/Career Areas Health and Medical Sciences.

Award Scholarship for use in postgraduate years; not renewable. *Number:* 5–10. *Amount:* $25,000.

Eligibility Requirements Applicant must be enrolled or expecting to enroll full-time at an institution or university. Available to U.S. and non-U.S. citizens.

Application Requirements Application, resume, references, research proposal, curriculum vitae. *Deadline:* September 1.

Contact Kym Liddick, Director of Research
    Program
    American Foundation for Urologic
    Disease, Inc.
    1128 North Charles Street
    Baltimore, MD 21201
    Phone: 410-468-1812
    Fax: 410-468-1808
    E-mail: kym@afud.org

NATIONAL INSTITUTE OF DIABETES, DIGESTIVE AND KIDNEY DISEASES/AFUD INTRAMURAL UROLOGY RESEARCH TRAINING PROGRAM • 456

Award for urologists with less than five years postdoctoral research experience not including clinical residency training. Provides opportunity to complete research project under senior investigator in Intramural Program of NIDDK or NCI. Provides intensive exposure to research experience using basic molecular cellular biologic techniques in urology. Applicants may be physicians in urology residency programs or have recently completed urology residency. Send duplicate application to: Dr. Leroy M. Nyberg, Director Urology Program, Division of Kidney, Urology, Hematology, NIDDC, Natcher Building, Room 6AS13D, Bethesda, MD 20892.

Academic/Career Areas Health and Medical Sciences.

Award Scholarship for use in postgraduate years; renewable. *Number:* 2. *Amount:* $45,000–$52,000.

Eligibility Requirements Applicant must be enrolled or expecting to enroll at an institution or university. Available to U.S. and non-U.S. citizens.

Application Requirements Resume, references, cover letter. *Deadline:* Continuous.

Contact Kym Liddick, Director of Research
    Program
    American Foundation for Urologic
    Disease, Inc.
    1128 North Charles Street
    Baltimore, MD 21201
    Phone: 410-468-1812
    Fax: 410-468-1808
    E-mail: kym@afud.org

NCI/AFUD INTRAMURAL UROLOGIC ONCOLOGY PH.D./POST DOCTORAL RESEARCH TRAINING PROGRAM • 457

This program is designed to train Ph.D. postdoctoral scientists in the growing field of urologic oncology. The program provides an opportunity for selected individuals to complete a research project under the direction of a Senior Investigator in the Intramural Program of the National Cancer Institute. Duplicate application must be sent to: Dr. W. Marston Linehan, Chief, Urologic Oncology Branch, National Cancer Institute, Building 10, Room 2B47, 10 Center Drive, MSC 1501, Bethesda, MD 20892-1501.

Academic/Career Areas Health and Medical Sciences.

Award Fellowship for use in postgraduate years; not renewable. *Amount:* $28,700–$35,900.

Eligibility Requirements Applicant must be enrolled or expecting to enroll at an institution or university. Available to U.S. and non-U.S. citizens.

Application Requirements Resume, references, cover letter, curriculum vitae. *Deadline:* Continuous.

Contact Kym Liddick, Director of Research
    Program
    American Foundation for Urologic
    Disease, Inc.
    1128 North Charles Street
    Baltimore, MD 21201
    Phone: 410-468-1812
    Fax: 410-468-1808
    E-mail: kym@afud.org

NCI/AFUD INTRAMURAL UROLOGIC ONCOLOGY RESEARCH TRAINING PROGRAM • 458

This program is designed to train urologic surgeons committed to academic careers in urologic oncology. Aims to instruct urologic oncologists in a combined modality approach to the treatment of urologic cancer patients including surgical treatment, chemotherapy, immunotherapy; and to provide a solid basis for the direct conduct of clinical and laboratory research. Duplicate application must be sent to: Dr. W. Marston Linehan, Chief, Urologic Oncology

Branch, National Cancer Institute, Building 10, Room 2B47, 10 Center Drive, MSC 1501, Bethesda, MD 20892-1501.

Academic/Career Areas Health and Medical Sciences.

Award Fellowship for use in postgraduate years; renewable. *Number:* up to 4. *Amount:* $52,000–$58,000.

Eligibility Requirements Applicant must be enrolled or expecting to enroll at an institution or university. Available to U.S. and non-U.S. citizens.

Application Requirements Resume, references, cover letter, curriculum vitae. *Deadline:* Continuous.

Contact Kym Liddick, Director of Research
　　　　　Program
　　　　　American Foundation for Urologic
　　　　　Disease, Inc.
　　　　　1128 North Charles Street
　　　　　Baltimore, MD 21201
　　　　　Phone: 410-468-1812
　　　　　Fax: 410-468-1808
　　　　　E-mail: kym@afud.org

AMERICAN HEART ASSOCIATION, MID-ATLANTIC RESEARCH CONSORTIUM
http://www.americanheart.org

MID-ATLANTIC AFFILIATE BEGINNING GRANT-IN-AID • 459

Annual $66,000 awards for MD, Ph.D., D.O., or equivalent initiating independent research careers in cardiovascular areas. Two-year award; applicant may apply for only one year. Awardees who have more than $100,000 of research support remaining from other sources are ineligible. Contact for application procedures and more information.

Academic/Career Areas Health and Medical Sciences.

Award Grant for use in postgraduate years; not renewable. *Number:* 20–25. *Amount:* $66,000–$132,000.

Eligibility Requirements Applicant must be enrolled or expecting to enroll at an institution or university and studying in District of Columbia, Maryland, North Carolina, South Carolina, or Virginia. Available to U.S. and non-U.S. citizens.

Application Requirements Application. *Deadline:* January 17.

Contact Mid-Atlantic Research Consortium
　　　　　American Heart Association, Mid-Atlantic
　　　　　Research Consortium
　　　　　415 North Charles Street
　　　　　Baltimore, MD 21201
　　　　　Phone: 410-685-7074
　　　　　Fax: 410-468-4219

MID-ATLANTIC AFFILIATE GRANT-IN-AID • 460

Two-year ($66,000 annually) award for faculty/staff of any rank, pursuing independent research broadly related to cardiovascular function and disease, stroke, or related clinical, basic science, behavioral, and public health problems. May not hold another AHA award concurrently. Contact for application procedures and further information.

Academic/Career Areas Health and Medical Sciences.

Award Grant for use in postgraduate years; not renewable. *Amount:* $66,000–$132,000.

Eligibility Requirements Applicant must be enrolled or expecting to enroll at an institution or university and studying in District of Columbia, Maryland, North Carolina, South Carolina, or Virginia. Available to U.S. and non-U.S. citizens.

Application Requirements Application. *Deadline:* January 17.

Contact Mid-Atlantic Research Consortium
　　　　　American Heart Association, Mid-Atlantic
　　　　　Research Consortium
　　　　　415 North Charles Street
　　　　　Baltimore, MD 21201
　　　　　Phone: 410-685-7074
　　　　　Fax: 410-468-4219

MID-ATLANTIC AFFILIATE PREDOCTORAL FELLOWSHIP AWARD • 461

Two-year stipend support of $12,000 per year, plus 10% fringe benefits ($1,200), plus $5,000 project support annually. Pre-doctoral M.D., Ph.D., D.O., or equivalent students seeking research training with a sponsor/mentor prior to embarking on a research career.

Academic/Career Areas Health and Medical Sciences.

Award Fellowship for use in graduate, or postgraduate years; not renewable. *Number:* 10–20. *Amount:* $18,200–$36,400.

Eligibility Requirements Applicant must be enrolled or expecting to enroll full-time at an institution or university and studying in District of Columbia, Maryland, North Carolina, South Carolina, or Virginia. Available to U.S. and non-U.S. citizens.

Application Requirements Application, transcript, must have a sponsor/mentor prior to applying. *Deadline:* January 17.

Contact Mid-Atlantic Research Consortium
　　　　　American Heart Association, Mid-Atlantic
　　　　　Research Consortium
　　　　　415 North Charles Street
　　　　　Baltimore, MD 21201
　　　　　Phone: 410-685-7074

PENNSYLVANIA-DELAWARE AFFILIATE BEGINNING GRANT-IN-AID • 462

Two-year ($50,000 annually) award for MD, Ph.D., D.O. or equivalent independent research careers. Research should be broadly related to cardiovascular function and disease, stroke, or to related clinical, basic science, behavioral, and public health problems. Scientists receiving $250,000 (direct cost) per fiscal year of research support from other sources are ineligible. Contact for application procedures and more information.

Academic/Career Areas Health and Medical Sciences.

Award Grant for use in postgraduate years; not renewable. *Amount:* $50,000–$100,000.

Eligibility Requirements Applicant must be enrolled or expecting to enroll at an institution or university and studying in Delaware or Pennsylvania. Available to U.S. and non-U.S. citizens.

Application Requirements Application. *Deadline:* January 17.

Contact Mid-Atlantic Research Consortium
American Heart Association, Mid-Atlantic
Research Consortium
415 North Charles Street
Baltimore, MD 21201
Phone: 410-685-7074
Fax: 410-468-4219

PENNSYLVANIA-DELAWARE AFFILIATE GRANT-IN-AID • 463

Two-year ($50,000 annually) award for full-time faculty/staff of any rank pursuing independent research broadly related to cardiovascular function and disease, stroke, or related clinical, basic science, behavioral, and public health problems. Must hold MD, Ph.D., DO or equivalent degree. Scientists receiving $300,000 (direct cost) per fiscal year of research support from other sources are ineligible. Contact for application procedures and more information.

Academic/Career Areas Health and Medical Sciences.

Award Grant for use in postgraduate years; not renewable. *Amount:* $50,000–$100,000.

Eligibility Requirements Applicant must be enrolled or expecting to enroll at an institution or university and studying in Delaware or Pennsylvania. Available to U.S. and non-U.S. citizens.

Application Requirements Application. *Deadline:* January 17.

Contact Mid-Atlantic Research Consortium
American Heart Association, Mid-Atlantic
Research Consortium
415 North Charles Street
Baltimore, MD 21201
Phone: 410-685-7074
Fax: 410-468-4219

PENNSYLVANIA-DELAWARE AFFILIATE POSTDOCTORAL FELLOWSHIP • 464

Two-year ($36,000 annually) award for individuals before they are ready for fully independent research. Must have M.D., Ph.D., D.O., or equivalent when fellowship is awarded. Not intended for individuals of faculty rank. May not hold another AHA award concurrently. Option to apply for a third year. Contact for application procedures, deadline, and further information.

Academic/Career Areas Health and Medical Sciences.

Award Fellowship for use in postgraduate years; not renewable. *Amount:* $36,000–$72,000.

Eligibility Requirements Applicant must be enrolled or expecting to enroll full-time at an institution or university and studying in Delaware or Pennsylvania. Available to U.S. and non-U.S. citizens.

Application Requirements Application. *Deadline:* January 17.

Contact Mid-Atlantic Research Consortium
American Heart Association, Mid-Atlantic
Research Consortium
415 North Charles Street
Baltimore, MD 21201
Phone: 410-685-7074
Fax: 410-468-4219

PENNSYLVANIA-DELAWARE AFFILIATE PREDOCTORAL FELLOWSHIP • 465

Three-month to two year stipend with annual maximum of $20,000. Pre-doctoral M.D., Ph.D., D.O, or equivalent students seeking research training with a sponsor/mentor prior to embarking on a research career.

Academic/Career Areas Health and Medical Sciences.

Award Fellowship for use in postgraduate years; not renewable. *Number:* 10–20. *Amount:* $20,000–$40,000.

Eligibility Requirements Applicant must be enrolled or expecting to enroll full-time at a four-year institution or university and studying in Delaware or Pennsylvania. Available to U.S. and non-U.S. citizens.

Application Requirements Application, transcript, must have sponsor/mentor before applying. *Deadline:* January 17.

Contact Mid-Atlantic Research Consortium
American Heart Association, Mid-Atlantic Research Consortium
415 North Charles Street
Baltimore, MD 21201

AMERICAN INSTITUTE OF THE HISTORY OF PHARMACY
http://www.aihp.org

GRADUATE STUDENT GRANTS-IN-AID IN HISTORY OF PHARMACY • 466

Must be enrolled in a master's or Ph.D. program in a U.S. college or university. Dissertation topic must be related to history of pharmacy or drugs. One-time award of up to $5000.

Academic/Career Areas Health and Medical Sciences; History.

Award Grant for use in graduate, or postgraduate years; not renewable. *Amount:* up to $5000.

Eligibility Requirements Applicant must be enrolled or expecting to enroll at a four-year institution or university. Available to U.S. citizens.

Application Requirements Application. *Deadline:* February 1.

Contact Beth Fisher, Program Manager
American Institute of the History of Pharmacy
777 Highland Avenue
Madison, WI 53705-2222
Phone: 608-262-5378
E-mail: info@aihp.org

AMERICAN LIVER FOUNDATION
http://www.liverfoundation.org

AMERICAN LIVER FOUNDATION POSTDOCTORAL RESEARCH FELLOWSHIPS
• *See number 183*

LIVER SCHOLAR AWARDS
• *See number 184*

AMERICAN OPTOMETRIC FOUNDATION
http://www.ezell.org

BIOCOMPATIBLES EYECARE INNOVATIVE RESEARCH AWARDS • 467

The Biocampatibles Research Awards are for research which expands or explores the current body of knowledge in the field of contact lenses and associated technology.

Academic/Career Areas Health and Medical Sciences.

Award Prize for use in graduate, or postgraduate years; not renewable. *Number:* 1–17. *Amount:* $2000–$5000.

Eligibility Requirements Applicant must be enrolled or expecting to enroll full-time at an institution or university. Available to U.S. and non-U.S. citizens.

Application Requirements Application, essay. *Deadline:* March 1.

Contact Christine Armstrong, Foundation Director
American Optometric Foundation
6110 Executive Boulevard, Suite 506
Rockville, MD 20852
Phone: 301-984-4734
Fax: 301-984-4737
E-mail: christine@aaoptom.org

GLENN A. FRY LECTURE AWARD • 468

This award is given to an outstanding vision scientist for significant work in the preceding year. Chosen by the American Academy of Optometry, the Glenn A. Fry lecturer is a featured speaker at the annual AAO meeting.

Academic/Career Areas Health and Medical Sciences.

Award Prize for use in postgraduate years; not renewable. *Number:* 1. *Amount:* $2500.

Eligibility Requirements Applicant must be enrolled or expecting to enroll full-time at an institution or university. Applicant or parent of applicant must have employment or volunteer experience in designated career field. Available to U.S. and non-U.S. citizens.

Application Requirements Autobiography, essay, references, transcript. *Deadline:* Continuous.

Contact Christine Armstrong, Foundation Director
American Optometric Foundation
6110 Executive Boulevard, Suite 506
Rockville, MD 20852
Phone: 301-984-4734
Fax: 301-984-4737
E-mail: christine@aaoptom.org

VISTAKON AWARD OF EXCELLENCE IN CONTACT LENS PATIENT CARE • 469

Open to any fourth-year student attending any school or college of optometry. Must have 3.0 GPA. Student's knowledge of subject matter and skillful, professional clinical contact lens patient care are considered. School makes selection and sends application to AOF.

Academic/Career Areas Health and Medical Sciences.

Award Scholarship for use in graduate years; not renewable. *Number:* 19. *Amount:* $1000.

American Optometric Foundation (continued)

Eligibility Requirements Applicant must be enrolled or expecting to enroll full-time at an institution or university. Applicant must have 3.0 GPA or higher. Available to U.S. and non-U.S. citizens.

Application Requirements References. *Deadline:* Continuous.

Contact Christine Armstrong, Foundation Director
American Optometric Foundation
6110 Executive Boulevard, Suite 506
Rockville, MD 20852
Phone: 301-984-4734
Fax: 301-984-4737
E-mail: christine@aaoptom.org

VISTAKON RESEARCH GRANTS • **470**

Two grants are awarded to optometrists or vision scientists to fund basic or clinical research in the area of soft disposable contact lenses. Submit proposal.

Academic/Career Areas Health and Medical Sciences.

Award Grant for use in graduate, or postgraduate years; not renewable. *Number:* 2. *Amount:* $10,000–$25,000.

Eligibility Requirements Applicant must be enrolled or expecting to enroll full or part-time at an institution or university. Applicant or parent of applicant must have employment or volunteer experience in designated career field. Available to U.S. and non-U.S. citizens.

Application Requirements Essay, financial need analysis, proposal on research topic. *Deadline:* August 1.

Contact Christine Armstrong, Foundation Director
American Optometric Foundation
6110 Executive Boulevard, Suite 506
Rockville, MD 20852
Phone: 301-984-4734
Fax: 301-984-4737
E-mail: christine@aacptom.org

WILLIAM C. EZELL FELLOWSHIP
• *See number 31*

AMERICAN PHYSIOLOGICAL SOCIETY
http://www.faseb.org/aps

CAROLINE TUM SUDEN/FRANCES A. HELLEBRANDT PROFESSIONAL OPPORTUNITY AWARD
• *See number 186*

PORTER PHYSIOLOGY FELLOWSHIPS
• *See number 187*

PROCTER AND GAMBLE PROFESSIONAL OPPORTUNITY AWARD
• *See number 188*

AMERICAN PSYCHIATRIC ASSOCIATION
http://www.psych.org

AMERICAN PSYCHIATRIC ASSOCIATION/ASTRA ZENECA MINORITY FELLOWSHIP PROGRAM • **471**

Two-year psychiatric fellowship provides means to engage in or expand activities that address culturally relevant aspects of mental health during recipient's second year of residency training. Fellows are assigned to work with an APA component that is of particular interest. Award covers travel expenses to APA meeting in September, the annual meeting in May, and other component-related meetings as appropriate. Fellows are selected on the basis of their commitment to serve underrepresented populations, their demonstrated leadership abilities, and their interest in the interrelationship between mental health/illness and trans-cultural factors. Must be U.S. citizen or permanent resident. Submit curriculum vitae. Contact for application packet and deadline information.

Academic/Career Areas Health and Medical Sciences.

Award Fellowship for use in postgraduate years; not renewable. *Number:* 10.

Eligibility Requirements Applicant must be enrolled or expecting to enroll full-time at an institution or university and must have an interest in leadership. Available to U.S. citizens.

Application Requirements Application, essay, interview, references, transcript, curriculum vitae. *Deadline:* January 31.

Contact Marilyn M. King, Program Manager
American Psychiatric Association
Office of Minority/National Affairs, 1400
K Street NW
Washington, DC 20005
Phone: 202-682-6096
Fax: 202-682-6837
E-mail: mking@psych.org

AMERICAN PSYCHIATRIC ASSOCIATION/CENTER FOR MENTAL HEALTH SERVICES MINORITY FELLOWSHIP PROGRAM • **472**

One-time award for psychiatric residents interested in areas of psychiatry where minority groups are underrepresented. Fellows are selected on the basis of their commitment to serve underrepresented populations, their demonstrated leadership abilities, and their interest in the interrelationship between mental health or illness and transcultural factors. Must be in at least second year of postgraduate training. Must be

U.S. citizen or permanent resident. Submit curriculum vitae. Number of awards varies.

Academic/Career Areas Health and Medical Sciences.

Award Fellowship for use in postgraduate years; not renewable. *Number:* 10.

Eligibility Requirements Applicant must be enrolled or expecting to enroll full-time at an institution or university. Available to U.S. citizens.

Application Requirements Application, essay, interview, references, transcript, curriculum vitae. *Deadline:* January 31.

Contact Marilyn M. King, Program Manager
American Psychiatric Association
Office of the Minority/National Affairs,
1400 K Street NW
Washington, DC 20005
Phone: 202-682-6096
Fax: 202-682-6837
E-mail: mking@psych.org

AMERICAN PSYCHOLOGICAL ASSOCIATION
http://www.apa.org/mfp

MINORITY FELLOWSHIP FOR HIV/AIDS RESEARCH TRAINING • 473

Renewable award for U.S. citizen or permanent resident enrolled full-time in doctoral program in psychology. Must be an ethnic minority member or committed to a career as a research scientist on HIV/AIDS issues related to ethnic minority mental health. Application is available at website.

Academic/Career Areas Health and Medical Sciences; Social Sciences.

Award Fellowship for use in graduate years; renewable.

Eligibility Requirements Applicant must be enrolled or expecting to enroll full-time at an institution or university. Available to U.S. citizens.

Application Requirements Application, essay, financial need analysis, references, transcript. *Deadline:* January 15.

Contact Dr. Kim Nickerson, Program Assistant
Director
American Psychological Association
750 First Street, NE
Washington, DC 20002-4242
Phone: 202-336-6027
Fax: 202-336-6012
E-mail: mpf@apa.org

MINORITY FELLOWSHIP FOR NEUROSCIENCE TRAINING
• *See number 189*

MINORITY FELLOWSHIP IN MENTAL HEALTH AND SUBSTANCE ABUSE SERVICES • 474

Renewable award for U.S. citizen or permanent resident enrolled full-time in APA-accredited doctoral program in psychology. Must be ethnic minority underrepresented in field or show commitment to career in psychology related to ethnic minority populations. Application available at website.

Academic/Career Areas Health and Medical Sciences; Social Sciences.

Award Fellowship for use in graduate years; renewable.

Eligibility Requirements Applicant must be enrolled or expecting to enroll full-time at an institution or university. Available to U.S. citizens.

Application Requirements Application, essay, financial need analysis, references, transcript. *Deadline:* January 15.

Contact Dr. Kim Nickerson, Program Assistant
Director
American Psychological Association
750 First Street, NE
Washington, DC 20002-4242
Phone: 202-336-6027
Fax: 202-336-6012
E-mail: mfp@apa.org

AMERICAN RESPIRATORY CARE FOUNDATION
http://www.aarc.org

GLAXO SMITH KLINE FELLOWSHIP FOR ASTHMA MANAGEMENT EDUCATION • 475

One-year fellowship to complete a project in asthma education. Application can be no more than twenty pages and must detail proposed project, budget, and resources. Prefer issues of asthma education, self management, and awareness. One-time award of $3500.

Academic/Career Areas Health and Medical Sciences; Nursing; Therapy/Rehabilitation.

Award Fellowship for use in graduate years; not renewable. *Number:* 1. *Amount:* $3500.

Eligibility Requirements Applicant must be enrolled or expecting to enroll at an institution or university. Available to U.S. and non-U.S. citizens.

Application Requirements Application, references, proposal/abstract.

Contact Diane Shearer, Administrative Coordinator
American Respiratory Care Foundation
11030 Ables Lane
Dallas, TX 75229-4593
Phone: 972-243-2272
Fax: 972-484-2720
E-mail: info@aarc.org

H. FREDERIC HELMHOLZ, JR., MD, EDUCATIONAL RESEARCH FUND • 476

Research grant for educational or credentialing research, master's thesis, or doctoral dissertation with practical value to the respiratory care profession. Prescribed proposal format. Write for deadlines. One-time award of up to $3000.

Academic/Career Areas Health and Medical Sciences; Therapy/Rehabilitation.

Award Grant for use in graduate, or postgraduate years; not renewable. *Amount:* up to $3000.

Eligibility Requirements Applicant must be enrolled or expecting to enroll at an institution or university. Available to U.S. and non-U.S. citizens.

Application Requirements Application, references.

Contact Diane Shearer, Administrative Coordinator
American Respiratory Care Foundation
11030 Ables Lane
Dallas, TX 75229-4593
Phone: 972-243-2272
Fax: 972-484-2720
E-mail: info@aarc.org

MONAGHAN/TRUDELL FELLOWSHIP FOR AEROSOL TECHNIQUE DEVELOPMENT
• See number 376

NBRC/A&P GARETT B. GISH, MS, RRT MEMORIAL POSTGRADUATE EDUCATION RECOGNITION AWARD • 477

Award to graduate student enrolled in an accredited degree program in respiratory care. Minimum 3.0 GPA is required. One-time award of $1500. Deadline: May 31.

Academic/Career Areas Health and Medical Sciences; Therapy/Rehabilitation.

Award Prize for use in graduate years; not renewable. *Number:* 1. *Amount:* $1500.

Eligibility Requirements Applicant must be enrolled or expecting to enroll full or part-time at an institution or university. Applicant must have 3.0 GPA or higher.

Application Requirements Application, essay, references, transcript. *Deadline:* May 31.

Contact Diane Shearer, Administrative Coordinator
American Respiratory Care Foundation
11030 Ables Lane
Dallas, TX 75229-4593
Phone: 972-243-2272
Fax: 972-484-2720
E-mail: info@aarc.org

RESPIRONICS FELLOWSHIP IN MECHANICAL VENTILATION
• See number 32

RESPIRONICS FELLOWSHIP IN NON-INVASIVE RESPIRATORY CARE • 478

Fellowship designed to foster projects dealing with non-invasive techniques to provide ventilatory support. Detail project in no more than twenty pages. Project can be device development or evaluation, cost effect analysis, or education program. Award of $1000, plus airfare, one night's lodging, and registration at AARC annual convention.

Academic/Career Areas Health and Medical Sciences; Therapy/Rehabilitation.

Award Fellowship for use in graduate years; not renewable. *Number:* 1. *Amount:* $1000.

Eligibility Requirements Applicant must be enrolled or expecting to enroll at an institution or university. Available to U.S. and non-U.S. citizens.

Application Requirements Application, references, project proposal. *Deadline:* May 31.

Contact Diane Shearer, Administrative Coordinator
American Respiratory Care Foundation
11030 Ables Lane
Dallax, TX 75229-4593
Phone: 972-243-2272
Fax: 972-484-2720
E-mail: info@aarc.org

WILLIAM F. MILLER, MD POSTGRADUATE EDUCATION RECOGNITION AWARD • 479

Award available to a respiratory care practitioner who has at least a baccalaureate degree with a minimum 3.0 GPA. Must be accepted into an advanced degree program and submit proof of acceptance. One-time award of $1500, plus airfare, one night's lodging, and registration for AARC International Respiratory Congress.

Academic/Career Areas Health and Medical Sciences; Therapy/Rehabilitation.

Award Prize for use in graduate years; not renewable. *Number:* 1. *Amount:* $1500.

Eligibility Requirements Applicant must be enrolled or expecting to enroll full or part-time at an institution or university. Applicant or parent of applicant must have employment or volunteer experience in designated career field. Applicant must have 3.0 GPA or higher. Available to U.S. and non-U.S. citizens.

Application Requirements Application, essay, references, transcript. *Deadline:* May 31.

Contact Diane Shearer, Administrative Coordinator
American Respiratory Care Foundation
11030 Ables Lane
Dallas, TX 75229-4593
Phone: 972-243-2272
Fax: 972-484-2720
E-mail: info@aarc.org

AMERICAN SOCIETY FOR MICROBIOLOGY
http://www.asmusa.org/

AMERICAN SOCIETY FOR MICROBIOLOGY/NCID POSTDOCTORAL RESEARCH PROGRAM
• *See number 190*

AMERICAN WATER WORKS ASSOCIATION
http://www.awwa.org

AMERICAN WATER WORKS ASSOCIATION/ LARSON AQUATIC RESEARCH SUPPORT SCHOLARSHIP
• *See number 46*

AMERICAN WATER WORKS ASSOCIATION/ THOMAS R. CAMP MEMORIAL SCHOLARSHIP
• *See number 47*

ARMENIAN RELIEF SOCIETY OF NORTH AMERICA INC.-REGIONAL OFFICE

ARMENIAN RELIEF SOCIETY GRADUATE SCHOLARSHIP PROGRAM
• *See number 224*

BLUE CROSS BLUE SHIELD OF MICHIGAN FOUNDATION
http://www.bcbsm.com/foundation

BLUE CROSS BLUE SHIELD OF MICHIGAN FOUNDATION STUDENT AWARD PROGRAM
• *See number 393*

CANADIAN BLOOD SERVICES
http://www.bloodservices.ca

CANADIAN BLOOD SERVICES POSTDOCTORAL FELLOWSHIP AWARD • **480**

Program fosters transfusion science careers in Canada. Two-year award. Includes salary, research allowance and benefits plan. Must hold a recent Ph.D., M.D., D.D.S., D.V.M., or equivalent. Must select and contact a Canadian Blood Services affiliated scientist to serve as Postdoctoral Fellowship supervisor. See website for more information. (http://www.bloodservices.ca)

Academic/Career Areas Health and Medical Sciences.

Award Fellowship for use in postgraduate years; renewable. *Number:* 1–6. *Amount:* $20,000.

Eligibility Requirements Applicant must be enrolled or expecting to enroll full-time at an institution or university. Available to U.S. and non-U.S. citizens.

Application Requirements Application, resume, references, transcript. *Deadline:* July 1.

Contact Cilla Perry, Manager of Research and Development
Canadian Blood Services
1800 Alta Vista Drive
Ottawa, ON K1G 4J5
Canada
Phone: 613-739-2408
Fax: 613-739-2426
E-mail: cilla.perry@bloodservices.ca

TRANSFUSION MEDICINE FELLOWSHIP AWARD • **481**

Two awards for physicians who are Canadian citizens or landed immigrants to acquire training for two years in transfusion medicine at a Canadian Blood Services Centre. Candidates must be in final year of preparation for certifying examinations by the Royal College of Physicians and Surgeons, or should be newly qualified in a specialty of the Royal College. One-time award of Can$54,000-Can$65,000.

Academic/Career Areas Health and Medical Sciences.

Award Fellowship for use in graduate, or postgraduate years; not renewable. *Number:* 2. *Amount:* $54,000–$65,000.

Eligibility Requirements Applicant must be Canadian citizenship; enrolled or expecting to enroll full-time at an institution or university; resident of Alberta, British Columbia, Manitoba, New Foundland, North Brunswick, North West Territories, Nova Scotia, Ontario, Prince Edward Island, Quebec, Saskatchewan, or Yukon and studying in Alberta, British Columbia, Manitoba, New Foundland, North Brunswick, North West Territories, Nova Scotia, Ontario, Prince Edward Island, Quebec, Saskatchewan, or Yukon.

Canadian Blood Services (continued)

Application Requirements Application, autobiography, references. *Deadline:* February 1.

Contact Cilla Perry, Manager of Research and Development
Canadian Blood Services
1800 Alta Vista Drive
Ottawa, ON K1G 4J5
Canada
Phone: 613-739-2408
Fax: 613-739-2201
E-mail: cilla.perry@bloodservices.ca

CANADIAN SOCIETY FOR MEDICAL LABORATORY SCIENCE
http://www.csmls.org

CANADIAN SOCIETY FOR MEDICAL LABORATORY SCIENCE FOUNDERS' FUND AWARDS
• *See number 408*

CENTER FOR RURAL HEALTH INITIATIVES- TEXAS
http://www.crhi.state.tx.us

TEXAS HEALTH SERVICE CORPS PROGRAM • 482

Program providing stipends for primary care residents who agree to practice in rural Texas counties upon completion of residency program. Must provide medical school diploma.

Academic/Career Areas Health and Medical Sciences.

Award Grant for use in postgraduate years; renewable. *Number:* 3–4. *Amount:* $50,000.

Eligibility Requirements Applicant must be enrolled or expecting to enroll full-time at an institution or university; resident of Texas and studying in Texas.

Application Requirements Application. *Deadline:* March 30.

Contact Susan Kolliopoulos, Program Administrator
Center for Rural Health Initiatives- Texas
PO Drawer 1708
Austin, TX 78767-1708
Phone: 512-479-8891
Fax: 512-479-8898
E-mail: crhi@crhi.state.tx.us

CHINESE AMERICAN MEDICAL SOCIETY (CAMS)
http://www.camsociety.org

CHINESE AMERICAN MEDICAL SOCIETY SCHOLARSHIP
• *See number 285*

COUNCIL ON SOCIAL WORK EDUCATION
http://www.cswe.org

COUNCIL ON SOCIAL WORK EDUCATION/ MENTAL HEALTH MINORITY RESEARCH FELLOWSHIP • 483

Renewable award for full-time graduate minority students with master's in social work to help obtain a doctoral degree and master research skills. Must be interested in a mental health research career. Must have minimum 3.0 GPA. Must be American citizen or have permanent resident status. Monthly stipends defray living expenses. Tuition support provided using the NIH formula. 100% up to $3000 and 60% of balance.

Academic/Career Areas Health and Medical Sciences; Social Sciences; Social Services.

Award Fellowship for use in graduate years; renewable. *Number:* 10–20. *Amount:* $1255–$3000.

Eligibility Requirements Applicant must be American Indian/Alaska Native, Asian/Pacific Islander, Black (non-Hispanic), or Hispanic and enrolled or expecting to enroll full-time at an institution or university. Applicant must have 3.0 GPA or higher. Available to U.S. citizens.

Application Requirements Application, autobiography, essay, financial need analysis, references, test scores, transcript. *Deadline:* February 28.

Contact Dr. E. Aracelis Francis, Director Minority Fellowship Program
Council on Social Work Education
1725 Duke Street, Suite 500
Alexandria, VA 22314-3457
Phone: 703-683-8080
Fax: 703-683-8099
E-mail: eafrancis@cswe.org

DOCTORAL FELLOWSHIPS IN SOCIAL WORK FOR ETHNIC MINORITY STUDENTS PREPARING FOR LEADERSHIP ROLES IN MENTAL HEALTH AND/OR SUB. ABUSE • 484

Renewable awards for American citizens or permanent residents who have MSW and are enrolled full-time in a doctoral social work program. Recipients required to engage in clinical services in specific areas of need for a period of time equal to the length of support, within two years after termination of award.

Academic/Career Areas Health and Medical Sciences; Social Sciences; Social Services.

Award Fellowship for use in graduate years; renewable. *Number:* 10–20. *Amount:* $979–$1800.

Eligibility Requirements Applicant must be American Indian/Alaska Native, Asian/Pacific Islander, Black (non-Hispanic), or Hispanic and enrolled or expecting to enroll full-time at an institution or university. Available to U.S. citizens.

Application Requirements Application, autobiography, essay, financial need analysis, references, test scores, transcript. *Deadline:* February 28.

Contact Dr. E. Aracelis Francis, Director, Minority Fellowship Programs
Council on Social Work Education
1725 Duke Street, Suite 500
Alexandria, VA 22314-3457
Phone: 703-683-8080
Fax: 703-683-8099
E-mail: eafrancis@cswe.org

CROHN'S AND COLITIS FOUNDATION OF AMERICA, INC
http://www.ccfa.org

CROHN'S AND COLITIS FOUNDATION OF AMERICA CAREER DEVELOPMENT AWARDS • 485

Renewable award to encourage research into the inflammatory bowel diseases and develop the potential of young, outstanding basic and/or clinical scientists. Must be employed within the U.S. by an institution engaged in health-care or health-related research and hold M.D. or Ph.D. Application deadlines: January 14 and July 1.

Academic/Career Areas Health and Medical Sciences.

Award Grant for use in graduate years; renewable. *Amount:* up to $40,000.

Eligibility Requirements Applicant must be enrolled or expecting to enroll at an institution or university.

Application Requirements Application, references.

Contact Director of Research and Education
Crohn's and Colitis Foundation of America, Inc
386 Park Avenue South, 17th Floor
New York, NY 10016-8804
Phone: 800-932-2423
Fax: 212-779-4098
E-mail: info@ccfa.org

CROHN'S AND COLITIS FOUNDATION OF AMERICA FIRST AWARD • 486

One-time award to provide a sufficient period of research support for newly independent biomedical investigators to initiate their own research. Must be employed within the U.S. by institution engaged in health-related research and hold Ph.D. or M.D. Application deadlines: January 14 and July 1.

Academic/Career Areas Health and Medical Sciences.

Award Grant for use in graduate years; not renewable. *Amount:* up to $69,000.

Eligibility Requirements Applicant must be enrolled or expecting to enroll at an institution or university.

Application Requirements Application, references.

Contact Director of Research and Education
Crohn's and Colitis Foundation of America, Inc
386 Park Avenue South, 17th Floor
New York, NY 10016-8804
Phone: 800-932-2423
Fax: 212-779-4098
E-mail: info@ccfa.org

CROHN'S AND COLITIS FOUNDATION OF AMERICA RESEARCH FELLOWSHIP AWARDS • 487

One-time award to encourage research in the basic biomedical and clinical sciences related to the prevention and care of inflammatory bowel diseases. Must be employed within the U.S. by an institution engaged in health-related research. Must hold Ph.D. or M.D. Application deadlines: January 14 and July 1.

Academic/Career Areas Health and Medical Sciences.

Award Grant for use in graduate years; not renewable. *Amount:* up to $30,000.

Eligibility Requirements Applicant must be enrolled or expecting to enroll at an institution or university.

Application Requirements Application.

Contact Director of Research and Education
Crohn's and Colitis Foundation of America, Inc
386 Park Avenue South, 17th Floor
New York, NY 10016-8804
Phone: 800-932-2423
Fax: 212-779-4098
E-mail: info@ccfa.org

CROHN'S AND COLITIS FOUNDATION OF AMERICA RESEARCH GRANT PROGRAM • 488

Renewable award to provide funds to enable established investigators to generate sufficient data to become competitive for funding from other sources. Must be employed by institution engaged in health-related research and hold Ph.D. or M.D. Application deadlines: January 14 and July 1.

Academic/Career Areas Health and Medical Sciences.

Award Grant for use in graduate years; renewable. *Amount:* up to $115,000.

Eligibility Requirements Applicant must be enrolled or expecting to enroll at an institution or university.

Crohn's and Colitis Foundation of America, Inc (continued)

Application Requirements Application, references.

Contact Director of Research and Education
Crohn's and Colitis Foundation of
America, Inc
386 Park Avenue South, 17th Floor
New York, NY 10016-8804
Phone: 800-932-2423
Fax: 212-779-4098
E-mail: info@ccfa.org

CROHN'S AND COLITIS FOUNDATION OF AMERICA STUDENT RESEARCH FELLOWSHIP AWARDS • 489

Awards for students at North American institutions to pursue research careers in inflammatory bowel diseases. Project must last at least ten weeks. Must have mentor. Must be working in U.S. laboratory. Submit research plan and curriculum vitae. One-time award of $2500. Application deadline: March 15. Co-sponsored by Solvay Pharmaceuticals.

Academic/Career Areas Health and Medical Sciences.

Award Scholarship for use in graduate years; not renewable. *Number:* up to 16. *Amount:* $2500.

Eligibility Requirements Applicant must be enrolled or expecting to enroll full-time at an institution or university.

Application Requirements Application. *Deadline:* March 15.

Contact Director of Research and Education
Crohn's and Colitis Foundation of
America, Inc
386 Park Avenue South, 17th Floor
New York, NY 10016-8804
Phone: 800-932-2423
Fax: 212-779-4098
E-mail: info@ccfa.org

DAMON RUNYON CANCER RESEARCH FOUNDATION
http://www.drcrf.org

DAMON RUNYON SCHOLAR AWARD • 490

Primary qualification is that applicant's scientific accomplishments show promise of future contributions that will lead to understanding the causes and mechanisms of cancer and to developing more effective cancer therapies and preventions. Five awards at $100,000 each for three years granted to researchers who show exceptional promise of scientific accomplishment. Applicants must be former Runyon-Winchell Fellows at the assistant professor level or physician scientists at the assistant professor level affiliated with a clinical department at institutions invited by the Fund to submit a nomination.

Academic/Career Areas Health and Medical Sciences.

Award Grant for use in postgraduate years; renewable. *Number:* 5. *Amount:* $100,000.

Eligibility Requirements Applicant must be enrolled or expecting to enroll full-time at an institution or university. Available to U.S. and non-U.S. citizens.

Application Requirements Application, references. *Deadline:* July 1.

Contact Clare Cahill, Director, Award Programs
Administration
Damon Runyon Cancer Research
Foundation
675 Third Avenue, 25th Floor
New York, NY 10017-5704
Phone: 212-697-9550
Fax: 212-697-4950
E-mail: awards@drcrf.org

POSTDOCTORAL RESEARCH FELLOWSHIPS FOR BASIC AND PHYSICIAN SCIENTISTS • 491

Fellowships encouraging all theoretical and experimental research that is relevant to the study of cancer and the search for cancer causes, mechanisms, therapies, and prevention. Must apply under the guidance of a sponsor. Submit application cover sheet, curriculum vitae of sponsor and applicant, letters from sponsor and applicant, research proposal, and letters of recommendation. Contact for further requirements and application deadlines.

Academic/Career Areas Health and Medical Sciences.

Award Fellowship for use in postgraduate years; renewable. *Number:* 60. *Amount:* $40,000.

Eligibility Requirements Applicant must be enrolled or expecting to enroll full-time at an institution or university. Available to U.S. and non-U.S. citizens.

Application Requirements References, proposal.

Contact Clare Cahill, Director, Award Programs
Administration
Damon Runyon Cancer Research
Foundation
676 Third Avenue, 25th Floor
New York, NY 10017-5704
Phone: 212-697-9550
Fax: 212-697-4950
E-mail: awards@drcrf.org

DEAFNESS RESEARCH FOUNDATION
http://www.drf.org

DEAFNESS RESEARCH FOUNDATION GRANTS • 492

Award for investigators conducting research on any aspect of the ear and its function. Applications from new investigators conducting research in generally unexplored areas are encouraged. Awards are in the amount of $20,000 or $50,000 per year. Investigators can apply for 1, 2 or 3 years. Second and third-year funding are based on progress reports. Write for further information. Available to non-U.S. citizens if institution is in the U.S.

Academic/Career Areas Health and Medical Sciences.

Award Grant for use in graduate, or postgraduate years; renewable. *Number:* 35–45. *Amount:* $20,000–$50,000.

Eligibility Requirements Applicant must be enrolled or expecting to enroll full or part-time at an institution or university. Available to U.S. and non-U.S. citizens.

Application Requirements Application. *Deadline:* June 1.

Contact Ms. Mychelle Balthazard, Director,
　　　　　NHRGC
　　　　　Deafness Research Foundation
　　　　　1050 17th Street, NW Suite 701
　　　　　Washington, DC 20036
　　　　　Phone: 202-289-5850 Ext. 1100
　　　　　Fax: 202-293-1805
　　　　　E-mail: mychelle@drf.org

OTOLOGICAL RESEARCH FELLOWSHIP FOR MEDICAL STUDENTS • 493

Must be sponsored by a department of otolaryngology that is conducting otological research. Available for one year block of time at end of third year of medical school only. Submit written leave of absence, research outline, curriculum vitae of sponsor or applicant. Available to non-U.S. citizens only if institution is in the U.S.

Academic/Career Areas Health and Medical Sciences.

Award Fellowship for use in graduate years; not renewable. *Number:* 3–5. *Amount:* up to $15,000.

Eligibility Requirements Applicant must be enrolled or expecting to enroll full-time at an institution or university. Available to U.S. and non-U.S. citizens.

Application Requirements Application, references, transcript, curriculum vitae, research outline, leave of absence. *Deadline:* November 1.

Contact Ms. Mychelle Balthazard, Director,
　　　　　NHRGC
　　　　　Deafness Research Foundation
　　　　　1050 17th Street, NW Suite 701
　　　　　Washington, DC 20036
　　　　　Phone: 202-289-5850 Ext. 1100
　　　　　Fax: 202-293-1805
　　　　　E-mail: mychelle@drf.org

DEBRA
http://www.debra.org.uk

DEBRA INTERNATIONAL RESEARCH GRANTS • 494

Debra International provides grants to scholars doing medical and scientific research on Epidermolysis Bullosa (EB). Grants may be used for remuneration for either full-time or part-time research workers, associated research expenses and the purchase of special equipment, as detailed in the former offers of the grant. Whatever the period of the grant, yearly continuation will depend upon receipt of a satisfactory annual interim report. For more information and application, visit http://www.debra-international.org.

Academic/Career Areas Health and Medical Sciences.

Award Grant for use in postgraduate years; renewable. *Number:* 20. *Amount:* $50,000.

Eligibility Requirements Applicant must be enrolled or expecting to enroll at an institution or university. Available to U.S. and non-U.S. citizens.

Application Requirements Application, references, proposal, curriculum vitae. *Deadline:* Continuous.

Contact DEBRA
　　　　　13 Wellington Business Park, Dukes Ride
　　　　　Crowthorne, Berkshire RG45-6LS
　　　　　United Kingdom

DELAWARE HIGHER EDUCATION COMMISSION
http://www.doe.state.de.us/high-ed

OPTOMETRIC INSTITUTIONAL AID • 495

Must be a legal resident of Delaware in a program that will license him/her as an optometrist in Delaware. Loan not to exceed cost of tuition fees, and other direct educational expense. Deadline: June 1.

Academic/Career Areas Health and Medical Sciences.

Award Forgivable loan for use in graduate years; renewable. *Number:* 4. *Amount:* $4000.

Eligibility Requirements Applicant must be enrolled or expecting to enroll full-time at an institution or university; resident of Delaware and studying in Delaware. Available to U.S. citizens.

Application Requirements Letter of acceptance from school. *Deadline:* June 1.

Contact Maureen Laffey, Associate Director
　　　　　Delaware Higher Education Commission
　　　　　820 North French Street
　　　　　Wilmington, DE 19801
　　　　　Phone: 302-577-3240
　　　　　Fax: 302-577-6765
　　　　　E-mail: dhec@state.de.us

DELTA SOCIETY
http://www.deltasociety.org

HARRIS SWEATT TRAVEL GRANT
• *See number 17*

EDUCATION AND RESEARCH FOUNDATION, SOCIETY OF NUCLEAR MEDICINE
http://www.snmerf.org

PILOT RESEARCH GRANTS • 496

One-time award for M.D.'s or PhD's to start research in nuclear medicine. Must submit abstract of project proposal and budget proposal. Visit website for additional information.

Academic/Career Areas Health and Medical Sciences; Nuclear Science.

Award Grant for use in postgraduate years; not renewable. *Amount:* up to $8000.

Eligibility Requirements Applicant must be enrolled or expecting to enroll at an institution or university. Available to U.S. and non-U.S. citizens.

Application Requirements Application. *Deadline:* November 15.

Contact Ms. Susan Weiss, Administrative Director
Education and Research Foundation,
Society of Nuclear Medicine
2300 Children's Plaza, #42
Chicago, IL 60614
Phone: 773-880-4663
Fax: 773-880-4455
E-mail: sweiss@snmerf.org

SOCIETY OF NUCLEAR MEDICINE STUDENT FELLOWSHIP AWARDS • 497

One-time award for medical or graduate students. Student may receive $1000 a month for up to three months working on a project in nuclear medicine under a preceptor. Must submit preceptor statement. Visit website for additional information.

Academic/Career Areas Health and Medical Sciences; Nuclear Science.

Award Fellowship for use in graduate years; not renewable. *Amount:* $3000.

Eligibility Requirements Applicant must be enrolled or expecting to enroll full-time at an institution or university. Available to U.S. and non-U.S. citizens.

Application Requirements Application, references. *Deadline:* November 15.

Contact Ms. Susan Weiss, Administrative Director
Education and Research Foundation,
Society of Nuclear Medicine
2300 Children's Plaza, #42
Chicago, IL 60614
Phone: 773-880-4663
Fax: 773-880-4455
E-mail: sweiss@snmerf.org

EDUCATIONAL AND RESEARCH FOUNDATION FOR THE AMERICAN ACADEMY OF FACIAL PLASTIC AND RECONSTRUCTIVE SURGERY (AAFPRS FOUNDATION)
http://www.aafprs.org

BEN SHUSTER MEMORIAL AWARD • 498

One-time prize for a resident or fellow in training who submits the best research paper in clinical work or research delivered at a national meeting between March 1 and the following February 28. Must be the sole or senior author and a member of the American Academy of Facial Plastic and Reconstructive Surgery.

Academic/Career Areas Health and Medical Sciences.

Award Prize for use in postgraduate years; not renewable. *Number:* 1. *Amount:* $1000.

Eligibility Requirements Applicant must be enrolled or expecting to enroll at an institution or university. Applicant or parent of applicant must be member of American Academy of Facial Plastic and Reconstructive Surgery. Applicant or parent of applicant must have employment or volunteer experience in designated career field.

Application Requirements Application. *Deadline:* February 28.

Contact Ann Holton, Director of Development,
Research and Humanitarian Programs
Educational and Research Foundation for
the American Academy of Facial
Plastic and Reconstructive Surgery
(AAFPRS Foundation)
310 South Henry Street
Alexandria, VA 22314
Phone: 703-299-9291
Fax: 703-299-8898
E-mail: info@aafprs.org

BERNSTEIN GRANT • 499

One-time award for an American Academy of Facial Plastic and Reconstructive Surgery fellow undertaking research that will advance plastic or reconstructive surgery. Research must be original and must be completed in three years. Write for more information. Must submit proposal.

Academic/Career Areas Health and Medical Sciences.

Award Grant for use in postgraduate years; not renewable. *Number:* 1. *Amount:* $25,000.

Eligibility Requirements Applicant must be enrolled or expecting to enroll at an institution or university. Applicant or parent of applicant must be member of American Academy of Facial Plastic and Reconstructive Surgery. Applicant or parent of applicant must have employment or volunteer experience in designated career field.

Application Requirements Application, financial need analysis, references. *Deadline:* December 15.

Contact Ann Holton, Director of Development,
   Research, and Human Programs
   Educational and Research Foundation for
   the American Academy of Facial
   Plastic and Reconstructive Surgery
   (AAFPRS Foundation)
   310 South Henry Street
   Alexandria, VA 22314
   Phone: 703-299-9291
   Fax: 703-299-8898
   E-mail: info@aafprs.org

EDUCATION & RESEARCH FOUNDATION FOR THE AMERICAN ACADEMY OF FACIAL PLASTIC AND RECONSTRUCTIVE SURGERY INVESTIGATOR DEVELOPMENT GRANT • 500

One-time grant to support work of young faculty members in facial plastic surgery conducting significant clinical or laboratory research and training residential surgeons in research. Must be members of the Academy. Must be a physician in a residence training program.

Academic/Career Areas Health and Medical Sciences.

Award Grant for use in postgraduate years; not renewable. *Number:* 1. *Amount:* $15,000.

Eligibility Requirements Applicant must be enrolled or expecting to enroll at an institution or university. Applicant or parent of applicant must be member of American Academy of Facial Plastic and Reconstructive Surgery. Applicant or parent of applicant must have employment or volunteer experience in designated career field.

Application Requirements Application, financial need analysis, references. *Deadline:* December 15.

Contact Ann Holton, Director of Development,
   Research, and Humanitarian
   Programs
   Educational and Research Foundation for
   the American Academy of Facial
   Plastic and Reconstructive Surgery
   (AAFPRS Foundation)
   310 South Henry Street
   Alexandria, VA 22314
   Phone: 703-299-9291
   Fax: 703-299-8898
   E-mail: info@aafprs.org

EDUCATION & RESEARCH FOUNDATION FOR THE AMERICAN ACADEMY OF FACIAL PLASTIC AND RECONSTRUCTIVE SURGERY RESIDENT RESEARCH GRANT • 501

One-time award to stimulate resident research in well-conceived and scientifically valid projects. Must be member of the Academy. Must be a physician in a residency training program interested in facial plastic and reconstructive surgery. Submit research proposal.

Academic/Career Areas Health and Medical Sciences.

Award Grant for use in postgraduate years; not renewable. *Number:* up to 3. *Amount:* $5000.

Eligibility Requirements Applicant must be enrolled or expecting to enroll at an institution or university. Applicant or parent of applicant must be member of American Academy of Facial Plastic and Reconstructive Surgery. Applicant or parent of applicant must have employment or volunteer experience in designated career field.

Application Requirements Application, financial need analysis, references. *Deadline:* December 15.

Contact Ann Holton, Director of Development,
   Research, and Humanitarian
   Programs
   Educational and Research Foundation for
   the American Academy of Facial
   Plastic and Reconstructive Surgery
   (AAFPRS Foundation)
   310 South Henry Street
   Alexandria, VA 22314
   Phone: 703-299-9291
   Fax: 703-299-8898
   E-mail: info@aafprs.org

EDUCATION. & RESEARCH FOUNDATION FOR THE AMERICAN ACADEMY OF FACIAL PLASTIC AND RECONSTRUCTIVE SURGERY COMMUNITY SERVICE AWARD • 502

Prize presented to an American Academy of Facial and Plastic Reconstructive Surgery member who has distinguished himself or herself by providing and/or

Educational and Research Foundation for the American Academy of Facial Plastic and Reconstructive Surgery (AAFPRS Foundation) (continued)

making possible free medical service to the poor. Must be nominated for award. One-time award.

Academic/Career Areas Health and Medical Sciences.

Award Prize for use in graduate years; not renewable. *Number:* 1.

Eligibility Requirements Applicant must be enrolled or expecting to enroll at an institution or university. Applicant or parent of applicant must be member of American Academy of Facial Plastic and Reconstructive Surgery. Applicant or parent of applicant must have employment or volunteer experience in designated career field. Available to U.S. and non-U.S. citizens.

Application Requirements Application. *Deadline:* February 28.

Contact Ann Holton, Director of Development, Research and Humanitarian Programs
Educational and Research Foundation for the American Academy of Facial Plastic and Reconstructive Surgery (AAFPRS Foundation)
310 South Henry Street
Alexandria, VA 22314
Phone: 703-299-9291
Fax: 703-299-8898
E-mail: info@aafprs.org

F. MARK RAFATY MEMORIAL AWARD • 503

Prize presented to an American Academy of Facial Plastic and Reconstructive Surgery member who has made an outstanding contribution to facial plastic and reconstructive surgery. Must be nominated for award. One-time award.

Academic/Career Areas Health and Medical Sciences.

Award Prize for use in graduate years; not renewable. *Number:* 1.

Eligibility Requirements Applicant must be enrolled or expecting to enroll at an institution or university. Applicant or parent of applicant must be member of American Academy of Facial Plastic and Reconstructive Surgery. Applicant or parent of applicant must have employment or volunteer experience in designated career field.

Application Requirements Application *Deadline:* February 28.

Contact Ann Holton, Director of Development, Research and Humanitarian Programs
Educational and Research Foundation for the American Academy of Facial Plastic and Reconstructive Surgery (AAFPRS Foundation)
310 South Henry Street
Alexandria, VA 22314
Phone: 703-299-9291
Fax: 703-299-8898
E-mail: info@aafprs.org

IRA TRESLEY RESEARCH AWARD • 504

Prize for the best original research in facial plastic surgery by an American Academy of Facial Plastic and Reconstructive Surgery member who has been board certified for at least three years. Papers presented at a national meeting between March 1 and February 28 are eligible. Submit proposal.

Academic/Career Areas Health and Medical Sciences.

Award Prize for use in postgraduate years; not renewable. *Number:* 1. *Amount:* $1000.

Eligibility Requirements Applicant must be enrolled or expecting to enroll at an institution or university. Applicant or parent of applicant must be member of American Academy of Facial Plastic and Reconstructive Surgery. Applicant or parent of applicant must have employment or volunteer experience in designated career field.

Application Requirements Application, proposal. *Deadline:* February 28.

Contact Ann Holton, Director of Development, Research and Humanitarian Programs
Educational and Research Foundation for the American Academy of Facial Plastic and Reconstructive Surgery (AAFPRS Foundation)
310 South Henry Street
Alexandria, VA 22314
Phone: 703-299-9291
Fax: 703-299-8898
E-mail: info@aafprs.org

JOHN DICKINSON TEACHER AWARD • 505

Prize honoring an American Academy of Facial Plastic Reconstructive Surgery fellow or member for sharing knowledge about facial plastic surgery with the effective use of audiovisuals in any one year. Must be nominated for award. One-time award.

Academic/Career Areas Health and Medical Sciences.

Award Prize for use in graduate years; not renewable. *Number:* 1.

Eligibility Requirements Applicant must be enrolled or expecting to enroll at an institution or university. Applicant or parent of applicant must be member of American Academy of Facial Plastic and Reconstructive Surgery. Applicant or parent of applicant must have employment or volunteer experience in designated career field.

Application Requirements Application. *Deadline:* February 28.

Contact Ann Holton, Director of Development,
Research and Humanitarian Programs
Educational and Research Foundation for
the American Academy of Facial
Plastic and Reconstructive Surgery
(AAFPRS Foundation)
310 South Henry Street
Alexandria, VA 22314
Phone: 703-299-9291
Fax: 703-299-8898
E-mail: info@aafprs.org

JOHN ORLANDO ROE AWARD • 506

One-time prize for a graduate fellow who submits the best clinical research paper during fellowship. Must be a member of the American Academy of Facial Plastic and Reconstructive Surgery. Write for more information.

Academic/Career Areas Health and Medical Sciences.

Award Prize for use in graduate years; not renewable. *Number:* 1. *Amount:* $1000.

Eligibility Requirements Applicant must be enrolled or expecting to enroll at an institution or university. Applicant or parent of applicant must be member of American Academy of Facial Plastic and Reconstructive Surgery. Applicant or parent of applicant must have employment or volunteer experience in designated career field.

Application Requirements Application. *Deadline:* February 28.

Contact Ann Holton, Director of Development,
Research and Humanitarian Programs
Educational and Research Foundation for
the American Academy of Facial
Plastic and Reconstructive Surgery
(AAFPRS Foundation)
310 South Henry Street
Alexandria, VA 22314
Phone: 703-299-9291
Fax: 703-299-8898
E-mail: info@aafprs.org

RESIDENCY TRAVEL AWARD • 507

Presented to the most outstanding paper in facial plastic and reconstructive surgery primarily authored by a resident or medical student in training. Paper must be submitted by June 1st for consideration and is to be presented at the annual fall meeting.

Academic/Career Areas Health and Medical Sciences.

Award Grant for use in postgraduate years; not renewable. *Number:* 1. *Amount:* $1000.

Eligibility Requirements Applicant must be enrolled or expecting to enroll full-time at an institution or university. Applicant or parent of applicant must have employment or volunteer experience in designated career field. Available to U.S. and Canadian citizens.

Application Requirements Application, applicant must enter a contest. *Deadline:* June 1.

Contact Ann Holton, Director of Development,
Research, and Humanitarian Program
Educational and Research Foundation for
the American Academy of Facial
Plastic and Reconstructive Surgery
(AAFPRS Foundation)
310 South Henry Street
Alexandria, VA 22314
Phone: 703-299-9291
Fax: 703-299-8890
E-mail: info@aafprs.org

SIR HAROLD DELF GILLIES AWARD • 508

One-time award for a graduate fellow who submits the best basic science research paper written during fellowship. Must be a member of the American Academy of Facial Plastic and Reconstructive Surgery. Write for more information.

Academic/Career Areas Health and Medical Sciences.

Award Prize for use in graduate years; not renewable. *Number:* up to 1. *Amount:* $1000.

Eligibility Requirements Applicant must be enrolled or expecting to enroll at an institution or university. Applicant or parent of applicant must be member of American Academy of Facial Plastic and Reconstructive Surgery. Applicant or parent of applicant must have employment or volunteer experience in designated career field.

Application Requirements Application. *Deadline:* February 28.

Contact Ann Holton, Director of Development,
Research and Humanitarian Programs
Educational and Research Foundation for
the American Academy of Facial
Plastic and Reconstructive Surgery
(AAFPRS Foundation)
310 South Henry Street
Alexandria, VA 22314
Phone: 703-299-9291
Fax: 703-299-8898
E-mail: info@aafprs.org

WILLIAM K. WRIGHT AWARD • 509

Prize presented to an American Academy of Facial Plastic and Reconstructive Surgery member who has made an outstanding contribution to facial plastic and reconstructive surgery. Must be nominated for award. One-time award.

Academic/Career Areas Health and Medical Sciences.

Award Prize for use in graduate years; not renewable. *Number:* 1.

Eligibility Requirements Applicant must be enrolled or expecting to enroll at an institution or university. Applicant or parent of applicant must be member of American Academy of Facial Plastic and Reconstructive Surgery. Applicant or parent of applicant must have employment or volunteer experience in designated career field.

Application Requirements Application. *Deadline:* February 28.

Contact Ann Holton, Director of Development,
Research and Humanitarian Programs
Educational and Research Foundation for
the American Academy of Facial
Plastic and Reconstructive Surgery
(AAFPRS Foundation)
310 South Henry Street
Alexandria, VA 22314
Phone: 703-299-9291
Fax: 703-299-8898
E-mail: info@aafprs.org

ELIZABETH GLASER PEDIATRIC AIDS FOUNDATION
http://www.pedaids.org

ELIZABETH GLASER SCIENTIST AWARD • 510

Award provides up to $650,000 in pediatrics HIV/AIDS research for five-year period. Up to five outstanding scientists funded each year. Must have M.D., Ph.D., D.D.S., or D.V.M. degree. Must be at assistant professor level or above. For additional information, visit website.

Academic/Career Areas Health and Medical Sciences.

Award Grant for use in postgraduate years; not renewable. *Number:* up to 5.

Eligibility Requirements Applicant must be enrolled or expecting to enroll at an institution or university. Available to U.S. and non-U.S. citizens.

Application Requirements Application. *Deadline:* October 3.

Contact Elizabeth Glaser Pediatric AIDS
Foundation
2950 31st Street, Suite 125
Santa Monica, CA 90405

RESEARCH GRANTS • 511

One or two year grant providing up to $80,000 per year for innovative pediatric HIV/AIDS research. Determination of duration of support will be decided by committee. Renewals for one-year grant are competitively reviewed, two-year grants are not renewable. Applicant must have full-time academic and/or institutional appointment. For additional information, see website.

Academic/Career Areas Health and Medical Sciences.

Award Grant for use in postgraduate years; not renewable. *Amount:* up to $80,000.

Eligibility Requirements Applicant must be enrolled or expecting to enroll full-time at an institution or university. Available to U.S. and non-U.S. citizens.

Application Requirements *Deadline:* November 8.

Contact Elizabeth Glaser Pediatric AIDS
Foundation
2950 31st Street, Suite 125
Santa Monica, CA 90405

SCHOLAR AWARDS • 512

Program created to encourage young investigators to select pediatric HIV/AIDS as a research focus for their career. Applicant must have two or three years of postdoctoral experience. Program provides two years of salary support, with possible third year renewal. Recipient must work with qualified sponsor. Tenured investigators are not eligible. For additional information, visit website.

Academic/Career Areas Health and Medical Sciences.

Award Grant for use in postgraduate years; renewable. *Amount:* $30,000–$48,000.

Eligibility Requirements Applicant must be enrolled or expecting to enroll at an institution or university. Available to U.S. and non-U.S. citizens.

Application Requirements *Deadline:* November 8.

Contact Elizabeth Glaser Pediatric AIDS
Foundation
2950 31st Street, Suite 125
Santa Monica, CA 90405

SHORT-TERM SCIENTIFIC AWARDS • 513

Grant provides up to $5,000 for travel and short-term study at U.S. institution. Focus must be pediatric HIV/AIDS research. Program facilitates critical research project. Recipient obtains preliminary data, learns new techniques in established laboratory, and may sponsor important workshop. For additional information, visit website.

Academic/Career Areas Health and Medical Sciences.

Award Grant for use in postgraduate years; not renewable. *Amount:* up to $5000.

Eligibility Requirements Applicant must be enrolled or expecting to enroll at an institution or university. Available to U.S. and non-U.S. citizens.

Application Requirements *Deadline:* November 8.

Contact Elizabeth Glaser Pediatric AIDS
Foundation
2950 31st Street, Suite 125
Santa Monica, CA 90405

EMERGENCY NURSES ASSOCIATION (ENA) FOUNDATION
http://www.ena.org/foundation

ENA FOUNDATION RESEARCH GRANTS #1 AND #2 • 514

Two grants to provide funding for research which will advance the specialized practice of emergency nursing. All relevant research topics will be considered. Priority funding will be given to studies relating to ENA/ENA Foundation Research Initiatives. Grant #1 deadline June 1, Grant #2 deadline October 1. Applicants must be ENA members for a minimum of 12 months.

Academic/Career Areas Health and Medical Sciences; Nursing.

Award Grant for use in graduate, or postgraduate years; not renewable. *Number:* 2. *Amount:* $10,000.

Eligibility Requirements Applicant must be enrolled or expecting to enroll at an institution or university. Applicant or parent of applicant must be member of Emergency Nurses Association. Available to U.S. and non-U.S. citizens.

Application Requirements Application.

Contact Emergency Nurses Association (ENA)
Foundation
915 Lee Street
Des Plaines, IL 60016
Phone: 847-460-4100

ENA FOUNDATION/EMERGENCY MEDICINE FOUNDATION TEAM RESEARCH GRANT • 515

Grants to facilitate collaborative research between physicians and nurses to improve clinical research in emergency care. Any registered nurse and physician team working in emergency care is eligible. See http://www.acep.org for more information and application (click on Research). The deadline for applications is January 11.

Academic/Career Areas Health and Medical Sciences; Nursing.

Award Grant for use in graduate, or postgraduate years; not renewable. *Number:* 1. *Amount:* $10,000.

Eligibility Requirements Applicant must be enrolled or expecting to enroll at an institution or university. Available to U.S. and non-U.S. citizens.

Application Requirements Application. *Deadline:* January 11.

Contact Emergency Medicine Foundation
Emergency Nurses Association (ENA)
Foundation
PO Box 619911
Dallas, TX 75261-9911
Phone: 972-550-0911

ENAF/SIGMA THETA TAU INTERNATIONAL RESEARCH GRANT • 516

The ENA Foundation and Sigma Theta Tau International have combined resources to offer this research grant. The purpose of the grant is to provide money for research that will advance the specialized practice of emergency nursing. All relevant research topics will be considered; priority will be given to studies relating to the ENA/ENA Foundation Research Initiatives.

Academic/Career Areas Health and Medical Sciences; Nursing.

Award Grant for use in graduate, or postgraduate years; not renewable. *Number:* 1. *Amount:* $6000.

Eligibility Requirements Applicant must be enrolled or expecting to enroll at a four-year institution or university. Available to U.S. and non-U.S. citizens.

Application Requirements Application. *Deadline:* February 1.

Contact Ellen Siciliano, Executive Assistant
Emergency Nurses Association (ENA)
Foundation
915 Lee Street
Des Plaines, IL 60016
Phone: 847-460-4100
Fax: 847-460-4005
E-mail: esiciliano@ena.org

EPILEPSY FOUNDATION
http://www.epilepsyfoundation.org

EPILEPSY FOUNDATION BEHAVIORAL SCIENCES RESEARCH TRAINING FELLOWSHIP
• *See number 318*

EPILEPSY FOUNDATION JUNIOR INVESTIGATOR RESEARCH GRANTS • 517

Award to support basic and clinical research in biological, behavioral, and social sciences with relation to epilepsy. Priority given to beginning investigators, to new or innovative projects, and to research relevant to developmental or pediatric aspects of epilepsy. One-year grant limited to $40,000. Deadline: September 5. Project must be completed in U.S. territories only.

Academic/Career Areas Health and Medical Sciences.

Epilepsy Foundation (continued)

Award Grant for use in postgraduate years; not renewable. *Number:* 2–15. *Amount:* up to $40,000.

Eligibility Requirements Applicant must be enrolled or expecting to enroll full or part-time at an institution or university. Available to U.S. citizens.

Application Requirements Application, autobiography, financial need analysis, references. *Deadline:* September 5.

Contact Cathy Morris, Administrative Coordinator,
        Programs and Research
        Epilepsy Foundation
        4351 Garden City Drive
        Landover, MD 20785
        Phone: 301-459-3700
        Fax: 301-577-4941
        E-mail: grants@efa.org

EPILEPSY FOUNDATION RESEARCH TRAINING FELLOWSHIP • 518

Award for physicians or Ph.D. neuroscientists who desire either basic or clinical postdoctoral epilepsy research experience. Preference given to applicants whose proposals have a pediatric or developmental emphasis. One-year fellowship carrying a $40,000 stipend. Deadline: September 5. Project must be carried out in U.S. or Canadian territories.

Academic/Career Areas Health and Medical Sciences.

Award Fellowship for use in postgraduate years; not renewable. *Amount:* up to $40,000.

Eligibility Requirements Applicant must be enrolled or expecting to enroll at an institution or university.

Application Requirements Application, autobiography, financial need analysis, references. *Deadline:* September 5.

Contact Cathy Morris, Administrative Coordinator,
        Programs and Research
        Epilepsy Foundation
        4351 Garden City Drive
        Landover, MD 20785
        Phone: 301-459-3700
        Fax: 301-577-4941
        E-mail: grants@efa.org

EPILEPSY FOUNDATION RESEARCH/CLINICAL TRAINING FELLOWSHIPS • 519

Award for individuals who have received M.D. and completed residency training. One-year training experience in either basic or clinical epilepsy research project, with equal emphasis on clinical training and clinical epileptology. Stipend of up to $40,000. Deadline: September 5. Project must be carried out in U.S. or Canadian territories.

Academic/Career Areas Health and Medical Sciences.

Award Fellowship for use in postgraduate years; not renewable. *Number:* 4–6. *Amount:* up to $40,000.

Eligibility Requirements Applicant must be enrolled or expecting to enroll at an institution or university.

Application Requirements Application, autobiography, financial need analysis, references. *Deadline:* September 5.

Contact Cathy Morris, Administrative Coordinator,
        Programs and Research
        Epilepsy Foundation
        4351 Garden City Drive
        Landover, MD 20785
        Phone: 301-459-3700
        Fax: 301-577-4941
        E-mail: grants@efa.org

FRITZ E. DREIFUSS INTERNATIONAL TRAVEL PROGRAM • 520

Promotes the exchange of medical and scientific information and expertise on epilepsy between the United States and other countries. The program provides an opportunity for a qualified candidate to spend from 3 to 6 weeks at a host institution. At least one party in the exchange must be from the United States. Applications may be submitted at any time. Funding from the Epilepsy Foundation is limited to payment of travel and incidental expenses.

Academic/Career Areas Health and Medical Sciences.

Award Fellowship for use in postgraduate years; not renewable.

Eligibility Requirements Applicant must be enrolled or expecting to enroll at an institution or university. Available to U.S. and non-U.S. citizens.

Application Requirements Application, autobiography, financial need analysis, references. *Deadline:* Continuous.

Contact Cathy Morris, Administrative Coordinator,
        Programs and Research
        Epilepsy Foundation
        4351 Garden City Drive
        Landover, MD 20785
        Phone: 301-459-3700
        Fax: 301-577-4941
        E-mail: grants@efa.org

FOUNDATION FOR CHIROPRACTIC EDUCATION AND RESEARCH
http://www.fcer.org

FOUNDATION FOR CHIROPRACTIC EDUCATION AND RESEARCH FELLOWSHIPS, SCHOLARSHIPS, AND RESIDENCY STIPENDS
• *See number 201*

FOUNDATION FOR SCIENCE AND DISABILITY
http://www.as.wvu.edu/~scidis/organize/fsd.html

GRANTS FOR DISABLED STUDENTS IN THE SCIENCES
• See number 54

FOUNDATION OF THE PENNSYLVANIA MEDICAL SOCIETY
http://www.pmsfoundation.org

DRS. SIEGFRIED AND VIGILANTE SCHOLARSHIP • 521

One-time award for a first year, medical student. The applicant must be a resident of Lehigh, Berks, or Northampton County in the state of Pennsylvania and be enrolled full-time in an accredited United States medical school. Must be U.S. citizen.

Academic/Career Areas Health and Medical Sciences.

Award Scholarship for use in graduate years; not renewable. *Number:* 1. *Amount:* $1000.

Eligibility Requirements Applicant must be enrolled or expecting to enroll full-time at a four-year institution or university and resident of Pennsylvania. Available to U.S. citizens.

Application Requirements Application, essay, references, enrollment verification letter from medical school. *Deadline:* September 30.

Contact Wendie Dunkin, Student Loan and Scholarship Assistant
Foundation of the Pennsylvania Medical Society
777 East Park Drive, PO Box 8820
Harrisburg, PA 17105-8820
Phone: 717-558-7750
Fax: 717-558-7818
E-mail: studentservices-foundation@pamedsoc.org

HEALTH PROFESSIONS EDUCATION FOUNDATION
http://www.healthprofessions.ca.gov

HEALTH PROFESSIONS EDUCATION LOAN REPAYMENT PROGRAM
• See number 287

HEALTH RESOURCES AND SERVICES ADMINISTRATION
http://www.bphr.hrsa.gov/nhsc

NATIONAL HEALTH SERVICES CORPS SCHOLARSHIP PROGRAM • 522

The NHSC Scholarship Program is not a general financial assistance program; a service obligation is required. Competitive scholarships are awarded to students in osteopathic and allopathic medicine, family nurse practitioner, nurse midwifery and physician assistant training programs who commit to providing primary health care in underserved areas throughout the United States. Must be a U.S. citizen.

Academic/Career Areas Health and Medical Sciences; Nursing.

Award Scholarship for use in graduate, or postgraduate years; renewable. *Number:* 300–350. *Amount:* $26,500–$130,000.

Eligibility Requirements Applicant must be enrolled or expecting to enroll full-time at an institution or university. Available to U.S. citizens.

Application Requirements Application, interview. *Deadline:* March 29.

Contact c/o IQ Solutions
Health Resources and Services Administration
Scholarships Programs Branch
4350 East West Highway, 10th Floor
Bethesda, MD 20814
Phone: 800-638-0824
E-mail: nhsc@iqsolutions.com

HEART AND STROKE FOUNDATION OF CANADA
http://www.hsf.ca/research

HEART AND STROKE FOUNDATION CAREER INVESTIGATOR AWARD • 523

Award available to individuals with an MD, Ph.D., or equivalent degree working in the field of cardiovascular and, or cerebrovascular disease who wish to make their research a full-time career. Applicants must provide proof of national recognition. Several renewal awards of varying amounts. Sponsored by the Heart and Stroke Foundations of Ontario and British Columbia and the Yukon and is tenable in these provinces only. See website for complete details.

Academic/Career Areas Health and Medical Sciences.

Award Scholarship for use in graduate years; renewable. *Amount:* $65,000.

Eligibility Requirements Applicant must be enrolled or expecting to enroll at an institution or university and studying in British Columbia, Ontario, or Yukon.

Application Requirements Application, essay, references, self-addressed stamped envelope, transcript. *Deadline:* August 31.

Contact Administrative Assistant, Research Department
Heart and Stroke Foundation of Canada
222 Queen Street, Suite 1402
Ottawa, ON K1P 5V9
Canada
Phone: 613-569-4361 Ext. 327
Fax: 613-569-3278

HEART AND STROKE FOUNDATION OF CANADA DOCTORAL RESEARCH AWARD • 524

Several awards for highly qualified graduate students enrolled in a Ph.D. program who are undertaking full-time research training in the cardiovascular or cerebrovascular fields. See website for complete details.

Academic/Career Areas Health and Medical Sciences.

Award Fellowship for use in graduate years; renewable. *Number:* 20–30. *Amount:* $19,000.

Eligibility Requirements Applicant must be enrolled or expecting to enroll full-time at an institution or university.

Application Requirements Application, essay, references, self-addressed stamped envelope, transcript. *Deadline:* November 1.

Contact Administrative Assistant, Research
Department
Heart and Stroke Foundation of Canada
222 Queen Street, Suite 1402
Ottawa, ON K1P 5V9
Canada
Phone: 613-569-4361 Ext. 327
Fax: 613-569-3278

HEART AND STROKE FOUNDATION OF CANADA GRANTS-IN-AID OF RESEARCH AND DEVELOPMENT • 525

Several grants available to support researchers in projects of experimental nature in cardiovascular or cerebrovascular development. Grants range from one to three years. See website for complete details.

Academic/Career Areas Health and Medical Sciences.

Award Grant for use in graduate, or postgraduate years; not renewable.

Eligibility Requirements Applicant must be enrolled or expecting to enroll at an institution or university.

Application Requirements Application, essay, references, self-addressed stamped envelope, transcript. *Deadline:* August 31.

Contact Administrative Assistant, Research
Department
Heart and Stroke Foundation of Canada
222 Queen Street, Suite 1402
Ottawa, ON K1P 5V9
Canada
Phone: 613-569-4361 Ext. 327
Fax: 613-569-3278

HEART AND STROKE FOUNDATION OF CANADA NURSING RESEARCH FELLOWSHIPS • 526

Several "in-training" awards for persons studying some area of cardiovascular, or cerebrovascular nursing. For master's degree candidates, the programs must include a thesis or project requirement. Desired applicants are nurses looking to further their education in their field. Renewable awards of varying amounts. See website for complete details.

Academic/Career Areas Health and Medical Sciences; Nursing.

Award Fellowship for use in graduate years; renewable. *Number:* 1–3. *Amount:* $25,000.

Eligibility Requirements Applicant must be enrolled or expecting to enroll full-time at an institution or university.

Application Requirements Application, references, self-addressed stamped envelope, transcript. *Deadline:* March 15.

Contact Administrative Assistant, Research
Department
Heart and Stroke Foundation of Canada
222 Queen Street, Suite 1402
Ottawa, ON K1P 5V9
Canada
Phone: 613-569-4361 Ext. 327
Fax: 613-569-3278

HEART AND STROKE FOUNDATION OF CANADA RESEARCH FELLOWSHIPS • 527

Several fellowships available to applicants with (or expecting) a Ph.D., MD, BM, DVM, or equivalent degree. Those with a medical degree may apply for study toward an M.Sc. or Ph.D. degree. Awardee may not be in receipt of another major award or have held a prior faculty appointment. Renewable awards of varying amounts. See website for complete details.

Academic/Career Areas Health and Medical Sciences.

Award Fellowship for use in graduate, or postgraduate years; renewable. *Number:* 10–20. *Amount:* $35,000–$45,000.

Eligibility Requirements Applicant must be enrolled or expecting to enroll full-time at an institution or university.

Application Requirements Application, essay, references, self-addressed stamped envelope, transcript. *Deadline:* November 1.

Contact Administrative Assistant, Research
Department
Heart and Stroke Foundation of Canada
222 Queen Street, Suite 1402
Ottawa, ON K1P 5V9
Canada
Phone: 613-569-4361 Ext. 327
Fax: 613-569-3278

HEART AND STROKE FOUNDATION OF CANADA RESEARCH SCHOLARSHIPS • 528

Several scholarships to those who have clearly demonstrated excellence during pre- and postdoctoral training in cardio or cerebrovascular research. Applicant must hold a Ph.D., MD, or equivalent degree and application must be initiated by the institution. See website for complete details. Research scholarships are tenable in Canada only.

Academic/Career Areas Health and Medical Sciences.

Award Scholarship for use in postgraduate years; not renewable. *Number:* 8–10.

Eligibility Requirements Applicant must be enrolled or expecting to enroll full-time at an institution or university.

Application Requirements Application, essay, references, self-addressed stamped envelope, transcript. *Deadline:* November 1.

Contact Administrative Assistant, Research
Department
Heart and Stroke Foundation of Canada
222 Queen Street, Suite 1402
Ottawa, ON K1P 5V9
Canada
Phone: 613-569-4361 Ext. 327
Fax: 613-569-3278

HEART AND STROKE FOUNDATION OF CANADA VISITING SCIENTIST PROGRAM • 529

One or more awards to senior individuals whose contribution and visit will be mutually rewarding to the host institution and the scientist. Intended for Canadians studying abroad or in Canada or for foreign visitors to Canada. Several awards of varying amounts for cardiovascular or cerebrovascular research.

Academic/Career Areas Health and Medical Sciences.

Award Fellowship for use in graduate, or postgraduate years; not renewable. *Amount:* $3000–$12,000.

Eligibility Requirements Applicant must be enrolled or expecting to enroll at an institution or university.

Application Requirements Application, essay, references, self-addressed stamped envelope. *Deadline:* December 14.

Contact Administrative Assistant, Research
Department
Heart and Stroke Foundation of Canada
222 Queen Street, Suite 1402
Ottawa, ON K1P 5V9
Canada
Phone: 613-569-4361 Ext. 327
Fax: 613-569-3278

HOSTESS COMMITTEE SCHOLARSHIPS/MISS AMERICA PAGEANT
http://www.missamerica.org

DR. AND MRS. DAVID B. ALLMAN MEDICAL SCHOLARSHIPS • 530

Scholarship for Miss America contestants who wish to enter field of medicine to become medical doctors. Award available to women who have competed within the Miss America system on the local, state, or national level from 1992 to the present, regardless of whether title was won. One or more scholarships are awarded annually, depending on qualifications of applicants. A new application must be submitted each year, previous applicants may apply. Applications must be received by June 30. Late or incomplete applications are not accepted.

Academic/Career Areas Health and Medical Sciences.

Award Scholarship for use in graduate years; not renewable. *Number:* 1.

Eligibility Requirements Applicant must be enrolled or expecting to enroll at an institution or university; female and must have an interest in beauty pageant. Available to U.S. citizens.

Application Requirements Application, essay, financial need analysis, references, test scores, transcript. *Deadline:* June 30.

Contact Hostess Committee Scholarships/Miss
America Pageant
Two Miss America Way, Suite 1000
Atlantic City, NJ 08401

HOWARD HUGHES MEDICAL INSTITUTE, OFFICE OF GRANTS AND SPECIAL PROGRAMS
http://www.hhmi.org

HOWARD HUGHES MEDICAL INSTITUTE PREDOCTORAL FELLOWSHIPS IN BIOLOGICAL SCIENCES
• *See number 203*

HOWARD HUGHES MEDICAL INSTITUTE RESEARCH TRAINING FELLOWSHIPS FOR MEDICAL STUDENTS
• *See number 204*

INTERNATIONAL DEVELOPMENT RESEARCH CENTER
http://www.idrc.ca/awards

AGROPOLIS
• *See number 10*

JANE COFFIN CHILDS MEMORIAL FUND FOR MEDICAL RESEARCH
http://www.jccfund.org

JANE COFFIN CHILDS MEMORIAL FUND FOR MEDICAL RESEARCH FELLOWSHIPS • 531

One-time fellowship for M.D.'s or PhD's for full-time studies in the medical and related sciences bearing on cancer. Award is for two to three years of research and applicant should have no more than one year of postdoctoral experience. Submit research proposal. Deadline: February 1.

Academic/Career Areas Health and Medical Sciences; Natural Sciences.

Award Fellowship for use in postgraduate years; not renewable. *Number:* 20–25. *Amount:* up to $121,500.

Eligibility Requirements Applicant must be enrolled or expecting to enroll full-time at an institution or university. Available to U.S. and non-U.S. citizens.

Application Requirements Application, references, research proposal. *Deadline:* February 1.

Contact Elizabeth Ford, Administrative Director
Jane Coffin Childs Memorial Fund for Medical Research
333 Cedar Street
New Haven, CT 06510
Phone: 203-785-4612
Fax: 203-785-3301

JAPANESE GOVERNMENT/THE MONBUSHO SCHOLARSHIP PROGRAM
http://embjapan.org/la

RESEARCH STUDENT SCHOLARSHIP
• *See number 13*

KANSAS BOARD OF REGENTS
http://www.kansasregents.com

KANSAS OPTOMETRY SERVICE PROGRAM • 532

This program is designed to encourage optometrists to establish Kansas practices. Kansas helps pay the difference between resident and nonresident tuition at eligible out-of-state institutions. Must be Kansas resident. Deadline: April 1.

Academic/Career Areas Health and Medical Sciences.

Award Forgivable loan for use in graduate years; renewable. *Number:* 30–40. *Amount:* $6500–$10,500.

Eligibility Requirements Applicant must be enrolled or expecting to enroll full-time at an institution or university and resident of Kansas. Available to U.S. citizens.

Application Requirements Application. *Deadline:* April 1.

Contact Diane Lindeman, Director of Student Financial Assistance
Kansas Board of Regents
1000 Southwest Jackson, Suite 520
Topeka, KS 66612-1368
Phone: 785-296-3517
Fax: 785-296-0983
E-mail: dlindeman@ksbor.org

OSTEOPATHIC SERVICE SCHOLARSHIP PROGRAM • 533

This program provides scholarships to Kansas residents who are osteopathic students and agree to practice one year in an underserved area in Kansas for each year of scholarship support. Deadline: May 15. Must be U.S. citizen.

Academic/Career Areas Health and Medical Sciences.

Award Forgivable loan for use in graduate years; renewable. *Number:* 25–35. *Amount:* $15,000.

Eligibility Requirements Applicant must be enrolled or expecting to enroll full-time at an institution or university; resident of Kansas and studying in Kansas. Available to U.S. citizens.

Application Requirements Application, essay, financial need analysis. *Deadline:* May 1.

Contact Diane Lindeman, Director of Student Financial Assistance
Kansas Board of Regents
1000 Southwest Jackson, Suite 520
Topeka, KS 66612-1368
Phone: 785-296-3517
Fax: 785-296-0983
E-mail: dlindeman@ksbor.org

LEUKEMIA & LYMPHOMA SOCIETY
http://www.leukemia-lymphoma.org

LEUKEMIA AND LYMPHOMA SOCIETY SCHOLAR AWARDS • 534

A career development program which provides support for basic and clinical research towards a cure or control of leukemia, lymphoma, and myeloma renewable for a period of five years. Program awards up to $100,000 per year.

Academic/Career Areas Health and Medical Sciences.

Award Fellowship for use in postgraduate years; renewable. *Amount:* up to $100,000.

Eligibility Requirements Applicant must be enrolled or expecting to enroll at an institution or university. Available to U.S. and non-U.S. citizens.

Application Requirements Application. *Deadline:* September 15.

Contact Director of Research Administration
Leukemia & Lymphoma Society
1311 Mamaroneck Avenue
White Plains, NY 11103

LEUKEMIA'S LYMPHOMA SOCIETY FELLOW AWARDS • 535

A career development program which provides support for basic and clinical research towards a cure or control of leukemia, lymphoma, and myeloma renewable for a period of three years. Program awards up to $40,000 per year.

Academic/Career Areas Health and Medical Sciences.

Award Fellowship for use in postgraduate years; renewable. *Amount:* up to $40,000.

Eligibility Requirements Applicant must be enrolled or expecting to enroll at an institution or university. Available to U.S. and non-U.S. citizens.

Application Requirements Application. *Deadline:* September 15.

Contact Director of Research Administration
Leukemia & Lymphoma Society
1311 Mamaroneck Avenue
White Plains, NY 11103

LEUKEMIA'S LYMPHOMA SOCIETY SPECIAL FELLOW AWARDS • 536

A career development program which provides support for basic and clinical research towards a cure or control of leukemia, lymphoma, and myeloma renewable for a period of three years. Program awards up to $50,000 a year.

Academic/Career Areas Health and Medical Sciences.

Award Fellowship for use in postgraduate years; renewable. *Amount:* up to $50,000.

Eligibility Requirements Applicant must be enrolled or expecting to enroll at an institution or university. Available to U.S. and non-U.S. citizens.

Application Requirements Application. *Deadline:* September 15.

Contact Director of Research Administration
Leukemia & Lymphoma Society
1311 Mamaroneck Avenue
White Plains, NY 11103

LIFE SCIENCES RESEARCH FOUNDATION
http://www.lsrf.org

POSTDOCTORAL FELLOWSHIPS
• *See number 208*

MACKENZIE FOUNDATION

MACKENZIE FOUNDATION AWARDS • 537

One-time award for students in California medical schools studying to be general practitioners. Award amounts depend on funds available and number of requests. California residence not required. Award for non-U.S. citizens only if they will be practicing medicine in the U.S. The financial aid office of each medical school distributes application forms to students regarded as potential candidates.

Academic/Career Areas Health and Medical Sciences.

Award Scholarship for use in graduate years; not renewable. *Amount:* $1500–$3500.

Eligibility Requirements Applicant must be enrolled or expecting to enroll full-time at an institution or university and studying in California. Available to U.S. and non-U.S. citizens.

Application Requirements Application, financial need analysis, references. *Deadline:* Continuous.

Contact Philip Irwin, Trustee
MacKenzie Foundation
400 South Hope Street, Suite 1853
Los Angeles, CA 90071-2899

MARCH OF DIMES BIRTH DEFECTS FOUNDATION - GRANTS ADMINISTRATION
http://www.modimes.org

BASIL O'CONNOR STARTER SCHOLAR RESEARCH AWARDS • 538

One-time award for young scientists who have just begun independent research careers. Must hold a recent faculty appointment. Research must be relevant to the interest of the March of Dimes. Submit letter of intent. Application must be postmarked by February 15. Candidates that are accepted will receive new application forms that must be postmarked by May 31. Visit website for more information.

Academic/Career Areas Health and Medical Sciences.

Award Grant for use in graduate, or postgraduate years; not renewable. *Amount:* up to $75,000.

Eligibility Requirements Applicant must be enrolled or expecting to enroll at an institution or university. Applicant or parent of applicant must have employment or volunteer experience in teaching. Available to U.S. and non-U.S. citizens.

March of Dimes Birth Defects Foundation - Grants Administration (continued)

Application Requirements Application, letter of nomination and abstract. *Deadline:* February 15.

Contact Dr. Michael Katz, Vice President, Research
March of Dimes Birth Defects Foundation
- Grants Administration
1275 Mamaroneck Avenue
White Plains, NY 10605
Phone: 914-997-4555
Fax: 914-997-4560
E-mail: researchgrants@modimes.org

MARCH OF DIMES RESEARCH GRANTS • 539

Awards for research scientists with faculty appointments or the equivalent at universities, hospitals, or research institutions. Research must be relevant to the interest of the March of Dimes. Submit letter of intent by April 30. Recipients may apply again. Application deadline is September 30. Research subjects appropriate for support by March of Dimes include basic biological processes governing development, genetics, clinical studies, studies of reproductive health, environmental toxicology, and social and behavioral studies. Visit website for additional information.

Academic/Career Areas Health and Medical Sciences.

Award Grant for use in graduate, or postgraduate years; not renewable.

Eligibility Requirements Applicant must be enrolled or expecting to enroll at an institution or university. Applicant or parent of applicant must have employment or volunteer experience in teaching. Available to U.S. and non-U.S. citizens.

Application Requirements Application, letter of intent. *Deadline:* September 30.

Contact Dr. Michael Katz, Vice President, Research
March of Dimes Birth Defects Foundation
- Grants Administration
1275 Mamaroneck Avenue
White Plains, NY 10605
Phone: 914-997-4555
Fax: 914-997-4560
E-mail: researchgrants@modimes.org

MARYLAND STATE HIGHER EDUCATION COMMISSION
http://www.mhec.state.md.us

LOAN ASSISTANCE REPAYMENT PROGRAM FOR PRIMARY CARE SERVICES • 540

Must be working at an eligible practice site in Maryland and be willing to provide at least two years of service. Provides assistance for repayment of loan debt to physicians and medical residents specializing in primary care in under-served areas.

Academic/Career Areas Health and Medical Sciences.

Award Forgivable loan for use in postgraduate years; renewable. *Number:* up to 25. *Amount:* $25,000–$30,000.

Eligibility Requirements Applicant must be enrolled or expecting to enroll at an institution or university; resident of Maryland and studying in Maryland. Applicant or parent of applicant must have employment or volunteer experience in designated career field. Available to U.S. citizens.

Application Requirements Application. *Deadline:* Continuous.

Contact Carla Rich, Scholarship Administration
Maryland State Higher Education
Commission
16 Francis Street
Annapolis, MD 21401-1781
Phone: 410-260-4513
Fax: 410-974-5994
E-mail: ssamail@mhec.state.md.us

MENNONITE HEALTH SERVICES
http://www.mhsonline.org

ELMER EDIGER MEMORIAL SCHOLARSHIP FUND • 541

Award for graduate student with vocational interest in the area of mental health, developmental disabilities, or related fields. Minimum 3.25 GPA required. Must be active member in a Mennonite, Brethren in Christ or Mennonite Brethren congregation.

Academic/Career Areas Health and Medical Sciences; Health Information Management/ Technology; Social Services; Special Education; Therapy/Rehabilitation.

Award Scholarship for use in graduate years; renewable. *Number:* 1. *Amount:* $1000–$1200.

Eligibility Requirements Applicant must be Brethren and enrolled or expecting to enroll full or part-time at an institution or university. Available to U.S. and Canadian citizens.

Application Requirements Application, autobiography, essay, financial need analysis, references, test scores, transcript. *Deadline:* February 1.

Contact Wendy Rohn, Office Manager
Mennonite Health Services
234 South Main Street, Suite 1
Goshen, IN 46526
Phone: 219-534-9689
Fax: 219-534-3254
E-mail: info@mhsonline.org

MILHEIM FOUNDATION FOR CANCER RESEARCH

MILHEIM FOUNDATION FOR CANCER RESEARCH PROJECT GRANTS IN ONCOLOGY • 542

Awards for graduate students to support research work in the prevention, treatment, and cure of cancer. Must reside within continental U.S. Grant request must be made in the name of a supporting institution. Write for application. One-time award of $1500-$20,000.

Academic/Career Areas Health and Medical Sciences; Health Information Management/Technology.

Award Grant for use in graduate years; not renewable. *Number:* 8–15. *Amount:* $1500–$20,000.

Eligibility Requirements Applicant must be enrolled or expecting to enroll full or part-time at an institution or university. Available to U.S. citizens.

Application Requirements Application. *Deadline:* March 15.

Contact Vicki Lillly, Trust Associate
Milheim Foundation for Cancer Research
918 17th Street, DN-CO-BB6T
Denver, CO 80202
Phone: 303-585-5915
Fax: 303-585-4144

MINNESOTA DEPARTMENT OF HEALTH
http://www.health.state.mn.us

MINNESOTA RURAL MIDLEVEL PRACTITIONER LOAN FORGIVENESS PROGRAM • 543

This program offers loan repayment to nurse practitioner, nurse midwife, nurse anesthetist, advance clinical nurse specialist, and physician assistant students who agree to practice in a designated rural area for a minimum two-year service obligation after completion of training. Candidates must apply while still in school. Up to eight selections are made annually contingent upon state funding.

Academic/Career Areas Health and Medical Sciences; Nursing.

Award Grant for use in graduate, or postgraduate years; not renewable. *Number:* up to 8. *Amount:* up to $3500.

Eligibility Requirements Applicant must be enrolled or expecting to enroll full or part-time at an institution or university. Available to U.S. citizens.

Application Requirements Application, essay. *Deadline:* December 1.

Contact Karen Welter
Minnesota Department of Health
121 East Seventh Place, Suite 460, PO Box 64975
St. Paul, MN 55164-0975
Phone: 651-282-6302
E-mail: karen.welter@health.state.mn.us

MINNESOTA RURAL PHYSICIAN LOAN FORGIVENESS PROGRAM • 544

Program funded to offer loan repayment to primary care medical residents who agree to practice in a designated rural area. Applicants must submit applications while in residency. Up to 12 selections per year contingent upon state funding.

Academic/Career Areas Health and Medical Sciences.

Award Grant for use in graduate, or postgraduate years; not renewable. *Number:* up to 12. *Amount:* up to $10,000.

Eligibility Requirements Applicant must be enrolled or expecting to enroll at an institution or university. Available to U.S. citizens.

Application Requirements Application, essay. *Deadline:* December 1.

Contact Karen Welter
Minnesota Department of Health
121 East Seventh Place, Suite 460, PO Box 64975
St. Paul, MN 55164-0975
Phone: 651-282-6302
E-mail: karen.welter@health.state.mn.us

MINNESOTA URBAN PHYSICIAN LOAN FORGIVENESS PROGRAM • 545

Program funded to offer loan repayment to primary care medical residents who agree to practice in a designated urban area. Applications must be submitted while applicants are still in residency. Up to 4 selections per year contingent upon state funding.

Academic/Career Areas Health and Medical Sciences.

Award Grant for use in graduate, or postgraduate years; not renewable. *Number:* up to 4. *Amount:* up to $10,000.

Eligibility Requirements Applicant must be enrolled or expecting to enroll at an institution or university. Available to U.S. citizens.

Minnesota Department of Health (continued)

Application Requirements Application, essay.
Deadline: December 1.

Contact Karen Welter
Minnesota Department of Health
121 East Seventh Place, Suite 460, PO
Box 64975
St. Paul, MN 55164-0975
Phone: 651-282-6302
E-mail: karen.welter@health.state.mn.us

MISSISSIPPI STATE STUDENT FINANCIAL AID
http://www.ihl.state.ms.us

GRADUATE AND PROFESSIONAL DEGREE LOAN/SCHOLARSHIP-MISSISSIPPI • 546

Renewable loan for Mississippi graduate students pursuing health-related degree programs not available at a Mississippi university. One year of service in Mississippi required for each year of loan. Eligible programs of study include the following: chiropractic medicine, podiatric medicine, orthotics or prosthetics.

Academic/Career Areas Health and Medical Sciences; Therapy/Rehabilitation.

Award Forgivable loan for use in graduate years; renewable. *Amount:* $7000.

Eligibility Requirements Applicant must be enrolled or expecting to enroll full-time at an institution or university and resident of Mississippi. Available to U.S. citizens.

Application Requirements Application, references, transcript. *Deadline:* March 31.

Contact Board of Trustees
Mississippi State Student Financial Aid
3825 Ridgewood Road
Jackson, MS 39211-6453

SOUTHERN REGIONAL EDUCATION BOARD LOAN/SCHOLARSHIP • 547

Award for Mississippi residents enrolled at accredited school of optometry or osteopathic medicine. Amount determined by Southern Regional Education Board. Renewable loan forgiven if student serves one year in Mississippi for each year loan is awarded.

Academic/Career Areas Health and Medical Sciences.

Award Forgivable loan for use in graduate years; renewable. *Amount:* up to $17,000.

Eligibility Requirements Applicant must be enrolled or expecting to enroll full-time at a four-year institution or university; resident of Mississippi and studying in Alabama, Florida, Tennessee, or Texas. Available to U.S. citizens.

Application Requirements Application, transcript.
Deadline: March 31.

Contact Board of Trustees
Mississippi State Student Financial Aid
3825 Ridgewood Road
Jackson, MS 39211-6453

MYASTHENIA GRAVIS FOUNDATION OF AMERICA, INC.
http://www.myasthenia.org

DR. HENRY R. VIETS MEDICAL STUDENT RESEARCH FELLOWSHIP
• *See number 210*

OSSERMAN/SOSIN/MCCLURE POSTDOCTORAL FELLOWSHIP
• *See number 211*

NASA IDAHO SPACE GRANT CONSORTIUM
http://www.uidaho.edu/nasa_isgc

NASA ID SPACE GRANT CONSORTIUM FELLOWSHIP PROGRAM
• *See number 60*

NATIONAL ARAB AMERICAN MEDICAL ASSOCIATION
http://www.naama.com

FOUNDATION SCHOLARSHIP
• *See number 290*

NATIONAL HEADACHE FOUNDATION
http://www.headaches.org

NATIONAL HEADACHE FOUNDATION RESEARCH GRANT • 548

One-time award to conduct research protocols that are objectively sound and whose results can contribute to the better understanding and treatment of headache and pain. Project must be conducted in U.S. Submit research proposal.

Academic/Career Areas Health and Medical Sciences.

Award Grant for use in graduate years; not renewable. *Number:* 8–12. *Amount:* $500–$15,000.

Eligibility Requirements Applicant must be enrolled or expecting to enroll full or part-time at an institution or university. Available to U.S. and Canadian citizens.

Application Requirements Application. *Deadline:* December 1.

Contact Suzanne Simons, Executive Director
National Headache Foundation
428 West St. James Place, 2nd Floor
Chicago, IL 60614-2750
Phone: 773-388-6399
Fax: 773-525-7357
E-mail: info@headaches.org

NATIONAL HEMOPHILIA FOUNDATION
http://www.hemophilia.org

NATIONAL HEMOPHILIA FOUNDATION JUDITH GRAHAM POOL POSTDOCTORAL FELLOWSHIP
• *See number 291*

NATIONAL HEMOPHILIA FOUNDATION LABORATORY GRANT • 549

Grants targeted to projects that would yield scientific information contributing to a cure for bleeding disorders such as hemophilia and von Wittebrand disease. Principal investigator must hold Ph.D., MD, or equivalent degree and have a full-time faculty position or equivalent. Institutions are the official recipients of grant up to $300,000 per year for three years.

Academic/Career Areas Health and Medical Sciences.

Award Grant for use in postgraduate years; renewable. *Amount:* up to $300,000.

Eligibility Requirements Applicant must be enrolled or expecting to enroll at an institution or university. Available to U.S. and non-U.S. citizens.

Application Requirements Application, description of proposed research project. *Deadline:* February 1.

Contact Rita Barsky, Assistant Director
National Hemophilia Foundation
116 West 32nd Street, 11th Floor
New York, NY 10001
Phone: 212-328-3730
Fax: 212-328-3788
E-mail: rbarsky@hemophilia.org

NATIONAL HEMOPHILIA FOUNDATION PHYSICAL THERAPY EXCELLENCE FELLOWSHIP • 550

$5000 fellowship for a physical therapist from an accredited physical therapy school currently working with patients with bleeding disorders. It is recommended that fellow be endorsed by a federally funded hemophilia treatment center. Submit application, letters of recommendation and description of proposed research project.

Academic/Career Areas Health and Medical Sciences.

Award Fellowship for use in postgraduate years; not renewable. *Number:* 1. *Amount:* $5000.

Eligibility Requirements Applicant must be enrolled or expecting to enroll at an institution or university.

Application Requirements Application, references, description of proposed research project. *Deadline:* April 1.

Contact Rita Barsky, Assistant Director
National Hemophilia Foundation
116 West 32nd Street, 11th Floor
New York, NY 10001
Phone: 212-328-3730
Fax: 212-328-3788
E-mail: rbarsky@hemophilia.org

NATIONAL MEDICAL FELLOWSHIPS, INC
http://www.nmf-online.org

BENN AND KATHLEEN GILMORE SCHOLARSHIP • 551

Scholarship is awarded annually to a rising, third-year African-American medical student. Candidates must demonstrate outstanding academic achievement, leadership, and be nominated by medical school deans. Must be resident of Michigan, Ohio, Indiana, Illinois, or the District of Columbia and must attend University of Michigan Medical School, Wayne State University School of Medicine, or Michigan State University College of Human Medicine. Applications are requested in October and the deadline for submission of all documents is November 23.

Academic/Career Areas Health and Medical Sciences.

Award Scholarship for use in graduate years; not renewable. *Number:* 1. *Amount:* $3000.

Eligibility Requirements Applicant must be Black (non-Hispanic); enrolled or expecting to enroll at an institution or university; resident of District of Columbia, Illinois, Indiana, Michigan, or Ohio; studying in Michigan and must have an interest in leadership. Available to U.S. citizens.

Application Requirements Essay, references, transcript. *Deadline:* November 23.

Contact Fellowship Coordinator
National Medical Fellowships, Inc
5 Hanover Square, 15th Floor
New York, NY 10004

C. R. BARD FOUNDATION PRIZE • 552

One-time award available to underrepresented minorities in senior year of medical school who intend to pursue careers in oncology, cardiology or urology. Students must be nominated by medical school deans and appropriate department chairs or directors for outstanding academic achievement and leadership. Curriculum vitae is required. Nominations are

National Medical Fellowships, Inc (continued)

requested in January and the deadline date for submission of all documents is February 15.

Academic/Career Areas Health and Medical Sciences.

Award Prize for use in graduate years; not renewable. *Number:* 1. *Amount:* $5000.

Eligibility Requirements Applicant must be American Indian/Alaska Native, Black (non-Hispanic), or Hispanic; enrolled or expecting to enroll full-time at an institution or university and must have an interest in leadership. Available to U.S. citizens.

Application Requirements References, transcript, curriculum vitae. *Deadline:* February 15.

Contact Fellowship Coordinator
National Medical Fellowships, Inc
5 Hanover Square, 15th Floor
New York, NY 10004

FELLOWSHIP PROGRAM IN ACADEMIC MEDICINE FOR MINORITY STUDENTS • 553

Thirty-five fellowships available to first through third-year underrepresented minority students attending accredited U.S. medical schools' who have demonstrated academic achievement and show promise for careers in bio-medical research and academic medicine. Fellows spend eight to twelve weeks working in a major research laboratory. Must be nominated by the dean of the medical school. One-time awards of $6000 each. Applicants are requested in September and the deadline for submission of documents is November 16.

Academic/Career Areas Health and Medical Sciences.

Award Fellowship for use in graduate years; not renewable. *Number:* 35. *Amount:* $6000.

Eligibility Requirements Applicant must be American Indian/Alaska Native, Black (non-Hispanic), or Hispanic and enrolled or expecting to enroll full-time at an institution or university. Available to U.S. citizens.

Application Requirements Application, essay, references, transcript. *Deadline:* November 16.

Contact Fellowship Coordinator
National Medical Fellowships, Inc
5 Hanover Square, 15th Floor
New York, NY 10004

FELLOWSHIP PROGRAM IN VIOLENCE PREVENTION FOR MINORITY MEDICAL STUDENTS • 554

Fellows participate in epidemiological research on violence under the supervision of senior researchers at CDC. Competition is open to second, third, or fourth year underrepresented minority medical students attending accredited U.S. medical schools. Candidates must demonstrate academic achievement, leadership and interest in violence prevention and education. Candidates must be recommended by the medical school deans.

Academic/Career Areas Health and Medical Sciences.

Award Fellowship for use in graduate years; not renewable. *Number:* 4. *Amount:* $5000.

Eligibility Requirements Applicant must be American Indian/Alaska Native, Black (non-Hispanic), or Hispanic; enrolled or expecting to enroll full-time at an institution or university and must have an interest in leadership. Available to U.S. citizens.

Application Requirements Application, references, transcript. *Deadline:* March 16.

Contact Fellowship Coordinator
National Medical Fellowships, Inc
5 Hanover Square, 15th Floor
New York, NY 10004

FRANKLIN C. MCLEAN AWARD • 555

This one-time award is National Medical Fellowship's oldest and most prestigious honor, presented to a graduating underrepresented minority medical student. Students must be nominated by their medical school dean for outstanding academic achievement, leadership and community service. Nominations are requested in June and the deadline for submission of all documents is July 30.

Academic/Career Areas Health and Medical Sciences.

Award Prize for use in graduate years; not renewable. *Number:* 1. *Amount:* $3000.

Eligibility Requirements Applicant must be American Indian/Alaska Native, Black (non-Hispanic), or Hispanic; enrolled or expecting to enroll full-time at an institution or university and must have an interest in leadership. Available to U.S. citizens.

Application Requirements References, transcript. *Deadline:* June 30.

Contact Fellowship Coordinator
National Medical Fellowships, Inc
5 Hanover Square, 15th Floor
New York, NY 10004

GERBER FELLOWSHIP IN PEDIATRIC NUTRITION • 556

Eligibility is limited to underrepresented minority medical students attending accredited U.S. medical schools and underrepresented minority residents participating in ongoing research in the area of pediatric nutrition. Candidates must be U.S. citizens.

Candidates must also demonstrate outstanding academic achievement, leadership, and the potential to make significant contributions to pediatric nutrition research. Candidates must be recommended by the medical school dean or director of graduate education. Applicant must submit curricula vitae. Nominations are requested in July and the deadline for submission of all documents is October 12.

Academic/Career Areas Health and Medical Sciences.

Award Fellowship for use in graduate years; not renewable. *Number:* 1. *Amount:* $3000.

Eligibility Requirements Applicant must be American Indian/Alaska Native, Black (non-Hispanic), or Hispanic; enrolled or expecting to enroll full-time at an institution or university and must have an interest in leadership. Available to U.S. citizens.

Application Requirements Application, references, transcript, curricula vitae. *Deadline:* October 12.

Contact Fellowship Coordinator
National Medical Fellowships, Inc
5 Hanover Square, 15th Floor
New York, NY 10004

HENRY G. HALLADAY AWARDS • 557

Five one-time awards available to African-American men who have been accepted into the first-year classes of accredited U.S. medical schools' and demonstrate exceptional financial need as well as having to overcome significant obstacles to obtain a medical education. Awards supplement National Medical Fellowship's general need-based scholarships. There is no special application for these awards. Recipients are selected from applicants of the need-based scholarships. The NMF need-based applications are available on line or through medical school.

Academic/Career Areas Health and Medical Sciences.

Award Scholarship for use in graduate years; not renewable. *Number:* 5. *Amount:* $760.

Eligibility Requirements Applicant must be Black (non-Hispanic); enrolled or expecting to enroll full-time at an institution or university and male. Available to U.S. citizens.

Application Requirements Financial need analysis. *Deadline:* June 29.

Contact Fellowship Coordinator
National Medical Fellowships, Inc
5 Hanover Square, 15th Floor
New York, NY 10004

HUGH J. ANDERSEN MEMORIAL SCHOLARSHIPS • 558

One-time award is for Minnesota residents or for students attending Minnesota medical schools. Can-

didates must be underrepresented minority students enrolled beyond their first-year in an accredited U.S. medical school. Candidates must demonstrate outstanding leadership, community service, and financial need. Students must be nominated by medical school deans and must submit personal essays. Nominations are requested in August and the deadline date for submission of all documents is September 28.

Academic/Career Areas Health and Medical Sciences.

Award Scholarship for use in graduate years; not renewable. *Number:* 2. *Amount:* $2500.

Eligibility Requirements Applicant must be American Indian/Alaska Native, Black (non-Hispanic), or Hispanic; enrolled or expecting to enroll full-time at an institution or university and must have an interest in leadership. Applicant or parent of applicant must have employment or volunteer experience in community service. Available to U.S. citizens.

Application Requirements Essay, financial need analysis, references, transcript. *Deadline:* September 28.

Contact Fellowship Coordinator
National Medical Fellowships, Inc
5 Hanover Square, 15th Floor
New York, NY 10004
Phone: 212-483-8880
Fax: 212-483-8897

IRVING GRAEF MEMORIAL SCHOLARSHIP • 559

One scholarship available to third-year, rising minority medical students who received NMF financial assistance during their second year. Candidates must be nominated by the dean for outstanding academic achievement and leadership. Applicants must submit personal essays. One renewable award of $2000 per year. Nominations requested in October and the deadline for submission of all documents is November 23.

Academic/Career Areas Health and Medical Sciences.

Award Scholarship for use in graduate years; renewable. *Number:* 1. *Amount:* $2000.

Eligibility Requirements Applicant must be American Indian/Alaska Native, Black (non-Hispanic), or Hispanic; enrolled or expecting to enroll full-time at an institution or university and must have an interest in leadership. Available to U.S. citizens.

Application Requirements Application, essay, financial need analysis, references, transcript. *Deadline:* November 23.

Contact Fellowship Coordinator
National Medical Fellowships, Inc
5 Hanover Square, 15th Floor
New York, NY 10004

JAMES H. ROBINSON M.D. MEMORIAL PRIZE IN SURGERY • 560

One award available to underrepresented minority students at accredited U.S. medical schools who will graduate during the academic year in which the award is made available. Students must be nominated by medical school deans and department of surgery chairpersons for outstanding performance in the surgical disciplines. One-time stipend of $500. Applicant must submit curriculum vitae with application. Nominations are requested in January and the deadline for submission of all documents is February 15.

Academic/Career Areas Health and Medical Sciences.

Award Prize for use in graduate years; not renewable. *Number:* 1. *Amount:* $500.

Eligibility Requirements Applicant must be American Indian/Alaska Native, Black (non-Hispanic), or Hispanic and enrolled or expecting to enroll full-time at an institution or university. Available to U.S. citizens.

Application Requirements References, transcript, curriculum vitae. *Deadline:* February 15.

Contact Fellowship Coordinator
National Medical Fellowships, Inc
5 Hanover Square, 15th Floor
New York, NY 10004

JOSIAH MACY JR. SUBSTANCE ABUSE FELLOWSHIP PROGRAM FOR MINORITY MEDICAL STUDENTS • 561

Fellowships available to second- and third-year underrepresented minority students attending accredited U.S. institutions that grant MD and DO degrees. Candidates must be nominated by medical school deans for academic excellence and show interest and promise for careers in biomedical and clinical sciences research, epidemiology and health policy. Program will involve students in 8-12 week rotations. Applications are requested in September and the deadline for submission of all documents is October 19.

Academic/Career Areas Health and Medical Sciences.

Award Fellowship for use in graduate years; not renewable. *Number:* up to 10. *Amount:* up to $6000.

Eligibility Requirements Applicant must be American Indian/Alaska Native, Black (non-Hispanic), or Hispanic; enrolled or expecting to enroll full-time at an institution or university and must have an interest in leadership. Applicant must have 3.0 GPA or higher. Available to U.S. citizens.

Application Requirements Application, essay, references, transcript. *Deadline:* October 19.

Contact Fellowship Coordinator
National Medical Fellowships, Inc
5 Hanover Square, 15th Floor
New York, NY 10004

METROPOLITAN LIFE FOUNDATION AWARDS PROGRAM FOR ACADEMIC EXCELLENCE IN MEDICINE • 562

Fourteen need-based scholarships available to second- and fourth-year underrepresented minority medical students who attend school or reside in selected cities in the following states: AZ, CA, CO, DC, FL, GA, IL, MA, NY, OH, OK, PA, RI, SC, NJ, CT and TX. Candidates must demonstrate outstanding academic achievement and leadership. Students must be nominated by medical school deans. Up to fourteen scholarships at $4000. Nominations are requested in October and the deadline for submission of all documents is November 26.

Academic/Career Areas Health and Medical Sciences.

Award Scholarship for use in graduate years; not renewable. *Number:* up to 14. *Amount:* up to $4000.

Eligibility Requirements Applicant must be American Indian/Alaska Native, Black (non-Hispanic), or Hispanic; enrolled or expecting to enroll full-time at an institution or university and resident of Arizona, California, Colorado, District of Columbia, Florida, Georgia, Illinois, Massachusetts, New York, Ohio, Oklahoma, Pennsylvania, Rhode Island, South Carolina, or Texas. Available to U.S. citizens.

Application Requirements Application, essay, financial need analysis, references, test scores, transcript. *Deadline:* November 26.

Contact Fellowship Coordinator
National Medical Fellowships, Inc
5 Hanover Square, 15th Floor
New York, NY 10004

NATIONAL MEDICAL ASSOCIATION MERIT SCHOLARSHIPS • 563

Several awards available to African-American medical students at an accredited MD or DO degree-granting school in the U.S. Students must request letters of recommendation from the dean of the medical school. Several one-time awards of $2250 each. Presented for outstanding academic achievement, exceptional leadership and community service. Applications are requested in May and the deadline for submission of all documents is June 18.

Academic/Career Areas Health and Medical Sciences.

Award Scholarship for use in graduate years; not renewable. *Number:* 6. *Amount:* $2250.

Eligibility Requirements Applicant must be Black (non-Hispanic); enrolled or expecting to enroll full-time at an institution or university and must have an interest in leadership. Available to U.S. citizens.

Application Requirements Application, essay, financial need analysis, references, transcript. *Deadline:* June 18.

Contact Fellowship Coordinator
National Medical Fellowships, Inc
5 Hanover Square, 15th Floor
New York, NY 10004

NATIONAL MEDICAL ASSOCIATION PATTI LA BELLE AWARD • 564

Award is presented for outstanding academic achievement, exceptional leadership and community service. Eligibility is limited to African-American medical students who are attending accredited MD or DO degree granting schools in the U.S.; applicants must be U.S. citizens. Applications are requested in May and the deadline for submission of all documents is June 18.

Academic/Career Areas Health and Medical Sciences.

Award Scholarship for use in graduate years; not renewable. *Number:* 1. *Amount:* $5000.

Eligibility Requirements Applicant must be Black (non-Hispanic); enrolled or expecting to enroll full-time at an institution or university and must have an interest in leadership. Available to U.S. citizens.

Application Requirements Application, essay, financial need analysis, references, transcript. *Deadline:* June 18.

Contact Fellowship Coordinator
National Medical Fellowships, Inc
5 Hanover Square
New York, NY 10004

NATIONAL MEDICAL ASSOCIATION SLACK AWARD FOR MEDICAL JOURNALISM • 565

Two one-time awards available to African-American medical students who are in an accredited MD or DO degree-granting school in the U.S. Students must request letter of recommendation from the dean and submit a sample of journalism work. Two one-time awards. Applications are requested in May and the deadline for submission of all documents is June 18.

Academic/Career Areas Health and Medical Sciences; Journalism.

Award Scholarship for use in graduate years; not renewable. *Number:* 2. *Amount:* $2500.

Eligibility Requirements Applicant must be Black (non-Hispanic); enrolled or expecting to enroll

full-time at an institution or university and must have an interest in writing. Available to U.S. citizens.

Application Requirements Application, essay, financial need analysis, references, transcript. *Deadline:* June 18.

Contact Fellowship Coordinator
National Medical Fellowships, Inc
5 Hanover Square, 15th Floor
New York, NY 10004

NATIONAL MEDICAL FELLOWSHIPS, INC. GENERAL NEED-BASED SCHOLARSHIP PROGRAMS • 566

Available to first- or second-year medical students who are either African-American, Alaskan Natives, Native Hawaiians, mainland Puerto Rican, Mexican-American, or Native American and who are in programs leading to MD or DO degrees. Based on need. Must be U.S. citizen. Must include verification of citizenship.

Academic/Career Areas Health and Medical Sciences.

Award Scholarship for use in graduate years; not renewable. *Amount:* $500–$2500.

Eligibility Requirements Applicant must be American Indian/Alaska Native, Black (non-Hispanic), or Hispanic and enrolled or expecting to enroll full-time at an institution or university. Available to U.S. citizens.

Application Requirements Application, essay, financial need analysis, references, test scores, transcript, verification of citizenship. *Deadline:* June 29.

Contact Fellowship Coordinator
National Medical Fellowships, Inc
5 Hanover Square, 15th Floor
New York, NY 10004
Phone: 212-483-8880
Fax: 212-483-8897

RALPH W. ELLISON MEMORIAL PRIZE • 567

One-time award presented to a graduating underrepresented minority medical student. Students must be nominated by their medical school deans for specific academic and leadership accomplishments and must submit a personal statement of at least 500 words. Nominations are requested in January and the deadline for submission of all documents is February 15.

Academic/Career Areas Health and Medical Sciences.

Award Prize for use in graduate years; not renewable. *Number:* 1. *Amount:* $500.

Eligibility Requirements Applicant must be American Indian/Alaska Native, Black (non-

National Medical Fellowships, Inc (continued)

Hispanic), or Hispanic; enrolled or expecting to enroll full-time at an institution or university and must have an interest in leadership. Available to U.S. citizens.

Application Requirements Application, essay, transcript. *Deadline:* February 15.

Contact Fellowship Coordinator
National Medical Fellowships, Inc
5 Hanover Square, 15th Floor
New York, NY 10004

WILLIAM AND CHARLOTTE CADBURY AWARD
• 568

One-time award is available to senior underrepresented minority students enrolled in accredited U.S. medical schools. Candidates must be nominated by the medical school deans for outstanding academic achievement and leadership. Nominations are requested in June and the deadline date for submission of all documents is July 30.

Academic/Career Areas Health and Medical Sciences.

Award Scholarship for use in graduate years; not renewable. *Number:* 1. *Amount:* $2000.

Eligibility Requirements Applicant must be American Indian/Alaska Native, Black (non-Hispanic), or Hispanic; enrolled or expecting to enroll full-time at an institution or university and must have an interest in leadership. Available to U.S. citizens.

Application Requirements Essay, references, transcript. *Deadline:* June 30.

Contact Fellowship Coordinator
National Medical Fellowships, Inc
5 Hanover Square, 15th Floor
New York, NY 10004

WYETH-AYERST LABORATORIES PRIZE IN WOMEN'S HEALTH
• 569

Candidates must be underrepresented minority women attending accredited medical schools in the U.S. Students must demonstrate exceptional achievement, leadership, and potential to make significant contributions in the field of women's health. Must include nominations from medical school deans, directors, or research mentor. Must submit curriculum vitae with application. Nominations are requested in January and the deadline for submission of all documents is February 15.

Academic/Career Areas Health and Medical Sciences.

Award Prize for use in graduate years; not renewable. *Number:* 2. *Amount:* $5000.

Eligibility Requirements Applicant must be American Indian/Alaska Native, Black (non-Hispanic), or Hispanic; enrolled or expecting to enroll full-time at an institution or university; female and must have an interest in leadership. Available to U.S. citizens.

Application Requirements References, transcript, curriculum vitae. *Deadline:* February 15.

Contact Fellowship Coordinator
National Medical Fellowships, Inc
5 Hanover Square, 15th Floor
New York, NY 10004

NATIONAL MILK PRODUCERS FEDERATION
http://www.nmpf.org

NATIONAL MILK PRODUCERS FEDERATION NATIONAL DAIRY LEADERSHIP SCHOLARSHIP PROGRAM
• *See number 5*

NATIONAL MULTIPLE SCLEROSIS SOCIETY
http://www.nationalmssociety.org

HARRY WEAVER NEUROSCIENCE SCHOLARSHIPS
• 570

Scholarships available to applicants with an MD, Ph.D., or equivalent degree to conduct research in the neurosciences. One-time award. Application deadline: 2/1.

Academic/Career Areas Health and Medical Sciences.

Award Scholarship for use in postgraduate years; not renewable. *Number:* 1–3. *Amount:* $50,000–$60,000.

Eligibility Requirements Applicant must be enrolled or expecting to enroll at an institution or university. Available to U.S. citizens.

Application Requirements Application. *Deadline:* February 1.

Contact National Multiple Sclerosis Society
733 Third Avenue
New York, NY 10017-3288

NATIONAL MULTIPLE SCLEROSIS SOCIETY BIOMEDICAL RESEARCH GRANTS
• 571

Grants available to established investigators for biomedical research. Must have an MD, Ph.D., or equivalent degree. One-time award. Application deadlines: February 1 and August 1.

Academic/Career Areas Health and Medical Sciences.

Award Grant for use in postgraduate years; not renewable. *Number:* 40–45. *Amount:* $80,000–$90,000.

Eligibility Requirements Applicant must be enrolled or expecting to enroll at an institution or university. Available to U.S. citizens.

Application Requirements Application.

Contact National Multiple Sclerosis Society
733 Third Avenue
New York, NY 10017-3288

NATIONAL MULTIPLE SCLEROSIS SOCIETY PATIENT MANAGEMENT CARE AND REHABILITATION GRANTS • 572

Grants for investigators with an MD, Ph.D., or equivalent degree to research patient management care and/or rehabilitation. One-time award of $80,000 per year. Application deadlines: February 1 and August 1.

Academic/Career Areas Health and Medical Sciences; Therapy/Rehabilitation.

Award Grant for use in postgraduate years; not renewable. *Number:* 2–3. *Amount:* $200,000–$300,000.

Eligibility Requirements Applicant must be enrolled or expecting to enroll at an institution or university. Available to U.S. citizens.

Application Requirements Application.

Contact National Multiple Sclerosis Society
733 Third Avenue
New York, NY 10017-3288

NATIONAL MULTIPLE SCLEROSIS SOCIETY PILOT RESEARCH GRANTS • 573

Grants for investigators with an MD, Ph.D., or equivalent degree. Several one-time awards for research in medicine. Application deadline: 2/1.

Academic/Career Areas Health and Medical Sciences.

Award Grant for use in postgraduate years; not renewable. *Number:* 25–27. *Amount:* $20,000–$25,000.

Eligibility Requirements Applicant must be enrolled or expecting to enroll at an institution or university. Available to U.S. citizens.

Application Requirements Application. *Deadline:* February 1.

Contact National Multiple Sclerosis Society
733 Third Avenue
New York, NY 10017-3288

NATIONAL MULTIPLE SCLEROSIS SOCIETY POSTDOCTORAL FELLOWSHIPS • 574

Renewable award to support research training in multiple sclerosis research for individuals with an MD, Ph.D., or equivalent degree. Several fellowships of $25,000-$30,000. Application deadline: 2/1.

Academic/Career Areas Health and Medical Sciences.

Award Fellowship for use in postgraduate years; renewable. *Number:* 30–40. *Amount:* $25,000–$30,000.

Eligibility Requirements Applicant must be enrolled or expecting to enroll at an institution or university. Available to U.S. citizens.

Application Requirements Application. *Deadline:* February 1.

Contact National Multiple Sclerosis Society
733 Third Avenue
New York, NY 10017-3288

NATIONAL MULTIPLE SCLEROSIS SOCIETY SENIOR FACULTY AWARDS • 575

One-time award for senior investigators with an MD, Ph.D. or equivalent degree in medicine. Application deadline: 2/1.

Academic/Career Areas Health and Medical Sciences.

Award Grant for use in postgraduate years; not renewable. *Number:* 1–2. *Amount:* $25,000–$30,000.

Eligibility Requirements Applicant must be enrolled or expecting to enroll at an institution or university. Available to U.S. citizens.

Application Requirements Application. *Deadline:* February 1.

Contact National Multiple Sclerosis Society
733 Third Avenue
New York, NY 10017-3288

NATIONAL SLEEP FOUNDATION
http://www.sleepfoundation.org

NATIONAL SLEEP FOUNDATION POSTDOCTORAL FELLOWSHIP PROGRAM
• *See number 213*

NEBRASKA HEALTH AND HUMAN SERVICES SYSTEM, OFFICE OF RURAL HEALTH

RURAL HEALTH SCHOLARSHIP PROGRAM
• *See number 292*

STATE OF NEBRASKA LOAN REPAYMENT PROGRAM FOR RURAL HEALTH PROFESSIONALS • 576

Physicians, nurse practitioners, physician assistants practicing internal medicine, family practice, pediatrics, obstetrics, gynecology, general surgery, and psychiatry eligible. Therapists, mental health professionals, dentists and pharmacists also eligible. Must commit to practicing three years in approved shortage area. To be used toward repayment of commercial or government educational loans.

Nebraska Health and Human Services System, Office of Rural Health (continued)

Academic/Career Areas Health and Medical Sciences; Nursing; Therapy/Rehabilitation.

Award Forgivable loan for use in graduate, or postgraduate years; not renewable. *Amount:* $10,000–$20,000.

Eligibility Requirements Applicant must be enrolled or expecting to enroll at an institution or university. Applicant or parent of applicant must have employment or volunteer experience in designated career field.

Application Requirements Application.

Contact Nebraska Health and Human Services
System, Office of Rural Health
301 Centennial Mall South PO Box 95044
Lincoln, NE 68509-5044
Phone: 402-471-2337

NEW JERSEY OSTEOPATHIC EDUCATION FOUNDATION
http://www.njosteo.com

NEW JERSEY OSTEOPATHIC EDUCATION FOUNDATION SCHOLARSHIP PROGRAM • 577

Award for New Jersey residents beginning their first year of a osteopathic medical program. Based on academic merit, financial need, and career potential. Must have minimum GPA of 3.0. Write for application deadline. One-time award of up to $10,000.

Academic/Career Areas Health and Medical Sciences.

Award Scholarship for use in graduate years; not renewable. *Number:* 4–10. *Amount:* $3000–$10,000.

Eligibility Requirements Applicant must be enrolled or expecting to enroll full-time at a four-year institution and resident of New Jersey. Applicant must have 3.0 GPA or higher. Available to U.S. citizens.

Application Requirements Application, essay, financial need analysis, interview, photo, references, test scores, transcript. *Deadline:* April 30.

Contact Frank Cagliari, Executive Director
New Jersey Osteopathic Education
Foundation
One Distribution Way
Monmouth Junction, NJ 08852-3001
Phone: 732-940-9000 Ext. 303
Fax: 732-940-8899
E-mail: njaops@njosteo.com

NEW MEXICO COMMISSION ON HIGHER EDUCATION
http://www.nmche.org

MEDICAL STUDENT LOAN-FOR-SERVICE PROGRAM • 578

Award for New Mexico residents accepted by or enrolled in public school of medicine in the U.S. Preference given to students attending UNM School of Medicine. Must practice as physician or physician assistant in designated health professional shortage area in New Mexico. Award dependent upon financial need but may not exceed $12,000 per year. Deadline: July 1. To apply call the Commission at the CHE Student Helpline: 1-800-279-9777.

Academic/Career Areas Health and Medical Sciences.

Award Forgivable loan for use in graduate years; not renewable. *Amount:* up to $12,000.

Eligibility Requirements Applicant must be enrolled or expecting to enroll full or part-time at a four-year institution or university and resident of New Mexico. Available to U.S. citizens.

Application Requirements Application, financial need analysis. *Deadline:* July 1.

Contact Barbara Serna, Clerk Specialist
New Mexico Commission on Higher
Education
PO Box 15910
Santa Fe, NM 87506-5910
Phone: 505-827-4026
Fax: 505-827-7392

NEW MEXICO HEALTH PROFESSIONAL LOAN REPAYMENT PROGRAM
• *See number 293*

OSTEOPATHIC MEDICAL STUDENT LOAN PROGRAM-NEW MEXICO • 579

Renewable award for New Mexico residents enrolled in accredited program of osteopathic education in the U.S. Must practice full-time in New Mexico. Loan may be repaid through service. Priority given to those with financial need. To apply call the Commission at the CHE Student Helpline: 1-800-279-9777.

Academic/Career Areas Health and Medical Sciences.

Award Forgivable loan for use in graduate years; renewable. *Amount:* up to $12,000.

Eligibility Requirements Applicant must be enrolled or expecting to enroll full or part-time at a four-year institution or university and resident of New Mexico. Available to U.S. citizens.

Application Requirements Application, financial need analysis, transcript. *Deadline:* July 1.

Contact Barbara Serna, Clerk Specialist
New Mexico Commission on Higher Education
PO Box 15910
Santa Fe, NM 87506-5910
Phone: 505-827-4026
Fax: 505-827-7392

NEW YORK STATE EDUCATION DEPARTMENT

REGENTS HEALTH CARE SCHOLARSHIPS FOR MEDICINE AND DENTISTRY-NEW YORK
• See number 294

REGENTS PHYSICIAN LOAN FORGIVENESS AWARD-NEW YORK • 580

Renewable award for New York resident licensed to practice medicine in New York. Must be within two years of completing residency or have completed residency within last five years. Must be U.S. citizen or permanent resident. Must practice medicine in a designated area of New York.

Academic/Career Areas Health and Medical Sciences.

Award Forgivable loan for use in postgraduate years; renewable. *Number:* up to 80. *Amount:* up to $10,000.

Eligibility Requirements Applicant must be enrolled or expecting to enroll at an institution or university; resident of New York and studying in New York. Available to U.S. citizens.

Application Requirements Application. *Deadline:* May 1.

Contact Lewis J. Hall, Coordinator
New York State Education Department
Room 1078 EBA
Albany, NY 12234
Phone: 518-486-1319
Fax: 518-486-5346

NORTH CAROLINA STATE EDUCATION ASSISTANCE AUTHORITY
http://www.cfnc.org

BOARD OF GOVERNORS MEDICAL SCHOLARSHIP PROGRAM • 581

Renewable award for students accepted to one of four medical schools in North Carolina. Must be a resident of North Carolina and be nominated by medical school for the award. Stipend of $5000 per year plus tuition and required fees is provided. Applicant must intend to practice medicine in North Carolina. Deadline is in April.

Academic/Career Areas Health and Medical Sciences.

Award Scholarship for use in graduate years; renewable. *Amount:* $12,000–$30,000.

Eligibility Requirements Applicant must be enrolled or expecting to enroll at an institution or university; resident of North Carolina and studying in North Carolina. Available to U.S. citizens.

Application Requirements Application, essay, financial need analysis, references, test scores, transcript.

Contact Bill Carswell, Manager of Scholarship and Grant Division
North Carolina State Education Assistance Authority
PO Box 13663
Research Triangle, NC 27709-3663

NORTHWEST OSTEOPATHIC MEDICAL FOUNDATION
http://www.nwosteo.org

NORTHWEST OSTEOPATHIC MEDICAL FOUNDATION RURAL ROTATION GRANTS • 582

Reimbursement grant available to osteopathic medical students who seek an experience in rural medicine in the Pacific Northwest. Grant recipients will serve a four week rotation in ambulatory primary care with an approved osteopathic physician. Write for deadlines and further information. Study must be in Alaska, Idaho, Montana, Oregon, or Washington.

Academic/Career Areas Health and Medical Sciences.

Award Grant for use in graduate years; not renewable. *Number:* up to 10. *Amount:* up to $500.

Eligibility Requirements Applicant must be enrolled or expecting to enroll at an institution or university and studying in Alaska, Idaho, Missouri, Oregon, or Washington.

Application Requirements Application, essay.

Contact Dennis Lavery, Executive Director
Northwest Osteopathic Medical Foundation
1410 SW Morrison Street, Suite 700
Portland, OR 97205
Phone: 503-222-7161
Fax: 503-222-2841
E-mail: lavery@nwosteo.org

NORTHWEST OSTEOPATHIC MEDICAL FOUNDATION SCHOLARSHIPS • 583

Scholarships available to residents of Northwest states and those who have lived, worked, or attended institutions of higher education in the Pacific Northwest. Based on prior/current academic work, evaluation of professional activity and aptitude for medical schoolwork and recommendations. Write for deadlines and further information. Must rank in upper quarter of class or have a minimum 3.5 GPA and include resume. Deadline: February 1.

Northwest Osteopathic Medical Foundation (continued)

Academic/Career Areas Health and Medical Sciences.

Award Scholarship for use in graduate years; not renewable. *Amount:* $1500–$6000.

Eligibility Requirements Applicant must be enrolled or expecting to enroll full-time at an institution or university and resident of Alaska, Idaho, Montana, Oregon, or Washington. Applicant must have 3.5 GPA or higher.

Application Requirements Application, driver's license, essay, references, transcript. *Deadline:* February 1.

Contact Dennis Lavery, Executive Director
Northwest Osteopathic Medical
Foundation
1410 SW Morrison Street, Suite 700
Portland, OR 97205
Phone: 503-222-7161
Fax: 503-222-2841
E-mail: lavery@nwosteo.org

OHIO BOARD OF REGENTS
http://www.regents.state.oh.us

PHYSICIAN LOAN REPAYMENT PROGRAM • 584

Renewable award that offers repayment of student loans for Ohio physicians who agree to practice in specialized areas in Ohio with limited access to medical care. Up to four years of student loan indebtedness may be canceled.

Academic/Career Areas Health and Medical Sciences.

Award Forgivable loan for use in graduate years; renewable. *Amount:* up to $20,000.

Eligibility Requirements Applicant must be enrolled or expecting to enroll at an institution or university; resident of Ohio and studying in Ohio. Applicant or parent of applicant must have employment or volunteer experience in designated career field.

Application Requirements Application. *Deadline:* Continuous.

Contact Barb Closser, Program Administrator
Ohio Board of Regents
PO Box 182452
Columbus, OH 43218-2452
Phone: 614-644-6629
Fax: 614-752-5903
E-mail: bclosser@regents.state.oh.us

OKLAHOMA EDUCATIONAL FOUNDATION FOR OSTEOPATHIC MEDICINE
http://www.okosteo.org

OKLAHOMA EDUCATIONAL FOUNDATION FOR OSTEOPATHIC MEDICINE ENDOWED STUDENT SCHOLARSHIP PROGRAM • 585

Nonrenewable award available to students attending osteopathic colleges. Applications are reviewed yearly. Write for specific deadlines. Must be Oklahoma resident.

Academic/Career Areas Health and Medical Sciences.

Award Scholarship for use in graduate years; not renewable. *Number:* 1–5. *Amount:* $2500.

Eligibility Requirements Applicant must be enrolled or expecting to enroll full-time at a four-year institution and resident of Oklahoma. Available to U.S. citizens.

Application Requirements Application, essay, financial need analysis, photo, references, transcript. *Deadline:* February 1.

Contact Dorothy Prophet, Foundation
Administrator
Oklahoma Educational Foundation for
Osteopathic Medicine
4848 North Lincoln Boulevard
Oklahoma City, OK 73105-3335
Phone: 405-528-4848
Fax: 405-528-6102
E-mail: dorothy@okosteo.org

ONS FOUNDATION
http://www.ons.org

ONS FOUNDATION ETHNIC MINORITY RESEARCHER AND MENTORSHIP GRANTS • 586

Two awards to encourage oncology nursing research by ethnic minority researchers. Beginning researchers' must use a mentor for consultative services. ONS Research Mentorship Program will help find mentor. One-time award of $4000 for the conduct of research and $1000 to mentor. Deadline: November 1.

Academic/Career Areas Health and Medical Sciences; Nursing.

Award Grant for use in graduate years; not renewable. *Number:* 2. *Amount:* $5000.

Eligibility Requirements Applicant must be American Indian/Alaska Native, Asian/Pacific Islander, Black (non-Hispanic), or Hispanic and enrolled or expecting to enroll at an institution or university.

Application Requirements Application. *Deadline:* November 1.

Contact ONS Foundation
501 Holiday Drive
Pittsburgh, PA 15220

ONS FOUNDATION NOVICE RESEARCHER AND MENTORSHIP GRANTS • 587

Two awards to encourage oncology nursing research by new, or novice investigators. Principal investigator must be AA, diploma, BSN, or master's prepared. Doctoral students not eligible. Must use a research mentor. ONS Research Mentorship Program will help find mentor. One-time award of $5000. Contact for application packet. Deadline: November 1.

Academic/Career Areas Health and Medical Sciences; Nursing.

Award Grant for use in graduate years; not renewable. *Number:* 2. *Amount:* $5000.

Eligibility Requirements Applicant must be enrolled or expecting to enroll at an institution or university.

Application Requirements Application. *Deadline:* November 1.

Contact ONS Foundation
501 Holiday Drive
Pittsburgh, PA 15220

ONS FOUNDATION ORTHO BIOTECH RESEARCH FELLOWSHIP • 588

One award to support short-term post-doctorate oncology-specific research training. Applicants must be registered nurses with interest in oncology and a completed doctoral degree in nursing or a related discipline. Must demonstrate how study with a senior investigator helps career. Previous fellows ineligible. Maximum $10,000 awarded to cover transportation, lodging, tuition, and other expenses. Up to $1700 to attend ONS Congress in following year is also awarded. Sponsoring institution of senior investigator receives $2000 to cover institutional costs and up to $8000 for salary support. Deadline: June 1.

Academic/Career Areas Health and Medical Sciences; Nursing.

Award Fellowship for use in postgraduate years; not renewable. *Number:* 1. *Amount:* up to $10,000.

Eligibility Requirements Applicant must be enrolled or expecting to enroll at an institution or university. Applicant or parent of applicant must have employment or volunteer experience in designated career field.

Application Requirements Application. *Deadline:* June 1.

Contact ONS Foundation
501 Holiday Drive
Pittsburgh, PA 15220

ONS FOUNDATION/AMERICAN BRAIN TUMOR ASSOCIATION GRANT • 589

One grant available to stimulate clinical research in neuro-oncology. One-time award of $5,000. Appli-

cant must be a registered nurse actively involved in some aspect of the care, education, or research of patients with cancer. Research must be clinically focused. Deadline: November 1.

Academic/Career Areas Health and Medical Sciences; Nursing.

Award Grant for use in graduate years; not renewable. *Number:* 1. *Amount:* $5000.

Eligibility Requirements Applicant must be enrolled or expecting to enroll at an institution or university. Applicant or parent of applicant must have employment or volunteer experience in designated career field.

Application Requirements Application. *Deadline:* November 1.

Contact ONS Foundation
501 Holiday Drive
Pittsburgh, PA 15220

ONS FOUNDATION/AVENTIS RESEARCH FELLOWSHIP • 590

One award to support short-term post-doctorate oncology-specific research training. Applicants must be registered nurses with interest in oncology and a completed doctoral degree in nursing or a related discipline. Must demonstrate how study with a senior investigator helps career. Previous fellows ineligible. Maximum $10,000 awarded to cover transportation, lodging, tuition, and other expenses. Up to $1700 to attend ONS Congress in following year is also awarded. Sponsoring institution of senior investigator receives $2000 to cover institutional costs and up to $8000 for salary support. Deadline: June 1.

Academic/Career Areas Health and Medical Sciences; Nursing.

Award Fellowship for use in postgraduate years; not renewable. *Number:* 1. *Amount:* up to $10,000.

Eligibility Requirements Applicant must be enrolled or expecting to enroll at an institution or university. Applicant or parent of applicant must have employment or volunteer experience in designated career field. Available to U.S. citizens.

Application Requirements Application. *Deadline:* June 1.

Contact ONS Foundation
501 Holiday Drive
Pittsburgh, PA 15220

ONS FOUNDATION/AVENTIS RESEARCH GRANT • 591

Two grants to registered nurses actively involved in an aspect of cancer patient care, education, or research. The principal investigator shall have less than a doctoral level of education and shall have received no previous research funding. Students are

ONS Foundation (continued)

eligible to seek funding for thesis or dissertation. One $8,500 and two $10,000 grants are awarded. Deadline: November 1.

Academic/Career Areas Health and Medical Sciences; Nursing.

Award Grant for use in graduate years; not renewable. *Number:* 1–3. *Amount:* $8500–$10,000.

Eligibility Requirements Applicant must be enrolled or expecting to enroll at an institution or university. Applicant or parent of applicant must have employment or volunteer experience in designated career field.

Application Requirements Application. *Deadline:* November 1.

Contact ONS Foundation
501 Holiday Drive
Pittsburgh, PA 15220

ONS FOUNDATION/BRISTOL-MYERS ONCOLOGY DIVISION COMMUNITY HEALTH RESEARCH GRANT • 592

Grants to encourage research in community-based health agencies such as community hospitals, physician's offices, and nursing homes. Principal investigator must be employed full-time as a registered nurse in community-based agency. One-time award of $5000, a plaque, and airfare to ONS Congress.

Academic/Career Areas Health and Medical Sciences; Nursing.

Award Grant for use in graduate years; not renewable. *Number:* 1. *Amount:* $5000.

Eligibility Requirements Applicant must be enrolled or expecting to enroll at an institution or university. Applicant or parent of applicant must have employment or volunteer experience in designated career field. Available to U.S. citizens.

Application Requirements Application. *Deadline:* November 1.

Contact ONS Foundation
501 Holiday Drive
Pittsburgh, PA 15220

ONS FOUNDATION/BRISTOL-MYERS ONCOLOGY DIVISION RESEARCH GRANT • 593

Grant to stimulate quality research in oncology nursing to improve cancer patient care. The applicant must be a registered nurse, actively involved in some aspect of cancer patient care, education, or research. One-time award of $7500, a plaque, and airfare to ONS Congress.

Academic/Career Areas Health and Medical Sciences; Nursing.

Award Grant for use in graduate years; not renewable. *Number:* 1. *Amount:* $7500.

Eligibility Requirements Applicant must be enrolled or expecting to enroll at an institution or university. Applicant or parent of applicant must have employment or volunteer experience in designated career field. Available to U.S. citizens.

Application Requirements Application. *Deadline:* November 1.

Contact ONS Foundation
501 Holiday Drive
Pittsburgh, PA 15220

ONS FOUNDATION/ONCOLOGY NURSING CERTIFICATION CORPORATION ONCOLOGY NURSING EDUCATION RESEARCH GRANT • 594

One-time award for a registered nurse actively involved in some aspect of cancer patient care, education, or research. Awarded to stimulate research in oncology nursing education to improve cancer patient care. One award of $7500. Deadline: November 1.

Academic/Career Areas Health and Medical Sciences; Nursing.

Award Grant for use in graduate years; not renewable. *Number:* 1. *Amount:* $7500.

Eligibility Requirements Applicant must be enrolled or expecting to enroll at an institution or university. Applicant or parent of applicant must have employment or volunteer experience in designated career field or teaching.

Application Requirements Application. *Deadline:* November 1.

Contact ONS Foundation
501 Holiday Drive
Pittsburgh, PA 15220

ONS FOUNDATION/ORTHO BIOTECH RESEARCH GRANT • 595

Four grants available to a registered nurses actively involved in some aspect of cancer patient care, education, or research. Research must be clinically focused and address one or more areas of nursing assessment and management of cancer and cancer treatment-related symptoms. One-time award of $8500. Deadline: November 1.

Academic/Career Areas Health and Medical Sciences; Nursing.

Award Grant for use in graduate years; not renewable. *Number:* 4. *Amount:* $8500.

Eligibility Requirements Applicant must be enrolled or expecting to enroll at an institution or university. Applicant or parent of applicant must have employment or volunteer experience in designated career field. Available to U.S. citizens.

Application Requirements Application. *Deadline:* November 1.

Contact ONS Foundation
501 Holiday Drive
Pittsburgh, PA 15220

ONS FOUNDATION/TRISH GREENE RESEARCH GRANT • 596

One grant to promote oncology nursing research in the area of pain assessment, and pain management. The applicant must be a registered nurse actively involved in some aspect of cancer patient care, education, or research. One-time award of $6000. A Purdue Frederick product must be used in at least one area of the treatments being employed.

Academic/Career Areas Health and Medical Sciences; Nursing.

Award Grant for use in graduate years; not renewable. *Number:* 1. *Amount:* $6000.

Eligibility Requirements Applicant must be enrolled or expecting to enroll at an institution or university. Applicant or parent of applicant must have employment or volunteer experience in designated career field.

Application Requirements Application. *Deadline:* November 1.

Contact ONS Foundation
501 Holiday Drive
Pittsburgh, PA 15220

OREGON STUDENT ASSISTANCE COMMISSION
http://www.osac.state.or.us

GAYLE AND HARVEY RUBIN SCHOLARSHIP • 597

Applicants must be enrolled in full-time graduate study toward MD, DDM or JD degree. Must apply annually for up to 9 quarters or their equivalent.

Academic/Career Areas Health and Medical Sciences; Law/Legal Services.

Award Scholarship for use in graduate years; not renewable.

Eligibility Requirements Applicant must be enrolled or expecting to enroll full-time at an institution or university and resident of Oregon. Available to U.S. citizens.

Application Requirements Application, essay, financial need analysis, transcript, activity chart. *Deadline:* March 1.

Contact Director of Grant Programs
Oregon Student Assistance Commission
1500 Valley River Drive, Suite 100
Eugene, OR 97401-7020
Phone: 800-452-8807 Ext. 7395
E-mail:
awardinfo@mercury.osac.state.or.us

JEANNETTE MOWERY SCHOLARSHIP
• *See number 295*

ORTHOPAEDIC RESEARCH AND EDUCATION FOUNDATION
http://www.oref.org

AAOS/OREF FELLOWSHIP IN HEALTH SERVICES RESEARCH • 598

One-time grant available to candidates who have completed an accredited North American orthopedic residency and are recommended by their department chair. Up to two two-year fellowships at up to $70,000 per year. Deadline is August 1.

Academic/Career Areas Health and Medical Sciences; Therapy/Rehabilitation.

Award Fellowship for use in postgraduate years; not renewable. *Number:* 1–2. *Amount:* up to $140,000.

Eligibility Requirements Applicant must be enrolled or expecting to enroll full or part-time at an institution or university. Available to U.S. and Canadian citizens.

Application Requirements Application, references. *Deadline:* August 1.

Contact Jean McGuire, Vice President of Grants
Orthopaedic Research and Education Foundation
6300 North River Road, Suite 700
Rosemont, IL 60018-4261
Phone: 847-384-4348
Fax: 847-698-7806
E-mail: mcguire@oref.org

OREF CAREER DEVELOPMENT AWARDS • 599

Several grants available to candidates who have completed a residency in orthopedic surgery doing research at a U.S. medical training center. Must submit letters of support as evidence of candidate's potential to develop as an investigator. Awards up to $75,000 per year for three years. Deadline is August 1.

Academic/Career Areas Health and Medical Sciences; Therapy/Rehabilitation.

Award Grant for use in postgraduate years; renewable. *Number:* 2–3. *Amount:* up to $75,000.

Eligibility Requirements Applicant must be enrolled or expecting to enroll at an institution or university.

Application Requirements Application, references. *Deadline:* August 1.

Contact Jean McGuire, Vice President of Grants
Orthopaedic Research and Education Foundation
6300 North River Road, Suite 700
Rosemont, IL 60018-4261
Phone: 847-384-4348
Fax: 847-698-7806
E-mail: mcguire@oref.org

OREF CLINICAL RESEARCH AWARD • 600

One award to recognize outstanding clinical research related to musculoskeletal disease or injury. Original manuscripts must be submitted by July 1. One-time award of up to $20,000. One manuscript will be chosen for award.

Academic/Career Areas Health and Medical Sciences; Therapy/Rehabilitation.

Award Prize for use in graduate years; not renewable. *Number:* 1. *Amount:* up to $20,000.

Eligibility Requirements Applicant must be enrolled or expecting to enroll at an institution or university.

Application Requirements *Deadline:* July 1.

Contact Jean McGuire, Vice President of Grants
Orthopaedic Research and Education
Foundation
6300 North River Road, Suite 700
Rosemont, IL 60018-4261
Phone: 847-384-4348
Fax: 847-698-7806
E-mail: mcguire@oref.org

OREF PROSPECTIVE CLINICAL RESEARCH GRANTS • 601

Several grants available to individuals at U.S. medical training centers for promising prospective clinical research projects. Grants of $50,000 per year renewable for up to three years. Deadline is August 1.

Academic/Career Areas Health and Medical Sciences; Therapy/Rehabilitation.

Award Grant for use in graduate years; renewable. *Number:* 1–2. *Amount:* up to $50,000.

Eligibility Requirements Applicant must be enrolled or expecting to enroll at an institution or university.

Application Requirements Application. *Deadline:* August 1.

Contact Jean McGuire, Vice President of Grants
Orthopaedic Research and Education
Foundation
6300 North River Road, Suite 700
Rosemont, IL 60018-4261
Phone: 847-384-4348
Fax: 847-698-7806
E-mail: mcguire@oref.org

OREF RESEARCH GRANTS • 602

Several grants available to individuals at U.S. medical training centers for musculoskeletal research. Grants of $50,000 per year renewable for up to two years. Deadline is August 1.

Academic/Career Areas Health and Medical Sciences; Therapy/Rehabilitation.

Award Grant for use in graduate years; renewable. *Number:* 9–12. *Amount:* up to $50,000.

Eligibility Requirements Applicant must be enrolled or expecting to enroll at an institution or university.

Application Requirements Application. *Deadline:* August 1.

Contact Jean McGuire, Vice President of Grants
Orthopaedic Research and Education
Foundation
6300 North River Road, Suite 700
Rosemont, IL 60018-4261
Phone: 847-384-4348
Fax: 847-698-7806
E-mail: mcguire@oref.org

OREF RESIDENT RESEARCH AWARDS • 603

Renewable award to enable orthopedic surgeons studying musculoskeletal problems to conduct research. Submit project budget with application. Research must be conducted at a U.S. medical training center. Deadline is August 1.

Academic/Career Areas Health and Medical Sciences.

Award Grant for use in graduate, or postgraduate years; not renewable. *Number:* 9–12. *Amount:* up to $15,000.

Eligibility Requirements Applicant must be enrolled or expecting to enroll at an institution or university.

Application Requirements Application, references. *Deadline:* August 1.

Contact Jean McGuire, Vice President of Grants
Orthopaedic Research and Education
Foundation
6300 North River Road, Suite 700
Rosemont, IL 60018-4261
Phone: 847-384-4348
Fax: 847-698-7806
E-mail: mcguire@oref.org

ZIMMER CAREER DEVELOPMENT AWARD • 604

Several one-time awards of $50,000 are available to eligible candidates who are currently completing formal orthopedic surgical training, and/or those currently enrolled in advanced surgical training. Applicants must submit letters to support a candidate's potential to develop as an investigator.

Academic/Career Areas Health and Medical Sciences; Therapy/Rehabilitation.

Award Grant for use in postgraduate years; not renewable. *Number:* 1–6. *Amount:* up to $50,000.

Eligibility Requirements Applicant must be enrolled or expecting to enroll at an institution or university.

Application Requirements Application, references. *Deadline:* August 1.

Contact Jean McGuire, Vice President of Grants
　　　　Orthopaedic Research and Education
　　　　Foundation
　　　　6300 North River Road, Suite 700
　　　　Rosemont, IL 60018-4261
　　　　Phone: 847-384-4348
　　　　Fax: 847-698-7806
　　　　E-mail: mcguire@oref.org

PARALYZED VETERANS OF AMERICA - SPINAL CORD RESEARCH FOUNDATION
http://www.pva.org/scrf

FELLOWSHIPS IN SPINAL CORD INJURY RESEARCH
• *See number 21*

PETRY-LOMB EDUCATION COMMITTEE

PETRY-LOMB SCHOLARSHIP/RESEARCH GRANT ● 605

Annual one-time scholarship/research grant awarded to an optometry student or graduate student in an accredited college of optometry. Award is based on financial need as determined by application and interview. Must be a student in good standing with a sincere desire to practice optometry in upstate New York after graduation. Applicants available at financial aid office at optometry school. Must be a resident of New York.

Academic/Career Areas Health and Medical Sciences.

Award Grant for use in graduate years; not renewable. *Number:* 1–3. *Amount:* $1000–$3000.

Eligibility Requirements Applicant must be enrolled or expecting to enroll full-time at an institution or university and resident of New York. Available to U.S. citizens.

Application Requirements Application, essay, financial need analysis, interview, references. *Deadline:* October 15.

Contact Dr. Michele Lagana, Chairperson
　　　　Petry-Lomb Education Committee
　　　　PO Box 63
　　　　Mendon, NY 14506

PFIZER, INC. - US PHARMACEUTICALS GROUP
http://www.physicianscientist.com

PFIZER /AMERICAN GERIATRICS SOCIETY POSTDOCTORAL FELLOWSHIPS ● 606

Two-year grants to two physician-scientists who wish to pursue original research in geriatrics outcomes research. Must have MD or DO degree and have completed at least one year of geriatric medicine, geropsychiatry, or geriatric neurology and be Board eligible. Please visit website for more details.

Academic/Career Areas Health and Medical Sciences.

Award Fellowship for use in postgraduate years; not renewable. *Amount:* $65,000.

Eligibility Requirements Applicant must be enrolled or expecting to enroll at an institution or university. Applicant or parent of applicant must have employment or volunteer experience in designated career field. Available to U.S. citizens.

Application Requirements Application, curriculum vitae, bibliography, research proposal. *Deadline:* December 1.

Contact Fellowship Administrator
　　　　Pfizer, Inc. - US Pharmaceuticals Group
　　　　Foundation for Health in Aging, The
　　　　Empire State Building, 350 Fifth
　　　　Avenue, Suite 801
　　　　New York, NY 10118
　　　　Phone: 800-247-4779

PFIZER POSTDOCTORAL FELLOWSHIP GRANTS ● 607

Research Fellowships available to applicants with an MD or DO degree. Two three-year awards of $65,000 per year in each of the following fields: biological psychiatry, cardiovascular medicine, infectious diseases and rheumatology/immunology. Must have arranged for an appointment to a U.S. medical school and have been accepted by a sponsor who is a full-time faculty member of the school. Cannot hold a tenure-track faculty position or its equivalent during first year of grant. 90% of professional time must be devoted to research. Other specific restrictions apply. Applicant must be sponsored at a U.S. medical school and must obtain permission to prepare an application from the dean of the medical school. Please visit website for more details.

Academic/Career Areas Health and Medical Sciences.

Award Grant for use in postgraduate years; not renewable. *Number:* 8. *Amount:* $65,000.

Eligibility Requirements Applicant must be enrolled or expecting to enroll at an institution or university. Applicant or parent of applicant must have employment or volunteer experience in designated career field. Available to U.S. citizens.

Application Requirements Application, C.V., bibliography, research proposal.

Contact Program Coordinator
　　　　Pfizer, Inc. - US Pharmaceuticals Group
　　　　33 Main Street
　　　　Old Saybrook, CT 06475
　　　　Phone: 800-201-1214

PFIZER POSTDOCTORAL FELLOWSHIPS IN NURSING RESEARCH • 608

Two fellowships of $65,000 per year for two years available to professional registered nurses who have earned a Ph.D., DrPH, or DNSc after 1995. Applicant must have arranged to conduct health outcomes research through an educational institution, a private research facility, or government agency in the US with a mentor who has a strong research and academic record. Must be US citizen or legal permanent resident. Write or call for additional requirements and guidelines.

Academic/Career Areas Health and Medical Sciences; Nursing.

Award Fellowship for use in postgraduate years; not renewable. *Number:* 2. *Amount:* $65,000.

Eligibility Requirements Applicant must be enrolled or expecting to enroll at an institution or university. Available to U.S. citizens.

Application Requirements Application, references, curriculum vitae, research proposal. *Deadline:* December 1.

Contact Program Coordinator
Pfizer, Inc. - US Pharmaceuticals Group
33 Main Street
Old Saybrook, CT 06475
Phone: 800-201-1214

PFIZER SCHOLARS GRANT FOR FACULTY DEVELOPMENT IN CLINICAL EPIDEMIOLOGY • 609

Two grants ($65,000 per year for three years) are available to individuals with an M.D. or other doctoral clinical degree. Completion of clinical training in specialty area required. Must have a designated sponsor at applicant's institution. A minimum of 80% or professional time must be devoted to research. Additional requirements must be met. Write for details. Must be U.S. citizen or legal permanent resident. Deadline April 6.

Academic/Career Areas Health and Medical Sciences.

Award Grant for use in postgraduate years; not renewable. *Number:* 2. *Amount:* $65,000.

Eligibility Requirements Applicant must be enrolled or expecting to enroll at an institution or university. Available to U.S. citizens.

Application Requirements Application, curriculum vitae, bibliography, research proposal. *Deadline:* April 6.

Contact Program Coordinator
Pfizer, Inc. - US Pharmaceuticals Group
33 Main Street
Old Saybrook, CT 06475
Phone: 800-201-1214

PFIZER/SOCIETY FOR WOMEN'S HEALTH RESEARCH SCHOLARS GRANTS FOR FACULTY DEVELOPMENT IN WOMEN'S HEALTH • 610

Three-year grant ($65,000 per year) enables medical school faculty members to pursue research in an area of serious disease affecting women, specifically cardiovascular diseases, mental health, and reproductive physiology. Applicants must hold M.D. or D.O. degree with twelve or less years of professional experience. Please visit website (http://www.physicianscientist.com) for more details.

Academic/Career Areas Health and Medical Sciences.

Award Grant for use in postgraduate years; not renewable. *Number:* 3. *Amount:* $65,000.

Eligibility Requirements Applicant must be enrolled or expecting to enroll at an institution or university. Available to U.S. citizens.

Application Requirements Application, references, research proposal, curriculum vitae. *Deadline:* December 1.

Contact Program Coordinator
Pfizer, Inc. - US Pharmaceuticals Group
33 Main Street
Old Saybrook, CT 06475
Phone: 800-201-1214

PLASTIC SURGERY EDUCATIONAL FOUNDATION
http://www.plasticsurgery.org

PLASTIC SURGERY BASIC RESEARCH GRANT • 611

One-time award to conduct research related to plastic and reconstructive surgery. Submit curriculum vitae, summary of previous work, budget, and statement of facilities where research will be performed.

Academic/Career Areas Health and Medical Sciences.

Award Grant for use in graduate years; not renewable. *Number:* 30–40. *Amount:* up to $5000.

Eligibility Requirements Applicant must be enrolled or expecting to enroll full or part-time at an institution or university. Available to U.S. and Canadian citizens.

Application Requirements Application, autobiography, references, summary of previous work, budget. *Deadline:* January 11.

Contact Mary Lewis, RN, Research Manager
Plastic Surgery Educational Foundation
444 East Algonquin Road
Arlington Heights, IL 60005
Phone: 847-228-9900 Ext. 354
Fax: 847-228-0628
E-mail: ml@plasticsurgery.org

PLASTIC SURGERY EDUCATIONAL FOUNDATION SCIENTIFIC ESSAY CONTEST • 612

Eight one-time cash awards for plastic surgeons in four categories: basic science, clinical research, investigator, and essay scholarship. Submit manuscript. Investigator award is presented to author(s) who is not a plastic surgeon but may be medical student, nurse, therapist or Ph.D. Deadline is February 16.

Academic/Career Areas Health and Medical Sciences.

Award Prize for use in graduate years; not renewable. *Number:* 8. *Amount:* $500–$3000.

Eligibility Requirements Applicant must be enrolled or expecting to enroll full or part-time at a four-year institution or university. Applicant or parent of applicant must have employment or volunteer experience in designated career field. Available to U.S. and non-U.S. citizens.

Application Requirements Autobiography, essay, manuscript. *Deadline:* February 16.

Contact Mary Lewis, RN, Research Manager
Plastic Surgery Educational Foundation
444 East Algonquin Road
Arlington Heights, IL 60005
Phone: 847-228-9900 Ext. 354
Fax: 847-228-0628
E-mail: ml@plasticsurgery.org

PLASTIC SURGERY RESEARCH FELLOWSHIP AWARD • 613

One-time award for the purpose of encouraging research and academic career development in plastic and reconstructive surgery. Submit research plan, statement of experience, and sponsoring PSEF member. Appropriate areas of research include cleft lips and palate/craniofacial surgery, and repair/ replacement of soft tissue loss due to trauma, disease or cancer, or as a result of congenital abnormalities.

Academic/Career Areas Health and Medical Sciences.

Award Fellowship for use in graduate years; not renewable. *Number:* 5. *Amount:* $30,000.

Eligibility Requirements Applicant must be enrolled or expecting to enroll full or part-time at an institution or university. Available to U.S. and non-U.S. citizens.

Application Requirements Application, autobiography, references, research plan. *Deadline:* December 14.

Contact Mary Lewis, RN, Research Manager
Plastic Surgery Educational Foundation
444 East Algonquin Road
Arlington Heights, IL 60005
Phone: 847-228-9900 Ext. 354
Fax: 847-228-0628
E-mail: ml@plasticsurgery.org

POPULATION COUNCIL
http://www.popcouncil.org

POPULATION COUNCIL FELLOWSHIPS IN THE SOCIAL SCIENCES, MID-CAREER LEVEL
• *See number 328*

POPULATION COUNCIL FELLOWSHIPS IN THE SOCIAL SCIENCES, POSTDOCTORAL LEVEL
• *See number 329*

POPULATION COUNCIL FELLOWSHIPS IN THE SOCIAL SCIENCES, PREDOCTORAL LEVEL
• *See number 330*

RADIOLOGICAL SOCIETY OF NORTH AMERICA
http://www.rsna.org/research

RADIOLOGICAL SOCIETY OF NORTH AMERICA MEDICAL STUDENT/SCHOLAR ASSISTANT • 614

Will provide promising medical students an opportunity to experience radiological research while assisting an RSNA research scholar. Applicants must be a citizen of a North American country or have permanent resident status and be nominated by a current RSNA research scholar grant recipient.

Academic/Career Areas Health and Medical Sciences.

Award Scholarship for use in graduate years; not renewable. *Amount:* $5000.

Eligibility Requirements Applicant must be enrolled or expecting to enroll full or part-time at an institution or university. Available to U.S. and Canadian citizens.

Application Requirements Application. *Deadline:* Continuous.

Contact Radiological Society of North America
820 Jorie Boulevard
Oak Brook, IL 60523-2251

RADIOLOGICAL SOCIETY OF NORTH AMERICA RESEARCH FELLOW • 615

To provide research opportunities for young investigators not yet professionally established in the radiological sciences and to gain further insight into scientific investigation and develop competence in research and educational techniques and methods. Applicant must be a citizen of a North American country or have permanent resident status, hold a degree of M.D., D.O., D.V.M., D.D.S., D.M.D. or the equivalent as recognized by the American Medical Association and be nearing the end of prescribed training and/or have completed the prerequisite training to sit for certifying exams.

Academic/Career Areas Health and Medical Sciences.

Award Grant for use in postgraduate years; renewable. *Amount:* $45,000.

Radiological Society of North America (continued)

Eligibility Requirements Applicant must be enrolled or expecting to enroll full or part-time at an institution or university. Available to U.S. and Canadian citizens.

Application Requirements Application. *Deadline:* January 9.

Contact Radiological Society of North America
820 Jorie Boulevard
Oak Brook, IL 60523-2251

RADIOLOGICAL SOCIETY OF NORTH AMERICA RESEARCH SCHOLAR • **616**

To support junior faculty members by freeing at least one-half of their time to gain experience in research early in their academic careers. Applicants must be citizen of a North American country or have permanent resident status, have completed advanced training, including doctorate, residency, fellowships, etc., be board certified or eligible to sit for certifying exams, be a faculty member of a North American educational institution at time of award commencement and be within five years of initial faculty appointment.

Academic/Career Areas Health and Medical Sciences.

Award Grant for use in postgraduate years; renewable. *Amount:* $75,000.

Eligibility Requirements Applicant must be enrolled or expecting to enroll full or part-time at an institution or university. Available to U.S. and Canadian citizens.

Application Requirements Application. *Deadline:* January 9.

Contact Radiological Society of North America
820 Jorie Boulevard
Oak Brook, IL 60523-2251

RADIOLOGICAL SOCIETY OF NORTH AMERICA RESEARCH SEED • **617**

To enable young investigators to gain experience in defining objectives and testing hypotheses before they apply for major grants from corporations, foundations and governmental agencies. Applicants must have completed all advanced training, be a full-time faculty member at a department of diagnostic radiology, radiation oncology or nuclear medicine and have not served as principal investigator or coinvestigator on grants or contracts totaling $50,000 or more in a single, calendar year.

Academic/Career Areas Health and Medical Sciences.

Award Grant for use in postgraduate years; not renewable. *Amount:* $30,000.

Eligibility Requirements Applicant must be enrolled or expecting to enroll at an institution or university. Available to U.S. and non-U.S. citizens.

Application Requirements Application.

Contact Radiological Society of North America
820 Jorie Boulevard
Oak Brook, IL 60523-2251

SARNOFF ENDOWMENT FOR CARDIOVASCULAR SCIENCE
http://www.sarnoffendowment.org

SARNOFF FELLOWSHIP PROGRAM • **618**

Gives medical students without extensive prior research experience the opportunity to spend a year conducting intensive work in a research laboratory at an institution other than their own. Each fellow will have a sponsor from his or her own institution and a Sarnoff Scientific Board member who will help in the choice of a preceptor and will serve as an advisor throughout the fellowship.

Academic/Career Areas Health and Medical Sciences.

Award Fellowship for use in graduate years; not renewable. *Number:* 1–18. *Amount:* $30,000.

Eligibility Requirements Applicant must be enrolled or expecting to enroll full-time at an institution or university. Available to U.S. and non-U.S. citizens.

Application Requirements Application, essay, references, transcript, curriculum vitae. *Deadline:* January 18.

Contact Dana Boyd, Executive Director
Sarnoff Endowment for Cardiovascular
Science
731 G2 Walker Road
Great Falls, VA 22066
Phone: 703-759-7600
Fax: 703-759-7838
E-mail: sarnoff@cais.com

SCOTTISH RITE CHARITABLE FOUNDATION
http://www.scottishritemasons-can.org/foundation

MAJOR RESEARCH GRANT FOR BIOMEDICAL RESEARCH INTO INTELLECTUAL IMPAIRMENT • **619**

Grant supports biomedical research into intellectual impairment. The focus of research should be on the causes and cure of the disease as opposed to the active treatment or palliative care. Applicants should be researchers who have or are offered at least a 3-year academic appointment at a Canadian university or research hospital. Must be Canadian citizen or permanent resident. Must carry out research in Canada. Write or visit website for additional details.

Academic/Career Areas Health and Medical Sciences.

Award Grant for use in postgraduate years; renewable. *Amount:* up to $35,000.

Eligibility Requirements Applicant must be Canadian citizenship; enrolled or expecting to enroll at an institution or university; resident of Alberta, British Columbia, Manitoba, Ontario, Quebec, or Saskatchewan and studying in Alberta, British Columbia, Manitoba, Ontario, Quebec, or Saskatchewan. Applicant or parent of applicant must have employment or volunteer experience in designated career field.

Application Requirements Application, research proposal. *Deadline:* April 30.

Contact Awards Committee
Scottish Rite Charitable Foundation
4 Queen Street South
Hamilton, ON L8P 3R3
Canada
Phone: 905-522-0033
Fax: 905-522-3716

RESEARCH INTO CAUSES, CURE, TREATMENT AND TREATMENT OF INTELLECTUAL IMPAIRMENT • 620

Awards support research focused on physical-biological and social aspects of intellectual impairment. Applicants should be enrolled in masters or doctoral program at Canadian university or research hospital. Must be Canadian citizen or permanent resident. Must carry out research in Canada. Write or visit website for additional information.

Academic/Career Areas Health and Medical Sciences.

Award Grant for use in graduate, or postgraduate years; renewable. *Amount:* up to $10,000.

Eligibility Requirements Applicant must be Canadian citizenship; enrolled or expecting to enroll at an institution or university; resident of Alberta, British Columbia, Manitoba, Ontario, Quebec, or Saskatchewan and studying in Alberta, British Columbia, Manitoba, Ontario, Quebec, or Saskatchewan. Applicant or parent of applicant must have employment or volunteer experience in designated career field.

Application Requirements Application, research proposal. *Deadline:* April 30.

Contact Awards Committee
Scottish Rite Charitable Foundation
4 Queen Street South
Hamilton, ON L8P 3R3
Canada
Phone: 905-522-0033
Fax: 905-522-3716

SENSE OF SMELL INSTITUTE
http://www.senseofsmell.org

SENSE OF SMELL INSTITUTE RESEARCH GRANTS
• *See number 214*

TOVA FELLOWSHIP
• *See number 101*

SOCIETY OF TOXICOLOGY
http://www.toxicology.org

COLGATE-PALMOLIVE AWARD FOR STUDENT RESEARCH
• *See number 215*

COLGATE-PALMOLIVE POSTDOCTORAL FELLOWSHIP
• *See number 216*

GRADUATE STUDENT FELLOWSHIP
• *See number 217*

GRADUATE STUDENT TRAVEL AWARDS
• *See number 218*

ROBERT L. DIXON INTERNATIONAL TRAVEL AWARD
• *See number 219*

SOT/ACC EARLY AWARD IN INHALATION TOXICOLOGY
• *See number 220*

STATE MEDICAL EDUCATION BOARD OF GEORGIA
http://www.communityhealth.state.ga.us

STATE MEDICAL EDUCATION BOARD SCHOLARSHIP PROGRAM • 621

Service repayable scholarship maximum of $18,000 per year for four years available to Georgia residents enrolled in U.S. medical school who display financial need. Repay by practicing medicine in rural Georgia one year for each year that loan is received. Service payment begins upon completion of residency training.

Academic/Career Areas Health and Medical Sciences.

Award Scholarship for use in postgraduate years; renewable. *Amount:* $18,000.

Eligibility Requirements Applicant must be enrolled or expecting to enroll full-time at an institution or university and resident of Georgia. Available to U.S. citizens.

State Medical Education Board of Georgia (continued)

Application Requirements Application, essay, financial need analysis, interview, photo, references, test scores, transcript. *Deadline:* May 15.

Contact Dr. Bruce Deighton, Executive Director
State Medical Education Board of Georgia
2 Northside 75, NW, Suite 220
Atlanta, GA 30318-7701
Phone: 404-352-6476
Fax: 404-352-6021
E-mail: bdeighton@dch.state.ga.us

STATE MEDICAL EDUCATION BOARD/GEORGIA LOAN REPAYMENT PROGRAM • 622

Loan program to repay medical education debts. Participants must practice in underserved areas in Georgia. Loan of $25,000 per year for two years, may be renewed for two additional years, to four-year maximum. Minimum two-year repayment. Must submit disclosure of debt. Deadlines: quarterly, on 15th day of first month.

Academic/Career Areas Health and Medical Sciences.

Award Forgivable loan for use in postgraduate years; not renewable. *Amount:* $50,000.

Eligibility Requirements Applicant must be enrolled or expecting to enroll full-time at an institution or university and studying in Georgia. Available to U.S. citizens.

Application Requirements Application, financial need analysis, references. *Deadline:* Continuous.

Contact Dr. Bruce Deighton, Executive Director
State Medical Education Board of Georgia
2 Northside 75, NW, Suite 220
Atlanta, GA 30318-7701
Phone: 404-352-6476
Fax: 404-352-6021
E-mail: bdeighton@dch.state.ga.us

STATE OF OKLAHOMA
http://www.pmtc.state.ok.us

OKLAHOMA PHYSICIAN MANPOWER TRAINING COMMISSION RESIDENT RURAL SCHOLARSHIP LOAN PROGRAM • 623

Renewable loan for family practice residents who are in first or second year of family practice training in an Oklahoma family practice or medical program. Loan is forgivable if student practices after graduation for one month in rural community per each month the loan was received. Write for application deadlines. Loan is $36,000 to be used over three years.

Academic/Career Areas Health and Medical Sciences.

Award Forgivable loan for use in graduate years; renewable. *Amount:* $36,000.

Eligibility Requirements Applicant must be enrolled or expecting to enroll full-time at an institution or university and studying in Oklahoma.

Application Requirements Application, references.

Contact Charlotte Ward, Physician Placement
Officer
State of Oklahoma
1140 Northwest 63rd Street, Suite 302
Oklahoma City, OK 73116
Phone: 405-843-5667
Fax: 405-843-5792
E-mail: pmtc@oklaosf.state.ok.us

OKLAHOMA PHYSICIAN MANPOWER TRAINING RURAL MEDICAL EDUCATION SCHOLARSHIP LOAN PROGRAM • 624

Renewable award for Oklahoma residents enrolled or accepted in medical college who plan to do residency in primary care. Loan forgiven if student practices in Oklahoma community with population of 7,500 or less for each year the loan was received. Scholarship totaling $42,000 for four years. Deadline: March 31.

Academic/Career Areas Health and Medical Sciences.

Award Forgivable loan for use in graduate years; renewable. *Amount:* $42,000.

Eligibility Requirements Applicant must be enrolled or expecting to enroll full-time at an institution or university and resident of Oklahoma.

Application Requirements Application, photo, references. *Deadline:* March 31.

Contact Charlotte Ward, Physician Placement
Officer
State of Oklahoma
1140 Northwest 63rd Street, Suite 302
Oklahoma City, OK 73116
Phone: 405-843-5667
Fax: 405-843-5792
E-mail: pmtc@oklaosf.state.ok.us

TEXAS HIGHER EDUCATION COORDINATING BOARD
http://www.collegefortexans.com

TEXAS HEALTH SERVICE CORPS PROGRAM: STIPENDS FOR RESIDENT PHYSICIANS • 625

For physicians pursuing primary care specialties who are willing to enter into a service agreement and work in a rural or other medically underserved area. Must be a Texas resident. Award is renewable up to five years. Applications taken on a continuous basis. Loan repayment funds to be used for undergraduate, graduate or medical education.

Academic/Career Areas Health and Medical Sciences.

Award Scholarship for use in graduate years; renewable. *Amount:* up to $15,000.

Eligibility Requirements Applicant must be enrolled or expecting to enroll full-time at an institution or university and studying in Oklahoma.

Application Requirements Application, references.

Contact Charlotte Ward, Physician Placement
Officer
State of Oklahoma
1140 Northwest 63rd Street, Suite 302
Oklahoma City, OK 73116
Phone: 405-843-5667
Fax: 405-843-5792
E-mail: pmtc@oklaosf.state.ok.us

Eligibility Requirements Applicant must be enrolled or expecting to enroll at an institution or university and resident of Texas. Applicant or parent of applicant must have employment or volunteer experience in designated career field.

Application Requirements Application. *Deadline:* Continuous.

Contact Rural Health Initiatives, THSC Program
Texas Higher Education Coordinating Board
PO Drawer 1708
Austin, TX 78767-1708

TEXAS PHYSICIAN EDUCATION LOAN REPAYMENT PROGRAM PART III (TX FAM. PRACTICE RES. TRAINING) • 626

Minimum $9000 award to repay loans acquired during undergraduate, graduate or medical education. Recipients must enter into contract and agree to practice at certain sites in Texas as a family practice physician. For complete information contact your residency program director or the Texas Higher Education Coordinating Board. Deadline is April 20.

Academic/Career Areas Health and Medical Sciences.

Award Forgivable loan for use in graduate, or postgraduate years; renewable. *Amount:* $9000.

Eligibility Requirements Applicant must be enrolled or expecting to enroll full-time at an institution or university and studying in Texas. Applicant or parent of applicant must have employment or volunteer experience in designated career field. Available to U.S. citizens.

Application Requirements Application. *Deadline:* April 20.

Contact Special Accounts Servicing Office
Texas Higher Education Coordinating Board
PO Box 12788
Austin, TX 78711-2788
Phone: 800-242-3062 Ext. 6367
E-mail: grantinfo@thecb.state.tx.us

THE CHRISTOPHER REEVE PARALYSIS FOUNDATION
http://www.crpf.org

CHRISTOPHER REEVE PARALYSIS FOUNDATION INDIVIDUAL GRANTS- TWO-YEAR AWARDS • 627

Two-year awards with a maximum funding level of $75,000 per year (direct and indirect costs, 10% maximum for the latter). The goals of this program are to (1) encourage promising new investigators to undertake research on regeneration and recovery, particularly with respect to the spinal cord; (2) encourage researchers who are well-established in other areas to transfer their efforts to spinal cord

research; and (3) enable researchers with novel ideas to test their ideas and develop pilot data for seeking larger awards from NIH and other funding sources. Application deadlines are June 15 and December 15.

Academic/Career Areas Health and Medical Sciences.

Award Grant for use in postgraduate years; renewable. *Amount:* up to $75,000.

Eligibility Requirements Applicant must be enrolled or expecting to enroll full or part-time at a four-year institution or university. Available to U.S. and non-U.S. citizens.

Application Requirements Application, curriculum vitae.

Contact Ms. Susan Howley, Research Director
The Christopher Reeve Paralysis Foundation
500 Morris Avenue
Springfield, NJ 07081
Phone: 973-379-2690
Fax: 973-912-9433
E-mail: showley@crpf.org

TOURETTE SYNDROME ASSOCIATION, INC.
http://tsa-usa.org

TOURETTE SYNDROME ASSOCIATION RESEARCH FUND • 628

Renewable award for research relevant to Tourette Syndrome. Research proposals should be in basic neuroscience or clinical studies related to the etiology, pathophysiology, and treatments of Tourette Syndrome. Several grants of up to $75000. Letter of intent to apply must be received by 10/20.

Academic/Career Areas Health and Medical Sciences.

Award Fellowship for use in postgraduate years; renewable. *Number:* 15–20. *Amount:* $5000–$75,000.

Eligibility Requirements Applicant must be enrolled or expecting to enroll full or part-time at an institution or university. Available to U.S. and non-U.S. citizens.

Application Requirements Application. *Deadline:* December 22.

Contact Sue Levi-Pearl, Vice President, Medical & Scientific Programs
Tourette Syndrome Association, Inc.
42-40 Bell Boulevard
Bayside, NY 11361-2874
Phone: 718-224-2999
Fax: 718-279-9596
E-mail: ts@tsa-usa.org

UNITED DAUGHTERS OF THE CONFEDERACY
http://www.hqudc.org

JUDGE WILLIAM M. BEARD SCHOLARSHIP • 629

Renewable award for full-time graduate student who is a descendant of a Confederate soldier enrolled in a School of History or School of Medicine. Must carry a minimum of 12 credit hours each semester and have a minimum 3.0 GPA. Submit letter of endorsement from sponsoring chapter of the United Daughters of the Confederacy.

Academic/Career Areas Health and Medical Sciences; History.

Award Scholarship for use in graduate years; renewable. *Number:* 1–2. *Amount:* $800–$1000.

Eligibility Requirements Applicant must be enrolled or expecting to enroll full-time at an institution or university. Applicant or parent of applicant must be member of United Daughters of the Confederacy. Applicant must have 3.0 GPA or higher. Available to U.S. citizens.

Application Requirements Application, essay, financial need analysis, photo, references, self-addressed stamped envelope, transcript. *Deadline:* February 15.

Contact Second Vice President General
United Daughters of the Confederacy
328 North Boulevard
Richmond, VA 23220-4057
Phone: 804-355-1636

UNITED NEGRO COLLEGE FUND
http://www.uncf.org

UNCF/PFIZER POSTDOCTORAL FELLOWSHIPS
• *See number 221*

UNITED STATES ARMY RECRUITING COMMAND
http://www.goarmy.com

ARMED FORCES HEALTH PROFESSIONS SCHOLARSHIP PROGRAM-ARMY
• *See number 23*

F.E. HEBERT FINANCIAL ASSISTANCE PROGRAM
• *See number 296*

UNIVERSITY OF MEDICINE AND DENTISTRY OF NJ SCHOOL OF OSTEOPATHIC MEDICINE
http://www.3.umdnj.edu/faidweb

M.L. KING PHYSICIAN/DENTIST SCHOLARSHIPS
• *See number 298*

WELLESLEY COLLEGE
http://www.wellesley.edu/CWS/

M.A. CARTLAND SHACKFORD MEDICAL FELLOWSHIP • 630

Fellowships are available for the study of medicine with view to general practice, not psychiatry. Open to women graduates of any American institution for graduate study for the coming year at any medical school. Based on merit and need.

Academic/Career Areas Health and Medical Sciences.

Award Fellowship for use in graduate years; not renewable. *Amount:* up to $9000.

Eligibility Requirements Applicant must be enrolled or expecting to enroll full-time at an institution or university and female. Available to U.S. citizens.

Application Requirements Application, financial need analysis, references, test scores, transcript. *Deadline:* January 3.

Contact Rose Crawford, Secretary to the
Committee on Graduate Fellowships
Wellesley College
106 Central Avenue, Green Hall 441
Wellesley, MA 02481
Phone: 781-283-3525
Fax: 781-283-3674
E-mail: cws-fellowships@wellesley.edu

SARAH PERRY WOOD MEDICAL FELLOWSHIP • 631

One or more awards available to alumnae of Wellesley College for the study of medicine. Deadline January 3.

Academic/Career Areas Health and Medical Sciences.

Award Fellowship for use in graduate, or postgraduate years; not renewable. *Amount:* up to $60,000.

Eligibility Requirements Applicant must be enrolled or expecting to enroll full-time at an institution or university and female. Available to U.S. citizens.

Application Requirements Application, essay, financial need analysis, resume, references, transcript. *Deadline:* January 3.

Contact Rose Crawford, Secretary to the
Committee on Graduate Fellowships
Wellesley College
106 Central Avenue, Green Hall 441
Wellesley, MA 02481-8200
Phone: 781-283-3525
Fax: 781-283-3674
E-mail: cws-fellowships@wellesley.edu

HEALTH INFORMATION MANAGEMENT/ TECHNOLOGY

AIR AND WASTE MANAGEMENT ASSOCIATION
http://www.awma.org

AIR AND WASTE MANAGEMENT ASSOCIATION SCHOLARSHIP ENDOWMENT TRUST FUND
• *See number 24*

ALBERT SCHWEITZER FELLOWSHIP
http://www.schweitzerfellowship.org

NEW HAMPSHIRE/VERMONT SCHWEITZER FELLOWS PROGRAM
• *See number 15*

AMERICAN FOUNDATION FOR UROLOGIC DISEASE, INC.
http://www.afud.org

AFUD/AUA HEALTH POLICY RESEARCH PROGRAM
• *See number 407*

BLUE CROSS BLUE SHIELD OF MICHIGAN FOUNDATION
http://www.bcbsm.com/foundation

BLUE CROSS BLUE SHIELD OF MICHIGAN FOUNDATION STUDENT AWARD PROGRAM
• *See number 393*

CANADIAN SOCIETY FOR MEDICAL LABORATORY SCIENCE
http://www.csmls.org

CANADIAN SOCIETY FOR MEDICAL LABORATORY SCIENCE FOUNDERS' FUND AWARDS
• *See number 408*

MENNONITE HEALTH SERVICES
http://www.mhsonline.org

ELMER EDIGER MEMORIAL SCHOLARSHIP FUND
• *See number 541*

MILHEIM FOUNDATION FOR CANCER RESEARCH

MILHEIM FOUNDATION FOR CANCER RESEARCH PROJECT GRANTS IN ONCOLOGY
• *See number 542*

NATIONAL MEDICAL FELLOWSHIPS, INC
http://www.nmf-online.org

W.K. KELLOGG FELLOWSHIP PROGRAM IN HEALTH POLICY RESEARCH
• *See number 409*

HEATING, AIR-CONDITIONING, AND REFRIGERATION MECHANICS

AMERICAN SOCIETY OF HEATING, REFRIGERATING, AND AIR CONDITIONING ENGINEERS, INC.
http://www.ashrae.org

AMERICAN SOCIETY OF HEATING, REFRIGERATING, AND AIR CONDITIONING RESEARCH GRANTS FOR GRADUATE STUDENTS • **632**

One-time award for full-time study in heating, ventilating, air-conditioning, and refrigeration. Participation of applicant and her/his adviser in ASHRAE is given strong consideration in selection of recipients. Submit application which includes description of research project, amount of grant needed, and information on institution and faculty adviser. Transcript required but does not have to be official. Application made by faculty adviser on behalf of student.

Academic/Career Areas Heating, Air-Conditioning, and Refrigeration Mechanics; Mechanical Engineering; Trade/Technical Specialties.

Award Grant for use in graduate years; not renewable. *Number:* 20–25. *Amount:* $7500.

Eligibility Requirements Applicant must be enrolled or expecting to enroll full-time at an institution or university. Available to U.S. citizens.

Application Requirements Application, references, transcript, description of research project. *Deadline:* December 15.

Contact Manager of Research
American Society of Heating,
Refrigerating, and Air Conditioning
Engineers, Inc.
1791 Tullie Circle, NE
Atlanta, GA 30329
Phone: 404-636-8400
Fax: 404-321-5478
E-mail: bseaton@ashrae.org

SENSE OF SMELL INSTITUTE
http://www.senseofsmell.org

TOVA FELLOWSHIP
• *See number 101*

HISTORIC PRESERVATION AND CONSERVATION

ARCHAEOLOGICAL INSTITUTE OF AMERICA
http://www.archaeological.org

ARCHAEOLOGICAL INSTITUTE OF AMERICA/ OLIVIA JAMES TRAVELING FELLOWSHIP
• See number 73

HARRIET AND LEON POMERANCE FELLOWSHIP
• See number 74

HELEN M. WOODRUFF FELLOWSHIP
• See number 75

WOODRUFF TRAVELING FELLOWSHIP
• See number 76

ASIAN CULTURAL COUNCIL
http://www.asianculturalcouncil.org

ASIAN ART AND RELIGION FELLOWSHIPS
• See number 90

FORD FOUNDATION FELLOWSHIPS
• See number 141

ATHENAEUM OF PHILADELPHIA
http://www.philaathenaeum.org

CHARLES E. PETERSON FELLOWSHIP
• See number 93

GETTY GRANT PROGRAM
http://www.getty.edu/grants

CONSERVATION GUEST SCHOLARS   • 633

Grants for established scholars and professionals that have attained distinction in conservation within their related fields. Scholars are in residence at the Getty Institute for three to nine months. Monthly stipend of $3500 is awarded during residency. Program provides opportunity for professionals to pursue scholarly research in interdisciplinary manner, across traditional boundaries, in areas of wide general interest to the international conservation community. See website for details.

Academic/Career Areas Historic Preservation and Conservation.

Award Grant for use in graduate, or postgraduate years; not renewable. *Amount:* $10,500–$31,500.

Eligibility Requirements Applicant must be enrolled or expecting to enroll at an institution or university; studying in California and must have an interest in museum/preservation work. Applicant or parent of applicant must have employment or volunteer experience in designated career field. Available to U.S. and non-U.S. citizens.

Application Requirements *Deadline:* November 1.

Contact Nancy Micklewright, Program Officer
Getty Grant Program
1200 Getty Center Drive, Suite 800
Los Angeles, CA 90049-1685
Phone: 310-440-7320
Fax: 310-440-7703
E-mail: researchgrants@getty.edu

HARRY S TRUMAN LIBRARY INSTITUTE
http://www.trumanlibrary.org

HARRY S. TRUMAN BOOK AWARD
• See number 324

HARRY S. TRUMAN LIBRARY INSTITUTE DISSERTATION YEAR FELLOWSHIPS
• See number 325

HARRY S. TRUMAN LIBRARY INSTITUTE RESEARCH GRANTS
• See number 326

HARRY S. TRUMAN LIBRARY INSTITUTE SCHOLAR'S AWARD
• See number 327

SMITHSONIAN INSTITUTION
http://www.si.edu/research+study

SMITHSONIAN INSTITUTION GRADUATE STUDENT FELLOWSHIPS   • 634

Fellowship of $3700 for a ten-week term at the Smithsonian. Applicants should be formally enrolled in a graduate program, have completed at least one semester of this program, and not yet been advanced to candidacy if in a Ph.D. program. Application deadline: January 15.

Academic/Career Areas Historic Preservation and Conservation; Museum Studies.

Award Fellowship for use in graduate years; not renewable. *Amount:* $3700.

Eligibility Requirements Applicant must be enrolled or expecting to enroll at an institution or university and studying in District of Columbia. Available to U.S. and non-U.S. citizens.

Application Requirements Application. *Deadline:* January 15.

Contact Pamela Hudson, Academic Programs
Specialist
Smithsonian Institution
Office of Fellowship and Grants,750 9th
Street, NW Suite 9300
Washington, DC 20560-0902
Phone: 202-275-0655
Fax: 202-275-0489
E-mail: siofg@ofg.si.edu

SMITHSONIAN INSTITUTION POSTDOCTORAL FELLOWSHIPS • 635

Postdoctoral fellowships available to study or conduct research in preservation or conservation sciences at the Conservation Analytical Laboratory. One-time award. Contact for application requirements. Offered to scholars who have held the doctoral degree or equivalent for less than seven years. Deadline: January 15.

Academic/Career Areas Historic Preservation and Conservation; Museum Studies.

Award Fellowship for use in postgraduate years; not renewable. *Amount:* $30,000.

Eligibility Requirements Applicant must be enrolled or expecting to enroll at an institution or university and studying in District of Columbia. Available to U.S. and non-U.S. citizens.

Application Requirements Application. *Deadline:* January 15.

Contact Pamela Hudson, Academic Programs
Specialist
Smithsonian Institution
Office of Fellowships and Grants, 750 9th
Street, NW Suite 9300
Washington, DC 20560-0902
E-mail: siofg@ofg.si.edu

SMITHSONIAN INSTITUTION PREDOCTORAL FELLOWSHIPS • 636

Award of $17,000 for doctoral candidates who have completed course work and examinations. Submit detailed proposal. Must have approval from applicant's university to conduct research in residence. Term of fellowship is 3 to 12 months.

Academic/Career Areas Historic Preservation and Conservation; Museum Studies.

Award Fellowship for use in graduate years; not renewable. *Amount:* $17,000.

Eligibility Requirements Applicant must be enrolled or expecting to enroll at an institution or university and studying in District of Columbia. Available to U.S. and non-U.S. citizens.

Application Requirements Application, proposal. *Deadline:* January 15.

Contact Pamela Hudson, Academic Programs
Specialist
Smithsonian Institution
Office of Fellowships and Grants, 750 9th
Street, NW Suite 9300
Washington, DC 20560-0902
Phone: 202-275-0655
E-mail: siofg@ofg.si.edu

SOCIETY OF ARCHITECTURAL HISTORIANS
http://www.sah.org

CARROLL L.V. MEEKS FELLOWSHIP
• *See number 104*

KEEPERS PRESERVATION EDUCATION FUND FELLOWSHIP • 637

Award for one graduate student of historic preservation to attend the annual meeting of the Society of Architectural Historians. Submit essay, references, and resume with application. One-time award of $500.

Academic/Career Areas Historic Preservation and Conservation.

Award Fellowship for use in graduate years; not renewable. *Number:* 1. *Amount:* $500.

Eligibility Requirements Applicant must be enrolled or expecting to enroll full-time at an institution or university. Available to U.S. and non-U.S. citizens.

Application Requirements Application, essay, resume, references. *Deadline:* November 15.

Contact Angela FitzSimmons, Director of Programs
Society of Architectural Historians
1385 North Astor Street
Chicago, IL 60610-2144
Phone: 312-573-1365
Fax: 312-573-1141
E-mail: afitzsimmons@sah.org

WINTERTHUR MUSEUM, GARDEN, AND LIBRARY
http://www.winterthur.org

NEH FELLOWSHIPS
• *See number 110*

WINTERTHUR RESEARCH FELLOWSHIPS
• *See number 111*

HISTORY

AMERICAN CENTER OF ORIENTAL RESEARCH
http://www.bu.edu/acor

NATIONAL ENDOWMENT FOR THE HUMANITIES POST-DOCTORAL RESEARCH FELLOWSHIPS
• *See number 65*

AMERICAN COUNCIL OF TEACHERS OF RUSSIAN
http://www.actr.org

TITLE VIII RESEARCH SCHOLAR AND COMBINED RESEARCH AND LANGUAGE STUDY PROGRAM
• *See number 114*

AMERICAN HISTORICAL ASSOCIATION
http://www.theaha.org

ALBERT J. BEVERIDGE GRANT FOR RESEARCH IN THE HISTORY OF THE WESTERN HEMISPHERE
• See number 115

BERNADETTE E. SCHMITT GRANTS FOR RESEARCH IN EUROPEAN, AFRICAN, OR ASIAN HISTORY
• See number 116

J. FRANKLIN JAMESON FELLOWSHIP IN AMERICAN HISTORY • 638

One-time, three-month fellowship at the Library of Congress to do research on a topic of American History. Must hold a Ph.D. earned within the last five years, but must not have published a book-length historical work. Submit curriculum vitae.

Academic/Career Areas History.

Award Fellowship for use in postgraduate years; not renewable. *Number:* 1. *Amount:* $10,000.

Eligibility Requirements Applicant must be enrolled or expecting to enroll full or part-time at an institution or university and studying in District of Columbia. Available to U.S. and non-U.S. citizens.

Application Requirements Application, references, curriculum vitae. *Deadline:* January 15.

Contact Fellowship Administrator
American Historical Association
400 A Street, SE
Washington, DC 20003
Phone: 202-544-2422
Fax: 202-544-8307
E-mail: aha@theaha.org

LITTLETON-GRISWOLD RESEARCH GRANTS • 639

Supports research in U.S. legal history and the general field of law and society. Applicants must be members of the association; preference to junior scholars and Ph.D. candidates. The grants are intended to further research in progress and may not be used for tuition or partial salary replacement. Submit curriculum vitae, 750-word project statement, and one-page bibliography with application. Contact for deadline information.

Academic/Career Areas History; Law/Legal Services; Social Sciences.

Award Grant for use in postgraduate years; not renewable.

Eligibility Requirements Applicant must be enrolled or expecting to enroll at an institution or university. Applicant or parent of applicant must be member of American Historical Association.

Application Requirements Application, essay, proposal, curriculum vitae, bibliography, statement of project support.

Contact Administrative Assistant
American Historical Association
400 A Street, SE
Washington, DC 20003
Phone: 202-544-2422 Ext. 104
Fax: 202-544-8307
E-mail: aha@theaha.org

MICHAEL KRAUS RESEARCH GRANTS IN HISTORY • 640

Supports research in American colonial history. Applicants must be members of the association; preference to junior scholars and Ph.D. candidates. The grants are intended to further research in progress and may not be used for tuition or partial salary replacement. Submit curriculum vitae, 750-word project statement, and one-page bibliography with application. Contact for deadline information.

Academic/Career Areas History.

Award Grant for use in postgraduate years; not renewable.

Eligibility Requirements Applicant must be enrolled or expecting to enroll at an institution or university. Applicant or parent of applicant must be member of American Historical Association.

Application Requirements Application, essay, resume, curriculum vitae, bibliography, project statement.

Contact Administrative Assistant
American Historical Association
400 A Street, SE
Washington, DC 20003
Phone: 202-544-2422 Ext. 104
Fax: 202-544-8307
E-mail: aha@theaha.org

NASA FELLOWSHIP IN AEROSPACE HISTORY
• See number 175

AMERICAN INSTITUTE OF THE HISTORY OF PHARMACY
http://www.aihp.org

GRADUATE STUDENT GRANTS-IN-AID IN HISTORY OF PHARMACY
• See number 466

AMERICAN SCHOOLS OF ORIENTAL RESEARCH (ASOR)
http://www.asor.org

MESOPOTAMIAN FELLOWSHIP
• See number 68

W.F. ALBRIGHT INSTITUTE OF ARCHAEOLOGICAL RESEARCH - JAMES A. MONTGOMERY FELLOW AND RESEARCH COORDINATOR
• *See number 69*

W.F. ALBRIGHT INSTITUTE OF ARCHAEOLOGICAL RESEARCH GEORGE A. BARTON FELLOWSHIP
• *See number 70*

W.F. ALBRIGHT INSTITUTE OF ARCHAEOLOGICAL RESEARCH/NATIONAL ENDOWMENT OF THE HUMANITIES FELLOWSHIPS
• *See number 71*

AMERICAN SOCIETY OF ARMS COLLECTORS

AMERICAN SOCIETY OF ARMS COLLECTORS SCHOLARSHIP
• *See number 138*

ARCHAEOLOGICAL INSTITUTE OF AMERICA
http://www.archaeological.org

ARCHAEOLOGICAL INSTITUTE OF AMERICA/ OLIVIA JAMES TRAVELING FELLOWSHIP
• *See number 73*

HARRIET AND LEON POMERANCE FELLOWSHIP
• *See number 74*

HELEN M. WOODRUFF FELLOWSHIP
• *See number 75*

WOODRUFF TRAVELING FELLOWSHIP
• *See number 76*

ARMENIAN RELIEF SOCIETY OF NORTH AMERICA INC.-REGIONAL OFFICE

ARMENIAN RELIEF SOCIETY GRADUATE SCHOLARSHIP PROGRAM
• *See number 224*

BRITISH LIBRARY
http://www.ihrinfo.ac.uk/maps/wallis.html

HELEN WALLIS FELLOWSHIP • **641**

One-time award confers recognition by the British Library to any scholar whose work will help promote the extended and complementary use of the British Library's book and cartographical collections in historical investigation. It offers unrestricted access to the British Library's collections on staff terms.

Academic/Career Areas History.

Award Scholarship for use in postgraduate years; not renewable. *Number:* 2. *Amount:* $300.

Eligibility Requirements Applicant must be enrolled or expecting to enroll full-time at an institution or university. Available to U.S. and non-U.S. citizens.

Application Requirements Application, autobiography, references. *Deadline:* May 1.

Contact Peter Barber, Head, MAP Collections
British Library
Map Library, 96 Euston Road
London NW1 2DB
United Kingdom
Phone: 44-207-412770 Ext. 1
Fax: 44-207-412778 Ext. 0
E-mail: peter.barber@bl.uk

CENTER FOR THE STUDY OF THE HISTORY OF NURSING
http://www.nursing.upenn.edu/history

ALICE FISHER SOCIETY HISTORICAL SCHOLARSHIP • **642**

One scholarship, available to those with masters and doctoral level preparation, to support residential study using the Center's collections. Selection based on evidence of interest in and aptitude for historical research related to nursing. One-time award offered every year. Application deadline: December 31.

Academic/Career Areas History; Nursing.

Award Scholarship for use in graduate years; not renewable. *Number:* 1. *Amount:* $2500.

Eligibility Requirements Applicant must be enrolled or expecting to enroll full or part-time at an institution or university. Available to U.S. and non-U.S. citizens.

Application Requirements Application. *Deadline:* December 31.

Contact Betsy Weiss, Administrative Assistant
Center for the Study of the History of Nursing
Nursing Education Building, 420 Guardian Drive
Philadelphia, PA 19104-6096
Phone: 215-898-4502
Fax: 215-573-2168
E-mail: ehweiss@nursing.upenn.edu

LILLIAN SHOLTIS BRUNNER SUMMER FELLOWSHIP • **643**

One fellowship available to graduate students to support residential study using the Center's collections. Selection based on evidence of preparation and/or productivity in historical research related to nursing. One-time award offered every year. Application deadline: December 30.

Academic/Career Areas History; Nursing.

Award Fellowship for use in graduate years; not renewable. *Number:* 1. *Amount:* $2500.

Center for the Study of the History of Nursing (continued)

Eligibility Requirements Applicant must be enrolled or expecting to enroll full or part-time at an institution or university.

Application Requirements Application. *Deadline:* December 30.

Contact Betsy Weiss, Administrative Assistant
Center for the Study of the History of Nursing
Nursing Education Building, 420 Guardian Drive
Philadelphia, PA 19104-6096
Phone: 215-898-4502

Award Fellowship for use in graduate, or postgraduate years; not renewable. *Number:* 8–12. *Amount:* $1600.

Eligibility Requirements Applicant must be enrolled or expecting to enroll at an institution or university and studying in Pennsylvania. Available to U.S. and non-U.S. citizens.

Application Requirements Application, essay, references. *Deadline:* March 31.

Contact Katherine Ludwig, Associate Librarian
David Library of the American Revolution
PO Box 748
Washington Crossing, PA 18977
Phone: 215-493-6776
Fax: 215-493-9276

CHARLES BABBAGE INSTITUTE
http://www.cbi.umn.edu

ADELLE AND ERWIN TOMASH FELLOWSHIP IN THE HISTORY OF INFORMATION PROCESSING
• *See number 267*

CHEMICAL HERITAGE FOUNDATION
http://www.chemheritage.org

BECKMAN CENTER FOR THE HISTORY OF CHEMISTRY RESEARCH TRAVEL GRANTS AT THE CHEMICAL HERITAGE FOUNDATION
• *See number 51*

CHINA TIMES CULTURAL FOUNDATION

CHINA TIMES CULTURAL FOUNDATION DOCTORAL DISSERTATION RESEARCH IN CHINESE STUDIES SCHOLARSHIPS
• *See number 122*

CULTURAL SERVICES OF THE FRENCH EMBASSY
http://www.frenchculture.org

CHATEAUBRIAND SCHOLARSHIP PROGRAM
• *See number 164*

DAVID LIBRARY OF THE AMERICAN REVOLUTION
http://www.dlar.org

FELLOWSHIPS FOR THE STUDY OF THE AMERICAN REVOLUTION •644

Fellowship for doctoral candidates and postdoctoral researchers for the study of American history and culture from 1750-1800. Fellowship takes place at David Library in Pennsylvania. Submit curriculum vitae and project description.

Academic/Career Areas History; Literature/English/Writing; Political Science; Social Sciences.

DUMBARTON OAKS
http://www.doaks.org

BLISS PRIZE FELLOWSHIP IN BYZANTINE STUDIES
• *See number 123*

DUMBARTON OAKS PROJECT GRANTS
• *See number 94*

RESIDENTIAL FELLOWSHIP IN BYZANTINE, PRE-COLUMBIAN, AND LANDSCAPE ARCHITECTURE STUDIES
• *See number 95*

FRENCH INSTITUTE OF WASHINGTON (INSTITUT FRANÇAIS DE WASHINGTON)
http://www.unc.edu/depts/institut

EDOUARD MOROT-SIR FELLOWSHIP IN LITERATURE
• *See number 165*

GILBERT CHINARD FELLOWSHIPS AND EDOUARD MOROT-SIR FELLOWSHIP IN LITERATURE
• *See number 166*

HARMON CHADBOURN RORISON FELLOWSHIP
• *See number 167*

FRIEDRICH EBERT FOUNDATION

EBERT FOUNDATION ADVANCED GRADUATE FELLOWSHIPS
• *See number 319*

EBERT FOUNDATION DOCTORAL RESEARCH FELLOWSHIP
• *See number 320*

EBERT FOUNDATION POSTDOCTORAL FELLOWSHIPS
• *See number 321*

GENERAL COMMISSION ON ARCHIVES AND HISTORY
http://www.gcah.org

ASIAN, BLACK, HISPANIC, AND NATIVE AMERICAN UNITED METHODIST HISTORY RESEARCH AWARDS • 645

One-time award promoting research and writing in the history of Asian Americans, African Americans, Latinos, and Native Americans in the United Methodist Church or its antecedents. Submit biographical information, project description, and budget plan with application.

Academic/Career Areas History; Religion/Theology.

Award Prize for use in graduate years; not renewable. *Number: 2. Amount: $1500.*

Eligibility Requirements Applicant must be enrolled or expecting to enroll full or part-time at an institution or university. Available to U.S. and non-U.S. citizens.

Application Requirements Autobiography. *Deadline:* December 31.

Contact Charles Yrigoyen Jr., General Secretary
General Commission on Archives and
History
PO Box 127
Madison, NJ 07940
Phone: 973-408-3189
Fax: 973-408-3909

WOMEN IN UNITED METHODIST HISTORY RESEARCH GRANT • 646

Grant is for seed money for projects related to the history of women in the United Methodist Church or its antecedents. Submit curriculum vitae, project description, timetable, budget, and three letters of recommendation.

Academic/Career Areas History; Religion/Theology.

Award Grant for use in graduate years; not renewable. *Number: 1–2. Amount: $500–$1000.*

Eligibility Requirements Applicant must be enrolled or expecting to enroll at an institution or university. Available to U.S. and non-U.S. citizens.

Application Requirements References. *Deadline:* December 31.

Contact Charles Yrigoyen Jr., General Secretary
General Commission on Archives and
History
PO Box 127
Madison, NJ 07940
Phone: 973-408-3189
Fax: 973-408-3909

WOMEN IN UNITED METHODIST HISTORY WRITING AWARD • 647

Contest is to encourage and reward excellence in research and writing on the history of women in the United Methodist Church or its antecedents. Manuscripts not to exceed 20 double-spaced, typewritten pages. One-time award of $250.

Academic/Career Areas History; Religion/Theology.

Award Prize for use in graduate years; not renewable. *Number: 1. Amount: $250.*

Eligibility Requirements Applicant must be enrolled or expecting to enroll at an institution or university. Available to U.S. citizens.

Application Requirements Applicant must enter a contest. *Deadline:* May 1.

Contact Charles Yrigoyen Jr., General Secretary
General Commission on Archives and
History
PO Box 127
Madison, NJ 07940
Phone: 973-408-3189
Fax: 973-408-3909

GERMAN ACADEMIC EXCHANGE SERVICE (DAAD)
http://www.daad.org

LEO BAECK INSTITUTE - DAAD GRANTS
• *See number 126*

HARRY S TRUMAN LIBRARY INSTITUTE
http://www.trumanlibrary.org

HARRY S. TRUMAN BOOK AWARD
• *See number 324*

HARRY S. TRUMAN LIBRARY INSTITUTE DISSERTATION YEAR FELLOWSHIPS
• *See number 325*

HARRY S. TRUMAN LIBRARY INSTITUTE RESEARCH GRANTS
• *See number 326*

HARRY S. TRUMAN LIBRARY INSTITUTE SCHOLAR'S AWARD
• *See number 327*

HUNTINGTON LIBRARY, ART COLLECTIONS, AND BOTANICAL GARDENS
http://www.huntington.org

HUNTINGTON RESEARCH AWARDS
• *See number 56*

JAPANESE GOVERNMENT/THE MONBUSHO SCHOLARSHIP PROGRAM
http://embjapan.org/la

RESEARCH STUDENT SCHOLARSHIP
• *See number 13*

JOHN F. KENNEDY LIBRARY FOUNDATION
http://www.jfklibrary.org

ARTHUR M. SCHLESINGER, JR. FELLOWSHIP • 648

Fellowship awarded to support applicants specializing in one of the following: Latin America or Western Hemisphere history, policy studies during the Kennedy Administration, or period from Roosevelt to Kennedy presidencies. Must include ten-page writing sample, project budget, and a vita. See application for further details.

Academic/Career Areas History; Political Science.

Award Fellowship for use in graduate years; not renewable. *Amount:* up to $5000.

Eligibility Requirements Applicant must be enrolled or expecting to enroll at an institution or university. Available to U.S. citizens.

Application Requirements Application, essay. *Deadline:* August 15.

Contact Grant and Fellowship Coordinator
John F. Kennedy Library Foundation
Columbia Point
Boston, MA 02125
Phone: 617-929-1200

KENNEDY RESEARCH GRANTS
• See number 100

MACKENZIE KING SCHOLARSHIPS BOARD

MACKENZIE KING TRAVELLING SCHOLARSHIPS
• See number 236

MARCUS CENTER OF THE AMERICAN JEWISH ARCHIVES
http://www.huc.edu/aja

AMERICAN JEWISH ARCHIVES DISSERTATION AND POSTDOCTORAL RESEARCH FELLOWSHIPS • 649

One-time award for postdoctoral candidates to write or conduct research for dissertation at the American Jewish Archives. Submit curriculum vitae, proposal, recommendation, and evidence of published research by March 1. Dissertation must be regarding the historical or sociological aspects of the American Jewish experience.

Academic/Career Areas History; Social Sciences.

Award Fellowship for use in postgraduate years; not renewable. *Amount:* $1000–$2000.

Eligibility Requirements Applicant must be enrolled or expecting to enroll at an institution or university and studying in Ohio. Available to U.S. and non-U.S. citizens.

Application Requirements References. *Deadline:* March 1.

Contact Kevin Proffitt, Director of Fellowship
Marcus Center of the American Jewish Archives
3101 Clifton Avenue
Cincinnati, OH 45220-2488
Phone: 513-221-1875
Fax: 513-221-7812

MASSACHUSETTS HISTORICAL SOCIETY
http://www.masshist.org

MASSACHUSETTS HISTORICAL SOCIETY RESEARCH FELLOWSHIP PROGRAM • 650

Eighteen research fellowships each year to independent scholars, advanced graduate students, or PhD's. Stipend of $1500 provided for four weeks of research which must be conducted in the Society's archives. Some fellowships target specific topics: African American Studies, Women's history, American Revolution. Prior familiarity with collections preferred.

Academic/Career Areas History; Humanities.

Award Fellowship for use in graduate, or postgraduate years; not renewable. *Number:* 20.

Eligibility Requirements Applicant must be enrolled or expecting to enroll part-time at an institution or university and studying in Massachusetts. Available to U.S. and non-U.S. citizens.

Application Requirements *Deadline:* March 1.

Contact Jean Powers, Editorial Assistant, Publications
Massachusetts Historical Society
1154 Boylston Street
Boston, MA 02215
Phone: 617-646-0513
Fax: 617-854-0074
E-mail: jpowers@masshist.org

NEW ENGLAND REGIONAL FELLOWSHIP CONSORTIUM GRANT • 651

The New England Regional Fellowship Consortium is a collaboration of 11 major cultural agencies. Each grant will provide a stipend of $5,000 for eight weeks of research at participating institutions. Applications are welcome from anyone with a serious need to use the collections and facilities of the organizations. The Consortium's grants are designed to encourage projects that draw on the resources of several agencies. Each award will be for research at a minimum of three different institutions. Fellows must work at each of these organizations for at least two weeks.

Academic/Career Areas History; Humanities.

Award Grant for use in graduate, or postgraduate years; not renewable. *Number:* 9. *Amount:* $5000.

Eligibility Requirements Applicant must be enrolled or expecting to enroll part-time at an institution or university and studying in Connecticut, Maine, Massachusetts, New Hampshire, Rhode Island, or Vermont. Available to U.S. and non-U.S. citizens.

Application Requirements References, curriculum vitae, project proposal. *Deadline:* February 1.

Contact Jean Powers, Editorial Assistant,
Publications
Massachusetts Historical Society
1154 Boylston Street
Boston, MA 02215
Phone: 617-646-0513
Fax: 617-854-0074
E-mail: jpowers@masshist.org

NATIONAL RESEARCH COUNCIL
http://www.nationalacademies.org/fellowships/

FORD FOUNDATION DISSERTATION FELLOWSHIPS FOR MINORITIES
• *See number 256*

FORD FOUNDATION POSTDOCTORAL FELLOWSHIP FOR MINORITIES
• *See number 257*

FORD FOUNDATION PREDOCTORAL FELLOWSHIPS FOR MINORITIES
• *See number 258*

ORGANIZATION OF AMERICAN HISTORIANS
http://www.oah.org

ERIK BARNOUW AWARD • 652

One-time award available to recognize outstanding reporting or programming on network or cable television, or in documentary film concerned with American history. Films completed since January 1 of application year are eligible. Entries should be submitted on 1/2 inch video. Winner receives a certificate. One copy of each entry must be received by each committee member by December 1.

Academic/Career Areas History.

Award Prize for use in graduate years; not renewable. *Number:* 1–2.

Eligibility Requirements Applicant must be enrolled or expecting to enroll at a four-year institution or university. Available to U.S. and non-U.S. citizens.

Application Requirements Applicant must enter a contest. *Deadline:* December 1.

Contact Kara Hamm, Award and Prize Committee
Coordinator
Organization of American Historians
112 North Bryan Avenue
Bloomington, IN 47408-4199
Phone: 812-855-9852
Fax: 812-855-0696
E-mail: awards@oah.org

LA PIETRA DISSERTATION TRAVEL FELLOWSHIP IN TRANSNATIONAL HISTORY • 653

Provides financial assistance to graduate students whose dissertation topics deal with aspects of American history beyond U.S. borders. Fellowship may be used for international travel to collections vital to dissertation research. Must be currently enrolled in U.S. or foreign graduate program. Deadline: December 1. Must send current c.v. indicating language proficiency.

Academic/Career Areas History.

Award Fellowship for use in graduate years; not renewable. *Number:* 1. *Amount:* $1250.

Eligibility Requirements Applicant must be enrolled or expecting to enroll at an institution or university. Available to U.S. and non-U.S. citizens.

Application Requirements Essay, references, 2-3 page project description. *Deadline:* December 1.

Contact Kara Hamm, Award and Prize Committee
Coordinator
Organization of American Historians
112 North Bryan Avenue
Bloomington, IN 47408-4199
Phone: 812-855-9852
Fax: 812-855-0696
E-mail: awards@oah.org

PHI ALPHA THETA HISTORY HONOR SOCIETY, INC.
http://www.phialphatheta.org

PHI ALPHA THETA DOCTORAL SCHOLARSHIPS • 654

Award for graduate members of Phi Alpha Theta to complete research leading to a Ph.D. in history. Must include transcript and references with application. Four one-time awards ranging from two at $750 to two at $1000.

Academic/Career Areas History.

Award Scholarship for use in graduate years; not renewable. *Number:* 4. *Amount:* $750–$1000.

Eligibility Requirements Applicant must be enrolled or expecting to enroll full-time at an institution or university. Applicant must have 3.0 GPA or higher. Available to U.S. and non-U.S. citizens.

Phi Alpha Theta History Honor Society, Inc. (continued)

Application Requirements Application, essay, references, transcript, dissertation prospectus, curriculum. *Deadline:* March 1.

Contact Graydon A. Tunstall Jr., Executive Director
Phi Alpha Theta History Honor Society, Inc.
SOC107, University of South Florida,
4202 East Fowler Avenue
Tampa, FL 33620-8100
Phone: 800-394-8195
Fax: 813-974-8215
E-mail: phialpha@cambio.acomp.usf.edu

Eligibility Requirements Applicant must be enrolled or expecting to enroll full-time at an institution or university. Applicant must have 3.0 GPA or higher. Available to U.S. and non-U.S. citizens.

Application Requirements References, 3 copies of dissertation. *Deadline:* May 31.

Contact Graydon A. Tunstall, Executive Director
Phi Alpha Theta History Honor Society, Inc.
SOC107, University of South Florida,
4202 East Fowler Avenue
Tampa, FL 33620-8100
Phone: 800-394-8195
Fax: 813-974-8215
E-mail: phialpha@cambio.acomp.usf.edu

PHI ALPHA THETA GRADUATE SCHOLARSHIPS • 655

One-time award for graduate student member of Phi Alpha Theta beginning studies for an MA degree in history. Must include transcript and references with application. A curriculum vitae is also required. Must rank in upper third of class or have minimum 3.0 GPA. Deadline is March 1.

Academic/Career Areas History.

Award Scholarship for use in graduate years; not renewable. *Number:* 5. *Amount:* $750–$1250.

Eligibility Requirements Applicant must be enrolled or expecting to enroll full-time at an institution or university. Applicant must have 3.0 GPA or higher. Available to U.S. and non-U.S. citizens.

Application Requirements Application, references, test scores, transcript, curriculum vitae. *Deadline:* March 1.

Contact Graydon A. Tunstall Jr., Executive Director
Phi Alpha Theta History Honor Society, Inc.
SOC107, University of South Florida,
4202 East Fowler Avenue
Tampa, FL 33620-8100
Phone: 800-394-8195
Fax: 813-974-8215
E-mail: phialpha@cambio.acomp.usf.edu

PHI ALPHA THETA/WESTERNERS INTERNATIONAL DOCTORAL DISSERTATION AWARD • 656

Available only to graduate student members of Phi Alpha Theta. Dissertation must have been written in the field of Western U.S. History. Co-sponsored by Westerners International. Deadline is May 31.

Academic/Career Areas History.

Award Prize for use in graduate years; not renewable. *Number:* 1. *Amount:* $500.

PHI BETA KAPPA SOCIETY
http://www.pbk.org

MARY ISABEL SIBLEY FELLOWSHIP FOR GREEK AND FRENCH STUDIES
• *See number 132*

PI GAMMA MU INTERNATIONAL HONOR SOCIETY IN SOCIETY SCIENCE
http://www.sckans.edu/~pgm

PI GAMMA MU SCHOLARSHIP
• *See number 273*

SWANN FOUNDATION FUND
http://www.lcweb.loc.gov/rr/print/swann/swann_foundation.html

SWANN FOUNDATION FUND FELLOWSHIP
• *See number 109*

UNITED DAUGHTERS OF THE CONFEDERACY
http://www.hqudc.org

JUDGE WILLIAM M. BEARD SCHOLARSHIP
• *See number 629*

UNITED NEGRO COLLEGE FUND
http://www.uncf.org

GEORGE S. LURCY CHARITABLE AND EDUCATIONAL TRUST
• *See number 405*

UNITED STATES ARMY CENTER OF MILITARY HISTORY
http://www.army.mil/cmh-pg

DISSERTATION YEAR FELLOWSHIP • 657

Two $9000 awards to support scholarly research and writing among qualified civilian graduate students who are not full-time employees of the federal government and whose dissertations focus on the history of war on land. Topics submitted should complement the Center's existing projects. Contact for complete information.

Academic/Career Areas History; Peace and Conflict Studies.

Award Fellowship for use in graduate years; not renewable. *Number:* 2. *Amount:* $9000.

Eligibility Requirements Applicant must be enrolled or expecting to enroll full or part-time at an institution or university. Available to U.S. citizens.

Application Requirements Application, essay, references, transcript. *Deadline:* January 15.

Contact Dr. Edgar F. Raines, Jr., Executive Secretary
United States Army Center of Military History
103 3rd Avenue
Ft. McNair, DC 20319-5058
Phone: 202-685-2094
Fax: 202-685-2077
E-mail: edgar.raines@hqda.army.mil

UNITED STATES INSTITUTE OF PEACE
http://www.usip.org

JENNINGS RANDOLPH SENIOR FELLOW AWARD
• See number 333

PEACE SCHOLAR DISSERTATION FELLOWSHIP
• See number 334

WELLESLEY COLLEGE
http://www.wellesley.edu/CWS/

EDNA V. MOFFETT FELLOWSHIP • 658

One or more fellowships available to young alumnae of Wellesley College for a first year study in history. Based on merit and need. For application and additional information visit the website at www.wellesley.edu/cws.

Academic/Career Areas History.

Award Fellowship for use in graduate years; not renewable. *Amount:* up to $12,000.

Eligibility Requirements Applicant must be enrolled or expecting to enroll full-time at an institution or university and female. Available to U.S. citizens.

Application Requirements Application, essay, financial need analysis, resume, references, transcript. *Deadline:* January 3.

Contact Rose Crawford, Secretary to the Committee on Graduate Fellowships
Wellesley College
106 Central Avenue, Green Hall 441
Wellesley, MA 02481-8200
Phone: 781-283-3525
Fax: 781-283-3674
E-mail: cws-fellowships@wellesley.edu

EUGENE L. COX FELLOWSHIP • 659

One or more fellowships available for graduate study in medieval or renaissance history and culture abroad or in the United States. Must be a graduate of Wellesley College. Award based on merit and need. E-mail inquiries to cws-fellowships@wellesley.edu.

Academic/Career Areas History.

Award Fellowship for use in graduate years; not renewable. *Amount:* up to $6000.

Eligibility Requirements Applicant must be enrolled or expecting to enroll full-time at an institution or university and female. Available to U.S. citizens.

Application Requirements Application, essay, financial need analysis, resume, references, transcript. *Deadline:* January 3.

Contact Rose Crawford, Secretary to the Committee on Graduate Fellowships
Wellesley College
106 Central Avenue, Green Hall 441
Wellesley, MA 02481-8200
Phone: 781-283-3525
Fax: 781-283-3674
E-mail: cws-fellowships@wellesley.edu

MARY MCEWEN SCHIMKE SCHOLARSHIP • 660

Supplemental one-time award for relief from household and childcare while pursuing graduate study preferably in literature and/or history, American studies. Open to women graduates over 30 years of age from any American institution. Based on need and merit.

Academic/Career Areas History; Literature/English/Writing.

Award Scholarship for use in graduate years; not renewable. *Amount:* up to $1000.

Eligibility Requirements Applicant must be age 31; enrolled or expecting to enroll full-time at an institution or university and female. Available to U.S. citizens.

Wellesley College (continued)

Application Requirements Application, financial need analysis, references, test scores, transcript. *Deadline:* January 3.

Contact Rose Crawford, Secretary to the
Committee on Graduate Fellowships
Wellesley College
106 Central Avenue, Green Hall 441
Wellesley, MA 02481
Phone: 781-283-3525
Fax: 781-283-3674
E-mail: cws-fellowships@wellesley.edu

THOMAS JEFFERSON FELLOWSHIP • **661**

One or more fellowships for advanced study in history. Must be Wellesley College graduate and demonstrate merit and need. More information and applications may be found at www.wellesley.edu/cws.

Academic/Career Areas History.

Award Fellowship for use in graduate years; not renewable. *Amount:* up to $9000.

Eligibility Requirements Applicant must be enrolled or expecting to enroll full-time at an institution or university and female. Available to U.S. citizens.

Application Requirements Application, essay, financial need analysis, resume, references, transcript. *Deadline:* January 3.

Contact Rose Crawford, Secretary to the
Committee on Graduate Fellowships
Wellesley College
106 Central Avenue, Green Hall 441
Wellesley, MA 02481-8200
Phone: 781-283-3525
Fax: 781-283-3674
E-mail: cws-fellowships@wellesley.edu

WESTERN ASSOCIATION OF WOMEN HISTORIANS
http://www.wawh.org

GRADUATE STUDENT FELLOWSHIP AWARD • **662**

Applicants must be members of Western Association of Women Historians for two years, advanced to candidacy, and writing the dissertation at the time of the application. The $1000 award may be used for any expenses related to the dissertation. Applications due February 15 for a June award.

Academic/Career Areas History.

Award Fellowship for use in graduate years; not renewable. *Number:* 1. *Amount:* $1000.

Eligibility Requirements Applicant must be enrolled or expecting to enroll full or part-time at an institution or university. Applicant or parent of

applicant must be member of Western Association of Women Historians. Available to U.S. and non-U.S. citizens.

Application Requirements Application. *Deadline:* February 15.

Contact Alexandra Nickliss, Graduate Student
Fellowship Chair
Western Association of Women
Historians
Department of Social Science, City
College of San Francisco, 50 Phelan
Avenue
San Francisco, CA 94112
E-mail: anicklis@ccsf.org

WINTERTHUR MUSEUM, GARDEN, AND LIBRARY
http://www.winterthur.org

LOIS F. MCNEIL DISSERTATION RESEARCH FELLOWSHIPS
• *See number 85*

NEH FELLOWSHIPS
• *See number 110*

WINTERTHUR RESEARCH FELLOWSHIPS
• *See number 111*

WOODROW WILSON NATIONAL FELLOWSHIP FOUNDATION
http://www.woodrow.org

ANDREW W. MELLON FELLOWSHIPS IN HUMANISTIC STUDIES
• *See number 134*

WOODROW WILSON NATIONAL FELLOWSHIP FOUNDATION DISSERTATION GRANTS IN WOMEN'S STUDIES
• *See number 135*

WOODROW WILSON POSTDOCTORAL FELLOWSHIPS IN THE HUMANITIES
• *See number 136*

HOME ECONOMICS

JAPANESE GOVERNMENT/THE MONBUSHO SCHOLARSHIP PROGRAM
http://embjapan.org/la

RESEARCH STUDENT SCHOLARSHIP
• *See number 13*

KAPPA OMICRON NU HONOR SOCIETY
http://www.kon.org

EILEEN C. MADDEX FELLOWSHIP
• *See number 386*

HETTIE M. ANTHONY FELLOWSHIP
• *See number 387*

KAPPA OMICRON NU NATIONAL ALUMNI CHAPTER GRANT
• *See number 388*

KAPPA OMICRON NU NATIONAL ALUMNI FELLOWSHIP
• *See number 389*

KAPPA OMICRON NU NEW INITIATIVES GRANT
• *See number 401*

MAUDE GILCHRIST FELLOWSHIP • **663**

Award for doctoral research in home economics or one of its specializations, to Kappa Omicron Nu member who has demonstrated scholarship, research, and leadership potential. Deadline: January 15.

Academic/Career Areas Home Economics.

Award Fellowship for use in graduate years; not renewable. *Number:* 1. *Amount:* $2000.

Eligibility Requirements Applicant must be enrolled or expecting to enroll at an institution or university and must have an interest in leadership. Available to U.S. and non-U.S. citizens.

Application Requirements Application. *Deadline:* January 15.

Contact Dorothy Mitstifer, Executive Director
Kappa Omicron Nu Honor Society
4990 Northwind Drive, Suite 140
East Lansing, MI 48823-5031
Phone: 517-351-8335
Fax: 517-351-8336
E-mail: dmitstifer@kon.org

OMICRON NU RESEARCH FELLOWSHIP • **664**

One-time award for doctoral research in home economics. Must be member of Kappa Omicron Nu who has demonstrated scholarship, research, and leadership potential. Deadline is January 15.

Academic/Career Areas Home Economics.

Award Fellowship for use in graduate years; not renewable. *Number:* 1. *Amount:* $2000.

Eligibility Requirements Applicant must be enrolled or expecting to enroll at an institution or university and must have an interest in leadership. Available to U.S. and non-U.S. citizens.

Application Requirements Application, references, transcript. *Deadline:* January 15.

Contact Dorothy Mitstifer, Executive Director
Kappa Omicron Nu Honor Society
4990 Northwind Drive, Suite 140
East Lansing, MI 48823-5031
Phone: 517-351-8335
Fax: 517-351-8336
E-mail: dmitstifer@kon.org

WINTERTHUR MUSEUM, GARDEN, AND LIBRARY
http://www.winterthur.org

NEH FELLOWSHIPS
• *See number 110*

WINTERTHUR RESEARCH FELLOWSHIPS
• *See number 111*

HORTICULTURE/ FLORICULTURE

AMERICAN CENTER OF ORIENTAL RESEARCH
http://www.bu.edu/acor

CAORC SENIOR FELLOWSHIP • **665**

Two- to six-month fellowships for senior post-doctoral scholars pursuing research or publications in the social sciences, humanities and associated disciplines relating to the Middle East. Must be U.S. citizen. Subject to funding.

Academic/Career Areas Horticulture/Floriculture; Social Sciences.

Award Fellowship for use in postgraduate years; not renewable. *Number:* 1–6. *Amount:* $26,700.

Eligibility Requirements Applicant must be enrolled or expecting to enroll at an institution or university. Available to U.S. citizens.

Application Requirements Application. *Deadline:* February 1.

Contact Dr. Donald Keller, Assistant Director
American Center of Oriental Research
656 Beacon Street, 5th Floor
Boston, MA 02215-2010
Phone: 617-353-6571
Fax: 617-353-6575
E-mail: acor@bu.ed

AMERICAN ORCHID SOCIETY
http://www.orchidweb.org

AMERICAN ORCHID SOCIETY/ORCHID RESEARCH GRANT
• *See number 185*

FIRST - FLORICULTURE INDUSTRY RESEARCH AND SCHOLARSHIP TRUST
http://www.firstinfloriculture.org

JOHN CAREW MEMORIAL SCHOLARSHIP
• *See number 8*

INTERNATIONAL DEVELOPMENT RESEARCH CENTER
http://www.idrc.ca/awards

AGROPOLIS
• See number 10

NATIONAL MILK PRODUCERS FEDERATION
http://www.nmpf.org

NATIONAL MILK PRODUCERS FEDERATION NATIONAL DAIRY LEADERSHIP SCHOLARSHIP PROGRAM
• See number 5

POTASH AND PHOSPHATE INSTITUTE
http://www.ppi-far.org

J. FIELDING REED FELLOWSHIPS
• See number 6

HOSPITALITY MANAGEMENT

KAPPA OMICRON NU HONOR SOCIETY
http://www.kon.org

EILEEN C. MADDEX FELLOWSHIP
• See number 386

HETTIE M. ANTHONY FELLOWSHIP
• See number 387

KAPPA OMICRON NU NATIONAL ALUMNI CHAPTER GRANT
• See number 388

KAPPA OMICRON NU NATIONAL ALUMNI FELLOWSHIP
• See number 389

NATIONAL TOURISM FOUNDATION
http://www.ntfonline.org

LURAY CAVERNS GRADUATE RESEARCH GRANT
• See number 402

HUMANITIES

ALEXANDER VON HUMBOLDT FOUNDATION
http://www.humboldt-foundation.de

TRANSCOOP PROGRAM
• See number 315

AMERICAN CENTER OF ORIENTAL RESEARCH
http://www.bu.edu/acor

CAORC FELLOWSHIPS • 666

Two- to six-month fellowships for pre-doctoral students and post-doctoral scholars. Fields of study include all areas of the humanities and social sciences. Topics should contribute to scholarship in Near Eastern Studies. Subject to funding. Must be U.S. citizen.

Academic/Career Areas Humanities; Social Sciences.

Award Fellowship for use in graduate, or postgraduate years; not renewable. *Number:* 6–15. *Amount:* $17,000.

Eligibility Requirements Applicant must be enrolled or expecting to enroll at an institution or university. Available to U.S. citizens.

Application Requirements Application, references, transcript. *Deadline:* February 1.

Contact Dr. Donald Keller, Assistant Director
American Center of Oriental Research
656 Beacon Street, 5th Floor
Boston, MA 02215-2010
Phone: 617-353-6571
Fax: 617-353-6575
E-mail: acor@bu.edu

AMERICAN COUNCIL OF LEARNED SOCIETIES (ACLS)
http://www.acls.org

AMERICAN COUNCIL OF LEARNED SOCIETIES FELLOWSHIPS FOR POSTDOCTORAL RESEARCH IN THE HUMANITIES • 667

One-time award for scholars holding Ph.D. or equivalent, U.S. citizen or permanent legal resident, to support postdoctoral research in all disciplines of the humanities and humanities-related social sciences. Scholars who have not held supported research leave for at least three years are eligible. Application deadline: October 1.

Academic/Career Areas Humanities; Social Sciences.

Award Fellowship for use in postgraduate years; not renewable. *Number:* up to 60. *Amount:* $30,000–$50,000.

Eligibility Requirements Applicant must be enrolled or expecting to enroll full-time at an institution or university. Available to U.S. citizens.

Application Requirements Application. *Deadline:* October 1.

Contact Office of Fellowships and Grants
American Council of Learned Societies (ACLS)
228 East 45th Street
New York, NY 10017-3398
Fax: 212-949-8058
E-mail: grants@acls.org

AMERICAN COUNCIL OF LEARNED SOCIETIES GRANTS FOR EAST EUROPEAN STUDIES-DISSERTATION FELLOWSHIPS
• *See number 113*

AMERICAN COUNCIL OF LEARNED SOCIETIES GRANTS FOR EAST EUROPEAN STUDIES-FELLOWSHIPS FOR POSTDOCTORAL RESEARCH
• **668**

One-time award for Ph.D. scholars to support research in the social sciences and humanities of Eastern Europe. Applicants must be U.S. citizens or permanent residents. Funds may be used to supplement sabbatical salaries or awards from other sources. Applicants deadline: November 1.

Academic/Career Areas Humanities; Social Sciences.

Award Fellowship for use in postgraduate years; not renewable. *Number:* 5–7. *Amount:* up to $25,000.

Eligibility Requirements Applicant must be enrolled or expecting to enroll full-time at an institution or university. Available to U.S. citizens.

Application Requirements Application. *Deadline:* November 1.

Contact Office of Fellowships and Grants
American Council of Learned Societies
(ACLS)
228 East 45th Street
New York, NY 10017-3398
Fax: 212-949-8058
E-mail: grants@acls.org

COMMITTEE ON SCHOLARLY COMMUNICATION-AMERICAN RESEARCH IN THE HUMANITIES IN THE PEOPLE'S REPUBLIC OF CHINA • **669**

Award for scholars in the humanities to do research in the People's Republic of China. Must be U.S. citizen or permanent resident who has lived continuously in the U.S. for at least 3 years by the time of the application deadline. Application deadline: November 15.

Academic/Career Areas Humanities.

Award Fellowship for use in postgraduate years; not renewable. *Number:* up to 5.

Eligibility Requirements Applicant must be enrolled or expecting to enroll full-time at an institution or university. Available to U.S. citizens.

Application Requirements Application. *Deadline:* November 15.

Contact Office of Fellowships and Grants
American Council of Learned Societies
(ACLS)
228 East 45th Street
New York, NY 10017-3398
Fax: 212-949-8058
E-mail: grants@acls.org

CONTEMPLATIVE PRACTICE FELLOWSHIPS
• *See number 162*

LIBRARY OF CONGRESS FELLOWSHIP IN INTERNATIONAL STUDIES • **670**

Supports postdoctoral research in all disciplines of the humanities and social sciences using the foreign language collections of the Library of Congress. Fellowships will be available for four to nine months each, with a stipend of $3,500 per month. Must be U.S. citizen or permanent resident. Preference given to scholar at an early stage of their career. Application deadline: November 1.

Academic/Career Areas Humanities; Social Sciences.

Award Fellowship for use in postgraduate years; not renewable. *Number:* up to 10. *Amount:* $14,000–$31,500.

Eligibility Requirements Applicant must be enrolled or expecting to enroll full-time at an institution or university. Available to U.S. citizens.

Application Requirements Application. *Deadline:* November 1.

Contact Office of Fellowships and Grants
American Council of Learned Societies
(ACLS)
228 East 45th Street
New York, NY 10017-3398
Fax: 212-949-8058
E-mail: grants@acls.org

AMERICAN COUNCIL OF TEACHERS OF RUSSIAN
http://www.actr.org

TITLE VIII RESEARCH SCHOLAR AND COMBINED RESEARCH AND LANGUAGE STUDY PROGRAM
• *See number 114*

AMERICAN HISTORICAL ASSOCIATION
http://www.theaha.org

ALBERT J. BEVERIDGE GRANT FOR RESEARCH IN THE HISTORY OF THE WESTERN HEMISPHERE
• *See number 115*

AMERICAN INSTITUTE OF PAKISTAN STUDIES

AMERICAN INSTITUTE OF PAKISTAN STUDIES GRADUATE STUDENT FELLOWSHIP • **671**

Four or more two- to four-month fellowships awarded to graduate students who have yet to complete course work towards a Ph.D.. Must have completed one or more years of graduate study towards MA or Ph.D. degree and demonstrate interest in topics related to Pakistan Studies. Must be

American Institute of Pakistan Studies (continued)

U.S. citizen. Award includes stipend of $1750 per month and travel expenses up to $2500.

Academic/Career Areas Humanities; Social Sciences.

Award Fellowship for use in graduate years; not renewable.

Eligibility Requirements Applicant must be enrolled or expecting to enroll at an institution or university and must have an interest in designated field specified by sponsor. Available to U.S. citizens.

Application Requirements Application, essay, references, transcript. *Deadline:* February 1.

Contact Charles Kennedy, Director
American Institute of Pakistan Studies
PO Box 7568
Winston-Salem, NC 27109
Phone: 336-758-5453
Fax: 336-758-6104
E-mail: ckennedy@wfu.edu

**AMERICAN INSTITUTE OF PAKISTAN STUDIES
POSTDOCTORAL FELLOWSHIP • 672**

Two or more two- to nine-month fellowships awarded to postdoctoral scholars pursuing work in Pakistan Studies. Must be U.S. citizen. Award includes stipend of $3550 per month plus travel expenses up to $2500.

Academic/Career Areas Humanities; Social Sciences.

Award Fellowship for use in postgraduate years; not renewable.

Eligibility Requirements Applicant must be enrolled or expecting to enroll at an institution or university and must have an interest in designated field specified by sponsor. Available to U.S. citizens.

Application Requirements Application, essay, references, transcript. *Deadline:* February 1.

Contact Charles Kennedy, Director
American Institute of Pakistan Studies
PO Box 7568
Winston-Salem, NC 27109
Phone: 336-758-5453
Fax: 336-758-6104
E-mail: ckennedy@wfu.edu

**AMERICAN INSTITUTE OF PAKISTAN STUDIES
PREDOCTORAL FELLOWSHIPS • 673**

One-time awards for pre-doctoral candidates to pursue research on Pakistan. Must be U.S. citizen and pursue a dissertation topic relevant to Pakistan studies. Submit application, transcripts, essay, and references by February 1. Award includes stipend of $2750 per month plus travel expenses of up to $2500.

Academic/Career Areas Humanities; Social Sciences.

Award Fellowship for use in graduate, or postgraduate years; not renewable. *Number:* 15. *Amount:* $9000.

Eligibility Requirements Applicant must be enrolled or expecting to enroll full-time at an institution or university and must have an interest in designated field specified by sponsor. Available to U.S. citizens.

Application Requirements Application, essay, references, transcript. *Deadline:* February 1.

Contact Charles Kennedy, Director
American Institute of Pakistan Studies
PO Box 7568
Winston-Salem, NC 27109
Phone: 336-758-5453
Fax: 336-758-6104
E-mail: ckennedy@wfu.edu

AMERICAN PHILOSOPHICAL SOCIETY
http://www.amphilsoc.org

**LIBRARY RESIDENT RESEARCH
FELLOWSHIP • 674**

One-time fellowships for independent scholars, Ph.D. or equivalent, and Ph.D. candidates in relevant field who live more than 75 miles from Philadelphia. Must be U.S. citizen or foreign national. One-month, two-months, or three-months award. Need three-page proposal. Check website for complete information: www.amphilsoc.org.

Academic/Career Areas Humanities.

Award Fellowship for use in graduate, or postgraduate years; not renewable. *Number:* 15–20. *Amount:* $2000.

Eligibility Requirements Applicant must be enrolled or expecting to enroll at an institution or university.

Application Requirements Application, essay, references, proposal. *Deadline:* March 1.

Contact Library Resident Research Fellowships
American Philosophical Society
105 South 5th Street
Philadelphia, PA 19106-3387

**PHILLIPS GRANTS FOR NATIVE AMERICAN
RESEARCH • 675**

One-time award for graduate research in linguistics or ethnohistory of Native American peoples north of Mexico-U.S. border. Provides funds for travel, fees, and other research costs. Not for educational use. Must be over 21. Several grants of up to $2000. Check website for complete information: www.amphilsoc.org.

Academic/Career Areas Humanities.

Award Grant for use in graduate, or postgraduate years; not renewable. *Number:* 15–20. *Amount:* up to $2000.

Eligibility Requirements Applicant must be age 22 and enrolled or expecting to enroll at an institution or university.

Application Requirements Application, references, proposal. *Deadline:* March 1.

Contact Phillips Fund
American Philosophical Society
104 South 5th Street
Philadelphia, PA 19106-3387

AMERICAN POLITICAL SCIENCE ASSOCIATION
http://www.apsanet.org

CONGRESSIONAL FELLOWSHIP FOR FEDERAL EXECUTIVES • 676

Nonrenewable fellowship for senior federal executive to engage in research on politics or government in joint program with APSA. Submit SF171 or resume.

Academic/Career Areas Humanities; Political Science; Social Sciences.

Award Fellowship for use in graduate, or postgraduate years; not renewable.

Eligibility Requirements Applicant must be enrolled or expecting to enroll at an institution or university. Applicant or parent of applicant must have employment or volunteer experience in designated career field. Available to U.S. citizens.

Application Requirements Application, essay, resume, references. *Deadline:* December 1.

Contact Dr. Jeffrey Biggs, Director
American Political Science Association
1527 New Hampshire Avenue, NW
Washington, DC 20036-1206
Phone: 202-483-2512
Fax: 202-483-2657

AMERICAN RESEARCH INSTITUTE IN TURKEY (ARIT)
http://www.mec.sas.upenn.edu/ARIT

ARIT MELLON RESEARCH FELLOWSHIPS FOR CENTRAL AND EASTERN EUROPEAN SCHOLARS IN TURKEY • 677

One-time award for Czech, Hungarian, Polish, Slovak, Rumanian and Bulgarian Ph.D. scholars to conduct advanced research in the humanities and social sciences. Research to be carried out in Turkey for two to three months. Include project statement, curriculum vitae, and letters of recommendation.

Academic/Career Areas Humanities; Social Sciences.

Award Fellowship for use in postgraduate years; not renewable. *Number:* 3–4. *Amount:* up to $11,500.

Eligibility Requirements Applicant must be Bulgarian, Hungarian, Polish, Rumanian, or Slavic/Czech citizenship and enrolled or expecting to enroll full-time at an institution or university. Available to citizens of countries other than the U.S. or Canada.

Application Requirements Application, essay, financial need analysis, references, research permit, project statement, curriculum vitae. *Deadline:* March 5.

Contact Nancy Leinwand, Administrator
American Research Institute in Turkey (ARIT)
University of Pennsylvania Museum
Philadelphia, PA 19104-6324
Phone: 215-898-3474
Fax: 215-898-0657
E-mail: leinwand@sas.upenn.edu

ARIT, HUMANITIES AND SOCIAL SCIENCE FELLOWSHIPS IN TURKEY • 678

One-time award for graduate and postdoctoral research in the humanities and social sciences, to be carried out in Turkey for periods of two months to one year. Must obtain permission of the Turkish Embassy to conduct research. Submit proposal, project budget, letters of reference, and curriculum vitae. Applicant must be affiliated with a U.S. or Canadian university or college or other institution for research or higher education.

Academic/Career Areas Humanities; Social Sciences.

Award Fellowship for use in graduate, or postgraduate years; not renewable. *Number:* 10–15. *Amount:* $4000–$16,000.

Eligibility Requirements Applicant must be enrolled or expecting to enroll full-time at an institution or university. Available to U.S. and non-U.S. citizens.

Application Requirements Application, essay, financial need analysis, references, transcript, permit for research in Turkey, proposal, curriculum vitae. *Deadline:* November 15.

Contact Nancy Leinwand, Administrator
American Research Institute in Turkey (ARIT)
University of Pennsylvania Museum
Philadelphia, PA 19104-6324
Phone: 215-898-3474
Fax: 215-898-0657
E-mail: leinwand@sas.upenn.edu

ARIT/NATIONAL ENDOWMENT FOR THE HUMANITIES FELLOWSHIPS FOR THE HUMANITIES IN TURKEY • 679

One-time award for postdoctoral research in the humanities and cultural history in Turkey. Four- to twelve-month tenure. Must be a U.S. citizen or a permanent resident of at least three years. Must be affiliated with a U.S. or Canadian university. Submit budget.

American Research Institute in Turkey (ARIT) (continued)

Academic/Career Areas Humanities.

Award Fellowship for use in postgraduate years; not renewable. *Number: 2–4. Amount:* $10,000–$30,000.

Eligibility Requirements Applicant must be enrolled or expecting to enroll full-time at a four-year institution or university. Available to U.S. citizens.

Application Requirements Application, essay, financial need analysis, references, research permit, budget. *Deadline:* November 15.

Contact Nancy Leinwand, Administrator
American Research Institute in Turkey
(ARIT)
University of Pennsylvania Museum
Philadelphia, PA 19104-6324
Phone: 215-898-3474
Fax: 215-898-0657
E-mail: leinwand@sas.upenn.edu

AMERICAN SCHOOLS OF ORIENTAL RESEARCH (ASOR)
http://www.asor.org

W.F. ALBRIGHT INSTITUTE OF ARCHAEOLOGICAL RESEARCH EDUCATION AND CULTURAL AFFAIRS JUNIOR RESEARCH FELLOWSHIP • 680

Fellowships available to U.S. citizens who are predoctoral students and recent Ph.D. recipients in Near East Studies. Research period is for 5-10 months. Application deadline is October 12.

Academic/Career Areas Humanities.

Award Fellowship for use in postgraduate years; not renewable. *Number: 3. Amount:* $16,000.

Eligibility Requirements Applicant must be enrolled or expecting to enroll at an institution or university. Available to U.S. citizens.

Application Requirements Application. *Deadline:* October 12.

Contact Dr. John R. Spencer, W. F. Albright
Institute of Archaeological Research
American Schools of Oriental Research
(ASOR)
20700 North Park Boulevard
University Heights, OH 44118
Phone: 216-397-4705
Fax: 216-397-4478
E-mail: spencer@jcu.edu

W.F. ALBRIGHT INSTITUTE OF ARCHAEOLOGICAL RESEARCH/COUNCIL OF AMERICAN OVERSEAS RESEARCH CENTERS FELLOWSHIPS FOR ADVANCED MULTICOUNTRY RESEARCH • 681

Fellowships for scholars pursuing research on broad questions of multi-country significance in the fields of humanities, social sciences, and related natural sciences in countries in the Near and Middle East and South Asia. Doctoral candidates and established scholars with U.S. citizenship are eligible to apply as individuals or in teams. Preference will be given to candidates examining comparative and/or cross-regional questions requiring research in two or more countries. Application deadline: December 31.

Academic/Career Areas Humanities; Natural Sciences; Social Sciences.

Award Fellowship for use in postgraduate years; not renewable. *Number: 8. Amount:* $6000–$9000.

Eligibility Requirements Applicant must be enrolled or expecting to enroll at an institution or university. Available to U.S. citizens.

Application Requirements Application. *Deadline:* December 31.

Contact The Council of American Overseas
Research Centers
American Schools of Oriental Research
(ASOR)
Smithsonian Institution, IC 3123 MRC 705
Washington, DC 20560
E-mail: caorc@caorc.org

ARCHAEOLOGICAL INSTITUTE OF AMERICA
http://www.archaeological.org

ARCHAEOLOGICAL INSTITUTE OF AMERICA/ OLIVIA JAMES TRAVELING FELLOWSHIP
• *See number 73*

HARRIET AND LEON POMERANCE FELLOWSHIP
• *See number 74*

HELEN M. WOODRUFF FELLOWSHIP
• *See number 75*

WOODRUFF TRAVELING FELLOWSHIP
• *See number 76*

ARCTIC INSTITUTE OF NORTH AMERICA
http://www.ucalgary.ca/aina

LORRAINE ALLISON SCHOLARSHIP
• *See number 118*

ASIAN CULTURAL COUNCIL
http://www.asianculturalcouncil.org

ASIAN CULTURAL COUNCIL FELLOWSHIPS
• *See number 91*

ASIAN CULTURAL COUNCIL HUMANITIES FELLOWSHIPS
• *See number 92*

ASIAN CULTURAL COUNCIL RESIDENCY PROGRAM IN ASIA
• See number 140

CENTER FOR HELLENIC STUDIES
http://www.chs.harvard.edu

CENTER FOR HELLENIC STUDIES FELLOWSHIPS
• See number 121

CHARLES BABBAGE INSTITUTE
http://www.cbi.umn.edu

ADELLE AND ERWIN TOMASH FELLOWSHIP IN THE HISTORY OF INFORMATION PROCESSING
• See number 267

CHINA TIMES CULTURAL FOUNDATION

CHINA TIMES CULTURAL FOUNDATION DOCTORAL DISSERTATION RESEARCH IN CHINESE STUDIES SCHOLARSHIPS
• See number 122

COUNCIL FOR EUROPEAN STUDIES
http://www.europanet.org

COUNCIL FOR EUROPEAN STUDIES PRE-DISSERTATION FELLOWSHIP
• 682

Pre-dissertation fellowships assist graduate students in making rapid progress on their dissertation projects by providing support to spend six to eight weeks in Europe exploring the feasibility of research ideas. For more information visit http://www.europanet.org. Applicants must be students whose home institutions are members of the Council for European Studies.

Academic/Career Areas Humanities; Social Sciences.

Award Fellowship for use in graduate years; not renewable. *Number:* 9–15. *Amount:* $4000.

Eligibility Requirements Applicant must be enrolled or expecting to enroll full-time at an institution or university. Available to U.S. citizens.

Application Requirements Application, essay, references. *Deadline:* February 1.

Contact Council for European Studies
420 West 118th Street
Mailcode 3310
New York, NY 10027

CULTURAL SERVICES OF THE FRENCH EMBASSY
http://www.frenchculture.org

CHATEAUBRIAND SCHOLARSHIP PROGRAM
• See number 164

D'ARCY MCNICKLE CENTER FOR AMERICAN INDIAN HISTORY
http://www.newberry.org

FRANCES C. ALLEN FELLOWSHIP
• 683

The Frances C. Allen Fellowship is designed for graduate or pre-professional women students of American Indian heritage for research at the Newberry Library in Chicago on topics appropriate to the Newberry Library's collections. Financial support varies according to need and may include travel expenses. Tenure of fellowship is from one month to a year. Each applicant must submit vita, description of research topic, and a budget of travel and research expenses. For more information and application visit website: www.newberry.org.

Academic/Career Areas Humanities.

Award Fellowship for use in graduate years; not renewable. *Number:* 1–3. *Amount:* $1200–$8000.

Eligibility Requirements Applicant must be American Indian/Alaska Native; enrolled or expecting to enroll full-time at an institution or university; female and studying in Illinois. Available to U.S. and non-U.S. citizens.

Application Requirements Application, essay, resume, references. *Deadline:* February 20.

Contact The Committee on Awards/Newberry Library
D'Arcy McNickle Center for American Indian History
60 West Walton Street
Chicago, IL 60610-3380
Phone: 312-255-3666
E-mail: research@newberry.org

DUMBARTON OAKS
http://www.doaks.org

BLISS PRIZE FELLOWSHIP IN BYZANTINE STUDIES
• See number 123

DUMBARTON OAKS PROJECT GRANTS
• See number 94

RESIDENTIAL FELLOWSHIP IN BYZANTINE, PRE-COLUMBIAN, AND LANDSCAPE ARCHITECTURE STUDIES
• See number 95

GERMAN ACADEMIC EXCHANGE SERVICE (DAAD)
http://www.daad.org

LEO BAECK INSTITUTE - DAAD GRANTS
• See number 126

GETTY GRANT PROGRAM
http://www.getty.edu/grants

GETTY SCHOLAR AND VISITING SCHOLAR GRANTS
• See number 145

Getty Grant Program (continued)

PREDOCTORAL AND POSTDOCTORAL FELLOWSHIPS
• *See number 147*

HAGLEY MUSEUM AND LIBRARY
http://www.hagley.org

HAGLEY MUSEUM AND LIBRARY GRANTS-IN-AID
• *See number 97*

HAGLEY/WINTERTHUR FELLOWSHIPS IN ARTS AND INDUSTRIES
• *See number 98*

HENRY BELIN DU PONT DISSERTATION FELLOWSHIP
• *See number 99*

INTERNATIONAL FOUNDATION FOR ETHICAL RESEARCH
http://www.ifer.org

FELLOWSHIPS IN ALTERNATIVES IN ETHICAL RESEARCH
• *See number 207*

INTERNATIONAL RESEARCH & EXCHANGES BOARD
http://www.irex.org

IREX INDIVIDUAL ADVANCED RESEARCH OPPORTUNITIES • 684

This program provides grants of two to nine months to Master's, pre-doctoral and postdoctoral scholars from the U.S. for individual long-term research in Central and Eastern Europe, the New Independent States, Turkey and Iran in the social sciences and humanities. Award is available to 3-year and permanent residents of the U.S.

Academic/Career Areas Humanities; Social Sciences.

Award Grant for use in graduate, or postgraduate years; not renewable. *Number:* 25–35. *Amount:* up to $30,000.

Eligibility Requirements Applicant must be enrolled or expecting to enroll full or part-time at an institution or university. Available to U.S. citizens.

Application Requirements Application, resume, references, transcript, proposal. *Deadline:* November 1.

Contact Information Assistant
International Research & Exchanges Board
2121 K Street, NW, Suite 700
Washington, DC 20037
Phone: 202-628-8188
Fax: 202-628-8189
E-mail: irex@irex.org

IREX SHORT-TERM TRAVEL GRANTS • 685

The short-term travel grants provide support to U.S. scholars for visits of up to two months to conduct postdoctoral research, or consult with colleagues in countries of Central and Eastern Europe, the New Independent States, and limited funding for Turkey and Iran. Must hold Ph.D. or other terminal degree. Award available to 3-year and permanent residents of the US.

Academic/Career Areas Humanities; Social Sciences.

Award Grant for use in postgraduate years; not renewable. *Amount:* up to $3000.

Eligibility Requirements Applicant must be enrolled or expecting to enroll at an institution or university. Available to U.S. citizens.

Application Requirements Application, resume, proposal. *Deadline:* February 1.

Contact Information Assistant
International Research & Exchanges Board
2121 K Street, NW, Suite 700
Washington, DC 20037
Phone: 202-628-8188
Fax: 202-628-8189
E-mail: irex@irex.org

REGIONAL SCHOLAR EXCHANGE PROGRAM (RSEP) • 686

Grants of up to nine months for U.S. university faculty and scholars at early stages of their careers, advanced graduate students and associate professors to conduct independent research in the humanities and social sciences at institutions in The New Independent States (NIS).

Academic/Career Areas Humanities; Social Sciences.

Award Grant for use in graduate, or postgraduate years; not renewable. *Number:* up to 10.

Eligibility Requirements Applicant must be enrolled or expecting to enroll at an institution or university. Available to U.S. citizens.

Application Requirements Application, resume, references, transcript, proposal. *Deadline:* January 15.

Contact Information Assistant
International Research & Exchanges Board
2121 K Street, NW, Suite 700
Washington, DC 20037
Phone: 202-628-8188
Fax: 202-628-8189
E-mail: irex@irex.org

JAPAN FOUNDATION
http://www.jfny.org

JAPAN FOUNDATION DOCTORAL FELLOWSHIP • 687

Award for doctoral candidates in the humanities and social sciences, as well as in other disciplines, who are conducting comparative research projects and need the opportunity to conduct research in Japan. Ten one-time awards. Must submit language evaluation.

Academic/Career Areas Humanities; Social Sciences.

Award Fellowship for use in graduate years; not renewable. *Number:* 10.

Eligibility Requirements Applicant must be enrolled or expecting to enroll at an institution or university and must have an interest in Japanese language. Available to U.S. citizens.

Application Requirements Application, essay, references, transcript. *Deadline:* November 1.

Contact Katherine Wearne, Program Assistant
Japan Foundation
152 West 57th Street, 39th Floor
New York, NY 10019
Phone: 212-489-0299
Fax: 212-489-0409
E-mail: katherine_wearne@jfny.org

JAPAN FOUNDATION RESEARCH FELLOWSHIP • 688

Awards for scholars, researchers, and professionals who wish to conduct research in Japan for periods ranging from two to twelve months. Ten one-time awards. Research must be related to the social sciences or humanities.

Academic/Career Areas Humanities; Social Sciences.

Award Fellowship for use in postgraduate years; not renewable. *Number:* 10.

Eligibility Requirements Applicant must be enrolled or expecting to enroll at an institution or university and must have an interest in Japanese language. Applicant or parent of applicant must have employment or volunteer experience in designated career field. Available to U.S. citizens.

Application Requirements Application, essay, references. *Deadline:* November 1.

Contact Katherine Wearne, Program Assistant
Japan Foundation
152 West 57th Street, 39th Floor
New York, NY 10019
Phone: 212-489-0299
Fax: 212-489-0409
E-mail: katherine_wearne@jfny.org

JAPAN FOUNDATION SHORT-TERM RESEARCH FELLOWSHIP • 689

Awards for scholars, researchers, and professionals who wish to conduct research in Japan for short-term periods ranging from 21 to 60 days. Ten one-time awards. Research must be related to the social sciences or humanities.

Academic/Career Areas Humanities; Social Sciences.

Award Fellowship for use in postgraduate years; not renewable. *Number:* 10.

Eligibility Requirements Applicant must be enrolled or expecting to enroll at an institution or university and must have an interest in Japanese language. Applicant or parent of applicant must have employment or volunteer experience in designated career field. Available to U.S. citizens.

Application Requirements Application, essay, references. *Deadline:* November 1.

Contact Katherine Wearne, Program Assistant
Japan Foundation
152 West 57th Street, 39th Floor
New York, NY 10019
Phone: 212-489-0299
Fax: 212-489-0409
E-mail: katerine_wearne@jfny.org

JAPANESE GOVERNMENT/THE MONBUSHO SCHOLARSHIP PROGRAM
http://embjapan.org/la

RESEARCH STUDENT SCHOLARSHIP
• *See number 13*

JOHN F. KENNEDY LIBRARY FOUNDATION
http://www.jfklibrary.org

HEMINGWAY RESEARCH GRANTS • 690

One-time grant for students to do research in the Hemingway Collection at the Kennedy Library. Preference given to dissertation research by Ph.D. candidates in newly opened or unused portions of the Collection. Submit application, curriculum vitae, proposal, budget, and letters of recommendation.

Academic/Career Areas Humanities; Literature/English/Writing; Social Sciences.

Award Grant for use in graduate years; not renewable. *Number:* 5. *Amount:* $200–$1000.

Eligibility Requirements Applicant must be enrolled or expecting to enroll at a four-year institution or university and studying in Massachusetts. Available to U.S. and non-U.S. citizens.

Application Requirements Application, references. *Deadline:* March 15.

Contact Grant and Fellowship Coordinator
John F. Kennedy Library Foundation
Columbia Point
Boston, MA 02125
Phone: 617-929-1200

KENNEDY RESEARCH GRANTS
• See number 100

MASSACHUSETTS HISTORICAL SOCIETY
http://www.masshist.org

MASSACHUSETTS HISTORICAL SOCIETY RESEARCH FELLOWSHIP PROGRAM
• See number 650

NEW ENGLAND REGIONAL FELLOWSHIP CONSORTIUM GRANT
• See number 651

MRS. GILES WHITING FOUNDATION
http://www.whitingfoundation.org

WHITING FELLOWSHIPS IN THE HUMANITIES   • 691

Offered at seven participating universities: Bryn Mawr College, University of Chicago, Columbia, Harvard, Princeton, Stanford, and Yale. For Ph.D. student in humanities in last year of dissertation writing. Recipients are selected by university. Submit applications to universities, not to Foundation.

Academic/Career Areas Humanities.

Award Fellowship for use in graduate years; not renewable. *Number:* 60. *Amount:* $17,000.

Eligibility Requirements Applicant must be enrolled or expecting to enroll at an institution or university and studying in California, Connecticut, Illinois, Massachusetts, New Jersey, New York, or Pennsylvania. Available to U.S. and non-U.S. citizens.

Application Requirements Application.

Contact Kellye Rosenheim, Associate Director
Mrs. Giles Whiting Foundation
1133 Avenue of the Americas, 22nd Floor
New York, NY 10036-6710
Phone: 212-336-2138

NATIONAL ACADEMY OF EDUCATION
http://www.nae.nyu.edu

NATIONAL ACADEMY OF EDUCATION/SPENCER POSTDOCTORAL FELLOWSHIP PROGRAM
• See number 360

NATIONAL GALLERY OF ART
http://www.nga.gov/resources/casva.htm

FELLOWSHIP PROGRAMS
• See number 154

NEWBERRY LIBRARY
http://www.newberry.org

FELLOWSHIPS IN THE HUMANITIES AT THE NEWBERRY LIBRARY   • 692

Fellowships at the Newberry Library provide assistance to researchers who wish to use the collections. Fellowships are residential; no funds are available for tuition or other educational expenses. Long-term fellowships are available to post-doctoral scholars for periods of six to eleven months. Short-term fellowships are available to Ph.D. candidates and post-doctoral scholars from outside Chicago who have a specific need for Newberry collections; tenure ranges from one week to two months. Deadlines: January 20 and February 20.

Academic/Career Areas Humanities.

Award Fellowship for use in graduate, or postgraduate years; not renewable. *Number:* 40–50. *Amount:* $300–$30,000.

Eligibility Requirements Applicant must be enrolled or expecting to enroll full-time at an institution or university and studying in Illinois. Available to U.S. and non-U.S. citizens.

Application Requirements Application, essay, resume, references. *Deadline:* January 20.

Contact Newberry Library
Committee on Awards
60 West Walton Street
Chicago, IL 60610-3380
Phone: 312-255-3666
Fax: 212-255-3680
E-mail: research@newberry.org

PHI BETA KAPPA SOCIETY
http://www.pbk.org

MARY ISABEL SIBLEY FELLOWSHIP FOR GREEK AND FRENCH STUDIES
• See number 132

SWANN FOUNDATION FUND
http://www.lcweb.loc.gov/rr/print/swann/swann_foundation.html

SWANN FOUNDATION FUND FELLOWSHIP
• See number 109

SWEDISH INFORMATION SERVICE
http://www.swedeninfo.com

BICENTENNIAL SWEDISH-AMERICAN EXCHANGE FUND TRAVEL GRANTS
• See number 133

UNITED STATES INSTITUTE OF PEACE
http://www.usip.org

JENNINGS RANDOLPH SENIOR FELLOW AWARD
• See number 333

PEACE SCHOLAR DISSERTATION FELLOWSHIP
• See number 334

WOODROW WILSON NATIONAL FELLOWSHIP FOUNDATION
http://www.woodrow.org

ANDREW W. MELLON FELLOWSHIPS IN HUMANISTIC STUDIES
• See number 134

CHARLOTTE W. NEWCOMBE DOCTORAL DISSERTATION FELLOWSHIPS • 693

Fellowships designed to encourage original and significant study of ethical or religious values in all fields of the humanities and social sciences. Award covers twelve months of full-time dissertation writing. Graduate schools asked to waive tuition for Newcombe Fellows.

Academic/Career Areas Humanities; Religion/Theology; Social Sciences.

Award Fellowship for use in graduate years; not renewable. *Number:* 35. *Amount:* $16,500.

Eligibility Requirements Applicant must be enrolled or expecting to enroll full-time at an institution or university. Available to U.S. and Canadian citizens.

Application Requirements Application, references, transcript, dissertation proposal, bibliography. *Deadline:* December 1.

Contact Sheila Walker, Program Assistant
Woodrow Wilson National Fellowship
Foundation
CN 5281
Princeton, NJ 08543-5281
E-mail: walker@woodrow.org

WOODROW WILSON NATIONAL FELLOWSHIP FOUNDATION DISSERTATION GRANTS IN WOMEN'S STUDIES
• See number 135

WOODROW WILSON POSTDOCTORAL FELLOWSHIPS IN THE HUMANITIES
• See number 136

INTERIOR DESIGN

DURRANT FOUNDATION
http://www.durant.com/foundation.html

DURRANT FOUNDATION SCHOLARSHIP/INTERNSHIP
• See number 96

INTERNATIONAL INTERIOR DESIGN ASSOCIATION (IIDA) FOUNDATION
http://www.iida.org

GRADUATE AND EDUCATOR RESEARCH AWARDS • 694

Two fellowship programs offered annually. One supports research on the value of interior design. Applicants must hold undergraduate degree in interior design, and be studying in a graduate-level interior design program. The other is awarded to Interior Design faculty for research to enhance Interior Design education. Applicants must be Interior Design Educators at FIDER-accredited schools.

Academic/Career Areas Interior Design.

Award Fellowship for use in graduate, or postgraduate years; not renewable. *Number:* 3–4. *Amount:* $2500–$5000.

Eligibility Requirements Applicant must be enrolled or expecting to enroll full or part-time at a four-year institution or university. Applicant or parent of applicant must have employment or volunteer experience in designated career field. Available to U.S. and non-U.S. citizens.

Application Requirements Application. *Deadline:* April 14.

Contact Eve Gutmann, Foundation Administrator
International Interior Design Association
(IIDA) Foundation
203 North Wabash, Suite 1800
Chicago, IL 60601
Phone: 312-443-9671
Fax: 312-641-5736
E-mail: egutmann@Ameritech.net

JOEL POLSKY-FIXTURES FURNITURE/IIDA FOUNDATION RESEARCH GRANT • 695

One-time funding of research projects that will net a tangible product providing long-term benefits as well as educational value to design professionals. Funds must be used to improve the interior design industry as a whole.

Academic/Career Areas Interior Design.

Award Grant for use in graduate, or postgraduate years; not renewable. *Number:* 1. *Amount:* $5000.

Eligibility Requirements Applicant must be enrolled or expecting to enroll full or part-time at an institution or university. Applicant or parent of applicant must have employment or volunteer experience in designated career field. Available to U.S. and non-U.S. citizens.

International Interior Design Association (IIDA) Foundation (continued)

Application Requirements Application.

Contact Eve Gutmann, Foundation Administrator
International Interior Design Association
(IIDA) Foundation
203 North Wabash
Chicago, IL 60601
Phone: 312-443-9671
Fax: 312-641-5736
E-mail: egutmann@ameritech.net

KAPPA OMICRON NU HONOR SOCIETY
http://www.kon.org

EILEEN C. MADDEX FELLOWSHIP
• *See number 386*

HETTIE M. ANTHONY FELLOWSHIP
• *See number 387*

KAPPA OMICRON NU NATIONAL ALUMNI CHAPTER GRANT
• *See number 388*

KAPPA OMICRON NU NATIONAL ALUMNI FELLOWSHIP
• *See number 389*

SENSE OF SMELL INSTITUTE
http://www.senseofsmell.org

TOVA FELLOWSHIP
• *See number 101*

WINTERTHUR MUSEUM, GARDEN, AND LIBRARY
http://www.winterthur.org

NEH FELLOWSHIPS
• *See number 110*

WINTERTHUR RESEARCH FELLOWSHIPS
• *See number 111*

INTERNATIONAL MIGRATION

POPULATION COUNCIL
http://www.popcouncil.org

POPULATION COUNCIL FELLOWSHIPS IN THE SOCIAL SCIENCES, MID-CAREER LEVEL
• *See number 328*

POPULATION COUNCIL FELLOWSHIPS IN THE SOCIAL SCIENCES, POSTDOCTORAL LEVEL
• *See number 329*

POPULATION COUNCIL FELLOWSHIPS IN THE SOCIAL SCIENCES, PREDOCTORAL LEVEL
• *See number 330*

UNITED STATES INSTITUTE OF PEACE
http://www.usip.org

JENNINGS RANDOLPH SENIOR FELLOW AWARD
• *See number 333*

PEACE SCHOLAR DISSERTATION FELLOWSHIP
• *See number 334*

INTERNATIONAL STUDIES

AMERICAN COUNCIL OF TEACHERS OF RUSSIAN
http://www.actr.org

TITLE VIII RESEARCH SCHOLAR AND COMBINED RESEARCH AND LANGUAGE STUDY PROGRAM
• *See number 114*

ARMENIAN RELIEF SOCIETY OF NORTH AMERICA INC.-REGIONAL OFFICE

ARMENIAN RELIEF SOCIETY GRADUATE SCHOLARSHIP PROGRAM
• *See number 224*

CHINA TIMES CULTURAL FOUNDATION

CHINA TIMES CULTURAL FOUNDATION DOCTORAL DISSERTATION RESEARCH IN CHINESE STUDIES SCHOLARSHIPS
• *See number 122*

INSTITUTE FOR CURRENT WORLD AFFAIRS
http://www.icwa.org

INSTITUTE OF CURRENT WORLD AFFAIRS/CRANE ROGERS FOUNDATION FELLOWSHIP • **696**

Self-designed, two-year fellowships for independent study in the Middle East or East Europe, to persons with superior writing skills and demonstrable motivation. Two deadlines: April 1 and September 1. Samples of writing must be submitted. Visit website for additional information.

Academic/Career Areas International Studies.

Award Fellowship for use in postgraduate years; not renewable. *Number:* 5. *Amount:* $5000–$25,000.

Eligibility Requirements Applicant must be age 35 or under; enrolled or expecting to enroll full-time at an institution or university and must have an interest in writing. Available to U.S. and non-U.S. citizens.

Application Requirements Application, resume, initial letter of interest. *Deadline:* April 1.

Contact Peter B. Martin, Executive Director
Institute for Current World Affairs
4 West Wheelock Street
Hanover, NH 03755
Phone: 603-643-5548
Fax: 603-643-9599
E-mail: icwa@valley.net

INTERNATIONAL DEVELOPMENT RESEARCH CENTER
http://www.idrc.ca/awards

CANADIAN WINDOW ON INTERNATIONAL DEVELOPMENT AWARDS • 697

Award of up to Can$20,000 for doctoral research that explores the relationship between Canadian aid, trade, immigration and diplomatic policy, and international development and the alleviation of global poverty. Applicant must be a Canadian citizen or permanent resident, be registered at a Canadian university, and be conducting the proposed research for a doctoral dissertation and have completed course work and passed comprehensive exams by the time of the award tenure. Contact for application procedures.

Academic/Career Areas International Studies.

Award Grant for use in graduate years; not renewable. *Number:* 2–3. *Amount:* up to $20,000.

Eligibility Requirements Applicant must be Canadian citizenship and enrolled or expecting to enroll full-time at an institution or university.

Application Requirements Application, financial need analysis, resume, references, transcript, letter from institution, proof of citizenship. *Deadline:* April 1.

Contact Danielle Reinhardt, Program Assistant
International Development Research
Center
PO Box 8500
Ottawa, ON K1G 3H9
Canada
Phone: 613-236-6163
Fax: 613-563-0815
E-mail: cta@idrc.ca

UNITED STATES INSTITUTE OF PEACE
http://www.usip.org

JENNINGS RANDOLPH SENIOR FELLOW AWARD
• See number 333

PEACE SCHOLAR DISSERTATION FELLOWSHIP
• See number 334

WOODROW WILSON NATIONAL FELLOWSHIP FOUNDATION
http://www.woodrow.org

THOMAS R. PICKERING GRADUATE FOREIGN AFFAIRS FELLOWSHIP PROGRAM
• See number 241

JOURNALISM

ARMENIAN RELIEF SOCIETY OF NORTH AMERICA INC.-REGIONAL OFFICE

ARMENIAN RELIEF SOCIETY GRADUATE SCHOLARSHIP PROGRAM
• See number 224

ASSOCIATION FOR EDUCATION IN JOURNALISM AND MASS COMMUNICATIONS
http://www.aejmc.org

ASSOCIATION FOR EDUCATION IN JOURNALISM AND MASS COMMUNICATIONS COMM. THEORY & METHODOLOGY DIVISION MINORITY DOCTORAL SCHOLARSHIPS
• See number 252

CHINA TIMES CULTURAL FOUNDATION

CHINA TIMES CULTURAL FOUNDATION DOCTORAL DISSERTATION RESEARCH IN CHINESE STUDIES SCHOLARSHIPS
• See number 122

INTERNATIONAL FOUNDATION FOR ETHICAL RESEARCH
http://www.ifer.org

FELLOWSHIPS IN ALTERNATIVES IN ETHICAL RESEARCH
• See number 207

JOHN F. KENNEDY LIBRARY FOUNDATION
http://www.jfklibrary.org

THEODORE C. SORENSEN FELLOWSHIP • 698

Fellowship for graduate student pursuing research in domestic policy, political journalism, polling, or press relations. Must use Kennedy Library to do at least part of research. Submit application, proposal, letters of recommendation, writing sample, budget plan, and curriculum vitae. One-time award of up to $3600.

Academic/Career Areas Journalism; Political Science.

John F. Kennedy Library Foundation (continued)

Award Fellowship for use in graduate years; not renewable. *Number:* 1. *Amount:* up to $3600.

Eligibility Requirements Applicant must be enrolled or expecting to enroll at an institution or university. Available to U.S. citizens.

Application Requirements Application, essay, references. *Deadline:* March 15.

Contact Grant and Fellowship Coordinator
John F. Kennedy Library Foundation
Columbia Point
Boston, MA 02125
Phone: 617-929-1200

NATIONAL ASSOCIATION OF BROADCASTERS
http://www.nab.org/Research/Grants/grants.asp

NATIONAL ASSOCIATION OF BROADCASTERS GRANTS FOR RESEARCH IN BROADCASTING
• *See number 254*

NATIONAL MEDICAL FELLOWSHIPS, INC
http://www.nmf-online.org

NATIONAL MEDICAL ASSOCIATION SLACK AWARD FOR MEDICAL JOURNALISM
• *See number 565*

NATIONAL PRESS PHOTOGRAPHERS FOUNDATION, INC.
http://www.nppa.org

KIT C. KING GRADUATE SCHOLARSHIP FUND
• **699**

Award of $500 for graduate student pursuing an advanced degree in journalism with an emphasis in photojournalism. Applicant must show proof of acceptance to photojournalism program. Submit portfolio and goal statement.

Academic/Career Areas Journalism; Photojournalism.

Award Scholarship for use in graduate years; not renewable. *Number:* 1. *Amount:* $500.

Eligibility Requirements Applicant must be enrolled or expecting to enroll full-time at a four-year institution or university. Available to U.S. citizens.

Application Requirements Application, essay, financial need analysis, portfolio, self-addressed stamped envelope, transcript. *Deadline:* March 1.

Contact Scott Sines, Managing Editor
National Press Photographers Foundation, Inc.
The Spokesman Review, West 999 Riverside Avenue
Spokane, WA 99210
Phone: 509-459-5405
E-mail: scotts@spokesman.com

PHILLIPS FOUNDATION
http://www.thephillipsfoundation.org

PHILLIPS FOUNDATION JOURNALISM FELLOWSHIP PROGRAM
• **700**

The program awards annual journalism fellowships to working print journalists with less than five years of professional experience. Winners undertake a one-year project of their choosing focusing on journalism supportive of American culture and a free society. Deadline: March 1.

Academic/Career Areas Journalism.

Award Fellowship for use in graduate, or postgraduate years; not renewable. *Number:* 3–5. *Amount:* $5000–$50,000.

Eligibility Requirements Applicant must be enrolled or expecting to enroll full or part-time at an institution or university. Applicant or parent of applicant must have employment or volunteer experience in journalism. Available to U.S. citizens.

Application Requirements Application, references. *Deadline:* March 1.

Contact John W. Farley, Secretary
Phillips Foundation
7811 Montrose Road, Suite 100
Potomac, MD 20854
Phone: 301-340-7788 Ext. 6090
Fax: 301-424-0245
E-mail: jfarley@phillips.com

QUILL AND SCROLL FOUNDATION
http://www.uiowa.edu/~quill-sc

LESTER BENZ MEMORIAL SCHOLARSHIP
• *See number 260*

SANTA CLARA UNIVERSITY SCHOOL OF LAW - COMPUTER AND HIGH TECHNOLOGY LAW JOURNAL
http://www.scu.edu/techlaw

SANTA CLARA UNIVERSITY SCHOOL OF LAW COMPUTER AND HIGH TECHNOLOGY LAW JOURNAL COMMENT CONTEST
• **701**

Current law students in the U.S. may submit a comment involving research and analysis on law and technology. Please call or contact website for more information.

Academic/Career Areas Journalism; Law/Legal Services.

Award Prize for use in graduate years; not renewable. *Number:* 3. *Amount:* $1000–$2000.

Eligibility Requirements Applicant must be enrolled or expecting to enroll full or part-time at an institution or university. Available to U.S. citizens.

Application Requirements Applicant must enter a contest, essay, 3 copies of essay, cover letter, disk with essay. *Deadline:* June 1.

Contact Santa Clara University School of Law - Computer and High Technology Law Journal
500 El Camino Real
Santa Clara, CA 95053
Phone: 408-554-4197

SWANN FOUNDATION FUND
http://www.lcweb.loc.gov/rr/print/swann/swann_foundation.html

SWANN FOUNDATION FUND FELLOWSHIP
• *See number 109*

UNITED METHODIST COMMUNICATIONS
http://www.umcom.org/scholarships

STOODY-WEST FELLOWSHIP FOR GRADUATE STUDY IN RELIGIOUS JOURNALISM
• *See number 261*

UNITED STATES INSTITUTE OF PEACE
http://www.usip.org

JENNINGS RANDOLPH SENIOR FELLOW AWARD
• *See number 333*

PEACE SCHOLAR DISSERTATION FELLOWSHIP
• *See number 334*

LANDSCAPE ARCHITECTURE

ATHENAEUM OF PHILADELPHIA
http://www.philaathenaeum.org

CHARLES E. PETERSON FELLOWSHIP
• *See number 93*

DUMBARTON OAKS
http://www.doaks.org

DUMBARTON OAKS PROJECT GRANTS
• *See number 94*

RESIDENTIAL FELLOWSHIP IN BYZANTINE, PRE-COLUMBIAN, AND LANDSCAPE ARCHITECTURE STUDIES
• *See number 95*

DURRANT FOUNDATION
http://www.durant.com/foundation.html

DURRANT FOUNDATION SCHOLARSHIP/ INTERNSHIP
• *See number 96*

HAGLEY MUSEUM AND LIBRARY
http://www.hagley.org

HAGLEY MUSEUM AND LIBRARY GRANTS-IN-AID
• *See number 97*

HAGLEY/WINTERTHUR FELLOWSHIPS IN ARTS AND INDUSTRIES
• *See number 98*

HENRY BELIN DU PONT DISSERTATION FELLOWSHIP
• *See number 99*

LANDSCAPE ARCHITECTURE FOUNDATION
http://www.LAprofession.org

DOUGLAS DOCKERY THOMAS FELLOWSHIP IN GARDEN HISTORY AND DESIGN • **702**

$4,000 Fellowship to assist graduate student with study and research at a leading American institution. Project study possibilities include investigating new techniques of garden restoration; studying how small gardens created by community groups have impacted public gardens; exploring and documenting physical, emotional and spiritual healing properties of the garden; and instigating the development of gardens that use ecological and regenerative concepts. Applications must be postmarked by January 15. Sponsored by the Garden Club of America.

Academic/Career Areas Landscape Architecture.

Award Fellowship for use in graduate years; not renewable. *Number:* 1. *Amount:* $4000.

Eligibility Requirements Applicant must be enrolled or expecting to enroll at an institution or university.

Application Requirements Application, resume, references, proposal and budget. *Deadline:* January 15.

Contact Melinda Sippel, Executive Assistant
Landscape Architecture Foundation
818 18th Street
Suite 810
Washington, DC 20006
Phone: 202-216-2356
Fax: 202-898-1185
E-mail: msippel@asla.org

SKIDMORE, OWINGS, AND MERRILL FOUNDATION
http://www.som.com

URBAN DESIGN TRAVELING FELLOWSHIP PROGRAM
• See number 103

WINTERTHUR MUSEUM, GARDEN, AND LIBRARY
http://www.winterthur.org

NEH FELLOWSHIPS
• See number 110

WINTERTHUR RESEARCH FELLOWSHIPS
• See number 111

LAW/LEGAL SERVICES

ALBERT SCHWEITZER FELLOWSHIP
http://www.schweitzerfellowship.org

NEW HAMPSHIRE/VERMONT SCHWEITZER FELLOWS PROGRAM
• See number 15

ALEXANDER VON HUMBOLDT FOUNDATION
http://www.humboldt-foundation.de

TRANSCOOP PROGRAM
• See number 315

AMERICAN ASSOCIATION OF LAW LIBRARIES
http://www.aallnet.org

AALL AND WEST GROUP GEORGE A. STRAIT MINORITY SCHOLARSHIP ENDOWMENT • 703

One-time award for minority graduate students who have library experience and are working toward an advanced degree to further law library career. Based on need.

Academic/Career Areas Law/Legal Services; Library Sciences.

Award Scholarship for use in graduate years; not renewable. *Amount:* $3500.

Eligibility Requirements Applicant must be American Indian/Alaska Native, Asian/Pacific Islander, Black (non-Hispanic), or Hispanic and enrolled or expecting to enroll full or part-time at a four-year institution or university. Available to U.S. and non-U.S. citizens.

Application Requirements Application, essay, financial need analysis, references, self-addressed stamped envelope, transcript. *Deadline:* April 1.

Contact Rachel Shaevel, Membership Coordinator
American Association of Law Libraries
53 West Jackson Boulevard, Suite 940
Chicago, IL 60604-3695
Phone: 312-939-4764 Ext. 10
Fax: 312-431-1097
E-mail: rshaevel@aall.org

JAMES F. CONNOLLY CONGRESSIONAL INFORMATION SCHOLARSHIP • 704

Awarded to a law librarian who is interested in pursuing a law degree. Preference given to a librarian who has demonstrated an interest in government publications.

Academic/Career Areas Law/Legal Services.

Award Scholarship for use in graduate years; not renewable.

Eligibility Requirements Applicant must be enrolled or expecting to enroll full or part-time at a four-year institution or university. Applicant or parent of applicant must have employment or volunteer experience in designated career field. Available to U.S. and non-U.S. citizens.

Application Requirements Application, essay, financial need analysis, references, self-addressed stamped envelope, transcript. *Deadline:* April 1.

Contact Rachel Shaevel, Membership Coordinator
American Association of Law Libraries
53 West Jackson Boulevard, Suite 940
Chicago, IL 60604-3695
Phone: 312-939-4764 Ext. 10
Fax: 312-431-1097
E-mail: rshaevel@aall.org

LEXIS NEXIS (TM) / JOHN R. JOHNSON MEMORIAL SCHOLARSHIP ENDOWMENT • 705

Candidates who apply for AALL Scholarships, Type I-IV, become automatically eligible to receive the award.

Academic/Career Areas Law/Legal Services; Library Sciences.

Award Scholarship for use in graduate years; not renewable.

Eligibility Requirements Applicant must be enrolled or expecting to enroll full or part-time at an institution or university. Available to U.S. and non-U.S. citizens.

Application Requirements Application, essay, financial need analysis, references, transcript.

Contact Rachel Shaevel, Membership Coordinator
American Association of Law Libraries
53 West Jackson Boulevard, Suite 940
Chicago, IL 60604
Phone: 312-939-4764 Ext. 10
Fax: 312-431-1097
E-mail: membership@aall.org

LIBRARY SCHOOL GRADUATES ATTENDING LAW SCHOOL • 706

One-time award for library school graduates in the process of working toward a law degree with no more than 36 credits remaining before qualifying for a law degree. Need-based.

Academic/Career Areas Law/Legal Services; Library Sciences.

Award Scholarship for use in graduate years; not renewable.

Eligibility Requirements Applicant must be enrolled or expecting to enroll full or part-time at a four-year institution or university. Available to U.S. and non-U.S. citizens.

Application Requirements Application, essay, financial need analysis, references, self-addressed stamped envelope, transcript. *Deadline:* April 1.

Contact Rachel Shaevel, Membership Coordinator
American Association of Law Libraries
53 West Jackson Boulevard, Suite 940
Chicago, IL 60604-3695
Phone: 312-939-4764 Ext. 10
Fax: 312-431-1097
E-mail: rshaevel@aall.org

TYPE I: LIBRARY DEGREE FOR LAW SCHOOL GRADUATES • 707

One-time award for graduates of law school who are degree candidates in an accredited library school. Preference given to AALL members and to those with law library experience. Based on need.

Academic/Career Areas Law/Legal Services; Library Sciences.

Award Scholarship for use in graduate years; not renewable.

Eligibility Requirements Applicant must be enrolled or expecting to enroll full or part-time at a four-year institution or university. Applicant or parent of applicant must be member of American Association of Law Librarians. Available to U.S. and non-U.S. citizens.

Application Requirements Application, essay, financial need analysis, references, self-addressed stamped envelope, transcript. *Deadline:* April 1.

Contact Rachel Shaevel, Membership Coordinator
American Association of Law Libraries
53 West Jackson Boulevard, Suite 940
Chicago, IL 60604-3695
Phone: 312-939-4764 Ext. 10
Fax: 312-431-1097
E-mail: rshaevel@aall.org

AMERICAN ASSOCIATION OF UNIVERSITY WOMEN (AAUW) EDUCATIONAL FOUNDATION
http://www.aauw.org

AAUW EDUCATIONAL FOUNDATION SELECTED PROFESSIONS FELLOWSHIPS
• *See number 87*

AMERICAN CENTER OF ORIENTAL RESEARCH
http://www.bu.edu/acor

NATIONAL ENDOWMENT FOR THE HUMANITIES POST-DOCTORAL RESEARCH FELLOWSHIPS
• *See number 65*

AMERICAN COUNCIL OF TEACHERS OF RUSSIAN
http://www.actr.org

TITLE VIII RESEARCH SCHOLAR AND COMBINED RESEARCH AND LANGUAGE STUDY PROGRAM
• *See number 114*

AMERICAN GEOPHYSICAL UNION
http://www.agu.org

AMERICAN GEOPHYSICAL UNION HORTON RESEARCH GRANT
• *See number 25*

AMERICAN HISTORICAL ASSOCIATION
http://www.theaha.org

LITTLETON-GRISWOLD RESEARCH GRANTS
• *See number 639*

AMERICAN JUDGES ASSOCIATION
http://www.aja.ncsc.dni.us/

LAW STUDENT ESSAY COMPETITION • 708

This is an essay competition for full-time law students studying at accredited law schools in the United States, Canada, and Mexico. A review committee rates the entries on their quality and their interest to the

American Judges Association (continued)

judiciary. Essays must be original and unpublished. 1st place: $3000. 2nd place: $1250. 3rd place: $1000.

Academic/Career Areas Law/Legal Services.

Award Prize for use in graduate years; not renewable. *Number:* 3. *Amount:* $1000–$3000.

Eligibility Requirements Applicant must be enrolled or expecting to enroll full-time at an institution or university. Available to U.S. and non-U.S. citizens.

Application Requirements Application, essay. *Deadline:* June 30.

Contact Shelley Rockwell, Association Management
Specialist
American Judges Association
300 Newport Avenue, PO Box 8798
Williamsburg, VA 23187-8798
Phone: 757-259-1841
Fax: 757-259-1520
E-mail: srockwell@ncsc.dni.us

ARMENIAN RELIEF SOCIETY OF NORTH AMERICA INC.-REGIONAL OFFICE

ARMENIAN RELIEF SOCIETY GRADUATE SCHOLARSHIP PROGRAM
• *See number 224*

ATTORNEY - CPA FOUNDATION
http://www.attorney-cpa.com/foundation.html

ATTORNEY-CPA FOUNDATION SCHOLARSHIPS
• *See number 225*

COMMUNITY ASSOCIATIONS INSTITUTE RESEARCH FOUNDATION
http://www.cairf.org

BYRON HANKE FELLOWSHIP FOR GRADUATE RESEARCH
• *See number 317*

COUNTY PROSECUTORS ASSOCIATION OF NEW JERSEY FOUNDATION

ANDREW K. RUOTOLO MEMORIAL SCHOLARSHIP • **709**

One-time award for New Jersey resident pursuing legal studies at a New Jersey post-secondary institution. Must be a U.S. citizen. Must be interested in law enforcement. Must exhibit an interest in and commitment to, enhancing the rights and well-being of children through child advocacy programs.

Academic/Career Areas Law/Legal Services.

Award Scholarship for use in graduate, or postgraduate years; not renewable. *Number:* 1. *Amount:* $2500.

Eligibility Requirements Applicant must be enrolled or expecting to enroll full or part-time at a four-year institution or university; resident of New Jersey and studying in New Jersey. Available to U.S. citizens.

Application Requirements Application, interview. *Deadline:* June 15.

Contact Irene Brown, Assistant Attorney General
County Prosecutors Association of New
Jersey Foundation
PO Box 085
Trenton, NJ 08625
Phone: 609-984-2814
Fax: 609-341-2077

HARRY Y. COTTON MEMORIAL SCHOLARSHIP • **710**

One-time award for New Jersey resident accepted for admission to law school. Must have an interest in pursuing a career as a prosecutor with an emphasis on domestic violence or hate crimes prosecutions. Must attend law school in New Jersey.

Academic/Career Areas Law/Legal Services.

Award Scholarship for use in graduate, or postgraduate years; not renewable. *Number:* 1. *Amount:* $2500.

Eligibility Requirements Applicant must be enrolled or expecting to enroll at a four-year institution or university; resident of New Jersey and studying in New Jersey. Available to U.S. citizens.

Application Requirements Application, financial need analysis, interview. *Deadline:* June 15.

Contact Irene Brown, Assistant Attorney General
County Prosecutors Association of New
Jersey Foundation
PO Box 085
Trenton, NJ 08625
Phone: 609-984-2814
Fax: 609-341-2077

OSCAR W. RITTENHOUSE MEMORIAL SCHOLARSHIP • **711**

One-time award for New Jersey resident pursuing legal studies at a New Jersey post-secondary institution. Must be U.S. citizen. Must be interested in law enforcement. Must have an interest in pursuing a career as a prosecutor.

Academic/Career Areas Law/Legal Services.

Award Scholarship for use in graduate, or postgraduate years; not renewable. *Number:* 1. *Amount:* $2500.

Eligibility Requirements Applicant must be enrolled or expecting to enroll full or part-time at a four-year institution or university; resident of New Jersey and studying in New Jersey. Available to U.S. citizens.

Application Requirements Application, financial need analysis, interview. *Deadline:* June 15.

Contact Irene Brown, Assistant Attorney General
County Prosecutors Association of New Jersey Foundation
PO Box 085
Trenton, NJ 08625
Phone: 609-984-2814
Fax: 609-341-2077

FEDERAL CIRCUIT BAR ASSOCIATION
http://www.fedcirbar.org

GEORGE HUTCHINSON WRITING COMPETITION • 712

The competition is open to law students enrolled in ABA accredited law schools. Entry to the competition is accomplished by submitting a paper that discusses a topic within the substance, procedure, or scope of jurisdiction of the Federal Circuit Court of Appeals.

Academic/Career Areas Law/Legal Services.

Award Prize for use in graduate years; not renewable. *Number:* 1–3. *Amount:* $500–$4000.

Eligibility Requirements Applicant must be enrolled or expecting to enroll full or part-time at an institution or university. Available to U.S. citizens.

Application Requirements Applicant must enter a contest, essay. *Deadline:* June 1.

Contact G. Peter Nichols, Chairman, George Hutchinson Writing Competition
Federal Circuit Bar Association
NBC Tower-3600 455 North City Front Plaza Drive
Chicago, IL 60611
Phone: 312-321-4200
Fax: 312-321-4299
E-mail: gpnichols@brinkshofer.com

FOOD AND DRUG LAW INSTITUTE
http://www.fdli.org

H. THOMAS AUSTERN FOOD AND DRUG LAW WRITING AWARD COMPETITION • 713

One-time award for law students interested in the food and drug law field. Must be enrolled in a JD program at an accredited U.S. law school and submit a forty-page paper that is an analysis of a current food and drug issue. Contact for guidelines. Prizes are: first place $1,500, second place $1,000, third place $500.

Academic/Career Areas Law/Legal Services.

Award Prize for use in graduate years; not renewable. *Number:* 3. *Amount:* $500–$1500.

Eligibility Requirements Applicant must be enrolled or expecting to enroll full-time at an institution or university. Available to U.S. and non-U.S. citizens.

Application Requirements Application, applicant must enter a contest. *Deadline:* May 17.

Contact M. Cathryn Butler, Academic Programs Coordinator
Food and Drug Law Institute
1000 Vermont Avenue, Suite 200
Washington, DC 20005-4903
Phone: 202-371-1420
Fax: 202-371-0649
E-mail: cat@fdli.org

FREDRIKSON AND BYRON FOUNDATION
http://www.fredlaw.com

FREDRIKSON AND BYRON FOUNDATION MINORITY SCHOLARSHIP • 714

One-time award to provide financial aid and work experience to minority law students. Must be currently enrolled in second semester of first year of law school at time of application. Based on academic performance and potential.

Academic/Career Areas Law/Legal Services.

Award Scholarship for use in graduate years; not renewable. *Number:* 1–2. *Amount:* $5000.

Eligibility Requirements Applicant must be American Indian/Alaska Native, Asian/Pacific Islander, Black (non-Hispanic), or Hispanic and enrolled or expecting to enroll full or part-time at an institution or university. Available to U.S. and non-U.S. citizens.

Application Requirements Application, essay, interview, resume, references, transcript. *Deadline:* April 1.

Contact Ms. Greta Larson, Recruiting Administrator
Fredrikson and Byron Foundation
1100 International Centre, 900 Second Avenue South
Minneapolis, MN 55402-3397
Phone: 612-347-7141
Fax: 612-347-7077
E-mail: glarson@fredlaw.com

GERMAN ACADEMIC EXCHANGE SERVICE (DAAD)
http://www.daad.org

GERMAN ACADEMIC EXCHANGE INTERNATIONAL LAWYERS PROGRAM • 715

Scholarships available to young lawyers to gain unique insight into the structure and function of German law during an eight-month program in Germany. Applicants must provide proof of a JD or LLB degree, proof of passing the bar examination,

German Academic Exchange Service (DAAD)
(continued)

and be under the age of 30. An excellent command of German is necessary. One-time award.

Academic/Career Areas Law/Legal Services.

Award Scholarship for use in postgraduate years; not renewable.

Eligibility Requirements Applicant must be age 29 or under; enrolled or expecting to enroll at an institution or university and must have an interest in German language. Available to U.S. and non-U.S. citizens.

Application Requirements Application, essay, photo, references, transcript, curriculum, DAAD language certificate, notarized copy of Board of Law Examiners' notification letter. *Deadline:* March 1.

Contact German Academic Exchange Service
        (DAAD)
        871 United Nations Plaza
        New York, NY 10017
        Phone: 212-758-3223
        Fax: 212-755-5780
        E-mail: daadny@daad.org

HOSTESS COMMITTEE SCHOLARSHIPS/MISS AMERICA PAGEANT
http://www.missamerica.org

LEONARD C. HORN AWARD FOR LEGAL STUDIES   •716

Scholarship for Miss America contestants pursuing career in field of law. Award available to women who have competed within the Miss America system on the local, state, or national level from 1992 to the present, regardless of whether title was won. One or more scholarships will be awarded annually, depending on the qualifications of the applicants. A new application must be submitted each year, previous applicants may apply. Applications must be received by June 30. Later or incomplete applications are not accepted.

Academic/Career Areas Law/Legal Services.

Award Grant for use in graduate years; not renewable. *Number:* 1.

Eligibility Requirements Applicant must be enrolled or expecting to enroll at an institution or university; female and must have an interest in beauty pageant. Available to U.S. citizens.

Application Requirements Application, essay, financial need analysis, references, test scores, transcript. *Deadline:* June 30.

Contact Hostess Committee Scholarships/Miss
        America Pageant
        Two Miss America Way, Suite 1000
        Atlantic City, NJ 08401

JAPANESE AMERICAN CITIZENS LEAGUE
http://www.jacl.org

JAPANESE AMERICAN CITIZENS LEAGUE LAW AWARDS   •717

One-time award for members of Japanese-American Citizens League, enrolled in or planning to enter an accredited law school. Send self-addressed stamped envelope for application, specifying application category.

Academic/Career Areas Law/Legal Services.

Award Scholarship for use in graduate, or postgraduate years; not renewable. *Number:* 2. *Amount:* $1000–$2500.

Eligibility Requirements Applicant must be enrolled or expecting to enroll full or part-time at an institution or university. Applicant or parent of applicant must be member of Japanese-American Citizens League. Available to U.S. and non-U.S. citizens.

Application Requirements Application, essay, references, self-addressed stamped envelope, transcript. *Deadline:* April 1.

Contact National JACL Scholarship & Awards
        Japanese American Citizens League
        1765 Sutter Street
        San Francisco, CA 94115
        Phone: 415-921-5225
        Fax: 415-931-4671
        E-mail: jacl@jacl.org

JAPANESE GOVERNMENT/THE MONBUSHO SCHOLARSHIP PROGRAM
http://embjapan.org/la

RESEARCH STUDENT SCHOLARSHIP
• *See number 13*

MACKENZIE KING SCHOLARSHIPS BOARD

MACKENZIE KING TRAVELLING SCHOLARSHIPS
• *See number 236*

MEXICAN AMERICAN LEGAL DEFENSE AND EDUCATIONAL FUND
http://www.maldef.org

MALDEF LAW SCHOOL SCHOLARSHIP PROGRAM   •718

Through its scholarship program, MALDEF seeks to increase the number of Latinos in the legal profession. The scholarships are based upon three primary factors: 1. demonstrated commitment to serve the Latino community through the legal profession; 2. financial need; and 3. academic achievement.

Academic/Career Areas Law/Legal Services.

Award Scholarship for use in graduate years; renewable. *Number:* 1–10. *Amount:* $1000–$6000.

Eligibility Requirements Applicant must be Hispanic and enrolled or expecting to enroll full-time at an institution or university. Available to U.S. and non-U.S. citizens.

Application Requirements Application, autobiography, essay, financial need analysis, resume, references, test scores, transcript. *Deadline:* June 30.

Contact Alicia Romero, Scholarship Coordinator
Mexican American Legal Defense and
Educational Fund
634 South Spring Street, 11th Floor
Los Angeles, CA 90014
Phone: 213-629-2512
Fax: 213-629-8016
E-mail: aromero@maldef.org

NAPABA LAW FOUNDATION
http://www.napaba.org

NAPABA LAW FOUNDATION PUBLIC SERVICE FELLOWSHIPS • 719

Awarded to a graduating law student to provide legal services to the Asian Pacific American community.

Academic/Career Areas Law/Legal Services.

Award Fellowship for use in graduate, or postgraduate years; not renewable. *Number:* 2. *Amount:* $5000.

Eligibility Requirements Applicant must be enrolled or expecting to enroll full-time at an institution or university. Available to U.S. and non-U.S. citizens.

Application Requirements Application, autobiography, essay, references, transcript, 501(c)(3) tax-exempt status letter from hosting organization. *Deadline:* March 31.

Contact Grace Yoo, Acting Executive Director
NAPABA Law Foundation
1341 G Street, NW, #500
Washington, DC 20005
Phone: 202-626-7693
Fax: 202-628-6327
E-mail: ed@napaba.org

NAPABA LAW FOUNDATION SCHOLARSHIPS • 720

Awarded to Asian Pacific American law students in recognition of their academic excellence, demonstrated leadership qualities, and commitment to the Asian Pacific American community.

Academic/Career Areas Law/Legal Services.

Award Scholarship for use in graduate years; not renewable. *Number:* 4–10. *Amount:* $2000–$5000.

Eligibility Requirements Applicant must be Asian/Pacific Islander; enrolled or expecting to enroll full-time at an institution or university and must have an interest in leadership. Available to U.S. and non-U.S. citizens.

Application Requirements Application, autobiography, essay, financial need analysis, references, transcript. *Deadline:* August 30.

Contact Grace Yoo, Acting Executive Director
NAPABA Law Foundation
1341 G Street, NW #500
Washington, DC 20005
Phone: 202-626-7693
Fax: 202-628-6327
E-mail: ed@napaba.org

OREGON STUDENT ASSISTANCE COMMISSION
http://www.osac.state.or.us

GAYLE AND HARVEY RUBIN SCHOLARSHIP
• *See number 597*

JEANNETTE MOWERY SCHOLARSHIP
• *See number 295*

PI GAMMA MU INTERNATIONAL HONOR SOCIETY IN SOCIETY SCIENCE
http://www.sckans.edu/~pgm

PI GAMMA MU SCHOLARSHIP
• *See number 273*

PUERTO RICAN LEGAL DEFENSE AND EDUCATION FUND
http://www.prldef.org/IPR

PUERTO RICAN BAR ASSOCIATION SCHOLARSHIP AWARD • 721

One-time award for Latino students attending law school in the U.S. Selection is based on financial need and academic promise. Must be in a JD degree program in an ABA-approved law school.

Academic/Career Areas Law/Legal Services.

Award Scholarship for use in graduate years; not renewable. *Number:* 5. *Amount:* $2000.

Eligibility Requirements Applicant must be of Hispanic heritage and enrolled or expecting to enroll at an institution or university. Applicant must have 2.5 GPA or higher. Available to U.S. citizens.

Puerto Rican Legal Defense and Education Fund (continued)

Application Requirements Application, essay, financial need analysis, resume, references, transcript, 1040 Tax Form. *Deadline:* November 15.

Contact Ileana Infante, Director, Education
Division
Puerto Rican Legal Defense and
Education Fund
99 Hudson Street, 14th Floor
New York, NY 10013
Phone: 212-739-7496
Fax: 212-431-4276
E-mail: education@prldef.org

PUERTO RICAN LEGAL DEFENSE AND EDUCATION FUND FR. JOSEPH FITZPATRICK SCHOLARSHIP PROGRAM • 722

One-time award for Latino students in their first or second year of law school. Based on academic standing, need, and demonstration of involvement in the Latino community. Contact address below for deadlines. Applicant must be in a JD program at a law school approved by the American Bar Association.

Academic/Career Areas Law/Legal Services.

Award Scholarship for use in graduate years; not renewable. *Number:* 5. *Amount:* up to $1500.

Eligibility Requirements Applicant must be of Hispanic heritage and enrolled or expecting to enroll at an institution or university. Applicant or parent of applicant must have employment or volunteer experience in community service. Applicant must have 2.5 GPA or higher. Available to U.S. citizens.

Application Requirements Application, essay, financial need analysis, resume, references, transcript, 1040 Tax Form. *Deadline:* January 1.

Contact Ileana Infante, Director, Education
Division
Puerto Rican Legal Defense and
Education Fund
99 Hudson Street, 14th Floor
New York, NY 10013
Phone: 212-739-7496
Fax: 212-431-4276
E-mail: education@prldef.org

RHODE ISLAND FOUNDATION
http://www.rifoundation.org

MARLYNNE GRABOYS WOOL SCHOLARSHIP • 723

One-time award for women with financial need who plan to attend graduate school to attain a law degree at an accredited institution. Must be a Rhode Island resident.

Academic/Career Areas Law/Legal Services.

Award Scholarship for use in graduate years; not renewable. *Number:* 1. *Amount:* $2000.

Eligibility Requirements Applicant must be enrolled or expecting to enroll at an institution or university; female and resident of Rhode Island.

Application Requirements Application, financial need analysis, self-addressed stamped envelope. *Deadline:* June 21.

Contact Libby Monahan, Scholarship Coordinator
Rhode Island Foundation
One Union Station
Providence, RI 02903
Phone: 401-274-4564
Fax: 401-272-1359

SANTA CLARA UNIVERSITY SCHOOL OF LAW - COMPUTER AND HIGH TECHNOLOGY LAW JOURNAL
http://www.scu.edu/techlaw

SANTA CLARA UNIVERSITY SCHOOL OF LAW COMPUTER AND HIGH TECHNOLOGY LAW JOURNAL COMMENT CONTEST
• *See number 701*

UNITED STATES INSTITUTE OF PEACE
http://www.usip.org

JENNINGS RANDOLPH SENIOR FELLOW AWARD
• *See number 333*

PEACE SCHOLAR DISSERTATION FELLOWSHIP
• *See number 334*

WELLESLEY COLLEGE
http://www.wellesley.edu/CWS/

MARGARET FREEMAN BOWERS FELLOWSHIP • 724

One or more fellowships for a first year of study in the fields of social work, law, or public policy/public administration, including MBA candidates with plans for a career in the field of social services. Preference will be given to candidates demonstrating financial need. Must be a graduate of Wellesley College.

Academic/Career Areas Law/Legal Services; Social Services.

Award Fellowship for use in graduate years; not renewable. *Amount:* up to $6000.

Eligibility Requirements Applicant must be enrolled or expecting to enroll full-time at an institution or university and female. Available to U.S. citizens.

Application Requirements Application, essay, financial need analysis, resume, references, transcript. *Deadline:* January 3.

Contact Rose Crawford, Secretary to the
Committee on Graduate Fellowships
Wellesley College
106 Central Avenue, Green Hall 441
Wellesley, MA 02481-8200
Phone: 781-283-3525
Fax: 781-283-3674
E-mail: cws-fellowships@wellesley.edu

LIBRARY SCIENCES

ALA-ALSC ASSOCIATION FOR LIBRARY SERVICE TO CHILDREN
http://www.ala.org/alsc./scholars.html

BOUND TO STAY BOUND SCHOLARSHIP • 725

Scholarship available to graduate students with an interest in library science. Submit transcripts, references, and self-addressed stamped envelope with application. One-time award. Deadline is March 1. Must have commitment to service for children.

Academic/Career Areas Library Sciences.

Award Scholarship for use in graduate, or postgraduate years; not renewable. *Number:* 3. *Amount:* $6000.

Eligibility Requirements Applicant must be enrolled or expecting to enroll full or part-time at an institution or university. Available to U.S. and Canadian citizens.

Application Requirements Application, references, self-addressed stamped envelope, transcript. *Deadline:* March 1.

Contact ALSC Scholarship Information
ALA-ALSC Association For Library
Service to Children
50 East Huron Street
Chicago, IL 60611
Phone: 312-280-2163
Fax: 312-944-7671
E-mail: alsc@ala.org

FREDERIC MELCHER SCHOLARSHIP • 726

Scholarship available to graduate students with an interest in library science. Submit transcripts, references, and self-addressed stamped envelope with application. One-time award. Deadline is March 1. Must have commitment to service for children.

Academic/Career Areas Library Sciences.

Award Scholarship for use in graduate, or postgraduate years; not renewable. *Number:* 2. *Amount:* $6000.

Eligibility Requirements Applicant must be enrolled or expecting to enroll full or part-time at an institution or university. Available to U.S. and Canadian citizens.

Application Requirements Application, references, self-addressed stamped envelope, transcript. *Deadline:* March 1.

Contact ALA-ALSC Association For Library Service
to Children
50 East Huron Street
Chicago, IL 60611
Phone: 312-280-2163
Fax: 312-944-7671
E-mail: alsc@ala.org

ALASKA LIBRARY ASSOCIATION
http://www.akla.org

ALASKA LIBRARY ASSOCIATION SCHOLARSHIP • 727

Minimum of $3000 grant available to a student enrolled in a graduate degree program in Library and Information Science in a university accredited by the American Library Association. Must commit to working in an Alaskan library for a minimum of one year after graduation. Must be a resident of Alaska.

Academic/Career Areas Library Sciences.

Award Scholarship for use in graduate years; not renewable. *Number:* 1. *Amount:* up to $3000.

Eligibility Requirements Applicant must be enrolled or expecting to enroll full or part-time at an institution or university and resident of Alaska. Available to U.S. citizens.

Application Requirements Application, essay, references, transcript, statement of intent to work in an Alaskan library. *Deadline:* January 15.

Contact Aja Markel Razumny, Library Development
Coordinator
Alaska Library Association
PO Box 110571
Juneau, AK 99811-0571
Phone: 907-465-2458
Fax: 907-465-2665
E-mail: aja_razumny@eed.state.ak.us

AMERICAN ASSOCIATION OF LAW LIBRARIES
http://www.aallnet.org

AALL AND WEST GROUP GEORGE A. STRAIT MINORITY SCHOLARSHIP ENDOWMENT
• See number 703

LAW LIBRARIANS IN CONTINUING EDUCATION COURSES • 728

Awarded to law librarians with a degree from an accredited library or law school who are registrants in

American Association of Law Libraries (continued)

continuing education courses related to law librarianship. Application deadlines are February 1, April 1, and October 1.

Academic/Career Areas Library Sciences.

Award Scholarship for use in graduate years; not renewable.

Eligibility Requirements Applicant must be enrolled or expecting to enroll full or part-time at a four-year institution or university. Applicant or parent of applicant must be member of American Association of Law Librarians. Applicant or parent of applicant must have employment or volunteer experience in designated career field. Available to U.S. and non-U.S. citizens.

Application Requirements Application, essay, financial need analysis, references, self-addressed stamped envelope, course description.

Contact Rachel Shaevel, Membership Coordinator
American Association of Law Libraries
53 West Jackson Boulevard, Suite 940
Chicago, IL 60604-3695
Phone: 312-939-4764 Ext. 10
Fax: 312-431-1097
E-mail: rshaevel@aall.org

LEXIS NEXIS (TM) / JOHN R. JOHNSON MEMORIAL SCHOLARSHIP ENDOWMENT
• *See number 705*

LIBRARY SCHOOL GRADUATES ATTENDING LAW SCHOOL
• *See number 706*

TYPE I: LIBRARY DEGREE FOR LAW SCHOOL GRADUATES
• *See number 707*

TYPE III: LIBRARY DEGREE FOR NON-LAW SCHOOL GRADUATES • 729

One-time award for college graduate with meaningful law library experience who is a degree candidate in an accredited library school. Preference given to AALL members. Based on need.

Academic/Career Areas Library Sciences.

Award Scholarship for use in graduate years; not renewable.

Eligibility Requirements Applicant must be enrolled or expecting to enroll full or part-time at a four-year institution or university. Applicant or parent of applicant must be member of American Association of Law Librarians. Available to U.S. and non-U.S. citizens.

Application Requirements Application, essay, financial need analysis, references, self-addressed stamped envelope, transcript. *Deadline:* April 1.

Contact Rachel Shaevel, Membership Coordinator
American Association of Law Libraries
53 West Jackson Boulevard, Suite 940
Chicago, IL 60604-3695
Phone: 312-939-4764 Ext. 10
Fax: 312-431-1097
E-mail: rshaevel@aall.org

AMERICAN SOCIETY FOR INFORMATION SCIENCE AND TECHNOLOGY
http://www.asis.org

INSTITUTE FOR SCIENTIFIC INFORMATION DOCTORAL DISSERTATION PROPOSAL SCHOLARSHIP
• *See number 262*

ISI OUTSTANDING INFORMATION SCIENCE TEACHER AWARD
• *See number 263*

UMI DOCTORAL DISSERTATION AWARD
• *See number 264*

BETA PHI MU, INTERNATIONAL LIBRARY AND INFORMATION SCIENCE HONOR SOCIETY
http://www.beta-phi-mu.org

BETA PHI MU DOCTORAL DISSERTATION SCHOLARSHIP • 730

Scholarship of $1500 for completion of doctoral dissertation. Must have completed all course work towards doctorate prior to receiving award. Submit resume and three references. Application available on website.

Academic/Career Areas Library Sciences.

Award Scholarship for use in postgraduate years; not renewable. *Number:* 1. *Amount:* $1500.

Eligibility Requirements Applicant must be enrolled or expecting to enroll full-time at an institution or university.

Application Requirements Application, essay, references, self-addressed stamped envelope. *Deadline:* March 15.

Contact Dr. Jane Robbins, Executive Director
Beta Phi Mu, International Library and
Information Science Honor Society
101 Louis Shores Building
Tallahassee, FL 32306-2100
E-mail: beta_phi_mu@lis.fsu.edu

BLANCHE E. WOOLLS SCHOLARSHIP • 731

Award of $1000 for graduate student accepted in ALA-accredited program to study library and information sciences. Must not have completed more than 12 semester hours of study by fall of year award is designated. Submit three references. Application available on website.

Academic/Career Areas Library Sciences.

Award Scholarship for use in graduate years; not renewable. *Number:* 1. *Amount:* $1000.

Eligibility Requirements Applicant must be enrolled or expecting to enroll full-time at an institution or university.

Application Requirements Application, essay, references, self-addressed stamped envelope. *Deadline:* March 15.

Contact Dr. Jane Robbins, Executive Director
Beta Phi Mu, International Library and
Information Science Honor Society
101 Louis Shores Building
Tallahassee, FL 32306-2100
E-mail: beta_phi_mu@lis.fsu.edu

EUGENE GARFIELD DOCTORAL DISSERTATION FELLOWSHIP • 732

Award is available to doctoral students who have completed course work and have an approved dissertation topic.

Academic/Career Areas Library Sciences.

Award Fellowship for use in graduate, or postgraduate years; not renewable. *Number:* 6. *Amount:* $3000.

Eligibility Requirements Applicant must be enrolled or expecting to enroll full-time at an institution or university. Available to U.S. and Canadian citizens.

Application Requirements Application, essay, references, letter from dean indicating approval of dissertation topic. *Deadline:* March 15.

Contact Dr. Jane Robbins, Executive Director
Beta Phi Mu, International Library and
Information Science Honor Society
101 Louis Shores Building
Tallahassee, FL 32306-2100
E-mail: beta_phi_mu@lis.fsu.edu

FRANK B. SESSA SCHOLARSHIP FOR CONTINUING EDUCATION • 733

Award of $750 for a member of Beta Phi Mu studying library and information science. Include resume and explanation of proposed study or research. Contact for further information. Application available on website.

Academic/Career Areas Library Sciences.

Award Scholarship for use in postgraduate years; not renewable. *Number:* 1. *Amount:* $750.

Eligibility Requirements Applicant must be enrolled or expecting to enroll at an institution or university. Applicant or parent of applicant must be member of Beta Phi Mu.

Application Requirements Application, essay, resume, references, self-addressed stamped envelope. *Deadline:* March 15.

Contact Dr. Jane Robbins, Executive Director
Beta Phi Mu, International Library and
Information Science Honor Society
101 Louis Shores Building
Tallahassee, FL 32306-2100
E-mail: beta_phi_mu@lis.fsu.edu

HAROLD LANCOUR SCHOLARSHIP FOR INTERNATIONAL STUDY • 734

Award of $1000 for graduate student in library and information sciences. Submit resume and explain relevance of proposed foreign study to work or schooling. Contact for further information. Application available on website.

Academic/Career Areas Library Sciences.

Award Scholarship for use in graduate years; not renewable. *Number:* 1. *Amount:* $1000.

Eligibility Requirements Applicant must be enrolled or expecting to enroll full-time at an institution or university.

Application Requirements Application, essay, resume, references, self-addressed stamped envelope. *Deadline:* March 15.

Contact Dr. Jane Robbins, Executive Director
Beta Phi Mu, International Library and
Information Science Honor Society
101 Louis Shores Building
Tallahassee, FL 32306-2100
E-mail: beta_phi_mu@lis.fsu.edu

SARAH REBECCA REED SCHOLARSHIP • 735

Scholarship of $1500 for a graduate student of library and information studies accepted into an ALA-accredited program. Must not have completed more than 12 semester hours by fall of acceptance. Submit five references. Application available on website.

Academic/Career Areas Library Sciences.

Award Scholarship for use in graduate years; not renewable. *Number:* 1. *Amount:* $1500.

Eligibility Requirements Applicant must be enrolled or expecting to enroll full-time at an institution or university.

Application Requirements Application, essay, references, self-addressed stamped envelope. *Deadline:* March 15.

Contact Dr. Jane Robbins, Executive Director
Beta Phi Mu, International Library and
Information Science Honor Society
101 Louis Shores Building
Tallahassee, FL 32306-2100
E-mail: beta_phi_mu@lis.fsu.edu

CANADIAN LIBRARY ASSOCIATION
http://www.cla.ca

CANADIAN LIBRARY ASSOCIATION DAFOE SCHOLARSHIPS • 736

One scholarship open to a college graduate entering an accredited Canadian library school. Application form, transcripts, reference, and proof of admission required. One-time award of Can$3000.

Academic/Career Areas Library Sciences.

Award Scholarship for use in graduate years; not renewable. *Number:* 1.

Eligibility Requirements Applicant must be enrolled or expecting to enroll at an institution or university. Available to U.S. and Canadian citizens.

Application Requirements Application, financial need analysis, references, transcript. *Deadline:* May 1.

Contact Brenda Shields, Scholarship and Awards
    Committee
    Canadian Library Association
    328 Frank Street
    Ottawa, ON K2P OX8
    Canada
    Phone: 613-232-9625 Ext. 318
    Fax: 613-563-9895

H. W. WILSON SCHOLARSHIP • 737

One scholarship awarded annually to a student entering an accredited library school. Canadian citizenship or landed immigrant status is required. Applicants considered on basis of academic standing and financial need. One-time award of Can$2000.

Academic/Career Areas Library Sciences.

Award Scholarship for use in graduate years; not renewable. *Number:* 1.

Eligibility Requirements Applicant must be of Canadian heritage and enrolled or expecting to enroll at an institution or university. Applicant must have 2.5 GPA or higher.

Application Requirements Application, financial need analysis. *Deadline:* May 1.

Contact Brenda Shields, Scholarship and Awards
    Committee
    Canadian Library Association
    328 Frank Street
    Ottawa, ON K2P OX8
    Canada
    Phone: 613-232-9625 Ext. 318
    Fax: 613-563-9895

LIBRARY RESEARCH AND DEVELOPMENT GRANTS • 738

One or more grants awarded annually to members of the Canadian Library Association for theoretical and applied research in library and information science.

Proposal required. Contact for application requirements. One-time award of up to Can$1000.

Academic/Career Areas Library Sciences.

Award Grant for use in graduate years; not renewable. *Number:* 1.

Eligibility Requirements Applicant must be enrolled or expecting to enroll at an institution or university. Applicant or parent of applicant must be member of Canadian Library Association. Available to U.S. and Canadian citizens.

Application Requirements Proposal. *Deadline:* Continuous.

Contact Brenda Shields, Scholarship and Awards
    Committee
    Canadian Library Association
    328 Frank Street
    Ottawa, ON K2P OX8
    Canada
    Phone: 613-232-9625 Ext. 318
    Fax: 613-563-9895

WORLD BOOK GRADUATE SCHOLARSHIP IN LIBRARY SCIENCE • 739

One scholarship available to a graduate student who is currently engaged in library work or who is planning to continue his or her library studies. Must be a Canadian citizen or landed immigrant. One-time award of Can$2500.

Academic/Career Areas Library Sciences.

Award Scholarship for use in graduate years; not renewable. *Number:* 1.

Eligibility Requirements Applicant must be of Canadian heritage and enrolled or expecting to enroll at an institution or university.

Application Requirements Application. *Deadline:* May 1.

Contact Brenda Shields, Scholarship and Awards
    Committee
    Canadian Library Association
    328 Frank Street
    Ottawa, ON K2P OX8
    Canada
    Phone: 613-232-9625 Ext. 318
    Fax: 613-563-9895

CONSORTIUM OF COLLEGE AND UNIVERSITY MEDIA CENTERS
http://www.ccumc.org

CONSORTIUM OF COLLEGE AND UNIVERSITY MEDIA CENTERS RESEARCH AWARDS
• *See number 253*

COUNCIL ON LIBRARY AND INFORMATION RESOURCES
http://www.clir.org

A.R. ZIPF FELLOWSHIP
• *See number 268*

DELAWARE HIGHER EDUCATION COMMISSION
http://www.doe.state.de.us/high-ed

LIBRARIAN INCENTIVE SCHOLARSHIP PROGRAM • 740

Renewable award for Delaware residents enrolled in graduate programs to pursue careers as librarians and archivists in Delaware libraries. Loan requires a service repayment in Delaware. Must have minimum 3.0 GPA.

Academic/Career Areas Library Sciences.

Award Forgivable loan for use in graduate years; renewable. *Number:* up to 10. *Amount:* up to $10,000.

Eligibility Requirements Applicant must be enrolled or expecting to enroll full-time at an institution or university and resident of Delaware. Applicant must have 3.0 GPA or higher. Available to U.S. citizens.

Application Requirements Application, essay, financial need analysis, test scores, transcript. *Deadline:* March 31.

Contact Maureen Laffey, Associate Director
Delaware Higher Education Commission
820 North French Street
Wilmington, DE 19801
Phone: 302-577-3240
Fax: 302-577-6765
E-mail: mlaffey@state.de.us

GEORGIA LIBRARY ASSOCIATION
http://www.library.gsu.edu/gla

GEORGIA LIBRARY ASSOCIATION HUBBARD SCHOLARSHIP • 741

One-time award to recruit librarians for Georgia and provide financial assistance toward completing a degree in library science. Must show proof of acceptance at an American Library Association-accredited library school. Residents of Georgia will be given preference.

Academic/Career Areas Library Sciences.

Award Scholarship for use in graduate years; not renewable. *Number:* 1. *Amount:* $3000.

Eligibility Requirements Applicant must be enrolled or expecting to enroll full or part-time at an institution or university and resident of Georgia. Available to U.S. and non-U.S. citizens.

Application Requirements Application, essay, references, transcript. *Deadline:* May 1.

Contact Susan Kendall, Vinings Library Manager
Georgia Library Association
GLA Administrative Services, PO Box 793
Rex, GA 30273-0793
Phone: 770-801-5330
Fax: 770-801-5319
E-mail: kendalls@cobbcat.org

HEWINS SCHOLARSHIP FUND
http://www.hartfordpl.lib.ct.us

CAROLINE M. HEWINS SCHOLARSHIP FOR CHILDREN'S LIBRARIANS • 742

This scholarship is open only to those who plan to specialize in library work with children. For graduate work only; four-year undergraduate degree required. One-time award of $4000. Deadline: March 1.

Academic/Career Areas Library Sciences.

Award Scholarship for use in graduate years; not renewable. *Number:* 1. *Amount:* $4000.

Eligibility Requirements Applicant must be enrolled or expecting to enroll at an institution or university. Available to U.S. citizens.

Application Requirements Application, transcript. *Deadline:* March 1.

Contact Louise Blalock, Chief Librarian
Hewins Scholarship Fund
Hartford Public Library, 500 Main Street
Hartford, CT 06103
Phone: 860-543-6280
Fax: 860-722-6900
E-mail: lblalock@hartfordpl.lib.ct.us

ILLINOIS STATE LIBRARY
http://www.library.sos.state.il.us

ILLINOIS STATE LIBRARY MASTER OF LIBRARY SCIENCE DEGREE SCHOLARSHIP • 743

One-time award for graduate students pursuing degrees in library sciences at ALA accredited universities. Must be a U.S. citizen and a resident of Illinois. Interview required. Minimum 3.0 GPA required.

Academic/Career Areas Library Sciences.

Award Scholarship for use in graduate years; not renewable. *Number:* 15. *Amount:* $7500.

Eligibility Requirements Applicant must be enrolled or expecting to enroll full or part-time at an institution or university and resident of Illinois. Applicant must have 3.0 GPA or higher. Available to U.S. citizens.

Application Requirements Application, essay, interview, references, transcript. *Deadline:* May 1.

Contact Patricia Norris, Associate Director
Illinois State Library
300 South Second Street
Springfield, IL 62701
Phone: 217-557-7259
Fax: 217-782-1877
E-mail: pnorris@ilsos.net

JOHN F. KENNEDY LIBRARY FOUNDATION
http://www.jfklibrary.org

KENNEDY RESEARCH GRANTS
• *See number 100*

LIBRARY AND INFORMATION TECHNOLOGY ASSOCIATION
http://www.lita.org

LIBRARY AND INFORMATION TECHNOLOGY ASSOCIATION/CHRISTIAN LAREW MEMORIAL SCHOLARSHIP IN LIBRARY AND INFORMATION TECHNOLOGY • 744

Designed to encourage the entry of qualified persons into the library and information technology field who plan to follow a career in that field and who demonstrate academic excellence, leadership, and a vision in pursuit of library and information technology.

Academic/Career Areas Library Sciences.

Award Scholarship for use in graduate years; not renewable. *Number:* 1. *Amount:* $3000.

Eligibility Requirements Applicant must be enrolled or expecting to enroll full-time at an institution or university. Available to U.S. and non-U.S. citizens.

Application Requirements Application, essay, references, transcript. *Deadline:* March 1.

Contact Scholarship Committee
Library and Information Technology
Association
50 East Huron Street
Chicago, IL 60611-2795
Phone: 312-280-4269
E-mail: lita@ala.org

LIBRARY AND INFORMATION TECHNOLOGY ASSOCIATION/GEAC SCHOLARSHIP • 745

Scholarship for those who plan to follow a career in library automation. Candidate must have applied for admission to a formal degree program of library education with emphasis on library automation leading to a master's degree. Leadership, work experience, and academic excellence are considered. Must submit personal statement. Renewable award of $2500.

Academic/Career Areas Library Sciences.

Award Scholarship for use in graduate years; not renewable. *Number:* 1. *Amount:* $2500.

Eligibility Requirements Applicant must be enrolled or expecting to enroll full-time at an institution or university. Available to U.S. and non-U.S. citizens.

Application Requirements Application, essay, references, transcript. *Deadline:* March 1.

Contact Scholarship Committee
Library and Information Technology
Association
50 East Huron Street
Chicago, IL 60611-2795
Phone: 312-280-4269
E-mail: lita@ala.org

LIBRARY AND INFORMATION TECHNOLOGY ASSOCIATION/LSSI MINORITY SCHOLARSHIP • 746

Award for minority students planning to follow a career in library automation. Candidate must have applied for admission to a formal degree program in library education with emphasis on library automation leading to a master's degree. Leadership skills, work experience, and academic excellence are considered. Must submit personal statement.

Academic/Career Areas Library Sciences.

Award Scholarship for use in graduate years; not renewable. *Number:* 1. *Amount:* $2500.

Eligibility Requirements Applicant must be American Indian/Alaska Native, Asian/Pacific Islander, Black (non-Hispanic), or Hispanic and enrolled or expecting to enroll full-time at an institution or university. Available to U.S. and Canadian citizens.

Application Requirements Application, essay, references, transcript. *Deadline:* March 1.

Contact Scholarship Committee
Library and Information Technology
Association
50 East Huron Street
Chicago, IL 60611-2795
Phone: 312-280-4269
E-mail: lita@ala.org

LIBRARY AND INFORMATION TECHNOLOGY ASSOCIATION/OCLC MINORITY SCHOLARSHIP • 747

Award for minority students planning to follow a career in library automation. Candidate must have applied for admission to a formal degree in library education with emphasis on library automation leading to a master's degree. Leadership skills, work experience, and academic excellence are considered. Must submit personal statement.

Academic/Career Areas Library Sciences.

Award Scholarship for use in graduate years; not renewable. *Number:* 1. *Amount:* $3000.

Eligibility Requirements Applicant must be American Indian/Alaska Native, Asian/Pacific Islander, Black (non-Hispanic), or Hispanic and enrolled or expecting to enroll full-time at an institution or university. Available to U.S. and Canadian citizens.

Application Requirements Application, essay, references, transcript. *Deadline:* March 1.

Contact Scholarship Committee
Library and Information Technology
Association
50 East Huron Street
Chicago, IL 60611-2795
Phone: 312-280-4269
E-mail: lita@ala.org

MASSACHUSETTS BLACK LIBRARIAN'S NETWORK

MASSACHUSETTS BLACK LIBRARIAN'S NETWORK SCHOLARSHIP IN HONOR OF JUNE MULLINS • 748

One-time award for black students entering a graduate program in library science or information science. Must attend an accredited four-year library science and information science school and have a minimum 3.5 GPA. Merit-based award of $500-$1000.

Academic/Career Areas Library Sciences.

Award Scholarship for use in graduate years; not renewable. *Number:* 2. *Amount:* $500–$1000.

Eligibility Requirements Applicant must be Black (non-Hispanic) and enrolled or expecting to enroll full or part-time at an institution or university. Applicant must have 3.5 GPA or higher. Available to U.S. citizens.

Application Requirements Application, essay, financial need analysis, references, self-addressed stamped envelope, test scores, transcript. *Deadline:* February 28.

Contact Mrs. Pearl Mosley, Scholarship
        Chairperson
        Massachusetts Black Librarian's Network
        17 Beech Glen Street
        Boston, MA 02119-1426

MEDICAL LIBRARY ASSOCIATION
http://www.mlanet.org

MEDICAL LIBRARY ASSOCIATION DOCTORAL FELLOWSHIP SPONSORED BY THE INSTITUTE FOR SCIENTIFIC INFORMATION • 749

One-time grant of $2000 for study in library science. Must be U.S. or Canadian citizen. Contact MLA for complete information.

Academic/Career Areas Library Sciences.

Award Fellowship for use in graduate years; not renewable. *Number:* 1. *Amount:* $2000.

Eligibility Requirements Applicant must be enrolled or expecting to enroll full or part-time at an institution or university. Available to U.S. and Canadian citizens.

Application Requirements Application, essay, references, transcript. *Deadline:* December 1.

Contact Lisa Fried, Coordinator, Research and
        Professional Recognition
        Medical Library Association
        65 E. Wacker Place, Suite 1900
        Chicago, IL 60601-7298
        Phone: 312-419-9094 Ext. 28
        Fax: 312-419-8950
        E-mail: mlapd2@mlahq.org

MEDICAL LIBRARY ASSOCIATION RESEARCH, DEVELOPMENT & DEMONSTRATION PROJECT GRANT • 750

Please contact the MLA for complete information. Must be U.S. or Canadian citizen. For graduate students and students who have earned a degree in library science. One-time award of $100-$1000.

Academic/Career Areas Library Sciences.

Award Grant for use in graduate years; not renewable. *Amount:* $100–$1000.

Eligibility Requirements Applicant must be enrolled or expecting to enroll at an institution or university. Available to U.S. and Canadian citizens.

Application Requirements Application, essay, references. *Deadline:* December 1.

Contact Lisa Fried, Coordinator, Research and
        Professional Recognition
        Medical Library Association
        65 E. Wacker Place, Suite 1900
        Chicago, IL 60601-7298
        Phone: 312-419-9094
        Fax: 312-419-8950
        E-mail: mlapd2@mlahq.org

MEDICAL LIBRARY ASSOCIATION SCHOLARSHIP • 751

Award for graduate study in library science at an ALA-accredited school. Must be U.S. or Canadian citizen. One-time award of $5000. Contact MLA for complete information.

Academic/Career Areas Library Sciences.

Award Scholarship for use in graduate years; not renewable. *Number:* 1. *Amount:* $5000.

Eligibility Requirements Applicant must be enrolled or expecting to enroll full or part-time at an institution or university. Available to U.S. and Canadian citizens.

Application Requirements Application, essay, references, transcript. *Deadline:* December 1.

Contact Lisa Fried, Coordinator, Research and
        Professional Recognition
        Medical Library Association
        65 E. Wacker Place, Suite 1900
        Chicago, IL 60601-7298
        Phone: 312-419-9094
        Fax: 312-419-8950
        E-mail: mlapd2@mlahq.org

MEDICAL LIBRARY ASSOCIATION SCHOLARSHIP FOR MINORITY STUDENTS • 752

Scholarship for minority graduate students to study at an ALA-accredited school for library science. Submit transcripts from all institutions attended, essay on career objectives, and references. One-time award of $5000.

Medical Library Association (continued)

Academic/Career Areas Library Sciences.

Award Scholarship for use in graduate years; not renewable. *Number:* 1. *Amount:* $5000.

Eligibility Requirements Applicant must be American Indian/Alaska Native, Asian/Pacific Islander, Black (non-Hispanic), or Hispanic and enrolled or expecting to enroll full or part-time at an institution or university.

Application Requirements Application, essay, references, transcript. *Deadline:* December 1.

Contact Lisa Fried, Coordinator, Research and
Professional Recognition
Medical Library Association
65 E. Wacker Place, Suite 1900
Chicago, IL 60601-7298
Phone: 312-419-9094
Fax: 312-419-8950
E-mail: mlapd2@mlahq.org

NEBRASKA LIBRARY ASSOCIATION
http://www.nol.org/home/NLA/

NEBRASKA LIBRARY ASSOCIATION LOUISE A. NIXON SCHOLARSHIP • 753

Award for students pursuing graduate level library education on a full- or part-time basis. Must be either resident of Nebraska, member of NLA, or employee, past or present, of Nebraska library, each for at least one year. Submit employment record, three letters of recommendation, estimated expenses, proof of acceptance. Deadline: April 15.

Academic/Career Areas Library Sciences.

Award Scholarship for use in graduate years; not renewable. *Number:* 3. *Amount:* $1000.

Eligibility Requirements Applicant must be enrolled or expecting to enroll full or part-time at an institution or university and resident of Nebraska. Applicant or parent of applicant must be member of Nebraska Library Association. Available to U.S. citizens.

Application Requirements Application, essay, references, transcript. *Deadline:* April 15.

Contact Dr. R. J. Pasco, Assistant Professor, Library
Science
Nebraska Library Association
Kayser Hall, 514 G, University of
Nebraska at Ohama
6001 Dodge
Omaha, NE 68182
Phone: 402-554-2119
Fax: 402-554-2125
E-mail: rpasco@unomaha.edu

NEW JERSEY LIBRARY ASSOCIATION SCHOLARSHIP COMMITTEE
http://www.njla.org

NEW JERSEY LIBRARY ASSOCIATION SCHOLARSHIPS • 754

These scholarships are offered for study leading to a graduate or postgraduate degree in librarianship. Awards are made on an evaluation of credentials and personal interviews with candidates. All awards are to be used for a graduate library education program that allows the graduate eligibility for a New Jersey Professional Librarian Certificate.

Academic/Career Areas Library Sciences.

Award Scholarship for use in graduate, or postgraduate years; not renewable. *Number:* 7. *Amount:* $500–$2000.

Eligibility Requirements Applicant must be enrolled or expecting to enroll full or part-time at a four-year institution or university and resident of New Jersey. Available to U.S. and non-U.S. citizens.

Application Requirements Application, essay, financial need analysis, interview, references, transcript.

Contact Patricia Tumulty, Executive Director
New Jersey Library Association
Scholarship Committee
PO Box 1534
Trenton, NJ 08607
Phone: 609-394-8032
Fax: 609-394-8164
E-mail: ptumulty@njla.org

NORTH CAROLINA LIBRARY ASSOCIATION
http://www.nclaonline.org

NORTH CAROLINA LIBRARY ASSOCIATION SCHOLARSHIPS • 755

Scholarships are available to a student entering library school for the first time, to a student currently enrolled in a library school program, to a practicing librarian who wishes to continue his or her studies. Factors to be considered in making the awards are academic excellence, potential for leadership and/or commitment to service, potential for evidence of commitment to a career in librarianship in North Carolina, and financial need. Must be a resident of North Carolina.

Academic/Career Areas Library Sciences.

Award Scholarship for use in graduate years; renewable. *Number:* 2. *Amount:* $1000.

Eligibility Requirements Applicant must be enrolled or expecting to enroll full or part-time at a four-year institution or university; resident of North Carolina and studying in North Carolina. Available to U.S. citizens.

Application Requirements Application, references.
Deadline: May 2.

Contact Sue Williams, Scholarship Committee
Chair
North Carolina Library Association
4646 Mail Service Center
Raleigh, NC 27699-4646
Phone: 336-627-1106
Fax: 336-623-1258
E-mail: swilliams@library.rcpl.org

PENNSYLVANIA LIBRARY ASSOCIATION
http://www.palibraries.org

PENNSYLVANIA LIBRARY ASSOCIATION SCHOLARSHIP
• **756**

Scholarship are given to graduate students who are Pennsylvania residents attending an accredited university. Eligible applicants will be studying library sciences. The deadline is May 15.

Academic/Career Areas Library Sciences.

Award Scholarship for use in graduate years; not renewable. *Amount:* $1500.

Eligibility Requirements Applicant must be enrolled or expecting to enroll full-time at an institution or university and resident of Pennsylvania. Available to U.S. citizens.

Application Requirements Application, financial need analysis, references. *Deadline:* May 15.

Contact Ellen Wharton, Administrative Assistant
Pennsylvania Library Association
3905 North Front Street
Harrisburg, PA 17110
Phone: 717-233-3113
Fax: 717-233-3121
E-mail: ellen@palibraries.org

TEXAS LIBRARY ASSOCIATION
http://www.txla.org

CENTURY SCHOLARSHIP
• **757**

Scholarship awarded to individuals with disabilities who are attending or have been admitted to an ALA (American Library Association) accredited library education program in Texas.

Academic/Career Areas Library Sciences.

Award Scholarship for use in graduate years; not renewable. *Number:* 1. *Amount:* $2000.

Eligibility Requirements Applicant must be enrolled or expecting to enroll full or part-time at a four-year institution or university and studying in Texas. Applicant must be hearing impaired, learning disabled, physically disabled, or visually impaired. Available to U.S. and non-U.S. citizens.

Application Requirements Application, transcript.
Deadline: February 15.

Contact Catherine Lee, Director of Administration
Texas Library Association
3355 Bee Cave Road, Suite 401
Austin, TX 78746
Phone: 512-328-1518
Fax: 512-328-8852
E-mail: catherinel@txla.org

GARRETT SCHOLARSHIP
• **758**

Scholarship awarded to Texas residents concentrating on studies in children's, young adult, or school librarianship. Awarded in odd-numbered years. Must be studying at Texas institution.

Academic/Career Areas Library Sciences.

Award Scholarship for use in graduate years; not renewable. *Number:* 1. *Amount:* $1000.

Eligibility Requirements Applicant must be enrolled or expecting to enroll full or part-time at a four-year institution or university; resident of Texas and studying in Texas. Available to U.S. citizens.

Application Requirements Application, transcript.
Deadline: February 15.

Contact Catherine Lee, Director of Administration
Texas Library Association
3355 Bee Cave Road, Suite 401
Austin, TX 78746
Phone: 512-328-1518
Fax: 512-328-8852
E-mail: catherinel@txla.org

RAY C. JANEWAY SCHOLARSHIP
• **759**

Scholarship awarded to a graduate student attending a Texas ALA (American Library Association) accredited library education program. Must be a resident of Texas.

Academic/Career Areas Library Sciences.

Award Scholarship for use in graduate years; not renewable. *Number:* 1. *Amount:* $2000.

Eligibility Requirements Applicant must be enrolled or expecting to enroll full or part-time at a four-year institution or university; resident of Texas and studying in Texas. Available to U.S. and non-U.S. citizens.

Application Requirements Application, transcript.
Deadline: February 15.

Contact Catherine Lee, Director of Administration
Texas Library Association
3355 Bee Cave Road, Suite 401
Austin, TX 78746
Phone: 512-328-1518
Fax: 512-328-8852
E-mail: catherinel@txla.org

SPECTRUM SCHOLARSHIP • 760

Applicant must be an American Library Association (ALA) Spectrum Scholar. Must also be enrolled in an ALA recognized master's degree program in library and information studies in Texas. Award restricted to Native American, Asian, African-American and Hispanic applicants. Visit website for additional information.

Academic/Career Areas Library Sciences.

Award Scholarship for use in graduate years; not renewable. *Amount:* $2000.

Eligibility Requirements Applicant must be American Indian/Alaska Native, Asian/Pacific Islander, Black (non-Hispanic), or Hispanic; enrolled or expecting to enroll full or part-time at a four-year institution or university and studying in Texas. Available to U.S. citizens.

Application Requirements Application, transcript. *Deadline:* February 15.

Contact Catherine Lee, Director of Administration
Texas Library Association
3355 Bee Cave Road, Suite 401
Austin, TX 78746
Phone: 512-328-1518
Fax: 512-328-8852
E-mail: catherinel@txla.org

VANDUSEN/BRADY SCHOLARSHIP • 761

Scholarship awarded in even numbered years to Texas residents pursuing graduate studies at a Texas institution leading to a career as an elementary school or children's librarian.

Academic/Career Areas Library Sciences.

Award Scholarship for use in graduate years; not renewable. *Number:* 1. *Amount:* $1000.

Eligibility Requirements Applicant must be enrolled or expecting to enroll full or part-time at a four-year institution or university; resident of Texas and studying in Texas. Available to U.S. and non-U.S. citizens.

Application Requirements Application, transcript. *Deadline:* February 15.

Contact Catherine Lee, Director of Administration
Texas Library Association
3355 Bee Cave Road, Suite 401
Austin, TX 78746
Phone: 512-328-1518
Fax: 512-328-8852
E-mail: catherinel@txla.org

TULSA LIBRARY TRUST
http://www.tulsalibrary.org

ALLIE BETH MARTIN SCHOLARSHIP AWARD • 762

One-time award of $4000 for graduate students pursuing a course of studies in library science. Must be resident of Oklahoma.

Academic/Career Areas Library Sciences.

Award Scholarship for use in graduate years; not renewable. *Number:* 1. *Amount:* $4000.

Eligibility Requirements Applicant must be enrolled or expecting to enroll full or part-time at an institution or university and resident of Oklahoma. Available to U.S. citizens.

Application Requirements Application, essay, resume, references, transcript. *Deadline:* June 15.

Contact Geraldine C. Hendon, Human Resources
Manager, Tulsa City-County Library
Tulsa Library Trust
400 Civic Center, 80 West Fourth Street
Tulsa, OK 74103
Phone: 918-596-7887
Fax: 918-596-2641
E-mail: ghendon@tulsalibrary.org

YOUTH SERVICES SECTION OF THE NEW YORK
http://www.nyla.org

ANN GIBSON SCHOLARSHIP • 763

To provide financial assistance to a person who has chosen to pursue graduate studies in New York that will lead to New York State certification as a youth service specialist in a public library or school library media center. Award restricted to New York residents.

Academic/Career Areas Library Sciences.

Award Scholarship for use in graduate years; not renewable. *Number:* 1. *Amount:* $1000.

Eligibility Requirements Applicant must be enrolled or expecting to enroll full or part-time at a four-year institution or university; resident of New York and studying in New York. Available to U.S. citizens.

Application Requirements Application, autobiography, references, transcript. *Deadline:* May 31.

Contact Cindy Rasely
Youth Services Section of the New York
Broome County Public Library, 185
Court Street
Binghamton, NY 13901
Phone: 607-778-6456
Fax: 607-778-1441
E-mail: rasely2000@yahoo.com

LITERATURE/ENGLISH/ WRITING

ALBERTA HERITAGE SCHOLARSHIP FUND
http://www.alis.gov.ab.ca/scholarships

ALBERTA FOUNDATION FOR THE ARTS GRADUATE LEVEL SCHOLARSHIPS
• *See number 160*

AMERICAN CENTER OF ORIENTAL RESEARCH
http://www.bu.edu/acor

NATIONAL ENDOWMENT FOR THE HUMANITIES POST-DOCTORAL RESEARCH FELLOWSHIPS
• See number 65

AMERICAN SCHOOLS OF ORIENTAL RESEARCH (ASOR)
http://www.asor.org

W.F. ALBRIGHT INSTITUTE OF ARCHAEOLOGICAL RESEARCH/NATIONAL ENDOWMENT OF THE HUMANITIES FELLOWSHIPS
• See number 71

CHILDREN'S LITERATURE ASSOCIATION
http://www.childlitassn.org

CHLA BEITER SCHOLARSHIPS FOR GRADUATE STUDENTS • 764

One-time award for research-related expenses, not for obtaining professional degree. Must submit proposal description and curriculum vitae. Must either be a member of the Children's Literature Association or join before receiving funds. Deadline: February 1. To receive a copy of the guidelines by mail, send a self-addressed stamped envelope.

Academic/Career Areas Literature/English/Writing.

Award Scholarship for use in graduate years; not renewable. *Number: 1–4. Amount: $250–$1000.*

Eligibility Requirements Applicant must be enrolled or expecting to enroll full or part-time at an institution or university and must have an interest in writing. Available to U.S. and non-U.S. citizens.

Application Requirements Application, references, self-addressed stamped envelope, curriculum vitae and proposal. *Deadline:* February 1.

Contact Scholarship Chair
Children's Literature Association
PO Box 138
Battle Creek, MI 49016-0138
Phone: 616-965-8180
Fax: 616-965-3568
E-mail: chla@mlc.lib.mi.us

DAVID LIBRARY OF THE AMERICAN REVOLUTION
http://www.dlar.org

FELLOWSHIPS FOR THE STUDY OF THE AMERICAN REVOLUTION
• See number 644

FRENCH INSTITUTE OF WASHINGTON (INSTITUT FRANÇAIS DE WASHINGTON)
http://www.unc.edu/depts/institut

EDOUARD MOROT-SIR FELLOWSHIP IN LITERATURE
• See number 165

GILBERT CHINARD FELLOWSHIPS AND EDOUARD MOROT-SIR FELLOWSHIP IN LITERATURE
• See number 166

HARMON CHADBOURN RORISON FELLOWSHIP
• See number 167

HUNTINGTON LIBRARY, ART COLLECTIONS, AND BOTANICAL GARDENS
http://www.huntington.org

HUNTINGTON RESEARCH AWARDS
• See number 56

INTERNATIONAL READING ASSOCIATION
http://www.reading.org

INTERNATIONAL READING ASSOCIATION HELEN M. ROBINSON AWARD • 765

One award to support doctoral students at the early stages of their dissertation research in the field of reading and literacy. Must be member of International Reading Association. One-time award of $1,000. Contact to obtain application procedures. Application deadline: June 15.

Academic/Career Areas Literature/English/Writing.

Award Grant for use in graduate years; not renewable. *Number: 1. Amount: $1000.*

Eligibility Requirements Applicant must be enrolled or expecting to enroll at an institution or university. Applicant or parent of applicant must be member of International Reading Association.

Application Requirements *Deadline:* January 15.

Contact Marcella Moore, Senior Secretary
International Reading Association
800 Barksdale Road, PO Box 8139
Newark, DE 19714-8139
Phone: 302-731-1600 Ext. 423
Fax: 302-731-1057
E-mail: research@reading.org

INTERNATIONAL READING ASSOCIATION JEANNE S. CHALL RESEARCH FELLOWSHIP • 766

One award to encourage and support doctoral research investigating issues in beginning research, readability, reading difficulty, and stages of reading development. Must be member of International

International Reading Association (continued)

Reading Association. One-time award of up to $6000. Contact to obtain application procedures. Application deadline: January 15.

Academic/Career Areas Literature/English/Writing.

Award Fellowship for use in graduate years; not renewable. *Number:* 1. *Amount:* up to $6000.

Eligibility Requirements Applicant must be enrolled or expecting to enroll at an institution or university. Applicant or parent of applicant must be member of International Reading Association.

Application Requirements Application. *Deadline:* January 15.

Contact Marcella Moore, Senior Secretary
International Reading Association
800 Barksdale Road, PO Box 8139
Newark, DE 19714-8139
Phone: 302-731-1600 Ext. 423
Fax: 302-731-1057
E-mail: research@reading.org

INTERNATIONAL READING ASSOCIATION OUTSTANDING DISSERTATION OF THE YEAR AWARD • 767

One award to recognize dissertations in the field of reading and literacy completed between May 15, 2000 and May 14, 2001. Must be member of International Reading Association. One-time award of $1000. Contact to obtain application procedures. Application deadline: October 1.

Academic/Career Areas Literature/English/Writing.

Award Prize for use in postgraduate years; not renewable. *Number:* 1. *Amount:* $1000.

Eligibility Requirements Applicant must be enrolled or expecting to enroll at an institution or university. Applicant or parent of applicant must be member of International Reading Association.

Application Requirements Application. *Deadline:* October 1.

Contact Marcella Moore, Senior Secretary
International Reading Association
800 Barksdale Road, PO Box 8139
Newark, DE 19714-8139
Phone: 302-731-1600 Ext. 423
Fax: 302-731-1057
E-mail: research@reading.org

READING/LITERACY RESEARCH FELLOWSHIP • 768

One award to provide support during the first five years after completing doctoral study to researcher outside U.S. and/or Canada who has shown exceptional promise in reading or literacy research. Must

be member of International Reading Association. One-time award of $1000. Contact to obtain application procedures.

Academic/Career Areas Literature/English/Writing.

Award Fellowship for use in postgraduate years; not renewable. *Number:* 1. *Amount:* $1000.

Eligibility Requirements Applicant must be enrolled or expecting to enroll full or part-time at an institution or university. Applicant or parent of applicant must be member of International Reading Association. Available to citizens of countries other than the U.S. or Canada.

Application Requirements Application. *Deadline:* January 15.

Contact Marcella Moore, Senior Secretary
International Reading Association
800 Barksdale Road, PO Box 8139
Newark, DE 19714-8139
Phone: 302-731-1600 Ext. 423
Fax: 302-731-1057
E-mail: research@reading.org

JAPANESE GOVERNMENT/THE MONBUSHO SCHOLARSHIP PROGRAM
http://embjapan.org/la

RESEARCH STUDENT SCHOLARSHIP
• *See number 13*

JOHN F. KENNEDY LIBRARY FOUNDATION
http://www.jfklibrary.org

HEMINGWAY RESEARCH GRANTS
• *See number 690*

KENNEDY RESEARCH GRANTS
• *See number 100*

MEMORIAL FOUNDATION FOR JEWISH CULTURE
http://www.mfjc.org

INTERNATIONAL FELLOWSHIPS IN JEWISH CULTURE PROGRAM
• *See number 128*

NATIONAL RESEARCH COUNCIL
http://www.nationalacademies.org/fellowships/

FORD FOUNDATION DISSERTATION FELLOWSHIPS FOR MINORITIES
• *See number 256*

FORD FOUNDATION POSTDOCTORAL FELLOWSHIP FOR MINORITIES
• *See number 257*

FORD FOUNDATION PREDOCTORAL FELLOWSHIPS FOR MINORITIES
• *See number 258*

PHI BETA KAPPA SOCIETY
http://www.pbk.org

MARY ISABEL SIBLEY FELLOWSHIP FOR GREEK AND FRENCH STUDIES
• *See number 132*

SWANN FOUNDATION FUND
http://www.lcweb.loc.gov/rr/print/swann/swann_foundation.html

SWANN FOUNDATION FUND FELLOWSHIP
• *See number 109*

UNITED NEGRO COLLEGE FUND
http://www.uncf.org

GEORGE S. LURCY CHARITABLE AND EDUCATIONAL TRUST
• *See number 405*

WELLESLEY COLLEGE
http://www.wellesley.edu/CWS/

MARY MCEWEN SCHIMKE SCHOLARSHIP
• *See number 660*

RUTH INGERSOLL GOLDMARK FELLOWSHIP
• **769**

One or more fellowships available to graduates of Wellesley College for graduate study in English literature, English composition or the Classics. Award based on need and merit. Information and applications available at www.wellesley.edu/cws.

Academic/Career Areas Literature/English/Writing.

Award Fellowship for use in graduate years; not renewable. *Amount:* up to $2000.

Eligibility Requirements Applicant must be enrolled or expecting to enroll full-time at an institution or university and female. Available to U.S. citizens.

Application Requirements Application, essay, financial need analysis, resume, references, transcript. *Deadline:* January 3.

Contact Rose Crawford, Secretary to the
Committee on Graduate Fellowships
Wellesley College
106 Central Avenue, Green Hall 441
Wellesley, MA 02481-8200
Phone: 781-283-3525
Fax: 781-283-3674
E-mail: cws-fellowships@wellesley.edu

VIDA DUTTON SCUDDER FELLOWSHIP • **770**

One or more fellowships available to alumnae of Wellesley College for study in the field of social science, political science or literature. Based on need and merit. Visit our website at www.wellesley.edu/cws for guidelines and application.

Academic/Career Areas Literature/English/Writing; Political Science; Social Sciences.

Award Fellowship for use in graduate years; not renewable. *Amount:* up to $10,000.

Eligibility Requirements Applicant must be enrolled or expecting to enroll full-time at an institution or university and female. Available to U.S. citizens.

Application Requirements Application, essay, financial need analysis, resume, references, transcript. *Deadline:* January 3.

Contact Rose Crawford, Secretary to the
Committee on Graduate Fellowships
Wellesley College
106 Central Avenue, Green Hall 441
Wellesley, MA 02481-8200
Phone: 781-283-3525
Fax: 781-283-3674
E-mail: cws-fellowships@wellesley.edu

WINTERTHUR MUSEUM, GARDEN, AND LIBRARY
http://www.winterthur.org

NEH FELLOWSHIPS
• *See number 110*

WINTERTHUR RESEARCH FELLOWSHIPS
• *See number 111*

WOODROW WILSON NATIONAL FELLOWSHIP FOUNDATION
http://www.woodrow.org

ANDREW W. MELLON FELLOWSHIPS IN HUMANISTIC STUDIES
• *See number 134*

WOODROW WILSON NATIONAL FELLOWSHIP FOUNDATION DISSERTATION GRANTS IN WOMEN'S STUDIES
• *See number 135*

WOODROW WILSON POSTDOCTORAL FELLOWSHIPS IN THE HUMANITIES
• *See number 136*

MATERIALS SCIENCE, ENGINEERING, AND METALLURGY

AFRICAN NETWORK OF SCIENTIFIC AND TECHNOLOGICAL INSTITUTIONS - ANSTI
http://www.ansti.org

AFRICAN NETWORK OF SCIENTIFIC AND TECHNOLOGICAL INSTITUTIONS POSTGRADUATE FELLOWSHIPS
• *See number 14*

AMERICAN INSTITUTE OF AERONAUTICS AND ASTRONAUTICS
http://www.aiaa.org

AIAA FOUNDATION GRADUATE AWARDS
• *See number 26*

AIAA FOUNDATION ORVILLE AND WILBUR WRIGHT AWARDS
• *See number 27*

AMERICAN NUCLEAR SOCIETY
http://www.ans.org

AMERICAN NUCLEAR SOCIETY GRADUATE SCHOLARSHIPS
• *See number 30*

ASSOCIATION FOR WOMEN IN SCIENCE EDUCATIONAL FOUNDATION
http://www.awis.org

ASSOCIATION FOR WOMEN IN SCIENCE PREDOCTORAL FELLOWSHIP
• *See number 77*

GEM CONSORTIUM
http://www.nd.edu/~gem

GEM PH.D. ENGINEERING FELLOWSHIP
• *See number 9*

MINERALS, METALS, AND MATERIALS SOCIETY (TMS)
http://www.tms.org

TMS OUTSTANDING STUDENT PAPER CONTEST— GRADUATE
• *See number 374*

NASA WYOMING SPACE GRANT CONSORTIUM
http://www.wyomingspacegrant.uwyo.edu

WYOMING NASA SPACE GRANT CONSORTIUM RESEARCH FELLOWSHIP
• *See number 61*

NATIONAL ACTION COUNCIL FOR MINORITIES IN ENGINEERING- NACME, INC.
http://www.nacme.org

SLOAN PH.D PROGRAM
• *See number 243*

NATIONAL PHYSICAL SCIENCE CONSORTIUM
http://www.npsc.org

NATIONAL PHYSICAL SCIENCE CONSORTIUM GRADUATE FELLOWSHIPS IN THE PHYSICAL SCIENCES
• *See number 244*

SOCIETY OF AUTOMOTIVE ENGINEERS
http://www.sae.org/students/stuschol.htm

SOCIETY OF AUTOMOTIVE ENGINEERS DOCTORAL SCHOLARS PROGRAM
• *See number 178*

MECHANICAL ENGINEERING

AMERICAN INSTITUTE OF AERONAUTICS AND ASTRONAUTICS
http://www.aiaa.org

AIAA FOUNDATION GRADUATE AWARDS
• *See number 26*

AIAA FOUNDATION ORVILLE AND WILBUR WRIGHT AWARDS
• *See number 27*

AMERICAN SOCIETY OF HEATING, REFRIGERATING, AND AIR CONDITIONING ENGINEERS, INC.
http://www.ashrae.org

AMERICAN SOCIETY OF HEATING, REFRIGERATING, AND AIR CONDITIONING RESEARCH GRANTS FOR GRADUATE STUDENTS
• *See number 632*

AMERICAN SOCIETY OF MECHANICAL ENGINEERS (ASME INTERNATIONAL)
http://www.asme.org/educate/aid

AMERICAN SOCIETY OF MECHANICAL ENGINEERS GRADUATE TEACHING FELLOWSHIP • 771

Renewable award for outstanding mechanical engineering Ph.D. students, especially women and minorities, to encourage them to pursue a documents in mechanical engineering and to select engineering education as a profession. Must be a member of the American Society of Mechanical Engineers and have a departmental commitment for a teaching assistantship.

Academic/Career Areas Mechanical Engineering.

Award Fellowship for use in graduate years; renewable. *Number:* 2–4. *Amount:* $5000.

Eligibility Requirements Applicant must be enrolled or expecting to enroll at an institution or university. Available to U.S. citizens.

Application Requirements Application, essay, references, test scores, transcript. *Deadline:* October 20.

Contact Ms. Theresa Oluwanifise, Administrative Assistant
American Society of Mechanical
Engineers (ASME International)
3 Park Avenue
New York, NY 10016-5990
Phone: 212-591-8131
Fax: 212-591-7143
E-mail: oluwanifiset@asme.org

AMERICAN SOCIETY OF MECHANICAL ENGINEERS SOLID WASTE PROCESSING DIVISION GRADUATE STUDY SCHOLARSHIP
• *See number 377*

ELISABETH M. AND WINCHELL M. PARSONS SCHOLARSHIP • 772

Grants given to students working toward a doctoral degree in mechanical engineering. Please visit website for additional information. Application deadline is March 15.

Academic/Career Areas Mechanical Engineering.

Award Scholarship for use in graduate years; not renewable. *Number:* 2. *Amount:* $2000.

Eligibility Requirements Applicant must be enrolled or expecting to enroll full-time at an institution or university. Available to U.S. citizens.

Application Requirements Application, resume, references, transcript. *Deadline:* March 15.

Contact Mrs. Michael G. Snyder
American Society of Mechanical
Engineers (ASME International)
102 Meadowridge Drive
Lynchburg, VA 24503-3829
Phone: 804-384-1057
E-mail: mrsnyder@aol.com

MARJORIE ROY ROTHERMEL SCHOLARSHIP • 773

One-time award for a student working towards a masters degree in mechanical engineering at an accredited U.S. institution. Must be a U.S. citizen and hold some grade of ASME membership.

Academic/Career Areas Mechanical Engineering.

Award Scholarship for use in graduate years; not renewable. *Number:* 6–8. *Amount:* $2000.

Eligibility Requirements Applicant must be enrolled or expecting to enroll full-time at an institution or university. Available to U.S. citizens.

Application Requirements Application, financial need analysis, references, self-addressed stamped envelope, transcript. *Deadline:* March 15.

Contact Ms. Theresa Oluwanifise, Administrative Assistant
American Society of Mechanical
Engineers (ASME International)
3 Park Avenue
New York, NY 10016-5990
Phone: 212-591-8131
Fax: 212-591-7143
E-mail: oluwanifiset@asme.org

RICE-CULLIMORE SCHOLARSHIP
• *See number 378*

ASSOCIATED WESTERN UNIVERSITIES, INC.
http://www.awu.org

ASSOCIATED WESTERN UNIVERSITIES FACULTY FELLOWSHIPS
• *See number 48*

ASSOCIATED WESTERN UNIVERSITIES GRADUATE RESEARCH FELLOWSHIPS
• *See number 49*

ASSOCIATED WESTERN UNIVERSITIES POSTGRADUATE FELLOWSHIP
• *See number 50*

DELAWARE VALLEY SPACE GRANT CONSORTIUM
http://www.delspace.org

NASA/DELAWARE VALLEY SPACE GRANT FELLOWSHIP
• *See number 52*

DURRANT FOUNDATION
http://www.durant.com/foundation.html

DURRANT FOUNDATION SCHOLARSHIP/ INTERNSHIP
• *See number 96*

FANNIE AND JOHN HERTZ FOUNDATION
http://www.hertzfoundation.org

FANNIE AND JOHN HERTZ FOUNDATION FELLOWSHIP
• *See number 53*

FOUNDATION FOR SCIENCE AND DISABILITY
http://www.as.wvu.edu/~scidis/organize/fsd.html

GRANTS FOR DISABLED STUDENTS IN THE SCIENCES
• *See number 54*

GEM CONSORTIUM
http://www.nd.edu/~gem

GEM PH.D. ENGINEERING FELLOWSHIP
• *See number 9*

INTERNATIONAL DESALINATION ASSOCIATION
http://www.ida.bm

INTERNATIONAL DESALINATION ASSOCIATION SCHOLARSHIP
• *See number 57*

NASA WYOMING SPACE GRANT CONSORTIUM
http://www.wyomingspacegrant.uwyo.edu

WYOMING NASA SPACE GRANT CONSORTIUM RESEARCH FELLOWSHIP
• *See number 61*

NATIONAL PHYSICAL SCIENCE CONSORTIUM
http://www.npsc.org

NATIONAL PHYSICAL SCIENCE CONSORTIUM GRADUATE FELLOWSHIPS IN THE PHYSICAL SCIENCES
• *See number 244*

SOCIETY OF AUTOMOTIVE ENGINEERS
http://www.sae.org/students/stuschol.htm

SOCIETY OF AUTOMOTIVE ENGINEERS DOCTORAL SCHOLARS PROGRAM
• *See number 178*

SOCIETY OF WOMEN ENGINEERS
http://www.swe.org

GENERAL MOTORS FOUNDATION GRADUATE SCHOLARSHIP
• *See number 245*

METEOROLOGY/ ATMOSPHERIC SCIENCE

AIR AND WASTE MANAGEMENT ASSOCIATION
http://www.awma.org

AIR AND WASTE MANAGEMENT ASSOCIATION SCHOLARSHIP ENDOWMENT TRUST FUND
• *See number 24*

AMERICAN GEOPHYSICAL UNION
http://www.agu.org

CONGRESSIONAL SCIENCE FELLOWSHIP PROGRAM
• *See number 299*

AMERICAN METEOROLOGICAL SOCIETY
http://www.ametsoc.org/AMS

AMERICAN METEOROLOGICAL SOCIETY GRADUATE HISTORY OF SCIENCE FELLOWSHIP • **774**

Goal of fellowship is to generate dissertation topic in the history of atmospheric, or related oceanic or hydrologic sciences. Award carries $15000 stipend and will support one year of dissertation research.

Academic/Career Areas Meteorology/Atmospheric Science.

Award Fellowship for use in graduate years; not renewable. *Amount:* $15,000.

Eligibility Requirements Applicant must be enrolled or expecting to enroll full-time at an institution or university. Available to U.S. citizens.

Application Requirements References, transcript, cover letter with vita, description of topic. *Deadline:* February 15.

Contact Donna Fernandez, Fellowship/Scholarship
Coordinator
American Meteorological Society
45 Beacon Street
Boston, MA 02108-3693
Phone: 617-227-2426 Ext. 246
Fax: 617-742-8718
E-mail: dfernand@ametsoc.org

AMERICAN METEOROLOGICAL SOCIETY/ INDUSTRY/GOVERNMENT GRADUATE FELLOWSHIPS
• *See number 28*

ASSOCIATED WESTERN UNIVERSITIES, INC.
http://www.awu.org

ASSOCIATED WESTERN UNIVERSITIES FACULTY FELLOWSHIPS
• *See number 48*

ASSOCIATED WESTERN UNIVERSITIES GRADUATE RESEARCH FELLOWSHIPS
• *See number 49*

ASSOCIATED WESTERN UNIVERSITIES POSTGRADUATE FELLOWSHIP
• *See number 50*

ASSOCIATION FOR WOMEN IN SCIENCE EDUCATIONAL FOUNDATION
http://www.awis.org

ASSOCIATION FOR WOMEN IN SCIENCE PREDOCTORAL FELLOWSHIP
• *See number 77*

DELAWARE VALLEY SPACE GRANT CONSORTIUM
http://www.delspace.org

NASA/DELAWARE VALLEY SPACE GRANT FELLOWSHIP
• *See number 52*

FANNIE AND JOHN HERTZ FOUNDATION
http://www.hertzfoundation.org

FANNIE AND JOHN HERTZ FOUNDATION FELLOWSHIP
• *See number 53*

JILA
http://jilawww.colorado.edu/

POSTDOCTORAL RESEARCH ASSOCIATESHIPS • 775

Research and applications in the fields of laser technology, optoelectronics, precision measurement, surface science and semiconductors, information and image processing, materials and process science, as well as basic research in atomic, molecular, and optical physics, gravitational physics, chemical physics, astrophysics, and geophysical measurements. Award is renewed based on continued eligibility. Award restricted for study in Colorado.

Academic/Career Areas Meteorology/Atmospheric Science; Physical Sciences and Math.

Award Fellowship for use in postgraduate years; renewable. *Number:* up to 15. *Amount:* $28,000–$36,000.

Eligibility Requirements Applicant must be enrolled or expecting to enroll full-time at an institution or university and studying in Colorado. Available to U.S. and non-U.S. citizens.

Application Requirements Application, references, transcript. *Deadline:* Continuous.

Contact Cheryl Glenn, Program Assistant
JILA
UCB440, University of Colorado
Boulder, CO 80309-0440
Phone: 303-492-7796
Fax: 303-492-5235
E-mail: jilavf@jila.colorado.edu

VISITING FELLOWSHIPS • 776

Fellowships for individuals (4-12 months) contributing to the fields of research and applications in laser technology, optoelectronics, precision measurement, surface science and semiconductors, information and image processing, and materials process science, as well as basic research in atomic, molecular and optical physics, precision measurement, gravitational physics, chemical physics, astrophysics, and geophysical measurements. Maximum $3500 per month. Award restricted for study in Colorado.

Academic/Career Areas Meteorology/Atmospheric Science; Physical Sciences and Math.

Award Fellowship for use in postgraduate years; not renewable. *Number:* 6–10. *Amount:* up to $3500.

Eligibility Requirements Applicant must be enrolled or expecting to enroll full-time at an institution or university and studying in Colorado. Available to U.S. and non-U.S. citizens.

JILA (continued)

Application Requirements Application, references. *Deadline:* November 1.

Contact Cheryl Glenn, Program Assistant
JILA
UCB 440, University of Colorado
Boulder, CO 80309-0440
Phone: 303-492-7796
Fax: 303-492-5235
E-mail: jilavrf@jila.colorado.edu

NATIONAL ACTION COUNCIL FOR MINORITIES IN ENGINEERING-NACME, INC.
http://www.nacme.org

SLOAN PH.D PROGRAM
• *See number 243*

NATIONAL CENTER FOR ATMOSPHERIC RESEARCH
http://www.asp.ucar.edu/

NATIONAL CENTER FOR ATMOSPHERIC RESEARCH POSTDOCTORAL RESEARCH FELLOWSHIP • **777**

One-time award for scientists just receiving Ph.D. and scientists with no more than four years postdoctoral experience. Fellowship is for two years. Submit curriculum vitae, abstract of doctoral thesis, list of publications, four reference letters, and statement of objectives in atmospheric science with application. Award restricted to use for study in Boulder, Colorado.

Academic/Career Areas Meteorology/Atmospheric Science.

Award Fellowship for use in postgraduate years; not renewable. *Number:* 8–10. *Amount:* $40,000–$42,000.

Eligibility Requirements Applicant must be enrolled or expecting to enroll at an institution or university and studying in Colorado. Available to U.S. and non-U.S. citizens.

Application Requirements Application, autobiography, essay, references, transcript. *Deadline:* January 5.

Contact Barbara Hansford, Coordinator, Advanced Study Program
National Center for Atmospheric Research
PO Box 3000
Boulder, CO 80307-3000
Phone: 303-497-1601
Fax: 303-497-1646
E-mail: barbm@ucar.edu

NATIONAL PHYSICAL SCIENCE CONSORTIUM
http://www.npsc.org

NATIONAL PHYSICAL SCIENCE CONSORTIUM GRADUATE FELLOWSHIPS IN THE PHYSICAL SCIENCES
• *See number 244*

NATIONAL SCIENCE FOUNDATION
http://www.nsf.gov/grfp

NATIONAL SCIENCE FOUNDATION GRADUATE RESEARCH FELLOWSHIPS
• *See number 62*

MUSEUM STUDIES

AMERICAN SOCIETY OF ARMS COLLECTORS

AMERICAN SOCIETY OF ARMS COLLECTORS SCHOLARSHIP
• *See number 138*

ASIAN CULTURAL COUNCIL
http://www.asianculturalcouncil.org

ASIAN ART AND RELIGION FELLOWSHIPS
• *See number 90*

ASIAN CULTURAL COUNCIL FELLOWSHIPS
• *See number 91*

ASIAN CULTURAL COUNCIL HUMANITIES FELLOWSHIPS
• *See number 92*

ASIAN CULTURAL COUNCIL RESIDENCY PROGRAM IN ASIA
• *See number 140*

FORD FOUNDATION FELLOWSHIPS
• *See number 141*

HAGLEY MUSEUM AND LIBRARY
http://www.hagley.org

HAGLEY MUSEUM AND LIBRARY GRANTS-IN-AID
• *See number 97*

HAGLEY/WINTERTHUR FELLOWSHIPS IN ARTS AND INDUSTRIES
• *See number 98*

HENRY BELIN DU PONT DISSERTATION FELLOWSHIP
• *See number 99*

METROPOLITAN MUSEUM OF ART
http://www.metmuseum.org

ANDREW W. MELLON FOUNDATION CONSERVATION FELLOWSHIP • 778

Conservation fellowship award is given to a student for training at the Metropolitan Museum of Art. Deadline: January 3. For masters degree and predoctoral applicants only.

Academic/Career Areas Museum Studies.

Award Fellowship for use in graduate, or postgraduate years; not renewable. *Amount:* $25,000.

Eligibility Requirements Applicant must be enrolled or expecting to enroll at an institution or university and studying in New York. Available to U.S. and non-U.S. citizens.

Application Requirements Essay, resume, references, transcript. *Deadline:* January 3.

Contact Marcie Karp, Coordinator of Fellowships
Metropolitan Museum of Art
1000 Fifth Avenue
New York, NY 10028
Phone: 212-650-2763
Fax: 212-396-5168
E-mail: marcie.karp@metmuseum.org

L.W. FROHLICH CHARITABLE TRUST FELLOWSHIP
• See number 59

SHERMAN FAIRCHILD FOUNDATION CONSERVATION FELLOWSHIP • 779

Annual conservation fellowship to qualified candidates from the U.S. and abroad who have already reached an advanced level of training or experience in museum conservation. For masters degree and pre-doctoral applicants only.

Academic/Career Areas Museum Studies.

Award Fellowship for use in graduate, or postgraduate years; not renewable. *Amount:* $25,000.

Eligibility Requirements Applicant must be enrolled or expecting to enroll full-time at an institution or university and studying in New York. Available to U.S. and non-U.S. citizens.

Application Requirements Essay, resume, references, transcript. *Deadline:* January 3.

Contact Marcie Karp, Coordinator of Fellowships
Metropolitan Museum of Art
1000 Fifth Avenue
New York, NY 10028
Phone: 212-650-2763
Fax: 212-396-5168
E-mail: marcie.karp@metmuseum.org

SMITHSONIAN INSTITUTION
http://www.si.edu/research+study

SMITHSONIAN INSTITUTION GRADUATE STUDENT FELLOWSHIPS
• See number 634

SMITHSONIAN INSTITUTION POSTDOCTORAL FELLOWSHIPS
• See number 635

SMITHSONIAN INSTITUTION PREDOCTORAL FELLOWSHIPS
• See number 636

SWANN FOUNDATION FUND
http://www.lcweb.loc.gov/rr/print/swann/swann_foundation.html

SWANN FOUNDATION FUND FELLOWSHIP
• See number 109

WELLESLEY COLLEGE
http://www.wellesley.edu/CWS/

HARRIET A. SHAW FELLOWSHIP
• See number 159

WINTERTHUR MUSEUM, GARDEN, AND LIBRARY
http://www.winterthur.org

NEH FELLOWSHIPS
• See number 110

WINTERTHUR RESEARCH FELLOWSHIPS
• See number 111

NATURAL RESOURCES

AMERICAN AGRICULTURAL ECONOMICS ASSOCIATION FOUNDATION
http://www.aaea.org

FARM CREDIT GRADUATE SCHOLARSHIP FOR THE STUDY OF YOUNG, BEGINNING OR SMALL FARMERS AND RANCHERS
• See number 1

OUTSTANDING DOCTORAL AND MASTER'S THESIS AWARDS
• See number 2

SYLVIA LANE MENTOR RESEARCH FELLOWSHIP FUND
• See number 3

AMERICAN FISHERIES SOCIETY
http://www.fisheries.org

J. FRANCES ALLEN SCHOLARSHIP AWARD
• See number 182

AMERICAN GEOPHYSICAL UNION
http://www.agu.org

AMERICAN GEOPHYSICAL UNION HORTON RESEARCH GRANT
- *See number 25*

AMERICAN WATER WORKS ASSOCIATION
http://www.awwa.org

AMERICAN WATER WORKS ASSOCIATION/ABEL WOLMAN FELLOWSHIP
- *See number 44*

AMERICAN WATER WORKS ASSOCIATION/ HOLLY A. CORNELL SCHOLARSHIP
- *See number 45*

AMERICAN WATER WORKS ASSOCIATION/ LARSON AQUATIC RESEARCH SUPPORT SCHOLARSHIP
- *See number 46*

AMERICAN WATER WORKS ASSOCIATION/ THOMAS R. CAMP MEMORIAL SCHOLARSHIP
- *See number 47*

ATLANTIC SALMON FEDERATION
http://www.asf.ca

ATLANTIC SALMON FEDERATION OLIN FELLOWSHIP
- *See number 16*

EDMUND NILES HUYCK PRESERVE AND BIOLOGICAL RESEARCH STATION
http://www.huyckpreserve.org

HUYCK STATION RESEARCH GRANTS
- *See number 18*

ENTOMOLOGICAL SOCIETY OF AMERICA
http://www.entsoc.org

NORMAND R. DUBOIS MEMORIAL SCHOLARSHIP
- *See number 197*

GEOLOGICAL SOCIETY OF AMERICA
http://www.geosociety.org

ARTHUR D. HOWARD RESEARCH GRANTS
- *See number 303*

J. HOOVER MACKIN RESEARCH GRANTS
- *See number 308*

GREAT LAKES COMMISSION
http://www.glc.org

GREAT LAKES COMMISSION - SEA GRANT FELLOWSHIP
- *See number 202*

HUDSON RIVER FOUNDATION
http://www.hudsonriver.org

HUDSON RIVER RESEARCH GRANTS
- *See number 206*

HUDSON RIVER NATIONAL ESTUARINE RESEARCH RESERVE
http://www.ocm.nos.noaa/nerr/fellow.html

NATIONAL ESTUARINE RESEARCH RESERVE GRADUATE FELLOWSHIP PROGRAM
- *See number 55*

INTERNATIONAL DEVELOPMENT RESEARCH CENTER
http://www.idrc.ca/awards

AGROPOLIS
- *See number 10*

IDRC DOCTORAL RESEARCH AWARD
- *See number 12*

INTERNATIONAL WOMEN'S FISHING ASSOCIATION SCHOLARSHIP TRUST
http://www.iwfa.org

INTERNATIONAL WOMEN'S FISHING ASSOCIATION GRADUATE SCHOLARSHIPS IN THE MARINE SCIENCES
- *See number 19*

NATIONAL MILK PRODUCERS FEDERATION
http://www.nmpf.org

NATIONAL MILK PRODUCERS FEDERATION NATIONAL DAIRY LEADERSHIP SCHOLARSHIP PROGRAM
- *See number 5*

RESOURCES FOR THE FUTURE
http://www.rff.org

GILBERT F. WHITE POSTDOCTORAL FELLOWSHIPS
- *See number 331*

JOSEPH L. FISHER DISSERTATION AWARDS
- *See number 332*

ROB & BESSIE WELDER WILDLIFE FOUNDATION

WILDLIFE RESEARCH SCHOLARSHIP
• See number 22

SAN FRANCISCO FOUNDATION
http://www.sff.org

SWITZER ENVIRONMENTAL FELLOWSHIPS • 780

Award for graduate students at California institutions who are pursuing studies to help reduce pollution of the environment or restore polluted natural resources. Must be nominated by professor and have completed one semester of environmental science. One-time award of $13,000.

Academic/Career Areas Natural Resources.

Award Fellowship for use in graduate years; not renewable. *Number:* 1–10. *Amount:* $13,000.

Eligibility Requirements Applicant must be enrolled or expecting to enroll full-time at an institution or university and studying in California. Available to U.S. citizens.

Application Requirements Application, essay, interview, resume, references, transcript. *Deadline:* January 31.

Contact Awards Coordinator
San Francisco Foundation
225 Bush Street, Suite 500
San Francisco, CA 94104-4224
Phone: 415-733-8500
E-mail: rec@sff.org

SOIL AND WATER CONSERVATION SOCIETY
http://www.swcs.org

SWCS KENNETH E. GRANT SCHOLARSHIP
• See number 313

NATURAL SCIENCES

AIR AND WASTE MANAGEMENT ASSOCIATION
http://www.awma.org

AIR AND WASTE MANAGEMENT ASSOCIATION SCHOLARSHIP ENDOWMENT TRUST FUND
• See number 24

AMERICAN FISHERIES SOCIETY
http://www.fisheries.org

J. FRANCES ALLEN SCHOLARSHIP AWARD
• See number 182

AMERICAN OIL CHEMISTS' SOCIETY
http://www.aocs.org

AMERICAN OIL CHEMISTS' SOCIETY HONORED STUDENT AWARDS • 781

One-time award for graduate students studying any area of science dealing with fats and oils, proteins, lipids, surfactants, detergents, or related materials to attend annual meeting of the American Oil Chemists' Society. Must submit abstract with application. Write for complete details.

Academic/Career Areas Natural Sciences.

Award Scholarship for use in graduate years; not renewable. *Number:* 1–20. *Amount:* $750–$1000.

Eligibility Requirements Applicant must be enrolled or expecting to enroll full-time at an institution or university. Available to U.S. and non-U.S. citizens.

Application Requirements Application, references, paper abstract. *Deadline:* October 15.

Contact Barbara Semeraro, Assistant to Area
Manager of Membership Services
American Oil Chemists' Society
PO Box 3489
Champaign, IL 61826-3489
Phone: 217-359-2344
Fax: 217-351-8091
E-mail: membership@aocs.org

AMERICAN SCHOOLS OF ORIENTAL RESEARCH (ASOR)
http://www.asor.org

W.F. ALBRIGHT INSTITUTE OF ARCHAEOLOGICAL RESEARCH/COUNCIL OF AMERICAN OVERSEAS RESEARCH CENTERS FELLOWSHIPS FOR ADVANCED MULTICOUNTRY RESEARCH
• See number 681

ASSOCIATION FOR WOMEN IN SCIENCE EDUCATIONAL FOUNDATION
http://www.awis.org

ASSOCIATION FOR WOMEN IN SCIENCE PREDOCTORAL FELLOWSHIP
• See number 77

BLUE CROSS BLUE SHIELD OF MICHIGAN FOUNDATION
http://www.bcbsm.com/foundation

BLUE CROSS BLUE SHIELD OF MICHIGAN FOUNDATION STUDENT AWARD PROGRAM
• See number 393

GERMAN ACADEMIC EXCHANGE SERVICE (DAAD)
http://www.daad.org

NSF-DAAD GRANTS FOR THE NATURAL, ENGINEERING, AND SOCIAL SCIENCES
• *See number 379*

GREAT LAKES COMMISSION
http://www.glc.org

GREAT LAKES COMMISSION - SEA GRANT FELLOWSHIP
• *See number 202*

HUDSON RIVER FOUNDATION
http://www.hudsonriver.org

HUDSON RIVER FOUNDATION GRADUATE FELLOWSHIPS
• *See number 205*

HUDSON RIVER RESEARCH GRANTS
• *See number 206*

HUDSON RIVER NATIONAL ESTUARINE RESEARCH RESERVE
http://www.ocm.nos.noaa/nerr/fellow.html

NATIONAL ESTUARINE RESEARCH RESERVE GRADUATE FELLOWSHIP PROGRAM
• *See number 55*

INTERNATIONAL DESALINATION ASSOCIATION
http://www.ida.bm

INTERNATIONAL DESALINATION ASSOCIATION SCHOLARSHIP
• *See number 57*

JANE COFFIN CHILDS MEMORIAL FUND FOR MEDICAL RESEARCH
http://www.jccfund.org

JANE COFFIN CHILDS MEMORIAL FUND FOR MEDICAL RESEARCH FELLOWSHIPS
• *See number 531*

L.S.B. LEAKEY FOUNDATION
http://www.leakeyfoundation.org

RESEARCH GRANTS
• *See number 79*

LIFE SCIENCES RESEARCH FOUNDATION
http://www.lsrf.org

POSTDOCTORAL FELLOWSHIPS
• *See number 208*

NASA WYOMING SPACE GRANT CONSORTIUM
http://www.wyomingspacegrant.uwyo.edu

WYOMING NASA SPACE GRANT CONSORTIUM RESEARCH FELLOWSHIP
• *See number 61*

NOVARTIS FOUNDATION
http://wwwl.novartisfound.org.uk/bursary.htm

NOVARTIS FOUNDATION BURSARY SCHEME
• *See number 20*

SOIL AND WATER CONSERVATION SOCIETY
http://www.swcs.org

SWCS KENNETH E. GRANT SCHOLARSHIP
• *See number 313*

NUCLEAR SCIENCE

AMERICAN NUCLEAR SOCIETY
http://www.ans.org

ALAN F. HENRY/PAUL A. GREEBLER SCHOLARSHIP
• *See number 29*

AMERICAN NUCLEAR SOCIETY GRADUATE SCHOLARSHIPS
• *See number 30*

VERNE R. DAPP SCHOLARSHIP • **782**

One award of $3000 available in odd number years. Must be full-time graduate student. Memorial scholarship. Application available on website.

Academic/Career Areas Nuclear Science.

Award Scholarship for use in graduate years; not renewable. *Number:* 1. *Amount:* $3000.

Eligibility Requirements Applicant must be enrolled or expecting to enroll full-time at a four-year institution. Available to U.S. citizens.

Application Requirements Application, references, transcript. *Deadline:* February 1.

Contact Scholarship Coordinator
American Nuclear Society
555 North Kensington Avenue
La Grange Park, IL 60526
Phone: 708-352-6611
Fax: 708-352-0499
E-mail: outreach@ans.org

ASSOCIATED WESTERN UNIVERSITIES, INC.
http://www.awu.org

ASSOCIATED WESTERN UNIVERSITIES FACULTY FELLOWSHIPS
• *See number 48*

ASSOCIATED WESTERN UNIVERSITIES GRADUATE RESEARCH FELLOWSHIPS
• *See number 49*

ASSOCIATED WESTERN UNIVERSITIES POSTGRADUATE FELLOWSHIP
• *See number 50*

EDUCATION AND RESEARCH FOUNDATION, SOCIETY OF NUCLEAR MEDICINE
http://www.snmerf.org

PILOT RESEARCH GRANTS
• *See number 496*

SOCIETY OF NUCLEAR MEDICINE STUDENT FELLOWSHIP AWARDS
• *See number 497*

FANNIE AND JOHN HERTZ FOUNDATION
http://www.hertzfoundation.org

FANNIE AND JOHN HERTZ FOUNDATION FELLOWSHIP
• *See number 53*

GEM CONSORTIUM
http://www.nd.edu/~gem

GEM PH.D. ENGINEERING FELLOWSHIP
• *See number 9*

NATIONAL ACADEMY FOR NUCLEAR TRAINING
http://www.nei.org

NATIONAL ACADEMY OF NUCLEAR TRAINING GRADUATE FELLOWSHIP • **783**

Fellowships are available to graduate students at U.S. colleges and universities studying nuclear engineering and/or power-generation health physics programs following a rigorous review of proposals submitted by the institution where they are enrolled. Eligible applicants must be U.S. citizens, full-time, in good academic standing and have no previous Academy fellowship support. For more information visit http://www.nei.org.

Academic/Career Areas Nuclear Science.

Award Fellowship for use in graduate years; not renewable. *Number:* 40. *Amount:* $14,000.

Eligibility Requirements Applicant must be enrolled or expecting to enroll full-time at an institution or university. Available to U.S. citizens.

Application Requirements Application, transcript.

Contact National Academy for Nuclear Training
Attn: Educational Assistance Program
700 Galleria Parkway, NW, Suite 100
Atlanta, GA 30339-5957

NATIONAL ACTION COUNCIL FOR MINORITIES IN ENGINEERING-NACME, INC.
http://www.nacme.org

SLOAN PH.D PROGRAM
• *See number 243*

NURSING

ALBERT SCHWEITZER FELLOWSHIP
http://www.schweitzerfellowship.org

NEW HAMPSHIRE/VERMONT SCHWEITZER FELLOWS PROGRAM
• *See number 15*

AMERICAN ASSOCIATION OF CRITICAL-CARE NURSES (AACN)
http://www.aacn.org

AACN CERTIFICATION CORPORATION RESEARCH GRANT • **784**

Grant supports research related to certified nursing practice. Must be member of AACN. Proposals due February 1.

Academic/Career Areas Nursing.

Award Grant for use in graduate years; not renewable. *Number:* up to 4. *Amount:* up to $10,000.

Eligibility Requirements Applicant must be enrolled or expecting to enroll full or part-time at an institution or university. Applicant or parent of applicant must be member of American Association of Critical Care Nurses. Available to U.S. and non-U.S. citizens.

Application Requirements Application, references, research proposal. *Deadline:* February 1.

Contact Director of Practice, Research, and Membership
American Association of Critical-Care Nurses (AACN)
101 Colombia
Aliso Viego, CA 92656
Phone: 800-899-2226
E-mail: info@aacn.org

AACN CRITICAL CARE RESEARCH GRANT • 785

One award for a registered nurse who is a member of the American Association of Critical Care Nurses. Submit research proposal relevant to critical care nursing practices. May not be used to meet requirements of an academic degree. One-time award of up to $15,000.

Academic/Career Areas Nursing.

Award Grant for use in graduate years; not renewable. *Number:* 1. *Amount:* up to $15,000.

Eligibility Requirements Applicant must be enrolled or expecting to enroll full or part-time at an institution or university. Applicant or parent of applicant must be member of American Association of Critical Care Nurses. Applicant or parent of applicant must have employment or volunteer experience in designated career field. Available to U.S. and non-U.S. citizens.

Application Requirements Application, references, research proposal. *Deadline:* February 1.

Contact Director of Practice, Research, and
　　　　　Membership
　　　　　American Association of Critical-Care
　　　　　Nurses (AACN)
　　　　　101 Columbia
　　　　　Aliso Viejo, CA 92656
　　　　　Phone: 800-899-2226
　　　　　E-mail: info@aacn.org

AACN EDUCATIONAL ADVANCEMENT SCHOLARSHIPS-GRADUATE • 786

One-time award for graduate students currently enrolled in a master's or doctoral nursing program. Must be AACN member with an active RN license who is currently or has recently worked in critical care. Must have 3.0 GPA. Supports members completing a graduate degree related to nursing practice. Program must be accredited by NLN or CCNE.

Academic/Career Areas Nursing.

Award Scholarship for use in graduate years; not renewable. *Number:* 50–100. *Amount:* $1500.

Eligibility Requirements Applicant must be enrolled or expecting to enroll full or part-time at a four-year institution or university. Applicant or parent of applicant must be member of American Association of Critical Care Nurses. Applicant or parent of applicant must have employment or volunteer experience in designated career field. Applicant must have 3.0 GPA or higher. Available to U.S. citizens.

Application Requirements Application, references, test scores, transcript. *Deadline:* April 1.

Contact American Association of Critical-Care
　　　　　Nurses (AACN)
　　　　　101 Columbia
　　　　　Aliso Viejo, CA 92656
　　　　　Phone: 800-899-2226

AACN-SIGMA THETA TAU CRITICAL CARE GRANT • 787

One award for a registered nurse to conduct research relevant to critical care nursing. Must be member of the American Association of Critical Care Nurses or Sigma Theta Tau. Proposal must be received by October 1. One-time award of up to $10,000.

Academic/Career Areas Nursing.

Award Grant for use in graduate years; not renewable. *Number:* 1. *Amount:* up to $10,000.

Eligibility Requirements Applicant must be enrolled or expecting to enroll full or part-time at an institution or university. Applicant or parent of applicant must be member of American Association of Critical Care Nurses or Sigma Theta Tau International. Applicant or parent of applicant must have employment or volunteer experience in designated career field. Available to U.S. and non-U.S. citizens.

Application Requirements Application, references, research proposal. *Deadline:* October 1.

Contact Director of Practice, Research, and
　　　　　Membership
　　　　　American Association of Critical-Care
　　　　　Nurses (AACN)
　　　　　101 Columbia
　　　　　Aliso Viejo, CA 92656
　　　　　Phone: 800-899-2226
　　　　　E-mail: info@aacn.org

AGILENT TECHNOLOGIES AMERICAN ASSOCIATION OF CRITICAL CARE NURSES RESEARCH GRANT • 788

One-time award for registered nurses who are members of the American Association of Critical Care Nurses to research a topic which addresses the information technology requirements of patient management in acute and critical care. Applications must be received by September 1.

Academic/Career Areas Nursing.

Award Grant for use in graduate years; not renewable. *Number:* 1. *Amount:* up to $35,000.

Eligibility Requirements Applicant must be enrolled or expecting to enroll full or part-time at an institution or university. Applicant or parent of applicant must be member of American Association of Critical Care Nurses. Applicant or parent of applicant must have employment or volunteer experience in designated career field. Available to U.S. citizens.

Application Requirements Application, references, proposal. *Deadline:* September 1.

Contact Director of Practice, Research and
Membership
American Association of Critical-Care
Nurses (AACN)
101 Columbia
Alisa Viejo, CA 92656
Phone: 800-899-2226
E-mail: info@.aaacn.org

AMERICAN ASSOCIATION OF CRITICAL CARE NURSES MENTORSHIP GRANT • 789

One-time award for registered nurse who is a novice researcher with current American Association of Critical Care Nurses membership to conduct research relevant to critical care nursing practice. Must be under guidance of a mentor who shows strong evidence of research expertise in proposed area of research. Proposals must be received by February 1.

Academic/Career Areas Nursing.

Award Grant for use in graduate years; not renewable. *Number:* 1. *Amount:* up to $10,000.

Eligibility Requirements Applicant must be enrolled or expecting to enroll full or part-time at an institution or university. Applicant or parent of applicant must be member of American Association of Critical Care Nurses. Applicant or parent of applicant must have employment or volunteer experience in designated career field. Available to U.S. and non-U.S. citizens.

Application Requirements Application, references, research proposal. *Deadline:* February 1.

Contact Director of Practice, Research, and
Membership
American Association of Critical-Care
Nurses (AACN)
101 Columbia
Aliso Viejo, CA 92656
E-mail: info@aacn.org

AMERICAN RESPIRATORY CARE FOUNDATION
http://www.aarc.org

GLAXO SMITH KLINE FELLOWSHIP FOR ASTHMA MANAGEMENT EDUCATION
• *See number 475*

BLUE CROSS BLUE SHIELD OF MICHIGAN FOUNDATION
http://www.bcbsm.com/foundation

BLUE CROSS BLUE SHIELD OF MICHIGAN FOUNDATION STUDENT AWARD PROGRAM
• *See number 393*

CENTER FOR THE STUDY OF THE HISTORY OF NURSING
http://www.nursing.upenn.edu/history

ALICE FISHER SOCIETY HISTORICAL SCHOLARSHIP
• *See number 642*

LILLIAN SHOLTIS BRUNNER SUMMER FELLOWSHIP
• *See number 643*

DELTA SOCIETY
http://www.deltasociety.org

HARRIS SWEATT TRAVEL GRANT
• *See number 17*

EMERGENCY NURSES ASSOCIATION (ENA) FOUNDATION
http://www.ena.org/foundation

EMERGENCY NURSES ASSOCIATION FOUNDATION ADVANCED NURSING PRACTICE SCHOLARSHIP #1 • 790

Up to $2500 awarded to current Emergency Nurses Association (ENA) member pursuing an advanced clinical practice degree to become a nurse practitioner or clinical nurse specialist. Application must be postmarked by April 1. Recipient will be notified June 1.

Academic/Career Areas Nursing.

Award Scholarship for use in graduate years; not renewable. *Number:* 1. *Amount:* $2500.

Eligibility Requirements Applicant must be enrolled or expecting to enroll full or part-time at an institution or university. Applicant or parent of applicant must be member of Emergency Nurses Association. Available to U.S. and non-U.S. citizens.

Application Requirements Application, transcript. *Deadline:* April 1.

Contact Emergency Nurses Association (ENA)
Foundation
915 Lee Street
Des Plaines, IL 60016

EMERGENCY NURSES ASSOCIATION FOUNDATION ADVANCED NURSING PRACTICE SCHOLARSHIP #2 • 791

Up to $2500 awarded to current Emergency Nurses Association (ENA) member pursuing an advanced clinical practice degree to become a nurse practitioner or clinical nurse specialist. Application must be postmarked by June 1. Recipient will be notified August 1.

Academic/Career Areas Nursing.

Award Scholarship for use in graduate years; not renewable. *Number:* 1. *Amount:* $2500.

Emergency Nurses Association (ENA)
Foundation (continued)

Eligibility Requirements Applicant must be enrolled or expecting to enroll full or part-time at an institution or university. Applicant or parent of applicant must be member of Emergency Nurses Association. Available to U.S. and non-U.S. citizens.

Application Requirements Application, transcript. *Deadline:* June 1.

Contact Emergency Nurses Association (ENA)
Foundation
915 Lee Street
Des Plaines, IL 60016

Academic/Career Areas Nursing.

Award Scholarship for use in graduate years; not renewable. *Number:* 1. *Amount:* up to $3000.

Eligibility Requirements Applicant must be enrolled or expecting to enroll full or part-time at an institution or university. Applicant or parent of applicant must be member of Emergency Nurses Association. Available to U.S. and non-U.S. citizens.

Application Requirements Application, transcript. *Deadline:* September 1.

Contact Emergency Nurses Association (ENA)
Foundation
915 Lee Street
Des Plaines, IL 60016

ENA FOUNDATION DOCTORAL SCHOLARSHIP
• 792

Up to $4000 awarded to a nurse pursuing a doctoral degree. Applicant must be a current Emergency Nurses Association (ENA) member. Application must be postmarked by September 1. Recipient will be notified November 1.

Academic/Career Areas Nursing.

Award Scholarship for use in postgraduate years; not renewable. *Number:* 1. *Amount:* up to $4000.

Eligibility Requirements Applicant must be enrolled or expecting to enroll full or part-time at an institution or university. Applicant or parent of applicant must be member of Emergency Nurses Association. Available to U.S. and non-U.S. citizens.

Application Requirements Application, transcript. *Deadline:* September 1.

Contact Emergency Nurses Association (ENA)
Foundation
915 Lee Street
Des Plaines, IL 60016

ENA FOUNDATION RESEARCH GRANTS #1 AND #2
• *See number 514*

ENA FOUNDATION/EMERGENCY MEDICINE FOUNDATION TEAM RESEARCH GRANT
• *See number 515*

ENAF/SIGMA THETA TAU INTERNATIONAL RESEARCH GRANT
• *See number 516*

KAREN O'NEIL ENDOWED ADVANCED NURSING PRACTICE SCHOLARSHIP
• 793

Maximum $3000 award for an emergency nurse pursuing an advanced degree. Application must be postmarked by September 1. Recipient will be notified November 1. Contact for additional information. Applicant must be ENA member for a minimum of 12 months prior to applying.

MEDTRONIC PHYSIO-CONTROL ADVANCED NURSING PRACTICE SCHOLARSHIP
• 794

Supported by Medtronic Physio-Control, this scholarship is intended for a nurse pursuing an advanced clinical practice degree to become a nurse practitioner or clinical nurse specialist. Priority for funding will be given to nurses focusing on cardiac nursing, including cardiac resuscitation. Applicant must be ENA member for a minimum of 12 months prior to applying.

Academic/Career Areas Nursing.

Award Scholarship for use in graduate years; not renewable. *Number:* 1. *Amount:* $3000.

Eligibility Requirements Applicant must be enrolled or expecting to enroll full or part-time at an institution or university. Applicant or parent of applicant must be member of Emergency Nurses Association. Available to U.S. and non-U.S. citizens.

Application Requirements Application, transcript. *Deadline:* June 1.

Contact Emergency Nurses Association (ENA)
Foundation
915 Lee Street
Des Plaines, IL 60016

EPILEPSY FOUNDATION
http://www.epilepsyfoundation.org

PREDOCTORAL RESEARCH TRAINING FELLOWSHIP
• *See number 200*

HEALTH PROFESSIONS EDUCATION FOUNDATION
http://www.healthprofessions.ca.gov

HEALTH PROFESSIONS EDUCATION LOAN REPAYMENT PROGRAM
• *See number 287*

HEALTH RESOURCES AND SERVICES ADMINISTRATION
http://www.bphr.hrsa.gov/nhsc

NATIONAL HEALTH SERVICES CORPS SCHOLARSHIP PROGRAM
• See number 522

HEART AND STROKE FOUNDATION OF CANADA
http://www.hsf.ca/research

HEART AND STROKE FOUNDATION OF CANADA NURSING RESEARCH FELLOWSHIPS
• See number 526

MARCH OF DIMES BIRTH DEFECTS FOUNDATION - GRANTS ADMINISTRATION
http://www.modimes.org

MARCH OF DIMES GRADUATE NURSING SCHOLARSHIP   • 795

One-time award to registered nurse currently enrolled in a graduate program or post-graduate in maternal-child nursing at the Master's or Doctorate level. Must be a member of ACNM, AWHONN or NANN.

Academic/Career Areas Nursing.

Award Scholarship for use in graduate, or postgraduate years; not renewable. *Number:* 4. *Amount:* $5000.

Eligibility Requirements Applicant must be enrolled or expecting to enroll full or part-time at an institution or university. Available to U.S. and non-U.S. citizens.

Application Requirements Application, essay, references, curriculum vitae. *Deadline:* January 15.

Contact Karen Kroder, Education Services Department
March of Dimes Birth Defects Foundation - Grants Administration
1275 Mamaroneck Avenue
White Plains, NY 10605
Phone: 914-997-4456
Fax: 914-997-4501
E-mail: kkroder@modimes.org

MATERNITY CENTER ASSOCIATION
http://www.maternitywise.org

HAZEL CORBIN GRANT   • 796

Applicant must be a registered nurse and accepted into an ACNM-accredited certified nurse-midwifery program. Must submit letter of acceptance. One-time award of up to $5000. Grant may be used for expenses associated with planned research. Grantees are encouraged to publish results of research supported by the Hazel Corbin Grant, and are required to provide MCA with a copy of the final report of the research and of any related publications. All reports must acknowledge MCA support.

Academic/Career Areas Nursing.

Award Grant for use in graduate years; not renewable. *Number:* 1. *Amount:* up to $5000.

Eligibility Requirements Applicant must be enrolled or expecting to enroll full-time at an institution or university. Available to U.S. citizens.

Application Requirements Application, essay, references. *Deadline:* August 1.

Contact Tahshann Richards, Program Associate
Maternity Center Association
281 Park Avenue South, 5th Floor
New York, NY 10010
Phone: 212-777-5000
Fax: 212-777-9320
E-mail: info@maternitywise.org

MENNONITE HEALTH SERVICES
http://www.mhsonline.org

MILLER-ERB NURSING DEVELOPMENT FUND   • 797

Priorities for the project funding shall be: 1) Loans for research and writing with a forgiveness clause when published and presented to Menonite constituency and others in the nursing field. 2) Graduate study loans with a forgiveness clause for service in Mennonite institutions. 3) Leadership training loans for nursing service with a forgiveness clause for service in Mennonite institutions. Other creative projects that support the philosophy of the Miller-Erb Nursing Development Fund.

Academic/Career Areas Nursing.

Award Forgivable loan for use in graduate years; renewable. *Number:* 4–6. *Amount:* $300–$2000.

Eligibility Requirements Applicant must be Brethren and enrolled or expecting to enroll full or part-time at an institution or university. Applicant must have 3.0 GPA or higher. Available to U.S. and non-U.S. citizens.

Application Requirements Application, autobiography, essay, financial need analysis, references, test scores, transcript. *Deadline:* February 1.

Contact Wendy Rohn, Office Manager
Mennonite Health Services
234 South Main Street, Suite. 1
Goshen, IN 46526
Phone: 219-534-9689
Fax: 219-534-3254
E-mail: wendy@mhsonline.org

MINNESOTA DEPARTMENT OF HEALTH
http://www.health.state.mn.us

MINNESOTA RURAL MIDLEVEL PRACTITIONER LOAN FORGIVENESS PROGRAM
• See number 543

MISSISSIPPI STATE STUDENT FINANCIAL AID
http://www.ihl.state.ms.us

MISSISSIPPI NURSING EDUCATION MSN PROGRAM • 798

Renewable scholarship for Mississippi graduate nursing students attending Mississippi universities. Must fulfill work obligation in Mississippi or pay back as a loan. Write for further details.

Academic/Career Areas Nursing.

Award Forgivable loan for use in graduate years; not renewable. *Amount:* up to $3000.

Eligibility Requirements Applicant must be enrolled or expecting to enroll full or part-time at an institution or university; resident of Mississippi and studying in Mississippi. Applicant must have 3.0 GPA or higher. Available to U.S. citizens.

Application Requirements Application, driver's license, financial need analysis, references, transcript. *Deadline:* March 31.

Contact Board of Trustees
Mississippi State Student Financial Aid
3825 Ridgewood Road
Jackson, MS 39211-6453

MYASTHENIA GRAVIS FOUNDATION OF AMERICA, INC.
http://www.myasthenia.org

MYASTHENIA GRAVIS FOUNDATION NURSES RESEARCH FELLOWSHIP • 799

Award for research pertaining to problems faced by myasthenia gravis patients. Candidates must be currently licensed as registered professional nurses. Submit research proposal, curriculum vitae, and letters of approval. One-time award of $1500-$3000.

Academic/Career Areas Nursing.

Award Fellowship for use in graduate, or postgraduate years; not renewable. *Number:* 1–4. *Amount:* $1500–$3000.

Eligibility Requirements Applicant must be enrolled or expecting to enroll full or part-time at an institution or university. Applicant or parent of applicant must have employment or volunteer experience in designated career field. Available to U.S. and non-U.S. citizens.

Application Requirements Application, autobiography, references, transcript, research proposal. *Deadline:* Continuous.

Contact Debora Boelz, Chief Executive
Myasthenia Gravis Foundation of
America, Inc.
5841 Cedar Lake Road
Suite 204
Minneapolis, MN 55416
Phone: 800-541-5454
Fax: 952-646-2028
E-mail: myastheniagravis@msn.com

NATIONAL ASSOCIATION OF PEDIATRIC NURSE PRACTITIONERS
http://www.napnap.org

NATIONAL ASSOCIATION OF PEDIATRIC NURSE PRACTITIONERS MCNEIL SCHOLARSHIPS • 800

Award for students enrolled in a pediatric nurse practitioner program. Must be registered nurse with work experience in pediatrics. Must demonstrate financial need and state rationale for seeking pediatric nurse practitioner education. Deadlines are May 30 and September 30.

Academic/Career Areas Nursing.

Award Scholarship for use in graduate years; not renewable. *Number:* 2. *Amount:* $2000.

Eligibility Requirements Applicant must be enrolled or expecting to enroll full or part-time at an institution or university. Applicant or parent of applicant must have employment or volunteer experience in designated career field. Available to U.S. and Canadian citizens.

Application Requirements Application, financial need analysis.

Contact Virginia Marx, Executive Secretary
National Association of Pediatric Nurse
Practitioners
1101 Kings Highway North, Suite 206
Cherry Hill, NJ 08034-1912
Phone: 856-667-1773
Fax: 856-667-7187
E-mail: napnap5@aol.com

NATIONAL HEMOPHILIA FOUNDATION
http://www.hemophilia.org

NATIONAL HEMOPHILIA FOUNDATION NURSING EXCELLENCE FELLOWSHIP • 801

Fellowship providing support for a registered nurse currently employed or interested in hemophilia care to conduct nursing research or clinical projects. Must be RN from an accredited nursing school enrolled in a graduate nursing program or practicing hemophilia nursing care. Submit application, letters of recommendation and description of proposed research project.

Academic/Career Areas Nursing.

Award Fellowship for use in graduate, or postgraduate years; not renewable. *Number:* 1. *Amount:* $10,000.

Eligibility Requirements Applicant must be enrolled or expecting to enroll at an institution or university.

Application Requirements Application, references, description of proposed research project. *Deadline:* April 1.

Contact Rita Barsky, Assistant Director
National Hemophilia Foundation
116 West 32nd Street, 11th Floor
New York, NY 10001
Phone: 212-328-3730
Fax: 212-328-3788
E-mail: rbarsky@hemophilia.org

NEBRASKA HEALTH AND HUMAN SERVICES SYSTEM, OFFICE OF RURAL HEALTH

STATE OF NEBRASKA LOAN REPAYMENT PROGRAM FOR RURAL HEALTH PROFESSIONALS
• See number 576

NEW MEXICO COMMISSION ON HIGHER EDUCATION
http://www.nmche.org

NEW MEXICO HEALTH PROFESSIONAL LOAN REPAYMENT PROGRAM
• See number 293

NORTH CAROLINA STATE EDUCATION ASSISTANCE AUTHORITY
http://www.cfnc.org

NURSE SCHOLARS PROGRAM— MASTER'S   • 802

Merit-based scholarship/loan program for North Carolina residents who are U.S. citizens and plan to enter the nursing profession full-time. Must plan to study in a North Carolina graduate program. Preference given to full-time students. Twelve months of service as a full-time nurse cancels one full year of support. Minimum of six months consecutive full-time employment with one employer is required to qualify for service cancellation. Contact nursing department at school student plans to attend for application and deadline.

Academic/Career Areas Nursing.

Award Forgivable loan for use in graduate years; not renewable. *Number:* up to 35. *Amount:* $3000–$6000.

Eligibility Requirements Applicant must be enrolled or expecting to enroll full or part-time at an institution or university; resident of North Carolina and studying in North Carolina. Available to U.S. citizens.

Contact Tony Bordeaux, Assistant Director, Health, Education and Welfare
North Carolina State Education Assistance Authority
PO Box 13663
Research Triangle, NC 27709-3663

NURSES' EDUCATION FUNDS, INC.
http://www.n-e-f.org

M. ELIZABETH CARNEGIE AND ESTELLE MASSEY OSBORNE SCHOLARSHIPS   • 803

Award for African-Americans who are registered nurses, members of national professional nursing organization, and are enrolled in or applying to a National League for Nursing-accredited graduate degree program in nursing. Must submit GRE or MAT scores. Write for application by February 1; include $10 for postage and handling. At the masters degree level, applicants will be supported for full-time study only. Doctoral study may be full-time or part-time.

Academic/Career Areas Nursing.

Award Scholarship for use in graduate years; not renewable. *Number:* 2. *Amount:* $2500–$10,000.

Eligibility Requirements Applicant must be Black (non-Hispanic); enrolled or expecting to enroll full or part-time at an institution or university and must have an interest in leadership. Applicant or parent of applicant must be member of any National Professional Nursing Association. Applicant or parent of applicant must have employment or volunteer experience in designated career field. Available to U.S. citizens.

Application Requirements Application, essay, references, test scores, transcript. *Fee:* $10. *Deadline:* March 1.

Contact Barbara Butler, Executive Director
Nurses' Education Funds, Inc.
555 West 57th Street
New York, NY 10019
Phone: 212-399-1428
Fax: 212-581-2368
E-mail: bbnef@aol.com

NURSING ECONOMIC$ FOUNDATION
http://www.ajj.com/services/pblshng/nej/default.htm

NURSING ECONOMIC$ FOUNDATION SCHOLARSHIPS   • 804

Up to four $5,000 scholarships are awarded to RNs in a master's or doctoral nursing program with an emphasis on administration or management at a school of nursing in the U.S. Applicant must plan to continue in the field of nursing with an interest in

Nursing Economic$ Foundation (continued)

nursing leadership, administration, or management. Citizens of other countries may apply as long as they attend U.S. institution.

Academic/Career Areas Nursing.

Award Scholarship for use in graduate years; not renewable. *Number:* 1–4. *Amount:* $5000.

Eligibility Requirements Applicant must be enrolled or expecting to enroll full or part-time at a four-year institution or university. Available to U.S. and non-U.S. citizens.

Application Requirements Application, resume, test scores, transcript. *Deadline:* May 1.

Contact Jo Ann Dinan, Executive Secretary
Nursing Economic$ Foundation
East Holly Avenue
Box 56
Pitman, NJ 08071-0056
Phone: 856-256-2318
Fax: 856-589-7463
E-mail: dinanj@ajj.com

NURSING FOUNDATION OF PENNSYLVANIA
http://www.psna.org

PAULINE THOMPSON CLINICAL RESEARCH AWARD • 805

Awards are given to a registered nurse enrolled in a graduate program who is conducting a clinical research project in nursing. The recipient will be the qualified applicant with the best-designed patient/client care research project. The applicant must be a member of the Pennsylvania State Nurses Association and a resident of Pennsylvania.

Academic/Career Areas Nursing.

Award Scholarship for use in graduate years; not renewable. *Number:* 2. *Amount:* $1000.

Eligibility Requirements Applicant must be enrolled or expecting to enroll at an institution or university and resident of Pennsylvania. Available to U.S. citizens.

Application Requirements Application, autobiography, essay, references, transcript. *Deadline:* May 10.

Contact Frances Manning, Executive Assistant
Nursing Foundation of Pennsylvania
2578 Interstate Drive
PO Box 68525
Harrisburg, PA 17106
Phone: 717-657-1222 Ext. 205
Fax: 717-657-3796
E-mail: psna@psna.org

ONS FOUNDATION
http://www.ons.org

ETHICS CAREER DEVELOPMENT AWARD • 806

One $3000 scholarship will be given to support a professional registered nurse in obtaining knowledge in clinical ethics by providing financial assistance to attend a continuing-education program that will further his or her professional goals and potential to contribute to oncology nursing. The candidate must be employed in oncology as a registered nurse working a minimum of 75% of his or her time in the area of research, clinical, administration education or advanced practice nursing and must possess a BSN or higher degree.

Academic/Career Areas Nursing.

Award Grant for use in graduate years; not renewable. *Number:* 1. *Amount:* $3000.

Eligibility Requirements Applicant must be enrolled or expecting to enroll at an institution or university. Available to U.S. and non-U.S. citizens.

Application Requirements *Deadline:* December 1.

Contact ONS Foundation
501 Holiday Drive
Pittsburgh, PA 15220-2749

NOVARTIS PHARMACEUTICALS POST-MASTER'S CERTIFICATE SCHOLARSHIPS • 807

One $3000 scholarship will be given to assist a nurse in furthering his or her education. Eligible applicants must be enrolled in (or applying to) a post-master's nurse practitioner certificate academic credit-bearing program in an NLN- or CCNE-accredited school of nursing. The candidate must also have a previous master's degree in nursing, a current license in and commitment to oncology nursing. Deadline: February 1.

Academic/Career Areas Nursing.

Award Scholarship for use in postgraduate years; not renewable. *Number:* 1. *Amount:* $3000.

Eligibility Requirements Applicant must be enrolled or expecting to enroll at an institution or university. Available to U.S. and non-U.S. citizens.

Application Requirements *Deadline:* February 1.

Contact ONS Foundation
501 Holiday Drive
Pittsburgh, PA 15220-2749

ONCOLOGY NURSING SOCIETY POST-MASTER'S CERTIFICATE SCHOLARSHIP • 808

One $3000 scholarship will be given to assist a nurse in furthering his or her education. Eligible applicants must be enrolled in (or applying to) a post-master's nurse practitioner certificate academic credit-bearing program in an NLN- or CCNE-accredited school of nursing. The candidate must also have a previous master's degree in nursing, a current license in and commitment to oncology nursing. Deadline: February 1.

Academic/Career Areas Nursing.

Award Scholarship for use in postgraduate years; not renewable. *Number:* 1. *Amount:* $3000.

Eligibility Requirements Applicant must be enrolled or expecting to enroll at an institution or university. Available to U.S. and non-U.S. citizens.

Application Requirements *Deadline:* February 1.

Contact ONS Foundation
501 Holiday Drive
Pittsburgh, PA 15220-2749

ONCOLOGY NURSING SOCIETY/AMGEN INC. EXCELLENCE IN PATIENT/PUBLIC EDUCATION AWARD • 809

One-time award for a registered nurse who is a member of the Oncology Nursing Society. Must have minimum two years experience in oncology nursing. Nominees should be oncology nurses who are involved in offering creative public or patient education. Deadline: August 15.

Academic/Career Areas Nursing.

Award Prize for use in graduate years; not renewable. *Amount:* $2000.

Eligibility Requirements Applicant must be enrolled or expecting to enroll at an institution or university. Applicant or parent of applicant must be member of Oncology Nursing Society. Applicant or parent of applicant must have employment or volunteer experience in designated career field.

Application Requirements Application. *Deadline:* August 15.

Contact ONS Foundation
501 Holiday Drive
Pittsburgh, PA 15220

ONCOLOGY NURSING SOCIETY/BRISTOL-MEYERS DISTINGUISHED RESEARCHER AWARD • 810

One-time award to recognize the contributions of a member who has conducted or promoted research enhancing oncology nursing. Must be member of ONS with a Ph.D. in nursing who demonstrates research and contributions to oncology nursing. Deadline: August 15.

Academic/Career Areas Nursing.

Award Prize for use in graduate years; not renewable. *Amount:* $3000.

Eligibility Requirements Applicant must be enrolled or expecting to enroll at an institution or university. Applicant or parent of applicant must be member of Oncology Nursing Society. Applicant or

parent of applicant must have employment or volunteer experience in designated career field. Available to U.S. citizens.

Application Requirements *Deadline:* August 15.

Contact ONS Foundation
501 Holiday Drive
Pittsburgh, PA 15220

ONS FOUNDATION DOCTORAL SCHOLARSHIPS • 811

Three scholarships available to registered nurses who have demonstrated interest and commitment to oncology nursing and who currently hold a license to practice as a registered nurse. Must be enrolled or applying to a doctoral nursing or related program. May not have previously received a doctoral scholarship from the Foundation. One-time award of $3000. Deadline: February 1.

Academic/Career Areas Nursing.

Award Scholarship for use in graduate, or postgraduate years; not renewable. *Number:* 3. *Amount:* $3000.

Eligibility Requirements Applicant must be enrolled or expecting to enroll full or part-time at an institution or university. Applicant or parent of applicant must have employment or volunteer experience in designated career field.

Application Requirements Application, references, transcript. *Deadline:* February 1.

Contact ONS Foundation
501 Holiday Drive
Pittsburgh, PA 15220

ONS FOUNDATION ETHNIC MINORITY MASTER'S SCHOLARSHIP • 812

Two awards for registered nurses with demonstrated interest in oncology nursing. Must be enrolled in a graduate nursing program in an NLN-accredited school, and must currently hold a license to practice as a registered nurse. Must be a minority student and not have received an MA scholarship. One-time award of $3000.

Academic/Career Areas Nursing.

Award Scholarship for use in graduate years; not renewable. *Number:* 2. *Amount:* $3000.

Eligibility Requirements Applicant must be American Indian/Alaska Native, Asian/Pacific Islander, Black (non-Hispanic), or Hispanic and enrolled or expecting to enroll full or part-time at an institution or university. Applicant or parent of applicant must have employment or volunteer experience in designated career field.

Application Requirements Application, transcript. *Deadline:* February 1.

Contact ONS Foundation
501 Holiday Drive
Pittsburgh, PA 15220

ONS FOUNDATION ETHNIC MINORITY RESEARCHER AND MENTORSHIP GRANTS
• *See number 586*

ONS FOUNDATION MASTER'S SCHOLARSHIP
• **813**

Nine awards for registered nurses with demonstrated interest in oncology. Must be currently enrolled in a graduate nursing program at an NLN-accredited school and currently hold a license to practice as a registered nurse. May be a full-time or part-time student. Must not have previously received an MA scholarship. One-time award of $3000. Deadline: February 1.

Academic/Career Areas Nursing.

Award Scholarship for use in graduate years; not renewable. *Number:* 9. *Amount:* $3000.

Eligibility Requirements Applicant must be enrolled or expecting to enroll full or part-time at an institution or university. Applicant or parent of applicant must have employment or volunteer experience in designated career field.

Application Requirements Application, transcript. *Deadline:* February 1.

Contact ONS Foundation
501 Holiday Drive
Pittsburgh, PA 15220

ONS FOUNDATION NOVICE RESEARCHER AND MENTORSHIP GRANTS
• *See number 587*

ONS FOUNDATION ORTHO BIOTECH RESEARCH FELLOWSHIP
• *See number 588*

ONS FOUNDATION SIGMA THETA TAU INTERNATIONAL RESEARCH GRANT
• **814**

One award for a registered nurse actively involved in some aspect of cancer patient care, education, or research. Must be a Sigma Theta Tau member. Author is encouraged to publish research results in Oncology Nursing Foundation or Sigma Theta Tau International publications. Research must be clinically focused. One-time award of $10,000. Deadline: November 1.

Academic/Career Areas Nursing.

Award Grant for use in graduate years; not renewable. *Number:* 1. *Amount:* $10,000.

Eligibility Requirements Applicant must be enrolled or expecting to enroll at an institution or university. Applicant or parent of applicant must be member of Sigma Theta Tau International. Applicant or parent of applicant must have employment or volunteer experience in designated career field.

Application Requirements Application. *Deadline:* November 1.

Contact ONS Foundation
501 Holiday Drive
Pittsburgh, PA 15220-2749

ONS FOUNDATION/AMERICAN BRAIN TUMOR ASSOCIATION GRANT
• *See number 589*

ONS FOUNDATION/AMGEN INC. RESEARCH GRANT
• **815**

One grant for a registered nurse actively involved in some aspect of cancer patient care, education, or research. Award to be used to support research. Research must be clinically focused. One-time award of $5,000. Deadline: November 1.

Academic/Career Areas Nursing.

Award Grant for use in graduate years; not renewable. *Number:* 1. *Amount:* $5000.

Eligibility Requirements Applicant must be enrolled or expecting to enroll at an institution or university. Applicant or parent of applicant must have employment or volunteer experience in designated career field.

Application Requirements Application. *Deadline:* November 1.

Contact ONS Foundation
501 Holiday Drive
Pittsburgh, PA 15220

ONS FOUNDATION/ANN OLSON MEMORIAL DOCTORAL SCHOLARSHIP
• **816**

One award for registered nurse with demonstrated interest in oncology nursing who is currently enrolled in or applying to doctoral nursing degree or related program. One-time award of $3000. Deadline: February 1.

Academic/Career Areas Nursing.

Award Scholarship for use in graduate, or postgraduate years; not renewable. *Number:* 1. *Amount:* $3000.

Eligibility Requirements Applicant must be enrolled or expecting to enroll full or part-time at an institution or university. Applicant or parent of applicant must have employment or volunteer experience in designated career field. Available to U.S. and non-U.S. citizens.

Application Requirements Application, references, transcript. *Deadline:* February 1.

Contact Bonny Revo, Executive Assistant
ONS Foundation
501 Holiday Drive
Pittsburgh, PA 15220
Phone: 412-921-7373 Ext. 278
Fax: 412-921-6565

ONS FOUNDATION/AVENTIS RESEARCH FELLOWSHIP
• *See number 590*

ONS FOUNDATION/AVENTIS RESEARCH GRANT
• *See number 591*

ONS FOUNDATION/BRISTOL-MYERS ONCOLOGY DIVISION COMMUNITY HEALTH RESEARCH GRANT
• *See number 592*

ONS FOUNDATION/BRISTOL-MYERS ONCOLOGY DIVISION RESEARCH GRANT
• *See number 593*

ONS FOUNDATION/NURSING CERTIFICATION CORPORATION MASTER'S SCHOLARSHIP • 817

Two awards for registered nurses with demonstrated interest in oncology nursing. Must be currently enrolled in a graduate nursing program at an NLN-accredited school and must currently hold a license to practice as a registered nurse. May be a full-time or part-time student. Must not have received any MA scholarship previously from Foundation. One-time award of $3000. Deadline: February 1.

Academic/Career Areas Nursing.

Award Scholarship for use in graduate years; not renewable. *Number:* 2. *Amount:* $3000.

Eligibility Requirements Applicant must be enrolled or expecting to enroll full or part-time at an institution or university. Applicant or parent of applicant must have employment or volunteer experience in designated career field. Available to U.S. citizens.

Application Requirements Application, transcript. *Deadline:* February 1.

Contact ONS Foundation
501 Holiday Drive
Pittsburgh, PA 15220

ONS FOUNDATION/ONCOLOGY NURSING CERTIFICATION CORPORATION ONCOLOGY NURSING EDUCATION RESEARCH GRANT
• *See number 594*

ONS FOUNDATION/ONCOLOGY NURSING CERTIFICATION CORPORATION ONCOLOGY NURSING RESEARCH GRANT • 818

One award for a registered nurse actively involved in some aspect of cancer patient care, education, or research. Award to improve cancer patient care. One-time award of $7500. Deadline: November 1.

Academic/Career Areas Nursing.

Award Scholarship for use in graduate years; not renewable. *Number:* 1. *Amount:* $7500.

Eligibility Requirements Applicant must be enrolled or expecting to enroll at an institution or

university. Applicant or parent of applicant must have employment or volunteer experience in designated career field.

Application Requirements Application. *Deadline:* November 1.

Contact ONS Foundation
501 Holiday Drive
Pittsburgh, PA 15220

ONS FOUNDATION/ORTHO BIOTECH RESEARCH GRANT
• *See number 595*

ONS FOUNDATION/PHARMACIA ONCOLOGY, INC. MASTER'S SCHOLARSHIP • 819

One-time award for registered nurse with demonstrated interest in oncology nursing who is currently enrolled in graduate nursing degree program that has application to oncology nursing. Must attend NLN-accredited school and may be full or part-time student. One award of $3000. Deadline: February 1.

Academic/Career Areas Nursing.

Award Scholarship for use in graduate years; not renewable. *Number:* 1. *Amount:* $3000.

Eligibility Requirements Applicant must be enrolled or expecting to enroll full or part-time at an institution or university. Applicant or parent of applicant must have employment or volunteer experience in designated career field. Available to U.S. and non-U.S. citizens.

Application Requirements Application, transcript. *Deadline:* February 1.

Contact ONS Foundation
501 Holiday Drive
Pittsburgh, PA 15220

ONS FOUNDATION/THOMAS JORDAN DOCTORAL SCHOLARSHIP • 820

One award to improve oncology nursing by assisting registered nurses in fulfilling their education. Must be currently enrolled in or applying to a doctoral nursing degree program. One-time award of $3000. One award available per level of education. Deadline: February 1.

Academic/Career Areas Nursing.

Award Scholarship for use in graduate years; not renewable. *Number:* 1. *Amount:* $3000.

Eligibility Requirements Applicant must be enrolled or expecting to enroll full or part-time at an institution or university. Applicant or parent of applicant must have employment or volunteer experience in designated career field. Available to U.S. and non-U.S. citizens.

ONS Foundation (continued)

Application Requirements Application, references, transcript. *Deadline:* February 1.

Contact ONS Foundation
501 Holiday Drive
Pittsburgh, PA 15220

ONS FOUNDATION/TRISH GREENE RESEARCH GRANT
• *See number 596*

ONS/KOMEN FOUNDATION EXCELLENCE IN BREAST CANCER EDUCATION AWARD • 821

To recognize and support dedication to educating the public or patients about breast cancer. Must be RN, member of ONS, and have educated the public on early detection devices and early detection screening programs. Deadline: August 15.

Academic/Career Areas Nursing.

Award Prize for use in graduate years; not renewable. *Number:* 1. *Amount:* $4000.

Eligibility Requirements Applicant must be enrolled or expecting to enroll at an institution or university. Applicant or parent of applicant must be member of Oncology Nursing Society. Applicant or parent of applicant must have employment or volunteer experience in designated career field.

Application Requirements Application. *Deadline:* August 15.

Contact ONS Foundation
501 Holiday Drive
Pittsburgh, PA 15220

ONS/MARY NOWOTNY EXCELLENCE IN CANCER NURSING EDUCATION AWARD • 822

To recognize and support excellence in cancer nursing education. Must be an RN and member of ONS with at least two years experience in oncology education. Must contribute to the development of professional oncology practice and meet needs for education in geographic area. Deadline: August 15.

Academic/Career Areas Nursing.

Award Prize for use in graduate years; not renewable. *Number:* 1. *Amount:* $2000.

Eligibility Requirements Applicant must be enrolled or expecting to enroll at an institution or university. Applicant or parent of applicant must be member of Oncology Nursing Society. Applicant or parent of applicant must have employment or volunteer experience in designated career field or teaching. Available to U.S. citizens.

Application Requirements Application. *Deadline:* August 15.

Contact ONS Foundation
501 Holiday Drive
Pittsburgh, PA 15220-2749

ONS/VARIAN EXCELLENCE IN RADIATION THERAPY NURSING AWARD • 823

One-time award to recognize and support excellence in radiation therapy nursing. Must be an RN and active ONS member. Should be a recognized expert in the field of radiation through publications, presentations, research, or peer review. Deadline: August 15.

Academic/Career Areas Nursing.

Award Prize for use in graduate years; not renewable. *Number:* 1. *Amount:* $1000.

Eligibility Requirements Applicant must be enrolled or expecting to enroll at an institution or university. Applicant or parent of applicant must be member of Oncology Nursing Society. Applicant or parent of applicant must have employment or volunteer experience in designated career field. Available to U.S. citizens.

Application Requirements Application. *Deadline:* August 15.

Contact ONS Foundation
501 Holiday Drive
Pittsburgh, PA 15220-2749

PFIZER, INC. - US PHARMACEUTICALS GROUP
http://www.physicianscientist.com

PFIZER POSTDOCTORAL FELLOWSHIPS IN NURSING RESEARCH
• *See number 608*

SIGMA THETA TAU INTERNATIONAL
http://www.nursingsociety.org

PATRICIA SMITH CHRISTENSEN SCHOLARSHIP • 824

One-time award given to assist graduate nursing student pursuing their education in the area of maternal child or pediatric nursing. Awarded once every two years (in odd-numbered years) to the student with the greatest demonstrated potential for advanced study and research. Preference will be given to a Canadian resident, other qualifications being equal.

Academic/Career Areas Nursing.

Award Scholarship for use in graduate, or postgraduate years; not renewable. *Number:* 1. *Amount:* $1000.

Eligibility Requirements Applicant must be enrolled or expecting to enroll at an institution or university. Applicant or parent of applicant must have employment or volunteer experience in designated career field. Available to U.S. and non-U.S. citizens.

Application Requirements Essay, references, transcript, curriculum vitae.

Contact Tara Bateman, Research Services Specialist
Sigma Theta Tau International
550 West North Street
Indianapolis, IN 46202
Phone: 888-634-7575
Fax: 317-634-8188
E-mail: research@stti.iupui.edu

ROSEMARY BERKEL CRISP RESEARCH AWARD
• 825

Grant to a registered nurse with a current license and a master's degree or higher. Award to support nursing research in the critical areas of women's health, oncology, and infant/child care. Must be a member of Sigma Theta Tau International. Some preference given to residents of Illinois, Missouri, Arkansas, Kentucky, and Tennessee. Submit proposal with application materials by December 1. This is a research grant, not to be used for educational expenses. Award money is received from the Harry L. Crisp II and Rosemary Berkel Crisp Foundation which is given to Sigma Theta Tau Internationals Research Endowment.

Academic/Career Areas Nursing.

Award Grant for use in postgraduate years; not renewable. *Number:* 1. *Amount:* up to $5000.

Eligibility Requirements Applicant must be enrolled or expecting to enroll at an institution or university. Applicant or parent of applicant must be member of Sigma Theta Tau International. Applicant or parent of applicant must have employment or volunteer experience in designated career field. Available to U.S. and non-U.S. citizens.

Application Requirements Application, references, proposal, IRB approval (as needed), budget. *Deadline:* December 1.

Contact Research Grant
Sigma Theta Tau International
550 West North Street
Indianapolis, IN 46202
Phone: 317-634-8171 Ext. 263
Fax: 317-634-8188
E-mail: research@stti.iupui.edu

SIGMA THETA TAU INTERNATIONAL / EMERGENCY NURSES ASSOCIATION FOUNDATION GRANT
• 826

Sigma Theta Tau International and the Emergency Nurses Association Foundation co-sponsor this award for qualified nurses. Principal Investigator is required to be a registered nurse. Team members may be from other disciplines. Principal Investigator is required to have a Master's Degree. Must submit a complete application with signed research agreement and be

ready to, or have already started the research project. This is a research grant, not to be used for educational expenses.

Academic/Career Areas Nursing.

Award Grant for use in postgraduate years; not renewable. *Number:* 1. *Amount:* up to $6000.

Eligibility Requirements Applicant must be enrolled or expecting to enroll at an institution or university. Applicant or parent of applicant must have employment or volunteer experience in designated career field. Available to U.S. and non-U.S. citizens.

Application Requirements Application, proposal. *Deadline:* February 1.

Contact ENA Foundation
Sigma Theta Tau International
915 Lee Street
Des Plaines, IL 60016-6569
Phone: 847-460-4100
Fax: 847-460-4005

SIGMA THETA TAU INTERNATIONAL SMALL RESEARCH GRANT
• 827

Grant for registered nurses with current license and master's degree. Grant has no specific focus, but is to encourage qualified nurses to contribute to the advancement of nursing through research. Submit proposal for pilot and/or developmental research with application materials by December 1. This is a research grant, not to be used for educational expenses.

Academic/Career Areas Nursing.

Award Grant for use in postgraduate years; not renewable. *Number:* 10–15. *Amount:* up to $5000.

Eligibility Requirements Applicant must be enrolled or expecting to enroll at an institution or university. Applicant or parent of applicant must have employment or volunteer experience in designated career field. Available to U.S. and non-U.S. citizens.

Application Requirements Application, references, proposal, IRB approval (as needed), budget. *Deadline:* December 1.

Contact Research Grants
Sigma Theta Tau International
550 West North Street
Indianapolis, IN 46202
Phone: 317-634-8171
Fax: 317-634-8188
E-mail: research@stti.iupui.edu

SIGMA THETA TAU INTERNATIONAL/ AMERICAN ASSOCIATION OF CRITICAL CARE NURSES CRITICAL CARE GRANT
• 828

Sigma Theta Tau International and the American Association of Critical Care Nurses co-sponsor this

Nursing

Sigma Theta Tau International (continued)

award for registered nurses with current license. Grant proposals must be relevant to critical care nursing practice. Must have received a Master's degree. This is a research grant, not to be used for educational expenses.

Academic/Career Areas Nursing.

Award Grant for use in postgraduate years; not renewable. *Number:* 1. *Amount:* up to $10,000.

Eligibility Requirements Applicant must be enrolled or expecting to enroll at an institution or university. Applicant or parent of applicant must have employment or volunteer experience in designated career field. Available to U.S. and non-U.S. citizens.

Application Requirements Application, proposal. *Deadline:* October 1.

Contact American Association of Critical Care Nurses
Sigma Theta Tau International
Department of Research 101 Colombia
Aliso Viejo, CA 92656-1491
Phone: 800-899-2226
Fax: 949-362-2020

SIGMA THETA TAU INTERNATIONAL/ ASSOCIATION OF OPERATING ROOM NURSES GRANT • 829

Sigma Theta Tau International and the Association of Operating Room Nurses co-sponsor this award for qualified nurses. Principal investigator required to be a registered nurse (with current license) in the perioperative setting or a registered nurse who demonstrates interest in or significant contributions to perioperative nursing practice. Must have, at a minimum, a master's degree in nursing. Membership in either organization is acceptable but not required. Submit a completed AORN research application. This is a research grant, not to be used for educational expenses.

Academic/Career Areas Nursing.

Award Grant for use in postgraduate years; not renewable. *Number:* 1. *Amount:* up to $10,000.

Eligibility Requirements Applicant must be enrolled or expecting to enroll at an institution or university. Applicant or parent of applicant must have employment or volunteer experience in designated career field. Available to U.S. and non-U.S. citizens.

Application Requirements Application, proposal. *Deadline:* April 1.

Contact Association of Operating Room Nurses
Sigma Theta Tau International
2170 South Parker Road, Suite 3000
Denver, CO 80231-5711
Phone: 800-755-2676 Ext. 277
Fax: 303-750-2927
E-mail: mparlapiano@aorn.org

SIGMA THETA TAU INTERNATIONAL/ ONCOLOGY NURSING SOCIETY GRANT • 830

Sigma Theta Tau International and the Oncology Nursing Society co-sponsor this award for a registered nurse actively involved in some aspect of cancer patient care, education, or research. Must have received a Master's Degree. Preference will be given to Sigma Theta Tau members, others qualifications being equal. This is a research grant, not to be used for educational expenses.

Academic/Career Areas Nursing.

Award Grant for use in postgraduate years; not renewable. *Number:* 1. *Amount:* up to $10,000.

Eligibility Requirements Applicant must be enrolled or expecting to enroll at an institution or university. Applicant or parent of applicant must have employment or volunteer experience in designated career field. Available to U.S. and non-U.S. citizens.

Application Requirements Application, proposal. *Deadline:* November 1.

Contact Oncology Nursing Foundation
Sigma Theta Tau International
501 Holiday Drive
Pittsburgh, PA 15220-2749
Phone: 412-921-7373
Fax: 412-921-6565

SIGMA THETA TAU INTERNATIONAL/ REHABILITATION NURSING FOUNDATION GRANT • 831

Sigma Theta Tau International and the Rehabilitation Nursing Foundation cosponsor this award for qualified nurses. Principal investigator is required to be a registered nurse in rehabilitation or a registered nurse who demonstrates interest in and significant contribution to rehabilitation nursing. Proposals that address the clinical practice, educational or administrative dimensions of rehabilitation nursing are requested. Quantitative and qualitative research projects will be accepted for review. Must have ability to complete project within two years of initial funding. Principal investigator must have a master's degree in nursing. This is a research grant, not to be used for educational expenses.

Academic/Career Areas Nursing.

Award Grant for use in postgraduate years; not renewable. *Number:* 1. *Amount:* up to $6000.

Eligibility Requirements Applicant must be enrolled or expecting to enroll at an institution or university. Applicant or parent of applicant must have employment or volunteer experience in designated career field. Available to U.S. and non-U.S. citizens.

Application Requirements Application, proposal. *Deadline:* April 1.

Contact Rehabilitation Nursing Foundation
Sigma Theta Tau International
4700 West Lake Avenue
Glenview, IL 60025
Phone: 800-229-7530
E-mail: info@rehabnurse.org

SIGMA THETA TAU INTERNATIONAL/AMERICAN ASSOCIATION OF DIABETES EDUCATORS GRANT • 832

Sigma Theta Tau International and the American Association of Diabetes Educators co-sponsor this award for qualified nurses. Principal Investigator must be a registered nurse. Team members may be from other disciplines. Must have received a Master's degree and have ability to complete project one year from funding date. Preference will be given to Sigma Theta Tau members, other qualifications being equal. This is a research grant, not to be used for educational expenses.

Academic/Career Areas Nursing.

Award Grant for use in postgraduate years; not renewable. *Number:* 1. *Amount:* up to $6000.

Eligibility Requirements Applicant must be enrolled or expecting to enroll at an institution or university. Applicant or parent of applicant must have employment or volunteer experience in designated career field. Available to U.S. and non-U.S. citizens.

Application Requirements Application, proposal. *Deadline:* October 1.

Contact AADE Foundation Awards
Sigma Theta Tau International
100 West Monroe Street, 4th Floor
Chicago, IL 60603

SIGMA THETA TAU INTERNATIONAL/AMERICAN NEPHROLOGY NURSES' ASSOCIATION GRANT • 833

Sigma Theta Tau International and the American Nephrology Nurses Association co-sponsor this award for registered nurse with current license. Must have received Master's degree. Preference will be given to Sigma Theta Tau members, other qualifications being equal. This is a research grant, not be used for educational expenses.

Academic/Career Areas Nursing.

Award Grant for use in postgraduate years; not renewable. *Number:* 1. *Amount:* up to $6000.

Eligibility Requirements Applicant must be enrolled or expecting to enroll at an institution or university. Applicant or parent of applicant must have employment or volunteer experience in designated career field. Available to U.S. and non-U.S. citizens.

Application Requirements Application, proposal. *Deadline:* October 31.

Contact c/o American Nephrology Nurses'
Association
Sigma Theta Tau International
East Holly Avenue, Box 56
Pitman, NJ 08071-0056
Phone: 856-256-2320

SIGMA THETA TAU INTERNATIONAL/AMERICAN NURSES FOUNDATION GRANT • 834

Sigma Theta Tau International and the American Nurses Foundation co-sponsors this award for registered nurses with current license. Must have received a Master's degree. Must have submitted a complete research application package. Must be ready to start the research project. Must have signed a Sigma Theta Tau research agreement. This is a research grant, not to be used for educational expenses. For off-numbered years, contact American Nurses Foundation. In even-numbered years, contact Sigma Theta Tau International.

Academic/Career Areas Nursing.

Award Grant for use in postgraduate years; not renewable. *Number:* 1. *Amount:* up to $7500.

Eligibility Requirements Applicant must be enrolled or expecting to enroll at an institution or university. Applicant or parent of applicant must have employment or volunteer experience in designated career field. Available to U.S. and non-U.S. citizens.

Application Requirements Application, proposal. *Deadline:* May 1.

Contact Sigma Theta Tau International
c/o American Nurses Foundation, 600
Maryland Avenue, S.W., Suite 100
West
Washington, DC 20024-2571
Phone: 202-651-7071
Fax: 202-651-7354

VIRGINIA HENDERSON/SIGMA THETA TAU INTERNATIONAL CLINICAL RESEARCH GRANT • 835

Biennial grant to a registered nurse actively involved in some aspect of health care delivery, education, or research in a clinical setting. Must have a master's degree in nursing and be a member of Sigma Theta Tau International. Purpose is to encourage the research career development of clinically-based nurses through support of clinically-oriented research. Submit proposal with application materials by December 1. This is an educational grant, not to be used for educational expenses. Award given out once every two years.

Academic/Career Areas Nursing.

Sigma Theta Tau International (continued)

Award Grant for use in postgraduate years; not renewable. *Number:* 1. *Amount:* up to $5000.

Eligibility Requirements Applicant must be enrolled or expecting to enroll at an institution or university. Applicant or parent of applicant must be member of Sigma Theta Tau International. Applicant or parent of applicant must have employment or volunteer experience in designated career field. Available to U.S. and non-U.S. citizens.

Application Requirements Application, references, proposal. *Deadline:* December 1.

Contact Research Grants
Sigma Theta Tau International
550 West North Street
Indianapolis, IN 46202
Phone: 317-634-8171
Fax: 317-634-8188
E-mail: research@stti.iupui.edu

SIGMA THETA TAU INTERNATIONAL/ AMERICAN NEPHROLOGY NURSES' ASSOCIATION
http://www.annanurse.org

SIGMA THETA TAU INTERNATIONAL/AMERICAN NEPHROLOGY NURSES' ASSOCIATION GRANT • 836

Grant to registered nurse with current license and Master's degree for research related to nephrology nursing practice. Other qualifications being equal, preference will be given to Sigma Theta Tau members. Submit proposal and application materials by November 1.

Academic/Career Areas Nursing.

Award Grant for use in postgraduate years; not renewable. *Number:* 1. *Amount:* up to $6000.

Eligibility Requirements Applicant must be enrolled or expecting to enroll at an institution or university. Applicant or parent of applicant must have employment or volunteer experience in designated career field. Available to U.S. citizens.

Application Requirements Application, references. *Deadline:* November 1.

Contact American Nephrology Nurses' Association
Sigma Theta Tau International/American Nephrology Nurses' Association
East Holly Avenue, Box 56
Pitman, NJ 08071-0056
Phone: 856-256-2320
Fax: 856-589-7463

UNITED DAUGHTERS OF THE CONFEDERACY
http://www.hqudc.org

SHIP ISLAND - MRS. J.O. JONES MEMORIAL SCHOLARSHIP • 837

Award for full-time graduate student who is a descendant of a Confederate soldier pursuing the study of nursing. Must carry a minimum of 12 credit hours each semester and have a minimum 3.0 GPA. Submit letter of endorsement from sponsoring chapter of the United Daughters of the Confederacy.

Academic/Career Areas Nursing.

Award Scholarship for use in graduate years; renewable. *Number:* 1–2. *Amount:* $800–$1000.

Eligibility Requirements Applicant must be enrolled or expecting to enroll full-time at an institution or university. Applicant or parent of applicant must be member of United Daughters of the Confederacy. Applicant must have 3.0 GPA or higher. Available to U.S. citizens.

Application Requirements Application, essay, financial need analysis, photo, references, self-addressed stamped envelope, transcript. *Deadline:* February 15.

Contact Second Vice President General
United Daughters of the Confederacy
328 North Boulevard
Richmond, VA 23220-4057
Phone: 804-355-1636

UNITED STATES ARMY RECRUITING COMMAND
http://www.goarmy.com

ARMED FORCES HEALTH PROFESSIONS SCHOLARSHIP PROGRAM-ARMY
• *See number 23*

UNIFORMED SERVICES UNIVERSITY OF HEALTH SCIENCES MASTER OF SCIENCE IN NURSE ANESTHESIA • 838

Students receive full pay and allowances commensurate with military rank during entire master's program. Tuition, fees and books paid by the Army. Active-duty Army obligation is four years upon completion of program. Must undergo physical examination.

Academic/Career Areas Nursing.

Award Scholarship for use in graduate years; not renewable. *Number:* 1–10.

Eligibility Requirements Applicant must be age 21-47 and enrolled or expecting to enroll at an institution or university. Available to U.S. citizens. Applicant must have served in the Army.

Application Requirements Application, references, transcript. *Deadline:* June 1.

Contact United States Army Recruiting Command
Health Services Directorate 1307 Third
Avenue
Fort Knox, KY 40121-2726

UNIVERSITY OF TEXAS-HOUSTON HEALTH SCIENCE MASTER OF SCIENCE DEGREE IN NURSE ANESTHESIA • 839

Award provides full pay and allowances commensurate with military rank during entire master's program. Tuition and fees paid by the Army. Reimbursed up to $300 a year for books. Active-duty obligation is four years upon completion of program. Must undergo physical examination. Ten one-time awards available.

Academic/Career Areas Nursing.

Award Scholarship for use in graduate years; not renewable. *Number:* 1–10.

Eligibility Requirements Applicant must be age 21-47 and enrolled or expecting to enroll at an institution or university. Available to U.S. citizens. Applicant must have served in the Army.

Application Requirements Application, interview, references, test scores, transcript. *Deadline:* June 1.

Contact United States Army Recruiting Command
Health Services Directorate 1307 Third
Avenue
Fort Knox, KY 40121-2726

VIRGINIA DEPARTMENT OF HEALTH, OFFICE OF HEALTH POLICY AND PLANNING
http://www.vdh.state.va.us/primcare/index.html

NURSE PRACTITIONERS/NURSE MIDWIFE PROGRAM SCHOLARSHIPS • 840

One-time award for nurse practitioner/nurse midwife students who have been residents of Virginia for at least one year. Must attend a full-time nursing program in Virginia. Recipient must agree to work in an underserved community in Virginia following graduation or in a nurse midwifery program in a nearby state. Recipient must work in this area for a period of years equal to the number of annual scholarships received. Minimum 3.0 GPA required.

Academic/Career Areas Nursing.

Award Scholarship for use in graduate, or postgraduate years; not renewable. *Amount:* $5000.

Eligibility Requirements Applicant must be enrolled or expecting to enroll full-time at a four-year institution or university; resident of Virginia and studying in Virginia. Applicant must have 3.0 GPA or higher. Available to U.S. citizens.

Application Requirements Application, references, transcript. *Deadline:* June 30.

Contact Norma Marrin, Business Manager
Virginia Department of Health, Office of
Health Policy and Planning
PO Box 2448
Richmond, VA 23218
Phone: 804-371-4090
Fax: 804-371-0116
E-mail: nmarrin@vdh.state.va.us

VISITING NURSE ASSOCIATION OF CENTRAL JERSEY
http://www.vnacj.org

MARCIA GRANUCCI MEMORIAL SCHOLARSHIP • 841

The Marcia Granucci Memorial Fund provides scholarships to graduate nursing students who intend to pursue an educational concentration in psychiatric/mental health or community health nursing. Requirements include New Jersey residency, part-time or full-time graduate status at a National League of Nursing (NLN)-accredited institution, current licensure, and a minimum 3.0 GPA.

Academic/Career Areas Nursing.

Award Scholarship for use in graduate years; renewable. *Number:* 1. *Amount:* $2000.

Eligibility Requirements Applicant must be enrolled or expecting to enroll full or part-time at an institution or university and resident of New Jersey. Applicant must have 3.0 GPA or higher. Available to U.S. and non-U.S. citizens.

Application Requirements Application, essay, interview, references, test scores, transcript. *Deadline:* May 15.

Contact Peter Rich, Director of Development
Visiting Nurse Association of Central
Jersey
141 Bodman Place
Red Bank, NJ 07701
Phone: 732-224-6760
Fax: 732-747-2822
E-mail: prich@vnacj.org

PEACE AND CONFLICT STUDIES

AMERICAN COUNCIL OF TEACHERS OF RUSSIAN
http://www.actr.org

TITLE VIII RESEARCH SCHOLAR AND COMBINED RESEARCH AND LANGUAGE STUDY PROGRAM
• *See number 114*

CHINA TIMES CULTURAL FOUNDATION

CHINA TIMES CULTURAL FOUNDATION DOCTORAL DISSERTATION RESEARCH IN CHINESE STUDIES SCHOLARSHIPS
• *See number 122*

UNITED STATES ARMY CENTER OF MILITARY HISTORY
http://www.army.mil/cmh-pg

DISSERTATION YEAR FELLOWSHIP
• *See number 657*

UNITED STATES INSTITUTE OF PEACE
http://www.usip.org

JENNINGS RANDOLPH SENIOR FELLOW AWARD
• *See number 333*

PEACE SCHOLAR DISSERTATION FELLOWSHIP
• *See number 334*

PERFORMING ARTS

ALBERTA HERITAGE SCHOLARSHIP FUND
http://www.alis.gov.ab.ca/scholarships

ALBERTA FOUNDATION FOR THE ARTS GRADUATE LEVEL SCHOLARSHIPS
• *See number 160*

ALPHA DELTA KAPPA FOUNDATION
http://www.alphadeltakappa.org

APHA DELTA KAPPA FOUNDATION FINE ARTS GRANTS
• *See number 161*

AMERICAN ORFF-SCHULWERK ASSOCIATION
http://www.aosa.org

AMERICAN ORFF-SCHULWERK ASSOCIATION RESEARCH GRANT
• *See number 347*

AOSA-TRAINING AND PROJECTS FUND
• *See number 348*

GUNILD KEETMAN ASSISTANCE FUND
• *See number 349*

SHIELDS-GILLESPIE SCHOLARSHIP
• *See number 350*

ASIAN CULTURAL COUNCIL
http://www.asianculturalcouncil.org

ASIAN ART AND RELIGION FELLOWSHIPS
• *See number 90*

ASIAN CULTURAL COUNCIL FELLOWSHIPS
• *See number 91*

ASIAN CULTURAL COUNCIL HUMANITIES FELLOWSHIPS
• *See number 92*

ASIAN CULTURAL COUNCIL RESIDENCY PROGRAM IN ASIA
• *See number 140*

FORD FOUNDATION FELLOWSHIPS
• *See number 141*

FONDATION DES ETATS-UNIS
http://www.feusa.org

HARRIET HALE WOOLLEY SCHOLARSHIP • **842**

The award finances the studies of musicians or visual artists in Paris. It is necessary to have an affiliation with a French institution or a recognized professional who will welcome the visiting artist. The deadline is January 31.

Academic/Career Areas Performing Arts.

Award Scholarship for use in graduate, or postgraduate years; not renewable. *Number:* 1–4. *Amount:* $4000–$8500.

Eligibility Requirements Applicant must be age 21-29; enrolled or expecting to enroll full-time at an institution or university and single. Applicant must have 2.5 GPA or higher. Available to U.S. citizens.

Application Requirements Application, essay, photo, portfolio, resume, references, self-addressed stamped envelope, transcript. *Deadline:* January 31.

Contact Terence Murphy, Director
Fondation des Etats-Unis
15, Boulevard Jourdan
Paris Cedex 14 75690
France
Phone: 33-1-5380688 Ext. 0
Fax: 33-1-5380689 Ext. 9
E-mail: fondusa@iway.fr

KURT WEILL FOUNDATION FOR MUSIC
http://www.kwf.org

KURT WEILL FOUNDATION FOR MUSIC GRANTS PROGRAM • **843**

One-time awards for uses that must perpetuate, either through performance or research, the legacy of Kurt Weill. Deadline is November 1. Write for more information.

Academic/Career Areas Performing Arts.

Award Grant for use in graduate years; not renewable. *Number:* 10–30. *Amount:* $750–$5000.

Eligibility Requirements Applicant must be enrolled or expecting to enroll at a four-year institution or university and must have an interest in music/singing. Available to U.S. and non-U.S. citizens.

Application Requirements Application. *Deadline:* November 1.

Contact Carolyn Weber, Associate Director for Program Administration
Kurt Weill Foundation for Music
7 East 20th Street
New York, NY 10003-1106
E-mail: kwfinfo@kwf.org

LOREN L. ZACHARY SOCIETY FOR THE PERFORMING ARTS

NATIONAL VOCAL COMPETITION FOR YOUNG OPERA SINGERS • 844

Competition for experienced opera singers pursuing a career. Women must be 21 to 33 years old; men must be 21-35. Held annually in New York and Los Angeles. Top prize is $10,000. Submit copy of birth certificate or passport. To request application, include self-addressed stamped envelope. Application fee: $35. 2002 New York deadline is January 29; Los Angeles deadline is March 16.

Academic/Career Areas Performing Arts.

Award Prize for use in graduate, or postgraduate years; not renewable. *Number:* 10.

Eligibility Requirements Applicant must be age 21-35; enrolled or expecting to enroll at an institution or university and must have an interest in music/singing. Available to U.S. and Canadian citizens.

Application Requirements Application, applicant must enter a contest, resume, self-addressed stamped envelope, copy of birth certificate or passport. *Fee:* $35.

Contact Nedra Zachary, Director of Competition
Loren L. Zachary Society for the Performing Arts
2250 Gloaming Way
Beverly Hills, CA 90210
Phone: 310-276-2731
Fax: 310-275-8245

PRINCESS GRACE FOUNDATION—USA
http://www.pgfusa.com

PRINCESS GRACE FELLOWSHIPS IN THEATER AND DANCE • 845

Theater and Dance fellowships are offered to new, full-time members of non-profit theater and dance companies. Fellowships help pay the artist's salary and are awarded to dancers, actors, designers, and directors. Must be a U.S. citizen or have permanent residence status. Must include video and nominator's statements. Deadlines: Theater - March 31 and Dance - April 30.

Academic/Career Areas Performing Arts.

Award Fellowship for use in postgraduate years; not renewable. *Number:* 5–10. *Amount:* $3000–$20,000.

Eligibility Requirements Applicant must be enrolled or expecting to enroll full-time at a four-year institution or university. Available to U.S. citizens.

Application Requirements Application, autobiography, essay, photo, portfolio, references, self-addressed stamped envelope. *Deadline:* April 30.

Contact Ms. Toby Boshak, Executive Director
Princess Grace Foundation—USA
150 East 58th Street, 21st Floor
New York, NY 10155
Phone: 212-317-1470
Fax: 212-317-1473
E-mail: tboshak@pgfusa.com

RHODE ISLAND FOUNDATION
http://www.rifoundation.org

ANTONIO CIRINO MEMORIAL ART EDUCATION FELLOWSHIP
• *See number 172*

SHASTRI INDO-CANADIAN INSTITUTE
http://www.ucalgary.ca/~sici

SHASTRI INDIA STUDIES SENIOR ARTS FELLOWSHIPS
• *See number 157*

SIGMA ALPHA IOTA PHILANTHROPIES, INC.
http://www.sai-national.org

GRADUATE SCHOLARSHIP IN MUSIC EDUCATION
• *See number 367*

SIGMA ALPHA IOTA DOCTORAL GRANT
• *See number 368*

SIGMA ALPHA IOTA GRADUATE PERFORMANCE AWARDS • 846

One-time award offered triennially to SAI members over 20 who are pursuing graduate study in field of music performance. Winners perform at national convention. Submit tape with required repertoire. Contact chapter for details. Four awards in each category (vocal; keyboard and percussion; strings; wind and brass) ranging from $1500 to $2000. Application fee: $25.

Academic/Career Areas Performing Arts.

Award Prize for use in graduate years; not renewable. *Number:* 8. *Amount:* $1500–$2000.

Sigma Alpha Iota Philanthropies, Inc. (continued)

Eligibility Requirements Applicant must be age 21; enrolled or expecting to enroll at an institution or university; female and must have an interest in music/singing. Available to U.S. and non-U.S. citizens.

Application Requirements Application, applicant must enter a contest, essay, references, transcript, tape. *Fee:* $25. *Deadline:* April 15.

Contact Ms. Ruth Sieber Johnson, Secretary
Sigma Alpha Iota Philanthropies, Inc.
7 Hickey Drive
Framingham, MA 01701-8812
Phone: 828-251-0606
Fax: 828-251-0644
E-mail: nh@sai-national.org

**SIGMA ALPHA IOTA SCHOLARSHIP FOR
CONDUCTORS** • **847**

One-time award offered triennially to SAI member who is enrolled in an accredited graduate program in music with an emphasis in conducting. Submit thirty-minute videotape of work. Contact your chapter for further details. Application fee: $25.

Academic/Career Areas Performing Arts.

Award Scholarship for use in graduate years; not renewable. *Number:* 1. *Amount:* $1000.

Eligibility Requirements Applicant must be enrolled or expecting to enroll at an institution or university; female and must have an interest in music/singing. Available to U.S. and non-U.S. citizens.

Application Requirements Application, essay, references, transcript, videotape. *Fee:* $25. *Deadline:* April 15.

Contact Ms. Ruth Sieber Johnson, Secretary
Sigma Alpha Iota Philanthropies, Inc.
7 Hickey Drive
Framingham, MA 01701-8812
Phone: 828-251-0606
Fax: 828-251-0644
E-mail: nh@sai-national.org

SWANN FOUNDATION FUND
http://www.lcweb.loc.gov/rr/print/swann/
swann_foundation.html

SWANN FOUNDATION FUND FELLOWSHIP
• *See number 109*

PHOTOJOURNALISM

**CONSORTIUM OF COLLEGE AND
UNIVERSITY MEDIA CENTERS**
http://www.ccumc.org

**CONSORTIUM OF COLLEGE AND UNIVERSITY
MEDIA CENTERS RESEARCH AWARDS**
• *See number 253*

**NATIONAL PRESS PHOTOGRAPHERS
FOUNDATION, INC.**
http://www.nppa.org

KIT C. KING GRADUATE SCHOLARSHIP FUND
• *See number 699*

**UNITED METHODIST
COMMUNICATIONS**
http://www.umcom.org/scholarships

**STOODY-WEST FELLOWSHIP FOR GRADUATE
STUDY IN RELIGIOUS JOURNALISM**
• *See number 261*

PHYSICAL SCIENCES AND
MATH

**AIR AND WASTE MANAGEMENT
ASSOCIATION**
http://www.awma.org

**AIR AND WASTE MANAGEMENT ASSOCIATION
SCHOLARSHIP ENDOWMENT TRUST FUND**
• *See number 24*

**AMERICAN ASSOCIATION OF
UNIVERSITY WOMEN (AAUW)
EDUCATIONAL FOUNDATION**
http://www.aauw.org

**AAUW EDUCATIONAL FOUNDATION SELECTED
PROFESSIONS FELLOWSHIPS**
• *See number 87*

ELEANOR ROOSEVELT TEACHER FELLOWSHIPS
• *See number 343*

**AMERICAN COUNCIL OF TEACHERS
OF RUSSIAN**
http://www.actr.org

**TITLE VIII RESEARCH SCHOLAR AND COMBINED
RESEARCH AND LANGUAGE STUDY PROGRAM**
• *See number 114*

AMERICAN GEOPHYSICAL UNION
http://www.agu.org

CONGRESSIONAL SCIENCE FELLOWSHIP PROGRAM
• *See number 299*

AMERICAN INSTITUTE OF AERONAUTICS AND ASTRONAUTICS
http://www.aiaa.org

AIAA FOUNDATION GRADUATE AWARDS
• *See number 26*

AIAA FOUNDATION ORVILLE AND WILBUR WRIGHT AWARDS
• *See number 27*

AMERICAN LIVER FOUNDATION
http://www.liverfoundation.org

AMERICAN LIVER FOUNDATION POSTDOCTORAL RESEARCH FELLOWSHIPS
• *See number 183*

LIVER SCHOLAR AWARDS
• *See number 184*

AMERICAN MATHEMATICAL SOCIETY
http://www.ams.org

AMERICAN MATHEMATICAL SOCIETY CENTENNIAL RESEARCH FELLOWSHIP • **848**

One-time fellowships will be awarded to researchers holding their doctoral degree for at least three years and not more than twelve years at the inception of the award. Preference will be given to candidates who have not had extensive fellowship support in the past. Applications should include a cogent plan indicating how the fellowship will be used. The plans should include travel to at least one other institution.

Academic/Career Areas Physical Sciences and Math.

Award Fellowship for use in postgraduate years; not renewable. *Number:* 1–3. *Amount:* $55,000.

Eligibility Requirements Applicant must be enrolled or expecting to enroll at an institution or university. Available to U.S. and Canadian citizens.

Application Requirements Application, references, short research plan. *Deadline:* December 1.

Contact Executive Director
American Mathematical Society
201 Charles Street
Providence, RI 02904-2294
Phone: 401-455-4000
Fax: 401-331-3842
E-mail: ams@ams.org

AMERICAN METEOROLOGICAL SOCIETY
http://www.ametsoc.org/AMS

AMERICAN METEOROLOGICAL SOCIETY/ INDUSTRY/GOVERNMENT GRADUATE FELLOWSHIPS
• *See number 28*

AMERICAN NUCLEAR SOCIETY
http://www.ans.org

AMERICAN NUCLEAR SOCIETY GRADUATE SCHOLARSHIPS
• *See number 30*

AMERICAN OPTOMETRIC FOUNDATION
http://www.ezell.org

WILLIAM C. EZELL FELLOWSHIP
• *See number 31*

AMERICAN PHILOSOPHICAL SOCIETY
http://www.amphilsoc.org

JOHN CLARKE SLATER FELLOWSHIP • **849**

One-time doctoral dissertation fellowship in the history of twentieth-century physical sciences. Must have passed preliminary examinations. Must be over 24. Must submit dissertation prospectus. Check website for complete information and forms: www. amphilsoc.org.

Academic/Career Areas Physical Sciences and Math.

Award Fellowship for use in graduate years; not renewable. *Number:* 1. *Amount:* $12,000.

Eligibility Requirements Applicant must be age 25 and enrolled or expecting to enroll at an institution or university.

Application Requirements Application, essay, references, transcript, dissertation prospectus. *Deadline:* December 1.

Contact Slater Fellowship Committee
American Philosophical Society
104 South 5th Street
Philadelphia, PA 19106-3387

AMERICAN PHYSIOLOGICAL SOCIETY
http://www.faseb.org/aps

CAROLINE TUM SUDEN/FRANCES A. HELLEBRANDT PROFESSIONAL OPPORTUNITY AWARD
• *See number 186*

PORTER PHYSIOLOGY FELLOWSHIPS
• *See number 187*

American Physiological Society (continued)

PROCTER AND GAMBLE PROFESSIONAL OPPORTUNITY AWARD
• *See number 188*

AMERICAN SOCIETY FOR PHOTOGRAMMETRY AND REMOTE SENSING
http://www.asprs.org

AMERICAN SOCIETY FOR PHOTOGRAMMETRY AND REMOTE SENSING OUTSTANDING PAPERS AWARDS
• *See number 33*

TA LIANG MEMORIAL AWARD
• *See number 34*

WILLIAM A. FISCHER MEMORIAL SCHOLARSHIP
• *See number 35*

AMERICAN VACUUM SOCIETY
http://www.avs.org

ALBERT NERKEN AWARD
• *See number 36*

AMERICAN VACUUM SOCIETY GRADUATE RESEARCH AWARD
• *See number 37*

GAEDE-LANGMUIR AWARD
• *See number 38*

JOHN A. THORNTON MEMORIAL AWARD AND LECTURE
• *See number 39*

MEDARD W. WELCH AWARD
• *See number 40*

NELLIE YEOH WHETTEN AWARD
• *See number 41*

PETER MARK MEMORIAL AWARD
• *See number 42*

RUSSELL AND SIGURD VARIAN FELLOWSHIP
• *See number 43*

ARKANSAS DEPARTMENT OF HIGHER EDUCATION
http://www.arscholarships.com

MINORITY MASTER'S FELLOWS PROGRAM
• *See number 351*

ARMED FORCES COMMUNICATIONS AND ELECTRONICS ASSOCIATION, EDUCATIONAL FOUNDATION
http://www.afcea.org

ARMED FORCES COMMUNICATIONS & ELECTRONICS ASSOCIATION EDUCATIONAL FOUNDATION FELLOWSHIP
• *See number 265*

ARMED FORCES COMMUNICATIONS AND ELECTRONICS ASSOCIATION RALPH W. SHRADER SCHOLARSHIPS
• *See number 266*

ASSOCIATED WESTERN UNIVERSITIES, INC.
http://www.awu.org

ASSOCIATED WESTERN UNIVERSITIES FACULTY FELLOWSHIPS
• *See number 48*

ASSOCIATED WESTERN UNIVERSITIES GRADUATE RESEARCH FELLOWSHIPS
• *See number 49*

ASSOCIATED WESTERN UNIVERSITIES POSTGRADUATE FELLOWSHIP
• *See number 50*

ASSOCIATION FOR WOMEN IN MATHEMATICS
http://www.awm-math.org/

ASSOCIATION FOR WOMEN IN MATHEMATICS WORKSHOP FOR GRADUATE STUDENTS AND POSTDOCTORAL MATHEMATICIANS   • **850**

Award for female graduate students and recent PhD's in math to attend the annual workshop in Florida. Graduate students must have begun work on thesis problem and present it at workshop. Post-doctorates present talks on research. Deadlines: March 1 and September 1.

Academic/Career Areas Physical Sciences and Math.

Award Grant for use in graduate, or postgraduate years; not renewable. *Number:* 20–40. *Amount:* $800–$1000.

Eligibility Requirements Applicant must be enrolled or expecting to enroll at an institution or university and female.

Application Requirements Application.

Contact Dawn V. Wheeler, Director of Marketing
Association for Women in Mathematics
4114 Computer and Space Sciences
   Building
College Park, MD 20742-2461

LOUISE HAY AWARD FOR EXCELLENCE IN MATHEMATICS EDUCATION • 851

One-time award for women to recognize outstanding achievements in any area of mathematics education, to be interpreted in the broadest possible sense. Must be nominated for award.

Academic/Career Areas Physical Sciences and Math.

Award Prize for use in postgraduate years; not renewable.

Eligibility Requirements Applicant must be enrolled or expecting to enroll at an institution or university and female. Applicant or parent of applicant must have employment or volunteer experience in teaching.

Application Requirements Nomination. *Deadline:* October 1.

Contact Dawn V. Wheeler, Director of Marketing
Association for Women in Mathematics
4114 Computer and Space Sciences Building
College Park, MD 20742-2461

TRAVEL GRANTS FOR WOMEN IN MATHEMATICS • 852

One-time award for women who recently received Ph.D. in mathematics to provide travel expenses to attend research conferences in their field. Submit description of recent research, curriculum vitae, and budget. Deadlines: February 1, May 1, and October 1.

Academic/Career Areas Physical Sciences and Math.

Award Grant for use in postgraduate years; not renewable. *Number:* 3–6. *Amount:* $1000–$2000.

Eligibility Requirements Applicant must be enrolled or expecting to enroll at an institution or university and female.

Contact Dawn V. Wheeler, Director of Marketing
Association for Women in Mathematics
4114 Computer and Space Sciences Building
College Park, MD 20742-2461

ASSOCIATION FOR WOMEN IN SCIENCE EDUCATIONAL FOUNDATION
http://www.awis.org

ASSOCIATION FOR WOMEN IN SCIENCE PREDOCTORAL FELLOWSHIP
• *See number 77*

CANADIAN NORTHERN STUDIES TRUST - ASSOCIATION OF CANADIAN UNIVERSITIES FOR NORTHERN STUDIES
http://www.cyberus.ca/~acuns

RESEARCH SUPPORT OPPORTUNITIES IN ARCTIC ENVIRONMENTAL STUDIES
• *See number 120*

CHEMICAL HERITAGE FOUNDATION
http://www.chemheritage.org

BECKMAN CENTER FOR THE HISTORY OF CHEMISTRY RESEARCH TRAVEL GRANTS AT THE CHEMICAL HERITAGE FOUNDATION
• *See number 51*

DELAWARE VALLEY SPACE GRANT CONSORTIUM
http://www.delspace.org

NASA/DELAWARE VALLEY SPACE GRANT FELLOWSHIP
• *See number 52*

EPILEPSY FOUNDATION
http://www.epilepsyfoundation.org

PREDOCTORAL RESEARCH TRAINING FELLOWSHIP
• *See number 200*

FANNIE AND JOHN HERTZ FOUNDATION
http://www.hertzfoundation.org

FANNIE AND JOHN HERTZ FOUNDATION DOCTORAL THESIS PRIZE • 853

Upon receiving their Ph.D., contestant may submit a copy of their thesis. No less than $1000 is awarded to exceptional entries. Awards are not given out every year and more than one award may be given out each year. The number and amount of awards given out depends on the quality of the entries. Entries will be judged on overall excellence and pertinence to high-impact applications of the physical sciences. Visit http://www.hertzfoundation.org/prize.html for more information.

Academic/Career Areas Physical Sciences and Math.

Award Prize for use in postgraduate years; not renewable. *Amount:* $1000.

Eligibility Requirements Applicant must be enrolled or expecting to enroll at an institution or university. Available to U.S. citizens.

Fannie and John Hertz Foundation (continued)

Application Requirements Applicant must enter a contest, thesis.

Contact Theresa Mattos, Administrative Assistant
Fannie and John Hertz Foundation
2456 Research Drive
Livermore, CA 94550
Phone: 925-373-1642
E-mail: askhertz@aol.com

FANNIE AND JOHN HERTZ FOUNDATION FELLOWSHIP
• *See number 53*

FOUNDATION FOR SCIENCE AND DISABILITY
http://www.as.wvu.edu/~scidis/organize/fsd.html

GRANTS FOR DISABLED STUDENTS IN THE SCIENCES
• *See number 54*

GEOLOGICAL SOCIETY OF AMERICA
http://www.geosociety.org

ARTHUR D. HOWARD RESEARCH GRANTS
• *See number 303*

J. HOOVER MACKIN RESEARCH GRANTS
• *See number 308*

HARRY S TRUMAN LIBRARY INSTITUTE
http://www.trumanlibrary.org

HARRY S. TRUMAN LIBRARY INSTITUTE SCHOLAR'S AWARD
• *See number 327*

HUNTINGTON LIBRARY, ART COLLECTIONS, AND BOTANICAL GARDENS
http://www.huntington.org

HUNTINGTON RESEARCH AWARDS
• *See number 56*

IMGIP/ICEOP
http://www.imgip.siu.edu

ILLINOIS MINORITY GRADUATE INCENTIVE PROGRAM FELLOWSHIP
• *See number 372*

JILA
http://jilawww.colorado.edu/

POSTDOCTORAL RESEARCH ASSOCIATESHIPS
• *See number 775*

VISITING FELLOWSHIPS
• *See number 776*

MYASTHENIA GRAVIS FOUNDATION OF AMERICA, INC.
http://www.myasthenia.org

DR. HENRY R. VIETS MEDICAL STUDENT RESEARCH FELLOWSHIP
• *See number 210*

OSSERMAN/SOSIN/MCCLURE POSTDOCTORAL FELLOWSHIP
• *See number 211*

NASA IDAHO SPACE GRANT CONSORTIUM
http://www.uidaho.edu/nasa_isgc

NASA ID SPACE GRANT CONSORTIUM FELLOWSHIP PROGRAM
• *See number 60*

NASA WYOMING SPACE GRANT CONSORTIUM
http://www.wyomingspacegrant.uwyo.edu

WYOMING NASA SPACE GRANT CONSORTIUM RESEARCH FELLOWSHIP
• *See number 61*

NATIONAL ACTION COUNCIL FOR MINORITIES IN ENGINEERING-NACME, INC.
http://www.nacme.org

SLOAN PH.D PROGRAM
• *See number 243*

NATIONAL PHYSICAL SCIENCE CONSORTIUM
http://www.npsc.org

NATIONAL PHYSICAL SCIENCE CONSORTIUM GRADUATE FELLOWSHIPS IN THE PHYSICAL SCIENCES
• *See number 244*

NATIONAL RESEARCH COUNCIL
http://www.nationalacademies.org/fellowships/

FORD FOUNDATION DISSERTATION FELLOWSHIPS FOR MINORITIES
• *See number 256*

FORD FOUNDATION POSTDOCTORAL FELLOWSHIP FOR MINORITIES
• *See number 257*

FORD FOUNDATION PREDOCTORAL FELLOWSHIPS FOR MINORITIES
• *See number 258*

NATIONAL SCIENCE FOUNDATION
http://www.nsf.gov/grfp

NATIONAL SCIENCE FOUNDATION GRADUATE RESEARCH FELLOWSHIPS
• *See number 62*

NATIONAL SCIENCE FOUNDATION MINORITY CAREER ADVANCEMENT AWARDS
• *See number 381*

NATIONAL SCIENCE FOUNDATION MINORITY RESEARCH PLANNING GRANTS
• *See number 382*

SCIENCE ADVANCEMENT PROGRAMS RESEARCH CORPORATION
http://www.rescorp.org

COTTRELL COLLEGE SCIENCE AWARDS • 854

Applicant must have a faculty appointment in a department of astronomy, chemistry or physics that offers at least baccalaureate, but not doctoral degrees. Preference is given to tenured or tenure-track faculty in all ranks. The potential of a proposed research project to add to fundamental scientific knowledge is a prime criterion in its evaluation as is its potential for developing into a long term viable program capable of attracting future support from other agencies. Visit http://www.rescorp.org for more information.

Academic/Career Areas Physical Sciences and Math.

Award Grant for use in postgraduate years; not renewable. *Amount:* $35,000.

Eligibility Requirements Applicant must be enrolled or expecting to enroll at a four-year institution or university.

Application Requirements Application, proposal.

Contact Science Advancement Programs Research
Corporation
101 North Wilmot Road, Suite 250
Tucson, AZ 85711

COTTRELL SCHOLARS AWARD • 855

Eligible applicants will be tenure track assistant professors in Ph.D.-granting departments of astronomy, chemistry, or physics. The proposal should consist of brief proposals for both research and teaching. Originality, feasibility, and the prospect for significant fundamental advances to science are the main criteria for the research plan. Contributions to education, especially at the undergraduate level, aspirations for teaching and the proposed strategies to achieve educational objectives are factors in the assessments of the teaching plan. Visit http://www.rescorp.org for more information.

Academic/Career Areas Physical Sciences and Math.

Award Grant for use in postgraduate years; not renewable. *Amount:* $75,000.

Eligibility Requirements Applicant must be enrolled or expecting to enroll at a four-year institution or university. Available to U.S. and non-U.S. citizens.

Application Requirements Application, proposal. *Deadline:* September 3.

Contact Science Advancement Programs Research
Corporation
101 North Wilmot Road, Suite 250
Tucson, AZ 85711

RESEARCH INNOVATION AWARDS • 856

Eligible applicants will be members in Ph.D.-granting departments of astronomy, chemistry, or physics at research universities in the US and Canada. Proposals should outline research that transcends the ordinary and offers promise for significant discoveries. These proposals will be judged on innovation of the proposed research including scientific significance, potential impact and feasibility. Visit http://www.rescorp.org for more information.

Academic/Career Areas Physical Sciences and Math.

Award Grant for use in postgraduate years; not renewable. *Amount:* $35,000.

Eligibility Requirements Applicant must be enrolled or expecting to enroll at a four-year institution or university. Available to U.S. and Canadian citizens.

Application Requirements Application, proposal. *Deadline:* May 1.

Contact Science Advancement Programs Research
Corporation
101 North Wilmot Road, Suite 250
Tucson, AZ 85711

SMITHSONIAN ASTROPHYSICAL OBSERVATORY
http://cfa-www.harvard.edu

FELLOWSHIPS AT THE SMITHSONIAN ASTROPHYSICAL OBSERVATORY • 857

Basic research in astronomy, astrophysics, geophysics, space science, science education. Must study in Arizona, Massachusetts, or Hawaii. Application deadline varies by fellowship.

Academic/Career Areas Physical Sciences and Math.

Award Fellowship for use in graduate, or postgraduate years; not renewable. *Number:* 6–10.

Smithsonian Astrophysical Observatory (continued)

Eligibility Requirements Applicant must be enrolled or expecting to enroll at an institution or university and studying in Arizona, Hawaii, or Massachusetts. Available to U.S. and non-U.S. citizens.

Application Requirements Application, references, description of proposed research.

Contact Dale Alianiello, Office of the Director
Smithsonian Astrophysical Observatory
60 Garden Street
Cambridge, MA 02138
Phone: 617-495-7103
Fax: 617-495-7105
E-mail: dalianiello@cfa.harvard.edu

POLITICAL SCIENCE

AMERICAN POLITICAL SCIENCE ASSOCIATION
http://www.apsanet.org

CONGRESSIONAL FELLOWSHIP FOR FEDERAL EXECUTIVES
• *See number 676*

CONGRESSIONAL FELLOWSHIP FOR JOURNALISTS
• *See number 250*

SMALL RESEARCH GRANT COMPETITION • **858**

Awards up to $2500 for faculty members at non-Ph.D. granting institutions or independent scholars with a Ph.D. who are also members of APSA. Research projects must address a significant problem in political science. A research design and explanation of how the project fits in the theoretical literature are essential components of the proposal. A 5 page project description, budget, CV, and title page must be sent between December 1 and February 1. For details, see website: http://www.apsanet.org/opps/ apsagrants.cfm.

Academic/Career Areas Political Science.

Award Grant for use in postgraduate years; not renewable. *Number:* 12–16. *Amount:* up to $2500.

Eligibility Requirements Applicant must be enrolled or expecting to enroll at an institution or university. Applicant or parent of applicant must be member of American Political Science Association.

Application Requirements Project proposal. *Deadline:* February 1.

Contact Sue Davis, Director, Small Research Grants
American Political Science Association
1527 New Hampshire Avenue, NW
Washington, DC 20036-1206
Phone: 202-483-2512
Fax: 202-483-2657
E-mail: grants@apsanet.org

ARMENIAN RELIEF SOCIETY OF NORTH AMERICA INC.-REGIONAL OFFICE

ARMENIAN RELIEF SOCIETY GRADUATE SCHOLARSHIP PROGRAM
• *See number 224*

CHINA TIMES CULTURAL FOUNDATION

CHINA TIMES CULTURAL FOUNDATION DOCTORAL DISSERTATION RESEARCH IN CHINESE STUDIES SCHOLARSHIPS
• *See number 122*

CULTURAL SERVICES OF THE FRENCH EMBASSY
http://www.frenchculture.org

CHATEAUBRIAND SCHOLARSHIP PROGRAM
• *See number 164*

DAVID LIBRARY OF THE AMERICAN REVOLUTION
http://www.dlar.org

FELLOWSHIPS FOR THE STUDY OF THE AMERICAN REVOLUTION
• *See number 644*

DIRKSEN CONGRESSIONAL CENTER
http://www.pekin.net/dirksen

CONGRESSIONAL RESEARCH AWARDS PROGRAM • **859**

Open to individuals with a serious interest in studying congress. Funds research in congressional leadership and the U.S. Congress. Award available to graduate students for dissertation research. Funds not available for tuition or room and board. Deadline is February 1.

Academic/Career Areas Political Science.

Award Grant for use in graduate, or postgraduate years; renewable. *Amount:* up to $3500.

Eligibility Requirements Applicant must be enrolled or expecting to enroll full or part-time at a four-year institution or university. Available to U.S. citizens.

Application Requirements Application, resume, references. *Deadline:* February 1.

Contact Frank Mackaman
Dirksen Congressional Center
301 South Fourth Street, Suite A
Pekin, IL 61554-4219
Phone: 309-347-7113
Fax: 309-347-6432
E-mail: fmackaman@pekin.net

EPILEPSY FOUNDATION
http://www.epilepsyfoundation.org

EPILEPSY FOUNDATION BEHAVIORAL SCIENCES RESEARCH TRAINING FELLOWSHIP
• See number 318

FRIEDRICH EBERT FOUNDATION

EBERT FOUNDATION ADVANCED GRADUATE FELLOWSHIPS
• See number 319

EBERT FOUNDATION DOCTORAL RESEARCH FELLOWSHIP
• See number 320

EBERT FOUNDATION POSTDOCTORAL FELLOWSHIPS
• See number 321

HARRY S TRUMAN LIBRARY INSTITUTE
http://www.trumanlibrary.org

HARRY S. TRUMAN BOOK AWARD
• See number 324

HARRY S. TRUMAN LIBRARY INSTITUTE DISSERTATION YEAR FELLOWSHIPS
• See number 325

HARRY S. TRUMAN LIBRARY INSTITUTE RESEARCH GRANTS
• See number 326

HARVARD UNIVERSITY CENTER FOR BASIC RESEARCH IN THE SOCIAL SCIENCES
http://www.cbrss.harvard.edu

CENTER FOR BASIC RESEARCH IN THE SOCIAL SCIENCES POSTDOCTORAL FELLOWSHIP • 860

One-year postdoctoral fellowships for scholars holding Ph.D. in political science, economics, political economy, statistics, or other social sciences. Must have received Ph.D. within the last five years. Fellows will conduct their own research and participate in year-long seminar with Center faculty. No teaching duties. Competitive stipend awarded. Submit application, C.V., 3 letters of reference, recent paper, and 2-page statement of planned research.

Academic/Career Areas Political Science; Social Sciences.

Award Fellowship for use in postgraduate years; not renewable.

Eligibility Requirements Applicant must be enrolled or expecting to enroll at an institution or university.

Application Requirements Application, references. *Deadline:* February 15.

Contact Administrative Assistant
Harvard University Center for Basic Research in the Social Sciences
34 Kirkland Street
Cambridge, MA 02138

INTERNATIONAL DEVELOPMENT RESEARCH CENTER
http://www.idrc.ca/awards

IDRC DOCTORAL RESEARCH AWARD
• See number 12

JOHN F. KENNEDY LIBRARY FOUNDATION
http://www.jfklibrary.org

ABBA SCHWARTZ FELLOWSHIPS • 861

Fellowships for graduate scholars pursuing research in immigration, refugee policy, or naturalization. Submit proposal, writing sample, application, project budget, curriculum vitae, and letters of recommendation by March 15. Must use Kennedy Library to do at least a portion of research. One-time award of up to $3100.

Academic/Career Areas Political Science; Social Sciences.

Award Fellowship for use in graduate years; not renewable. *Number:* 1. *Amount:* up to $3100.

Eligibility Requirements Applicant must be enrolled or expecting to enroll at an institution or university. Available to U.S. citizens.

Application Requirements Application, essay, references. *Deadline:* March 15.

Contact Grant and Fellowship Coordinator
John F. Kennedy Library Foundation
Columbia Point
Boston, MA 02125
Phone: 617-929-1200

ARTHUR M. SCHLESINGER, JR. FELLOWSHIP
• See number 648

KENNEDY RESEARCH GRANTS
• See number 100

MARJORIE KOVLER FELLOWSHIP • 862

One-time fellowship of $2500 awarded to support a graduate scholar in the production of work in the area of foreign intelligence and the presidency or a related topic. Must include ten-page writing sample, project budget, and a vita. See application for further details.

Academic/Career Areas Political Science.

Award Fellowship for use in graduate years; not renewable. *Number:* 1. *Amount:* $2500.

John F. Kennedy Library Foundation (continued)

Eligibility Requirements Applicant must be enrolled or expecting to enroll at an institution or university. Available to U.S. citizens.

Application Requirements Application, essay. *Deadline:* March 15.

Contact Grant and Fellowship Coordinator
John F. Kennedy Library Foundation
Columbia Point
Boston, MA 02125
Phone: 617-929-1200

THEODORE C. SORENSEN FELLOWSHIP
• *See number 698*

MACKENZIE KING SCHOLARSHIPS BOARD

MACKENZIE KING TRAVELLING SCHOLARSHIPS
• *See number 236*

NATIONAL RESEARCH COUNCIL
http://www.nationalacademies.org/fellowships/

FORD FOUNDATION DISSERTATION FELLOWSHIPS FOR MINORITIES
• *See number 256*

FORD FOUNDATION POSTDOCTORAL FELLOWSHIP FOR MINORITIES
• *See number 257*

FORD FOUNDATION PREDOCTORAL FELLOWSHIPS FOR MINORITIES
• *See number 258*

PI GAMMA MU INTERNATIONAL HONOR SOCIETY IN SOCIETY SCIENCE
http://www.sckans.edu/~pgm

PI GAMMA MU SCHOLARSHIP
• *See number 273*

RESOURCES FOR THE FUTURE
http://www.rff.org

GILBERT F. WHITE POSTDOCTORAL FELLOWSHIPS
• *See number 331*

JOSEPH L. FISHER DISSERTATION AWARDS
• *See number 332*

UNITED STATES INSTITUTE OF PEACE
http://www.usip.org

JENNINGS RANDOLPH SENIOR FELLOW AWARD
• *See number 333*

PEACE SCHOLAR DISSERTATION FELLOWSHIP
• *See number 334*

WELLESLEY COLLEGE
http://www.wellesley.edu/CWS/

VIDA DUTTON SCUDDER FELLOWSHIP
• *See number 770*

WOODROW WILSON NATIONAL FELLOWSHIP FOUNDATION
http://www.woodrow.org

ANDREW W. MELLON FELLOWSHIPS IN HUMANISTIC STUDIES
• *See number 134*

THOMAS R. PICKERING GRADUATE FOREIGN AFFAIRS FELLOWSHIP PROGRAM
• *See number 241*

WOODROW WILSON NATIONAL FELLOWSHIP FOUNDATION DISSERTATION GRANTS IN WOMEN'S STUDIES
• *See number 135*

WOODROW WILSON POSTDOCTORAL FELLOWSHIPS IN THE HUMANITIES
• *See number 136*

RELIGION/THEOLOGY

AMERICAN ACADEMY OF RELIGION
http://www.aarweb.org

AMERICAN ACADEMY OF RELIGION RESEARCH ASSISTANCE AND COLLABORATIVE RESEARCH GRANTS • **863**

One-time award for members of the American Academy of Religion to conduct independent or collaborative research projects. Not available for dissertation research. Awardee must be a member of AAR for at least three years. Write for more information or consult website.

Academic/Career Areas Religion/Theology.

Award Grant for use in graduate years; not renewable. *Number:* 10–20. *Amount:* $500–$5000.

Eligibility Requirements Applicant must be enrolled or expecting to enroll at an institution or university. Applicant or parent of applicant must be member of American Academy of Religion. Available to U.S. and non-U.S. citizens.

Application Requirements Project description, curriculum vitae. *Deadline:* August 1.

Contact Anne Kentch, Office Manager
American Academy of Religion
825 Houston Mill Road, Suite 300
Atlanta, GA 30329-4075
Phone: 404-727-7920
Fax: 404-727-7959
E-mail: info@aarweb.org

AMERICAN CENTER OF ORIENTAL RESEARCH
http://www.bu.edu/acor

NATIONAL ENDOWMENT FOR THE HUMANITIES POST-DOCTORAL RESEARCH FELLOWSHIPS
• *See number 65*

AMERICAN SCHOOLS OF ORIENTAL RESEARCH (ASOR)
http://www.asor.org

W.F. ALBRIGHT INSTITUTE OF ARCHAEOLOGICAL RESEARCH - JAMES A. MONTGOMERY FELLOW AND RESEARCH COORDINATOR
• *See number 69*

W.F. ALBRIGHT INSTITUTE OF ARCHAEOLOGICAL RESEARCH GEORGE A. BARTON FELLOWSHIP
• *See number 70*

W.F. ALBRIGHT INSTITUTE OF ARCHAEOLOGICAL RESEARCH/NATIONAL ENDOWMENT OF THE HUMANITIES FELLOWSHIPS
• *See number 71*

ASIAN CULTURAL COUNCIL
http://www.asianculturalcouncil.org

ASIAN ART AND RELIGION FELLOWSHIPS
• *See number 90*

ASIAN CULTURAL COUNCIL FELLOWSHIPS
• *See number 91*

ASIAN CULTURAL COUNCIL HUMANITIES FELLOWSHIPS
• *See number 92*

DUMBARTON OAKS
http://www.doaks.org

BLISS PRIZE FELLOWSHIP IN BYZANTINE STUDIES
• *See number 123*

RESIDENTIAL FELLOWSHIP IN BYZANTINE, PRE-COLUMBIAN, AND LANDSCAPE ARCHITECTURE STUDIES
• *See number 95*

EVANGELICAL LUTHERAN CHURCH IN AMERICA/DIVISION FOR MINISTRY
http://elca.org/dm/te/grants.html

EVANGELICAL LUTHERAN CHURCH IN AMERICA EDUCATIONAL GRANT PROGRAM • 864

Awards available to graduate students pursuing an advanced academic theological education degree (Ph.D. or Th.D.). Limited to members of the Evangelical Lutheran Church in America. Priority given to minorities and women. Award of $500-$5000 is renewable up to four years and also for fifth-year dissertation.

Academic/Career Areas Religion/Theology.

Award Grant for use in graduate years; renewable. *Number:* up to 60. *Amount:* $500–$5000.

Eligibility Requirements Applicant must be Lutheran and enrolled or expecting to enroll full or part-time at an institution or university. Available to U.S. citizens.

Application Requirements Application, financial need analysis, references. *Deadline:* March 15.

Contact Dr. Jonathan Strandjord, Director for
Theological Education
Evangelical Lutheran Church in America/
Division for Ministry
8765 West Higgins Road
Chicago, IL 60631-4195
Phone: 773-380-2873
Fax: 773-380-2829
E-mail: jstrandj@elca.org

FUND FOR THEOLOGICAL EDUCATION, INC. (FTE)
http://www.thefund.org

DISSERTATION FELLOWS PROGRAM • 865

Fellowship is for African American students in Ph.D. or Th.D. programs in religious or theological studies whose dissertation proposal has been approved and who are ready to write full-time by the fall of the award year. Award includes $15,000 stipend and attendance at a summer conference. Applicants must be U.S. citizens.

Academic/Career Areas Religion/Theology.

Award Fellowship for use in graduate years; not renewable. *Number:* 10. *Amount:* $15,000.

Eligibility Requirements Applicant must be Christian; Black (non-Hispanic) and enrolled or expecting to enroll full-time at a four-year institution or university. Available to U.S. citizens.

Fund for Theological Education, Inc.
(FTE) (continued)

Application Requirements Application, essay, financial need analysis, resume, references, test scores, transcript, dissertation prospectus. *Deadline:* February 1.

Contact Dr. Sharon Watson Fluker, Director,
Expanding Horizons Partnership
Fund for Theological Education, Inc.
(FTE)
825 Houston Mill Road, Suite 250
Atlanta, GA 30329
Phone: 404-727-1450
Fax: 404-727-1490
E-mail: sfluker@thefund.org

DOCTORAL FELLOWS PROGRAM • 866

Fellowship for African American students entering their first year of Ph.D. or Th.D. work in religious or theological studies. Currently enrolled students are ineligible. Applicants must be U.S. citizens. Award includes $15,000 stipend and attendance at a summer conference.

Academic/Career Areas Religion/Theology.

Award Fellowship for use in graduate years; renewable. *Number:* 11. *Amount:* $15,000.

Eligibility Requirements Applicant must be Christian; Black (non-Hispanic) and enrolled or expecting to enroll full-time at a four-year institution or university. Available to U.S. citizens.

Application Requirements Application, essay, financial need analysis, resume, references, test scores, transcript. *Deadline:* March 1.

Contact Dr. Sharon Watson Fluker, Director,
Expanding Horizons Partnership
Fund for Theological Education, Inc.
(FTE)
825 Houston Mill Road, Suite 250
Atlanta, GA 30329
Phone: 404-727-1450
Fax: 404-727-1490
E-mail: sfluker@thefund.org

MINISTRY FELLOWS PROGRAM • 867

Fellowship for students entering first year of a Master of Divinity program in the fall at an ATS-accredited seminary. Applicants must be U.S. or Canadian citizens. Award includes a $5000 stipend for a summer project, attendance at an FTE summer conference, and ongoing enrichment opportunities.

Academic/Career Areas Religion/Theology.

Award Fellowship for use in graduate years; not renewable. *Number:* 40. *Amount:* $5000.

Eligibility Requirements Applicant must be Christian; age 35 or under and enrolled or expecting

to enroll full-time at an institution or university. Available to U.S. and Canadian citizens.

Application Requirements Application, essay, resume, references, transcript. *Deadline:* April 1.

Contact Ms. Melissa Wiginton, Director,
Partnership for Excellence
Fund for Theological Education, Inc.
(FTE)
825 Houston Mill Road, Suite 250
Atlanta, GA 30329
Phone: 404-727-1450
Fax: 404-727-1490
E-mail: mwigint@thefund.org

NORTH AMERICAN DOCTORAL FELLOWS PROGRAM • 868

Fellowship for racial ethnic minority students enrolled in Ph.D. or Th.D. programs in religious or theological studies. Applicants must be citizens or permanent residents of the U.S. or Canada. Award includes a stipend of up to $7500.

Academic/Career Areas Religion/Theology.

Award Fellowship for use in graduate years; not renewable. *Number:* 10–12. *Amount:* $5000–$10,000.

Eligibility Requirements Applicant must be Christian; American Indian/Alaska Native, Asian/Pacific Islander, Black (non-Hispanic), or Hispanic and enrolled or expecting to enroll full-time at a four-year institution or university. Available to U.S. and Canadian citizens.

Application Requirements Application, essay, financial need analysis, resume, references, transcript. *Deadline:* March 1.

Contact Dr. Sharon Watson Fluker, Director,
Expanding Horizons Partnership
Fund for Theological Education, Inc.
(FTE)
825 Houston Mill Road, Suite 250
Atlanta, GA 30329
Phone: 404-727-1450
Fax: 404-727-1490
E-mail: sfluker@thefund.org

GENERAL COMMISSION ON ARCHIVES AND HISTORY
http://www.gcah.org

ASIAN, BLACK, HISPANIC, AND NATIVE AMERICAN UNITED METHODIST HISTORY RESEARCH AWARDS
• *See number 645*

WOMEN IN UNITED METHODIST HISTORY RESEARCH GRANT
• *See number 646*

WOMEN IN UNITED METHODIST HISTORY WRITING AWARD
• *See number 647*

HISPANIC THEOLOGICAL INITIATIVE
http://www.htiprogram.org

HISPANIC THEOLOGICAL INITIATIVE
DISSERTATION YEAR GRANT • 869

The HTI will award nine (9) one-year dissertation fellowships per year throughout the life of the program to applicants who are ABD (All But Dissertation). Each award will be for an average of $16,000 for a period of one academic year. It is expected that the applicant completes his/her dissertation at the end of the award year. This grant is not renewable and cannot be extended beyond the designated award year.

Academic/Career Areas Religion/Theology.

Award Grant for use in graduate years; not renewable. *Number:* 9. *Amount:* $16,000.

Eligibility Requirements Applicant must be Christian; of Hispanic heritage and enrolled or expecting to enroll full-time at an institution or university. Available to U.S. citizens.

Application Requirements Application, portfolio, resume, references, dissertation proposal, approval and timeline. *Deadline:* January 11.

Contact Joanne Rodriguez, Associate Director
Hispanic Theological Initiative
12 Library Place
Princeton, NJ 08540
Phone: 609-252-1721
Fax: 609-252-1738
E-mail: hti@ptsem.edu

HISPANIC THEOLOGICAL INITIATIVE DOCTORAL
GRANT • 870

The HTI will award nine (9) outstanding Latino/a doctoral students a $13,000 grant each year during the life of the program. This award is for full-time doctoral students (Ph.D., Ed.D., Th.D. or equivalent only) and requires that the student's institution partners with HTI in providing the student with a tuition scholarship.

Academic/Career Areas Religion/Theology.

Award Grant for use in graduate years; renewable. *Number:* 9. *Amount:* $13,000.

Eligibility Requirements Applicant must be Christian; of Hispanic heritage and enrolled or expecting to enroll full-time at an institution or university. Available to U.S. citizens.

Application Requirements Application, autobiography, essay, resume, references, test scores, transcript, list of publications in print. *Deadline:* December 7.

Contact Joanne Rodriguez, Associate Director
Hispanic Theological Initiative
12 Library Place
Princeton, NJ 08540
Phone: 609-252-1721
Fax: 609-252-1738
E-mail: hti@ptsem.edu

HISPANIC THEOLOGICAL INITIATIVE SPECIAL
MENTORING GRANT • 871

Provides six awardees with a mentor each for one year and with $1,000 networking funds that are set aside for networking activities. It is offered when students have finished all of their Ph.D. course work and are preparing for exams or when students have been awarded a stipend which will be withdrawn or diminished if the student receives other funds.

Academic/Career Areas Religion/Theology.

Award Grant for use in graduate years; not renewable. *Number:* 6. *Amount:* $5000.

Eligibility Requirements Applicant must be Christian; of Hispanic heritage and enrolled or expecting to enroll full-time at an institution or university. Available to U.S. citizens.

Application Requirements Application, references, transcript. *Deadline:* January 11.

Contact Joanne Rodriguez, Associate Director
Hispanic Theological Initiative
12 Library Place
Princeton, NJ 08540
Phone: 609-252-1721
Fax: 609-252-1738
E-mail: hti@ptsem.edu

INTERNATIONAL ORDER OF THE
KING'S DAUGHTERS AND SONS

INTERNATIONAL ORDER OF THE KING'S
DAUGHTERS AND SONS STUDENT MINISTRY
SCHOLARSHIP • 872

Merit-based award available to graduate students, with a minimum 3.0 GPA, who are pursuing a career in the ministry, Master of Divinity only. School or seminary must be accredited by Association of Theological Schools in the U.S. or Canada. U.S. and Canadian citizens only. Send self-addressed stamped envelope with application request. Submit cassette of two five-minute discussions. Several one-time awards ranging from $500 to $1000. Application requests accepted January 1-March 31 only.

Academic/Career Areas Religion/Theology.

Award Scholarship for use in graduate years; not renewable. *Number:* 30–36. *Amount:* $500–$1000.

International Order of the King's Daughters and Sons (continued)

Eligibility Requirements Applicant must be Christian and enrolled or expecting to enroll at an institution or university. Applicant must have 3.0 GPA or higher. Available to U.S. and Canadian citizens.

Application Requirements Application, autobiography, essay, financial need analysis, photo, references, self-addressed stamped envelope, transcript. *Deadline:* April 30.

Contact Headquarters Office
International Order of the King's
Daughters and Sons
PO Box 1017
Chautauqua, NY 14722-1017
Phone: 716-357-4951

JEWISH FOUNDATION FOR EDUCATION OF WOMEN
http://www.jfew.org

FELLOWSHIP PROGRAM FOR EMIGRES PURSUING CAREERS IN JEWISH EDUCATION
• *See number 358*

MEMORIAL FOUNDATION FOR JEWISH CULTURE
http://www.mfjc.org

INTERNATIONAL FELLOWSHIPS IN JEWISH CULTURE PROGRAM
• *See number 128*

MEMORIAL FOUNDATION FOR JEWISH CULTURE INTERNATIONAL DOCTORAL SCHOLARSHIP
• *See number 130*

MEMORIAL FOUNDATION FOR JEWISH CULTURE SCHOLARSHIPS FOR POST-RABBINICAL STUDENTS • **873**

One-time award for post-rabbinical students for use in furthering their studies. This award is open to non-U.S. citizens and is not restricted to use in the U.S. Write for application. Deadline is October 31.

Academic/Career Areas Religion/Theology.

Award Scholarship for use in graduate years; not renewable. *Amount:* $1000–$3000.

Eligibility Requirements Applicant must be Jewish and enrolled or expecting to enroll full-time at an institution or university.

Application Requirements Application, photo, references. *Deadline:* October 31.

Contact Dr. Jerry Hochbaum, Executive Vice
President
Memorial Foundation for Jewish Culture
15 East 26th Street, Room 1703
New York, NY 10010
Phone: 212-679-4074

NATIONAL RESEARCH COUNCIL
http://www.nationalacademies.org/fellowships/

FORD FOUNDATION DISSERTATION FELLOWSHIPS FOR MINORITIES
• *See number 256*

FORD FOUNDATION POSTDOCTORAL FELLOWSHIP FOR MINORITIES
• *See number 257*

FORD FOUNDATION PREDOCTORAL FELLOWSHIPS FOR MINORITIES
• *See number 258*

PHI BETA KAPPA SOCIETY
http://www.pbk.org

MARY ISABEL SIBLEY FELLOWSHIP FOR GREEK AND FRENCH STUDIES
• *See number 132*

PRESBYTERIAN CHURCH (USA)
http://www.pcusa.org/highered

CONTINUING EDUCATION GRANT PROGRAM • **874**

Renewable grants for professional church workers who are serving congregations of less than 250 members. Must be a minister or lay professional in the Presbyterian Church (U.S.A.) for at least three years and planning to seek advanced degree, or professional development courses leading to certification.

Academic/Career Areas Religion/Theology.

Award Grant for use in graduate, or postgraduate years; renewable. *Amount:* $100–$2000.

Eligibility Requirements Applicant must be Presbyterian and enrolled or expecting to enroll at an institution or university. Applicant or parent of applicant must have employment or volunteer experience in designated career field. Available to U.S. citizens.

Application Requirements Application, financial need analysis, references. *Deadline:* Continuous.

Contact Laura Bryan, Program Assistant
Presbyterian Church (USA)
100 Witherspoon Street
Louisville, KY 40202-1396
Phone: 888-728-7228 Ext. 5735
Fax: 502-569-8766
E-mail: lbryan@ctr.pcusa.org

NATIVE AMERICAN SEMINARY SCHOLARSHIP
• **875**

One-time award for Alaska Natives, and Native Americans pursuing theological education. Must be a member of the Presbyterian Church (U.S.A.), and a U.S. citizen. Write for more information. Must have minimum 2.5 GPA.

Academic/Career Areas Religion/Theology.

Award Scholarship for use in graduate years; not renewable. *Number:* 5–10. *Amount:* $500–$1500.

Eligibility Requirements Applicant must be Presbyterian; American Indian/Alaska Native and enrolled or expecting to enroll at an institution or university. Applicant must have 2.5 GPA or higher. Available to U.S. citizens.

Application Requirements Application, financial need analysis, references, transcript. *Deadline:* Continuous.

Contact Maria Alvarez, Program Associate
Presbyterian Church (USA)
100 Witherspoon Street
Louisville, KY 40202-1396
Phone: 888-728-7228 Ext. 5760
Fax: 502-569-8766
E-mail: fcook@ctr.pcusa.org

PRESBYTERIAN STUDY GRANT • 876

Award for member of Presbyterian Church (U.S.A.) who is preparing for professional church occupation. Must be recommended by financial aid officer at theological institution. Must be U.S. citizen. Inquire for eligibility. Must rank in upper half of class or have a minimum 2.5 GPA. Renewal is possible.

Academic/Career Areas Religion/Theology.

Award Grant for use in graduate years; not renewable. *Amount:* $500–$2000.

Eligibility Requirements Applicant must be Presbyterian and enrolled or expecting to enroll full-time at an institution or university. Applicant must have 2.5 GPA or higher. Available to U.S. citizens.

Application Requirements Application, financial need analysis, references, transcript. *Deadline:* Continuous.

Contact Maria Alvarez, Program Associate
Presbyterian Church (USA)
100 Witherspoon Street
Louisville, KY 40202-1396
Phone: 888-728-7228 Ext. 5776
Fax: 502-569-8766
E-mail: fcook@ctr.pcusa.org

RACIAL ETHNIC LEADERSHIP SUPPLEMENTAL GRANT • 877

Award for minority member of Presbyterian Church (U.S.A.) preparing for professional church occupation. Must be recommended by financial aid officer at theological institution. Must be U.S. citizen. Inquire for eligibility. Must rank in upper half of class or have a minimum 2.5 GPA.

Academic/Career Areas Religion/Theology.

Award Grant for use in graduate years; not renewable. *Number:* up to 100. *Amount:* $500–$1500.

Eligibility Requirements Applicant must be Presbyterian; American Indian/Alaska Native, Asian/Pacific Islander, Black (non-Hispanic), or Hispanic and enrolled or expecting to enroll full-time at an institution or university. Applicant must have 2.5 GPA or higher. Available to U.S. citizens.

Application Requirements Application, financial need analysis, references, transcript. *Deadline:* Continuous.

Contact Maria Alvarez, Program Associate
Presbyterian Church (USA)
100 Witherspoon Street
Louisville, KY 40202-1396
Phone: 888-728-7228 Ext. 5776
Fax: 502-569-8766
E-mail: fcook@ctr.pcusa.org

RIVERSIDE PRESBYTERIAN CHURCH
http://www.rpcjax.org

DAISY AND EUGENE HALE MEMORIAL FUND • 878

Helps defray costs in pursuing religious education in theological seminaries for the purpose of becoming a minister in the Presbyterian Church. Must be resident of Florida.

Academic/Career Areas Religion/Theology.

Award Scholarship for use in graduate years; renewable. *Number:* 8–16. *Amount:* $500–$4000.

Eligibility Requirements Applicant must be Presbyterian; enrolled or expecting to enroll full-time at an institution or university and resident of Florida. Available to U.S. and non-U.S. citizens.

Application Requirements Application, autobiography, essay, financial need analysis, photo, references, transcript. *Deadline:* April 1.

Contact Mrs. Lois Ward, Chair
Riverside Presbyterian Church
849 Park Street
Jacksonville, FL 32204-3394
Phone: 904-355-4585
Fax: 904-355-4508
E-mail: office@rpcjax.org

UNITED METHODIST CHURCH
http://www.umc.org/

GEORGIA HARKNESS SCHOLARSHIPS • 879

One-time award for female preparing for ordained ministry as an elder in the United Methodist Church. Must be 35 or older and enrolled in an accredited school of theology and working toward a basic seminary degree. Must study full-time.

United Methodist Church (continued)

Academic/Career Areas Religion/Theology.

Award Scholarship for use in graduate years; not renewable.

Eligibility Requirements Applicant must be Methodist; age 35; enrolled or expecting to enroll full-time at an institution or university and female. Available to U.S. citizens.

Application Requirements Application, essay, references, transcript. *Deadline:* March 1.

Contact Sandy Walker, Coordinator for Continuing
　　　　　Education in Ministry
　　　　　United Methodist Church
　　　　　PO Box 340007
　　　　　Nashville, TN 37203-0007
　　　　　Phone: 615-340-7409
　　　　　E-mail: swalker@gbhem.org

UNITED METHODIST COMMUNICATIONS
http://www.umcom.org/scholarships

STOODY-WEST FELLOWSHIP FOR GRADUATE STUDY IN RELIGIOUS JOURNALISM
• *See number 261*

VERNE CATT MCDOWELL CORPORATION

VERNE CATT MC DOWELL CORPORATION SCHOLARSHIP • **880**

Scholarships for graduate theological studies to ministers ordained or studying to meet the requirements to be ordained as a minister in the Christian Church (Disciple of Christ) denomination. Applicant must be admitted into a professional degree program at a graduate institution of theological education. Application is due May 1.

Academic/Career Areas Religion/Theology.

Award Scholarship for use in graduate years; renewable. *Number:* 6–8. *Amount:* $3000.

Eligibility Requirements Applicant must be Disciple of Christ and enrolled or expecting to enroll full or part-time at an institution or university. Available to U.S. citizens.

Application Requirements Application, financial need analysis, interview, references, transcript. *Deadline:* May 1.

Contact Emily Killin, Business Manager
　　　　　Verne Catt McDowell Corporation
　　　　　PO Box 1336
　　　　　Albany, OR 97321-0440
　　　　　Phone: 541-926-6829

WOODROW WILSON NATIONAL FELLOWSHIP FOUNDATION
http://www.woodrow.org

ANDREW W. MELLON FELLOWSHIPS IN HUMANISTIC STUDIES
• *See number 134*

CHARLOTTE W. NEWCOMBE DOCTORAL DISSERTATION FELLOWSHIPS
• *See number 693*

WOODROW WILSON NATIONAL FELLOWSHIP FOUNDATION DISSERTATION GRANTS IN WOMEN'S STUDIES
• *See number 135*

WOODROW WILSON POSTDOCTORAL FELLOWSHIPS IN THE HUMANITIES
• *See number 136*

SCIENCE, TECHNOLOGY, AND SOCIETY

AIR AND WASTE MANAGEMENT ASSOCIATION
http://www.awma.org

AIR AND WASTE MANAGEMENT ASSOCIATION SCHOLARSHIP ENDOWMENT TRUST FUND
• *See number 24*

AMERICAN AGRICULTURAL ECONOMICS ASSOCIATION FOUNDATION
http://www.aaea.org

FARM CREDIT GRADUATE SCHOLARSHIP FOR THE STUDY OF YOUNG, BEGINNING OR SMALL FARMERS AND RANCHERS
• *See number 1*

OUTSTANDING DOCTORAL AND MASTER'S THESIS AWARDS
• *See number 2*

SYLVIA LANE MENTOR RESEARCH FELLOWSHIP FUND
• *See number 3*

AMERICAN ASSOCIATION OF UNIVERSITY WOMEN (AAUW) EDUCATIONAL FOUNDATION
http://www.aauw.org

ELEANOR ROOSEVELT TEACHER FELLOWSHIPS
• *See number 343*

AMERICAN INSTITUTE OF AERONAUTICS AND ASTRONAUTICS
http://www.aiaa.org

AIAA FOUNDATION GRADUATE AWARDS
• See number 26

AIAA FOUNDATION ORVILLE AND WILBUR WRIGHT AWARDS
• See number 27

AMERICAN SOCIETY OF ARMS COLLECTORS

AMERICAN SOCIETY OF ARMS COLLECTORS SCHOLARSHIP
• See number 138

ARKANSAS DEPARTMENT OF HIGHER EDUCATION
http://www.arscholarships.com

MINORITY MASTER'S FELLOWS PROGRAM
• See number 351

CHARLES BABBAGE INSTITUTE
http://www.cbi.umn.edu

ADELLE AND ERWIN TOMASH FELLOWSHIP IN THE HISTORY OF INFORMATION PROCESSING
• See number 267

DELAWARE VALLEY SPACE GRANT CONSORTIUM
http://www.delspace.org

NASA/DELAWARE VALLEY SPACE GRANT FELLOWSHIP
• See number 52

HUDSON RIVER FOUNDATION
http://www.hudsonriver.org

HUDSON RIVER FOUNDATION GRADUATE FELLOWSHIPS
• See number 205

IMGIP/ICEOP
http://www.imgip.siu.edu

ILLINOIS MINORITY GRADUATE INCENTIVE PROGRAM FELLOWSHIP
• See number 372

INTERNATIONAL DEVELOPMENT RESEARCH CENTER
http://www.idrc.ca/awards

IDRC DOCTORAL RESEARCH AWARD
• See number 12

JOHN G. BENE FELLOWSHIP IN COMMUNITY FORESTRY • 881

One-time award for Canadian graduate students undertaking research on the relationship of forest resources to the social, economic, and environmental welfare of people in developing countries. Submit curriculum vitae and proof of Canadian citizenship. Award is up to Can$15,000. Write for complete requirements and application guidelines, proof of Canadian citizenship or permanent residency required. Deadline is March 1.

Academic/Career Areas Science, Technology and Society.

Award Fellowship for use in graduate years; not renewable. *Number:* 1. *Amount:* up to $15,000.

Eligibility Requirements Applicant must be Canadian citizenship and enrolled or expecting to enroll full-time at an institution or university.

Application Requirements Application, autobiography, essay, financial need analysis, resume, references, transcript, letter from institution. *Deadline:* March 1.

Contact Danielle Reinhardt, Program Assistant
International Development Research
Center
PO Box 8500
Ottawa, ON K1G 3H9
Canada
Phone: 613-236-6163
Fax: 613-563-0815
E-mail: cta@idrc.ca

L.S.B. LEAKEY FOUNDATION
http://www.leakeyfoundation.org

RESEARCH GRANTS
• See number 79

NASA IDAHO SPACE GRANT CONSORTIUM
http://www.uidaho.edu/nasa_isgc

NASA ID SPACE GRANT CONSORTIUM FELLOWSHIP PROGRAM
• See number 60

NATIONAL ACTION COUNCIL FOR MINORITIES IN ENGINEERING-NACME, INC.
http://www.nacme.org

SLOAN PH.D PROGRAM
• See number 243

SENSE OF SMELL INSTITUTE
http://www.senseofsmell.org

SENSE OF SMELL INSTITUTE RESEARCH GRANTS
• See number 214

TOVA FELLOWSHIP
• See number 101

SOCIAL SCIENCES

AFRICAN AMERICAN SUCCESS FOUNDATION, INC.
http://www.blacksuccessfoundation.org

LYDIA DONALDSON TUTT-JONES MEMORIAL AWARD
• See number 112

ALEXANDER VON HUMBOLDT FOUNDATION
http://www.humboldt-foundation.de

TRANSCOOP PROGRAM
• See number 315

AMERICAN AGRICULTURAL ECONOMICS ASSOCIATION FOUNDATION
http://www.aaea.org

OUTSTANDING DOCTORAL AND MASTER'S THESIS AWARDS
• See number 2

SYLVIA LANE MENTOR RESEARCH FELLOWSHIP FUND
• See number 3

AMERICAN CENTER OF ORIENTAL RESEARCH
http://www.bu.edu/acor

CAORC FELLOWSHIPS
• See number 666

CAORC SENIOR FELLOWSHIP
• See number 665

AMERICAN COUNCIL OF LEARNED SOCIETIES (ACLS)
http://www.acls.org

AMERICAN COUNCIL OF LEARNED SOCIETIES FELLOWSHIPS FOR POSTDOCTORAL RESEARCH IN THE HUMANITIES
• See number 667

AMERICAN COUNCIL OF LEARNED SOCIETIES GRANTS FOR EAST EUROPEAN STUDIES-DISSERTATION FELLOWSHIPS
• See number 113

AMERICAN COUNCIL OF LEARNED SOCIETIES GRANTS FOR EAST EUROPEAN STUDIES-FELLOWSHIPS FOR POSTDOCTORAL RESEARCH
• See number 668

CONTEMPLATIVE PRACTICE FELLOWSHIPS
• See number 162

LIBRARY OF CONGRESS FELLOWSHIP IN INTERNATIONAL STUDIES
• See number 670

AMERICAN GEOPHYSICAL UNION
http://www.agu.org

AMERICAN GEOPHYSICAL UNION HORTON RESEARCH GRANT
• See number 25

AMERICAN HISTORICAL ASSOCIATION
http://www.theaha.org

LITTLETON-GRISWOLD RESEARCH GRANTS
• See number 639

AMERICAN INSTITUTE OF PAKISTAN STUDIES

AMERICAN INSTITUTE OF PAKISTAN STUDIES GRADUATE STUDENT FELLOWSHIP
• See number 671

AMERICAN INSTITUTE OF PAKISTAN STUDIES POSTDOCTORAL FELLOWSHIP
• See number 672

AMERICAN INSTITUTE OF PAKISTAN STUDIES PREDOCTORAL FELLOWSHIPS
• See number 673

AMERICAN POLITICAL SCIENCE ASSOCIATION
http://www.apsanet.org

CONGRESSIONAL FELLOWSHIP FOR FEDERAL EXECUTIVES
• See number 676

AMERICAN PSYCHOLOGICAL ASSOCIATION
http://www.apa.org/mfp

MINORITY FELLOWSHIP FOR HIV/AIDS RESEARCH TRAINING
• See number 473

MINORITY FELLOWSHIP FOR MENTAL HEALTH RESEARCH • 882

Renewable award for U.S. citizen or permanent resident enrolled full-time in doctoral program in psychology and committee to a career in mental health or psychological research as it relates to ethnic minority populations. Application available at website.

Academic/Career Areas Social Sciences.

Award Fellowship for use in graduate years; renewable.

Eligibility Requirements Applicant must be enrolled or expecting to enroll full-time at an institution or university. Available to U.S. citizens.

Application Requirements Application, essay, financial need analysis, references, transcript. *Deadline:* January 15.

Contact Dr. Kim Nickerson, Program Assistant
Director
American Psychological Association
750 First Street, NE
Washington, DC 20002-4242
Phone: 202-336-6027
Fax: 202-336-6012
E-mail: mfp@apa.org

MINORITY FELLOWSHIP IN MENTAL HEALTH AND SUBSTANCE ABUSE SERVICES
• See number 474

AMERICAN RESEARCH INSTITUTE IN TURKEY (ARIT)
http://www.mec.sas.upenn.edu/ARIT

ARIT MELLON RESEARCH FELLOWSHIPS FOR CENTRAL AND EASTERN EUROPEAN SCHOLARS IN TURKEY
• See number 677

ARIT, HUMANITIES AND SOCIAL SCIENCE FELLOWSHIPS IN TURKEY
• See number 678

AMERICAN SCHOOLS OF ORIENTAL RESEARCH (ASOR)
http://www.asor.org

MESOPOTAMIAN FELLOWSHIP
• See number 68

W.F. ALBRIGHT INSTITUTE OF ARCHAEOLOGICAL RESEARCH/COUNCIL OF AMERICAN OVERSEAS RESEARCH CENTERS FELLOWSHIPS FOR ADVANCED MULTICOUNTRY RESEARCH
• See number 681

W.F. ALBRIGHT INSTITUTE OF ARCHAEOLOGICAL RESEARCH/NATIONAL ENDOWMENT OF THE HUMANITIES FELLOWSHIPS
• See number 71

W.F. ALRBIGHT INSTITUTE OF ARCHAEOLOGICAL RESEARCH SAMUEL H. KRESS JOINT ATHENS-JERUSALEM FELLOWSHIP
• See number 72

ARCTIC INSTITUTE OF NORTH AMERICA
http://www.ucalgary.ca/aina

LORRAINE ALLISON SCHOLARSHIP
• See number 118

ASSOCIATION FOR INSTITUTIONAL RESEARCH
http://www.airweb.org

AIR RESEARCH GRANTS-IMPROVING INSTITUTIONAL RESEARCH IN POSTSECONDARY EDUCATION INSTITUTIONS
• See number 352

DISSERTATION SUPPORT GRANT- IMPROVING INSTITUTIONAL RESEARCH IN POSTSECONDARY EDUCATIONAL INSTITUTIONS
• See number 353

SUMMER DATA POLICY INSTITUTE
• See number 354

ASSOCIATION FOR WOMEN IN SCIENCE EDUCATIONAL FOUNDATION
http://www.awis.org

ASSOCIATION FOR WOMEN IN SCIENCE PREDOCTORAL FELLOWSHIP
• See number 77

BLUE CROSS BLUE SHIELD OF MICHIGAN FOUNDATION
http://www.bcbsm.com/foundation

BLUE CROSS BLUE SHIELD OF MICHIGAN FOUNDATION STUDENT AWARD PROGRAM
• See number 393

CENTER FOR HELLENIC STUDIES
http://www.chs.harvard.edu

CENTER FOR HELLENIC STUDIES FELLOWSHIPS
• *See number 121*

CHINA TIMES CULTURAL FOUNDATION

CHINA TIMES CULTURAL FOUNDATION DOCTORAL DISSERTATION RESEARCH IN CHINESE STUDIES SCHOLARSHIPS
• *See number 122*

COMMUNITY ASSOCIATIONS INSTITUTE RESEARCH FOUNDATION
http://www.cairf.org

BYRON HANKE FELLOWSHIP FOR GRADUATE RESEARCH
• *See number 317*

COUNCIL FOR EUROPEAN STUDIES
http://www.europanet.org

COUNCIL FOR EUROPEAN STUDIES PRE-DISSERTATION FELLOWSHIP
• *See number 682*

COUNCIL ON SOCIAL WORK EDUCATION
http://www.cswe.org

COUNCIL ON SOCIAL WORK EDUCATION/ MENTAL HEALTH MINORITY RESEARCH FELLOWSHIP
• *See number 483*

DOCTORAL FELLOWSHIPS IN SOCIAL WORK FOR ETHNIC MINORITY STUDENTS PREPARING FOR LEADERSHIP ROLES IN MENTAL HEALTH AND/OR SUB. ABUSE
• *See number 484*

CULTURAL SERVICES OF THE FRENCH EMBASSY
http://www.frenchculture.org

CHATEAUBRIAND SCHOLARSHIP PROGRAM
• *See number 164*

DAVID LIBRARY OF THE AMERICAN REVOLUTION
http://www.dlar.org

FELLOWSHIPS FOR THE STUDY OF THE AMERICAN REVOLUTION
• *See number 644*

EPILEPSY FOUNDATION
http://www.epilepsyfoundation.org

EPILEPSY FOUNDATION BEHAVIORAL SCIENCES RESEARCH TRAINING FELLOWSHIP
• *See number 318*

PREDOCTORAL RESEARCH TRAINING FELLOWSHIP
• *See number 200*

FRENCH INSTITUTE OF WASHINGTON (INSTITUT FRANÇAIS DE WASHINGTON)
http://www.unc.edu/depts/institut

EDOUARD MOROT-SIR FELLOWSHIP IN LITERATURE
• *See number 165*

GILBERT CHINARD FELLOWSHIPS AND EDOUARD MOROT-SIR FELLOWSHIP IN LITERATURE
• *See number 166*

HARMON CHADBOURN RORISON FELLOWSHIP
• *See number 167*

FRIEDRICH EBERT FOUNDATION

EBERT FOUNDATION ADVANCED GRADUATE FELLOWSHIPS
• *See number 319*

EBERT FOUNDATION DOCTORAL RESEARCH FELLOWSHIP
• *See number 320*

EBERT FOUNDATION POSTDOCTORAL FELLOWSHIPS
• *See number 321*

GERMAN ACADEMIC EXCHANGE SERVICE (DAAD)
http://www.daad.org

LEO BAECK INSTITUTE - DAAD GRANTS
• *See number 126*

NSF-DAAD GRANTS FOR THE NATURAL, ENGINEERING, AND SOCIAL SCIENCES
• *See number 379*

GETTY GRANT PROGRAM
http://www.getty.edu/grants

GETTY SCHOLAR AND VISITING SCHOLAR GRANTS
• *See number 145*

PREDOCTORAL AND POSTDOCTORAL FELLOWSHIPS
• *See number 147*

GOVERNMENT FINANCE OFFICERS ASSOCIATION
http://www.GFOA.org

PUBLIC EMPLOYEE RETIREMENT RESEARCH AND ADMINISTRATION SCHOLARSHIP
• *See number 230*

HARVARD UNIVERSITY CENTER FOR BASIC RESEARCH IN THE SOCIAL SCIENCES
http://www.cbrss.harvard.edu

CENTER FOR BASIC RESEARCH IN THE SOCIAL SCIENCES POSTDOCTORAL FELLOWSHIP
• *See number 860*

HUDSON RIVER NATIONAL ESTUARINE RESEARCH RESERVE
http://www.ocm.nos.noaa/nerr/fellow.html

NATIONAL ESTUARINE RESEARCH RESERVE GRADUATE FELLOWSHIP PROGRAM
• *See number 55*

INTERNATIONAL DEVELOPMENT RESEARCH CENTER
http://www.idrc.ca/awards

AGROPOLIS
• *See number 10*

IDRC DOCTORAL RESEARCH AWARD
• *See number 12*

INTERNATIONAL FOUNDATION FOR ETHICAL RESEARCH
http://www.ifer.org

FELLOWSHIPS IN ALTERNATIVES IN ETHICAL RESEARCH
• *See number 207*

INTERNATIONAL RESEARCH & EXCHANGES BOARD
http://www.irex.org

IREX INDIVIDUAL ADVANCED RESEARCH OPPORTUNITIES
• *See number 684*

IREX SHORT-TERM TRAVEL GRANTS
• *See number 685*

JOHN J. AND NANCY LEE ROBERTS FELLOWSHIP PROGRAM • **883**

A single grant of up to $50,000 for research projects lasting up to 18 months. This program supports cutting-edge research in the social sciences in Eastern Europe, the NIS, China, Mongolia, Turkey, Afghani-stan, Pakistan, and Iran for scholars with Ph.D. or equivalent terminal degrees. Collaborative research programs involving international colleagues are strongly encouraged.

Academic/Career Areas Social Sciences.

Award Grant for use in postgraduate years; not renewable. *Number:* 1. *Amount:* up to $50,000.

Eligibility Requirements Applicant must be enrolled or expecting to enroll at an institution or university. Available to U.S. citizens.

Application Requirements Application, references, C.V., proposal, and budget. *Deadline:* April 15.

Contact Information Assistant
International Research & Exchanges Board
2121 K Street, NW, Suite 700
Washington, DC 20037
Phone: 202-628-8188
Fax: 202-628-8189
E-mail: irex@irex.org

REGIONAL SCHOLAR EXCHANGE PROGRAM (RSEP)
• *See number 686*

JAPAN FOUNDATION
http://www.jfny.org

JAPAN FOUNDATION DOCTORAL FELLOWSHIP
• *See number 687*

JAPAN FOUNDATION RESEARCH FELLOWSHIP
• *See number 688*

JAPAN FOUNDATION SHORT-TERM RESEARCH FELLOWSHIP
• *See number 689*

JAPANESE GOVERNMENT/THE MONBUSHO SCHOLARSHIP PROGRAM
http://embjapan.org/la

RESEARCH STUDENT SCHOLARSHIP
• *See number 13*

JOHN F. KENNEDY LIBRARY FOUNDATION
http://www.jfklibrary.org

ABBA SCHWARTZ FELLOWSHIPS
• *See number 861*

HEMINGWAY RESEARCH GRANTS
• *See number 690*

KENNEDY RESEARCH GRANTS
• *See number 100*

MACKENZIE KING SCHOLARSHIPS BOARD

MACKENZIE KING TRAVELLING SCHOLARSHIPS
• See number 236

MARCUS CENTER OF THE AMERICAN JEWISH ARCHIVES
http://www.huc.edu/aja

AMERICAN JEWISH ARCHIVES DISSERTATION AND POSTDOCTORAL RESEARCH FELLOWSHIPS
• See number 649

NATIONAL ACADEMY OF EDUCATION
http://www.nae.nyu.edu

NATIONAL ACADEMY OF EDUCATION/SPENCER POSTDOCTORAL FELLOWSHIP PROGRAM
• See number 360

NATIONAL ASSOCIATION OF THE DEAF
http://www.nad.org

WILLIAM C. STOKOE SCHOLARSHIPS
• See number 255

NATIONAL HEMOPHILIA FOUNDATION
http://www.hemophilia.org

NATIONAL HEMOPHILIA FOUNDATION SOCIAL WORK EXCELLENCE FELLOWSHIP • 884

Fellowship for MSW from an accredited school of social work or student in a DSW program or applicant. Must have a master's degree in social work related field, be licensed by the State to practice as a master's level clinical social worker, and work in a bleeding disorder program. Proposed project must have relevance to current practice in bleeding disorders.

Academic/Career Areas Social Sciences.

Award Fellowship for use in postgraduate years; not renewable. *Number:* 1. *Amount:* $10,000.

Eligibility Requirements Applicant must be enrolled or expecting to enroll at an institution or university.

Application Requirements Application, references, description of proposed research project. *Deadline:* April 1.

Contact Rita Barsky, Assistant Director
National Hemophilia Foundation
116 West 32nd Street, 11th Floor
New York, NY 10001
Phone: 212-328-3730
Fax: 212-328-3788
E-mail: rbarsky@hemophilia.org

NATIONAL RESEARCH COUNCIL
http://www.nationalacademies.org/fellowships/

FORD FOUNDATION DISSERTATION FELLOWSHIPS FOR MINORITIES
• See number 256

FORD FOUNDATION POSTDOCTORAL FELLOWSHIP FOR MINORITIES
• See number 257

FORD FOUNDATION PREDOCTORAL FELLOWSHIPS FOR MINORITIES
• See number 258

NATIONAL SLEEP FOUNDATION
http://www.sleepfoundation.org

NATIONAL SLEEP FOUNDATION POSTDOCTORAL FELLOWSHIP PROGRAM
• See number 213

PHI BETA KAPPA SOCIETY
http://www.pbk.org

MARY ISABEL SIBLEY FELLOWSHIP FOR GREEK AND FRENCH STUDIES
• See number 132

PI GAMMA MU INTERNATIONAL HONOR SOCIETY IN SOCIETY SCIENCE
http://www.sckans.edu/~pgm

PI GAMMA MU SCHOLARSHIP
• See number 273

POPULATION COUNCIL
http://www.popcouncil.org

POPULATION COUNCIL FELLOWSHIPS IN THE SOCIAL SCIENCES, MID-CAREER LEVEL
• See number 328

POPULATION COUNCIL FELLOWSHIPS IN THE SOCIAL SCIENCES, POSTDOCTORAL LEVEL
• See number 329

POPULATION COUNCIL FELLOWSHIPS IN THE SOCIAL SCIENCES, PREDOCTORAL LEVEL
• See number 330

RADCLIFFE INSTITUTE FOR ADVANCED STUDY-MURRAY RESEARCH CENTER
http://www.radcliffe.edu/murray

ADOLESCENT AND YOUTH DISSERTATION AWARD • 885

The goal of the program is to support research on youth and adolescent development. Proposals focusing on "youth as a resource" or positive attributes and strengths of youth are especially encouraged. Projects drawing on the center's data will be given priority, although the use of the center's resources is not a requirement. For details visit http://www.radcliff.edu/murray.

Academic/Career Areas Social Sciences.

Award Grant for use in graduate years; not renewable. *Number:* 4. *Amount:* $5000.

Eligibility Requirements Applicant must be enrolled or expecting to enroll full or part-time at an institution or university. Available to U.S. and non-U.S. citizens.

Application Requirements Application, references, proposal, timetable, budget, CV, cover letter. *Deadline:* April 1.

Contact Veronic Aghayan, Grants Administrator
Radcliffe Institute for Advanced Study-
Murray Research Center
10 Garden Street
Cambridge, MA 02138
Phone: 617-495-8140
E-mail: mrc@radcliffe.edu

BLOCK DISSERTATION AWARD • 886

Grants to support women graduate students studying the psychological development of girls or women. Proposals should focus on sex and gender differences or some developmental issue of particular concern to American females. Priority given to projects that draw on data resources of Murray Research Center. See http://www.radcliffe.edu for details.

Academic/Career Areas Social Sciences.

Award Grant for use in graduate years; not renewable. *Number:* 1. *Amount:* $5000.

Eligibility Requirements Applicant must be enrolled or expecting to enroll full or part-time at an institution or university and female. Available to U.S. and non-U.S. citizens.

Application Requirements Application, references, proposal, timetable, budget, curriculum vitae. *Deadline:* April 1.

Contact Veronic Aghayan, Grants Administrator
Radcliffe Institute for Advanced Study-
Murray Research Center
10 Garden Street
Cambridge, MA 02138
Phone: 617-495-8140
E-mail: mrc@radcliffe.edu

MURRAY DISSERTATION AWARD • 887

Grants to support graduate students doing research in the social and behavioral sciences. Dissertation topic should focus on some aspect of "the study of lives," concentrating on issues in human development or personality for populations within the U.S. Preference

given to projects drawing on the center's data. See http://www.radcliffe.edu for details.

Academic/Career Areas Social Sciences.

Award Grant for use in graduate years; not renewable. *Number:* 4. *Amount:* $5000.

Eligibility Requirements Applicant must be enrolled or expecting to enroll full or part-time at an institution or university. Available to U.S. and non-U.S. citizens.

Application Requirements Application, references, proposal, timetable, budget, curriculum vitae. *Deadline:* April 1.

Contact Veronic Aghayan, Grants Administrator
Radcliffe Institute for Advanced Study-
Murray Research Center
10 Garden Street
Cambridge, MA 02138
Phone: 617-495-8140
E-mail: mrc@radcliffe.edu

OBSERVATIONAL STUDIES DISSERTATION AWARD • 888

Award to encourage students' use of observational studies data which evaluates impact and effectiveness of two welfare intervention programs. Dissertation proposals must be approved by advisor or committee before application is submitted. See website for details. Applicants must have received a Ph.D. or other doctoral or terminal degree prior to time of application. Application deadlines are October 15 and March 15.

Academic/Career Areas Social Sciences.

Award Grant for use in postgraduate years; not renewable. *Number:* 2. *Amount:* up to $10,000.

Eligibility Requirements Applicant must be enrolled or expecting to enroll full or part-time at an institution or university. Available to U.S. and non-U.S. citizens.

Application Requirements Application, references, proposal, timetable, budget, curriculum vitae.

Contact Grants Administrator
Radcliffe Institute for Advanced Study-
Murray Research Center
10 Garden Street
Cambridge, MA 02138
Phone: 617-495-8140
E-mail: mrc@radcliffe.edu

RADCLIFFE POSTDOCTORAL RESEARCH SUPPORT PROGRAM- STUDYING DIVERSE LIVES • 889

Grants are available for social science researchers who have received their PhD in the past ten years. Research should focus on data with racially and ethnically diverse sample to use in their work who have received their doctorate within the last ten years.

Radcliffe Institute for Advanced Study-Murray Research Center (continued)

Proposed projects must draw on data from the Murray Center's Diversity Archive. Deadlines: February 1 and October 15.

Academic/Career Areas Social Sciences.

Award Grant for use in postgraduate years; not renewable. *Number:* 3. *Amount:* up to $10,000.

Eligibility Requirements Applicant must be enrolled or expecting to enroll at an institution or university. Available to U.S. and non-U.S. citizens.

Application Requirements Application.

Contact Grants Administrator
Radcliffe Institute for Advanced Study-Murray Research Center
10 Garden Street
Cambridge, MA 02138
Phone: 617-495-8140
E-mail: mrc@radcliffe.edu

RESOURCES FOR THE FUTURE
http://www.rff.org

GILBERT F. WHITE POSTDOCTORAL FELLOWSHIPS
• *See number 331*

JOSEPH L. FISHER DISSERTATION AWARDS
• *See number 332*

SENSE OF SMELL INSTITUTE
http://www.senseofsmell.org

SENSE OF SMELL INSTITUTE RESEARCH GRANTS
• *See number 214*

TOVA FELLOWSHIP
• *See number 101*

SWEDISH INFORMATION SERVICE
http://www.swedeninfo.com

BICENTENNIAL SWEDISH-AMERICAN EXCHANGE FUND TRAVEL GRANTS
• *See number 133*

UNITED STATES INSTITUTE OF PEACE
http://www.usip.org

JENNINGS RANDOLPH SENIOR FELLOW AWARD
• *See number 333*

PEACE SCHOLAR DISSERTATION FELLOWSHIP
• *See number 334*

W. E. UPJOHN INSTITUTE FOR EMPLOYMENT RESEARCH
http://www.upjohninst.org

UPJOHN INSTITUTE DISSERTATION AWARD
• *See number 335*

UPJOHN INSTITUTE GRANT PROGRAM
• *See number 336*

UPJOHN INSTITUTE MINI-GRANT PROGRAM
• *See number 337*

WELLESLEY COLLEGE
http://www.wellesley.edu/CWS/

VIDA DUTTON SCUDDER FELLOWSHIP
• *See number 770*

WOODROW WILSON NATIONAL FELLOWSHIP FOUNDATION
http://www.woodrow.org

CHARLOTTE W. NEWCOMBE DOCTORAL DISSERTATION FELLOWSHIPS
• *See number 693*

THOMAS R. PICKERING GRADUATE FOREIGN AFFAIRS FELLOWSHIP PROGRAM
• *See number 241*

WOODROW WILSON NATIONAL FELLOWSHIP FOUNDATION DISSERTATION GRANTS IN WOMEN'S STUDIES
• *See number 135*

WORLD BANK
http://www.worldbank.org/wbi/scholarships

ROBERT S. MCNAMARA FELLOWSHIP
• *See number 339*

SOCIAL SERVICES

AMERICAN COUNCIL OF TEACHERS OF RUSSIAN
http://www.actr.org

TITLE VIII RESEARCH SCHOLAR AND COMBINED RESEARCH AND LANGUAGE STUDY PROGRAM
• *See number 114*

COUNCIL ON SOCIAL WORK EDUCATION
http://www.cswe.org

COUNCIL ON SOCIAL WORK EDUCATION/ MENTAL HEALTH MINORITY RESEARCH FELLOWSHIP
• *See number 483*

DOCTORAL FELLOWSHIPS IN SOCIAL WORK FOR ETHNIC MINORITY STUDENTS PREPARING FOR LEADERSHIP ROLES IN MENTAL HEALTH AND/OR SUB. ABUSE
• See number 484

DELTA SOCIETY
http://www.deltasociety.org

HARRIS SWEATT TRAVEL GRANT
• See number 17

EPILEPSY FOUNDATION
http://www.epilepsyfoundation.org

EPILEPSY FOUNDATION BEHAVIORAL SCIENCES RESEARCH TRAINING FELLOWSHIP
• See number 318

MENNONITE HEALTH SERVICES
http://www.mhsonline.org

ELMER EDIGER MEMORIAL SCHOLARSHIP FUND
• See number 541

NATIONAL ASSOCIATION OF JUNIOR AUXILIARIES, INC.
http://www.najanet.org

NATIONAL ASSOCIATION OF JUNIOR AUXILIARIES GRADUATE SCHOLARSHIP PROGRAM
• See number 361

OREGON STUDENT ASSISTANCE COMMISSION
http://www.osac.state.or.us

OREGON SCHOLARSHIP FUND GRADUATE STUDENT AWARD
• See number 362

PI GAMMA MU INTERNATIONAL HONOR SOCIETY IN SOCIETY SCIENCE
http://www.sckans.edu/~pgm

PI GAMMA MU SCHOLARSHIP
• See number 273

WELLESLEY COLLEGE
http://www.wellesley.edu/CWS/

MARGARET FREEMAN BOWERS FELLOWSHIP
• See number 724

SPECIAL EDUCATION

AMERICAN LEGION AUXILIARY, DEPARTMENT OF NEBRASKA

AMERICAN LEGION AUXILIARY DEPARTMENT OF NEBRASKA GRADUATE SCHOLARSHIPS
• See number 345

AMERICAN LEGION AUXILIARY, DEPARTMENT OF NEW MEXICO

NEW MEXICO PAST PRESIDENTS SCHOLARSHIP FOR TEACHERS OF EXCEPTIONAL CHILDREN • 890

One-time award for residents of New Mexico to provide additional special education training to teach exceptional children in New Mexico. Contact for additional information.

Academic/Career Areas Special Education.

Award Scholarship for use in graduate years; not renewable. *Number:* up to 1. *Amount:* up to $250.

Eligibility Requirements Applicant must be enrolled or expecting to enroll full or part-time at an institution or university and resident of New Mexico. Applicant or parent of applicant must have employment or volunteer experience in teaching. Available to U.S. citizens.

Application Requirements Application. *Deadline:* March 1.

Contact Loreen Jorgensen, Scholarship Director
American Legion Auxiliary, Department of New Mexico
1215 Mountain Road, NE
Albuquerque, NM 87102
Phone: 505-242-9918

AMERICAN LEGION AUXILIARY, DEPARTMENT OF WISCONSIN
http://www.amlegionauxwi.org

CHILD WELFARE SCHOLARSHIPS
• See number 346

DELTA SOCIETY
http://www.deltasociety.org

HARRIS SWEATT TRAVEL GRANT
• See number 17

GEORGIA STUDENT FINANCE COMMISSION
http://www.gsfc.org

GEORGIA HOPE TEACHER SCHOLARSHIP PROGRAM
• See number 356

KNIGHTS OF COLUMBUS

BISHOP CHARLES P. GRECO GRADUATE FELLOWSHIP PROGRAM
• See number 359

MENNONITE HEALTH SERVICES
http://www.mhsonline.org

ELMER EDIGER MEMORIAL SCHOLARSHIP FUND
• See number 541

NATIONAL ASSOCIATION OF JUNIOR AUXILIARIES, INC.
http://www.najanet.org

NATIONAL ASSOCIATION OF JUNIOR AUXILIARIES GRADUATE SCHOLARSHIP PROGRAM
• See number 361

SPORTS-RELATED

NATIONAL COLLEGIATE ATHLETIC ASSOCIATION
http://www.ncaa.org

ETHNIC MINORITY AND WOMEN'S ENHANCEMENT SCHOLARSHIP • 891

One-time awards to ethnic minorities and to women are available annually to college graduates who will be entering into the first year of their initial postgraduate studies. The applicant must be seeking admission or have been accepted into a sports administration or related program that will assist in obtaining a career in intercollegiate athletics (athletics administrator, coach, athletic trainer or other career that provides a direct service to intercollegiate athletics).

Academic/Career Areas Sports-related.

Award Scholarship for use in graduate years; not renewable. *Number:* 30. *Amount:* $6000.

Eligibility Requirements Applicant must be enrolled or expecting to enroll full-time at a four-year institution or university and must have an interest in athletics/sports. Available to U.S. citizens.

Application Requirements Application, essay, resume, references, transcript. *Deadline:* February 15.

Contact Arthur Hightower, Professional
Development Coordinator
National Collegiate Athletic Association
700 West Washington Avenue
PO Box 6222
Indianapolis, IN 46206-6222
Phone: 317-917-6222
Fax: 317-917-6336
E-mail: ahightower@ncaa.org

SENSE OF SMELL INSTITUTE
http://www.senseofsmell.org

SENSE OF SMELL INSTITUTE RESEARCH GRANTS
• See number 214

TOVA FELLOWSHIP
• See number 101

WOMEN'S SPORTS FOUNDATION
http://www.womenssportsfoundation.org

DOROTHY HARRIS SCHOLARSHIP • 892

One-time award to provide support to female graduate students in physical education, sport management, sport psychology, or sport sociology. Must be a U.S. citizen.

Academic/Career Areas Sports-related.

Award Scholarship for use in graduate years; not renewable. *Number:* 1–3. *Amount:* $1500.

Eligibility Requirements Applicant must be enrolled or expecting to enroll full-time at a four-year institution or university and female. Available to U.S. citizens.

Application Requirements Application, references, transcript. *Deadline:* December 31.

Contact Women's Sports Foundation
Eisenhower Park
East Meadow, NY 11554
Phone: 800-227-3988
E-mail: wosport@aol.com

SURVEYING; SURVEYING TECHNOLOGY, CARTOGRAPHY, OR GEOGRAPHIC INFORMATION SCIENCE

AMERICAN CONGRESS ON SURVEYING AND MAPPING
http://www.acsm.net

AMERICAN ASSOCIATION FOR GEODETIC SURVEYING GRADUATE FELLOWSHIP • 893

Award of $2000 for graduate student pursuing studies in geodetic surveying or geodesy. Must be a member of the American Congress on Surveying and Mapping. Preference given to applicants having at least two years of employment experience in the surveying profession.

Academic/Career Areas Surveying; Surveying Technology, Cartography, or Geographic Information Science.

Award Fellowship for use in graduate years; not renewable. *Amount:* $2000.

Eligibility Requirements Applicant must be enrolled or expecting to enroll at an institution or university. Applicant or parent of applicant must be member of American Congress on Surveying and Mapping.

Application Requirements Application, essay, references, transcript. *Deadline:* December 1.

Contact Scholarship Information
American Congress on Surveying and
 Mapping
6 Montgomery Village Avenue
Suite 403
Gaithersburg, MD 20879

THERAPY/REHABILITATION

AMERICAN ORFF-SCHULWERK ASSOCIATION
http://www.aosa.org

AMERICAN ORFF-SCHULWERK ASSOCIATION RESEARCH GRANT
• *See number 347*

AOSA-TRAINING AND PROJECTS FUND
• *See number 348*

GUNILD KEETMAN ASSISTANCE FUND
• *See number 349*

SHIELDS-GILLESPIE SCHOLARSHIP
• *See number 350*

AMERICAN RESPIRATORY CARE FOUNDATION
http://www.aarc.org

GLAXO SMITH KLINE FELLOWSHIP FOR ASTHMA MANAGEMENT EDUCATION
• *See number 475*

H. FREDERIC HELMHOLZ, JR., MD, EDUCATIONAL RESEARCH FUND
• *See number 476*

MONAGHAN/TRUDELL FELLOWSHIP FOR AEROSOL TECHNIQUE DEVELOPMENT
• *See number 376*

NBRC/A&P GARETT B. GISH, MS, RRT MEMORIAL POSTGRADUATE EDUCATION RECOGNITION AWARD
• *See number 477*

RESPIRONICS FELLOWSHIP IN MECHANICAL VENTILATION
• *See number 32*

RESPIRONICS FELLOWSHIP IN NON-INVASIVE RESPIRATORY CARE
• *See number 478*

WILLIAM F. MILLER, MD POSTGRADUATE EDUCATION RECOGNITION AWARD
• *See number 479*

BLUE CROSS BLUE SHIELD OF MICHIGAN FOUNDATION
http://www.bcbsm.com/foundation

BLUE CROSS BLUE SHIELD OF MICHIGAN FOUNDATION STUDENT AWARD PROGRAM
• *See number 393*

CALIFORNIA ASSOCIATION OF MARRIAGE AND FAMILY THERAPISTS EDUCATIONAL FOUNDATION
http://www.camft.org/

CALIFORNIA ASSOCIATION OF MARRIAGE AND FAMILY THERAPISTS EDUCATIONAL FOUNDATION SCHOLARSHIPS　● **894**

Awards for graduate students pursuing studies in marriage or family therapy. Membership in the California Association of Marriage and Family Therapists is encouraged. Preference given to California residents and those studying in California. Submit transcript, essay, and statement of financial need with application. One-time award of $1000.

Academic/Career Areas Therapy/Rehabilitation.

Award Scholarship for use in graduate years; not renewable. *Number:* 4. *Amount:* $1000.

Eligibility Requirements Applicant must be enrolled or expecting to enroll full or part-time at an institution or university. Available to U.S. citizens.

Application Requirements Application, essay, financial need analysis, transcript. *Deadline:* January 25.

Contact Patti Tice, Member Services Director
California Association of Marriage and
 Family Therapists Educational
 Foundation
7901 Raytheon Road
San Diego, CA 92111-1606
Phone: 858-292-2638
Fax: 858-292-2666
E-mail: pattit@camft.org

CLINTON E. PHILLIPS SCHOLARSHIP　● **895**

Award for graduate students pursuing studies in marriage or family therapy. Membership in the California Association of Marriage and Family Therapists is encouraged. Preference given to California residents and those studying in California. Submit transcript, essay, and statement of financial need with application. One-time award of $1000.

Academic/Career Areas Therapy/Rehabilitation.

California Association of Marriage and Family Therapists Educational Foundation (continued)

Award Scholarship for use in graduate years; not renewable. *Number:* 1. *Amount:* $1000.

Eligibility Requirements Applicant must be enrolled or expecting to enroll full or part-time at an institution or university. Available to U.S. citizens.

Application Requirements Application, essay, financial need analysis, transcript. *Deadline:* February 25.

Contact Patti Tice, Member Services Director
   California Association of Marriage and
    Family Therapists Educational
    Foundation
   7901 Raytheon Road
   San Diego, CA 92111-1606
   Phone: 858-292-2638
   Fax: 858-292-2666
   E-mail: pattit@camft.org

RONALD D. LUNCEFORD SCHOLARSHIP   • 896

Award for graduate students pursuing studies in marriage or family therapy. Membership in the California Association of Marriage and Family Therapists is encouraged. Preference given to California residents and those studying in California. Submit transcript, essay, and statement of financial need with application. One-time award of $1000.

Academic/Career Areas Therapy/Rehabilitation.

Award Scholarship for use in graduate years; not renewable. *Number:* 1. *Amount:* $1000.

Eligibility Requirements Applicant must be enrolled or expecting to enroll full or part-time at an institution or university. Available to U.S. citizens.

Application Requirements Application, essay, financial need analysis, transcript. *Deadline:* January 25.

Contact Patti Tice, Member Services Director
   California Association of Marriage and
    Family Therapists Educational
    Foundation
   7901 Raytheon Road
   San Diego, CA 92111-1606
   Phone: 858-292-2638
   Fax: 858-292-2666
   E-mail: pattit@camft.org

DELAWARE HIGHER EDUCATION COMMISSION
http://www.doe.state.de.us/high-ed

SPEECH LANGUAGE PATHOLOGIST INCENTIVE PROGRAM   • 897

Renewable loan for Delaware students pursuing graduate programs for speech or language pathology

licenses. Must be U.S. citizen and demonstrate financial need. Must have minimum 3.0 GPA. Loan requires a service repayment in Delaware.

Academic/Career Areas Therapy/Rehabilitation.

Award Forgivable loan for use in graduate years; renewable. *Number:* 1–10. *Amount:* up to $10,000.

Eligibility Requirements Applicant must be enrolled or expecting to enroll full-time at an institution or university and resident of Delaware. Applicant must have 3.0 GPA or higher. Available to U.S. citizens.

Application Requirements Application, essay, financial need analysis, test scores, transcript. *Deadline:* March 31.

Contact Maureen Laffey, Associate Director
   Delaware Higher Education Commission
   820 North French Street
   Wilmington, DE 19801
   Phone: 302-577-3240
   Fax: 302-577-6765
   E-mail: mlaffey@state.de.us

DELTA SOCIETY
http://www.deltasociety.org

HARRIS SWEATT TRAVEL GRANT
• *See number 17*

GENERAL FEDERATION OF WOMEN'S CLUBS OF MASSACHUSETTS

GENERAL FEDERATION OF WOMEN'S CLUBS OF MASSACHUSETTS COMMUNICATION DISORDER SCHOLARSHIPS   • 898

Award for a graduate student studying communication disorders. Must be Massachusetts resident. Write for further information. Submit a personal statement of no more than 500 words addressing professional goals and financial need. Must have a letter of endorsement from the president of the GFWC of MA in the community of your legal residence.

Academic/Career Areas Therapy/Rehabilitation.

Award Scholarship for use in graduate years; not renewable. *Number:* 1. *Amount:* $800.

Eligibility Requirements Applicant must be enrolled or expecting to enroll at an institution or university and resident of Massachusetts.

Application Requirements Application, autobiography, interview, references, self-addressed stamped envelope, transcript. *Deadline:* March 1.

Contact Jane Howard, Scholarship Chairperson
   General Federation of Women's Clubs of
    Massachusetts
   PO Box 679
   Sudbury, MA 01776-0679
   Phone: 781-444-9105

MENNONITE HEALTH SERVICES
http://www.mhsonline.org

ELMER EDIGER MEMORIAL SCHOLARSHIP FUND
• *See number 541*

MISSISSIPPI STATE STUDENT FINANCIAL AID
http://www.ihl.state.ms.us

GRADUATE AND PROFESSIONAL DEGREE LOAN/SCHOLARSHIP-MISSISSIPPI
• *See number 546*

NATIONAL MULTIPLE SCLEROSIS SOCIETY
http://www.nationalmssociety.org

NATIONAL MULTIPLE SCLEROSIS SOCIETY PATIENT MANAGEMENT CARE AND REHABILITATION GRANTS
• *See number 572*

NATIONAL STRENGTH AND CONDITIONING ASSOCIATION
http://www.nsca-lift.org

NATIONAL STRENGTH AND CONDITIONING ASSOCIATION STUDENT RESEARCH GRANT • **899**

One-time award for NSCA member graduate students, researching areas of strength and conditioning. Submit letter of intent by February 3 and grant application by March 17. Must submit abstract.

Academic/Career Areas Therapy/Rehabilitation.

Award Grant for use in graduate years; not renewable. *Number:* 1–6. *Amount:* $500–$2500.

Eligibility Requirements Applicant must be enrolled or expecting to enroll full-time at a four-year institution or university. Applicant or parent of applicant must be member of National Strength and Conditioning Association. Available to U.S. and non-U.S. citizens.

Application Requirements Application, essay, financial need analysis, photo, references, transcript. *Deadline:* March 17.

Contact Karri Baker, Membership Director
National Strength and Conditioning Association
PO Box 9908
Colorado Springs, CO 80932-0908
Phone: 719-632-6722
Fax: 719-632-6367
E-mail: nsca@nsca-lift.org

NEBRASKA HEALTH AND HUMAN SERVICES SYSTEM, OFFICE OF RURAL HEALTH

STATE OF NEBRASKA LOAN REPAYMENT PROGRAM FOR RURAL HEALTH PROFESSIONALS
• *See number 576*

ORTHOPAEDIC RESEARCH AND EDUCATION FOUNDATION
http://www.oref.org

AAOS/OREF FELLOWSHIP IN HEALTH SERVICES RESEARCH
• *See number 598*

OREF CAREER DEVELOPMENT AWARDS
• *See number 599*

OREF CLINICAL RESEARCH AWARD
• *See number 600*

OREF PROSPECTIVE CLINICAL RESEARCH GRANTS
• *See number 601*

OREF RESEARCH GRANTS
• *See number 602*

ZIMMER CAREER DEVELOPMENT AWARD
• *See number 604*

PARALYZED VETERANS OF AMERICA - SPINAL CORD RESEARCH FOUNDATION
http://www.pva.org/scrf

FELLOWSHIPS IN SPINAL CORD INJURY RESEARCH
• *See number 21*

SENSE OF SMELL INSTITUTE
http://www.senseofsmell.org

SENSE OF SMELL INSTITUTE RESEARCH GRANTS
• *See number 214*

TOVA FELLOWSHIP
• *See number 101*

SIGMA ALPHA IOTA PHILANTHROPIES, INC.
http://www.sai-national.org

SIGMA ALPHA IOTA DOCTORAL GRANT
• *See number 368*

TRADE/TECHNICAL SPECIALTIES

AMERICAN SOCIETY OF HEATING, REFRIGERATING, AND AIR CONDITIONING ENGINEERS, INC.
http://www.ashrae.org

AMERICAN SOCIETY OF HEATING, REFRIGERATING, AND AIR CONDITIONING RESEARCH GRANTS FOR GRADUATE STUDENTS
• *See number 632*

ASIAN CULTURAL COUNCIL
http://www.asianculturalcouncil.org

*ASIAN CULTURAL COUNCIL RESIDENCY
PROGRAM IN ASIA*
• *See number 140*

**NATIONAL MILK PRODUCERS
FEDERATION**
http://www.nmpf.org

*NATIONAL MILK PRODUCERS FEDERATION
NATIONAL DAIRY LEADERSHIP SCHOLARSHIP
PROGRAM*
• *See number 5*

SOCIETY OF WOMEN ENGINEERS
http://www.swe.org

*GENERAL MOTORS FOUNDATION GRADUATE
SCHOLARSHIP*
• *See number 245*

TRANSPORTATION

**INSTITUTE OF INDUSTRIAL
ENGINEERS**
http://www.iieet.org

E.J. SIERLEJA MEMORIAL SCHOLARSHIP • **900**

One-time award of $600 available to graduate students pursuing advanced studies in the area of transportation. Priority consideration is given to students focusing on rail transportation. Must be a member of the Institute of Industrial Engineers, have had a minimum GPA of 3.4 as an undergraduate, and be nominated by a department head.

Academic/Career Areas Transportation.

Award Fellowship for use in graduate years; not renewable. *Number:* 1. *Amount:* $600.

Eligibility Requirements Applicant must be enrolled or expecting to enroll full-time at a four-year institution or university. Applicant or parent of applicant must be member of Institute of Industrial Engineers.

Application Requirements Application, references, nomination. *Deadline:* November 30.

Contact Sherry Richards, Chapter Operations
Assistant
Institute of Industrial Engineers
25 Technology Park
Norcross, GA 30092-2988
Phone: 770-449-0461 Ext. 140
Fax: 770-263-8532
E-mail: srichards@iienet.org

**TRANSPORTATION ASSOCIATION OF
CANADA**
http://www.tac-atc.ca

*TRANSPORTATION ASSOCIATION OF CANADA
SCHOLARSHIPS*
• *See number 249*

TRAVEL/TOURISM

**AMERICAN SOCIETY OF TRAVEL
AGENTS (ASTA) FOUNDATION**
http://www.astanet.com

A.L. SIMMONS SCHOLARSHIP FUND • **901**

One-time award for graduate students pursuing master's or doctoral degrees with emphasis on travel or tourism. Must have minimum 2.5 GPA, as well as a previously submitted paper on travel or tourism. Must relate paper to travel agents. Write for application by sending a self-addressed stamped business-size envelope or go to www.astanet.com for requirements and application form.

Academic/Career Areas Travel/Tourism.

Award Scholarship for use in graduate, or postgraduate years; not renewable. *Number:* 2. *Amount:* $2000.

Eligibility Requirements Applicant must be enrolled or expecting to enroll full or part-time at a four-year institution or university. Applicant must have 2.5 GPA or higher. Available to U.S. and non-U.S. citizens.

Application Requirements Application, essay, references, self-addressed stamped envelope, transcript. *Deadline:* July 31.

Contact Myriam Lechuga, Manager
American Society of Travel Agents
(ASTA) Foundation
1101 King Street
Alexandria, VA 22314-2187
Phone: 703-739-2782
Fax: 703-684-8319
E-mail: scholarship@astahq.com

NATIONAL TOURISM FOUNDATION
http://www.ntfonline.org

LURAY CAVERNS GRADUATE RESEARCH GRANT
• *See number 402*

VISITING SCHOLAR AWARDS • **902**

Award for two educators, one from a four-year institution, one from a two-year institution. Recipients will meet with NTA/NTF staff at NTA Headquarters for three days in August. Recipients will also be invited to participate in NTA's annual convention. Room, board, and airfare for both events are provided by the Foundation. Submit curriculum vitae, letter of support from a colleague or Department Chair, and one-to-two-page document explaining why program would help you educate students, what you hope to learn, how your expertise would complement your Visiting Scholar experience, and highlights of the travel and tourism program at your institution.

Academic/Career Areas Travel/Tourism.

Award Scholarship for use in postgraduate years; not renewable. *Number:* 2.

Eligibility Requirements Applicant must be enrolled or expecting to enroll at an institution or university. Applicant or parent of applicant must have employment or volunteer experience in teaching. Available to U.S. citizens.

Application Requirements Essay, curriculum vitae, letter of support. *Deadline:* April 15.

Contact Assistant Executive Director
National Tourism Foundation
546 East Main Street
Lexington, KY 40508-3071
Phone: 800-682-8886 Ext. 4265
Fax: 859-226-4437

WINTERTHUR MUSEUM, GARDEN, AND LIBRARY
http://www.winterthur.org

NEH FELLOWSHIPS
• *See number 110*

WINTERTHUR RESEARCH FELLOWSHIPS
• *See number 111*

TV/RADIO BROADCASTING

CONSORTIUM OF COLLEGE AND UNIVERSITY MEDIA CENTERS
http://www.ccumc.org

CONSORTIUM OF COLLEGE AND UNIVERSITY MEDIA CENTERS RESEARCH AWARDS
• *See number 253*

NATIONAL ASSOCIATION OF BROADCASTERS
http://www.nab.org/Research/Grants/grants.asp

NATIONAL ASSOCIATION OF BROADCASTERS GRANTS FOR RESEARCH IN BROADCASTING
• *See number 254*

UNITED METHODIST COMMUNICATIONS
http://www.umcom.org/scholarships

STOODY-WEST FELLOWSHIP FOR GRADUATE STUDY IN RELIGIOUS JOURNALISM
• *See number 261*

UNITED STATES INSTITUTE OF PEACE
http://www.usip.org

JENNINGS RANDOLPH SENIOR FELLOW AWARD
• *See number 333*

PEACE SCHOLAR DISSERTATION FELLOWSHIP
• *See number 334*

NONACADEMIC/NONCAREER CRITERIA

CIVIC, PROFESSIONAL, SOCIAL, OR UNION AFFILIATION

AMERICAN ASSOCIATION OF LAW LIBRARIES
http://www.aallnet.org

LIBRARY SCHOOL GRADUATES SEEKING A NON-LAW DEGREE • 903

Awarded to library school graduates who are degree candidates in an area, other than law, which will be beneficial to the development of a professional career in law librarianship. Scholarship restricted to members of AALL. Evidence of financial need must be submitted.

Award Scholarship for use in graduate years; not renewable.

Eligibility Requirements Applicant must be enrolled or expecting to enroll full or part-time at a four-year institution or university. Applicant or parent of applicant must be member of American Association of Law Librarians. Available to U.S. and non-U.S. citizens.

Application Requirements Application, essay, financial need analysis, references, self-addressed stamped envelope, transcript. *Deadline:* April 1.

Contact Rachel Shaevel, Membership Coordinator
American Association of Law Libraries
53 West Jackson Boulevard, Suite 940
Chicago, IL 60604-3695
Phone: 312-939-4764 Ext. 10
Fax: 312-431-1097
E-mail: rshaevel@aall.org

AMERICAN NUMISMATIC SOCIETY
http://www.amnumsoc.org

AMERICAN NUMISMATIC SOCIETY GRADUATE SEMINAR • 904

Nonrenewable awards available to members of the American Numismatic Society to support graduate research. Contact ANS for details. Visit website for latest information.

Award Scholarship for use in graduate years; not renewable. *Number:* 6. *Amount:* up to $2500.

Eligibility Requirements Applicant must be enrolled or expecting to enroll full or part-time at an institution or university. Applicant or parent of applicant must be member of American Numismatic Society. Available to U.S. and Canadian citizens.

Application Requirements Application, references, transcript. *Deadline:* March 1.

Contact Ms. Tarnisha Smart, Membership
Secretary/Development
American Numismatic Society
Broadway at 155th Street
New York, NY 10032
Phone: 212-234-3130
Fax: 212-234-3381
E-mail: info@amnumsoc.org

AMERICAN NUMISMATIC SOCIETY/FRANCES M. SCHWARTZ FELLOWSHIP • 905

Fellowship supports work and study of numismatic and museum methodology at the American Numismatic Society. Students will learn to perform curatorial tasks in the Greek, Roman, and Byzantine departments. Applicants must have BA or equivalent. Stipend varies with term of tenure but will not exceed $2000. Visit website for latest information.

Award Fellowship for use in graduate years; not renewable. *Number:* 1. *Amount:* up to $2000.

Eligibility Requirements Applicant must be enrolled or expecting to enroll full or part-time at an institution or university and must have an interest in numismatics. Applicant or parent of applicant must be member of American Numismatic Society. Available to U.S. citizens.

Application Requirements Application, references, transcript. *Deadline:* March 1.

Contact Tarnisha Smart, Membership Secretary/
Development
American Numismatic Society
Broadway at 155th Street
New York, NY 10032
Phone: 212-234-3130
Fax: 212-234-3381
E-mail: info@amnumsoc.org

CIVIL AIR PATROL, USAF AUXILIARY
http://www.capnhq.gov

CIVIL AIR PATROL GRADUATE SCHOLARSHIPS • 906

Scholarship of $750-$1000 awarded to an active member of the Civil Air Patrol pursuing a graduate degree in any field of study. Not open to the general public.

Award Scholarship for use in graduate years; not renewable. *Number:* 1–5. *Amount:* $750–$1000.

Eligibility Requirements Applicant must be enrolled or expecting to enroll full-time at a four-year institution or university. Applicant or parent of applicant must be member of Civil Air Patrol. Available to U.S. citizens.

Application Requirements Application, essay, photo, references, transcript. *Deadline:* January 31.

Contact Registrar
Civil Air Patrol, USAF Auxiliary
105 South Hansell Street
Maxwell Air Force Base, AL 36112-6332
Phone: 334-953-4238
Fax: 334-953-6699
E-mail: cpr@cap.af.mil

DELTA DELTA DELTA FOUNDATION
http://www.tridelta.org

DELTA DELTA DELTA GRADUATE SCHOLARSHIP • 907

Scholarship awarded to alumnae members attending graduate school. All scholarship winners must complete application materials provided by the Foundation. All applicants must be highly involved in TriDelta and in their communities, they must also have achieved academic excellence.

Award Scholarship for use in graduate years; not renewable. *Number:* 8. *Amount:* $3000.

Eligibility Requirements Applicant must be enrolled or expecting to enroll full-time at an institution or university and female. Applicant or parent of applicant must have employment or volunteer experience in community service. Available to U.S. citizens.

Application Requirements Application, references, transcript. *Deadline:* January 25.

Contact Joyce Allen
Delta Delta Delta Foundation
PO Box 5987
Arlington, TX 76005
Phone: 817-633-8001
Fax: 817-652-0212
E-mail: jallen@trideltaeo.org

DELTA GAMMA FOUNDATION
http://www.deltagamma.org

DELTA GAMMA FOUNDATION FELLOWSHIPS • 908

One-time awards for graduate and postgraduate study. Candidates must be female and members of Delta Gamma Fraternity. Deadline: April 1.

Award Fellowship for use in graduate, or postgraduate years; not renewable. *Amount:* $2500.

Eligibility Requirements Applicant must be enrolled or expecting to enroll full-time at a four-year institution or university and female. Available to U.S. and Canadian citizens.

Application Requirements Application, autobiography, essay, photo, references, self-addressed stamped envelope, transcript. *Deadline:* April 1.

Contact Debbie Sayre, Assistant to the Development Director
Delta Gamma Foundation
3250 Riverside Drive, PO Box 21397
Columbus, OH 43221-0397
Phone: 614-481-8169
Fax: 614-481-0133
E-mail: debbie@deltagamma.org

FLEET RESERVE ASSOCIATION
http://www.fra.org

NOLAN/BARANSKI/GLEZEN SCHOLARSHIPS • 909

Eligible applicants are dependent children, grandchildren, and spouses of FRA members in good standing and members in good standing of the FRA. Preference given to applicants enrolled in courses of study at the post graduate level.

Award Scholarship for use in postgraduate years; not renewable. *Number:* 3. *Amount:* $5000.

Eligibility Requirements Applicant must be enrolled or expecting to enroll full-time at an institution or university. Applicant or parent of applicant must be member of Fleet Reserve Association/Auxiliary. Available to U.S. citizens. Applicant or parent must meet one or more of the following requirements: Coast Guard, Marine Corp, or Navy experience; retired from active duty; disabled or killed as a result of military service; prisoner of war; or missing in action.

Application Requirements Application, financial need analysis, references, transcript. *Deadline:* April 15.

Contact Scholarship Information
Fleet Reserve Association
125 North West Street
Alexandria, VA 22314
Phone: 703-683-1400
E-mail: fra@fra.org

GOLDEN KEY INTERNATIONAL HONOUR SOCIETY
http://goldenkey.gsu.edu

GRADUATE SCHOLARSHIP • 910

Graduate scholarships are given to students in twelve different areas of graduate study. Minimum 3.5 GPA required. Must be a member of Golden Key International Honor Society to be eligible for awards. Please visit website (http://goldenkey.gsu.edu) for more information.

Award Scholarship for use in graduate years; not renewable. *Number:* 12. *Amount:* $10,000.

Golden Key International Honour Society (continued)

Eligibility Requirements Applicant must be enrolled or expecting to enroll full-time at an institution or university. Applicant or parent of applicant must be member of Golden Key National Honor Society. Applicant must have 3.5 GPA or higher. Available to U.S. and non-U.S. citizens.

Application Requirements Application, essay, interview, transcript.

Contact Michelle Boone, Director of Scholarships
 and Awards
 Golden Key International Honour Society
 1189 Ponce de Leon Avenue
 Atlanta, GA 30306-4624
 Phone: 404-377-2400
 E-mail: mboone@goldenkey.gsu.edu

JAPANESE AMERICAN CITIZENS LEAGUE
http://www.jacl.org

JAPANESE AMERICAN CITIZENS LEAGUE GRADUATE SCHOLARSHIPS • 911

One-time award for scholars currently enrolled in or planning to enter an accredited graduate school. Must be member of Japanese-American Citizens League. Send self-addressed stamped envelope for application, specifying application category.

Award Scholarship for use in graduate, or postgraduate years; not renewable. *Number:* 7–10. *Amount:* $1000–$5000.

Eligibility Requirements Applicant must be enrolled or expecting to enroll full or part-time at a four-year institution or university. Applicant or parent of applicant must be member of Japanese-American Citizens League. Available to U.S. and non-U.S. citizens.

Application Requirements Application, essay, references, self-addressed stamped envelope, transcript. *Deadline:* April 1.

Contact National JACL Scholarship & Awards
 Japanese American Citizens League
 1765 Sutter Street
 San Francisco, CA 94115
 Phone: 415-921-5225
 Fax: 415-931-4671
 E-mail: jacl@jacl.org

KAPPA GAMMA PI
http://www.kappagammapi.org

ELENA LUCREZIA CORNARO PISCOPIA SCHOLARSHIP FOR GRADUATE STUDIES • 912

One-time awards for graduate studies are open to members of Kappa Gamma Pi, the National Catholic College Graduate Honor Society. They are awarded

annually and may be applied as needed for graduate expenses at any accredited university. Deadline: April 20.

Award Scholarship for use in graduate, or postgraduate years; not renewable. *Number:* 2–4. *Amount:* $3000.

Eligibility Requirements Applicant must be enrolled or expecting to enroll full or part-time at an institution or university. Available to U.S. and non-U.S. citizens.

Application Requirements Application, essay, financial need analysis, references. *Deadline:* April 20.

Contact Kathleen Hughes Fisher, Cornaro
 Scholarship Chair
 Kappa Gamma Pi
 3464 Barristers Keepe Circle
 Fairfax, VA 22031
 Phone: 703-383-4857
 Fax: 703-383-4859
 E-mail: khfisher@starpower.net

KAPPA KAPPA GAMMA FOUNDATION
http://www.kappakappagamma.org

KAPPA KAPPA GAMMA FOUNDATION GRADUATE SCHOLARSHIPS • 913

Kappa Kappa Gamma Foundation Scholarships are available only to members of Kappa Kappa Gamma. For complete information and application materials, send self-addressed stamped envelope. Please note chapter membership on request. Must have a minimum 3.0 GPA. Deadline: February 1.

Award Scholarship for use in graduate years; not renewable. *Number:* 40–50. *Amount:* $3000.

Eligibility Requirements Applicant must be enrolled or expecting to enroll full-time at an institution or university and female. Applicant must have 3.0 GPA or higher. Available to U.S. and Canadian citizens.

Application Requirements Application, autobiography, essay, financial need analysis, references, self-addressed stamped envelope, transcript. *Deadline:* February 1.

Contact Judy Parker, Administrative Director
 Kappa Kappa Gamma Foundation
 PO Box 38
 Columbus, OH 43216-0038
 Phone: 614-228-6515
 Fax: 614-228-6303

NATIONAL ACADEMIC ADVISING ASSOCIATION
http://www.nacada.ksu.edu

NATIONAL ACADEMIC ADVISING ASSOCIATION SCHOLARSHIP • 914

Available to members of National Academic Advising Association enrolled in a graduate program. Must have been an academic adviser for at least two years. Write for information and application. One-time award of $500-$1000.

Award Scholarship for use in graduate years; not renewable. *Number:* 1–5. *Amount:* $500–$1000.

Eligibility Requirements Applicant must be enrolled or expecting to enroll full or part-time at an institution or university. Applicant or parent of applicant must be member of National Academic Advising Association. Available to U.S. and non-U.S. citizens.

Application Requirements Application, essay, references, transcript. *Deadline:* March 4.

Contact NACADA National Awards Program
National Academic Advising Association
2323 Anderson Avenue, Suite 225
Manhattan, KS 66502-2912

ORGANIZATION OF AMERICAN HISTORIANS
http://www.oah.org

HORACE SAMUEL & MARION GALBRAITH MERRILL TRAVEL GRANTS IN TWENTIETH-CENTURY AMERICAN POLITICAL HISTORY • 915

Grant promotes access of younger scholars to Washington DC region's primary source collections in late nineteenth and twentieth-century American political history. Stipends of $500 to $3000 are awarded to underwrite travel and lodging expenses for members of Organization of American Historians who are working toward completion of a dissertation or a first book. Application deadline is December 1.

Award Grant for use in graduate, or postgraduate years; not renewable. *Amount:* $500–$3000.

Eligibility Requirements Applicant must be enrolled or expecting to enroll at a four-year institution or university. Applicant or parent of applicant must be member of Organization of American Historians. Available to U.S. and non-U.S. citizens.

Application Requirements *Deadline:* December 1.

Contact Kara Hamm, Award and Prize Committee
Coordinator
Organization of American Historians
112 North Bryan Avenue
Bloomington, IN 47408-4199
Phone: 812-855-9852
Fax: 812-855-0696
E-mail: awards@oah.org

RESERVE OFFICERS ASSOCIATION OF THE US
http://www.roa.org

HENRY J. REILLY MEMORIAL SCHOLARSHIP-GRADUATE • 916

Award for active or associate Reserve Officers Association members enrolled in graduate and doctoral programs. Must provide proof of Master's degree or acceptance in doctoral program. Must submit curriculum vitae, letters of recommendation, and resume with application. Must be U.S. citizen.

Award Scholarship for use in graduate, or postgraduate years; not renewable. *Number:* 25–35. *Amount:* $500.

Eligibility Requirements Applicant must be enrolled or expecting to enroll full or part-time at a four-year institution or university. Applicant or parent of applicant must be member of Reserve Officers Association. Available to U.S. citizens. Applicant or parent must meet one or more of the following requirements: general military experience; retired from active duty; disabled or killed as a result of military service; prisoner of war; or missing in action.

Application Requirements Application, references, test scores, transcript, curriculum vitae. *Deadline:* April 10.

Contact Ms. Mickey Hagen, Coordinator of
Applications
Reserve Officers Association of the US
1 Constitution Avenue, NE
Washington, DC 20002-5655
Phone: 202-479-2200
Fax: 202-479-0416
E-mail: mhagen@roa.org

UNITED DAUGHTERS OF THE CONFEDERACY
http://www.hqudc.org

MALCOLM M. BERGLUND SCHOLARSHIP • 917

Renewable award for graduate student who is a descendant of a Confederate soldier, sailor or marine. Must be enrolled in an accredited college or university and carry a minimum of 12 hours credit each semester. Minimum 3.0 GPA required. Submit letter of endorsement from sponsoring chapter of the United Daughters of the Confederacy.

Award Scholarship for use in graduate years; renewable. *Number:* 1–3. *Amount:* $800–$1000.

Eligibility Requirements Applicant must be enrolled or expecting to enroll full-time at a four-year institution or university. Applicant or parent of applicant must be member of United Daughters of the Confederacy. Applicant must have 3.0 GPA or higher. Available to U.S. citizens.

Application Requirements Application, essay, financial need analysis, photo, references, self-addressed stamped envelope, transcript. *Deadline:* February 15.

Contact Second Vice President General
United Daughters of the Confederacy
328 North Boulevard
Richmond, VA 23220-4057
Phone: 804-355-1636

EMPLOYMENT/VOLUNTEER EXPERIENCE

ALABAMA COMMISSION ON HIGHER EDUCATION
http://www.ache.state.al.us

TECHNOLOGY SCHOLARSHIP PROGRAM FOR ALABAMA TEACHERS   • 918

Scholarship not to exceed graduate tuition and fees at an approved Alabama institution. Must be full-time certified Alabama teacher enrolled in courses that incorporate new technology into curriculum. Required courses must be completed or scholarship must be repaid.

Award Grant for use in graduate years; renewable. *Number:* 500–900. *Amount:* $442–$717.

Eligibility Requirements Applicant must be enrolled or expecting to enroll at an institution or university; resident of Alabama and studying in Alabama. Applicant or parent of applicant must have employment or volunteer experience in teaching. Applicant must have 3.0 GPA or higher. Available to U.S. citizens.

Application Requirements Application.

Contact Dr. William Wall, Associate Executive
Director for Student Assistance,
ACHE
Alabama Commission on Higher
Education
PO Box 302000
Montgomery, AL 36130-2000

DELTA DELTA DELTA FOUNDATION
http://www.tridelta.org

DELTA DELTA DELTA GRADUATE SCHOLARSHIP
• *See number 907*

FINANCE AUTHORITY OF MAINE
http://www.famemaine.com

MAINE DENTAL EDUCATION LOAN REPAYMENT PROGRAM   • 919

Program is intended to increase access to dental care to underserved populations in Maine by providing repayment of dental education loans for dental service providers. Recipients must provide dental services regardless of a patient's ability to pay. Repayment is available at the rate of $20,000 per year of services for up to 4 years for outstanding education loan debt. See website for details. (http://www.famemaine.com)

Award Forgivable loan for use in postgraduate years; not renewable. *Amount:* $20,000.

Eligibility Requirements Applicant must be enrolled or expecting to enroll at an institution or university and resident of Maine. Applicant or parent of applicant must have employment or volunteer experience in designated career field. Available to U.S. citizens.

Application Requirements Application.

Contact Thomas Patenaude, Program Officer
Finance Authority of Maine
5 Community Drive
Augusta, ME 04332-0949
Phone: 800-228-3734
Fax: 207-623-3263
E-mail: tom@famemaine.com

GERMAN ACADEMIC EXCHANGE SERVICE (DAAD)
http://www.daad.org

LEARN GERMAN IN GERMANY FOR FACULTY   • 920

Offers support for faculty members who wish to attend intensive language courses at Goethe Institutes. The four- and eight-week courses are offered from May to November. Faculty members who teach in the fields of English, German or other modern languages or literatures are not eligible. Applicant must have basic knowledge of German. The Grant includes course fees, room and partial board. Application deadline: January 31.

Award Grant for use in postgraduate years; not renewable.

Eligibility Requirements Applicant must be enrolled or expecting to enroll at an institution or university and must have an interest in German language. Applicant or parent of applicant must have employment or volunteer experience in teaching. Available to U.S. and Canadian citizens.

Application Requirements Application, essay, photo, curriculum vitae, language evaluation. *Deadline:* January 31.

Contact German Academic Exchange Service
(DAAD)
871 United Nations Plaza
New York, NY 10017
Phone: 212-758-3223
Fax: 212-755-5780
E-mail: daadny@daad.org

ORGANIZATION OF AMERICAN HISTORIANS
http://www.oah.org

RICHARD W. LEOPOLD PRIZE   • 921

Biennial one-time award available for the best book written by a historian connected with federal, state, or municipal government in foreign policy, military affairs, or historical activities of the federal government or biography in one of the aforementioned areas. Winner must have been employed in a government position for at least five years. Each entry must be published between January 1, 2002 and

December 31, 2003 for 2004 award. One copy of each entry must be received by each member of the prize committee by October 1 of odd-numbered years (2001). Final page proofs accepted for books published after September 1 and before January 1 of the following year. Bound copy of final page proofs must be submitted by January 7. Contact for addresses. Author of winning books will receive $1500.

Award Prize for use in graduate years; not renewable. *Number:* 1. *Amount:* $1500.

Eligibility Requirements Applicant must be enrolled or expecting to enroll at a four-year institution or university. Applicant or parent of applicant must have employment or volunteer experience in designated career field. Available to U.S. and non-U.S. citizens.

Application Requirements Applicant must enter a contest. *Deadline:* October 1.

Contact Kara Hamm, Award and Prize Committee
Coordinator
Organization of American Historians
112 North Bryan Avenue
Bloomington, IN 47408-4199
Phone: 812-855-9852
Fax: 812-855-0696
E-mail: awards@oah.org

PI LAMBDA THETA, INC.
http://www.pilambda.org

NADEEN BURKEHOLDER WILLIAMS MUSIC SCHOLARSHIP • 922

The scholarship provides $1000 to an outstanding K-12 teacher who is pursuing a graduate degree at an accredited college or university and who is either a music education teacher or applies music systematically in teaching another subject. Minimum 3.5 GPA required.

Award Scholarship for use in graduate years; not renewable. *Number:* 1–5. *Amount:* $1000.

Eligibility Requirements Applicant must be enrolled or expecting to enroll full or part-time at an institution or university and must have an interest in music. Applicant or parent of applicant must have employment or volunteer experience in teaching. Applicant must have 3.5 GPA or higher. Available to U.S. and non-U.S. citizens.

Application Requirements Application, essay, portfolio, resume, references. *Deadline:* February 10.

Contact Pam Todd, Manager, Member Services
Pi Lambda Theta, Inc.
4101 East 3rd Street, PO Box 6626
Bloomington, IN 47407-6626
Phone: 812-339-3411
Fax: 812-339-3462
E-mail: endowment@pilambda.org

ROTARY FOUNDATION OF ROTARY INTERNATIONAL
http://www.rotary.org

ROTARY FOUNDATION GRANTS FOR UNIVERSITY TEACHERS TO SERVE IN DEVELOPING COUNTRIES • 923

One-time award for a university teacher to teach at a university in a low-income country. Rotary Foundation members and relatives of members are eligible. Contact the nearest Rotary Club regarding local deadlines.

Award Grant for use in postgraduate years; not renewable. *Amount:* $12,500–$22,500.

Eligibility Requirements Applicant must be enrolled or expecting to enroll at an institution or university. Applicant or parent of applicant must have employment or volunteer experience in teaching.

Application Requirements Application, essay, interview, references.

Contact Scholarship Program
Rotary Foundation of Rotary
International
1560 Sherman Avenue
Evanston, IL 60203

IMPAIRMENT

GALLAUDET UNIVERSITY ALUMNI ASSOCIATION
http://www.gallaudet.edu/~alumweb

GALLAUDET UNIVERSITY ALUMNI ASSOCIATION GRADUATE FELLOWSHIP FUND • 924

One-time award for deaf or hard-of-hearing doctoral-level students. Submit application, transcript, financial aid form, references, and audiogram. Write for more information and to request application form.

Award Fellowship for use in postgraduate years; not renewable. *Number:* 10–20. *Amount:* $500–$5000.

Eligibility Requirements Applicant must be enrolled or expecting to enroll full or part-time at a four-year institution or university. Applicant must be hearing impaired. Available to U.S. and non-U.S. citizens.

Application Requirements Application, financial need analysis, references, transcript, audiogram. *Deadline:* April 20.

Contact Ms. Daphne Cox McGregor, Associate
Director
Gallaudet University Alumni Association
800 Florida Avenue, NE
Washington, DC 20002-3695
Phone: 202-651-5060
Fax: 202-651-5062
E-mail: daphne.mcgregor@gallaudet.edu

JEWISH BRAILLE INSTITUTE
http://www.jewishbraille.org

SCHOLARSHIPS FOR BLIND JEWISH COMMUNITY PROFESSIONALS • **925**

Scholarships are made available to blind and visually impaired students preparing for professional careers in the Jewish community such as rabbis, cantors, and Jewish communal workers. Applicants are required to show need.

Award Scholarship for use in graduate years; not renewable. *Number:* 1. *Amount:* $10,000–$50,000.

Eligibility Requirements Applicant must be enrolled or expecting to enroll full or part-time at a four-year institution or university. Applicant must be visually impaired.

Application Requirements Application, financial need analysis, interview, references, transcript. *Deadline:* Continuous.

Contact Dr. Ellen Isler, Executive Vice President
Jewish Braille Institute
110 East 30th Street
New York, NY 10016
Phone: 212-889-2525
Fax: 212-689-3692
E-mail: admin@jewishbraille.org

ROY JOHNSON TRUST FUND

ROY JOHNSON TRUST FUND • **926**

Award for graduate school tuition expenses for legally blind college students, attending an accredited college or university in the state of Michigan. Non-U.S. citizens must have bachelor's degree from U.S. college or university. Must submit eye report, proof of acceptance into graduate school, and a copy of financial aid form from your college/university. Deadline: May 31.

Award Scholarship for use in graduate years; not renewable. *Number:* 4–15. *Amount:* $250–$2000.

Eligibility Requirements Applicant must be enrolled or expecting to enroll at a four-year institution or university and studying in Michigan. Applicant must be visually impaired. Available to U.S. and non-U.S. citizens.

Application Requirements Application, financial need analysis, references, transcript. *Deadline:* May 31.

Contact James Buscetta, Administrator
Roy Johnson Trust Fund
PO Box 30652
Lansing, MI 48909
Phone: 517-373-0579
Fax: 517-335-5140

MILITARY SERVICE: COAST GUARD

FLEET RESERVE ASSOCIATION
http://www.fra.org

NOLAN/BARANSKI/GLEZEN SCHOLARSHIPS
• *See number 909*

MILITARY SERVICE: GENERAL

RESERVE OFFICERS ASSOCIATION OF THE US
http://www.roa.org

HENRY J. REILLY MEMORIAL SCHOLARSHIP-GRADUATE
• *See number 916*

MILITARY SERVICE: MARINES

FLEET RESERVE ASSOCIATION
http://www.fra.org

NOLAN/BARANSKI/GLEZEN SCHOLARSHIPS
• *See number 909*

MILITARY SERVICE: NAVY

NOLAN/BARANSKI/GLEZEN SCHOLARSHIPS
• *See number 909*

NATIONALITY OR ETHNIC HERITAGE

ALBERTA HERITAGE SCHOLARSHIP FUND
http://www.alis.gov.ab.ca/scholarships

ALBERTA UKRAINIAN CENTENNIAL COMMEMORATIVE SCHOLARSHIPS • **927**

Award to provide academic opportunities for student from Ukraine to study in Alberta and for student from Alberta to study in Ukraine. Scholarships are for graduate level study and will be awarded every second year. Deadline: February 1. Must be ranked in upper third of class or have a minimum 3.0 GPA.

Award Scholarship for use in graduate years; not renewable. *Number:* 2.

Eligibility Requirements Applicant must be Canadian or Ukrainian citizenship and enrolled or expecting to enroll full-time at an institution or university. Applicant must have 3.0 GPA or higher. Available to Canadian and non-U.S. citizens.

Application Requirements Application, essay, references, transcript. *Deadline:* February 1.

Contact Alberta Heritage Scholarship Fund
9940 106th Street, 9th Floor, Box 28000
Station Main
Edmonton, AB T5J 4R4
Canada
Phone: 780-427-8640
Fax: 780-422-4516
E-mail: heritage@gov.ab.ca

GOVERNMENT OF ALBERTA GRADUATE SCHOLARSHIPS AND FELLOWSHIPS • 928

Awards to provide incentive and means for Canadians to pursue graduate study at Alberta post-secondary institutions. Nominations made by each graduate faculty in Alberta. Scholarships valued at up to Can$9300, fellowships at up to Can$10,500. Consult faculty of graduate studies for deadline. Must be a resident of Alberta, Canada.

Award Scholarship for use in graduate years; not renewable. *Number:* 140. *Amount:* $9300–$10,500.

Eligibility Requirements Applicant must be Canadian citizenship; enrolled or expecting to enroll full-time at an institution or university; resident of Alberta and studying in Alberta. Applicant must have 3.0 GPA or higher.

Application Requirements Application.

Contact Alberta Heritage Scholarship Fund
9940 106th Street, 9th Floor, Box 28000
Station Main
Edmonton, AB T5J 4R4
Canada
Phone: 780-427-8640
Fax: 780-422-4516
E-mail: heritage@gov.ab.ca

RALPH STEINHAUER AWARDS OF DISTINCTION • 929

Award to recognize exceptional academic achievement of students studying within Alberta. Must be Canadian resident enrolled or intending to enroll at an institution in Alberta. Awards valued at Can$15,000 for study at master's level and Can$20,000 for doctoral level study. Deadline: February 1. Must rank in upper quarter of class or have a minimum 3.5 GPA.

Award Scholarship for use in graduate, or postgraduate years; not renewable. *Number:* 15. *Amount:* $15,000–$20,000.

Eligibility Requirements Applicant must be Canadian citizenship; enrolled or expecting to enroll full-time at an institution or university and studying in Alberta. Applicant must have 3.5 GPA or higher.

Application Requirements Application, essay, references, transcript. *Deadline:* February 1.

Contact Alberta Heritage Scholarship Fund
9940 106th Street 9th Floor, Box 28000
Station Main
Edmonton, AB T5J 4R4
Canada
Phone: 780-427-8640
Fax: 780-422-4516
E-mail: heritage@gov.ab.ca

SIR JAMES LOUGHEED AWARDS OF DISTINCTION • 930

Awards to recognize academic excellence and provide Albertans with the opportunity for advanced study at institutions outside of Alberta. Awards valued at Can$15,000 for master's and Can$20,000 for doctoral level study. Deadline: February 1. Must be a resident of Alberta, Canada. Must be ranked in upper quarter of class or have a minimum 3.5 GPA.

Award Scholarship for use in graduate years; not renewable. *Number:* 15. *Amount:* $15,000–$20,000.

Eligibility Requirements Applicant must be Canadian citizenship; enrolled or expecting to enroll full-time at an institution or university and resident of Alberta. Applicant must have 3.5 GPA or higher.

Application Requirements Application, essay, references, transcript. *Deadline:* February 1.

Contact Alberta Heritage Scholarship Fund
9940 106th Street, 9th Floor, Box 28000
Station Main
Edmonton, AB T5J 4R4
Canada
Phone: 780-427-8640
Fax: 780-422-4516
E-mail: heritage@gov.ab.ca

AMERICAN INDIAN GRADUATE CENTER
http://www.aigc.com

AMERICAN INDIAN GRADUATE CENTER (AIGC) GRADUATE FELLOWSHIP • 931

Must be enrolled member of federally recognized American Indian tribe or Alaskan Native group in the U.S., or possess one quarter degree Indian blood. Must be pursuing or planning to pursue master's or doctorate degree. Must apply for campus-based aid through federal financial aid process at university financial aid office.

Award Fellowship for use in graduate years; renewable.

Eligibility Requirements Applicant must be American Indian/Alaska Native and enrolled or expecting to enroll full-time at an institution or university. Available to U.S. citizens.

American Indian Graduate Center (continued)

Application Requirements Application, essay, financial need analysis, Tribal Eligibility Certificate. *Fee:* $15. *Deadline:* June 3.

Contact Marveline Vallo, Academic Advisor
American Indian Graduate Center
4520 Montgomery NE
Albuquerque, NM 87109
Phone: 505-881-4584 Ext. 108
Fax: 505-884-0427
E-mail: marveline@aigc.com

AMERICAN INSTITUTE OF CERTIFIED PUBLIC ACCOUNTANTS
http://www.aicpa.org

FELLOWSHIPS FOR MINORITY DOCTORAL STUDENTS • 932

Fellowships are available to minority students enrolled in a doctoral program with a concentration in accounting. Must have earned a master's degree and/or completed a minimum of three years full-time experience in the practice of accounting. Recipients of the fellowship will attend school on a full-time basis.

Award Fellowship for use in graduate years; renewable. *Amount:* $12,000.

Eligibility Requirements Applicant must be American Indian/Alaska Native, Black (non-Hispanic), or Hispanic and enrolled or expecting to enroll full-time at an institution or university. Available to U.S. citizens.

Application Requirements Application, references, transcript. *Deadline:* April 1.

Contact Scholarship Coordinator
American Institute of Certified Public
Accountants
1211 Avenue of the Americas
New York, NY 10036-8775
Phone: 212-596-6270
E-mail: educat@aicpa.org

AMERICAN SCHOOLS OF ORIENTAL RESEARCH (ASOR)
http://www.asor.org

W.F. ALBRIGHT INSTITUTE OF ARCHEAOLOGICAL RESEARCH ANDREW W. MELLON FOUNDATION FELLOWSHIPS • 933

Three month fellowships open to Bulgarian, Czech, Hungarian, Polish, Romanian and Slovak scholars. Candidates should not permanently reside outside these six countries and should have obtained a doctorate by the time the fellowship is awarded. Fellows are expected to reside at the Albright Institute of Archaeological Research in Ohio if room is available. Application deadline: April 1.

Award Fellowship for use in postgraduate years; not renewable. *Number:* 3. *Amount:* $11,500.

Eligibility Requirements Applicant must be Bulgarian, Hungarian, Polish, Rumanian, or Slavic/Czech citizenship; enrolled or expecting to enroll at an institution or university and studying in Ohio. Available to citizens of countries other than the U.S. or Canada.

Application Requirements Application. *Deadline:* April 1.

Contact Dr. John R. Spencer, W. F. Albright
Institute of Archaeological Research
American Schools of Oriental Research
(ASOR)
20700 North Park Boulevard
University Heights, OH 44118
Phone: 216-397-4705
Fax: 216-397-4478
E-mail: spencer@jcu.edu

AMERICAN SOCIOLOGICAL ASSOCIATION
http://www.asanet.org

GRADUATE FELLOWSHIP PROGRAM FOR UNDERREPRESENTED MINORITIES • 934

With its emphasis on research training and professional development, the MFP provides resources and support to promote success and excellence among predoctoral minority students. Fellows receive a package of assistance that includes financial support, mentoring, direct research training, access to professional networks, and continuing guidance and evaluation. Must maintain a 3.0 GPA. Deadline: January 31.

Award Fellowship for use in graduate years; renewable. *Number:* 12. *Amount:* $16,500.

Eligibility Requirements Applicant must be American Indian/Alaska Native, Asian/Pacific Islander, Black (non-Hispanic), or Hispanic and enrolled or expecting to enroll full-time at an institution or university. Applicant must have 3.0 GPA or higher. Available to U.S. citizens.

Application Requirements Application, essay, financial need analysis, resume, references, transcript. *Deadline:* January 31.

Contact Dr. Alfonso Latoni, Director, Minority
Affairs Program
American Sociological Association
1307 New York Avenue, NW,
Suite 700
Washington, DC 20005-4701
Phone: 202-383-9005 Ext. 321
Fax: 202-638-0882
E-mail: latoni@asanet.org

AMERICAN-SCANDINAVIAN FOUNDATION
http://www.amscan.org

AWARDS FOR ADVANCED STUDY OR RESEARCH IN THE USA • 935

Awards for graduate and postgraduate research in the U.S. available to citizens of Denmark, Finland, Iceland, Norway, and Sweden. Preference given to dissertation-level research.

Award Scholarship for use in graduate, or postgraduate years; not renewable. *Number:* 60–80. *Amount:* $1000–$20,000.

Eligibility Requirements Applicant must be Danish, Finnish, Icelandic, Norwegian, or Swedish citizenship and enrolled or expecting to enroll at an institution or university. Available to citizens of countries other than the U.S. or Canada.

Application Requirements Application, references, transcript. *Deadline:* Continuous.

Contact Ellen McKey, Director of Fellowships and Grants
American-Scandinavian Foundation
58 Park Avenue
New York, NY 10016
Phone: 212-879-9779
Fax: 212-249-3444
E-mail: emckey@amscan.org

ASSOCIATION ON AMERICAN INDIAN AFFAIRS, INC.
http://www.indian-affairs.org

SEQUOYAH GRADUATE FELLOWSHIPS FOR AMERICAN INDIANS AND ALASKAN NATIVES • 936

Renewable award for American Indian and Alaskan Native full-time students who are working toward graduate degree. Applicant must be 1/4 degree Indian blood from federally recognized tribe. Must include certificate of enrollment and blood quantum from tribe with application. For additional information, see website.

Award Scholarship for use in graduate years; renewable.

Eligibility Requirements Applicant must be American Indian/Alaska Native and enrolled or expecting to enroll full-time at a four-year institution or university. Available to U.S. citizens.

Application Requirements Application, essay, financial need analysis, transcript. *Deadline:* September 10.

Contact Association on American Indian Affairs, Inc.
PO Box 268
Sisseton, SD 57262
Phone: 605-698-3998
Fax: 605-698-3316

CANADIAN BLOOD SERVICES
http://www.bloodservices.ca

RESEARCH FELLOWSHIP IN HEMOSTATIS • 937

Fellowship is generally held within four years of completion of clinical fellowship training in an appropriate specialty. Submit statement from work supervisor, curriculum vitae, a cover letter from CBS/University Hospital indicating endorsement of application, proposed outline of research, long-range career plans and summary of educational form RFH 2000. One-time award of Can$50000 . Application is available on website. Co-sponsored by Novo Nordisk.

Award Fellowship for use in postgraduate years; not renewable. *Number:* 1. *Amount:* $50,000.

Eligibility Requirements Applicant must be Canadian citizenship; enrolled or expecting to enroll part-time at an institution or university and resident of Alberta, British Columbia, Manitoba, New Foundland, North Brunswick, North West Territories, Nova Scotia, Ontario, Prince Edward Island, Quebec, Saskatchewan, or Yukon.

Application Requirements Application, autobiography, references. *Deadline:* November 1.

Contact Cilla Perry, Manager, Research and Development
Canadian Blood Services
1800 Alta Vista Drive
Ottawa, ON K1G 4J5
Canada
Phone: 613-739-2408
Fax: 613-739-2201
E-mail: cilla.perry@bloodservices.ca

CANADIAN NORTHERN STUDIES TRUST - ASSOCIATION OF CANADIAN UNIVERSITIES FOR NORTHERN STUDIES
http://www.cyberus.ca/~acuns

CANADIAN NORTHERN STUDIES POLAR COMMISSION SCHOLARSHIP • 938

Scholarship awarded for excellence in research at master's or doctorate level for 12-month period. Recipient's research must include field work in Polar regions. Preference given to candidates involved in interdisciplinary research. Must be Canadian citizen or permanent resident. Apply using the application form for studentships in Northern studies.

Award Scholarship for use in graduate, or postgraduate years; not renewable. *Number:* 1. *Amount:* $10,000.

Eligibility Requirements Applicant must be Canadian citizenship and enrolled or expecting to enroll at an institution or university.

Canadian Northern Studies Trust - Association of Canadian Universities for Northern Studies (continued)

Application Requirements Application. *Deadline:* January 31.

Contact Sandra Malcolm, Executive Officer
Canadian Northern Studies Trust -
Association of Canadian Universities
for Northern Studies
405 -17 York Street
Ottawa, ON K1N 9J6
Canada
Phone: 613-562-0515
Fax: 613-562-0533
E-mail: acuns@cyberus.ca

ELIZABETH TUCKERMAN FOUNDATION

ELIZABETH TUCKEMAN SCHOLARSHIP FOUNDATION • 939

Nonrenewable educational grants to persons domiciled in Wales who have graduated from college or university in U.K. or U.S. and who desire to further postgraduate education at college or university in U.S. Must apply through financial aid office of school where enrolled.

Award Scholarship for use in graduate years; not renewable. *Amount:* $5000–$40,000.

Eligibility Requirements Applicant must be of Welsh heritage and enrolled or expecting to enroll at a four-year institution. Available to U.S. citizens.

Application Requirements Financial need analysis, transcript. *Deadline:* June 15.

Contact Elizabeth Tuckerman Foundation
333 South Grand Avenue, Suite 540
Los Angeles, CA 90071

FLORIDA BOARD OF EDUCATION, DIVISION OF COLLEGES AND UNIVERSITIES
http://www.fldcu.org

DELORES A. AUZENNE FELLOWSHIP FOR GRADUATE STUDY • 940

Available for minority students pursuing full-time graduate study at one of the four-year public institutions in the Florida university system. Must have at least a 3.0 GPA. Renewable award. Contact the Equal Opportunity Office at each of the ten public state universities.

Award Scholarship for use in graduate years; renewable. *Number:* 60. *Amount:* $2500–$5000.

Eligibility Requirements Applicant must be American Indian/Alaska Native, Asian/Pacific Islander, Black (non-Hispanic), or Hispanic; enrolled or expecting to enroll full-time at an

institution or university and studying in Florida. Applicant must have 3.0 GPA or higher. Available to U.S. citizens.

Application Requirements Application, transcript. *Deadline:* May 31.

Contact Lynda Page
Florida Board of Education, Division of
Colleges and Universities
Florida Education Center, Suite 1548
Tallahassee, FL 32399-1950
Phone: 850-201-7180
Fax: 850-201-7195
E-mail: lynda.page@fldcu.org

IMGIP/ICEOP
http://www.imgip.siu.edu

ILLINOIS CONSORTIUM FOR EDUCATIONAL OPPORTUNITY PROGRAM FELLOWSHIP • 941

Overall intent of ICEOP is to increase the number of underrepresented faculty and staff at Illinois institutions of higher education and higher education governing boards. Requires minimum GPA of 2.75 in the last sixty hours of undergraduate work or over a 3.2 in at least 9 hours of graduate study.

Award Fellowship for use in graduate years; renewable. *Number:* 160–170. *Amount:* $12,500.

Eligibility Requirements Applicant must be American Indian/Alaska Native, Asian/Pacific Islander, Black (non-Hispanic), or Hispanic; enrolled or expecting to enroll full or part-time at an institution or university; resident of Illinois and studying in Illinois. Available to U.S. citizens.

Application Requirements Application, essay, financial need analysis, references, test scores, transcript. *Deadline:* February 15.

Contact Ms. Jane Meuth, IMGIP/ICEOP
Administrator
IMGIP/ICEOP
Woody Hall C-224, Southern Illinois
University
Carbondale, IL 62901-4723
Phone: 618-453-4558
Fax: 618-453-1800
E-mail: fellows@siu.edu

KOSCIUSZKO FOUNDATION
http://www.kosciuszkofoundation.org

KOSCIUSZKO FOUNDATION TUITION SCHOLARSHIP • 942

This scholarship is reserved for U.S. citizens of Polish descent, Poles who are permanent residents in the U.S., and for Americans engaged in study of Polish subjects. Minimum 3.0 GPA required. Must submit a personal statement. Application fee: $25. Several one-time scholarships ranging from $1000 to $5000.

See website for complete details. Tuition scholarship application is available for download from September through December.

Award Scholarship for use in graduate years; not renewable. *Number:* 100–160. *Amount:* $1000–$5000.

Eligibility Requirements Applicant must be of Polish heritage; enrolled or expecting to enroll full-time at a four-year institution or university and must have an interest in Polish language. Applicant must have 3.0 GPA or higher. Available to U.S. citizens.

Application Requirements Application, essay, financial need analysis, photo, references, transcript, personal statement. *Fee:* $25. *Deadline:* January 15.

Contact Ms. Addy Tymczyszyn, Grants Department
Kosciuszko Foundation
15 East 65th Street
New York, NY 10021-6595
Phone: 212-734-2130 Ext. 210

LI FOUNDATION, INC.
http://www.lifoundation.org

LI FOUNDATION FELLOWSHIPS   • 943

Fellowship assists deserving Chinese graduate and post-graduate students and scholars who are sponsored by selected institutions for one to two years of study and training in the U.S. Grant provides $20,000 annually to cover cost of living, professional expenses to attend a professional meeting, and return transportation to China.

Award Fellowship for use in graduate, or postgraduate years; not renewable. *Number:* 20. *Amount:* $20,000.

Eligibility Requirements Applicant must be of Chinese heritage and Chinese citizenship; Asian/Pacific Islander and enrolled or expecting to enroll full-time at an institution or university. Available to citizens of countries other than the U.S. or Canada.

Application Requirements Application, autobiography, references, test scores, transcript. *Deadline:* March 15.

Contact Administrative Officer
Li Foundation, Inc.
57 Glen Street, Suite 1
Glen Cove, NY 11547
Phone: 516-676-1315
Fax: 516-676-2539

NATIONAL WELSH-AMERICAN FOUNDATION
http://www.wales-usa.org

EXCHANGE SCHOLARSHIP   • 944

Limited to colleges/universities in Wales only. Applicant must have a Welsh background through birth and be willing to promote Welsh-American relations both here and abroad. Requested to consider becoming a member of NWAF upon completion of

study. Required to complete four-year college study in USA. Applicant must be 21 years of age or up.

Award Scholarship for use in graduate years; not renewable. *Number:* 1. *Amount:* $5000.

Eligibility Requirements Applicant must be of Welsh heritage; age 21 and enrolled or expecting to enroll full-time at a four-year institution or university. Available to U.S. citizens.

Application Requirements Application, autobiography, references, test scores. *Deadline:* March 1.

Contact Dr. Phillip Davies, Chairman, Scholarship Committee
National Welsh-American Foundation
24 Essex Road
Scotch Plains, NJ 07076
Phone: 908-594-6827
Fax: 908-889-5888
E-mail: philip_davies@merck.com

NORWAY-AMERICA ASSOCIATION
http://www.noram.no

NORWAY-AMERICA ASSOCIATION GRADUATE RESEARCH SCHOLARSHIPS   • 945

One-time award for Norwegian citizens to pursue graduate study in the U.S. Must be working toward a Master's or Ph.D. For all majors.

Award Scholarship for use in graduate years; not renewable. *Number:* 25. *Amount:* $2000–$20,000.

Eligibility Requirements Applicant must be Norwegian citizenship and enrolled or expecting to enroll full-time at a four-year institution or university. Available to citizens of countries other than the U.S. or Canada.

Application Requirements Application.

Contact Cheryl Storo, Director of Scholarship Program
Norway-America Association
Radhusgaten 23 B, 0158
Oslo
Norway
E-mail: namerika@online.no

OLD DOMINION UNIVERSITY

OLD DOMINION UNIVERSITY PRESIDENT'S GRADUATE FELLOWSHIP   • 946

The President's Graduate Fellowship program is to diversify the population of faculty members who hold the terminal degree in critical academic areas by providing financial support to persons from underrepresented groups as they earn their terminal degree. Qualifications of the applicant, as well as the needs of academic departments, are considered in selecting fellows. The normal stipend period is up to three years during which the fellow receives a monthly stipend and a tuition and fees allowance. Upon completion of the degree, fellows agree to serve

Old Dominion University (continued)

in a tenure-track position at Old Dominion University for at least three years.

Award Fellowship for use in graduate years; renewable. *Number:* 1–3. *Amount:* $25,000–$30,000.

Eligibility Requirements Applicant must be American Indian/Alaska Native, Asian/Pacific Islander, Black (non-Hispanic), or Hispanic and enrolled or expecting to enroll full-time at an institution or university. Applicant must have 3.0 GPA or higher. Available to U.S. citizens.

Application Requirements Application, essay, resume, references, transcript. *Deadline:* February 1.

Contact Jean Martin, Administrative Assistant
Old Dominion University
Office of Research/Grad Studies
Norfolk, VA 23529-0013
Phone: 757-683-6411
Fax: 757-683-3004
E-mail: jmartin@odu.edu

ORGANIZATION OF AMERICAN HISTORIANS
http://www.oah.org

HUGGINS-QUARLES AWARD • 947

Annual one-time award for minority graduate students at the dissertation research stage of their Ph.D. program in history. The student should submit a letter from the dissertation adviser, a two-page abstract of the dissertation project, and a budget. Application deadline December 1.

Award Prize for use in graduate years; not renewable. *Amount:* up to $1000.

Eligibility Requirements Applicant must be American Indian/Alaska Native, Asian/Pacific Islander, Black (non-Hispanic), or Hispanic and enrolled or expecting to enroll at a four-year institution or university. Available to U.S. and non-U.S. citizens.

Application Requirements Application. *Deadline:* December 1.

Contact Kara Hamm, Award and Prize Committee Coordinator
Organization of American Historians
112 North Bryan Avenue
Bloomington, IN 47408-4199
Phone: 812-855-9852
Fax: 812-855-0696
E-mail: awards@oah.org

SAINT ANDREWS SOCIETY OF THE STATE OF NEW YORK
http://www.standrewssocietyny.org

SAINT ANDREWS SOCIETY OF THE STATE OF NEW YORK SCHOLARSHIP FOR GRADUATE STUDY • 948

One-time award for graduate study in Scotland. Must be of Scottish descent and preferably reside within 250-mile radius of New York. Based on academic achievement, extracurricular activities, character, leadership, financial need, and statement of personal objectives. Minimum 2.5 GPA required. Candidates should possess qualifications which will enable them to be good ambassadors for the U.S. while in Scotland. One applicant from an institution will be considered. President of undergraduate institution must endorse one student as most qualified.

Award Scholarship for use in graduate years; not renewable. *Number:* 2. *Amount:* $15,000.

Eligibility Requirements Applicant must be of Scottish heritage; enrolled or expecting to enroll full-time at an institution or university and resident of Connecticut, Delaware, District of Columbia, Maine, Maryland, Massachusetts, New Hampshire, New Jersey, New York, North Carolina, Pennsylvania, Rhode Island, Vermont, or Virginia. Applicant must have 2.5 GPA or higher. Available to U.S. citizens.

Application Requirements Application, essay, financial need analysis, references, test scores, transcript. *Deadline:* December 15.

Contact Jane Stephens, Office Manager
Saint Andrews Society of the State of New York
150 East 55th Street
New York, NY 10022
Phone: 212-223-4248 Ext. 16
Fax: 212-223-0748
E-mail: standrewsny@msn.com

SHASTRI INDO-CANADIAN INSTITUTE
http://www.ucalgary.ca/~sici

SHASTRI CANADIAN STUDIES DOCTORAL RESEARCH FELLOWSHIPS FOR INDIAN SCHOLARS • 949

Research fellowships available to students enrolled in a doctoral program at an Indian university to conduct research on Canada. Recipients must submit an interim and a final report. One-time awards of varying amounts. Must be citizen of India.

Award Fellowship for use in graduate years; not renewable. *Number:* 2–3. *Amount:* $5800–$11,300.

Eligibility Requirements Applicant must be Indian citizenship and enrolled or expecting to enroll full-time at an institution or university. Available to citizens of countries other than the U.S. or Canada.

Application Requirements Application. *Deadline:* October 31.

Contact Programme Officer
Shastri Indo-Canadian Institute
5 Bhai Vir Singh Marg
New Delhi 110-001
India
Phone: 91-11-3746417
Fax: 91-11-3746416
E-mail: sici@vsnl.com

SHASTRI CANADIAN STUDIES FACULTY ENRICHMENT FELLOWSHIP FOR INDIAN SCHOLARS • 950

Faculty enrichment fellowships available to Indian university professors to assist them in developing and teaching new courses on Canada or expanding new courses. Fellows must complete a final report and attend a week-long summer institute. Four- to five-week awards of varying amounts.

Award Fellowship for use in postgraduate years; not renewable. *Number:* 7–10. *Amount:* $5700.

Eligibility Requirements Applicant must be of Indian heritage and enrolled or expecting to enroll full-time at an institution or university. Available to citizens of countries other than the U.S. or Canada.

Application Requirements Application. *Deadline:* October 31.

Contact Programme Officer
Shastri Indo-Canadian Institute
5 Bhai Vir Singh Marg
New Delhi 110-001
India
Phone: 91-11-3746417
Fax: 91-11-3746416
E-mail: sici@vsnl.com

SHASTRI CANADIAN STUDIES FACULTY RESEARCH FELLOWSHIPS FOR INDIAN SCHOLARS • 951

Faculty research fellowships help support research by Indian scholars who are committed to the promotion of Canadian studies at their own institution in India. Recipients must contribute to the pedagogical material on Canada in India through scholarly publications. One-time award for four to five weeks of study.

Award Fellowship for use in postgraduate years; not renewable. *Number:* 7–10. *Amount:* $5700.

Eligibility Requirements Applicant must be of Indian heritage and enrolled or expecting to enroll full-time at an institution or university. Available to citizens of countries other than the U.S. or Canada.

Application Requirements Application. *Deadline:* October 31.

Contact Programme Officer
Shastri Indo-Canadian Institute
5 Bhai Vir Singh Marg
New Delhi 110-001
India
Phone: 91-11-3746417
Fax: 91-11-3746416
E-mail: sici@vsnl.com

SHASTRI INDIA STUDIES FACULTY FELLOWSHIPS • 952

Fellowships available to Canadian scholars with full- or part-time appointments at a Canadian institution of higher education. Scholars may apply for research or training fellowships in India. One-time grants of varying amounts.

Award Fellowship for use in postgraduate years; not renewable.

Eligibility Requirements Applicant must be of Canadian heritage and enrolled or expecting to enroll at an institution or university. Available to Canadian citizens.

Application Requirements Application, photo. *Deadline:* June 30.

Contact Programme Officer
Shastri Indo-Canadian Institute
2500 University Drive, NW
Calgary, AB T2N 1N4
Canada
Phone: 403-220-7467
Fax: 403-289-0100
E-mail: sici@ucalgary.ca

SHASTRI INDIA STUDIES POSTDOCTORAL RESEARCH FELLOWSHIPS • 953

Research fellowships open to scholars who have completed a Ph.D. and wish to do research in India. Applicants need not have an academic position, but awards will not be made after five years beyond the receipt of the doctorate. Three-to-twelve-months awards of varying amounts. Must be Canadian citizen or permanent resident.

Award Fellowship for use in postgraduate years; not renewable.

Eligibility Requirements Applicant must be of Canadian heritage and enrolled or expecting to enroll at an institution or university. Available to Canadian citizens.

Shastri Indo-Canadian Institute (continued)

Application Requirements Application, photo.
Deadline: June 30.

Contact Programme Officer
Shastri Indo-Canadian Institute
2500 University Drive, NW
Calgary, AB T2N 1N4
Canada
Phone: 403-220-7467
Fax: 403-289-0100
E-mail: sici@ucalgary.ca

SHASTRI INDIA STUDIES STUDENT FELLOWSHIPS
• 954

Fellowships available to students specializing in India who are at thesis level in a graduate degree program. Students may apply for research, language training, or degree fellowships to be undertaken in India. Several one-time awards of varying amounts. Must be Canadian resident.

Award Fellowship for use in graduate years; not renewable.

Eligibility Requirements Applicant must be of Canadian heritage and enrolled or expecting to enroll at an institution or university. Available to Canadian citizens.

Application Requirements Application, photo, references, transcript. *Deadline:* June 30.

Contact Programme Officer
Shastri Indo-Canadian Institute
2500 University Drive, NW
Calgary, AB T2N 1N4
Canada
Phone: 403-220-7467
Fax: 403-289-0100
E-mail: sici@ucalgary.ca

SWISS BENEVOLENT SOCIETY OF NEW YORK
http://www.swissbenevolentny.com

ZIMMERMANN SCHOLARSHIPS
• 955

Merit award to academically outstanding graduate and post-graduate students. Must submit proof of Swiss parentage of nationality. Must reside in New York, New Jersey, Connecticut, Pennsylvania or Delaware. Application deadline is March 31.

Award Grant for use in graduate, or postgraduate years; not renewable. *Number:* 1–5. *Amount:* $5000.

Eligibility Requirements Applicant must be of Swiss heritage; enrolled or expecting to enroll full-time at an institution or university and resident of Connecticut, Delaware, New Jersey, New York, or Pennsylvania. Applicant must have 3.5 GPA or higher. Available to U.S. citizens.

Application Requirements Application, references, test scores, transcript, proof of Swiss parentage.
Deadline: March 31.

Contact Anne Marie Gilman, Scholarship Director
Swiss Benevolent Society of New York
608 Fifth Avenue, #309
New York, NY 10020
Phone: 212-246-0655
Fax: 212-246-1366
E-mail: info@swissbenevolentny.com

UNITED NEGRO COLLEGE FUND
http://www.uncf.org

GLAXOSMITHKLINE SCIENCE ACHIEVEMENT AWARDS
• 956

Four $3000 scholarships to graduates of a UNCF member college or university with science-related majors who are enrolled or planning to enroll in a graduate degree program at any American college or university. Minimum 3.0 GPA required.

Award Scholarship for use in graduate years; not renewable. *Number:* 4. *Amount:* up to $3000.

Eligibility Requirements Applicant must be Black (non-Hispanic) and enrolled or expecting to enroll at an institution or university. Applicant must have 3.0 GPA or higher.

Application Requirements Application.

Contact Program Services Department
United Negro College Fund
8260 Willow Oaks Corporate Drive
Fairfax, VA 22031

WEXNER FOUNDATION
http://www.wexnerfoundation.org

WEXNER GRADUATE FELLOWSHIP PROGRAM
• 957

Fellowships are awarded to North American college graduates who plan to enter qualifying graduate programs in preparation for careers in Jewish education, Jewish communal service, the Rabbinate, the Cantorate or Jewish studies. Fellowships cover full academic tuition, required fees and a generous living stipend. Fellowships are granted for full-time graduate study in qualifying academic programs. They are granted for a two-year term and may be renewed for up to two additional years.

Award Fellowship for use in graduate years; renewable. *Number:* 20.

Eligibility Requirements Applicant must be Jewish; of Hebrew heritage and enrolled or expecting to enroll full-time at a four-year institution or university. Available to U.S. and Canadian citizens.

Application Requirements Application, essay, interview, photo, references, test scores, transcript. *Deadline:* February 1.

Contact Rabbi. Elka Abrahamson, Director,
Graduate Fellowship Program
Wexner Foundation
6525 West Campus Oval
Suite 110
New Albany, OH 43054
Phone: 614-939-6060
Fax: 614-939-6066
E-mail: eabrahamson@wexner.net

RELIGIOUS AFFILIATION

MUSTARD SEED FOUNDATION
http://www.msfdn.org

HARVEY FELLOWS PROGRAM ● 958

Award for Christian graduate students who plan to enter culturally influential vocations in which there is currently little Christian leadership. Must enroll in a top-five-ranked program. Competitive and extensive application required. Submit a work sample from major area of study.

Award Fellowship for use in graduate years; renewable. *Number:* 15–25. *Amount:* $15,000.

Eligibility Requirements Applicant must be Christian and enrolled or expecting to enroll full-time at an institution or university. Available to U.S. and non-U.S. citizens.

Application Requirements Application, essay, resume, references, test scores, transcript, work sample. *Deadline:* November 15.

Contact Mr. Duane Grobman, Director of
Scholarships
Mustard Seed Foundation
3330 North Washington Boulevard, #100
Arlington, VA 59604-4267
Phone: 703-524-5650
Fax: 703-524-5643

WEXNER FOUNDATION
http://www.wexnerfoundation.org

WEXNER GRADUATE FELLOWSHIP PROGRAM
● *See number 957*

STATE/PROVINCE OF RESIDENCE

ALABAMA COMMISSION ON HIGHER EDUCATION
http://www.ache.state.al.us

TECHNOLOGY SCHOLARSHIP PROGRAM FOR ALABAMA TEACHERS
● *See number 918*

ALBERTA HERITAGE SCHOLARSHIP FUND
http://www.alis.gov.ab.ca/scholarships

GOVERNMENT OF ALBERTA GRADUATE SCHOLARSHIPS AND FELLOWSHIPS
● *See number 928*

RALPH STEINHAUER AWARDS OF DISTINCTION
● *See number 929*

SIR JAMES LOUGHEED AWARDS OF DISTINCTION
● *See number 930*

AMERICAN ANTIQUARIAN SOCIETY
http://www.americanantiquarian.org

AAS SHORT-TERM FELLOWSHIPS ● 959

Short-term fellowships which support 1 to 3 months of residence in the Society's library. These fellowships are available for scholars holding the Ph.D. and for doctoral candidates engaged in dissertation research. See website for further information.

Award Fellowship for use in graduate, or postgraduate years; not renewable. *Number:* 20–30. *Amount:* $1000–$3000.

Eligibility Requirements Applicant must be enrolled or expecting to enroll at an institution or university and studying in Massachusetts. Available to U.S. and non-U.S. citizens.

Application Requirements Application, references. *Deadline:* January 15.

Contact Director of Scholarly Programs
American Antiquarian Society
185 Salisbury Street
Worcester, MA 01609-1634
Phone: 508-755-5221
Fax: 508-754-9069
E-mail: csloat@mwa.org

AAS-NATIONAL ENDOWMENT FOR THE HUMANITIES FELLOWSHIPS AND MELLON POSTDOCTORAL RESEARCH FELLOWSHIPS ● 960

Long-term, postdoctoral fellowships support four to twelve months' residence in the Society's library. These long-term awards are intended for scholars beyond the doctorate, for which senior and mid-career scholars are particularly encouraged to apply. See website for further information.

Award Fellowship for use in postgraduate years; not renewable. *Number:* 3–5. *Amount:* $15,000–$40,000.

Eligibility Requirements Applicant must be enrolled or expecting to enroll at a four-year institution or university and studying in Massachusetts. Available to U.S. citizens.

American Antiquarian Society (continued)

Application Requirements Application, references. *Deadline:* January 15.

Contact Caroline F. Sloat, Director of Scholarly Programs
American Antiquarian Society
185 Salisbury Street
Worcester, MA 01609-1634
Phone: 508-755-5221
Fax: 508-754-9069
E-mail: csloat@mwa.org

AMERICAN SCHOOLS OF ORIENTAL RESEARCH (ASOR)
http://www.asor.org

W.F. ALBRIGHT INSTITUTE OF ARCHEAOLOGICAL RESEARCH ANDREW W. MELLON FOUNDATION FELLOWSHIPS
• *See number 933*

CANADIAN BLOOD SERVICES
http://www.bloodservices.ca

CANADIAN BLOOD SERVICES GRADUATE FELLOWSHIP PROGRAM • **961**

Awards for graduate students who are undertaking full-time research training leading to a Ph.D. degree. Submit statement from work supervisor, title and summary of research, proposal/proposed research plan, transcripts, and if needed proof of entitlement to work in Canada on form GFP-01. Award for a total of Can$20000. The initial term of the fellowship is two years with possible renewal for an additional two years upon reapplication. Applications are available on website and are accepted twice annually: July 31 for funding September 1; November 15 for funding January 1.

Award Fellowship for use in graduate years; not renewable. *Number:* 1–6. *Amount:* $20,000.

Eligibility Requirements Applicant must be enrolled or expecting to enroll full-time at an institution or university and resident of Alberta, British Columbia, Manitoba, New Foundland, North Brunswick, North West Territories, Nova Scotia, Ontario, Prince Edward Island, Quebec, Saskatchewan, or Yukon. Available to Canadian citizens.

Application Requirements Application, references, transcript.

Contact Cilla Perry, Manager, Research and Development
Canadian Blood Services
1800 Alta Vista Drive
Ottawa, ON K1G 4J5
Canada
Phone: 613-739-2408
Fax: 613-739-2201
E-mail: cilla.perry@bloodservices.com

RESEARCH FELLOWSHIP IN HEMOSTATIS
• *See number 937*

FINANCE AUTHORITY OF MAINE
http://www.famemaine.com

MAINE DENTAL EDUCATION LOAN REPAYMENT PROGRAM
• *See number 919*

FLORIDA BOARD OF EDUCATION, DIVISION OF COLLEGES AND UNIVERSITIES
http://www.fldcu.org

DELORES A. AUZENNE FELLOWSHIP FOR GRADUATE STUDY
• *See number 940*

FLORIDA DEPARTMENT OF HEALTH

NURSING STUDENT LOAN FORGIVENESS PROGRAM • **962**

Forgivable loan available to LPNs, RNs, and ARNPs who are out of school and working full time at a designated facility. Program assists with repaying loans taken to subsidize nursing education. Pays 25 percent (up to $4,000) per year of outstanding debt for a maximum of four years. Contact for information. Deadlines: March 1, June 1, September 1, and December 1.

Award Forgivable loan for use in postgraduate years; renewable. *Amount:* up to $4000.

Eligibility Requirements Applicant must be enrolled or expecting to enroll at an institution or university; resident of Florida and studying in Florida. Available to U.S. and non-U.S. citizens.

Application Requirements Application.

Contact Florida Department of Health
Division of EMS and Community Health Resources
4052 Bald Cypress Way, Mail Bin C-15
Tallahassee, FL 32399-1735

FOREST HISTORY SOCIETY
http://www.foresthistory.org

ALFRED D. BELL, JR. FELLOWSHIP • **963**

One-time award for travel expenses for qualified researchers to visit and use the facilities of the Forest History Society Library and Archives. Research strengths are forest history, conservation history, the forestry profession, U.S. land management agencies.

Award Fellowship for use in graduate, or postgraduate years; not renewable. *Number:* 5–7. *Amount:* up to $850.

Eligibility Requirements Applicant must be enrolled or expecting to enroll full or part-time at an institution or university and studying in North Carolina. Available to U.S. and non-U.S. citizens.

Application Requirements Application, resume. *Deadline:* Continuous.

Contact Cheryl Oakes, Librarian/Archivist
Forest History Society
701 Wm. Vickers Avenue
Durham, NC 27701-3162
Phone: 919-682-9319
Fax: 919-682-2349
E-mail: coakes@duke.edu

GENERAL FEDERATION OF WOMEN'S CLUBS OF MASSACHUSETTS

GENERAL FEDERATION OF WOMEN'S CLUBS OF MASSACHUSETTS MEMORIAL EDUCATION FELLOWSHIP • 964

Must be a female graduate student maintaining residence in Massachusetts for at least five years and must submit a letter of endorsement from president of the sponsoring General Federation of Women's Clubs of Massachusetts club. Applicable fields of study vary yearly. Submit a personal statement of no more than 500 words addressing professional goals and financial need.

Award Fellowship for use in graduate years; not renewable. *Amount:* $3000.

Eligibility Requirements Applicant must be enrolled or expecting to enroll at an institution or university; female and resident of Massachusetts.

Application Requirements Application, autobiography, interview, references, self-addressed stamped envelope, transcript. *Deadline:* March 1.

Contact Marianne Norman, Chairman of Trustees
General Federation of Women's Clubs of Massachusetts
PO Box 679, 245 Dutton Road
Sudbury, MA 01776-0679
Phone: 781-665-0676

HERBERT HOOVER PRESIDENTIAL LIBRARY ASSOCIATION
http://www.hooverassoc.org

HERBERT HOOVER PRESIDENTIAL LIBRARY ASSOCIATION TRAVEL GRANT PROGRAM • 965

One-time competitive travel grants help graduate and post-graduate researchers travel to West Branch, Iowa to conduct research in the archives of the Herbert Hoover Presidential Library Association.

Award Grant for use in graduate, or postgraduate years; not renewable. *Amount:* $500–$1500.

Eligibility Requirements Applicant must be enrolled or expecting to enroll full or part-time at a four-year institution or university and studying in Iowa. Available to U.S. and non-U.S. citizens.

Application Requirements Application, references. *Deadline:* March 1.

Contact Patricia Hand, Academic Programs Manager
Herbert Hoover Presidential Library Association
PO Box 696
West Branch, IA 52245
Phone: 319-643-5327
Fax: 319-643-2391
E-mail: info@hooverassociation.org

HERBERT SCOVILLE JR. PEACE FELLOWSHIP PROGRAM
http://www.clw.org/scoville/

HERBERT SCOVILLE JR. PEACE FELLOWSHIP • 966

Spring and fall fellowships awarded to recent outstanding college graduates interested in public advocacy. Applicants are selected to work with nonprofit, public-interest organizations addressing peace and security issues. Prospective fellows should demonstrate excellent academic accomplishments and experience with public-interest activism or advocacy. Scoville fellowship provides a stipend of $1800 per month for up to eight months. Preference is given to U.S. citizens, however foreign nationals residing in the U.S. may also apply. Spring deadline, October 22; fall deadline, February 1. Visit website for further information (http://www.clw.org).

Award Fellowship for use in graduate years; not renewable. *Number:* 6–8. *Amount:* $10,800–$14,400.

Eligibility Requirements Applicant must be enrolled or expecting to enroll at an institution or university and studying in District of Columbia. Available to U.S. and non-U.S. citizens.

Application Requirements Essay, references, transcript.

Contact Paul Revsine, Program Director
Herbert Scoville Jr. Peace Fellowship Program
110 Maryland Avenue, NE Suite 409
Washington, DC 20002
Phone: 202-543-4100

IMGIP/ICEOP
http://www.imgip.siu.edu

ILLINOIS CONSORTIUM FOR EDUCATIONAL OPPORTUNITY PROGRAM FELLOWSHIP
• *See number 941*

KANSAS BOARD OF REGENTS
http://www.kansasregents.com

DISTINGUISHED SCHOLAR PROGRAM • 967

This program was created to encourage Kansas Brasenose, Chevening, Fulbright, Madison, Marshall,

Kansas Board of Regents (continued)

Mellon, Rhodes and Truman scholars from Kansas to continue graduate studies at Kansas public universities. Deadline: April 1.

Award Scholarship for use in graduate, or postgraduate years; renewable. *Number:* 1–5.

Eligibility Requirements Applicant must be enrolled or expecting to enroll full-time at an institution or university; resident of Kansas and studying in Kansas. Applicant must have 3.5 GPA or higher. Available to U.S. citizens.

Application Requirements Application, essay, references, transcript. *Deadline:* April 1.

Contact Diane Lindeman, Director of Student Financial Assistance
Kansas Board of Regents
1000 Southwest Jackson, Suite 520
Topeka, KS 66612-1368
Phone: 785-296-3517
Fax: 785-296-0983
E-mail: dlindeman@ksbor.org

JAMES B. PEARSON FELLOWSHIP • 968

This program was established to encourage graduate students from Kansas public universities to experience the global perspective gained from study abroad. Minimum 3.5 GPA required. Deadline: April 1. Must be a U.S. citizen.

Award Scholarship for use in graduate, or postgraduate years; not renewable. *Number:* 3–15. *Amount:* $1000–$8000.

Eligibility Requirements Applicant must be enrolled or expecting to enroll full-time at an institution or university and resident of Kansas. Applicant must have 3.5 GPA or higher. Available to U.S. citizens.

Application Requirements Application, essay, interview, references, transcript. *Deadline:* April 1.

Contact Diane Lindeman, Director of Student Financial Assistance
Kansas Board of Regents
1000 Southwest Jackson, Suite 520
Topeka, KS 66612-1368
Phone: 785-296-3517
Fax: 785-296-0983
E-mail: dlindeman@ksbor.org

MICHIGAN SOCIETY OF FELLOWS
http://www.rackham.umich.edu/Faculty/society.html

MICHIGAN SOCIETY OF FELLOWS FELLOWSHIP • 969

Fellows are appointed as Assistant Professors/Postdoctoral Scholars. They are to be in residence at Ann Arbor during the academic years of the fellowship. They teach for one year, attend monthly

society meetings, and devote the remaining time to their independent research or artistic projects. Application fee is $30.

Award Fellowship for use in postgraduate years; not renewable. *Number:* 4. *Amount:* $42,000.

Eligibility Requirements Applicant must be enrolled or expecting to enroll at an institution or university and studying in Michigan. Available to U.S. and non-U.S. citizens.

Application Requirements Application, references, transcript. *Fee:* $30. *Deadline:* October 2.

Contact Administrative Assistant
Michigan Society of Fellows
University of Michigan, 3030 Rackham Building
915 East Washington Street
Ann Arbor, MI 48109-1070
Phone: 734-763-1259
E-mail: society.of.fellows@umich.edu

NASA FLORIDA SPACE GRANT CONSORTIUM
http://fsgc.engr.ucf.edu

SPACE GRANT FELLOWSHIP PROGRAM • 970

Program designed to reward and attract the best and brightest of U.S. citizens to space-related Masters and Doctoral studies and careers. Minimum 3.5 GPA required. Fellowship strictly for study at NASA Florida Space Center.

Award Fellowship for use in graduate years; renewable. *Number:* 3–4. *Amount:* $12,000–$20,000.

Eligibility Requirements Applicant must be enrolled or expecting to enroll full-time at an institution or university and studying in Florida. Applicant must have 3.5 GPA or higher. Available to U.S. citizens.

Application Requirements Application, essay, references, test scores, transcript. *Deadline:* March 1.

Contact Dr. Jaydeep Mukherjee, Administrator
NASA Florida Space Grant Consortium
Mail Stop: FSGC
Kennedy Space Center, FL 32899
Phone: 321-452-4301
Fax: 321-449-0739
E-mail: jmukherj@mail.vcf.edu

NASA SOUTH CAROLINA SPACE GRANT CONSORTIUM
http://www.cofc.edu/~scsgrant

GRADUATE RESEARCH PROGRAM • 971

Graduate student must be enrolled at SCSG member institutions. Applicants can be focused on any field that can be related to one of NASA's 5 enterprises. Deadline varies, usually in January or into early spring. See website for additional information: www.cofc.edu/~scsgrant. Must be U.S. citizen.

Award Fellowship for use in graduate years; renewable. *Number:* 3. *Amount:* $10,000.

Eligibility Requirements Applicant must be enrolled or expecting to enroll full-time at a four-year institution or university and studying in South Carolina. Available to U.S. citizens.

Application Requirements Application, references, transcript, research proposal.

Contact Tara Scozzaro, Program Manager
NASA South Carolina Space Grant
Consortium
College of Charleston, Department of
Geology
66 George Street
Charleston, SC 29424
Phone: 843-953-5463
Fax: 843-953-5446
E-mail: tara@loki.cofc.edu

NATIONAL SEA GRANT COLLEGE PROGRAM OFFICE
http://www.nsgo.seagrant.org/

DEAN JOHN KNAUSS MARINE POLICY FELLOWSHIP • 972

The program matches highly qualified graduate students with hosts in the legislative branch or the executive branch in the Washington, D.C. area for a one-year paid fellowship. Available to students in a graduate or professional degree program in a marine-related field. Applicant must be enrolled in U.S. accredited school. Contact for deadline information.

Award Fellowship for use in graduate years; not renewable. *Number:* 25–35. *Amount:* $38,000.

Eligibility Requirements Applicant must be enrolled or expecting to enroll full or part-time at an institution or university and studying in District of Columbia, Maryland, or Virginia. Available to U.S. and non-U.S. citizens.

Application Requirements Application, autobiography, essay, interview, references, transcript.

Contact Ms. Nikola Garber, Knauss Fellowship
Program Manager
National Sea Grant College Program
Office
1315 East-West Highway, 11th Floor,
R/SG, Room 11718
Silver Spring, MD 20910
Phone: 301-713-2431 Ext. 124
Fax: 301-713-0799
E-mail: nikola.garber@noaa.gov

NEW MEXICO COMMISSION ON HIGHER EDUCATION
http://www.nmche.org

MINORITY DOCTORAL ASSISTANCE LOAN-FOR-SERVICE PROGRAM • 973

Several loans available to increase the number of ethnic minorities and women available to teach in academic disciplines in which they are underrepresented. Must have a bachelor's or master's degree from New Mexico four-year public post-secondary institution and be accepted for enrollment as full-time doctoral student at eligible institution. As condition of the loan, recipient is required to teach at sponsoring New Mexico institution for a minimum of one year for each year loan is awarded. Several renewable loans for up to $25,000 per year. Deadline is in January.

Award Forgivable loan for use in graduate years; renewable. *Amount:* up to $25,000.

Eligibility Requirements Applicant must be enrolled or expecting to enroll full-time at a four-year institution or university; resident of New Mexico and studying in New Mexico. Available to U.S. citizens.

Application Requirements Application, essay, references, transcript.

Contact Barbara Serna, Clerk Specialist
New Mexico Commission on Higher
Education
PO Box 15910
Santa Fe, NM 87506-5910
Phone: 505-827-4026
Fax: 505-827-7392

NORTH DAKOTA DEPARTMENT OF PUBLIC INSTRUCTION
http://www.dpi.state.nd.us

PRESIDENT'S AWARD FOR EXCELLENCE IN MATH AND SCIENCE TEACHING • 974

Fellowship award of $7500 for part-time graduate student or post-graduate. Must be a U.S. citizen and a North Dakota resident. Applicant must submit with application: transcript, recommendations, and portfolio.

Award Fellowship for use in graduate, or postgraduate years; not renewable. *Number:* 1. *Amount:* $7500.

Eligibility Requirements Applicant must be enrolled or expecting to enroll part-time at a four-year institution or university and resident of North Dakota. Available to U.S. citizens.

Application Requirements Application, portfolio, references, transcript.

Contact North Dakota Department of Public
Instruction
600 East Boulevard Avenue
Department 201
Bismarck, ND 58505-0440

OHIO BOARD OF REGENTS
http://www.regents.state.oh.us

REGENTS GRADUATE/PROFESSIONAL FELLOWSHIP PROGRAM • 975

Available to Ohio residents pursuing a graduate or professional degree in Ohio immediately following graduation with a bachelor's degree. Must enroll full-time. Renewable for an additional year.

Award Fellowship for use in graduate years; renewable. *Number:* 70–80. *Amount:* up to $3500.

Eligibility Requirements Applicant must be enrolled or expecting to enroll full-time at an institution or university; resident of Ohio and studying in Ohio. Available to U.S. citizens.

Application Requirements Application, essay, interview, references, test scores, transcript. *Deadline:* March 1.

Contact Barbara Metheney, Program Administrator
Ohio Board of Regents
PO Box 182452
Columbus, OH 43218-2452
Phone: 614-752-9535
Fax: 614-752-5903
E-mail: bmethene@regents.state.oh.us

OREGON STUDENT ASSISTANCE COMMISSION
http://www.osac.state.or.us

RAY KAGELER SCHOLARSHIP • 976

One-time award for graduate school students who are members of a credit union affiliated with Oregon Credit Union League. Contact website for application procedures, requirements, and deadlines.

Award Scholarship for use in graduate years; not renewable.

Eligibility Requirements Applicant must be enrolled or expecting to enroll at an institution or university; resident of Oregon and must have an interest in designated field specified by sponsor. Available to U.S. citizens.

Application Requirements Application, essay, financial need analysis, references, transcript, activity chart. *Deadline:* March 1.

Contact Director of Grant Programs
Oregon Student Assistance Commission
1500 Valley River Drive, Suite 100
Eugene, OR 97401-7020
Phone: 800-452-8807 Ext. 7395
E-mail:
awardinfo@mercury.osac.state.or.us

ROY JOHNSON TRUST FUND

ROY JOHNSON TRUST FUND
• *See number 926*

SAINT ANDREWS SOCIETY OF THE STATE OF NEW YORK
http://www.standrewssocietyny.org

SAINT ANDREWS SOCIETY OF THE STATE OF NEW YORK SCHOLARSHIP FOR GRADUATE STUDY
• *See number 948*

SWISS BENEVOLENT SOCIETY OF NEW YORK
http://www.swissbenevolentny.com

ZIMMERMANN SCHOLARSHIPS
• *See number 955*

TEXAS HIGHER EDUCATION COORDINATING BOARD
http://www.collegefortexans.com

KENNETH H. ASHWORTH FELLOWSHIP PROGRAM • 977

One-time award to Texas residents enrolled as a graduate student in public affairs, public service or public administration. Must intend to work in Texas after completing graduate studies. Must attend a Texas institution.

Award Fellowship for use in graduate years; not renewable. *Number:* 1. *Amount:* $2000.

Eligibility Requirements Applicant must be enrolled or expecting to enroll at an institution or university; resident of Texas and studying in Texas.

Application Requirements Application, financial need analysis. *Deadline:* February 20.

Contact Grants and Special Programs Office
Texas Higher Education Coordinating Board
PO Box 12788
Austin, TX 78711
Phone: 800-242-3062
E-mail: grantinfo@thecb.state.tx.us

VIRGINIA HISTORICAL SOCIETY
http://www.vahistorical.org

MELLON RESEARCH FELLOWSHIP • 978

Supports research in the collections of the Virginia Historical Society.

Award Fellowship for use in graduate, or postgraduate years; not renewable. *Number:* 20–40. *Amount:* $150–$500.

Eligibility Requirements Applicant must be enrolled or expecting to enroll full-time at a four-year institution or university and studying in Virginia. Available to U.S. and non-U.S. citizens.

Application Requirements Application, essay, references. *Deadline:* January 15.

Contact Dr. Nelson Lankford, Editor
Virginia Historical Society
Box 7311
Richmond, VA 23221
Phone: 804-342-9672
Fax: 804-355-2399
E-mail: nelson@vahistorical.org

WESTERN INTERSTATE COMMISSION FOR HIGHER EDUCATION
http://www.wiche.edu

WESTERN REGIONAL GRADUATE PROGRAM • 979

Over 100 master or doctoral programs at thirty-five institutions in fourteen states are designated Western Regional Graduate Programs. Nonresident tuition differentials are waived for students granted admission. Available to residents of Alaska, Arizona, Colorado, Hawaii, Idaho, Montana, Nevada, New Mexico, North Dakota, Oregon, South Dakota, Utah, Washington, and Wyoming.

Award Scholarship for use in graduate years; renewable.

Eligibility Requirements Applicant must be enrolled or expecting to enroll at a four-year institution; resident of Alaska, Arizona, Colorado, Hawaii, Idaho, Montana, Nevada, New Mexico, North Dakota, Oregon, South Dakota, Utah, Washington, or Wyoming and studying in Alaska, Arizona, Colorado, Hawaii, Idaho, Montana, New Mexico, North Dakota, Oregon, South Dakota, Utah, or Washington. Available to U.S. citizens.

Application Requirements Application.

Contact Sandy Jackson, Program Coordinator
Western Interstate Commission for
Higher Education
PO Box 9752
Boulder, CO 80301-9752
Phone: 303-541-0210
Fax: 303-541-0291
E-mail: info-sep@wiche.edu

TALENT/AREAS OF INTEREST

AMERICAN NUMISMATIC SOCIETY
http://www.amnumsoc.org

AMERICAN NUMISMATIC SOCIETY/FRANCES M. SCHWARTZ FELLOWSHIP
• *See number 905*

DONALD GROVES FUND • 980

One-time award to promote publication in the field of early American numismatics involving material

dating no later than 1800. Provides money for travel and other expenses associated with research costs. Submit outline of proposed research, method of accomplishing research, funding requested, and specific uses to which funding will be put.

Award Scholarship for use in graduate years; not renewable. *Number:* 1. *Amount:* $2000–$3000.

Eligibility Requirements Applicant must be enrolled or expecting to enroll full or part-time at an institution or university and must have an interest in numismatics. Available to U.S. citizens.

Application Requirements Application, financial need analysis, outline of proposed research. *Deadline:* March 1.

Contact Dr. Ute Wartenberg, Executive Director
American Numismatic Society
Broadway at 155th Street
New York, NY 10032
Phone: 212-234-3130
Fax: 212-234-3381
E-mail: wartenberg@amnumsoc.org

AMERICAN PHILOSOPHICAL SOCIETY
http://www.amphilsoc.org

DALAND FELLOWSHIP FOR RESEARCH IN CLINICAL INVESTIGATION • 981

Candidates expected to have held M.D. or MD/Ph.D. degree for less than six years. Intended to be first post-clinical fellowship, but each case decided on its merits. Preference given to candidates with less than two years post-doctoral training. Complete information and forms are at www.amphilsoc.org.

Award Fellowship for use in postgraduate years; not renewable. *Number:* 2. *Amount:* $50,000.

Eligibility Requirements Applicant must be enrolled or expecting to enroll at an institution or university and must have an interest in designated field specified by sponsor. Available to U.S. citizens.

Application Requirements Application, photo, resume, references. *Deadline:* September 1.

Contact Daland Fund Committee
American Philosophical Society
104 South 5th Street
Philadelphia, PA 19106-3387

AMERICAN SOCIETY FOR INFORMATION SCIENCE AND TECHNOLOGY
http://www.asis.org

PRATT-SEVERN BEST STUDENT RESEARCH PAPER AWARD • 982

Award is to encourage student research and writing in the field of information science. Any student in a Masters degree-granting institution can submit a paper. Doctoral theses are not eligible. Papers submitted must fall into the scope of JASIS and must

American Society for Information Science and Technology (continued)

be endorsed by a faculty sponsor for submission to the contest. Papers submitted should be original manuscripts (not previously published) and should not be submitted to other publications or groups while they are being considered by the Jury.

Award Prize for use in graduate years; not renewable. *Number:* 1.

Eligibility Requirements Applicant must be enrolled or expecting to enroll at an institution or university and must have an interest in writing. Available to U.S. citizens.

Application Requirements Application, references. *Deadline:* June 15.

Contact Vanessa Foss, Awards Coordinator
American Society for Information Science and Technology
1320 Fenwick Lane, Suite 510
Silver Spring, MD 20910
Phone: 301-495-0900
Fax: 301-495-0810
E-mail: vfoss@asis.org

BOYS & GIRLS CLUBS OF AMERICA

ROBERT W. WOODRUFF FELLOWSHIP • 983

Award to encourage professional growth within the Boys and Girls Club movement

Award Fellowship for use in graduate years; not renewable. *Number:* 1–2. *Amount:* up to $15,000.

Eligibility Requirements Applicant must be enrolled or expecting to enroll at an institution or university and must have an interest in designated field specified by sponsor. Available to U.S. citizens.

Application Requirements Application. *Fee:* $25. *Deadline:* June 16.

Contact Jerry Latham, Director, Training and Professional Development
Boys & Girls Clubs of America
1230 West Peachtree Street, NW
Atlanta, GA 30309

GERMAN ACADEMIC EXCHANGE SERVICE (DAAD)
http://www.daad.org

GERMAN ACADEMIC EXCHANGE SERVICE (DAAD) DEUTSCHLANDJAHR SCHOLARSHIPS FOR GRADUATING SENIORS • 984

Scholarships available to U.S. and Canadian citizens who are about to complete their bachelors degree. Only students in their senior year of undergraduate study may apply. Recipients will be required to enroll at a German public institution of higher education and complete at least two scheine per semester. Must have a good command of German. Scholarship is open to students in all fields except medicine. Application deadline: January 15.

Award Scholarship for use in graduate years; not renewable.

Eligibility Requirements Applicant must be enrolled or expecting to enroll full or part-time at an institution or university and must have an interest in German language. Available to U.S. and Canadian citizens.

Application Requirements Application. *Deadline:* January 15.

Contact German Academic Exchange Service (DAAD)
871 United Nations Plaza
New York, NY 10017
Phone: 212-758-3223
Fax: 212-755-5780
E-mail: daadny@daad.org

GERMAN ACADEMIC EXCHANGE SERVICE (DAAD) GRADUATE SCHOLARSHIPS FOR STUDY AND /OR RESEARCH IN GERMANY • 985

One-time scholarships available to graduate students pursuing their masters or doctorate for study and/or research prior to completing their degree. Scholarship is open to all fields except medicine. Contact for specific details. Application deadline for performing musicians and fine artists: November 1. Application deadline for all other fields: January 15.

Award Scholarship for use in graduate, or postgraduate years; not renewable.

Eligibility Requirements Applicant must be enrolled or expecting to enroll full or part-time at an institution or university and must have an interest in German language. Available to U.S. and non-U.S. citizens.

Application Requirements Application.

Contact German Academic Exchange Service (DAAD)
871 United Nations Plaza
New York, NY 10017
Phone: 212-758-3223
Fax: 212-755-5780
E-mail: daadny@daad.org

LEARN GERMAN IN GERMANY FOR FACULTY
• *See number 920*

RESEARCH GRANTS FOR RECENT PH.D.s & PH.D. CANDIDATES • 986

Grant available to Ph.D. candidates and recent Ph.D. recipients to carry out dissertation or postdoctoral research at libraries, archives, institutes or laboratories in Germany for a period of one to six months during the calendar year. PhD's (up to two years after degree) not older than 35 and Ph.D. candidates not older than 32 are eligible. One-time award. Applicants should possess adequate knowledge of German language to carry out proposed research. Deadline: August 1.

Award Grant for use in graduate, or postgraduate years; not renewable.

Eligibility Requirements Applicant must be enrolled or expecting to enroll at an institution or university and must have an interest in German language. Available to U.S. and Canadian citizens.

Application Requirements Application, photo, references, transcript, curriculum vitae. *Deadline:* August 1.

Contact German Academic Exchange Service
(DAAD)
871 United Nations Plaza
New York, NY 10017
Phone: 212-758-3223
Fax: 212-755-5780
E-mail: daadny@daad.org

SUMMER LANGUAGE COURSES AT GOETHE INSTITUTES • 987

Scholarships available to graduate students to attend intensive eight-week language courses at Goethe Institutes in Germany during the summer. Graduate students enrolled full-time may apply. Students in the fields of English, German or any other modern languages or literature are not eligible. Applicants must have completed three semesters of college-level German or the equivalent and should be under age 33. One-time awards. Scholarship covers tuition, room, partial board, health and accident insurance, and a small travel subsidy.

Award Scholarship for use in graduate years; not renewable.

Eligibility Requirements Applicant must be age 32 or under; enrolled or expecting to enroll full-time at an institution or university and must have an interest in German language. Available to U.S. and Canadian citizens.

Application Requirements Application, essay, photo, references, transcript, curriculum vitae, DAAD German language certificate. *Deadline:* January 31.

Contact German Academic Exchange Service
(DAAD)
871 United Nations Plaza
New York, NY 10017
Phone: 212-758-3223
Fax: 212-755-5780
E-mail: daadny@daad.org

KOSCIUSZKO FOUNDATION
http://www.kosciuszkofoundation.org

GRADUATE AND POSTGRADUATE STUDIES AND RESEARCH IN POLAND PROGRAM • 988

Award for graduate students or faculty members for study or research in Poland. Submit research proposal

with application. Must be U.S. citizen or permanent resident. Must submit a letter from adviser, an invitation letter from Polish institution, and complete a physician's certificate. Must have working knowledge of Polish language. Application available for download from September through December. Application fee: $50. Deadline is December 15. See website for complete details http://www.kosciuszkofoundation.org.

Award Grant for use in graduate, or postgraduate years; not renewable. *Number:* 10–13. *Amount:* $1000–$2250.

Eligibility Requirements Applicant must be enrolled or expecting to enroll full-time at an institution or university and must have an interest in Polish language. Available to U.S. citizens.

Application Requirements Application, interview, photo, references, research proposal. *Fee:* $50. *Deadline:* December 15.

Contact Ms. Addy Tymczyszyn, Grants Department
Kosciuszko Foundation
15 East 65th Street
New York, NY 10021-6595
Phone: 212-734-2130 Ext. 210

KOSCIUSZKO FOUNDATION TUITION SCHOLARSHIP
• See number 942

NATIONAL ASSOCIATION FOR CAMPUS ACTIVITIES

NATIONAL ASSOCIATION FOR CAMPUS ACTIVITIES EAST COAST GRADUATE STUDENT SCHOLARSHIP • 989

Scholarships will be given to graduate students in student personnel services or a related area. Must provide proof of acceptance into an accredited graduate school within the NACA East Coast Region. Applicants must demonstrate experience and involvement in campus activities and be committed to pursuing a career as a campus activities professional.

Award Scholarship for use in graduate years; not renewable.

Eligibility Requirements Applicant must be enrolled or expecting to enroll at an institution or university and must have an interest in leadership. Available to U.S. citizens.

Application Requirements Application, essay, resume, references, transcript. *Deadline:* May 30.

Contact National Association for Campus Activities
13 Harbison Way
Columbia, SC 29212-3401

NATIONAL ASSOCIATION FOR CAMPUS ACTIVITIES FOUNDATION GRADUATE SCHOLARSHIPS • 990

Scholarships will be given to graduates of a four-year college or university with a minimum GPA of 2.5

National Association for Campus Activities (continued)

who is matriculating into a master's or doctoral degree program in student personnel services or a related area. Must provide proof of enrollment in an accredited graduate school and demonstrate experience and involvement in campus activities and be committed to pursuing a career as a campus activities professional.

Award Scholarship for use in graduate years; not renewable. *Number:* 3.

Eligibility Requirements Applicant must be enrolled or expecting to enroll at an institution or university and must have an interest in leadership. Applicant must have 2.5 GPA or higher. Available to U.S. citizens.

Application Requirements Application, essay, references, transcript. *Deadline:* May 30.

Contact National Association for Campus Activities
13 Harbison Way
Columbia, SC 29212-3401

NATIONAL COLLEGIATE ATHLETIC ASSOCIATION
http://www.ncaa.org

NCAA POSTGRADUATE SCHOLARSHIP • 991

Students must be nominated in the academic year in which they complete their final season of eligibility for intercollegiate athletics under NCAA legislation. Must have excelled academically and athletically. Minimum 3.2 GPA required. Must intend to continue academic work as a graduate student. Deadlines vary.

Award Scholarship for use in graduate years; not renewable. *Number:* up to 174. *Amount:* $5000.

Eligibility Requirements Applicant must be enrolled or expecting to enroll full or part-time at a four-year institution or university and must have an interest in athletics/sports. Available to U.S. and non-U.S. citizens.

Application Requirements Application, references, test scores, transcript.

Contact Arthur Hightower, Professional
Development Coordinator
National Collegiate Athletic Association
700 West Washington Avenue
PO Box 6222
Indianapolis, IN 46206-6222
Phone: 317-917-6222
Fax: 317-917-6336
E-mail: ahightower@ncaa.org

NATIONAL SCULPTURE SOCIETY
http://www.nationalsculpture.org

NATIONAL SCULPTURE SOCIETY ALEX J. ETTL GRANT • 992

Grant awarded to a figurative or realist sculptor who has demonstrated a commitment to sculpting and an outstanding ability through his or her life's work. Must submit photos of work. Not available to NSS members. This is a life time achievement award.

Award Prize for use in postgraduate years; not renewable. *Number:* 1. *Amount:* $4000–$5000.

Eligibility Requirements Applicant must be enrolled or expecting to enroll at an institution or university and must have an interest in art. Available to U.S. citizens.

Application Requirements Autobiography, self-addressed stamped envelope, photographs of work. *Deadline:* January 8.

Contact Gwen Pier, Executive Director
National Sculpture Society
237 Park Avenue
New York, NY 10017
Phone: 212-764-5645
Fax: 212-764-5651
E-mail: nss1893@aol.com

OREGON STUDENT ASSISTANCE COMMISSION
http://www.osac.state.or.us

RAY KAGELER SCHOLARSHIP
• *See number 976*

ORGANIZATION OF AMERICAN HISTORIANS
http://www.oah.org

FOREIGN-LANGUAGE BOOK PRIZE AND DAVID THELEN PRIZE • 993

The OAH awards a prize annually for the best article and biennially awards a prize for the best book on American history that have been published in languages other than English. The winner will receive $1,000 and a certificate. The winning article will be published in the Journal of American History. Eligible books or articles should be concerned with the past (recent or distant) or with issues of continuity and change. Entries should also be concerned with events or processes that began, developed, or ended in what is now the United States.

Award Prize for use in graduate years; not renewable. *Number:* up to 4. *Amount:* up to $1000.

Eligibility Requirements Applicant must be enrolled or expecting to enroll at a four-year institution or university and must have an interest in foreign language. Available to U.S. and non-U.S. citizens.

Application Requirements Applicant must enter a contest.

Contact Kara Hamm, Award and Prize Committee
Coordinator
Organization of American Historians
112 North Bryan Avenue
Bloomington, IN 47408-4199
Phone: 812-855-9852
Fax: 812-855-0696
E-mail: awards@aoh.org

PI LAMBDA THETA, INC.
http://www.pilambda.org

NADEEN BURKEHOLDER WILLIAMS MUSIC SCHOLARSHIP
• *See number 922*

SINFONIA FOUNDATION
http://www.sinfonia.org

RESEARCH ASSISTANCE GRANTS • 994

Awards grant to individual conducting scholarly research in music. Must be related to American music or music in America. Must show previous writing and research or knowledge of field to be researched.

Award Grant for use in graduate, or postgraduate years; not renewable. *Number:* 1. *Amount:* $1000.

Eligibility Requirements Applicant must be enrolled or expecting to enroll full or part-time at an institution or university and must have an interest in music. Available to U.S. and non-U.S. citizens.

Application Requirements Application, essay, financial need analysis, portfolio, references. *Deadline:* March 1.

Contact Cheri Spicer, Executive Assistant
Sinfonia Foundation
10600 Old State Road 905-510 5th Street, SW
Evansville, IN 47711
Phone: 812-867-2433
Fax: 812-867-0633

WELLESLEY COLLEGE
http://www.wellesley.edu/CWS/

ANNE LOUISE BARRETT FELLOWSHIP • 995

Fellowships are available to graduating seniors and alumnae of Wellesley College only. Must be pursuing graduate research, preferably in music with emphasis on study or research in musical theory, composition, or the history of music abroad or in the United States. Merit and need will be considered. Information available by e-mail: cws-fellowships@wellesley.edu.

Award Fellowship for use in graduate years; not renewable. *Amount:* up to $13,000.

Eligibility Requirements Applicant must be enrolled or expecting to enroll at an institution or university; female and must have an interest in music. Available to U.S. citizens.

Application Requirements Application, essay, financial need analysis, resume, references, transcript. *Deadline:* January 3.

Contact Rose Crawford, Secretary to the
Committee on Graduate Fellowships
Wellesley College
106 Central Avenue, Green Hall 441
Wellesley, MA 02481-8200
Phone: 781-283-3525
Fax: 781-283-3674
E-mail: cws-fellowships@wellesley.edu

MISCELLANEOUS CRITERIA

ACADEMY FOR EDUCATIONAL DEVELOPMENT
http://www.aed.org

NATIONAL SECURITY EDUCATION PROGRAM DAVID L. BOREN GRADUATE FELLOWSHIPS • 996

Provides U.S. graduate students with support for overseas study and limited domestic tuition to pursue the study of languages, cultures, and world regions deemed critical to U.S. national security. Excluded is study of Western Europe, Canada, Australia, and New Zealand. Award recipients incur a requirement to work for an agency or office of the federal government involved in national security affairs or in the field of higher education in an area of study for which the fellowship was awarded, in that order of precedence.

Award Fellowship for use in graduate years; not renewable. *Number:* 80–90. *Amount:* up to $20,000.

Eligibility Requirements Applicant must be enrolled or expecting to enroll full or part-time at an institution or university. Available to U.S. citizens.

Application Requirements Application, applicant must enter a contest, essay, references, transcript. *Deadline:* February 1.

Contact Program Staff
Academy for Educational Development
1825 Connecticut Avenue, NW
Washington, DC 20009
Phone: 800-498-9360
E-mail: nsep@aed.org

NEW VOICES: A NATIONAL FELLOWSHIP PROGRAM • 997

Enables graduates to work for at least two years in nonprofits addressing social justice issues. In addition to salary and benefits, Fellows may apply for up to $6,000 to cover student loans or other approvable expenses. Fellows also receive $1,500/year to support professional development activities. Visit website for additional information. A fellow and a nonprofit apply together as a team.

Award Fellowship for use in graduate, or postgraduate years; not renewable. *Number:* 15. *Amount:* $35,000–$50,000.

Eligibility Requirements Applicant must be enrolled or expecting to enroll at a four-year institution or university. Available to U.S. and non-U.S. citizens.

Application Requirements Application, essay, resume. *Deadline:* January 15.

Contact Ken Williams, Director, New Voices
Academy for Educational Development
1825 Connecticut Avenue, NW
Washington, DC 20009
Phone: 202-884-8051
Fax: 202-884-8407
E-mail: newvoice@aed.org

ALBERTA HERITAGE SCHOLARSHIP FUND
http://www.alis.gov.ab.ca/scholarships

ALBERTA UKRAINIAN CENTENNIAL COMMEMORATIVE SCHOLARSHIPS
• *See number 927*

ALEXANDER VON HUMBOLDT FOUNDATION
http://www.humboldt-foundation.de

GERMAN CHANCELLOR SCHOLARSHIP PROGRAM • 998

Each year the foundation awards 10 scholarships to young U.S. citizens from any profession or field of study who show outstanding potential for future leadership. Selected scholars represent the private, public, not-for-profit, cultural and academic sectors. The program provides for a stay of one year in Germany for professional development, study or research. Applicant must be under 35 years of age.

Award Scholarship for use in graduate, or postgraduate years; not renewable. *Number:* up to 10.

Eligibility Requirements Applicant must be age 34 or under and enrolled or expecting to enroll full or part-time at an institution or university. Available to U.S. citizens.

Application Requirements Application, essay, resume, references, transcript. *Deadline:* October 31.

Contact Dr. Robert Grathwol, Director
Alexander von Humboldt Foundation
US Liaison Office, 1012 14th Street, NW, Suite 301
Washington, DC 20005
Phone: 202-783-1907
Fax: 202-783-1908
E-mail: avh@bellatlantic.net

HUMBOLDT RESEARCH FELLOWSHIP PROGRAM • 999

The Humbolt Research Fellowship Program supports highly qualified scholars of all nationalities and disciplines so that they may carry out long-term research projects in Germany.

Award Fellowship for use in postgraduate years; not renewable. *Number:* 600.

Eligibility Requirements Applicant must be age 39 or under and enrolled or expecting to enroll at an institution or university. Available to U.S. and non-U.S. citizens.

Application Requirements Application, essay, resume, references, transcript. *Deadline:* Continuous.

Contact Dr. Robert Grathwol, Director, US Liaison Office
Alexander von Humboldt Foundation
1012 14th Street NW, Suite 301
Washington, DC 20005
Phone: 202-783-1907
Fax: 202-783-1908
E-mail: avh@bellatlantic.net

AMERICAN ACADEMY OF CHILD AND ADOLESCENT PSYCHIATRY (AACAP)
http://www.aacap.org

AACAP/PFIZER TRAVEL GRANTS • 1000

Each travel grant will provide $800 to help defray the cost of attending the AACAP's 49th Annual Meeting in San Francisco, CA, October 22-27, 2002. Applicants must be child and adolescent, psychiatry residents at the time of the Annual Meeting. Additional information can be located at http://www.aacap.org/awards/announcm.htm.

Award Grant for use in postgraduate years; not renewable. *Number:* 50. *Amount:* $800.

Eligibility Requirements Applicant must be enrolled or expecting to enroll full-time at an institution or university. Available to U.S. and non-U.S. citizens.

Application Requirements *Deadline:* August 1.

Contact Crissie Renner, Research Assistant
American Academy of Child and
Adolescent Psychiatry (AACAP)
3615 Wisconsin Avenue, NW
Washington, DC 20016
Phone: 202-966-7300 Ext. 105
Fax: 202-966-2891
E-mail: crenner@aacap.org

AMERICAN ANTIQUARIAN SOCIETY
http://www.americanantiquarian.org

ACLS FREDERICK BURKHARDT RESIDENTIAL FELLOWSHIPS FOR RECENTLY TENURED SCHOLARS • 1001

Humanists at institutions in the U.S. and Canada are eligible to apply after they have become tenured. Fellowships provide a year of academic leave with a $65,000 stipend. Must apply directly to American Council of Learned Societies. See website at http://www.acls.org/burkguid for complete details.

Award Fellowship for use in postgraduate years; not renewable. *Amount:* $65,000.

Eligibility Requirements Applicant must be enrolled or expecting to enroll at an institution or university. Available to U.S. citizens.

Application Requirements Application. *Deadline:* October 1.

Contact Office of Fellowships and Grants, ACLS
American Antiquarian Society
228 East 45th Street
New York, NY 10017-3398
Fax: 212-949-8058
E-mail: grants@acls.org

AMERICAN ASSOCIATION OF NEUROSCIENCE NURSES
http://www.aann.org

NEUROSCIENCE NURSING FOUNDATION GWEN BREIGER MEMORIAL SCHOLARSHIP IN ADVANCED PRACTICE NURSING • 1002

Scholarship available to registered nurse seeking master's degree or post-master's certificate at an NLN accredited institution. Must submit letter of school acceptance along with application, transcript and copy of current RN license.

Award Scholarship for use in graduate, or postgraduate years; not renewable.

Eligibility Requirements Applicant must be enrolled or expecting to enroll at an institution or university. Applicant must have 3.0 GPA or higher. Available to U.S. citizens.

Application Requirements Application, transcript, letter of school acceptance. *Deadline:* February 15.

Contact Scholarship Program
American Association of Neuroscience
Nurses
4700 West Lake Avenue
Glenview, IL 60025-1485

AMERICAN ASSOCIATION OF UNIVERSITY WOMEN (AAUW) EDUCATIONAL FOUNDATION
http://www.aauw.org

AAUW EDUCATIONAL FOUNDATION AMERICAN DISSERTATION FELLOWSHIP • 1003

One-year dissertation fellowship for women who are U.S. citizens or permanent residents. Must submit proposal. Award for full-time study or research. Filing fee is $30. Winners must be in the final stages of dissertation writing at the time of the fellowship.

Award Fellowship for use in graduate years; not renewable. *Number:* up to 51. *Amount:* $20,000.

Eligibility Requirements Applicant must be enrolled or expecting to enroll full-time at an institution or university and female. Available to U.S. citizens.

American Association of University Women (AAUW) Educational Foundation (continued)

Application Requirements Application, references, transcript, proposal. *Fee:* $30. *Deadline:* November 15.

Contact Customer Service Center
American Association of University Women (AAUW) Educational Foundation
2201 North Dodge Street
Iowa City, IA 52243-4030
E-mail: aauw@act.org

Application Requirements Application, references. *Fee:* $25. *Deadline:* December 15.

Contact Customer Service Center
American Association of University Women (AAUW) Educational Foundation
2201 North Dodge Street, Department 177
Iowa City, IA 52243-4030
Phone: 319-337-1716
E-mail: foundation@aauw.org

AAUW EDUCATIONAL FOUNDATION AMERICAN POSTDOCTORAL FELLOWSHIP • 1004

One-year nonrenewable postdoctoral fellowship for women who are U.S. citizens or permanent residents. Must submit proposal. Award for postdoctoral candidates completing dissertations or women scholars seeking funds for postdoctoral research leave from accredited institutions. Filing fee is $35.

Award Fellowship for use in postgraduate years; not renewable. *Number:* up to 18. *Amount:* $30,000.

Eligibility Requirements Applicant must be enrolled or expecting to enroll full-time at an institution or university and female. Available to U.S. citizens.

Application Requirements Application, references, transcript, proposal. *Fee:* $35. *Deadline:* November 15.

Contact Customer Services Center
American Association of University Women (AAUW) Educational Foundation
2201 North Dodge Street
Iowa City, IA 52243-4030
E-mail: aauw@act.org

AAUW EDUCATIONAL FOUNDATION INTERNATIONAL FELLOWSHIPS • 1006

Nonrenewable awards for international women (non-U.S. citizens and non-residents) to further their education at graduate and postgraduate level in the U.S. for one year. Must have strong commitment to cause of women and girls worldwide. Application fee is $20.

Award Fellowship for use in graduate, or postgraduate years; not renewable. *Number:* up to 47. *Amount:* $18,000–$30,000.

Eligibility Requirements Applicant must be enrolled or expecting to enroll full-time at a four-year institution or university and female. Available to Canadian and non-U.S. citizens.

Application Requirements Application, references, test scores, transcript, proposal. *Fee:* $20.

Contact Customer Service Office
American Association of University Women (AAUW) Educational Foundation
2201 North Dodge Street
Iowa City, IA 52243-4030
E-mail: aauw@act.org

AAUW EDUCATIONAL FOUNDATION CAREER DEVELOPMENT GRANTS • 1005

One-time awards for women pursuing post-baccalaureate degrees. Must be a U.S. citizen or permanent resident. Candidate must have a bachelor's degree and must have earned her last degree prior to June 30, 1998. Application fee: $25. Not available for doctoral study. Special consideration given to AAUW members, women of color, women pursuing their first advanced degree, or to those with credentials in nontraditional fields.

Award Grant for use in graduate years; not renewable. *Number:* 60–65. *Amount:* $2000–$8000.

Eligibility Requirements Applicant must be enrolled or expecting to enroll full or part-time at a four-year institution or university and female. Available to U.S. citizens.

AAUW EDUCATIONAL FOUNDATION SUMMER/ SHORT -TERM PUBLICATION GRANTS • 1007

Six publication grants to fund women college and university faculty and independent researchers to prepare research for publication. Applicants may be tenure track, part-time, temporary faculty, or independent scholars and researchers, either new or established. Must be available for eight consecutive weeks of final writing, editing, and responding to issues raised in critical reviews.

Award Fellowship for use in postgraduate years; not renewable. *Number:* up to 6. *Amount:* up to $6000.

Eligibility Requirements Applicant must be enrolled or expecting to enroll full-time at an institution or university and female. Available to U.S. citizens.

Application Requirements Application, references, transcript, proposal. *Fee:* $30. *Deadline:* November 15.

Contact Customer Service Center
American Association of University
Women (AAUW) Educational
Foundation
2201 North Dodge Street
Iowa City, IA 52243-4030
E-mail: aauw@act.org

AMERICAN CENTER OF ORIENTAL RESEARCH
http://www.bu.edu/acor

KENNETH W. RUSSELL FELLOWSHIP • 1008

Award to support graduate student for participation in ACOR-supported archaeological project which has passed an academic review process, or ACOR-funded archaeological research project.

Award Fellowship for use in graduate years; not renewable. *Number:* 1. *Amount:* $1500.

Eligibility Requirements Applicant must be enrolled or expecting to enroll at an institution or university. Available to U.S. and non-U.S. citizens.

Application Requirements Application, references, transcript. *Deadline:* February 1.

Contact Dr. Donald Keller, Assistant Director
American Center of Oriental Research
656 Beacon Street, 5th Floor
Boston, MA 02215-2010
Phone: 617-353-6571
Fax: 617-353-6575
E-mail: acor@bu.edu

PIERRE AND PATRICIA BIKAI FELLOWSHIP • 1009

Awarded to a graduate student of any nationality who will reside at ACOR for a period of one or two months. Must participate in an archaeological project in Jordan. The award includes room and board at ACOR and a monthly stipend of $400.

Award Fellowship for use in graduate years; not renewable. *Number:* 1. *Amount:* $400.

Eligibility Requirements Applicant must be enrolled or expecting to enroll at an institution or university. Available to U.S. and non-U.S. citizens.

Application Requirements Application, references, transcript. *Deadline:* February 1.

Contact Dr. Donald Keller, Assistant Director
American Center of Oriental Research
656 Beacon Street, 5th Floor
Boston, MA 02215-2010
Phone: 617-353-6571
Fax: 617-353-6575
E-mail: acor@bu.edu

AMERICAN FOUNDATION FOR PHARMACEUTICAL EDUCATION
http://www.afpenet.org

KAPPA EPSILON/AFPE/NELLIE WAKEMAN FIRST YEAR GRADUATE FELLOWSHIP • 1010

Applicant must in final year of a pharmacy college B.S. or Pharm.D. program or have completed a pharmacy degree. At time of application, Kappa Epsilon member must be in good standing with the Fraternity and be planning to pursue a Doctor of Philosophy degree, Masters degree, or combined Residency/Masters degree program at U.S. College or School of Pharmacy. Legal aliens enrolled in U.S. institutions are eligible. Applicants may reapply for up to three years. Minimum 3.5 GPA required. Financial need also required.

Award Fellowship for use in postgraduate years; not renewable. *Number:* 1. *Amount:* $4000.

Eligibility Requirements Applicant must be enrolled or expecting to enroll full-time at an institution or university. Applicant must have 3.5 GPA or higher. Available to U.S. and non-U.S. citizens.

Application Requirements Application, resume, references, test scores, transcript. *Deadline:* February 15.

Contact Robert M. Bachman, President
American Foundation for Pharmaceutical
Education
One Church Street, Suite 202
Rockville, MD 20850
Phone: 301-738-2160
Fax: 301-738-2161
E-mail: afpe@worldnet.att.net

PHI LAMBDA SIGMA- GLAXCO SMITH KLINE-AFPE FIRST YEAR GRADUATE SCHOLARSHIP • 1011

Applicant must be in final year of pharmacy college B.S. or Pharm.D. program and be a member of Phi Lambda Sigma. Recipient will be invited to attend award ceremony during the Annual Meeting of Phi Lambda Sigma, held during the annual meeting of the American Pharmaceutical Association. U.S. citizenship or permanent resident status is required.

Award Scholarship for use in postgraduate years; not renewable. *Number:* 1. *Amount:* $7500.

Eligibility Requirements Applicant must be enrolled or expecting to enroll full-time at an institution or university. Available to U.S. citizens.

American Foundation for Pharmaceutical Education (continued)

Application Requirements Application, essay, resume, references, test scores, transcript. *Deadline:* February 15.

Contact Robert M. Bachman, President
American Foundation for Pharmaceutical Education
One Church Street, Suite 202
Rockville, MD 20850
Phone: 301-738-2160
Fax: 301-738-2161
E-mail: afpe@worldnet.att.net

RHO CHI-SCHERING PLOUGH-AFPE FIRST YEAR GRADUATE FELLOWSHIP • 1012

Applicant must be senior pharmacy student enrolled in dual-degree pathway leading to professional degree in pharmacy and the Ph.D. program. Applicant may also be first year graduate student entering graduate Ph.D. program at accredited school or college of pharmacy. Must be member of Rho Chi Honor society. Recipient will be invited to attend award ceremony during the Annual Meeting of Rho Chi, held during the annual meeting of the American Pharmaceutical Association. US citizenship or permanent resident status is required.

Award Fellowship for use in postgraduate years; not renewable. *Number:* 1. *Amount:* $7500.

Eligibility Requirements Applicant must be enrolled or expecting to enroll full-time at an institution or university. Available to U.S. citizens.

Application Requirements Application, essay, financial need analysis, resume, references, test scores, transcript. *Deadline:* February 15.

Contact Robert M. Bachman, President
American Foundation for Pharmaceutical Education
One Church Street, Suite 202
Rockville, MD 20850
Phone: 301-738-2160
Fax: 301-738-2161
E-mail: afpe@worldnet.att.net

AMERICAN INSTITUTE OF CERTIFIED PUBLIC ACCOUNTANTS
http://www.aicpa.org

JOHN L. CAREY SCHOLARSHIPS • 1013

Each year up to seven scholarships are awarded to liberal arts degree holders pursuing graduate studies in accounting who, in the opinion of the AICPA's Selection Committee, show significant potential to become successful practitioners. The selection is based on demonstrated outstanding academic achievement, leadership and future career interest.

Award Scholarship for use in graduate years; renewable. *Number:* up to 7. *Amount:* $5000.

Eligibility Requirements Applicant must be enrolled or expecting to enroll full-time at an institution or university. Available to U.S. citizens.

Application Requirements Application, essay, resume, references, test scores, transcript. *Deadline:* April 1.

Contact Leticia Romeo, Coordinator
American Institute of Certified Public Accountants
1211 Avenue of Americas
New York, NY 10036
Phone: 212-596-6221
Fax: 212-596-6292
E-mail: educat@aicpa.org

AMERICAN INSTITUTE OF INDIAN STUDIES
http://www.indiastudies.org

JUNIOR FELLOWSHIPS • 1014

One-time awards for graduate students enrolled in American universities to do dissertation research in India. Application fee: $25. Deadline: July 1.

Award Fellowship for use in graduate years; not renewable.

Eligibility Requirements Applicant must be enrolled or expecting to enroll at an institution or university.

Application Requirements Application, essay, references, transcript. *Fee:* $25. *Deadline:* July 1.

Contact Administrator
American Institute of Indian Studies
1130 East 59th Street
Chicago, IL 60637
Phone: 773-702-8638
Fax: 773-702-6636
E-mail: aiis@uchicago.edu

AMERICAN PHILOSOPHICAL SOCIETY
http://www.amphilsoc.org

FRANKLIN RESEARCH GRANT PROGRAM • 1015

Applicants normally expected to have doctorate, but applications are accepted from persons whose publications display equivalent scholarly achievement. Grants not for pre-doctoral study or research. Proposals in the area of journalistic or other writing for the general readership not accepted. Deadline is October 1. Complete information and forms are at www.amphilsoc.org. Applicants must consult website first.

Award Grant for use in postgraduate years; not renewable. *Amount:* up to $6000.

Eligibility Requirements Applicant must be enrolled or expecting to enroll at an institution or university. Available to U.S. citizens.

Application Requirements Application, references. *Deadline:* October 1.

Contact Committee on Research
American Philosophical Society
104 South 5th Street
Philadelphia, PA 19106-3387

AMERICAN SCHOOLS OF ORIENTAL RESEARCH (ASOR)
http://www.asor.org

CYPRUS AMERICAN ARCHAEOLOGICAL RESEARCH INSTITUTE ANITA CECIL O'DONOVAN FELLOWSHIP • 1016

One to three month fellowship to assist in partial payment of essential expenses for a graduate student to conduct research in Cyprus. Residence at The Cyprus American Archaeological Research Institute is mandatory. One-time award of $750. Application deadline: Feburary 1.

Award Fellowship for use in graduate years; not renewable. *Number:* 1. *Amount:* $750.

Eligibility Requirements Applicant must be enrolled or expecting to enroll at an institution or university. Available to U.S. citizens.

Application Requirements Application, project statement. *Deadline:* February 1.

Contact CAARI at Boston University
American Schools of Oriental Research
(ASOR)
656 Beacon Street, 5th Floor
Boston, MA 02215
Fax: 617-353-6575
E-mail: caari@bu.edu

AMERICAN SOCIETY OF SAFETY ENGINEERS (ASSE) FOUNDATION
http://www.asse.org/foundat.htm

ASSE- JAMES P. KOHN MEMORIAL SCHOLARSHIP • 1017

Scholarships for students pursuing a graduate degree program in occupational safety. Completion of 9 current semester hours or more and minimum GPA of 3.5 required. Deadline is December 1.

Award Scholarship for use in graduate years; not renewable. *Number:* 1. *Amount:* $2000.

Eligibility Requirements Applicant must be enrolled or expecting to enroll full-time at an institution or university. Applicant must have 3.5 GPA or higher. Available to U.S. and non-U.S. citizens.

Application Requirements Application, essay, references, transcript. *Deadline:* December 1.

Contact Customer Service Department
American Society of Safety Engineers
(ASSE) Foundation
1800 East Oakton Street
Des Plaines, IL 60018
Phone: 847-699-2929
Fax: 847-296-9220

ASSE- THOMPSON SCHOLARSHIP FOR WOMEN IN SAFETY • 1018

This scholarship is for women pursuing post-baccalaureate education in safety engineering, safety management, occupational health nursing, occupational medicine, risk management, ergonomics, industrial hygiene, fire safety, environmental safety, environmental health or other safety related fields. Completion of at least 9 current semester hours and minimum GPA of 3.5 required. Deadline is December 1.

Award Scholarship for use in graduate years; not renewable. *Number:* 1. *Amount:* $1000.

Eligibility Requirements Applicant must be enrolled or expecting to enroll full-time at an institution or university and female. Applicant must have 3.5 GPA or higher. Available to U.S. and non-U.S. citizens.

Application Requirements Application, essay, references, transcript. *Deadline:* December 1.

Contact Customer Service Department
American Society of Safety Engineers
(ASSE) Foundation
1800 East Oakton Street
Des Plaines, IL 60018
Phone: 847-699-2929
Fax: 847-296-9220

DELMAR E. TALLY PROFESSIONAL DEVELOPMENT GRANT • 1019

This grant is to provide financial support to ASSE members for their participation in recognized safety, health and environmental certification study courses, professional development seminars and educational conferences to improve their professional credentials. Applications are due December 1 and April 1.

Award Grant for use in graduate years; not renewable. *Amount:* $1000.

Eligibility Requirements Applicant must be enrolled or expecting to enroll at an institution or university. Available to U.S. citizens.

American Society of Safety Engineers (ASSE) Foundation (continued)

Application Requirements Application.

Contact Customer Service Department
American Society of Safety Engineers
(ASSE) Foundation
1800 East Oakton Street
Des Plaines, IL 60018
Phone: 847-699-2929
Fax: 847-296-9220

FORD MOTOR COMPANY SCHOLARSHIP-GRADUATE • 1020

Scholarships for women pursuing a graduate degree in occupational safety. Completion of 9 current semester hours and minimum GPA of 3.5 required. Deadline is December 1.

Award Scholarship for use in graduate years; not renewable. *Number:* 1. *Amount:* $3375.

Eligibility Requirements Applicant must be enrolled or expecting to enroll full-time at an institution or university and female. Applicant must have 3.5 GPA or higher. Available to U.S. and non-U.S. citizens.

Application Requirements Application, essay, references, transcript. *Deadline:* December 1.

Contact Customer Service Department
American Society of Safety Engineers
(ASSE) Foundation
1800 East Oakton Street
Des Plaines, IL 60018
Phone: 847-699-2929
Fax: 847-296-9220

AMERICAN-SCANDINAVIAN FOUNDATION
http://www.amscan.org

AWARDS FOR ADVANCED STUDY OR RESEARCH IN THE USA
• *See number 935*

AWARDS FOR STUDY IN SCANDINAVIA • 1021

Fellowships valued at $18,000 and grants valued at $3000 for graduate research in a Scandinavian country. Applicants are encouraged to be competent in chosen country's language. Preference given to dissertation level research. Must be U.S. citizen. One-time award. Application fee: $10.

Award Scholarship for use in graduate, or postgraduate years; not renewable. *Number:* 25–35. *Amount:* $3000–$18,000.

Eligibility Requirements Applicant must be enrolled or expecting to enroll at an institution or university. Available to U.S. citizens.

Application Requirements Application, references, transcript. *Fee:* $10. *Deadline:* November 1.

Contact Ellen McKey, Director of Fellowships and
Grants
American-Scandinavian Foundation
58 Park Avenue
New York, NY 10016
Phone: 212-879-9779
Fax: 212-249-3444
E-mail: emckey@amscan.org

ARCTIC INSTITUTE OF NORTH AMERICA
http://www.ucalgary.ca/aina

AINA GRANTS-IN-AID • 1022

Awards are aimed at young investigators, especially graduate students, to provide funding to augment their research. Must be a member of the Arctic Institute of North America. Applications focused on the natural sciences and social sciences in the North are encouraged.

Award Grant for use in graduate years; not renewable. *Amount:* $1000.

Eligibility Requirements Applicant must be enrolled or expecting to enroll at an institution or university.

Application Requirements Proposal, budget. *Deadline:* February 1.

Contact Dr. Erich H. Follmann, Institute of Arctic
Biology
Arctic Institute of North America
University of Alaska, PO Box 757000
Fairbanks, AK 99775-7000
Phone: 907-474-7338
Fax: 907-474-6967
E-mail: ffehf@uaf.edu

ASSOCIATION OF ASPHALT PAVING TECHNOLOGIES
http://www.asphalttechnology.org

ASSOCIATION OF ASPHALT PAVING TECHNOLOGIES SCHOLARSHIP • 1023

Scholarship for graduate students specializing in some aspect of asphalt technology. Students are usually sponsored by a member of AAPT.

Award Scholarship for use in graduate years; not renewable. *Number:* 2–3. *Amount:* $1500–$3000.

Eligibility Requirements Applicant must be enrolled or expecting to enroll full or part-time at a four-year institution or university. Applicant must have 3.0 GPA or higher. Available to U.S. and non-U.S. citizens.

Application Requirements Application, resume, references, transcript. *Deadline:* May 1.

Contact Eugene Skok, Jr., Secretary-Treasurer
Association of Asphalt Paving
Technologies
400 Selby Avenue, Suite 1
St. Paul, MN 55102
Phone: 651-293-9188
Fax: 651-293-9193
E-mail:
aapt.asphalttechnology@worldnet.att.net

ASSOCIATION OF MOVING IMAGE ARCHIVISTS
http://www.amianet.org

ASSOCIATION OF MOVING IMAGE ARCHIVISTS SCHOLARSHIP PROGRAM • 1024

The AMIA Scholarship Program is designated for students wishing to pursue careers in moving image archiving. Currently, the program awards three scholarships. Funds are sent to the recipients' educational institutions to help cover the cost of tuition or registration fees. Minimum 3.0 GPA required.

Award Scholarship for use in graduate, or postgraduate years; not renewable. *Number:* 3. *Amount:* $4000.

Eligibility Requirements Applicant must be enrolled or expecting to enroll full-time at an institution or university. Applicant must have 3.0 GPA or higher. Available to U.S. and non-U.S. citizens.

Application Requirements Application, essay, references, transcript. *Deadline:* May 1.

Contact Oksana Dykyj, Scholarship Program
Coordinator
Association of Moving Image Archivists
c/o 8949 Wilshire Boulevard
Beverly Hills, CA 90211
Phone: 310-550-1300
Fax: 310-550-1363
E-mail: oksana@vax2.concordia.ca

THE KODAK FELLOWSHIP IN FILM PRESERVATION • 1025

The Kodak Fellowship in Film Preservation is a unique program to help foster the education and training of the next generation of moving image archivists. Includes a $4,000 scholarship, a six-week internship at Kodak and other film restoration facilities in Los Angeles, and complimentary registration to the AMIA conference in Portland. Minimum 3.0 GPA required.

Award Fellowship for use in graduate, or postgraduate years; not renewable. *Number:* 1. *Amount:* $4000.

Eligibility Requirements Applicant must be enrolled or expecting to enroll full-time at an institution or university. Applicant must have 3.0 GPA or higher. Available to U.S. and non-U.S. citizens.

Application Requirements Application, essay, references, transcript. *Deadline:* May 1.

Contact Oksana Dykyj, Scholarship Program
Coordinator
Association of Moving Image Archivists
c/o 8949 Wilshire Boulevard
Beverly Hills, CA 90211
Phone: 310-550-1300
E-mail: oksana@vax2.concordia.ca

AUDIOLOGY FOUNDATION OF AMERICA
http://www.audfound.org

AUDIOLOGY FOUNDATION OF AMERICA'S OUTSTANDING AUD STUDENT AWARD • 1026

The Audiology Foundation of America's Outstanding AuD Student Award provides funds for students pursuing the Doctor of Audiology (AuD) degree from institutions in the U.S. or Canada and who are entering the third year of an AuD program. Students are recognized for their academic achievement and professional potential.

Award Fellowship for use in graduate years; not renewable. *Number:* 2. *Amount:* $4500.

Eligibility Requirements Applicant must be enrolled or expecting to enroll full-time at a four-year institution or university. Applicant must have 3.5 GPA or higher. Available to U.S. and Canadian citizens.

Application Requirements Application, essay, photo, references, self-addressed stamped envelope, test scores, transcript, nomination by AuD program director, clinical evaluation forms. *Deadline:* April 1.

Contact Mary Wilson, Managing Assistant Director
Audiology Foundation of America
207 North Street, Suite 103
West Lafayette, IN 47906
Phone: 765-743-6283
Fax: 765-743-9283
E-mail: mary@auffound.org

CANADIAN NORTHERN STUDIES TRUST - ASSOCIATION OF CANADIAN UNIVERSITIES FOR NORTHERN STUDIES
http://www.cyberus.ca/~acuns

CANADIAN NORTHERN STUDIES POLAR COMMISSION SCHOLARSHIP
• *See number 938*

CENTER FOR GAY AND LESBIAN STUDIES (C.L.A.G.S.)
http://www.clags.org

CLAGS FELLOWSHIP • 1027

A fellowship for a graduate student, an academic, or an independent scholar for work on a dissertation, first, or second book. Open to intellectuals both within and outside the academy who have demonstrated a commitment to the field of LGBTQ studies. The fellowship can be used for research, travel, or writing support.

Award Fellowship for use in graduate, or postgraduate years; not renewable. *Number:* 1. *Amount:* $5000.

Eligibility Requirements Applicant must be enrolled or expecting to enroll at an institution or university.

Application Requirements References, proposal, curriculum vitae. *Deadline:* November 15.

Contact Preston Bautista, Office Staff
Center for Gay and Lesbian Studies
(C.L.A.G.S.)
365 Fifth Avenue
Room 7115
New York, NY 10016
Phone: 212-817-1955
Fax: 212-817-1567
E-mail: clags@gc.cuny.edu

MARTIN DUBERMAN FELLOWSHIP • 1028

Fellowship is open to applicants from any country doing scholarly research on the lesbian/gay/bisexual or transgender experience. University affiliation is not necessary, but applicant must be able to show a prior contribution to the field of lesbian/gay/bisexual/transgender studies. Adjudication is by independent panel.

Award Fellowship for use in graduate years; not renewable. *Number:* 1. *Amount:* $7500.

Eligibility Requirements Applicant must be enrolled or expecting to enroll at an institution or university.

Application Requirements References, proposal, evidence of prior contribution to the field. *Deadline:* November 15.

Contact Preston Bautista, Office Staff
Center for Gay and Lesbian Studies
(C.L.A.G.S.)
365 Fifth Avenue, Room 7115
New York, NY 10016
Phone: 212-817-1955
Fax: 212-817-1567
E-mail: clags@gc.cuny.edu

CITIZENS' SCHOLARSHIP FOUNDATION OF AMERICA
http://www.csfa.org

EMPLOYEE MANAGEMENT ASSOCIATION FOUNDATION FELLOWSHIP PROGRAM • 1029

Fellowship aids and encourages students of demonstrated ability that are preparing for careers in Human Resources in generalist or employment/staffing capacity. Applicants maybe full-time undergraduate seniors that have been accepted into accredited graduate program, current graduate students, or experienced degree holders returning to graduate level program. Application deadline is in January.

Award Fellowship for use in graduate years; not renewable. *Amount:* $5000.

Eligibility Requirements Applicant must be enrolled or expecting to enroll full-time at an institution or university. Available to U.S. citizens.

Application Requirements Application.

Contact Scholarship Management Services, CSFA
Citizens' Scholarship Foundation of
America
1505 Riverview Road, PO Box 297
St. Peter, MN 56082
Phone: 507-931-1682
E-mail: info_sms@csfa.org

COUNCIL FOR INTERNATIONAL EXCHANGE OF SCHOLARS
http://www.cies.org

FULBRIGHT SCHOLAR PROGRAM FOR FACULTY AND PROFESSIONALS • 1030

The Council for International Exchange of Scholars (CIES) is a private organization founded in 1947 to assist the U.S. government in administering the Fulbright Scholar Program for Faculty and Professionals. CIES sends some 800 U.S. academics and professionals abroad each year and brings some 800 foreign academics and professionals to the U.S. to lecture and do research. CIES is affiliated with the Institute of International Education (IIE). Information about the Fulbright Scholar Program is available at http://www.cies.org.

Award Grant for use in postgraduate years; not renewable. *Number:* 800.

Eligibility Requirements Applicant must be enrolled or expecting to enroll at an institution or university. Available to U.S. citizens.

Application Requirements Application, resume, references, project statement. *Deadline:* August 1.

Contact Council for International Exchange of
Scholars
3007 Tilden Street NW, Suite 5L
Washington, DC 20008
Phone: 202-686-4000
Fax: 202-362-3442
E-mail: apprequest@cies.iie.org

CUSHMAN FOUNDATION FOR FORAMINIFERAL RESEARCH
http://www.cushforams.niu.edu

JOSEPH A. CUSHMAN AWARDS FOR STUDENT RESEARCH • 1031

Awards partially support graduate research dealing with foraminifera or allied groups. Proposals are judged on scientific merit and financial need.

Award Grant for use in graduate years; not renewable. *Number:* 1–6. *Amount:* up to $1000.

Eligibility Requirements Applicant must be enrolled or expecting to enroll full or part-time at an institution or university. Available to U.S. and non-U.S. citizens.

Application Requirements Financial need analysis, references, summary of research project, curriculum vitae, budget. *Deadline:* September 15.

Contact Jennifer Jett, Secretary/Treasurer
Cushman Foundation for Foraminiferal Research
National Museum of National History,
MRC-121 Department of Paleobiology
Washington, DC 20560-0121
Phone: 202-357-1390
Fax: 202-786-2832
E-mail: jett.jennifer@nmnh.si.edu

WILLIAM V. SLITER AWARD FOR STUDENT RESEARCH • 1032

Award to partially support graduate student research dealing with foraminifera or allied organisms. Proposals are judged on scientific merit and financial need.

Award Grant for use in graduate years; not renewable. *Number:* 1. *Amount:* up to $1000.

Eligibility Requirements Applicant must be enrolled or expecting to enroll full or part-time at an institution or university. Available to U.S. and non-U.S. citizens.

Application Requirements Financial need analysis, references, research summary, curriculum vitae. *Deadline:* September 15.

Contact Jennifer Jett, Secretary/Treasurer
Cushman Foundation for Foraminiferal Research
National Museum of National History,
MRC-121 Department of Paleobiology
Washington, DC 20560-0121
Phone: 202-357-1390
Fax: 202-786-2832
E-mail: jett.jennifer@nmnh.si.edu

ENTOMOLOGICAL SOCIETY OF AMERICA
http://www.entsoc.org

GRADUATE AWARD FOR LEADERSHIP IN ENTOMOLOGY • 1033

A $2,000 leadership award acknowledges Master's students who exhibit exceptional interest in the study and application of entomology through outstanding research and leadership skills. As applied entomology continues to adjust and change with new developments in technology, people with exceptional leadership skills and vision will be required to address the significant challenges of establishing science-based pest management solutions.

Award Prize for use in graduate years; not renewable. *Amount:* $2000.

Eligibility Requirements Applicant must be enrolled or expecting to enroll at an institution or university.

Application Requirements Application. *Deadline:* July 1.

Contact Education Committee
Entomological Society of America
9301 Annapolis Road
Suite 300
Lanham, MD 20706-3115
Phone: 301-731-4535 Ext. 3029
Fax: 301-731-4538
E-mail: awards@entsoc.org

EXPLORERS CLUB
http://www.explorers.org

EXPLORATION FUND GRANTS • 1034

Grants award primarily to graduate students in amounts up to $1200 for the support of exploration and field research. Applications will be judged on the scientific and practical merit of the proposal, the competence of the investigator, and the appropriateness of the budget. Must include signed liability waiver.

Award Grant for use in graduate years; not renewable. *Amount:* up to $1200.

Eligibility Requirements Applicant must be enrolled or expecting to enroll at an institution or university.

Application Requirements Application. *Deadline:* January 31.

Contact Odalis Martinez, Administrative Assistant
Explorers Club
46 East 70th Street
New York, NY 10021
Phone: 212-628-8383
Fax: 212-288-4449
E-mail: odalmart@aol.com

GEORGE MITCHELL SCHOLARSHIPS/ US-IRELAND ALLIANCE
http://www.MitchellScholar.org

GEORGE MITCHELL SCHOLARSHIPS • 1035

Scholarship provides for a year of full-time post-graduate study at any university in Ireland or Northern Ireland. Must be U.S. citizen under 31 years old. Deadline for application is October 10.

Award Scholarship for use in postgraduate years; not renewable. *Number:* 12.

Eligibility Requirements Applicant must be age 18-30 and enrolled or expecting to enroll full-time at an institution or university. Available to U.S. citizens.

Application Requirements Application, essay, interview, photo, references, transcript. *Deadline:* October 10.

Contact Dell Pendergrast, Director, Mitchell
  Scholarships
  George Mitchell Scholarships/US-Ireland
  Alliance
  1747 Pennsylvania Avenue NW
  12th Floor
  Washington, DC 20006
  Phone: 202-261-7354
  Fax: 202-785-6687
  E-mail: dpenderg@aol.com

GERMAN ACADEMIC EXCHANGE SERVICE (DAAD)
http://www.daad.org

GERMAN ACADEMIC EXCHANGE SERVICE (DAAD)/AMERICAN INSTITUTE FOR CONTEMPORARY GERMAN STUDIES (AICGS) GRANT • 1036

Fellowship available to assist doctoral candidates, recent PhD's, and junior faculty working on topics dealing with postwar Germany. Funds provided for summer residency at the American Institute for Contemporary German Studies (AICGS) in Washington, DC. Application deadline: April 15.

Award Fellowship for use in postgraduate years; not renewable.

Eligibility Requirements Applicant must be enrolled or expecting to enroll full or part-time at an institution or university.

Application Requirements Application. *Deadline:* April 15.

Contact AICGS
  German Academic Exchange Service
  (DAAD)
  1400 16th Street, NW, Suite 420
  Washington, DC 20036-2217
  Phone: 202-332-9312
  Fax: 202-265-9531
  E-mail: info@aicgs.org

GERMAN ACADEMIC EXCHANGE SERVICE STUDY VISIT RESEARCH GRANTS FOR FACULTY • 1037

Grants available to scholars and scientists to pursue research at German institutions. A minimum of two years of teaching and/or research experience after the Ph.D. or equivalent and a research record in proposed field are required. One-time award. Deadlines: August 1 and February 1.

Award Grant for use in postgraduate years; not renewable.

Eligibility Requirements Applicant must be enrolled or expecting to enroll at an institution or university. Available to U.S. and Canadian citizens.

Application Requirements Application, photo, curriculum vitae, project description, letter(s) of invitation.

Contact German Academic Exchange Service
  (DAAD)
  871 United Nations Plaza
  New York, NY 10017
  Phone: 212-758-3223
  Fax: 212-755-5780
  E-mail: daadny@daad.org

GERMAN MARSHALL FUND OF THE UNITED STATES
http://www.gmfus.org

GMF RESEARCH SUPPORT PROGRAM • 1038

Grants for advanced research to improve the understanding of significant contemporary, economic, political and social developments relating to Europe, European integration and U.S.-Europe relations. For current information, see website at http://www.gmfu.org.

Award Grant for use in graduate, or postgraduate years; not renewable.

Eligibility Requirements Applicant must be enrolled or expecting to enroll at an institution or university. Available to U.S. citizens.

Application Requirements Application, references.

Contact German Marshall Fund of the United
  States
  11 Dupont Circle N.W., Suite 750
  Washington, DC 20036
  Phone: 202-745-3950
  Fax: 202-265-1662
  E-mail: info@gmfus.org

GOLF COURSE SUPERINTENDENTS ASSOCIATION OF AMERICA
http://www.gcsaa.org

GOLF COURSE SUPERINTENDENTS ASSOCIATION OF AMERICA WATSON FELLOWSHIP PROGRAM • 1039

Students must be enrolled and registered in post-graduate studies in a field related to turfgrass science and/or golf course management. Includes candidates for master's or doctoral degrees. Should plan to pursue a career in research, instruction or extension in a university setting.

Award Fellowship for use in graduate, or postgraduate years; not renewable. *Number:* 4. *Amount:* $5000.

Eligibility Requirements Applicant must be enrolled or expecting to enroll full-time at an institution or university. Available to U.S. and non-U.S. citizens.

Application Requirements Application, essay, resume, references, transcript, summary of research projects, activities. *Deadline:* October 1.

Contact Pam Smith, Scholarship Coordinator
Golf Course Superintendents Association of America
1421 Research Park Drive
Lawrence, KS 66049-3859
Phone: 800-472-7878 Ext. 678
Fax: 785-832-3673
E-mail: psmith@gcsaa.org

HARVARD TRAVELLERS CLUB

HARVARD TRAVELLERS CLUB GRANTS • 1040

Approximately three grants made each year to persons with projects that involve intelligent travel and exploration. The travel must be intimately involved with research and/or exploration. Prefer applications from persons working on advanced degrees.

Award Grant for use in graduate, or postgraduate years; not renewable. *Number:* 3–4. *Amount:* $500–$1000.

Eligibility Requirements Applicant must be enrolled or expecting to enroll at a four-year institution or university. Available to U.S. and non-U.S. citizens.

Application Requirements Application, financial need analysis, resume. *Deadline:* March 31.

Contact Mr. George P. Bates, Trustee
Harvard Travellers Club
PO Box 190
Canton, MA 02021-0190
Phone: 781-821-0400
Fax: 781-828-4254

HEART AND STROKE FOUNDATION OF BRITISH COLUMBIA AND YUKON
http://www.hsf.ca/research

HEART AND STROKE FOUNDATION OF BRITISH COLUMBIA AND YUKON PROJECT GRANTS • 1041

Award to provide support for three or more investigators in undertaking collaborative, multidisciplinary research. Each component grant-in-aid must be based in British Columbia. Grant is renewable and normally awarded for four years. Letter of Intent must be submitted by May 15; full application form, by September 30.

Award Grant for use in postgraduate years; renewable. *Number:* 10. *Amount:* $72,838.

Eligibility Requirements Applicant must be enrolled or expecting to enroll full or part-time at an institution or university. Available to U.S. and Canadian citizens.

Application Requirements Application.

Contact Odie Geiger, Manager of Research
Heart and Stroke Foundation of British Columbia and Yukon
1212 West Broadway
Vancouver, BC V6H 3V2
Canada
Phone: 604-737-3401
Fax: 604-736-8732
E-mail: ogeiger@hsf.bc.ca

HELEN HAY WHITNEY FOUNDATION
http://www.hhwf.org

HELEN HAY WHITNEY FOUNDATION FELLOWSHIP • 1042

The Helen Hay Whitney Foundation supports early Postdoctoral Research Training in all Basic Biomedical Sciences. Visit http://www.hhwf.org for more information. Deadline is August 15.

Award Fellowship for use in postgraduate years; renewable. *Number:* 19–21. *Amount:* $39,000.

Eligibility Requirements Applicant must be enrolled or expecting to enroll full-time at an institution or university. Available to U.S. and non-U.S. citizens.

Application Requirements Application, autobiography, interview, resume, references, transcript. *Deadline:* August 15.

Contact Robert Weinberger, Administrative Director
Helen Hay Whitney Foundation
450 East 63rd Street
New York, NY 10021-7928
Phone: 212-751-8228
Fax: 212-688-6794
E-mail: hhwf@earthlink.net

INDUSTRIAL DESIGNERS SOCIETY OF AMERICA
http://www.idsa.org

DAVID H. LUI MEMORIAL GRADUATE SCHOLARSHIP IN PRODUCT DESIGN • 1043

Two one-time awards of approximately $2000 each awarded to full-time graduate students studying industrial design. Must be U.S. citizen and submit 20 visual examples of work.

Industrial Designers Society of America (continued)

Award Scholarship for use in graduate years; not renewable. *Number:* 2. *Amount:* $2000.

Eligibility Requirements Applicant must be enrolled or expecting to enroll full-time at a four-year institution or university. Available to U.S. citizens.

Application Requirements Application, references, transcript, 20 visual examples of work, letter of intent. *Deadline:* May 1.

Contact Heather Behnke, Program Manager
Industrial Designers Society of America
45195 Business Court, #250
Dulles, VA 20166-6717
Phone: 703-707-6000
Fax: 703-787-8501
E-mail: heatherb@idsa.org

INDUSTRIAL DESIGNERS SOCIETY OF AMERICA GIANNINOTO GRADUATE SCHOLARSHIP • 1044

One-time award to a U.S. citizen or permanent U.S. resident either applying to or currently enrolled in an industrial design graduate school program. Must submit 20 visual examples of work and study full-time.

Award Scholarship for use in graduate years; not renewable. *Number:* 1. *Amount:* $2000.

Eligibility Requirements Applicant must be enrolled or expecting to enroll full-time at a four-year institution or university. Available to U.S. citizens.

Application Requirements Application, references, transcript, letter of intent, 20 visual examples of work. *Deadline:* May 1.

Contact Cordelia Chu-Mason, Program Manager
Industrial Designers Society of America
45195 Business Court, Suite 250
Dulles, VA 20166-6717
Phone: 703-707-6000
Fax: 703-787-8501
E-mail: cordeliac@idsa.org

INSTITUTE FOR CURRENT WORLD AFFAIRS
http://www.icwa.org

JOHN MILLER MUSSER MEMORIAL FOREST AND SOCIETY FELLOWSHIP • 1045

Applicants must hold graduate degrees in forestry or forest-related specialties. Fellowship provides opportunity to broaden understanding of relationship of forest-resource problems to humans. Competition opens in September.

Award Fellowship for use in postgraduate years; not renewable.

Eligibility Requirements Applicant must be age 35 or under and enrolled or expecting to enroll full-time at an institution or university. Available to U.S. and non-U.S. citizens.

Application Requirements Application, resume.

Contact Peter Martin, Executive Director
Institute for Current World Affairs
4 West Wheelock Street
Hanover, NH 03755
Phone: 603-643-5548
Fax: 603-643-9599
E-mail: icwa@valley.net

INSTITUTE FOR HUMANE STUDIES
http://www.theihs.org

HAYEK FUND FOR SCHOLARS • 1046

Awards of up to $1000 to young scholars who are engaged in career development activities such as presentations at conferences, research at archives or libraries, or distribution of published articles.

Award Grant for use in graduate, or postgraduate years; not renewable. *Amount:* up to $1000.

Eligibility Requirements Applicant must be enrolled or expecting to enroll full or part-time at a four-year institution or university. Available to U.S. and non-U.S. citizens.

Application Requirements Resume, list of expenses, letter explaining project. *Deadline:* Continuous.

Contact Hayek Fund for Scholars Coordinator
Institute for Humane Studies
3401 North Fairfax Drive, Suite 440
Arlington, VA 22201-4432
Phone: 703-993-4880
Fax: 703-993-4890
E-mail: ihs@gmu.edu

INSTITUTE OF INTERNATIONAL EDUCATION (FULBRIGHT PROGRAM)
http://www.iie.org/fulbright

FULBRIGHT FULL GRANTS • 1047

Grants will be awarded for programs of study or research that will require one academic year. Applicants must be U.S. citizens and hold a B.A degree. Preference given to candidates whose higher education was received primarily in the U.S. Must have sufficient proficiency in language of host country. Must have good health. Please visit website for additional information and participating countries.

Award Grant for use in graduate, or postgraduate years; not renewable. *Number:* up to 950.

Eligibility Requirements Applicant must be enrolled or expecting to enroll full-time at an institution or university. Available to U.S. citizens.

Application Requirements Application, proposed study or project. *Deadline:* October 25.

Contact US Student Programs
Institute of International Education
(Fulbright Program)
809 United Nations Plaza
New York, NY 10017-3580

FULBRIGHT TRAVEL GRANTS • 1048

Travel grants are available only to Germany, Hungary, Italy, or Korea. They are available to supplement an award from a non-IIE source that does not provide funds for travel or to supplement a student's own funds for study. Travel grants provide round-trip transportation to the country where the student will pursue studies for an academic year, supplemental health and accident insurance, and the cost of an orientation course abroad, if applicable.

Award Grant for use in graduate, or postgraduate years; not renewable.

Eligibility Requirements Applicant must be enrolled or expecting to enroll full-time at an institution or university. Available to U.S. citizens.

Application Requirements Application. *Deadline:* October 25.

Contact US Student Programs
Institute of International Education
(Fulbright Program)
809 United Nations Plaza
New York, NY 10017-3580

INTERNATIONAL RESEARCH & EXCHANGES BOARD
http://www.irex.org

BLACK AND CASPIAN SEA COLLABORATIVE RESEARCH PROGRAM • 1049

Grants of up to $25,000 to a collaborative team of graduate and/or postgraduate scholars conducting research for up to one year, focusing on issues of practical relevance and current interest to academic, corporate, and policymaking communities. The collaboration team must consist of a minimum of 3 people: at least one U.S. citizen or permanent resident and at least 2 citizens and current residents of two different countries of the Black and Caspian Sea region at time of application.

Award Grant for use in graduate, or postgraduate years; not renewable. *Amount:* up to $25,000.

Eligibility Requirements Applicant must be enrolled or expecting to enroll at an institution or university. Available to U.S. and non-Canadian citizens.

Application Requirements Application, references, curriculum vitae and proposal. *Deadline:* May 1.

Contact Information Assistant
International Research & Exchanges
Board
2121 K Street, NW, Suite 700
Washington, DC 20037
Phone: 202-628-8188
Fax: 202-628-8189
E-mail: irex@irex.org

JAMES J. HILL RESEARCH LIBRARY
http://www.jjhill.org

JAMES J. HILL RESEARCH GRANTS • 1050

Awards to support research in James J. Hill and Louis W. Hill Papers.

Award Grant for use in graduate, or postgraduate years; renewable. *Number:* 2–4. *Amount:* up to $2000.

Eligibility Requirements Applicant must be enrolled or expecting to enroll part-time at a four-year institution or university. Available to U.S. and non-U.S. citizens.

Application Requirements References, estimated budget, research plan/outline. *Deadline:* November 1.

Contact W. Thomas White, Curator
James J. Hill Research Library
80 West Fourth Street
St. Paul, MN 55102
Phone: 651-265-5441
E-mail: twhite@jjhill.org

LEMMERMANN FOUNDATION
http://lemmermann.nexus.it/lemmermann/

LEMMERMANN GRANT • 1051

The Lemmermann Foundation awards scholarships to post-graduate university students who need to study in Rome to carry out research concerning Rome and the Roman culture from the pre-Roman Period to the present day in the classical studies field. Application deadlines: 3/15 and 9/15.

Award Grant for use in postgraduate years; not renewable. *Number:* up to 12. *Amount:* $1400–$2800.

Eligibility Requirements Applicant must be age 25-35 and enrolled or expecting to enroll full or part-time at an institution or university. Available to U.S. and non-U.S. citizens.

Lemmermann Foundation (continued)

Application Requirements Application, autobiography, photo, references.

Contact Valentina Nardo, Senior Assistant
Lemmermann Foundation
c/o Studio Associato Romanelli via
Cosseria, 5
Roma 00192
Italy
Phone: 39-6-3630208 Ext. 2
Fax: 39-6-3221788
E-mail: lemmermann@mail.nexus.it

MACKENZIE KING SCHOLARSHIPS BOARD

MACKENZIE KING OPEN SCHOLARSHIP • 1052

Award for graduates of Canadian universities pursuing graduate study in any discipline in any country. Include transcript and references with application. Minimum 3.5 GPA required. One-time award of Can$7,500.

Award Scholarship for use in graduate years; not renewable. *Number:* 1. *Amount:* $7500.

Eligibility Requirements Applicant must be enrolled or expecting to enroll full-time at an institution or university. Applicant must have 3.5 GPA or higher.

Application Requirements Application, references, transcript. *Deadline:* February 1.

Contact J. Blom, Professor of Law and Chair of
Selection Committee
MacKenzie King Scholarships Board
1822 East Mall
Vancouver, BC V6T 1Z1
Canada
Phone: 604-822-4564
Fax: 602-822-8108
E-mail: blom@law.ubc.ca

MARGARET MCNAMARA MEMORIAL FUND
http://www.worldbank.org/yournet

MARGARET MCNAMARA MEMORIAL FUND FELLOWSHIPS • 1053

One-time awards for female students from developing countries enrolled in accredited graduate programs relating to women and children. Must be attending an accredited institution in the U.S. Candidates must plan to return to their countries within two years. Must be over 25 years of age. U.S. citizens are not eligible.

Award Grant for use in graduate, or postgraduate years; not renewable. *Number:* 5–6. *Amount:* $11,000.

Eligibility Requirements Applicant must be age 25; enrolled or expecting to enroll full-time at a four-year institution or university and female. Available to citizens of countries other than the U.S. or Canada.

Application Requirements Application, essay, financial need analysis, photo, references, transcript. *Deadline:* February 1.

Contact Hilary Welch, Chairman, M.M.M.F.
Selection Committee
Margaret McNamara Memorial Fund
1818 H Street, NW
Washington, DC 20433
Phone: 202-473-8751
Fax: 202-522-3142
E-mail: mmmf@worldbank.org

MINISTRY OF THE FLEMISH COMMUNITY
http://www.diplobel.org/usa

FELLOWSHIP OF THE FLEMISH COMMUNITY • 1054

A ten month fellowship is available to American college students holding a Bachelor's or Master's degree who wish to further their education in Belgium. Eligible candidates will be under 35 years-old. The fellowship provides a monthly stipend of approximately 27.200 Belgian Francs, partrial tuition reimbursement and health insurance and public liability insurance in accordance with Belgian law. For more information visit http://www.diplobel.org/usa.

Award Fellowship for use in graduate years; not renewable. *Number:* 5.

Eligibility Requirements Applicant must be enrolled or expecting to enroll at an institution or university. Available to U.S. citizens.

Application Requirements Application, essay, references, transcript. *Deadline:* January 31.

Contact Ministry of the Flemish Community
Embassy of Belgium, 3330 Garfield Street
NW
Washington, DC 20008

MISSOURI BOTANICAL GARDEN
http://www.mobot.org

ANNE S. CHATHAM FELLOWSHIP IN MEDICAL BOTANY • 1055

Fellowship is open to Ph.D. candidates and recent PhD's to promote the study of medicinal botany. The fellowship was established to protect and preserve knowledge about the medicinal use of plants, and thus prevent the disappearance of plants with therapeutic potential. Providing this research opportunity for botanist can, in turn, assist medical science in its ability to protect lives and develop new medicines.

Award Fellowship for use in graduate, or postgraduate years; not renewable. *Number:* 1. *Amount:* $4000.

Eligibility Requirements Applicant must be enrolled or expecting to enroll full or part-time at an institution or university. Available to U.S. and non-U.S. citizens.

Application Requirements Autobiography, essay, financial need analysis, references. *Deadline:* January 15.

Contact James Miller, Curator and Head, Applied
Research Department
Missouri Botanical Garden
PO Box 299
St. Louis, MO 63166-0299
Phone: 314-577-9503
Fax: 314-577-0800
E-mail: james.miller@mobot.org

NATIONAL ACADEMIC ADVISING ASSOCIATION
http://www.nacada.ksu.edu

NATIONAL ACADEMIC ADVISING ASSOCIATION RESEARCH GRANTS • 1056

Practicing professionals (administrators and faculty), as well as graduate students seeking support for dissertation research, are eligible. Award does not support indirect or overhead costs. Submit research proposal.

Award Grant for use in graduate, or postgraduate years; not renewable. *Number:* 1–5. *Amount:* up to $5000.

Eligibility Requirements Applicant must be enrolled or expecting to enroll full or part-time at a four-year institution or university. Available to U.S. and non-U.S. citizens.

Application Requirements Application. *Deadline:* June 10.

Contact Deborah M. Kirkwood, Assistant Dean of
Instruction
National Academic Advising Association
Genesee Community College, Wyoming
Campus Center at Arcade, 25 Edward
Street
Arcade, NY 14009-1012
Phone: 716-492-5265
Fax: 716-345-6804
E-mail: ddkirkwood@genesee.suny.edu

NATIONAL ALLIANCE FOR RESEARCH ON SCHIZOPHRENIA AND DEPRESSION
http://www.narsad.org

NATIONAL ALLIANCE FOR RESEARCH ON SCHIZOPHRENIA AND DEPRESSION DISTINGUISHED INVESTIGATOR AWARD • 1057

This grant offers up to $100,000 for a one-year period and is intended for established scientists who maintain peer reviewed competitively funded scientific programs. The program is intended to facilitate innovative research opportunities and supports basic and/or clinical investigators, but research must be relevent to schizophrenia, major affective disorders or other serious mental illnesses including research with bipolar disease, borderline disorders with depression and suicide, and research with children.

Award Grant for use in postgraduate years; not renewable. *Amount:* up to $100,000.

Eligibility Requirements Applicant must be enrolled or expecting to enroll at an institution or university. Available to U.S. citizens.

Application Requirements Application, references, proposal. *Deadline:* May 15.

Contact Audra Moran, Director, Research Grants
Program
National Alliance for Research on
Schizophrenia and Depression
60 Cutter Mill Road, Suite 404
Great Neck, NY 11021-3196
Phone: 516-829-5576
Fax: 516-487-6930
E-mail: amoran@narsad.org

NATIONAL ALLIANCE FOR RESEARCH ON SCHIZOPHRENIA AND DEPRESSION INDEPENDENT INVESTIGATOR AWARD • 1058

This grant offers up to $50,000 a year for two years and is intended for scientists at the associate professor level with national competitive support as a principal investigator. The program is intended to facilitate innovative research opportunities and supports basic and/or clinical investigators, but research must be relevant to schizophrenia, major affective disorders or other serious mental illnesses including research with bipolar disease, borderline disorders with depression and suicide, and research with children.

Award Grant for use in postgraduate years; renewable. *Amount:* up to $50,000.

Eligibility Requirements Applicant must be enrolled or expecting to enroll at an institution or university. Available to U.S. citizens.

Application Requirements Application, references, proposal. *Deadline:* March 5.

Contact Audra Moran, Director, Research Grants
Program
National Alliance for Research on
Schizophrenia and Depression
60 Cutter Mill Road, Suite 404
Great Neck, NY 11021-3196
Phone: 516-829-5576
Fax: 516-487-6930
E-mail: amoran@narsad.org

NATIONAL ALLIANCE FOR RESEARCH ON SCHIZOPHRENIA AND DEPRESSION YOUNG INVESTIGATOR AWARD • 1059

This grant offers up to $30,000 a year for up to two years to enable promising investigators to either extend their research fellowship training or to begin careers as independent research faculty. The program is intended to facilitate innovative research opportunities and supports basic and/or clinical investigators, but research must be relevant to schizophrenia, major affective disorders or other serious mental illnesses including research with bipolar disease, borderline disorders with depression and suicide, and research with children.

Award Grant for use in postgraduate years; renewable. *Number:* 15. *Amount:* up to $30,000.

Eligibility Requirements Applicant must be enrolled or expecting to enroll at an institution or university. Available to U.S. citizens.

Application Requirements Application, references, proposal. *Deadline:* July 25.

Contact Audra Moran, Director, Research Grants Program
National Alliance for Research on Schizophrenia and Depression
60 Cutter Mill Road, Suite 404
Great Neck, NY 11021-3196
Phone: 516-829-5576
Fax: 516-487-6930
E-mail: amoran@narsad.org

NATIONAL ASSOCIATION FOR GIFTED CHILDREN
http://www.nagc.org

HOLLINGWORTH AWARD COMPETITION • 1060

International competition for publishable research proposals concerning gifted and talented young people. Projects may be sponsored by universities, school systems, individual schools, or public agencies. Professors, educational administrators, psychologists, teachers, graduate students or other professional individuals are welcome to apply. Must include 8 copies of approved research proposal, 8 copies of 200-word abstract, a signed statement of approval from the sponsoring institution, and a self-addressed stamped postcard. Deadline: 1/15. Visit website for more information

Award Grant for use in graduate, or postgraduate years; not renewable. *Number:* 1. *Amount:* $2000.

Eligibility Requirements Applicant must be enrolled or expecting to enroll at a four-year institution or university. Available to U.S. and non-U.S. citizens.

Application Requirements Application. *Deadline:* January 15.

Contact Mr. Peter Rosenstein, Executive Director
National Association for Gifted Children
1707 L Street, NW, Suite 550
Washington, DC 20036
Phone: 202-785-4268

NATIONAL BLOOD FOUNDATION

SCIENTIFIC RESEARCH GRANT PROGRAM • 1061

The mission of the National Blood Foundation is to fund basic and applied scientific research, operational research projects, professional education, technical training in all aspects of blood banking, transfusion medicine, and tissue transplantation. Renewable award for up to 2 years. $50,000 awarded per year. $150 application fee.

Award Grant for use in postgraduate years; renewable. *Number:* up to 1. *Amount:* $50,000–$100,000.

Eligibility Requirements Applicant must be enrolled or expecting to enroll full-time at an institution or university. Available to U.S. and non-U.S. citizens.

Application Requirements Application. *Fee:* $150. *Deadline:* December 3.

Contact Charles U. Birdie, Executive Director
National Blood Foundation
8101 Glenbrook Road
Bethesda, MD 20814-2747
Phone: 301-215-6552
Fax: 301-907-0895
E-mail: chuck@aabb.org

NATIONAL HEMOPHILIA FOUNDATION
http://www.hemophilia.org

NATIONAL HEMOPHILIA FOUNDATION CAREER DEVELOPMENT AWARD • 1062

Up to three grants of $70,000 for candidates holding MD, Ph.D., or equivalent degree. Must be an assistant professor or equivalent with up to six years of experience since completion of training. Applicant is expected to spend at least 90% of the working time on research. Submit application, letters of recommendation and description of proposed research project.

Award Grant for use in postgraduate years; renewable. *Number:* 1–3. *Amount:* $70,000.

Eligibility Requirements Applicant must be enrolled or expecting to enroll at an institution or university. Available to U.S. and non-U.S. citizens.

Application Requirements Application, references, description of proposed research project. *Deadline:* February 1.

Contact Rita Barsky, Assistant Director
National Hemophilia Foundation
116 West 32nd Street, 11th Floor
New York, NY 10001
Phone: 212-328-3730
Fax: 212-328-3788
E-mail: rbarsky@hemophilia.org

NATIONAL TRAINING SYSTEMS ASSOCIATION
http://www.iitsec.org

INTERSERVICE/INDUSTRY TRAINING, SIMULATION AND EDUCATION CONFERENCE SCHOLARSHIP • 1063

The scholarship's intent is to stimulate interest and university participation in preparing individuals for leadership in the Simulation, Training and Education industry. Must include proof of U.S. citizenship.

Award Scholarship for use in graduate years; not renewable. *Number:* 1–2. *Amount:* $10,000.

Eligibility Requirements Applicant must be enrolled or expecting to enroll full or part-time at an institution or university. Available to U.S. citizens.

Application Requirements Essay, resume, references, transcript, proof of U.S. citizenship. *Deadline:* March 1.

Contact Ms. Barbara McDaniel, Director, Conferences and Programs
National Training Systems Association
2111 Wilson Boulevard
Arlington, VA 22201-3061
Phone: 703-247-2569
Fax: 703-243-1659
E-mail: bmcdaniel@ndia.org

NATIONAL WOMEN'S STUDIES ASSOCIATION
http://www.nwsa.org

GRADUATE SCHOLARSHIP IN WOMEN'S STUDIES • 1064

Applicant must be engaged in research or writing stage of a master's thesis or Ph.D. dissertation in interdisciplinary field of women's studies. Project must enhance NWSA mission. Only those who are members of NWSA at time of application may apply. Application must include three recommendations.

Award Scholarship for use in graduate, or postgraduate years; not renewable. *Number:* 1. *Amount:* $1000.

Eligibility Requirements Applicant must be enrolled or expecting to enroll full or part-time at a four-year institution or university. Available to U.S. and non-U.S. citizens.

Application Requirements Application, financial need analysis, references, 2-3 page abstract. *Deadline:* February 15.

Contact Loretta Younger, National Executive Administrator
National Women's Studies Association
7100 Baltimore Avenue, Suite 500
College Park, MD 20740
Phone: 301-403-0525
Fax: 301-403-4137
E-mail: nwsa@umail.umd.edu

JEWISH CAUCUS PRIZE • 1065

One-time award given to a graduate student who is enrolled full-time and has a special interest in the lives, work and culture of Jewish women. Submit two letters of recommendation.

Award Prize for use in graduate years; not renewable. *Number:* 1. *Amount:* $1000.

Eligibility Requirements Applicant must be enrolled or expecting to enroll full-time at an institution or university.

Application Requirements Application, essay, references. *Deadline:* March 15.

Contact Loretta Younger, National Executive Administrator
National Women's Studies Association
7100 Baltimore Avenue, Suite 500
College Park, MD 20740
Phone: 301-403-0525
Fax: 301-403-4137
E-mail: nwsa@umail.umd.edu

NATIONAL WOMEN'S STUDIES SCHOLARSHIP IN LESBIAN STUDIES • 1066

Award open to students in research or writing phase of master's thesis or Ph.D. dissertation in lesbian studies. Preference given to NWSA members. Three letters of recommendation must be submitted with application.

Award Scholarship for use in graduate, or postgraduate years; not renewable. *Number:* 1. *Amount:* $500.

Eligibility Requirements Applicant must be enrolled or expecting to enroll full or part-time at an institution or university.

Application Requirements Application, references, 2-3 page abstract. *Deadline:* February 15.

Contact Loretta Younger, National Executive Administrator
National Women's Studies Association
7100 Baltimore Avenue, Suite 500
College Park, MD 20740
Phone: 301-403-0525
Fax: 301-403-4137
E-mail: nwsa@umail.umd.edu

NATSO FOUNDATION
http://www.natsofoundation.org

UNIVERSITY RESEARCH GRANT • 1067

Funding for a project focusing on specific aspects of the truckstop/ Travel Plaza Industry e.g. fueling, dining habits, and demographics. See website for complete details.

Award Grant for use in graduate, or postgraduate years; not renewable. *Number:* 1–5. *Amount:* $10,000.

Eligibility Requirements Applicant must be enrolled or expecting to enroll at an institution or university. Available to U.S. and non-U.S. citizens.

Application Requirements Application, proposals consisting of title pg., study plan, bib., C.V., and budget. *Deadline:* Continuous.

Contact Program Manager
NATSO Foundation
1199 North Fairfax Street, Suite 801
Alexandria, VA 22314
E-mail: foundation@natso.com

NORWAY-AMERICA ASSOCIATION
http://www.noram.no

NORWAY-AMERICA ASSOCIATION GRADUATE RESEARCH SCHOLARSHIPS
• *See number 945*

NORWEGIAN MARSHALL FUND • 1068

Funds are to support Americans invited to come to Norway to conduct post-graduate study or research in areas of mutual importance to Norway and the United States. From 5 to 15 individual grants in various fields have been awarded each year for nearly 20 years. Applicants must be citizens of the US who have arranged with a Norwegian sponsor or research institution to pursue a research project or program in Norway.

Award Grant for use in postgraduate years; not renewable. *Number:* 5–15. *Amount:* $1500–$4500.

Eligibility Requirements Applicant must be enrolled or expecting to enroll at an institution or university. Available to U.S. citizens.

Application Requirements Application, references. *Deadline:* March 23.

Contact Cheryl Storo, Director of Scholarship Program
Norway-America Association
Radhusgaten 23 B, 0158
Oslo
Norway
E-mail: namerika@online.no

NORWEGIAN INFORMATION SERVICE

NORWEGIAN INFORMATION SERVICE TRAVEL GRANTS • 1069

Travel grants available to citizens and residents of the US that are members of NORTANA. Grants are financial assistance for teachers and graduate students visiting Norway for study and research purposes. Write or e-mail for additional information. There is no application form.

Award Grant for use in graduate, or postgraduate years; not renewable. *Amount:* $750–$1500.

Eligibility Requirements Applicant must be enrolled or expecting to enroll at a four-year institution or university. Available to U.S. citizens.

Application Requirements Resume, outline of subject to be studied in Norway. *Deadline:* February 15.

Contact Norwegian Information Service
835 Third Avenue, 38th Floor
New York, NY 10022-7584
Phone: 212-421-7333
E-mail: cg.newyork@mfa.no

ORGANIZATION OF AMERICAN HISTORIANS
http://www.oah.org

ABC-CLIO AMERICA: HISTORY AND LIFE AWARD • 1070

One-time biannual award available to recognize journal literature advancing new perspectives on accepted interpretations or previously unconsidered topics in American History. Individuals and editors may submit nominations. Entries must be published between November 16, 2000 and November 15, 2002 for 2003 award. One copy of each entry must be received by each member of the award committee by December 1 of even-numbered years. One prize of $750.

Award Prize for use in graduate years; not renewable. *Number:* 1. *Amount:* $750.

Eligibility Requirements Applicant must be enrolled or expecting to enroll at a four-year institution or university. Available to U.S. and non-U.S. citizens.

Application Requirements Applicant must enter a contest, essay. *Deadline:* December 1.

Contact Kara Hamm, Award Prize Committee Coordinator
Organization of American Historians
112 North Bryan Avenue
Bloomington, IN 47408-4199
Phone: 812-855-9852
Fax: 812-855-0696
E-mail: awards@oah.org

AVERY O. CRAVEN AWARD • 1071

Annual, one-time award for the most original book on the coming of the Civil War, Civil War years, or the Era of Reconstruction, with the exception of works of purely military history. Each entry must be published between January 1 and December 31. One copy of each entry must be received by each member of the prize committee by October 1 of the year in which the book was published.

Award Prize for use in graduate years; not renewable. *Number:* 1. *Amount:* $500.

Eligibility Requirements Applicant must be enrolled or expecting to enroll at a four-year institution or university. Available to U.S. and non-U.S. citizens.

Application Requirements Applicant must enter a contest. *Deadline:* October 1.

Contact Kara Hamm, Award and Prize Committee
Coordinator
Organization of American Historians
112 North Bryan Avenue
Bloomington, IN 47408-4199
Phone: 812-855-9852
Fax: 812-855-0696
E-mail: awards@oah.org

ELLIS W. HAWLEY PRIZE • 1072

One-time $500 annual award available for the best book on the political economy, politics, or institutions of the U.S., concerning its domestic or international affairs, from the Civil War to the present. Copy of each entry must be received by each member of award committee by October 1 of the year in which the book was published. Eligible works shall include book-length historical studies written in English.

Award Prize for use in graduate years; not renewable. *Number:* 1. *Amount:* $500.

Eligibility Requirements Applicant must be enrolled or expecting to enroll at a four-year institution or university. Available to U.S. and non-U.S. citizens.

Application Requirements Applicant must enter a contest. *Deadline:* October 1.

Contact Kara Hamm, Award and Prize Committee
Coordinator
Organization of American Historians
112 North Bryan Avenue
Bloomington, IN 47408-4199
Phone: 812-855-9852
Fax: 812-855-0696
E-mail: awards@oah.org

FREDERICK JACKSON TURNER AWARD • 1073

This award has been given annually since 1959 for an author's first book on some significant phase of American history and also to the press that submits and publishes it. The winning press receives a certificate and a complimentary ad for the book in the Journal of American History. The author receives $1,000, a certificate, and a medal. The deadline for receipt of entries is October 1.

Award Prize for use in graduate years; not renewable. *Number:* 1. *Amount:* $1000.

Eligibility Requirements Applicant must be enrolled or expecting to enroll at a four-year institution or university. Available to U.S. and non-U.S. citizens.

Application Requirements Applicant must enter a contest. *Deadline:* October 1.

Contact Kara Hamm, Award and Prize Committee
Coordinator
Organization of American Historians
112 North Bryan Avenue
Bloomington, IN 47408-4199
Phone: 812-855-9852
Fax: 812-855-0696
E-mail: awards@oah.org

JAMES A. RAWLEY PRIZE • 1074

Annual one-time award for a book dealing with the history of race relations in the U.S. One copy of each entry must be received by each member of prize committee by October 1. Final page proofs accepted for books published after October 1 and before January 1 of the following year. Bound copy of final page proofs must be submitted by January 7. Author of winning book receives $1000 and publisher receives certificate of merit.

Award Prize for use in graduate years; not renewable. *Number:* 1. *Amount:* $1000.

Eligibility Requirements Applicant must be enrolled or expecting to enroll at a four-year institution or university. Available to U.S. and non-U.S. citizens.

Application Requirements Applicant must enter a contest. *Deadline:* October 1.

Contact Kara Hamm, Award and Prize Committee
Coordinator
Organization of American Historians
112 North Bryan Avenue
Bloomington, IN 47408-4199
Phone: 812-855-9852
Fax: 812-855-0696
E-mail: awards@oah.org

JAMESTOWN SCHOLARS: NEW DISSERTATION FELLOWSHIPS FROM THE NATIONAL PARK SERVICE AND ORGANIZATION OF AMERICAN HISTORIANS • 1075

One-time fellowship award supporting Ph.D. research with focus on the development and legacy of 17th

Organization of American Historians (continued)

century Jamestown. For U.S. graduate students pursuing PhD's in history, American studies, and related fields.

Award Fellowship for use in graduate years; not renewable. *Number:* 1. *Amount:* $5000.

Eligibility Requirements Applicant must be enrolled or expecting to enroll at a four-year institution or university. Available to U.S. citizens.

Application Requirements *Deadline:* December 15.

Contact Kara Hamm, Award and Prize Committee
      Coordinator
      Organization of American Historians
      112 North Bryan Avenue
      Bloomington, IN 47408-4199
      Phone: 812-855-9852
      Fax: 812-855-0696
      E-mail: awards@oah.org

LERNER-SCOTT DISSERTATION PRIZE • 1076

One annual award for the best doctoral dissertation in U.S. women's history. Must submit letter of support from a faculty member at the degree granting institution, an abstract, table of contents, and sample chapter from the dissertation. Deadline for submissions is December 1.

Award Prize for use in graduate years; not renewable. *Number:* 1. *Amount:* $1000.

Eligibility Requirements Applicant must be enrolled or expecting to enroll at a four-year institution or university. Available to U.S. and non-U.S. citizens.

Application Requirements Application, applicant must enter a contest. *Deadline:* December 1.

Contact Kara Hamm, Award and Prize Committee
      Coordinator
      Organization of American Historians
      112 North Bryan Avenue
      Bloomington, IN 47408-4199
      Phone: 812-855-9852
      Fax: 812-855-0696
      E-mail: awards@oah.org

LOUIS PELZER MEMORIAL AWARD • 1077

Annual one-time award for the best essay in American History by a graduate student at any level in any field. Entries may not exceed 7,000 words and the winning entry will be published in the Journal of American History. Submit entries in quadruplicate with a separate cover sheet stating author's name and graduate program. One prize of $500. Essay must be received by December 1.

Award Prize for use in graduate years; not renewable. *Number:* 1. *Amount:* $500.

Eligibility Requirements Applicant must be enrolled or expecting to enroll at a four-year institution or university. Available to U.S. and non-U.S. citizens.

Application Requirements Applicant must enter a contest, essay. *Deadline:* December 1.

Contact Kara Hamm, Award and Prize Committee
      Coordinator
      Organization of American Historians
      112 North Bryan Avenue
      Bloomington, IN 47408-4199
      Phone: 812-855-9852
      Fax: 812-855-0696
      E-mail: awards@oah.org

MARY K. BONSTEEL TACHAN PRE-COLLEGIATE TEACHING AWARD • 1078

One award available to pre-collegiate teacher for exceptional performance in advancing history or social studies education. Submit a cover letter, curriculum vitae, samples of written work, narrative describing the goals and effects of candidate's work, and names of three references. Complete application must be no more than 25 double-spaced pages. Application materials deadline December 1.

Award Prize for use in graduate years; not renewable. *Number:* 1. *Amount:* $750.

Eligibility Requirements Applicant must be enrolled or expecting to enroll at a four-year institution or university. Available to U.S. and non-U.S. citizens.

Application Requirements Application, references. *Deadline:* December 1.

Contact Kara Hamm, Award and Prize Committee
      Coordinator
      Organization of American Historians
      112 North Bryan Avenue
      Bloomington, IN 47408-4199
      Phone: 812-855-9852
      Fax: 812-855-0696
      E-mail: awards@oah.org

MERLE CURTI AWARD • 1079

One-time award available for the best book in the field of American social history and intellectual history. One prize of $1000. Award is given for social history and one prize of $1,000 is given for intellectual history. Final page proofs accepted for books published after October 1 and before January 1 of the following year. Bound copy of final page proofs must be submitted by January 7. Publisher will be honored with a certificate of merit. Cultural history submissions may be considered in either intellectual or social history categories.

Award Prize for use in graduate years; not renewable. *Number:* 2. *Amount:* $1000.

Eligibility Requirements Applicant must be enrolled or expecting to enroll at a four-year institution or university. Available to U.S. and non-U.S. citizens.

Application Requirements Applicant must enter a contest, essay. *Deadline:* December 1.

Contact Kara Hamm, Award and Prize Committee
      Coordinator
      Organization of American Historians
      112 North Bryan Avenue
      Bloomington, IN 47408-4199
      Phone: 812-855-9852
      Fax: 812-855-0696
      E-mail: awards@oah.org

Eligibility Requirements Applicant must be enrolled or expecting to enroll at a four-year institution or university. Available to U.S. and non-U.S. citizens.

Application Requirements Applicant must enter a contest. *Deadline:* October 1.

Contact Kara Hamm, Award and Prize Committee
Coordinator
Organization of American Historians
112 North Bryan Avenue
Bloomington, IN 47408-4199
Phone: 812-855-9852
Fax: 812-855-0696
E-mail: awards@oah.org

RAY ALLEN BILLINGTON PRIZE • 1080

One award available biannually for the best book in American frontier history; defined broadly so as to include the pioneer periods of all geographical areas and comparison between American frontiers and others. One copy of each entry must be received by each member of the prize committee by October 1 of even-numbered years. Final page proofs accepted for books published after October 1 and before January 1 of the following year. Bound copy of final page proofs must be submitted by January 7. Author of winning book will receive $1000 and publisher will receive a certificate of merit.

Award Prize for use in graduate years; not renewable. *Number:* 1. *Amount:* $1000.

Eligibility Requirements Applicant must be enrolled or expecting to enroll at a four-year institution or university. Available to U.S. and non-U.S. citizens.

Application Requirements Applicant must enter a contest. *Deadline:* October 1.

Contact Kara Hamm, Award and Prize Committee
Coordinator
Organization of American Historians
112 North Bryan Avenue
Bloomington, IN 47408-4199
Phone: 812-855-9852
Fax: 812-855-0696
E-mail: awards@oah.org

SHORT-TERM RESIDENCIES FOR US HISTORIANS IN JAPANESE UNIVERSITIES • 1081

One-time award for 3 selected scholars of U.S. history to give lecturers and seminars at Japanese university. Program lasts for 2 weeks. Award covers airfare, housing, and daily expenses. Applicants must be members of the OAH and scholars of American history or culture. Application deadline December 1.

Award Grant for use in graduate years; not renewable.

Eligibility Requirements Applicant must be enrolled or expecting to enroll at a four-year institution or university. Available to U.S. citizens.

Application Requirements *Deadline:* December 1.

Contact Kara Hamm, Award and Prize Committee
Coordinator
Organization of American Historians
112 North Bryan Avenue
Bloomington, IN 47408-4199
Phone: 812-855-9852
Fax: 812-855-0696
E-mail: awards@oah.org

ORISE SCIENCE AND ENGINEERING EDUCATION (SEE)
http://www.atmos.anl.gov/GCEP/

GLOBAL CHANGE EDUCATION PROGRAM-GRADUATE RESEARCH ENVIRONMENTAL FELLOWSHIP • 1082

Fellowship will support graduate students in biological and environmental research-funded collaborative global change research involving universities and national laboratories. The fellowships, renewable for up to three years, will support doctoral candidates in various global change research areas. Applicants will be required to submit a five-page description of proposed research, letters of recommendation from two mentors and an outside individual, and undergraduate and graduate transcripts. Application: deadline February 1.

Award Fellowship for use in graduate, or postgraduate years; renewable. *Number:* 10–30. *Amount:* $18,000–$30,000.

Eligibility Requirements Applicant must be enrolled or expecting to enroll full-time at a four-year institution or university. Applicant must have 3.0 GPA or higher. Available to U.S. citizens.

Application Requirements Application, essay, references, test scores, transcript, research statement, research mentor. *Deadline:* February 1.

Contact Milton J. Constantin, Program Manager
ORISE Science and Engineering
Education (SEE)
Orise-See, M.S.-36, PO Box 117
Oak Ridge, TN 37831-0117
Phone: 865-576-7009
Fax: 865-241-9445
E-mail: contanm@orau.gov

OSTEOGENESIS IMPERFECTA FOUNDATION
http://www.oif.org/

OSTEOGENESIS IMPERFECTA FOUNDATION FELLOWSHIP AWARD • 1083

Fellowships available for young investigators working to develop expertise in OI research. The deadline is November 1.

Osteogenesis Imperfecta Foundation (continued)

Award Fellowship for use in postgraduate years; renewable. *Amount:* $50,000.

Eligibility Requirements Applicant must be enrolled or expecting to enroll full-time at an institution or university. Available to U.S. and non-U.S. citizens.

Application Requirements Application. *Deadline:* November 1.

Contact Heller An Shapiro, Executive Director
Osteogenesis Imperfecta Foundation
Attention: Research Grants
804 West Diamond Avenue, Suite 210
Gaithersburg, MD 20878
Phone: 301-947-0083
Fax: 301-947-0456
E-mail: bonelink@oif.org

PEO INTERNATIONAL PEACE SCHOLARSHIP FUND
http://www.peointernational.org

PEO INTERNATIONAL PEACE SCHOLARSHIP • 1084

The International Peace Scholarship Fund is a program, which provides scholarships for selected women from other countries for graduate study in the United States and Canada. An applicant must be qualified for admission to full-time graduate study, working toward a graduate degree in the college or university of her choice in the United States or Canada.

Award Scholarship for use in graduate years; renewable. *Number:* 160–170. *Amount:* $6000.

Eligibility Requirements Applicant must be enrolled or expecting to enroll full-time at a four-year institution or university and female. Available to citizens of countries other than the U.S. or Canada.

Application Requirements Application, autobiography, financial need analysis, references, transcript.

Contact Carolyn Larson, Project Supervisor
PEO International Peace Scholarship
Fund
PEO Sisterhood Executive Office
3700 Grand Avenue
Des Moines, IA 50312
Phone: 515-255-3153
Fax: 515-255-3820

PFIZER, INC. - US PHARMACEUTICALS GROUP
http://www.physicianscientist.com

AMERICAN FEDERATION FOR AGING RESEARCH/PFIZER RESEARCH GRANTS IN AGING • 1085

Four grants awarded to support projects by junior faculty involving basic, clinical, or epidemiological research. Applicants must hold M.D. or D.O. degree. Preference given to applicants in the first or second year of junior faculty appointment. Please visit website (http://www.physicianscientist.com) for more details.

Award Grant for use in postgraduate years; not renewable. *Number:* 4. *Amount:* $50,000.

Eligibility Requirements Applicant must be enrolled or expecting to enroll at an institution or university. Available to U.S. citizens.

Application Requirements Application.

Contact AFAR, Grant Coordinator
Pfizer, Inc. - US Pharmaceuticals Group
70 West 40th Street
New York, NY 10018
Phone: 212-703-9977
Fax: 212-997-0330

PI LAMBDA THETA, INC.
http://www.pilambda.org

JANET ISHIKAWA- DANIEL FULLMER SCHOLARSHIP IN COUNSELING • 1086

The scholarship provides $1,000 to outstanding students pursuing graduate degrees in counseling or counseling psychology. Applicant should display leadership potential and be involved in extracurricular activities. A cumulative GPA of at least 3.5 taken during the junior or senior years of the undergraduate degree program and, if applicable, in all courses taken while enrolled in a graduate program is required.

Award Scholarship for use in graduate years; not renewable. *Number:* 1. *Amount:* $1000.

Eligibility Requirements Applicant must be enrolled or expecting to enroll full or part-time at an institution or university. Applicant must have 3.5 GPA or higher. Available to U.S. and non-U.S. citizens.

Application Requirements Application, resume, references, transcript. *Deadline:* February 10.

Contact Pam Todd, Manager, Member Services
Pi Lambda Theta, Inc.
4101 East 3rd Street
PO Box 6626
Bloomington, IN 47407-6626
Phone: 812-339-3411
Fax: 812-339-3462
E-mail: endowment@pilambda.org

RADCLIFFE INSTITUTE FOR ADVANCED STUDY-MURRAY RESEARCH CENTER
http://www.radcliffe.edu/murray

ADOLESCENT AND YOUTH RESEARCH AWARD • 1087

Grants up to $5000 will be awarded to applicants who have a PhD. Awards will support research using data sets containing samples with youth and adolescents archived at the center. Funds are provided for travel to the center, duplicating, computer time, assistance in coding data and other research expenses. Deadlines: October 15 and March 15.

Award Grant for use in postgraduate years; not renewable. *Amount:* up to $5000.

Eligibility Requirements Applicant must be enrolled or expecting to enroll at an institution or university. Available to U.S. and non-U.S. citizens.

Application Requirements Application, references.

Contact Grants Administrator
Radcliffe Institute for Advanced Study-Murray Research Center
10 Garden Street
Cambridge, MA 02138
Phone: 617-495-8140
E-mail: mrc@radcliffe.edu

RADIOLOGICAL SOCIETY OF NORTH AMERICA
http://www.rsna.org/research

RADIOLOGICAL SOCIETY OF NORTH AMERICA EDUCATIONAL SCHOLAR PROGRAM GRANT • 1088

To fund board certified individuals in radiology or related disciplines who hold degree of M.D. and who are seeking an opportunity to develop their expertise in the discipline of education in the radiological sciences. Applicants must be citizens of a North American country or have permanent resident status. Grants are open to board certified individuals in radiology or related disciplines who hold a degree of M.D. with a demonstrated interest in teaching and where pursuit of advanced training in education will impact the future education of radiologists.

Award Grant for use in postgraduate years; renewable. *Amount:* up to $75,000.

Eligibility Requirements Applicant must be enrolled or expecting to enroll at an institution or university. Available to U.S. and Canadian citizens.

Application Requirements Application. *Deadline:* June 1.

Contact Radiological Society of North America
820 Jorie Boulevard
Oak Brook, IL 60523-2251

RADIOLOGICAL SOCIETY OF NORTH AMERICA RESEARCH RESIDENT • 1089

To provide opportunities for radiology residents to gain further insight into scientific investigation or to develop competence in research and educational techniques and methods. Applicants must be a citizen of a North American country or have permanent resident status, possess an academic degree acceptable for a radiology residency, be in residency program at the time of application and have not served as principal investigator or coinvestigator on grants or contracts totaling $50,000 or more in a single calendar year.

Award Grant for use in postgraduate years; not renewable. *Amount:* $30,000.

Eligibility Requirements Applicant must be enrolled or expecting to enroll at an institution or university. Available to U.S. and Canadian citizens.

Application Requirements Application. *Deadline:* January 9.

Contact Radiological Society of North America
820 Jorie Boulevard
Oak Brook, IL 60523-2251

RESOURCES FOR THE FUTURE
http://www.rff.org

RFF FELLOWSHIPS IN ENVIRONMENTAL REGULATORY IMPLEMENTATION • 1090

Supports scholarly research to document the implementation and outcomes of environmental regulations. To inform regulators, industry, and others of assumptions of environmental law and policies. Case studies of any environmental regulation implementation within the last 50 years in the United States will be considered.

Award Fellowship for use in postgraduate years; not renewable. *Number:* 2. *Amount:* $50,000–$80,000.

Eligibility Requirements Applicant must be enrolled or expecting to enroll full-time at an institution or university. Available to U.S. citizens.

Application Requirements Essay, resume, references. *Deadline:* January 4.

Contact Molly Macauley, Senior Fellow and Director, Academic Programs
Resources for the Future
1616 P Street NW
Washington, DC 20036-0014
Phone: 202-328-5000

SHASTRI INDO-CANADIAN INSTITUTE
http://www.ucalgary.ca/~sici

SHASTRI CANADIAN STUDIES DOCTORAL RESEARCH FELLOWSHIPS FOR INDIAN SCHOLARS
• *See number 949*

SOCIETY FOR THE TEACHING OF PSYCHOLOGY
http://www.teachpsych.org

STP TEACHING AWARDS PROGRAM   • 1091

One-time award given annually to psychology teachers at two and four year schools, high school teachers, and graduate student instructors in psychology. The deadline is November 1.

Award Prize for use in graduate, or postgraduate years; not renewable. *Number:* 4. *Amount:* $750.

Eligibility Requirements Applicant must be enrolled or expecting to enroll full or part-time at a four-year institution or university. Available to U.S. and Canadian citizens.

Application Requirements Application, essay, portfolio, references. *Deadline:* January 11.

Contact Dana Dunn, Chair, Teaching Awards
  Committee
  Society for the Teaching of Psychology
  Department of Psychology, Moravian
  College
  Bethlehem, PA 18018
  Phone: 610-861-1562
  E-mail: dunn@moravian.edu

SOCIETY OF NAVAL ARCHITECTS & MARINE ENGINEERS
http://www.sname.org

SOCIETY OF NAVAL ARCHITECTS AND MARINE ENGINEERS GRADUATE SCHOLARSHIPS   • 1092

These one-time scholarships are open to US, Canadian and International applicants. Study must take place in approved schools in the US or Canada. Society membership required one year prior to application. Awards are made for one year of study leading to a Master's Degree in naval architecture, marine engineering, ocean engineering or in fields directly related to the marine industry. For more information visit http://www.sname.org. Deadline is January 31.

Award Scholarship for use in graduate years; not renewable. *Number:* 6. *Amount:* $12,000.

Eligibility Requirements Applicant must be enrolled or expecting to enroll at an institution or university. Available to U.S. and non-U.S. citizens.

Application Requirements Application. *Deadline:* February 1.

Contact Chairman, Scholarship Committee
  Society of Naval Architects & Marine
  Engineers
  601 Pavonia Avenue
  Jersey City, NJ 07306

THOMAS J. WATSON FELLOWSHIP PROGRAM
http://www.watsonfellowship.org

THOMAS J. WATSON FELLOWSHIP PROGRAM   • 1093

Open to graduating college seniors at participating institutions. Must be nominated by institution. One-time award to enable college graduates of great promise to engage in year of independent study and travel abroad following graduation. Must submit proposal, personal statement to college committee.

Award Fellowship for use in graduate years; not renewable. *Number:* up to 60. *Amount:* $22,000–$31,000.

Eligibility Requirements Applicant must be enrolled or expecting to enroll full-time at a four-year institution or university. Available to U.S. and non-U.S. citizens.

Application Requirements Application, essay, interview, photo, references, transcript. *Deadline:* November 5.

Contact Mr. Norvelle E. Brasch, Executive Director
  Thomas J. Watson Fellowship Program
  293 South Main Street
  Providence, RI 02903
  Phone: 401-274-1952
  Fax: 401-274-1954

WELLESLEY COLLEGE
http://www.wellesley.edu/CWS/

ALICE FREEMAN PALMER FELLOWSHIPS   • 1094

One or more fellowships available to Wellesley alumnae for study or research abroad or in the United States. The holder must be no more than 26 years of age at the time of her appointment, and unmarried throughout the whole of her tenure. Fellowships awarded on basis of merit and need. Web site: www.wellesley.edu/cws contains guidelines and application.

Award Fellowship for use in graduate years; not renewable. *Amount:* up to $23,000.

Eligibility Requirements Applicant must be age 26 or under; enrolled or expecting to enroll full-time at an institution or university and single female. Available to U.S. citizens.

Application Requirements Application, essay, financial need analysis, resume, references, transcript. *Deadline:* January 3.

Contact Rose Crawford, Secretary to the
  Committee on Graduate Fellowships
  Wellesley College
  106 Central Avenue, Green Hall 441
  Wellesley, MA 02481-8200
  Phone: 781-283-3525
  Fax: 781-283-3674
  E-mail: cws-fellowships@wellesley.edu

FANNY BULLOCK WORKMAN FELLOWSHIP
• 1095

One or more awards available to alumnae of Wellesley College for graduate study in any field. Recommendations and resume required.

Award Fellowship for use in graduate years; not renewable. *Amount:* up to $14,000.

Eligibility Requirements Applicant must be enrolled or expecting to enroll full-time at an institution or university and female. Available to U.S. citizens.

Application Requirements Application, essay, financial need analysis, resume, references, transcript. *Deadline:* January 3.

Contact Rose Crawford, Secretary to the
Committee on Graduate Fellowships
Wellesley College
106 Central Avenue, Green Hall 441
Wellesley, MA 02481-8200
Phone: 781-283-3525
Fax: 781-283-3674
E-mail: cws-fellowships@wellesley.edu

HORTON-HALLOWELL FELLOWSHIP • 1096

One or more fellowships available to graduates of Wellesley College for study in any field. Preference given to applicants who are in the last two years of candidacy for Ph.D. or equivalent or for private research. Based on need and merit.

Award Fellowship for use in graduate, or postgraduate years; not renewable. *Amount:* up to $9000.

Eligibility Requirements Applicant must be enrolled or expecting to enroll full-time at an institution or university and female. Available to U.S. citizens.

Application Requirements Application, essay, financial need analysis, resume, references, transcript. *Deadline:* January 3.

Contact Rose Crawford, Secretary to the
Committee on Graduate Fellowships
Wellesley College
106 Central Avenue, Green Hall 441
Wellesley, MA 02481-8200
Phone: 781-283-3525
Fax: 781-283-3674
E-mail: cws-fellowships@wellesley.edu

MARY ELVIRA STEVEN TRAVELLING FELLOWSHIP
• 1097

One or more fellowships available to alumnae of Wellesley College for a full year of travel or study outside the United States. Any scholarly, artistic, or cultural purpose may be considered. Candidates must be at least 25 years of age in the year of application. Application forms may be obtained from the Alumnae Office. The application and supporting material should be returned by December 15.

Award Fellowship for use in graduate years; not renewable. *Amount:* up to $20,000.

Eligibility Requirements Applicant must be age 25; enrolled or expecting to enroll at an institution or university and female. Available to U.S. citizens.

Application Requirements Application, essay, financial need analysis, resume, references, transcript. *Deadline:* December 15.

Contact Alumnae Office
Wellesley College
106 Central Street
Wellesley, MA 02481-8201

WHITEHALL FOUNDATION, INC.
http://www.whitehall.org

WHITEHALL FOUNDATION GRANTS-IN-AID • 1098

The Grants-in-Aid program is designed for researchers at the assistant professor level who experience difficulty in competing for research funds because they have not yet become firmly established. Grants-in-Aid will also be made to senior scientists. All applications will be judged on the scientific merit and innovative aspects of the proposal, as well as on past performance and evidence of the applicant's continued productivity. Grants-in-Aid are awarded for a one-year period and do not exceed $30,000. Visit http://www.whitehall.org for details.

Award Grant for use in graduate, or postgraduate years; not renewable. *Amount:* up to $30,000.

Eligibility Requirements Applicant must be enrolled or expecting to enroll at an institution or university. Available to U.S. citizens.

Application Requirements Letter of intent.

Contact Whitehall Foundation, Inc.
PO Box 3423
Palm Beach, FL 33480

WHITEHALL FOUNDATION RESEARCH GRANT
• 1099

Research grants are available to established scientists of all ages working at accredited institutions in the United States in the area of neurobiology. Applications will be judged on the scientific merit and the innovative aspects of the proposal as well as on the competence of the applicant. Research grants of up to three years will be provided. A renewal grant with a maximum of two years is possible, but it will be awarded on a competitive basis. Research grants will not be awarded to investigators who have already received, or expect to receive, substantial support from other sources, even if it is for an unrelated purpose. Research grants normally range from $30,000 to $75,000 per year. Visit www.whitehall.org for details.

Whitehall Foundation, Inc. (continued)

Award Grant for use in graduate, or postgraduate years; renewable. *Amount:* $30,000–$75,000.

Eligibility Requirements Applicant must be enrolled or expecting to enroll at a four-year institution or university. Available to U.S. citizens.

Application Requirements Letter of intent.

Contact Whitehall Foundation, Inc.
PO Box 3423
Palm Beach, FL 33480

WOMAN'S SEAMEN'S FRIEND SOCIETY OF CONNECTICUT, INC.

FINANCIAL SUPPORT FOR GRADUATE WORK IN THE MARINE SCIENCES • 1100

Awards up to $1,500 to assist graduate students conducting research in the Marine Sciences. Priority given to students working on the first two years of their research. Deadline for summer session studies or research is March 15; deadline for next regular academic year is April 1.

Award Grant for use in graduate years; not renewable. *Amount:* $500–$1500.

Eligibility Requirements Applicant must be enrolled or expecting to enroll full-time at a four-year institution or university. Available to U.S. citizens.

Application Requirements Application, financial need analysis, references, transcript.

Contact Woman's Seamen's Friend Society of Connecticut, Inc.
291 Whitney Avenue
Suite 203
New Haven, CT 06511

WORLD BANK
http://www.worldbank.org/wbi/scholarships

JOINT JAPAN/WORLD BANK GRADUATE SCHOLARSHIP PROGRAM • 1101

Renewable award for nationals of a World Bank member country under 45 years old accepted into a graduate program in a World Bank member country. Open to all academic disciplines with preference given to economic development. Award not available to U.S. or Canadian citizens.

Award Scholarship for use in graduate years; renewable. *Number:* 300. *Amount:* up to $30,000.

Eligibility Requirements Applicant must be age 25-45 and enrolled or expecting to enroll full-time at an institution or university. Available to citizens of countries other than the U.S. or Canada.

Application Requirements Application, autobiography, resume, references, transcript. *Deadline:* April 1.

Contact Abdul Al-Mashat, Administrator
World Bank
1818 H Street, NW
Washington, DC 20433
Phone: 202-473-6414
Fax: 202-522-4036
E-mail: aalmashat@worldbank.org

AWARD NAME INDEX

A.L. Medlin Scholarship • 301
A.L. Simmons Scholarship Fund • 901
A.R. Zipf Fellowship • 268
AACAP George Tarjan Award • 419
AACAP Irving Philips Award • 420
AACAP Jeanne Spurlock Minority Medical Student Clinical
    Fellowship in Child and Adolescent Psychiatry • 421
AACAP Jeanne Spurlock Research Fellowship in Drug
    Abuse and Addiction for Minority Medical Students
    • 422
AACAP Pilot Research Award Supported by Eli Lilly and
    Company • 423
AACAP Presidential Scholar Awards • 424
AACAP Rieger Psychodynamic Psychotherapy Award • 425
AACAP Rieger Service Program Award for Excellence • 426
AACAP Robinson/Cunningham Awards • 427
AACAP Sidney Berman Award • 428
AACAP Simon Wile Award • 429
AACAP/Pfizer Travel Grants • 1000
AACN Certification Corporation Research Grant • 784
AACN Critical Care Research Grant • 785
AACN Educational Advancement Scholarships-Graduate
    • 786
AACN-Sigma Theta Tau Critical Care Grant • 787
AADR Student Research Fellowships • 278
AALL and West Group George A. Strait Minority
    Scholarship Endowment • 703
AAOS/OREF Fellowship in Health Services Research • 598
AAS Short-term Fellowships • 959
AAS-National Endowment for the Humanities Fellowships
    and Mellon Postdoctoral Research Fellowships • 960
AAUW Educational Foundation American Dissertation
    Fellowship • 1003
AAUW Educational Foundation American Postdoctoral
    Fellowship • 1004
AAUW Educational Foundation Career Development
    Grants • 1005
AAUW Educational Foundation International Fellowships
    • 1006
AAUW Educational Foundation Selected Professions
    Fellowships • 87
AAUW Educational Foundation Summer/Short -Term
    Publication Grants • 1007
Abba Schwartz Fellowships • 861
ABC-CLIO America: History and Life Award • 1070
ACLS Frederick Burkhardt Residential Fellowships for
    Recently Tenured Scholars • 1001
ACTR Summer Russian Language Teacher Program • 344
Adelle and Erwin Tomash Fellowship in the History of
    Information Processing • 267
Adolescent and Youth Dissertation Award • 885
Adolescent and Youth Research Award • 1087
African Network of Scientific and Technological Institutions
    Postgraduate Fellowships • 14
AFUD/AUA Health Policy Research Program • 407
AFUD/AUA MD Post Resident Research Program • 452
AFUD/AUA Ph.D. Post Doctoral Research Program • 453
AFUD/AUA Practicing Urologist Research Award • 454
AGA R. Robert and Sally D. Funderburg Research Scholar
    Award in Gastric Biology related to Cancer • 410
AGC Education and Research Foundation Graduate
    Scholarships • 247

Agilent Technologies American Association of Critical Care
    Nurses Research Grant • 788
AGROPOLIS • 10
AIA, New York Chapter, Stewardson Keefe LeBraun Travel
    Grant • 88
AIA, New York Chpater, Arnold W. Brunner Grant • 89
AIAA Foundation Graduate Awards • 26
AIAA Foundation Orville and Wilbur Wright Awards • 27
AIIS 9-month Language Program • 403
AINA Grants-in-Aid • 1022
Air and Waste Management Association Scholarship
    Endowment Trust Fund • 24
AIR Research Grants-Improving Institutional Research in
    Postsecondary Education Institutions • 352
Alan F. Henry/Paul A. Greebler Scholarship • 29
Alaska Library Association Scholarship • 727
Albert G. Richards Graduate Student Research Grant • 274
Albert H. Marckwardt Travel Grants • 369
Albert J. Beveridge Grant for Research in the History of the
    Western Hemisphere • 115
Albert Nerken Award • 36
Alberta Foundation for the Arts Graduate Level
    Scholarships • 160
Alberta Ukrainian Centennial Commemorative Scholarships
    • 927
Alexander Sisson Award • 302
Alfred C. Fones Scholarship • 281
Alfred D. Bell, Jr. Fellowship • 963
Alice Fisher Society Historical Scholarship • 642
Alice Freeman Palmer Fellowships • 1094
Allie Beth Martin Scholarship Award • 762
Alpha Epsilon Iota Scholarship • 418
Amelia Earhart Fellowship Awards • 180
American Academy of Family Physicians Foundation
    Research Stimulation Grant • 430
American Academy of Family Physicians Foundation/
    American Academy of Family Physicians Research
    Grant Awards • 431
American Academy of Religion Research Assistance and
    Collaborative Research Grants • 863
American Association for Geodetic Surveying Graduate
    Fellowship • 893
American Association for Health Education Barbara A.
    Cooley Scholarship • 340
American Association for Health Education Delbert
    Oberteuffer Scholarship • 341
American Association for Health Education Marion B.
    Pollock Fellowship • 342
American Association of Critical Care Nurses Mentorship
    Grant • 789
American Association of Neurological Surgeons William P.
    Van Wagenen Fellowship • 434
American Brain Tumor Association Research Fellowship
    Awards • 439
American College of Obstetricians and Gynecologists
    Research Award in Adolescent Health • 441
American College of Obstetricians and Gynecologists/3M
    Pharmaceuticals Research Award in Lower Genital
    Infections • 442
American College of Obstetricians and Gynecologists/
    CYTYC Corporation Research Award for the
    Prevention of Cervical Cancer • 443

Associated Western Universities Graduate Research Fellowships • 49

Associated Western Universities Postgraduate Fellowship • 50

Association for Education in Journalism and Mass Communications Comm.Theory & Methodology Division Minority Doctoral Scholarships • 252

Association for Women in Mathematics Workshop for Graduate Students and Postdoctoral Mathematicians • 850

Association for Women in Science Predoctoral Fellowship • 77

Association of Asphalt Paving Technologies Scholarship • 1023

Association of Moving Image Archivists Scholarship Program • 1024

Association on American Indian Affairs, Inc. • 163

Atlantic Salmon Federation Olin Fellowship • 16

Attorney-CPA Foundation Scholarships • 225

Audiology Foundation of America's Outstanding AUD Student Award • 1026

Avery O. Craven Award • 1071

Awards for Advanced Study or Research in the USA • 935

Awards for Study in Scandinavia • 1021

Basil O'Connor Starter Scholar Research Awards • 538

Beckman Center for the History of Chemistry Research Travel Grants at the Chemical Heritage Foundation • 51

Ben Shuster Memorial Award • 498

Benn and Kathleen Gilmore Scholarship • 551

Bernadette E. Schmitt Grants for Research in European, African, or Asian History • 116

Bernstein Grant • 499

Beta Phi Mu Doctoral Dissertation Scholarship • 730

Bicentennial Swedish-American Exchange Fund Travel Grants • 133

Biocompatibles Eyecare Innovative Research Awards • 467

Bishop Charles P. Greco Graduate Fellowship Program • 359

Black and Caspian Sea Collaborative Research Program • 1049

Blakemore Freeman Fellowships for Advanced Study of Asian Languages • 404

Blanche E. Woolls Scholarship • 731

Bliss Prize Fellowship in Byzantine Studies • 123

Block Dissertation Award • 886

Blue Cross Blue Shield of Michigan Foundation Student Award Program • 393

Board of Governors Medical Scholarship Program • 581

Bound to Stay Bound Scholarship • 725

Bruce L. "Biff" Reed Award • 304

Byron Hanke Fellowship for Graduate Research • 317

C. R. Bard Foundation Prize • 552

Cadogan Fellowship • 173

California Association of Marriage and Family Therapists Educational Foundation Scholarships • 894

Canadian Blood Services Graduate Fellowship Program • 961

Canadian Blood Services Postdoctoral Fellowship Award • 480

Canadian Library Association DaFoe Scholarships • 736

Canadian Northern Studies Polar Commission Scholarship • 938

Canadian Northern Studies Trust Studentships in Northern Studies • 119

Canadian Society for Medical Laboratory Science Founders' Fund Awards • 408

Canadian Window on International Development Awards • 697

CAORC Fellowships • 666

CAORC Senior Fellowship • 665

Caroline M. Hewins Scholarship for Children's Librarians • 742

Caroline tum Suden/Frances A. Hellebrandt Professional Opportunity Award • 186

Carroll L.V. Meeks Fellowship • 104

Center for Basic Research in the Social Sciences Postdoctoral Fellowship • 860

Center for Hellenic Studies Fellowships • 121

Century Scholarship • 757

Charles E. Peterson Fellowship • 93

Charles V. Cleghorn Graduate Accounting School Scholarship • 237

Charlotte W. Newcombe Doctoral Dissertation Fellowships • 693

Chateaubriand Scholarship Program • 164

Chester Dale Fellowships • 83

Chicago Institute of Architecture and Urbanism Award • 102

Child Welfare Scholarships • 346

China Times Cultural Foundation Doctoral Dissertation Research in Chinese Studies Scholarships • 122

Chinese American Medical Society Scholarship • 285

ChLA Beiter Scholarships for Graduate Students • 764

Christopher Reeve Paralysis Foundation Individual Grants-Two-Year Awards • 627

Civil Air Patrol Graduate Scholarships • 906

CLAGS Fellowship • 1027

Claude C. Albritton Jr. Scholarships • 78

Clinton E. Phillips Scholarship • 895

Colgate-Palmolive Award for Student Research • 215

Colgate-Palmolive Postdoctoral Fellowship • 216

Collaborative Research Grants • 143

Committee on Scholarly Communication- American Research in the Humanities in the People's Republic of China • 669

ConAgra Fellowship in Child Nutrition • 390

Congressional Fellowship for Federal Executives • 676

Congressional Fellowship for Journalists • 250

Congressional Research Awards Program • 859

Congressional Science Fellowship Program • 299

Conservation Guest Scholars • 633

Consortium Fellowship • 226

Consortium of College and University Media Centers Research Awards • 253

Contemplative Practice Fellowships • 162

Continuing Education Grant Program • 874

Cottrell College Science Awards • 854

Cottrell Scholars Award • 855

Council for European Studies Pre-dissertation Fellowship • 682

Council on Social Work Education/Mental Health Minority Research Fellowship • 483

Crohn's and Colitis Foundation of America Career Development Awards • 485

Crohn's and Colitis Foundation of America First Award • 486

Crohn's and Colitis Foundation of America Research Fellowship Awards • 487

Crohn's and Colitis Foundation of America Research Grant Program • 488

Crohn's and Colitis Foundation of America Student Research Fellowship Awards • 489

Curatorial Research Fellowships • 144

Cyprus American Archaeological Research Institute Anita Cecil O'Donovan Fellowship • 1016

Daisy and Eugene Hale Memorial Fund • 878

Daland Fellowship for Research in Clinical Investigation • 981

Damon Runyon Scholar Award • 490

Daniel B. Goldberg Scholarship • 229

David H. Lui Memorial Graduate Scholarship in Product Design • 1043

Davidson Family Fellowship Program • 139

Deafness Research Foundation Grants • 492

Dean John Knauss Marine Policy Fellowship • 972

DEBRA International Research Grants • 494

Delmar E. Tally Professional Development Grant • 1019

Deloitte and Touche Doctoral Fellowship • 227

Delores A. Auzenne Fellowship for Graduate Study • 940

Radiological Society of North America Medical Student/ Scholar Assistant • 614

Radiological Society of North America Research Fellow • 615

Radiological Society of North America Research Resident • 1089

Radiological Society of North America Research Scholar • 616

Radiological Society of North America Research Seed • 617

Radiology Centennial Scholarship • 276

Ralph Steinhauer Awards of Distinction • 929

Ralph W. Ellison Memorial Prize • 567

Ray Allen Billington Prize • 1080

Ray C. Janeway Scholarship • 759

Ray Kageler Scholarship • 976

Reading/Literacy Research Fellowship • 768

Regents Graduate/Professional Fellowship Program • 975

Regents Health Care Scholarships for Medicine and Dentistry-New York • 294

Regents Physician Loan Forgiveness Award-New York • 580

Regional Scholar Exchange Program (RSEP) • 686

Research Assistance Grants • 994

Research Fellowship in Hemostatis • 937

Research Fellowship Program • 373

Research Grants • 365

Research Grants • 79

Research Grants • 511

Research Grants for Recent PhD's & Ph.D. Candidates • 986

Research Grants for Research into Risk and Insurance Economics • 323

Research Innovation Awards • 856

Research into Causes, Cure, Treatment and Treatment of Intellectual Impairment • 620

Research Student Scholarship • 13

Research Support Opportunities in Arctic Environmental Studies • 120

Residency Travel Award • 507

Residential Fellowship in Byzantine, Pre-Columbian, and Landscape Architecture Studies • 95

Respironics Fellowship in Mechanical Ventilation • 32

Respironics Fellowship in Non-Invasive Respiratory Care • 478

RFF Fellowships in Environmental Regulatory Implementation • 1090

Rho Chi-Schering Plough-AFPE First Year Graduate Fellowship • 1012

Rice-Cullimore Scholarship • 378

Richard W. Leopold Prize • 921

Robert D. Watkins Minority Graduate Research Fellowship • 191

Robert H. Rumler Scholarship • 231

Robert K. Fahnestock Memorial Award • 311

Robert L. Dixon International Travel Award • 219

Robert S. McNamara Fellowship • 339

Robert W. Woodruff Fellowship • 983

Ronald D. Lunceford Scholarship • 896

Rosann S. Berry Annual Meeting Fellowship • 106

Rosemary Berkel Crisp Research Award • 825

Rotary Foundation Grants for University Teachers to Serve in Developing Countries • 923

Roy Johnson Trust Fund • 926

Rural Health Scholarship Program • 292

Russell and Sigurd Varian Fellowship • 43

Ruth Crymes Fellowship for Graduate Study • 370

Ruth Ingersoll Goldmark Fellowship • 769

S.E. Dwornik Student Paper Awards • 312

Saint Andrews Society of the State of New York Scholarship for Graduate Study • 948

Santa Clara University School of Law Computer and High Technology Law Journal Comment Contest • 701

Sarah Perry Wood Medical Fellowship • 631

Sarah Rebecca Reed Scholarship • 735

Sarnoff Fellowship Program • 618

Scholar Awards • 512

Scholarships for Blind Jewish Community Professionals • 925

Scientific Research Grant Program • 1061

Sense of Smell Institute Research Grants • 214

Sequoyah Graduate Fellowships for American Indians and Alaskan Natives • 936

Shastri Canadian Studies Doctoral Research Fellowships for Indian Scholars • 949

Shastri Canadian Studies Faculty Enrichment Fellowship for Indian Scholars • 950

Shastri Canadian Studies Faculty Research Fellowships for Indian Scholars • 951

Shastri India Studies Faculty Fellowships • 952

Shastri India Studies Postdoctoral Research Fellowships • 953

Shastri India Studies Senior Arts Fellowships • 157

Shastri India Studies Student Fellowships • 954

Sherman Fairchild Foundation Conservation Fellowship • 779

Shields-Gillespie Scholarship • 350

Ship Island - Mrs. J.O. Jones Memorial Scholarship • 837

Short-term Residencies for US Historians in Japanese Universities • 1081

Short-Term Scientific Awards • 513

Sigma Alpha Iota Doctoral Grant • 368

Sigma Alpha Iota Graduate Performance Awards • 846

Sigma Alpha Iota Scholarship for Conductors • 847

Sigma Phi Alpha Graduate Scholarship • 284

Sigma Theta Tau International /Emergency Nurses Association Foundation Grant • 826

Sigma Theta Tau International Small Research Grant • 827

Sigma Theta Tau International/ American Association of Critical Care Nurses Critical Care Grant • 828

Sigma Theta Tau International/ Association of Operating Room Nurses Grant • 829

Sigma Theta Tau International/ Oncology Nursing Society Grant • 830

Sigma Theta Tau International/ Rehabilitation Nursing Foundation Grant • 831

Sigma Theta Tau International/American Association of Diabetes Educators Grant • 832

Sigma Theta Tau International/American Nephrology Nurses' Association Grant • 836

Sigma Theta Tau International/American Nephrology Nurses' Association Grant • 833

Sigma Theta Tau International/American Nurses Foundation Grant • 834

Sir Harold Delf Gillies Award • 508

Sir James Lougheed Awards of Distinction • 930

Sloan Ph.D Program • 243

Small Research Grant Competition • 858

Smithsonian Institution Graduate Student Fellowships • 634

Smithsonian Institution Postdoctoral Fellowships • 635

Smithsonian Institution Predoctoral Fellowships • 636

Snodgrass Memorial Research Award • 199

Society of Automotive Engineers Doctoral Scholars Program • 178

Society of Flavor Chemists Memorial Graduate Fellowship • 400

Society of Naval Architects and Marine Engineers Graduate Scholarships • 1092

Society of Nuclear Medicine Student Fellowship Awards • 497

SOT/ACC Early Award in Inhalation Toxicology • 220

Southern Regional Education Board Loan/Scholarship • 547

Space Grant Fellowship Program • 970

Spectrum Scholarship • 760

Speech Language Pathologist Incentive Program • 897

Spiro Kostof Annual Meeting Fellowship • 107

Stanley C. Hollander Best Retailing Paper Competition • 223

State Medical Education Board Scholarship Program • 621

State Medical Education Board/Georgia Loan Repayment Program • 622

SPONSOR INDEX

Sponsor Index

Harvard University Center for Basic Research in the Social Sciences • 860
Health Professions Education Foundation • 287
Health Resources and Services Administration • 522
Heart and Stroke Foundation of British Columbia and Yukon • 1041
Heart and Stroke Foundation of Canada • 523, 524, 525, 526, 527, 528, 529
Helen Hay Whitney Foundation • 1042
Herbert Hoover Presidential Library Association • 965
Herbert Scoville Jr. Peace Fellowship Program • 966
Hewins Scholarship Fund • 742
Hispanic Theological Initiative • 869, 870, 871
Holstein Association USA, Inc. • 231
Hostess Committee Scholarships/Miss America Pageant • 530, 716
Howard Hughes Medical Institute, Office of Grants and Special Programs • 203, 204
Hudson River Foundation • 205, 206
Hudson River National Estuarine Research Reserve • 55
Huntington Library, Art Collections, and Botanical Gardens • 56
Illinois State Library • 743
Illinois Student Assistance Commission (ISAC) • 269
IMGIP/ICEOP • 372, 941
Industrial Designers Society of America • 1043, 1044
Institute for Current World Affairs • 696, 1045
Institute for Humane Studies • 1046
Institute for Supply Management • 232, 233
Institute of Food Technologists • 394, 395, 396, 397, 398, 399, 400
Institute of Industrial Engineers • 380, 900
Institute of International Education (Fulbright Program) • 1047, 1048
International Desalination Association • 57
International Development Research Center • 10, 11, 12, 697, 881
International Foundation for Ethical Research • 207
International Interior Design Association (IIDA) Foundation • 694, 695
International Order of the King's Daughters and Sons • 872
International Reading Association • 765, 766, 767, 768
International Research & Exchanges Board • 684, 685, 686, 883, 1049
International Union for Vacuum Science, Technique and Applications • 58
International Women's Fishing Association Scholarship Trust • 19
Jacki Tuckfield Memorial Graduate Business Scholarship Fund • 234
James J. Hill Research Library • 1050
Jane Coffin Childs Memorial Fund for Medical Research • 531
Japan Foundation • 687, 688, 689
Japan-America Society of Washington, DC • 357
Japanese American Citizens League • 717, 911
Japanese Government/The Monbusho Scholarship Program • 13
Jewish Braille Institute • 925
Jewish Foundation for Education of Women • 358
JILA • 775, 776
John F. Kennedy Library Foundation • 100, 648, 690, 698, 861, 862
Kansas Board of Regents • 532, 533, 967, 968
Kappa Gamma Pi • 912
Kappa Kappa Gamma Foundation • 913
Kappa Omicron Nu Honor Society • 386, 387, 388, 389, 401, 663, 664
Knights of Columbus • 359
Kosciuszko Foundation • 942, 988
KPMG Foundation • 235
Krell Institute • 270
Kurt Weill Foundation for Music • 843
L.S.B. Leakey Foundation • 79

Lambda Alpha National Collegiate Honors Society for Anthropology • 80, 81
Landscape Architecture Foundation • 702
Lemmermann Foundation • 1051
Leukemia & Lymphoma Society • 534, 535, 536
Li Foundation, Inc. • 943
Library and Information Technology Association • 744, 745, 746, 747
Life Sciences Research Foundation • 208
Loren L. Zachary Society for the Performing Arts • 844
MacKenzie Foundation • 537
MacKenzie King Scholarships Board • 236, 1052
March of Dimes Birth Defects Foundation - Grants Administration • 538, 539, 795
Marcus Center of the American Jewish Archives • 649
Margaret McNamara Memorial Fund • 1053
Maryland State Higher Education Commission • 288, 540
Massachusetts Black Librarian's Network • 748
Massachusetts Historical Society • 650, 651
Maternity Center Association • 796
Medical Library Association • 749, 750, 751, 752
Memorial Foundation for Jewish Culture • 127, 128, 129, 130, 873
Mennonite Health Services • 541, 797
Metropolitan Museum of Art • 59, 82, 83, 148, 149, 150, 151, 152, 153, 168, 169, 778, 779
Mexican American Legal Defense and Educational Fund • 718
Michigan Society of Fellows • 969
Milheim Foundation for Cancer Research • 542
Minerals, Metals, and Materials Society (TMS) • 374
Ministry of the Flemish Community • 1054
Minnesota Department of Health • 289, 543, 544, 545
Mississippi State Student Financial Aid • 546, 547, 798
Missouri Botanical Garden • 1055
Montana Space Grant Consortium • 177
Mountain Lake Biological Station • 209
Mrs. Giles Whiting Foundation • 691
Mustard Seed Foundation • 958
Myasthenia Gravis Foundation of America, Inc. • 210, 211, 799
NAPABA Law Foundation • 719, 720
NASA Florida Space Grant Consortium • 970
NASA Idaho Space Grant Consortium • 60
NASA South Carolina Space Grant Consortium • 971
NASA Wyoming Space Grant Consortium • 61
National Academic Advising Association • 914, 1056
National Academy for Nuclear Training • 783
National Academy of Education • 360
National Action Council for Minorities in Engineering-NACME, Inc. • 243
National Alliance for Research on Schizophrenia and Depression • 1057, 1058, 1059
National Arab American Medical Association • 290
National Association for Campus Activities • 989, 990
National Association for Gifted Children • 1060
National Association of Broadcasters • 254
National Association of Junior Auxiliaries, Inc. • 361
National Association of Pediatric Nurse Practitioners • 800
National Association of the Deaf • 255
National Blood Foundation • 1061
National Center for Atmospheric Research • 777
National Collegiate Athletic Association • 891, 991
National Gallery of Art • 154
National Headache Foundation • 548
National Hemophilia Foundation • 291, 549, 550, 801, 884, 1062
National Medical Fellowships, Inc • 409, 551, 552, 553, 554, 555, 556, 557, 558, 559, 560, 561, 562, 563, 564, 565, 566, 567, 568, 569
National Milk Producers Federation • 5
National Multiple Sclerosis Society • 570, 571, 572, 573, 574, 575
National Physical Science Consortium • 244
National Press Photographers Foundation, Inc. • 699

National Research Council • 212, 256, 257, 258
National Science Foundation • 62, 381, 382
National Sculpture Society • 992
National Sea Grant College Program Office • 972
National Sleep Foundation • 213
National Strength and Conditioning Association • 899
National Tourism Foundation • 402, 902
National Training Systems Association • 1063
National Welsh-American Foundation • 944
National Women's Studies Association • 1064, 1065, 1066
NATSO Foundation • 1067
Nebraska Health and Human Services System, Office of Rural Health • 292, 576
Nebraska Library Association • 753
New Jersey Library Association Scholarship Committee • 754
New Jersey Osteopathic Education Foundation • 577
New Mexico Commission on Higher Education • 293, 578, 579, 973
New York State Education Department • 294, 580
Newberry Library • 692
North Carolina Library Association • 755
North Carolina State Education Assistance Authority • 581, 802
North Dakota Department of Public Instruction • 974
Northwest Osteopathic Medical Foundation • 582, 583
Norway-America Association • 945, 1068
Norwegian Information Service • 1069
Norwegian-American Historical Association • 131
Novartis Foundation • 20
Nurses' Education Funds, Inc. • 803
Nursing Economic$ Foundation • 804
Nursing Foundation of Pennsylvania • 805
Ohio Board of Regents • 584, 975
Oklahoma Educational Foundation for Osteopathic Medicine • 585
Old Dominion University • 946
ONS Foundation • 586, 587, 588, 589, 590, 591, 592, 593, 594, 595, 596, 806, 807, 808, 809, 810, 811, 812, 813, 814, 815, 816, 817, 818, 819, 820, 821, 822, 823
Oregon Student Assistance Commission • 295, 362, 597, 976
Organization of American Historians • 652, 653, 915, 921, 947, 993, 1070, 1071, 1072, 1073, 1074, 1075, 1076, 1077, 1078, 1079, 1080, 1081
ORISE Science and Engineering Education (SEE) • 1082
Orthopaedic Research and Education Foundation • 598, 599, 600, 601, 602, 603, 604
Osteogenesis Imperfecta Foundation • 1083
Pacific Telecommunications Council • 259
Paralyzed Veterans of America - Spinal Cord Research Foundation • 21
Pennsylvania Institute of Certified Public Accountants • 237, 238
Pennsylvania Library Association • 756
PEO International Peace Scholarship Fund • 1084
Petry-Lomb Education Committee • 605
Pfizer, Inc. - US Pharmaceuticals Group • 606, 607, 608, 609, 610, 1085
Phi Alpha Theta History Honor Society, Inc. • 654, 655, 656
Phi Beta Kappa Society • 132
Phi Delta Kappa International • 363
Phillips Foundation • 700
Pi Gamma Mu International Honor Society in Society Science • 273
Pi Lambda Theta, Inc. • 364, 365, 922, 1086
Pitt Rivers Museum • 84
Plastic Surgery Educational Foundation • 611, 612, 613
Pollock-Krasner Foundation, Inc. • 170
Population Council • 328, 329, 330
Posey Foundation • 171
Potash and Phosphate Institute • 6
Presbyterian Church (USA) • 874, 875, 876, 877
Princess Grace Foundation—USA • 845

Puerto Rican Legal Defense and Education Fund • 721, 722
Quill and Scroll Foundation • 260
Radcliffe Institute for Advanced Study-Murray Research Center • 885, 886, 887, 888, 889, 1087
Radiological Society of North America • 614, 615, 616, 617, 1088, 1089
Reserve Officers Association of the US • 916
Resources for the Future • 331, 332, 1090
Rhode Island Foundation • 172, 723
Riverside Presbyterian Church • 878
Rob & Bessie Welder Wildlife Foundation • 22
Rotary Foundation of Rotary International • 923
Roy Johnson Trust Fund • 926
Saint Andrews Society of the State of New York • 948
Samuel H. Kress Foundation • 155, 156
San Francisco Foundation • 173, 174, 780
Santa Clara University School of Law - Computer and High Technology Law Journal • 701
Sarnoff Endowment for Cardiovascular Science • 618
School for International Training/English Teaching Fellows Program • 366
Science Advancement Programs Research Corporation • 854, 855, 856
Scottish Rite Charitable Foundation • 619, 620
Sense of Smell Institute • 101, 214
Shastri Indo-Canadian Institute • 157, 949, 950, 951, 952, 953, 954
Sigma Alpha Iota Philanthropies, Inc. • 367, 368, 846, 847
Sigma Theta Tau International • 824, 825, 826, 827, 828, 829, 830, 831, 832, 833, 834, 835
Sigma Theta Tau International/American Nephrology Nurses' Association • 836
Sinfonia Foundation • 994
Skidmore, Owings, and Merrill Foundation • 102, 103, 248
Smithsonian Astrophysical Observatory • 857
Smithsonian Institution • 634, 635, 636
Society for the Teaching of Psychology • 1091
Society of Architectural Historians • 104, 105, 106, 107, 637
Society of Automotive Engineers • 178
Society of Manufacturing Engineers Education Foundation • 383
Society of Naval Architects & Marine Engineers • 1092
Society of Toxicology • 215, 216, 217, 218, 219, 220
Society of Women Engineers • 245, 271, 272
Soil and Water Conservation Society • 313
State Farm Companies Foundation • 239
State Medical Education Board of Georgia • 621, 622
State of Oklahoma • 623, 624
Steedman Governing Committee • 108
Swann Foundation Fund • 109
Swedish Information Service • 133
Swiss Benevolent Society of New York • 955
Tau Beta Pi Association • 384
Teachers of English to Speakers of Other Languages (TESOL) • 369, 370, 371
Texas Higher Education Coordinating Board • 625, 626, 977
Texas Library Association • 757, 758, 759, 760, 761
Thomas J. Watson Fellowship Program • 1093
Tourette Syndrome Association, Inc. • 628
Transportation Association of Canada • 249
Tulsa Library Trust • 762
United Daughters of the Confederacy • 629, 837, 917
United Methodist Church • 879
United Methodist Communications • 261
United Negro College Fund • 179, 221, 405, 956
United States Army Center of Military History • 657
United States Army Recruiting Command • 23, 296, 297, 838, 839
United States Institute of Peace • 333, 334
University of Medicine and Dentistry of NJ School of Osteopathic Medicine • 298
Verne Catt McDowell Corporation • 880
Virginia Department of Health, Office of Health Policy and Planning • 840

Sponsor Index

ACADEMIC FIELDS/CAREER GOALS INDEX

Agribusiness
Farm Credit Graduate Scholarship for the Study of Young, Beginning or Small Farmers and Ranchers • 1
J. Fielding Reed Fellowships • 6
National Milk Producers Federation National Dairy Leadership Scholarship Program • 5
National Wool Growers Memorial Fellowship • 4
Outstanding Doctoral and Master's Thesis Awards • 2
Sylvia Lane Mentor Research Fellowship Fund • 3

Agriculture
AGROPOLIS • 10
American Wine Society Educational Foundation Scholarship Program • 7
Farm Credit Graduate Scholarship for the Study of Young, Beginning or Small Farmers and Ranchers • 1
Forage Crops in Sustainably Managed Agroecosystems: The Bentley Fellowship • 11
GEM Ph.D. Engineering Fellowship • 9
IDRC Doctoral Research Award • 12
J. Fielding Reed Fellowships • 6
John Carew Memorial Scholarship • 8
National Milk Producers Federation National Dairy Leadership Scholarship Program • 5
National Wool Growers Memorial Fellowship • 4
Outstanding Doctoral and Master's Thesis Awards • 2
Research Student Scholarship • 13
Sylvia Lane Mentor Research Fellowship Fund • 3

Animal/Veterinary Sciences
African Network of Scientific and Technological Institutions Postgraduate Fellowships • 14
AGROPOLIS • 10
Armed Forces Health Professions Scholarship Program-Army • 23
Atlantic Salmon Federation Olin Fellowship • 16
Fellowships in Spinal Cord Injury Research • 21
Harris Sweatt Travel Grant • 17
Huyck Station Research Grants • 18
International Women's Fishing Association Graduate Scholarships in the Marine Sciences • 19
National Milk Producers Federation National Dairy Leadership Scholarship Program • 5
National Wool Growers Memorial Fellowship • 4
New Hampshire/Vermont Schweitzer Fellows Program • 15
Novartis Foundation Bursary Scheme • 20
Wildlife Research Scholarship • 22

Applied Sciences
African Network of Scientific and Technological Institutions Postgraduate Fellowships • 14
AIAA Foundation Graduate Awards • 26
AIAA Foundation Orville and Wilbur Wright Awards • 27
Air and Waste Management Association Scholarship Endowment Trust Fund • 24
Alan F. Henry/Paul A. Greebler Scholarship • 29
Albert Nerken Award • 36

American Geophysical Union Horton Research Grant • 25
American Meteorological Society/Industry/Government Graduate Fellowships • 28
American Nuclear Society Graduate Scholarships • 30
American Society for Photogrammetry and Remote Sensing Outstanding Papers Awards • 33
American Vacuum Society Graduate Research Award • 37
American Water Works Association/Abel Wolman Fellowship • 44
American Water Works Association/Holly A. Cornell Scholarship • 45
American Water Works Association/Larson Aquatic Research Support Scholarship • 46
American Water Works Association/Thomas R. Camp Memorial Scholarship • 47
Associated Western Universities Faculty Fellowships • 48
Associated Western Universities Graduate Research Fellowships • 49
Associated Western Universities Postgraduate Fellowship • 50
Beckman Center for the History of Chemistry Research Travel Grants at the Chemical Heritage Foundation • 51
Fannie and John Hertz Foundation Fellowship • 53
Gaede-Langmuir Award • 38
Grants for Disabled Students in the Sciences • 54
Huntington Research Awards • 56
IDRC Doctoral Research Award • 12
International Desalination Association Scholarship • 57
John A. Thornton Memorial Award and Lecture • 39
L.W. Frohlich Charitable Trust Fellowship • 59
Medard W. Welch Award • 40
NASA ID Space Grant Consortium Fellowship Program • 60
NASA/Delaware Valley Space Grant Fellowship • 52
National Estuarine Research Reserve Graduate Fellowship Program • 55
National Milk Producers Federation National Dairy Leadership Scholarship Program • 5
National Science Foundation Graduate Research Fellowships • 62
Nellie Yeoh Whetten Award • 41
Novartis Foundation Bursary Scheme • 20
Peter Mark Memorial Award • 42
Respironics Fellowship in Mechanical Ventilation • 32
Russell and Sigurd Varian Fellowship • 43
Ta Liang Memorial Award • 34
Welch Foundation Scholarship • 58
William A. Fischer Memorial Scholarship • 35
William C. Ezell Fellowship • 31
Wyoming NASA Space Grant Consortium Research Fellowship • 61

Archaeology
Andrew W. Mellon Fellowships • 82
Archaeological Institute of America/Olivia James Traveling Fellowship • 73

Archaeology (continued)

Association for Women in Science Predoctoral Fellowship • 77
Chester Dale Fellowships • 83
Claude C. Albritton Jr. Scholarships • 78
Harrell Family Fellowship • 63
Harriet and Leon Pomerance Fellowship • 74
Helen M. Woodruff Fellowship • 75
Ilse and George Hanfmann Fellowship • 66
James A. Swan Fund • 84
Kress Fellowship in the Art and Archaeology of Jordan • 64
Kress/ARIT Predoctoral Fellowship in the History of Art and Archaeology • 67
Lambda Alpha National Collegiate Honor Society for Anthropology Scholarship Award • 80
Lambda Alpha National Collegiate Honor Society of Anthropology Graduate Research Grant • 81
Lois F. McNeil Dissertation Research Fellowships • 85
Mesopotamian Fellowship • 68
National Endowment for the Humanities Post-Doctoral Research Fellowships • 65
Research Grants • 79
W.F. Albright Institute of Archaeological Research - James A. Montgomery Fellow and Research Coordinator • 69
W.F. Albright Institute of Archaeological Research George A. Barton Fellowship • 70
W.F. Albright Institute of Archaeological Research/National Endowment of the Humanities Fellowships • 71
W.F. Alrbight Institute of Archaeological Research Samuel H. Kress Joint Athens-Jerusalem Fellowship • 72
Woodruff Traveling Fellowship • 76

Architecture

AAUW Educational Foundation Selected Professions Fellowships • 87
AGROPOLIS • 10
AIA, New York Chapter, Stewardson Keefe LeBraun Travel Grant • 88
AIA, New York Chpater, Arnold W. Brunner Grant • 89
American Institute of Architects/American Hospital Association Fellowship in Health Facilities Design • 86
Andrew W. Mellon Fellowships • 82
Archaeological Institute of America/Olivia James Traveling Fellowship • 73
Asian Art and Religion Fellowships • 90
Asian Cultural Council Fellowships • 91
Asian Cultural Council Humanities Fellowships • 92
Carroll L.V. Meeks Fellowship • 104
Charles E. Peterson Fellowship • 93
Chester Dale Fellowships • 83
Chicago Institute of Architecture and Urbanism Award • 102
Dumbarton Oaks Project Grants • 94
Durrant Foundation Scholarship/Internship • 96
Edilia and Francois-Auguste de Montequin Fellowship in Iberian and Latin American Architecture • 105
GEM Ph.D. Engineering Fellowship • 9
Hagley Museum and Library Grants-in-Aid • 97
Hagley/Winterthur Fellowships in Arts and Industries • 98
Harriet and Leon Pomerance Fellowship • 74
Helen M. Woodruff Fellowship • 75
Henry Belin du Pont Dissertation Fellowship • 99
Kennedy Research Grants • 100
Kress Fellowship in the Art and Archaeology of Jordan • 64
Kress/ARIT Predoctoral Fellowship in the History of Art and Archaeology • 67
Lois F. McNeil Dissertation Research Fellowships • 85
NEH Fellowships • 110
Residential Fellowship in Byzantine, Pre-Columbian, and Landscape Architecture Studies • 95
Rosann S. Berry Annual Meeting Fellowship • 106
Spiro Kostof Annual Meeting Fellowship • 107
Steedman Traveling Fellowship in Architecture • 108
Swann Foundation Fund Fellowship • 109

Tova Fellowship • 101
Urban Design Traveling Fellowship Program • 103
W.F. Alrbight Institute of Archaeological Research Samuel H. Kress Joint Athens-Jerusalem Fellowship • 72
Winterthur Research Fellowships • 111

Area/Ethnic Studies

Albert J. Beveridge Grant for Research in the History of the Western Hemisphere • 115
American Council of Learned Societies Grants for East European Studies-Dissertation Fellowships • 113
American Institute of Indian Studies Research Fellowships • 117
Andrew W. Mellon Fellowships in Humanistic Studies • 134
Asian Cultural Council Fellowships • 91
Asian Cultural Council Humanities Fellowships • 92
Bernadette E. Schmitt Grants for Research in European, African, or Asian History • 116
Bicentennial Swedish-American Exchange Fund Travel Grants • 133
Bliss Prize Fellowship in Byzantine Studies • 123
Canadian Northern Studies Trust Studentships in Northern Studies • 119
Center for Hellenic Studies Fellowships • 121
China Times Cultural Foundation Doctoral Dissertation Research in Chinese Studies Scholarships • 122
Dumbarton Oaks Project Grants • 94
Einar and Eva Lund Haugen Memorial Scholarship • 131
Frederick Douglas Postdoctoral Fellowship • 124
Frederick Douglass Institute For African And African-American Studies Predoctoral Dissertation Fellowship • 125
IDRC Doctoral Research Award • 12
International Doctoral Scholarships for Studies Specializing in Jewish Fields • 127
International Fellowships in Jewish Culture Program • 128
International Fellowships in Jewish Studies • 129
Leo Baeck Institute - DAAD Grants • 126
Lorraine Allison Scholarship • 118
Lydia Donaldson Tutt-Jones Memorial Award • 112
Mary Isabel Sibley Fellowship for Greek and French Studies • 132
Memorial Foundation for Jewish Culture International Doctoral Scholarship • 130
Research Student Scholarship • 13
Research Support Opportunities in Arctic Environmental Studies • 120
Residential Fellowship in Byzantine, Pre-Columbian, and Landscape Architecture Studies • 95
Swann Foundation Fund Fellowship • 109
Title VIII Research Scholar and Combined Research and Language Study Program • 114
Woodrow Wilson National Fellowship Foundation Dissertation Grants in Women's Studies • 135
Woodrow Wilson Postdoctoral Fellowships in the Humanities • 136

Art History

American Society of Arms Collectors Scholarship • 138
Andrew W. Mellon Fellowships • 82
Andrew W. Mellon Fellowships in Humanistic Studies • 134
Annette Kade Fellowship • 148
Archaeological Institute of America/Olivia James Traveling Fellowship • 73
Asian Art and Religion Fellowships • 90
Asian Cultural Council Fellowships • 91
Asian Cultural Council Humanities Fellowships • 92
Asian Cultural Council Residency Program in Asia • 140
Bliss Prize Fellowship in Byzantine Studies • 123
Carroll L.V. Meeks Fellowship • 104
Chester Dale Fellowships • 83
Collaborative Research Grants • 143
Curatorial Research Fellowships • 144

Arts

Aviation/Aerospace

Biology

American Geophysical Union Horton Research Grant • 25
American Water Works Association/Academic Achievement
  Awards • 246
Associated Western Universities Faculty Fellowships • 48
Associated Western Universities Graduate Research
  Fellowships • 49
Associated Western Universities Postgraduate Fellowship
  • 50
Durrant Foundation Scholarship/Internship • 96
Fannie and John Hertz Foundation Fellowship • 53
GEM Ph.D. Engineering Fellowship • 9
Grants for Disabled Students in the Sciences • 54
International Desalination Association Scholarship • 57
NASA/Delaware Valley Space Grant Fellowship • 52
Sloan Ph.D Program • 243
Structural Engineering Traveling Fellowship Program • 248
Transportation Association of Canada Scholarships • 249
Wyoming NASA Space Grant Consortium Research
  Fellowship • 61

Communications

AGROPOLIS • 10
Association for Education in Journalism and Mass
  Communications Comm.Theory & Methodology
  Division Minority Doctoral Scholarships • 252
China Times Cultural Foundation Doctoral Dissertation
  Research in Chinese Studies Scholarships • 122
Congressional Fellowship for Journalists • 250
Consortium of College and University Media Centers
  Research Awards • 253
Ford Foundation Dissertation Fellowships for Minorities
  • 256
Ford Foundation Postdoctoral Fellowship for Minorities
  • 257
Ford Foundation Predoctoral Fellowships for Minorities
  • 258
Lester Benz Memorial Scholarship • 260
Milton E. Cooper/Young AFCEAN Graduate School
  Scholarship • 251
National Association of Broadcasters Grants for Research in
  Broadcasting • 254
Pacific Telecommunications Council Essay Prize
  Competition • 259
Stoody-West Fellowship for Graduate Study in Religious
  Journalism • 261
William C. Stokoe Scholarships • 255

Computer Science/Data Processing

A.R. Zipf Fellowship • 268
AAUW Educational Foundation Selected Professions
  Fellowships • 87
Adelle and Erwin Tomash Fellowship in the History of
  Information Processing • 267
African Network of Scientific and Technological Institutions
  Postgraduate Fellowships • 14
Armed Forces Communications & Electronics Association
  Educational Foundation Fellowship • 265
Armed Forces Communications and Electronics Association
  Ralph W. Shrader Scholarships • 266
Arthur F. Quern Information Technology Grant • 269
Associated Western Universities Faculty Fellowships • 48
Associated Western Universities Graduate Research
  Fellowships • 49
Associated Western Universities Postgraduate Fellowship
  • 50
Association for Women in Science Predoctoral Fellowship
  • 77
Fannie and John Hertz Foundation Fellowship • 53
Ford Foundation Predoctoral Fellowships for Minorities
  • 258
GEM Ph.D. Engineering Fellowship • 9
Grants for Disabled Students in the Sciences • 54
High-Performance Computer Science Graduate Fellowship
  • 270
IDRC Doctoral Research Award • 12

Institute for Scientific Information Doctoral Dissertation
  Proposal Scholarship • 262
ISI Outstanding Information Science Teacher Award • 263
Lydia I. Pickup Memorial Scholarship • 271
Microsoft Corporation Graduate Scholarships • 272
Milton E. Cooper/Young AFCEAN Graduate School
  Scholarship • 251
NASA ID Space Grant Consortium Fellowship Program
  • 60
National Physical Science Consortium Graduate Fellowships
  in the Physical Sciences • 244
Sloan Ph.D Program • 243
UMI Doctoral Dissertation Award • 264

Criminal Justice/Criminology

Durrant Foundation Scholarship/Internship • 96
Kennedy Research Grants • 100
Pi Gamma Mu Scholarship • 273

Dental Health/Services

AADR Student Research Fellowships • 278
Albert G. Richards Graduate Student Research Grant • 274
Alfred C. Fones Scholarship • 281
American Dental Association Endowment and Assistance
  Fund Dental Student Scholarship Program • 279
American Dental Association Endowment and Assistance
  Fund Minority Dental Student Scholarship Program
  • 280
American Dental Hygienists' Association Institute Graduate
  Scholarship Program • 282
American Dental Hygienists' Association Institute Research
  Grant • 283
Armed Forces Health Professions Scholarship Program-
  Army • 23
Chinese American Medical Society Scholarship • 285
F.E. Hebert Financial Assistance Program • 296
Foundation Scholarship • 290
Health Professions Education Loan Repayment Program
  • 287
Health Professions Loan Repayment • 297
Howard Riley Paper Graduate Student Oral and
  Maxillofacial Radiology Award • 275
Jeannette Mowery Scholarship • 295
M.L. King Physician/Dentist Scholarships • 298
Maine Dental Education Loan Program • 286
Maryland Dent-Care Loan Assistance Repayment Program
  • 288
Minnesota Dental Loan Forgiveness Program • 289
National Hemophilia Foundation Judith Graham Pool
  Postdoctoral Fellowship • 291
New Hampshire/Vermont Schweitzer Fellows Program • 15
New Mexico Health Professional Loan Repayment Program
  • 293
Radiology Centennial Scholarship • 276
Regents Health Care Scholarships for Medicine and
  Dentistry-New York • 294
Research Student Scholarship • 13
Rural Health Scholarship Program • 292
Sigma Phi Alpha Graduate Scholarship • 284
William H. Rollins Award • 277

Earth Science

A.L. Medlin Scholarship • 301
African Network of Scientific and Technological Institutions
  Postgraduate Fellowships • 14
Air and Waste Management Association Scholarship
  Endowment Trust Fund • 24
Alexander Sisson Award • 302
American Geophysical Union Horton Research Grant • 25
Arthur D. Howard Research Grants • 303
Associated Western Universities Faculty Fellowships • 48
Associated Western Universities Graduate Research
  Fellowships • 49
Associated Western Universities Postgraduate Fellowship
  • 50

National Association of Junior Auxiliaries Graduate
Scholarship Program • 361
National Science Foundation Graduate Research Fellowships
• 62
Oregon Scholarship Fund Graduate Student Award • 362
Phi Delta Kappa International Graduate Fellowships in
Educational Leadership • 363
Research Grants • 365
Ruth Crymes Fellowship for Graduate Study • 370
Sense of Smell Institute Research Grants • 214
Shields-Gillespie Scholarship • 350
Sigma Alpha Iota Doctoral Grant • 368
Summer Data Policy Institute • 354
Swann Foundation Fund Fellowship • 109
Teachers of English to Speakers of Other Languages
Research Interest Section/Heinle & Heinle
Distinguished Research Award • 371
Tova Fellowship • 101
Washington-Tokyo Public Service Fellowship Program
• 357
William C. Stokoe Scholarships • 255

Electrical Engineering/Electronics

AAUW Educational Foundation Selected Professions
Fellowships • 87
Adelle and Erwin Tomash Fellowship in the History of
Information Processing • 267
African Network of Scientific and Technological Institutions
Postgraduate Fellowships • 14
AIAA Foundation Graduate Awards • 26
AIAA Foundation Orville and Wilbur Wright Awards • 27
Armed Forces Communications & Electronics Association
Educational Foundation Fellowship • 265
Armed Forces Communications and Electronics Association
Ralph W. Shrader Scholarships • 266
Associated Western Universities Postgraduate Fellowship
• 50
Durrant Foundation Scholarship/Internship • 96
Fannie and John Hertz Foundation Fellowship • 53
GEM Ph.D. Engineering Fellowship • 9
Grants for Disabled Students in the Sciences • 54
Illinois Minority Graduate Incentive Program Fellowship
• 372
International Desalination Association Scholarship • 57
Milton E. Cooper/Young AFCEAN Graduate School
Scholarship • 251
NASA ID Space Grant Consortium Fellowship Program
• 60
NASA/Delaware Valley Space Grant Fellowship • 52
National Physical Science Consortium Graduate Fellowships
in the Physical Sciences • 244
Sloan Ph.D Program • 243
Society of Automotive Engineers Doctoral Scholars Program
• 178
Welch Foundation Scholarship • 58
Wyoming NASA Space Grant Consortium Research
Fellowship • 61

Engineering-Related Technologies

AAUW Educational Foundation Selected Professions
Fellowships • 87
African Network of Scientific and Technological Institutions
Postgraduate Fellowships • 14
Air and Waste Management Association Scholarship
Endowment Trust Fund • 24
Fellowships in Spinal Cord Injury Research • 21
Ford Foundation Dissertation Fellowships for Minorities
• 256
Ford Foundation Postdoctoral Fellowship for Minorities
• 257
Ford Foundation Predoctoral Fellowships for Minorities
• 258
Gilbert F. White Postdoctoral Fellowships • 331
Illinois Minority Graduate Incentive Program Fellowship
• 372

International Desalination Association Scholarship • 57
Joseph L. Fisher Dissertation Awards • 332
NASA/Delaware Valley Space Grant Fellowship • 52
Pacific Telecommunications Council Essay Prize
Competition • 259
Research Fellowship Program • 373
Sloan Ph.D Program • 243
Society of Automotive Engineers Doctoral Scholars Program
• 178
TMS Outstanding Student Paper Contest—Graduate • 374
Transportation Association of Canada Scholarships • 249
Wyoming NASA Space Grant Consortium Research
Fellowship • 61

Engineering/Technology

AAUW Educational Foundation Selected Professions
Fellowships • 87
Adelle and Erwin Tomash Fellowship in the History of
Information Processing • 267
African Network of Scientific and Technological Institutions
Postgraduate Fellowships • 14
AGROPOLIS • 10
AIAA Foundation Graduate Awards • 26
AIAA Foundation Orville and Wilbur Wright Awards • 27
Air and Waste Management Association Scholarship
Endowment Trust Fund • 24
Alan F. Henry/Paul A. Greebler Scholarship • 29
Albert Nerken Award • 36
American Geophysical Union Horton Research Grant • 25
American Meteorological Society/Industry/Government
Graduate Fellowships • 28
American Nuclear Society Graduate Scholarships • 30
American Society for Photogrammetry and Remote Sensing
Outstanding Papers Awards • 33
American Society of Mechanical Engineers Solid Waste
Processing Division Graduate Study Scholarship • 377
American Vacuum Society Graduate Research Award • 37
American Water Works Association/Abel Wolman
Fellowship • 44
American Water Works Association/Holly A. Cornell
Scholarship • 45
Armed Forces Communications & Electronics Association
Educational Foundation Fellowship • 265
Armed Forces Communications and Electronics Association
Ralph W. Shrader Scholarships • 266
Associated Western Universities Faculty Fellowships • 48
Associated Western Universities Graduate Research
Fellowships • 49
Associated Western Universities Postgraduate Fellowship
• 50
Association for Women in Science Predoctoral Fellowship
• 77
Fannie and John Hertz Foundation Fellowship • 53
Fellowships in Spinal Cord Injury Research • 21
Gaede-Langmuir Award • 38
Gardner Fund • 300
GEM Ph.D. Engineering Fellowship • 9
General Motors Foundation Graduate Scholarship • 245
Gilberth Memorial Fellowship • 380
Graduate Fellowship Award • 375
Grants for Disabled Students in the Sciences • 54
Hudson River Foundation Graduate Fellowships • 205
Illinois Minority Graduate Incentive Program Fellowship
• 372
Institute for Supply Management Dissertation Grant
Program • 232
International Desalination Association Scholarship • 57
John A. Thornton Memorial Award and Lecture • 39
Lydia I. Pickup Memorial Scholarship • 271
Medard W. Welch Award • 40
Monaghan/Trudell Fellowship for Aerosol Technique
Development • 376
Montana Space Grant Felllowship Program • 177
NASA Fellowship in Aerospace History • 175

Engineering/Technology (continued)

NASA ID Space Grant Consortium Fellowship Program • 60
NASA/Delaware Valley Space Grant Fellowship • 52
National Science Foundation Graduate Research Fellowships • 62
National Science Foundation Minority Career Advancement Awards • 381
National Science Foundation Minority Research Planning Grants • 382
Nellie Yeoh Whetten Award • 41
NSF-DAAD Grants for the Natural, Engineering, and Social Sciences • 379
Pacific Telecommunications Council Essay Prize Competition • 259
Peter Mark Memorial Award • 42
Research Fellowship Program • 373
Research Student Scholarship • 13
Rice-Cullimore Scholarship • 378
Russell and Sigurd Varian Fellowship • 43
Sloan Ph.D Program • 243
Society of Automotive Engineers Doctoral Scholars Program • 178
Ta Liang Memorial Award • 34
Tau Beta Pi Fellowships for Graduate Study in Engineering • 384
TMS Outstanding Student Paper Contest—Graduate • 374
Transportation Association of Canada Scholarships • 249
Wayne Kay Graduate Fellowship • 383
Welch Foundation Scholarship • 58
William A. Fischer Memorial Scholarship • 35

Fashion Design

Eileen C. Maddex Fellowship • 386
Hettie M. Anthony Fellowship • 387
Kappa Omicron Nu National Alumni Chapter Grant • 388
Kappa Omicron Nu National Alumni Fellowship • 389
Lincoln Food Service Grant for Innovations in School Food Service • 385

Filmmaking

Antonio Cirino Memorial Art Education Fellowship • 172
Chateaubriand Scholarship Program • 164
Consortium of College and University Media Centers Research Awards • 253
Ford Foundation Fellowships • 141
Shastri India Studies Senior Arts Fellowships • 157
Virginia Museum of Fine Arts Graduate Fellowship Program • 158

Food Science/Nutrition

African Network of Scientific and Technological Institutions Postgraduate Fellowships • 14
American Wine Society Educational Foundation Scholarship Program • 7
Blue Cross Blue Shield of Michigan Foundation Student Award Program • 393
ConAgra Fellowship in Child Nutrition • 390
Eileen C. Maddex Fellowship • 386
Gerber Endowment in Pediatric Nutrition • 394
Graduate Fellowship Award • 375
Hettie M. Anthony Fellowship • 387
Hubert Humphrey Research Grant • 391
IDRC Doctoral Research Award • 12
Institute of Food Technologists Carbohydrate Division Graduate Fellowship • 395
Institute of Food Technologists Food Packaging Division Graduate Fellowship • 396
Institute of Food Technologists Graduate Fellowships • 397
Institute of Food Technologists Refrigerated & Frozen Foods Division Graduate Fellowship • 398
Institute of Food Technologists Sensory Evaluation Division Silver Celebration Graduate Fellowship • 399
Kappa Omicron Nu National Alumni Chapter Grant • 388

Kappa Omicron Nu National Alumni Fellowship • 389
Kappa Omicron Nu New Initiatives Grant • 401
Lincoln Food Service Grant for Innovations in School Food Service • 385
National Milk Producers Federation National Dairy Leadership Scholarship Program • 5
New Hampshire/Vermont Schweitzer Fellows Program • 15
Professional Growth Scholarship • 392
Society of Flavor Chemists Memorial Graduate Fellowship • 400
Tova Fellowship • 101

Food Service/Hospitality

Eileen C. Maddex Fellowship • 386
Hettie M. Anthony Fellowship • 387
Hubert Humphrey Research Grant • 391
Kappa Omicron Nu National Alumni Chapter Grant • 388
Kappa Omicron Nu National Alumni Fellowship • 389
Luray Caverns Graduate Research Grant • 402
Professional Growth Scholarship • 392

Foreign Language

ACTR Summer Russian Language Teacher Program • 344
AIIS 9-month Language Program • 403
American Institute of Indian Studies Research Fellowships • 117
Andrew W. Mellon Fellowships in Humanistic Studies • 134
Asian Cultural Council Fellowships • 91
Asian Cultural Council Humanities Fellowships • 92
Bicentennial Swedish-American Exchange Fund Travel Grants • 133
Blakemore Freeman Fellowships for Advanced Study of Asian Languages • 404
China Times Cultural Foundation Doctoral Dissertation Research in Chinese Studies Scholarships • 122
Ford Foundation Dissertation Fellowships for Minorities • 256
Ford Foundation Postdoctoral Fellowship for Minorities • 257
Ford Foundation Predoctoral Fellowships for Minorities • 258
George S. Lurcy Charitable and Educational Trust • 405
Mary Isabel Sibley Fellowship for Greek and French Studies • 132
Minority Master's Fellows Program • 351
National Endowment for the Humanities Post-Doctoral Research Fellowships • 65
Thomas R. Pickering Graduate Foreign Affairs Fellowship Program • 241
Title VIII Research Scholar and Combined Research and Language Study Program • 114
Woodrow Wilson Postdoctoral Fellowships in the Humanities • 136

Geography

James W. Bourque Studentship in Northern Geography • 406
W.F. Albright Institute of Archaeological Research - James A. Montgomery Fellow and Research Coordinator • 69
W.F. Albright Institute of Archaeological Research George A. Barton Fellowship • 70

Graphics/Graphic Arts/Printing

Swann Foundation Fund Fellowship • 109

Health Administration

AFUD/AUA Health Policy Research Program • 407
Blue Cross Blue Shield of Michigan Foundation Student Award Program • 393
Canadian Society for Medical Laboratory Science Founders' Fund Awards • 408
New Hampshire/Vermont Schweitzer Fellows Program • 15
W.K. Kellogg Fellowship Program in Health Policy Research • 409

Health and Medical Sciences

Health Information Management/Technology

Health Information Management/Technology (continued)

Blue Cross Blue Shield of Michigan Foundation Student Award Program • 393
Canadian Society for Medical Laboratory Science Founders' Fund Awards • 408
Elmer Ediger Memorial Scholarship Fund • 541
Milheim Foundation for Cancer Research Project Grants in Oncology • 542
New Hampshire/Vermont Schweitzer Fellows Program • 15
W.K. Kellogg Fellowship Program in Health Policy Research • 409

Heating, Air-Conditioning, and Refrigeration Mechanics

American Society of Heating, Refrigerating, and Air Conditioning Research Grants for Graduate Students • 632
Tova Fellowship • 101

Historic Preservation and Conservation

Archaeological Institute of America/Olivia James Traveling Fellowship • 73
Asian Art and Religion Fellowships • 90
Carroll L.V. Meeks Fellowship • 104
Charles E. Peterson Fellowship • 93
Conservation Guest Scholars • 633
Ford Foundation Fellowships • 141
Harriet and Leon Pomerance Fellowship • 74
Harry S. Truman Book Award • 324
Harry S. Truman Library Institute Dissertation Year Fellowships • 325
Harry S. Truman Library Institute Research Grants • 326
Harry S. Truman Library Institute Scholar's Award • 327
Helen M. Woodruff Fellowship • 75
Keepers Preservation Education Fund Fellowship • 637
NEH Fellowships • 110
Smithsonian Institution Graduate Student Fellowships • 634
Smithsonian Institution Postdoctoral Fellowships • 635
Smithsonian Institution Predoctoral Fellowships • 636
Winterthur Research Fellowships • 111
Woodruff Traveling Fellowship • 76

History

Adelle and Erwin Tomash Fellowship in the History of Information Processing • 267
Albert J. Beveridge Grant for Research in the History of the Western Hemisphere • 115
Alice Fisher Society Historical Scholarship • 642
American Jewish Archives Dissertation and Postdoctoral Research Fellowships • 649
American Society of Arms Collectors Scholarship • 138
Andrew W. Mellon Fellowships in Humanistic Studies • 134
Archaeological Institute of America/Olivia James Traveling Fellowship • 73
Armenian Relief Society Graduate Scholarship Program • 224
Arthur M. Schlesinger, Jr. Fellowship • 648
Asian, Black, Hispanic, and Native American United Methodist History Research Awards • 645
Beckman Center for the History of Chemistry Research Travel Grants at the Chemical Heritage Foundation • 51
Bernadette E. Schmitt Grants for Research in European, African, or Asian History • 116
Bliss Prize Fellowship in Byzantine Studies • 123
Chateaubriand Scholarship Program • 164
China Times Cultural Foundation Doctoral Dissertation Research in Chinese Studies Scholarships • 122
Dissertation Year Fellowship • 657
Dumbarton Oaks Project Grants • 94
Ebert Foundation Advanced Graduate Fellowships • 319
Ebert Foundation Doctoral Research Fellowship • 320
Ebert Foundation Postdoctoral Fellowships • 321

Edna V. Moffett Fellowship • 658
Edouard Morot-sir Fellowship in Literature • 165
Erik Barnouw Award • 652
Eugene L. Cox Fellowship • 659
Fellowships for the Study of the American Revolution • 644
Ford Foundation Dissertation Fellowships for Minorities • 256
Ford Foundation Postdoctoral Fellowship for Minorities • 257
Ford Foundation Predoctoral Fellowships for Minorities • 258
George S. Lurcy Charitable and Educational Trust • 405
Gilbert Chinard Fellowships and Edouard Morot-Sir Fellowship in Literature • 166
Graduate Student Fellowship Award • 662
Graduate Student Grants-in-Aid in History of Pharmacy • 466
Harmon Chadbourn Rorison Fellowship • 167
Harriet and Leon Pomerance Fellowship • 74
Harry S. Truman Book Award • 324
Harry S. Truman Library Institute Dissertation Year Fellowships • 325
Harry S. Truman Library Institute Research Grants • 326
Harry S. Truman Library Institute Scholar's Award • 327
Helen M. Woodruff Fellowship • 75
Helen Wallis Fellowship • 641
Huntington Research Awards • 56
J. Franklin Jameson Fellowship in American History • 638
Jennings Randolph Senior Fellow Award • 333
Judge William M. Beard Scholarship • 629
Kennedy Research Grants • 100
La Pietra Dissertation Travel Fellowship in Transnational History • 653
Leo Baeck Institute - DAAD Grants • 126
Lillian Sholtis Brunner Summer Fellowship • 643
Littleton-Griswold Research Grants • 639
Lois F. McNeil Dissertation Research Fellowships • 85
MacKenzie King Travelling Scholarships • 236
Mary Isabel Sibley Fellowship for Greek and French Studies • 132
Mary McEwen Schimke Scholarship • 660
Massachusetts Historical Society Research Fellowship Program • 650
Mesopotamian Fellowship • 68
Michael Kraus Research Grants in History • 640
NASA Fellowship in Aerospace History • 175
National Endowment for the Humanities Post-Doctoral Research Fellowships • 65
NEH Fellowships • 110
New England Regional Fellowship Consortium Grant • 651
Peace Scholar Dissertation Fellowship • 334
Phi Alpha Theta Doctoral Scholarships • 654
Phi Alpha Theta Graduate Scholarships • 655
Phi Alpha Theta/Westerners International Doctoral Dissertation Award • 656
Pi Gamma Mu Scholarship • 273
Research Student Scholarship • 13
Residential Fellowship in Byzantine, Pre-Columbian, and Landscape Architecture Studies • 95
Swann Foundation Fund Fellowship • 109
Thomas Jefferson Fellowship • 661
Title VIII Research Scholar and Combined Research and Language Study Program • 114
W.F. Albright Institute of Archaeological Research - James A. Montgomery Fellow and Research Coordinator • 69
W.F. Albright Institute of Archaeological Research George A. Barton Fellowship • 70
W.F. Albright Institute of Archaeological Research/National Endowment of the Humanities Fellowships • 71
Winterthur Research Fellowships • 111
Women in United Methodist History Research Grant • 646
Women in United Methodist History Writing Award • 647
Woodrow Wilson National Fellowship Foundation Dissertation Grants in Women's Studies • 135

Literature/English/Writing

Materials Science, Engineering, and Metallurgy

Mechanical Engineering

Meteorology/Atmospheric Science

Harris Sweatt Travel Grant • 17
Hazel Corbin Grant • 796
Health Professions Education Loan Repayment Program
• 287
Heart and Stroke Foundation of Canada Nursing Research
Fellowships • 526
Karen O'Neil Endowed Advanced Nursing Practice
Scholarship • 793
Lillian Sholtis Brunner Summer Fellowship • 643
M. Elizabeth Carnegie and Estelle Massey Osborne
Scholarships • 803
March of Dimes Graduate Nursing Scholarship • 795
Marcia Granucci Memorial Scholarship • 841
Medtronic Physio-Control Advanced Nursing Practice
Scholarship • 794
Miller-Erb Nursing Development Fund • 797
Minnesota Rural Midlevel Practitioner Loan Forgiveness
Program • 543
Mississippi Nursing Education MSN Program • 798
Myasthenia Gravis Foundation Nurses Research Fellowship
• 799
National Association of Pediatric Nurse Practitioners
McNeil Scholarships • 800
National Health Services Corps Scholarship Program • 522
National Hemophilia Foundation Nursing Excellence
Fellowship • 801
New Hampshire/Vermont Schweitzer Fellows Program • 15
New Mexico Health Professional Loan Repayment Program
• 293
Novartis Pharmaceuticals Post-Master's Certificate
Scholarships • 807
Nurse Practitioners/Nurse Midwife Program Scholarships
• 840
Nurse Scholars Program— Master's • 802
Nursing Economic$ Foundation Scholarships • 804
Oncology Nursing Society Post-Master's Certificate
Scholarship • 808
Oncology Nursing Society/AMGEN Inc. Excellence in
Patient/Public Education Award • 809
Oncology Nursing Society/Bristol-Meyers Distinguished
Researcher Award • 810
ONS Foundation Doctoral Scholarships • 811
ONS Foundation Ethnic Minority Master's Scholarship
• 812
ONS Foundation Ethnic Minority Researcher and
Mentorship Grants • 586
ONS Foundation Master's Scholarship • 813
ONS Foundation Novice Researcher and Mentorship Grants
• 587
ONS Foundation Ortho Biotech Research Fellowship • 588
ONS Foundation Sigma Theta Tau International Research
Grant • 814
ONS Foundation/American Brain Tumor Association Grant
• 589
ONS Foundation/AMGEN Inc. Research Grant • 815
ONS Foundation/Ann Olson Memorial Doctoral
Scholarship • 816
ONS Foundation/Aventis Research Fellowship • 590
ONS Foundation/Aventis Research Grant • 591
ONS Foundation/Bristol-Myers Oncology Division
Community Health Research Grant • 592
ONS Foundation/Bristol-Myers Oncology Division Research
Grant • 593
ONS Foundation/Nursing Certification Corporation
Master's Scholarship • 817
ONS Foundation/Oncology Nursing Certification
Corporation Oncology Nursing Education Research
Grant • 594
ONS Foundation/Oncology Nursing Certification
Corporation Oncology Nursing Research Grant • 818
ONS Foundation/Ortho Biotech Research Grant • 595
ONS Foundation/Pharmacia Oncology, Inc. Master's
Scholarship • 819
ONS Foundation/Thomas Jordan Doctoral Scholarship
• 820

ONS Foundation/Trish Greene Research Grant • 596
ONS/Komen Foundation Excellence in Breast Cancer
Education Award • 821
ONS/Mary Nowotny Excellence in Cancer Nursing
Education Award • 822
ONS/Varian Excellence in Radiation Therapy Nursing
Award • 823
Patricia Smith Christensen Scholarship • 824
Pauline Thompson Clinical Research Award • 805
Pfizer Postdoctoral Fellowships in Nursing Research • 608
Predoctoral Research Training Fellowship • 200
Rosemary Berkel Crisp Research Award • 825
Ship Island - Mrs. J.O. Jones Memorial Scholarship • 837
Sigma Theta Tau International /Emergency Nurses
Association Foundation Grant • 826
Sigma Theta Tau International Small Research Grant • 827
Sigma Theta Tau International/ American Association of
Critical Care Nurses Critical Care Grant • 828
Sigma Theta Tau International/ Association of Operating
Room Nurses Grant • 829
Sigma Theta Tau International/ Oncology Nursing Society
Grant • 830
Sigma Theta Tau International/ Rehabilitation Nursing
Foundation Grant • 831
Sigma Theta Tau International/American Association of
Diabetes Educators Grant • 832
Sigma Theta Tau International/American Nephrology
Nurses' Association Grant • 836
Sigma Theta Tau International/American Nephrology
Nurses' Association Grant • 833
Sigma Theta Tau International/American Nurses
Foundation Grant • 834
State of Nebraska Loan Repayment Program for Rural
Health Professionals • 576
Uniformed Services University of Health Sciences Master of
Science in Nurse Anesthesia • 838
University of Texas-Houston Health Science Master of
Science Degree in Nurse Anesthesia • 839
Virginia Henderson/Sigma Theta Tau International Clinical
Research Grant • 835

Peace and Conflict Studies

China Times Cultural Foundation Doctoral Dissertation
Research in Chinese Studies Scholarships • 122
Dissertation Year Fellowship • 657
Jennings Randolph Senior Fellow Award • 333
Peace Scholar Dissertation Fellowship • 334
Title VIII Research Scholar and Combined Research and
Language Study Program • 114

Performing Arts

Alberta Foundation for the Arts Graduate Level
Scholarships • 160
American Orff-Schulwerk Association Research Grant • 347
Antonio Cirino Memorial Art Education Fellowship • 172
AOSA-Training and Projects Fund • 348
Apha Delta Kappa Foundation Fine Arts Grants • 161
Asian Art and Religion Fellowships • 90
Asian Cultural Council Fellowships • 91
Asian Cultural Council Humanities Fellowships • 92
Asian Cultural Council Residency Program in Asia • 140
Ford Foundation Fellowships • 141
Graduate Scholarship in Music Education • 367
Gunild Keetman Assistance Fund • 349
Harriet Hale Woolley Scholarship • 842
Kurt Weill Foundation for Music Grants Program • 843
National Vocal Competition for Young Opera Singers • 844
Princess Grace Fellowships in Theater and Dance • 845
Shastri India Studies Senior Arts Fellowships • 157
Shields-Gillespie Scholarship • 350
Sigma Alpha Iota Doctoral Grant • 368
Sigma Alpha Iota Graduate Performance Awards • 846
Sigma Alpha Iota Scholarship for Conductors • 847
Swann Foundation Fund Fellowship • 109

Performing Arts (continued)

Photojournalism

Consortium of College and University Media Centers Research Awards • 253

Kit C. King Graduate Scholarship Fund • 699

Stoody-West Fellowship for Graduate Study in Religious Journalism • 261

Physical Sciences and Math

AAUW Educational Foundation Selected Professions Fellowships • 87

AIAA Foundation Graduate Awards • 26

AIAA Foundation Orville and Wilbur Wright Awards • 27

Air and Waste Management Association Scholarship Endowment Trust Fund • 24

Albert Nerken Award • 36

American Liver Foundation Postdoctoral Research Fellowships • 183

American Mathematical Society Centennial Research Fellowship • 848

American Meteorological Society/Industry/Government Graduate Fellowships • 28

American Nuclear Society Graduate Scholarships • 30

American Society for Photogrammetry and Remote Sensing Outstanding Papers Awards • 33

American Vacuum Society Graduate Research Award • 37

Armed Forces Communications & Electronics Association Educational Foundation Fellowship • 265

Armed Forces Communications and Electronics Association Ralph W. Shrader Scholarships • 266

Arthur D. Howard Research Grants • 303

Associated Western Universities Faculty Fellowships • 48

Associated Western Universities Graduate Research Fellowships • 49

Associated Western Universities Postgraduate Fellowship • 50

Association for Women in Mathematics Workshop for Graduate Students and Postdoctoral Mathematicians • 850

Association for Women in Science Predoctoral Fellowship • 77

Beckman Center for the History of Chemistry Research Travel Grants at the Chemical Heritage Foundation • 51

Caroline tum Suden/Frances A. Hellebrandt Professional Opportunity Award • 186

Congressional Science Fellowship Program • 299

Cottrell College Science Awards • 854

Cottrell Scholars Award • 855

Dr. Henry R. Viets Medical Student Research Fellowship • 210

Eleanor Roosevelt Teacher Fellowships • 343

Fannie and John Hertz Foundation Doctoral Thesis Prize • 853

Fannie and John Hertz Foundation Fellowship • 53

Fellowships at the Smithsonian Astrophysical Observatory • 857

Ford Foundation Dissertation Fellowships for Minorities • 256

Ford Foundation Postdoctoral Fellowship for Minorities • 257

Ford Foundation Predoctoral Fellowships for Minorities • 258

Gaede-Langmuir Award • 38

Grants for Disabled Students in the Sciences • 54

Harry S. Truman Library Institute Scholar's Award • 327

Huntington Research Awards • 56

Illinois Minority Graduate Incentive Program Fellowship • 372

J. Hoover Mackin Research Grants • 308

John A. Thornton Memorial Award and Lecture • 39

John Clarke Slater Fellowship • 849

Liver Scholar Awards • 184

Louise Hay Award for Excellence in Mathematics Education • 851

Medard W. Welch Award • 40

Minority Master's Fellows Program • 351

NASA ID Space Grant Consortium Fellowship Program • 60

NASA/Delaware Valley Space Grant Fellowship • 52

National Physical Science Consortium Graduate Fellowships in the Physical Sciences • 244

National Science Foundation Graduate Research Fellowships • 62

National Science Foundation Minority Career Advancement Awards • 381

National Science Foundation Minority Research Planning Grants • 382

Nellie Yeoh Whetten Award • 41

Osserman/Sosin/McClure Postdoctoral Fellowship • 211

Peter Mark Memorial Award • 42

Porter Physiology Fellowships • 187

Postdoctoral Research Associateships • 775

Predoctoral Research Training Fellowship • 200

Procter and Gamble Professional Opportunity Award • 188

Research Innovation Awards • 856

Research Support Opportunities in Arctic Environmental Studies • 120

Russell and Sigurd Varian Fellowship • 43

Sloan Ph.D Program • 243

Ta Liang Memorial Award • 34

Title VIII Research Scholar and Combined Research and Language Study Program • 114

Travel Grants for Women in Mathematics • 852

Visiting Fellowships • 776

William A. Fischer Memorial Scholarship • 35

William C. Ezell Fellowship • 31

Wyoming NASA Space Grant Consortium Research Fellowship • 61

Political Science

Abba Schwartz Fellowships • 861

Andrew W. Mellon Fellowships in Humanistic Studies • 134

Armenian Relief Society Graduate Scholarship Program • 224

Arthur M. Schlesinger, Jr. Fellowship • 648

Center for Basic Research in the Social Sciences Postdoctoral Fellowship • 860

Chateaubriand Scholarship Program • 164

China Times Cultural Foundation Doctoral Dissertation Research in Chinese Studies Scholarships • 122

Congressional Fellowship for Federal Executives • 676

Congressional Fellowship for Journalists • 250

Congressional Research Awards Program • 859

Ebert Foundation Advanced Graduate Fellowships • 319

Ebert Foundation Doctoral Research Fellowship • 320

Ebert Foundation Postdoctoral Fellowships • 321

Epilepsy Foundation Behavioral Sciences Research Training Fellowship • 318

Fellowships for the Study of the American Revolution • 644

Ford Foundation Dissertation Fellowships for Minorities • 256

Ford Foundation Postdoctoral Fellowship for Minorities • 257

Ford Foundation Predoctoral Fellowships for Minorities • 258

Gilbert F. White Postdoctoral Fellowships • 331

Harry S. Truman Book Award • 324

Harry S. Truman Library Institute Dissertation Year Fellowships • 325

Harry S. Truman Library Institute Research Grants • 326

IDRC Doctoral Research Award • 12

Jennings Randolph Senior Fellow Award • 333

Joseph L. Fisher Dissertation Awards • 332

Kennedy Research Grants • 100

MacKenzie King Travelling Scholarships • 236

Marjorie Kovler Fellowship • 862

Peace Scholar Dissertation Fellowship • 334
Pi Gamma Mu Scholarship • 273
Small Research Grant Competition • 858
Theodore C. Sorensen Fellowship • 698
Thomas R. Pickering Graduate Foreign Affairs Fellowship
  Program • 241
Vida Dutton Scudder Fellowship • 770
Woodrow Wilson National Fellowship Foundation
  Dissertation Grants in Women's Studies • 135
Woodrow Wilson Postdoctoral Fellowships in the
  Humanities • 136

Religion/Theology

American Academy of Religion Research Assistance and
  Collaborative Research Grants • 863
Andrew W. Mellon Fellowships in Humanistic Studies
  • 134
Asian Art and Religion Fellowships • 90
Asian Cultural Council Fellowships • 91
Asian Cultural Council Humanities Fellowships • 92
Asian, Black, Hispanic, and Native American United
  Methodist History Research Awards • 645
Bliss Prize Fellowship in Byzantine Studies • 123
Charlotte W. Newcombe Doctoral Dissertation Fellowships
  • 693
Continuing Education Grant Program • 874
Daisy and Eugene Hale Memorial Fund • 878
Dissertation Fellows Program • 865
Doctoral Fellows Program • 866
Evangelical Lutheran Church in America Educational Grant
  Program • 864
Fellowship Program for Emigres Pursuing Careers in Jewish
  Education • 358
Ford Foundation Dissertation Fellowships for Minorities
  • 256
Ford Foundation Postdoctoral Fellowship for Minorities
  • 257
Ford Foundation Predoctoral Fellowships for Minorities
  • 258
Georgia Harkness Scholarships • 879
Hispanic Theological Initiative Dissertation Year Grant
  • 869
Hispanic Theological Initiative Doctoral Grant • 870
Hispanic Theological Initiative Special Mentoring Grant
  • 871
International Fellowships in Jewish Culture Program • 128
International Order of the King's Daughters and Sons
  Student Ministry Scholarship • 872
Mary Isabel Sibley Fellowship for Greek and French Studies
  • 132
Memorial Foundation for Jewish Culture International
  Doctoral Scholarship • 130
Memorial Foundation for Jewish Culture Scholarships for
  Post-Rabbinical Students • 873
Ministry Fellows Program • 867
National Endowment for the Humanities Post-Doctoral
  Research Fellowships • 65
Native American Seminary Scholarship • 875
North American Doctoral Fellows Program • 868
Presbyterian Study Grant • 876
Racial Ethnic Leadership Supplemental Grant • 877
Residential Fellowship in Byzantine, Pre-Columbian, and
  Landscape Architecture Studies • 95
Stoody-West Fellowship for Graduate Study in Religious
  Journalism • 261
Verne Catt Mc Dowell Corporation Scholarship • 880
W.F. Albright Institute of Archaeological Research - James
  A. Montgomery Fellow and Research Coordinator • 69
W.F. Albright Institute of Archaeological Research George
  A. Barton Fellowship • 70
W.F. Albright Institute of Archaeological Research/National
  Endowment of the Humanities Fellowships • 71
Women in United Methodist History Research Grant • 646
Women in United Methodist History Writing Award • 647

Woodrow Wilson National Fellowship Foundation
  Dissertation Grants in Women's Studies • 135
Woodrow Wilson Postdoctoral Fellowships in the
  Humanities • 136

Science, Technology, and Society

Adelle and Erwin Tomash Fellowship in the History of
  Information Processing • 267
AIAA Foundation Graduate Awards • 26
AIAA Foundation Orville and Wilbur Wright Awards • 27
Air and Waste Management Association Scholarship
  Endowment Trust Fund • 24
American Society of Arms Collectors Scholarship • 138
Eleanor Roosevelt Teacher Fellowships • 343
Farm Credit Graduate Scholarship for the Study of Young,
  Beginning or Small Farmers and Ranchers • 1
Hudson River Foundation Graduate Fellowships • 205
IDRC Doctoral Research Award • 12
Illinois Minority Graduate Incentive Program Fellowship
  • 372
John G. Bene Fellowship in Community Forestry • 881
Minority Master's Fellows Program • 351
NASA ID Space Grant Consortium Fellowship Program
  • 60
NASA/Delaware Valley Space Grant Fellowship • 52
Outstanding Doctoral and Master's Thesis Awards • 2
Research Grants • 79
Sense of Smell Institute Research Grants • 214
Sloan Ph.D Program • 243
Sylvia Lane Mentor Research Fellowship Fund • 3
Tova Fellowship • 101

Social Sciences

Abba Schwartz Fellowships • 861
Adolescent and Youth Dissertation Award • 885
AGROPOLIS • 10
AIR Research Grants-Improving Institutional Research in
  Postsecondary Education Institutions • 352
American Council of Learned Societies Fellowships for
  Postdoctoral Research in the Humanities • 667
American Council of Learned Societies Grants for East
  European Studies-Dissertation Fellowships • 113
American Council of Learned Societies Grants for East
  European Studies-Fellowships for Postdoctoral Research
  • 668
American Geophysical Union Horton Research Grant • 25
American Institute of Pakistan Studies Graduate Student
  Fellowship • 671
American Institute of Pakistan Studies Postdoctoral
  Fellowship • 672
American Institute of Pakistan Studies Predoctoral
  Fellowships • 673
American Jewish Archives Dissertation and Postdoctoral
  Research Fellowships • 649
ARIT Mellon Research Fellowships for Central and Eastern
  European Scholars in Turkey • 677
ARIT, Humanities and Social Science Fellowships in Turkey
  • 678
Association for Women in Science Predoctoral Fellowship
  • 77
Bicentennial Swedish-American Exchange Fund Travel
  Grants • 133
Block Dissertation Award • 886
Blue Cross Blue Shield of Michigan Foundation Student
  Award Program • 393
Byron Hanke Fellowship for Graduate Research • 317
CAORC Fellowships • 666
CAORC Senior Fellowship • 665
Center for Basic Research in the Social Sciences
  Postdoctoral Fellowship • 860
Center for Hellenic Studies Fellowships • 121
Charlotte W. Newcombe Doctoral Dissertation Fellowships
  • 693
Chateaubriand Scholarship Program • 164

Surveying; Surveying Technology, Cartography, or Geographic Information Science

American Association for Geodetic Surveying Graduate Fellowship • 893

Therapy/Rehabilitation

AAOS/OREF Fellowship in Health Services Research • 598
American Orff-Schulwerk Association Research Grant • 347
AOSA-Training and Projects Fund • 348
Blue Cross Blue Shield of Michigan Foundation Student Award Program • 393
California Association of Marriage and Family Therapists Educational Foundation Scholarships • 894
Clinton E. Phillips Scholarship • 895
Elmer Ediger Memorial Scholarship Fund • 541
Fellowships in Spinal Cord Injury Research • 21
General Federation of Women's Clubs of Massachusetts Communication Disorder Scholarships • 898
Glaxo Smith Kline Fellowship for Asthma Management Education • 475
Graduate and Professional Degree Loan/Scholarship-Mississippi • 546
Gunild Keetman Assistance Fund • 349
H. Frederic Helmholz, Jr., MD, Educational Research Fund • 476
Harris Sweatt Travel Grant • 17
Monaghan/Trudell Fellowship for Aerosol Technique Development • 376
National Multiple Sclerosis Society Patient Management Care and Rehabilitation Grants • 572
National Strength and Conditioning Association Student Research Grant • 899
NBRC/A&P Garett B. Gish, MS, RRT Memorial Postgraduate Education Recognition Award • 477
OREF Career Development Awards • 599
OREF Clinical Research Award • 600
OREF Prospective Clinical Research Grants • 601
OREF Research Grants • 602
Respironics Fellowship in Mechanical Ventilation • 32

Respironics Fellowship in Non-Invasive Respiratory Care • 478
Ronald D. Lunceford Scholarship • 896
Sense of Smell Institute Research Grants • 214
Shields-Gillespie Scholarship • 350
Sigma Alpha Iota Doctoral Grant • 368
Speech Language Pathologist Incentive Program • 897
State of Nebraska Loan Repayment Program for Rural Health Professionals • 576
Tova Fellowship • 101
William F. Miller, MD Postgraduate Education Recognition Award • 479
Zimmer Career Development Award • 604

Trade/Technical Specialties

American Society of Heating, Refrigerating, and Air Conditioning Research Grants for Graduate Students • 632
Asian Cultural Council Residency Program in Asia • 140
General Motors Foundation Graduate Scholarship • 245
National Milk Producers Federation National Dairy Leadership Scholarship Program • 5

Transportation

E.J. Sierleja Memorial Scholarship • 900
Transportation Association of Canada Scholarships • 249

Travel/Tourism

A.L. Simmons Scholarship Fund • 901
Luray Caverns Graduate Research Grant • 402
NEH Fellowships • 110
Visiting Scholar Awards • 902
Winterthur Research Fellowships • 111

TV/Radio Broadcasting

Consortium of College and University Media Centers Research Awards • 253
Jennings Randolph Senior Fellow Award • 333
National Association of Broadcasters Grants for Research in Broadcasting • 254
Peace Scholar Dissertation Fellowship • 334
Stoody-West Fellowship for Graduate Study in Religious Journalism • 261

CIVIC, PROFESSIONAL, SOCIAL, OR UNION AFFILIATION INDEX

American Academy of Child and Adolescent Psychiatry
AACAP George Tarjan Award • 419
AACAP Irving Philips Award • 420
AACAP Pilot Research Award Supported by Eli Lilly and Company • 423
AACAP Presidential Scholar Awards • 424
AACAP Rieger Psychodynamic Psychotherapy Award • 425
AACAP Rieger Service Program Award for Excellence • 426
AACAP Robinson/Cunningham Awards • 427
AACAP Sidney Berman Award • 428
AACAP Simon Wile Award • 429

American Academy of Facial Plastic and Reconstructive Surgery
Ben Shuster Memorial Award • 498
Bernstein Grant • 499
Education & Research Foundation for the American Academy of Facial Plastic and Reconstructive Surgery Investigator Development Grant • 500
Education & Research Foundation for the American Academy of Facial Plastic and Reconstructive Surgery Resident Research Grant • 501
Education. & Research Foundation for the American Academy of Facial Plastic and Reconstructive Surgery Community Service Award • 502
F. Mark Rafaty Memorial Award • 503
Ira Tresley Research Award • 504
John Dickinson Teacher Award • 505
John Orlando Roe Award • 506
Sir Harold Delf Gillies Award • 508
William K. Wright Award • 509

American Academy of Religion
American Academy of Religion Research Assistance and Collaborative Research Grants • 863

American Association of Critical Care Nurses
AACN Certification Corporation Research Grant • 784
AACN Critical Care Research Grant • 785
AACN Educational Advancement Scholarships-Graduate • 786
AACN-Sigma Theta Tau Critical Care Grant • 787
Agilent Technologies American Association of Critical Care Nurses Research Grant • 788
American Association of Critical Care Nurses Mentorship Grant • 789

American Association of Law Librarians
Law Librarians in Continuing Education Courses • 728
Library School Graduates Seeking a Non-Law Degree • 903
Type I: Library Degree for Law School Graduates • 707
Type III: Library Degree for Non-Law School Graduates • 729

American Congress on Surveying and Mapping
American Association for Geodetic Surveying Graduate Fellowship • 893

American Dental Hygienist's Association
Alfred C. Fones Scholarship • 281
American Dental Hygienists' Association Institute Graduate Scholarship Program • 282
American Dental Hygienists' Association Institute Research Grant • 283
Sigma Phi Alpha Graduate Scholarship • 284

American Historical Association
Albert J. Beveridge Grant for Research in the History of the Western Hemisphere • 115
Bernadette E. Schmitt Grants for Research in European, African, or Asian History • 116
Littleton-Griswold Research Grants • 639
Michael Kraus Research Grants in History • 640

American Legion or Auxiliary
Child Welfare Scholarships • 346

American Numismatic Society
American Numismatic Society Graduate Seminar • 904
American Numismatic Society/Frances M. Schwartz Fellowship • 905

American Orff-Schulwerk Association
American Orff-Schulwerk Association Research Grant • 347
AOSA-Training and Projects Fund • 348
Gunild Keetman Assistance Fund • 349
Shields-Gillespie Scholarship • 350

American Physiological Society
Caroline tum Suden/Frances A. Hellebrandt Professional Opportunity Award • 186
Procter and Gamble Professional Opportunity Award • 188

American Political Science Association
Small Research Grant Competition • 858

American School Food Service Association
Hubert Humphrey Research Grant • 391
Lincoln Food Service Grant for Innovations in School Food Service • 385
Professional Growth Scholarship • 392

American Schools of Oriental Research
Mesopotamian Fellowship • 68

American Society for Microbiology
Robert D. Watkins Minority Graduate Research Fellowship • 191

American Society for Photogrammetry and Remote Sensing

Ta Liang Memorial Award • 34
William A. Fischer Memorial Scholarship • 35

Any National Professional Nursing Association

M. Elizabeth Carnegie and Estelle Massey Osborne Scholarships • 803

Beta Phi Mu

Frank B. Sessa Scholarship for Continuing Education • 733

Canadian Library Association

Library Research and Development Grants • 738

Canadian Society for Medical Laboratory Science

Canadian Society for Medical Laboratory Science Founders' Fund Awards • 408

Civil Air Patrol

Civil Air Patrol Graduate Scholarships • 906

Emergency Nurses Association

Emergency Nurses Association Foundation Advanced Nursing Practice Scholarship #1 • 790
Emergency Nurses Association Foundation Advanced Nursing Practice Scholarship #2 • 791
ENA Foundation Doctoral Scholarship • 792
ENA Foundation Research Grants #1 and #2 • 514
Karen O'Neil Endowed Advanced Nursing Practice Scholarship • 793
Medtronic Physio-Control Advanced Nursing Practice Scholarship • 794

Entomological Society of America

Henry and Sylvia Richardson Research Grant • 194
John Henry Comstock Graduate Student Award • 196
Snodgrass Memorial Research Award • 199

Fleet Reserve Association/Auxiliary

Nolan/Baranski/Glezen Scholarships • 909

Geological Society of America

A.L. Medlin Scholarship • 301
Alexander Sisson Award • 302
Arthur D. Howard Research Grants • 303
Bruce L. "Biff" Reed Award • 304
Claude C. Albritton Jr. Scholarships • 78
Geological Society of America Student Research Grants • 305
Gretchen L. Blechschmidt Award • 306
Harold T. Stearns Fellowship Award • 307
J. Hoover Mackin Research Grants • 308
John T. Dillon Alaska Research Award • 309
Lipman Research Award • 310
Robert K. Fahnestock Memorial Award • 311
S.E. Dwornik Student Paper Awards • 312

Golden Key National Honor Society

Graduate Scholarship • 910

Greek Organization

Delta Delta Delta Graduate Scholarship • 907
Delta Gamma Foundation Fellowships • 908
Elena Lucrezia Cornaro Piscopia Scholarship For Graduate Studies • 912
Kappa Kappa Gamma Foundation Graduate Scholarships • 913
Research Grants • 365

Institute of Food Technologists

Institute of Food Technologists Food Packaging Division Graduate Fellowship • 396

Institute of Industrial Engineers

E.J. Sierleja Memorial Scholarship • 900
Gilberth Memorial Fellowship • 380

International Reading Association

International Reading Association Helen M. Robinson Award • 765
International Reading Association Jeanne S. Chall Research Fellowship • 766
International Reading Association Outstanding Dissertation of the Year Award • 767
Reading/Literacy Research Fellowship • 768

Japanese-American Citizens League

Japanese American Citizens League Graduate Scholarships • 911
Japanese American Citizens League Law Awards • 717

Knights of Columbus

Bishop Charles P. Greco Graduate Fellowship Program • 359

National Academic Advising Association

National Academic Advising Association Scholarship • 914

National Strength and Conditioning Association

National Strength and Conditioning Association Student Research Grant • 899

Nebraska Library Association

Nebraska Library Association Louise A. Nixon Scholarship • 753

Oncology Nursing Society

Oncology Nursing Society/AMGEN Inc. Excellence in Patient/Public Education Award • 809
Oncology Nursing Society/Bristol-Meyers Distinguished Researcher Award • 810
ONS/Komen Foundation Excellence in Breast Cancer Education Award • 821
ONS/Mary Nowotny Excellence in Cancer Nursing Education Award • 822
ONS/Varian Excellence in Radiation Therapy Nursing Award • 823

Organization of American Historians

Horace Samuel & Marion Galbraith Merrill Travel Grants in Twentieth-Century American Political History • 915

Other Student Academic Clubs

American Society of Mechanical Engineers Graduate Teaching Fellowship • 771
American Society of Mechanical Engineers Solid Waste Processing Division Graduate Study Scholarship • 377
Elisabeth M. and Winchell M. Parsons Scholarship • 772
Graduate Scholarship in Music Education • 367
Kappa Omicron Nu New Initiatives Grant • 401
Marjorie Roy Rothermel Scholarship • 773
Maude Gilchrist Fellowship • 663
Omicron Nu Research Fellowship • 664
Phi Alpha Theta Doctoral Scholarships • 654
Phi Alpha Theta Graduate Scholarships • 655
Phi Alpha Theta/Westerners International Doctoral Dissertation Award • 656
Phi Delta Kappa International Graduate Fellowships in Educational Leadership • 363
Pi Gamma Mu Scholarship • 273
Rice-Cullimore Scholarship • 378
Sigma Alpha Iota Doctoral Grant • 368

Civic, Professional, Social, or Union Affiliation Index

Sigma Alpha Iota Graduate Performance Awards • 846
Sigma Alpha Iota Scholarship for Conductors • 847
Tau Beta Pi Fellowships for Graduate Study in Engineering • 384

Reserve Officers Association

Henry J. Reilly Memorial Scholarship-Graduate • 916

Sigma Theta Tau International

AACN-Sigma Theta Tau Critical Care Grant • 787
ONS Foundation Sigma Theta Tau International Research Grant • 814
Rosemary Berkel Crisp Research Award • 825
Virginia Henderson/Sigma Theta Tau International Clinical Research Grant • 835

Society of Architectural Historians

Carroll L.V. Meeks Fellowship • 104
Rosann S. Berry Annual Meeting Fellowship • 106
Spiro Kostof Annual Meeting Fellowship • 107

Soil and Water Conservation Society

SWCS Kenneth E. Grant Scholarship • 313

Teachers of English to Speakers of Other Languages

Albert H. Marckwardt Travel Grants • 369
Ruth Crymes Fellowship for Graduate Study • 370
Teachers of English to Speakers of Other Languages Research Interest Section/Heinle & Heinle Distinguished Research Award • 371

United Daughters of the Confederacy

Judge William M. Beard Scholarship • 629
Malcolm M. Berglund Scholarship • 917
Ship Island - Mrs. J.O. Jones Memorial Scholarship • 837

Western Association of Women Historians

Graduate Student Fellowship Award • 662

EMPLOYMENT/VOLUNTEER EXPERIENCE INDEX

Community Service
Delta Delta Delta Graduate Scholarship • 907
Graduate Student Scholar Award • 364
Hugh J. Andersen Memorial Scholarships • 558
Mead Johnson Awards for Graduate Education in Family
Practice • 432
Puerto Rican Legal Defense and Education Fund Fr. Joseph
Fitzpatrick Scholarship Program • 722

Designated Career Field
AACN Critical Care Research Grant • 785
AACN Educational Advancement Scholarships-Graduate
• 786
AACN-Sigma Theta Tau Critical Care Grant • 787
Agilent Technologies American Association of Critical Care
Nurses Research Grant • 788
Albert Nerken Award • 36
American Association of Critical Care Nurses Mentorship
Grant • 789
American Brain Tumor Association Research Fellowship
Awards • 439
American Orchid Society/Orchid Research Grant • 185
American Orff-Schulwerk Association Research Grant • 347
AOSA-Training and Projects Fund • 348
Ben Shuster Memorial Award • 498
Bernstein Grant • 499
Congressional Fellowship for Federal Executives • 676
Conservation Guest Scholars • 633
Continuing Education Grant Program • 874
Curatorial Research Fellowships • 144
Ebert Foundation Postdoctoral Fellowships • 321
Education & Research Foundation for the American
Academy of Facial Plastic and Reconstructive Surgery
Investigator Development Grant • 500
Education & Research Foundation for the American
Academy of Facial Plastic and Reconstructive Surgery
Resident Research Grant • 501
Education. & Research Foundation for the American
Academy of Facial Plastic and Reconstructive Surgery
Community Service Award • 502
F. Mark Rafaty Memorial Award • 503
George S. Lurcy Charitable and Educational Trust • 405
Glenn A. Fry Lecture Award • 468
Graduate and Educator Research Awards • 694
Gunild Keetman Assistance Fund • 349
Henry and Sylvia Richardson Research Grant • 194
Ira Tresley Research Award • 504
James F. Connolly Congressional Information Scholarship
• 704
Japan Foundation Research Fellowship • 688
Japan Foundation Short-Term Research Fellowship • 689
Joel Polsky-Fixtures Furniture/IIDA Foundation Research
Grant • 695
John Dickinson Teacher Award • 505
John Orlando Roe Award • 506
Law Librarians in Continuing Education Courses • 728

Loan Assistance Repayment Program for Primary Care
Services • 540
M. Elizabeth Carnegie and Estelle Massey Osborne
Scholarships • 803
Maine Dental Education Loan Repayment Program • 919
Major Research Grant for Biomedical Research into
Intellectual Impairment • 619
Medard W. Welch Award • 40
Milton E. Cooper/Young AFCEAN Graduate School
Scholarship • 251
Myasthenia Gravis Foundation Nurses Research Fellowship
• 799
National Association of Pediatric Nurse Practitioners
McNeil Scholarships • 800
Neuroscience Nursing Foundation Research Grant • 437
Neuroscience Nursing Foundation Clinical Research
Fellowship Program • 438
New Mexico Health Professional Loan Repayment Program
• 293
Oncology Nursing Society/AMGEN Inc. Excellence in
Patient/Public Education Award • 809
Oncology Nursing Society/Bristol-Meyers Distinguished
Researcher Award • 810
ONS Foundation Doctoral Scholarships • 811
ONS Foundation Ethnic Minority Master's Scholarship
• 812
ONS Foundation Master's Scholarship • 813
ONS Foundation Ortho Biotech Research Fellowship • 588
ONS Foundation Sigma Theta Tau International Research
Grant • 814
ONS Foundation/American Brain Tumor Association Grant
• 589
ONS Foundation/AMGEN Inc. Research Grant • 815
ONS Foundation/Ann Olson Memorial Doctoral
Scholarship • 816
ONS Foundation/Aventis Research Fellowship • 590
ONS Foundation/Aventis Research Grant • 591
ONS Foundation/Bristol-Myers Oncology Division
Community Health Research Grant • 592
ONS Foundation/Bristol-Myers Oncology Division Research
Grant • 593
ONS Foundation/Nursing Certification Corporation
Master's Scholarship • 817
ONS Foundation/Oncology Nursing Certification
Corporation Oncology Nursing Education Research
Grant • 594
ONS Foundation/Oncology Nursing Certification
Corporation Oncology Nursing Research Grant • 818
ONS Foundation/Ortho Biotech Research Grant • 595
ONS Foundation/Pharmacia Oncology, Inc. Master's
Scholarship • 819
ONS Foundation/Thomas Jordan Doctoral Scholarship
• 820
ONS Foundation/Trish Greene Research Grant • 596
ONS/Komen Foundation Excellence in Breast Cancer
Education Award • 821

ONS/Mary Nowotny Excellence in Cancer Nursing Education Award • 822

ONS/Varian Excellence in Radiation Therapy Nursing Award • 823

Patricia Smith Christensen Scholarship • 824

Pfizer /American Geriatrics Society Postdoctoral Fellowships • 606

Pfizer Postdoctoral Fellowship Grants • 607

Physician Loan Repayment Program • 584

Plastic Surgery Educational Foundation Scientific Essay Contest • 612

Pollock-Krasner Grants • 170

Research into Causes, Cure, Treatment and Treatment of Intellectual Impairment • 620

Residency Travel Award • 507

Richard W. Leopold Prize • 921

Rosemary Berkel Crisp Research Award • 825

Rural Health Scholarship Program • 292

Shields-Gillespie Scholarship • 350

Sigma Theta Tau International /Emergency Nurses Association Foundation Grant • 826

Sigma Theta Tau International Small Research Grant • 827

Sigma Theta Tau International/ American Association of Critical Care Nurses Critical Care Grant • 828

Sigma Theta Tau International/ Association of Operating Room Nurses Grant • 829

Sigma Theta Tau International/ Oncology Nursing Society Grant • 830

Sigma Theta Tau International/ Rehabilitation Nursing Foundation Grant • 831

Sigma Theta Tau International/American Association of Diabetes Educators Grant • 832

Sigma Theta Tau International/American Nephrology Nurses' Association Grant • 836

Sigma Theta Tau International/American Nephrology Nurses' Association Grant • 833

Sigma Theta Tau International/American Nurses Foundation Grant • 834

Sir Harold Delf Gillies Award • 508

State of Nebraska Loan Repayment Program for Rural Health Professionals • 576

Steedman Traveling Fellowship in Architecture • 108

Texas Health Service Corps Program: Stipends for Resident Physicians • 625

Texas Physician Education Loan Repayment Program Part III (TX Fam. Practice Res. Training) • 626

Virginia Henderson/Sigma Theta Tau International Clinical Research Grant • 835

Vistakon Research Grants • 470

Washington-Tokyo Public Service Fellowship Program • 357

William F. Miller, MD Postgraduate Education Recognition Award • 479

William K. Wright Award • 509

Food Service

Hubert Humphrey Research Grant • 391

Lincoln Food Service Grant for Innovations in School Food Service • 385

Professional Growth Scholarship • 392

Helping Handicapped

Bishop Charles P. Greco Graduate Fellowship Program • 359

Journalism

Congressional Fellowship for Journalists • 250

Lester Benz Memorial Scholarship • 260

Phillips Foundation Journalism Fellowship Program • 700

Teaching

AGA R. Robert and Sally D. Funderburg Research Scholar Award in Gastric Biology related to Cancer • 410

American Gasteroenterological Association Elsevier Research Initiative Award • 411

American Gasteroenterological Association June and Donald O. Castell, MD. Esophageal Clinical Research Award • 412

American Gasteroenterological Association Miles and Shirley Fiterman Foundation Basic Research Awards • 413

American Gasteroenterological Association Research Scholar Awards • 414

American Gasteroenterological Association Research Scholar Awards for Underrepresented Minorities • 415

American Gasteroenterological Merck Clinical Research Career Development Award • 416

Associated Western Universities Faculty Fellowships • 48

Basil O'Connor Starter Scholar Research Awards • 538

Ebert Foundation Postdoctoral Fellowships • 321

Eleanor Roosevelt Teacher Fellowships • 343

English Language Fellow Program • 366

Excellence in Aviation Education Award • 176

Exceptional Student Education Training Grant for Teachers • 355

ISI Outstanding Information Science Teacher Award • 263

Learn German in Germany for Faculty • 920

Lester Benz Memorial Scholarship • 260

Louise Hay Award for Excellence in Mathematics Education • 851

March of Dimes Research Grants • 539

Nadeen Burkeholder Williams Music Scholarship • 922

National Science Foundation Minority Career Advancement Awards • 381

National Science Foundation Minority Research Planning Grants • 382

New Mexico Past Presidents Scholarship for Teachers of Exceptional Children • 890

ONS Foundation/Oncology Nursing Certification Corporation Oncology Nursing Education Research Grant • 594

ONS/Mary Nowotny Excellence in Cancer Nursing Education Award • 822

Rotary Foundation Grants for University Teachers to Serve in Developing Countries • 923

Technology Scholarship Program for Alabama Teachers • 918

Visiting Scholar Awards • 902

IMPAIRMENT INDEX

Hearing Impaired
Century Scholarship • 757
Gallaudet University Alumni Association Graduate
   Fellowship Fund • 924
Grants for Disabled Students in the Sciences • 54
William C. Stokoe Scholarships • 255

Learning Disabled
Century Scholarship • 757
Grants for Disabled Students in the Sciences • 54

Physically Disabled
Century Scholarship • 757
Grants for Disabled Students in the Sciences • 54

Visually Impaired
Century Scholarship • 757
Grants for Disabled Students in the Sciences • 54
Roy Johnson Trust Fund • 926
Scholarships for Blind Jewish Community Professionals
   • 925

MILITARY SERVICE INDEX

Army

Armed Forces Health Professions Scholarship Program-
Army • 23
F.E. Hebert Financial Assistance Program • 296
Health Professions Loan Repayment • 297
Uniformed Services University of Health Sciences Master of
Science in Nurse Anesthesia • 838
University of Texas-Houston Health Science Master of
Science Degree in Nurse Anesthesia • 839

Coast Guard

Nolan/Baranski/Glezen Scholarships • 909

General

American Legion Auxiliary Department of Nebraska
Graduate Scholarships • 345
Henry J. Reilly Memorial Scholarship-Graduate • 916

Marine Corp

Nolan/Baranski/Glezen Scholarships • 909

Navy

Nolan/Baranski/Glezen Scholarships • 909

NATIONALITY OR ETHNIC HERITAGE INDEX

African

African Network of Scientific and Technological Institutions Postgraduate Fellowships • 14

Arab

Foundation Scholarship • 290

Armenian

Armenian Relief Society Graduate Scholarship Program • 224

Bulgarian

ARIT Mellon Research Fellowships for Central and Eastern European Scholars in Turkey • 677

W.F. Albright Institute of Archeaological Research Andrew W. Mellon Foundation Fellowships • 933

Canadian

Alberta Foundation for the Arts Graduate Level Scholarships • 160

Alberta Ukrainian Centennial Commemorative Scholarships • 927

Canadian Northern Studies Polar Commission Scholarship • 938

Canadian Northern Studies Trust Studentships in Northern Studies • 119

Canadian Society for Medical Laboratory Science Founders' Fund Awards • 408

Canadian Window on International Development Awards • 697

Forage Crops in Sustainably Managed Agroecosystems: The Bentley Fellowship • 11

Government of Alberta Graduate Scholarships and Fellowships • 928

H. W. Wilson Scholarship • 737

IDRC Doctoral Research Award • 12

James W. Bourque Studentship in Northern Geography • 406

John G. Bene Fellowship in Community Forestry • 881

Major Research Grant for Biomedical Research into Intellectual Impairment • 619

Ralph Steinhauer Awards of Distinction • 929

Research Fellowship in Hemostatis • 937

Research into Causes, Cure, Treatment and Treatment of Intellectual Impairment • 620

Research Support Opportunities in Arctic Environmental Studies • 120

Shastri India Studies Faculty Fellowships • 952

Shastri India Studies Postdoctoral Research Fellowships • 953

Shastri India Studies Senior Arts Fellowships • 157

Shastri India Studies Student Fellowships • 954

Sir James Lougheed Awards of Distinction • 930

Transfusion Medicine Fellowship Award • 481

Transportation Association of Canada Scholarships • 249

World Book Graduate Scholarship in Library Science • 739

Chinese

Li Foundation Fellowships • 943

Danish

Awards for Advanced Study or Research in the USA • 935

Finnish

Awards for Advanced Study or Research in the USA • 935

French

Annette Kade Fellowship • 148

German

Annette Kade Fellowship • 148

Hebrew

Wexner Graduate Fellowship Program • 957

Hispanic

Hispanic Theological Initiative Dissertation Year Grant • 869

Hispanic Theological Initiative Doctoral Grant • 870

Hispanic Theological Initiative Special Mentoring Grant • 871

Puerto Rican Bar Association Scholarship Award • 721

Puerto Rican Legal Defense and Education Fund Fr. Joseph Fitzpatrick Scholarship Program • 722

W.F. Albright Institute of Archeaological Research Andrew W. Mellon Foundation Fellowships • 933

Hungarian

ARIT Mellon Research Fellowships for Central and Eastern European Scholars in Turkey • 677

Icelandic

Awards for Advanced Study or Research in the USA • 935

Indian

Shastri Canadian Studies Doctoral Research Fellowships for Indian Scholars • 949

Shastri Canadian Studies Faculty Enrichment Fellowship for Indian Scholars • 950

Shastri Canadian Studies Faculty Research Fellowships for Indian Scholars • 951

Norwegian

Awards for Advanced Study or Research in the USA • 935

Norway-America Association Graduate Research Scholarships • 945

Of the Former Soviet Union

Fellowship Program for Emigres Pursuing Careers in Jewish Education • 358

Polish

ARIT Mellon Research Fellowships for Central and Eastern European Scholars in Turkey • 677

RELIGIOUS AFFILIATION INDEX

Brethren
Elmer Ediger Memorial Scholarship Fund • 541
Miller-Erb Nursing Development Fund • 797

Christian
Dissertation Fellows Program • 865
Doctoral Fellows Program • 866
Harvey Fellows Program • 958
Hispanic Theological Initiative Dissertation Year Grant • 869
Hispanic Theological Initiative Doctoral Grant • 870
Hispanic Theological Initiative Special Mentoring Grant • 871
International Order of the King's Daughters and Sons Student Ministry Scholarship • 872
Ministry Fellows Program • 867
North American Doctoral Fellows Program • 868

Disciple of Christ
Verne Catt Mc Dowell Corporation Scholarship • 880

Jewish
Memorial Foundation for Jewish Culture Scholarships for Post-Rabbinical Students • 873
Wexner Graduate Fellowship Program • 957

Lutheran
Evangelical Lutheran Church in America Educational Grant Program • 864

Methodist
Georgia Harkness Scholarships • 879

Presbyterian
Continuing Education Grant Program • 874
Daisy and Eugene Hale Memorial Fund • 878
Native American Seminary Scholarship • 875
Presbyterian Study Grant • 876
Racial Ethnic Leadership Supplemental Grant • 877

Roman Catholic
Bishop Charles P. Greco Graduate Fellowship Program • 359

STATE/PROVINCE OF RESIDENCE INDEX

Alabama
National Association of Junior Auxiliaries Graduate Scholarship Program • 361
Technology Scholarship Program for Alabama Teachers • 918

Alaska
Alaska Library Association Scholarship • 727
Northwest Osteopathic Medical Foundation Scholarships • 583
Western Regional Graduate Program • 979

Alberta
Alberta Foundation for the Arts Graduate Level Scholarships • 160
Canadian Blood Services Graduate Fellowship Program • 961
Government of Alberta Graduate Scholarships and Fellowships • 928
Major Research Grant for Biomedical Research into Intellectual Impairment • 619
Research Fellowship in Hemostatis • 937
Research into Causes, Cure, Treatment and Treatment of Intellectual Impairment • 620
Sir James Lougheed Awards of Distinction • 930
Transfusion Medicine Fellowship Award • 481

Arizona
Metropolitan Life Foundation Awards Program for Academic Excellence in Medicine • 562
Western Regional Graduate Program • 979

Arkansas
Minority Master's Fellows Program • 351
National Association of Junior Auxiliaries Graduate Scholarship Program • 361

British Columbia
Canadian Blood Services Graduate Fellowship Program • 961
Major Research Grant for Biomedical Research into Intellectual Impairment • 619
Research Fellowship in Hemostatis • 937
Research into Causes, Cure, Treatment and Treatment of Intellectual Impairment • 620
Transfusion Medicine Fellowship Award • 481

California
Health Professions Education Loan Repayment Program • 287
Metropolitan Life Foundation Awards Program for Academic Excellence in Medicine • 562

Colorado
Metropolitan Life Foundation Awards Program for Academic Excellence in Medicine • 562
Western Regional Graduate Program • 979

Connecticut
Fellowship Program for Emigres Pursuing Careers in Jewish Education • 358
Lambaréné Schweitzer Fellows Program • 417
Saint Andrews Society of the State of New York Scholarship for Graduate Study • 948
Zimmermann Scholarships • 955

Delaware
Librarian Incentive Scholarship Program • 740
Optometric Institutional Aid • 495
Saint Andrews Society of the State of New York Scholarship for Graduate Study • 948
Speech Language Pathologist Incentive Program • 897
Zimmermann Scholarships • 955

District of Columbia
Benn and Kathleen Gilmore Scholarship • 551
Metropolitan Life Foundation Awards Program for Academic Excellence in Medicine • 562
Saint Andrews Society of the State of New York Scholarship for Graduate Study • 948

Florida
Daisy and Eugene Hale Memorial Fund • 878
Jacki Tuckfield Memorial Scholarship • 234
Metropolitan Life Foundation Awards Program for Academic Excellence in Medicine • 562
Nursing Student Loan Forgiveness Program • 962

Georgia
Georgia HOPE Teacher Scholarship Program • 356
Georgia Library Association Hubbard Scholarship • 741
Metropolitan Life Foundation Awards Program for Academic Excellence in Medicine • 562
State Medical Education Board Scholarship Program • 621

Hawaii
Western Regional Graduate Program • 979

Idaho
Northwest Osteopathic Medical Foundation Scholarships • 583
Western Regional Graduate Program • 979

Illinois
Arthur F. Quern Information Technology Grant • 269
Benn and Kathleen Gilmore Scholarship • 551
Illinois Consortium for Educational Opportunity Program Fellowship • 941
Illinois State Library Master of Library Science Degree Scholarship • 743
Metropolitan Life Foundation Awards Program for Academic Excellence in Medicine • 562

Indiana
Benn and Kathleen Gilmore Scholarship • 551

Kansas

Distinguished Scholar Program • 967
James B. Pearson Fellowship • 968
Kansas Optometry Service Program • 532
Osteopathic Service Scholarship Program • 533

Louisiana

National Association of Junior Auxiliaries Graduate
   Scholarship Program • 361

Maine

Lambaréné Schweitzer Fellows Program • 417
Maine Dental Education Loan Program • 286
Maine Dental Education Loan Repayment Program • 919
Saint Andrews Society of the State of New York Scholarship
   for Graduate Study • 948

Manitoba

Canadian Blood Services Graduate Fellowship Program
   • 961
Major Research Grant for Biomedical Research into
   Intellectual Impairment • 619
Research Fellowship in Hemostatis • 937
Research into Causes, Cure, Treatment and Treatment of
   Intellectual Impairment • 620
Transfusion Medicine Fellowship Award • 481

Maryland

Loan Assistance Repayment Program for Primary Care
   Services • 540
Maryland Dent-Care Loan Assistance Repayment Program
   • 288
Saint Andrews Society of the State of New York Scholarship
   for Graduate Study • 948

Massachusetts

General Federation of Women's Clubs of Massachusetts
   Communication Disorder Scholarships • 898
General Federation of Women's Clubs of Massachusetts
   Memorial Education Fellowship • 964
Lambaréné Schweitzer Fellows Program • 417
Metropolitan Life Foundation Awards Program for
   Academic Excellence in Medicine • 562
Saint Andrews Society of the State of New York Scholarship
   for Graduate Study • 948

Michigan

Benn and Kathleen Gilmore Scholarship • 551

Mississippi

Graduate and Professional Degree Loan/Scholarship-
   Mississippi • 546
Mississippi Nursing Education MSN Program • 798
National Association of Junior Auxiliaries Graduate
   Scholarship Program • 361
Southern Regional Education Board Loan/Scholarship • 547

Missouri

National Association of Junior Auxiliaries Graduate
   Scholarship Program • 361

Montana

Northwest Osteopathic Medical Foundation Scholarships
   • 583
Western Regional Graduate Program • 979

Nebraska

American Legion Auxiliary Department of Nebraska
   Graduate Scholarships • 345
Nebraska Library Association Louise A. Nixon Scholarship
   • 753
Rural Health Scholarship Program • 292

Nevada

Western Regional Graduate Program • 979

New Foundland

Canadian Blood Services Graduate Fellowship Program
   • 961
Research Fellowship in Hemostatis • 937
Transfusion Medicine Fellowship Award • 481

New Hampshire

Lambaréné Schweitzer Fellows Program • 417
New Hampshire/Vermont Schweitzer Fellows Program • 15
Saint Andrews Society of the State of New York Scholarship
   for Graduate Study • 948

New Jersey

Andrew K. Ruotolo Memorial Scholarship • 709
Fellowship Program for Emigres Pursuing Careers in Jewish
   Education • 358
Harry Y. Cotton Memorial Scholarship • 710
M.L. King Physician/Dentist Scholarships • 298
Marcia Granucci Memorial Scholarship • 841
New Jersey Library Association Scholarships • 754
New Jersey Osteopathic Education Foundation Scholarship
   Program • 577
Oscar W. Rittenhouse Memorial Scholarship • 711
Saint Andrews Society of the State of New York Scholarship
   for Graduate Study • 948
Zimmermann Scholarships • 955

New Mexico

Medical Student Loan-For-Service Program • 578
Minority Doctoral Assistance Loan-For-Service Program
   • 973
New Mexico Past Presidents Scholarship for Teachers of
   Exceptional Children • 890
Osteopathic Medical Student Loan Program-New Mexico
   • 579
Western Regional Graduate Program • 979

New York

Ann Gibson Scholarship • 763
Fellowship Program for Emigres Pursuing Careers in Jewish
   Education • 358
Leo and Julia Forchheimer Fellowship • 169
Metropolitan Life Foundation Awards Program for
   Academic Excellence in Medicine • 562
Petry-Lomb Scholarship/Research Grant • 605
Regents Health Care Scholarships for Medicine and
   Dentistry-New York • 294
Regents Physician Loan Forgiveness Award-New York • 580
Saint Andrews Society of the State of New York Scholarship
   for Graduate Study • 948
Zimmermann Scholarships • 955

North Brunswick

Canadian Blood Services Graduate Fellowship Program
   • 961
Research Fellowship in Hemostatis • 937
Transfusion Medicine Fellowship Award • 481

North Carolina

Board of Governors Medical Scholarship Program • 581
North Carolina Library Association Scholarships • 755
Nurse Scholars Program— Master's • 802
Saint Andrews Society of the State of New York Scholarship
   for Graduate Study • 948

North Dakota

President's Award for Excellence in Math and Science
   Teaching • 974
Western Regional Graduate Program • 979

North West Territories

Canadian Blood Services Graduate Fellowship Program
   • 961
Research Fellowship in Hemostatis • 937
Transfusion Medicine Fellowship Award • 481

TALENT/AREAS OF INTEREST INDEX

Art

Apha Delta Kappa Foundation Fine Arts Grants • 161
Asian Cultural Council Fellowships • 91
Asian Cultural Council Residency Program in Asia • 140
Davidson Family Fellowship Program • 139
Graduate Arts Scholarship • 171
Hagley/Winterthur Fellowships in Arts and Industries • 98
National Sculpture Society Alex J. Ettl Grant • 992

Athletics/Sports

Ethnic Minority and Women's Enhancement Scholarship • 891
NCAA Postgraduate Scholarship • 991

Beauty Pageant

Dr. and Mrs. David B. Allman Medical Scholarships • 530
Leonard C. Horn Award for Legal Studies • 716

Designated Field Specified by Sponsor

American Institute of Pakistan Studies Graduate Student Fellowship • 671
American Institute of Pakistan Studies Postdoctoral Fellowship • 672
American Institute of Pakistan Studies Predoctoral Fellowships • 673
American Society of Arms Collectors Scholarship • 138
Daland Fellowship for Research in Clinical Investigation • 981
Ray Kageler Scholarship • 976
Robert W. Woodruff Fellowship • 983

Foreign Language

Blakemore Freeman Fellowships for Advanced Study of Asian Languages • 404
Foreign-Language Book Prize and David Thelen Prize • 993

French Language

Chateaubriand Scholarship Program • 164
Lambaréné Schweitzer Fellows Program • 417
Mary Isabel Sibley Fellowship for Greek and French Studies • 132

German Language

Ebert Foundation Advanced Graduate Fellowships • 319
Ebert Foundation Doctoral Research Fellowship • 320
Ebert Foundation Postdoctoral Fellowships • 321
German Academic Exchange International Lawyers Program • 715
German Academic Exchange Service (DAAD) Deutschlandjahr Scholarships for Graduating Seniors • 984
German Academic Exchange Service (DAAD) Graduate Scholarships for Study and /or Research in Germany • 985
Learn German in Germany for Faculty • 920
Research Grants for Recent PhD's & Ph.D. Candidates • 986

Summer Language Courses at Goethe Institutes • 987

Greek Language

Mary Isabel Sibley Fellowship for Greek and French Studies • 132

Japanese Language

Japan Foundation Doctoral Fellowship • 687
Japan Foundation Research Fellowship • 688
Japan Foundation Short-Term Research Fellowship • 689
Research Student Scholarship • 13

Leadership

American Psychiatric Association/Astra Zeneca Minority Fellowship Program • 471
Benn and Kathleen Gilmore Scholarship • 551
C. R. Bard Foundation Prize • 552
Eileen C. Maddex Fellowship • 386
Fellowship Program in Violence Prevention for Minority Medical Students • 554
Franklin C. McLean Award • 555
General Motors Foundation Graduate Scholarship • 245
Gerber Fellowship in Pediatric Nutrition • 556
Graduate Student Scholar Award • 364
Hettie M. Anthony Fellowship • 387
Hugh J. Andersen Memorial Scholarships • 558
Irving Graef Memorial Scholarship • 559
Josiah Macy Jr. Substance Abuse Fellowship Program for Minority Medical Students • 561
Kappa Omicron Nu National Alumni Chapter Grant • 388
Kappa Omicron Nu National Alumni Fellowship • 389
Kappa Omicron Nu New Initiatives Grant • 401
M. Elizabeth Carnegie and Estelle Massey Osborne Scholarships • 803
Maude Gilchrist Fellowship • 663
Mead Johnson Awards for Graduate Education in Family Practice • 432
NAPABA Law Foundation Scholarships • 720
National Association for Campus Activities East Coast Graduate Student Scholarship • 989
National Association for Campus Activities Foundation Graduate Scholarships • 990
National Medical Association Merit Scholarships • 563
National Medical Association Patti La Belle Award • 564
Omicron Nu Research Fellowship • 664
Ralph W. Ellison Memorial Prize • 567
Thomas R. Pickering Graduate Foreign Affairs Fellowship Program • 241
William and Charlotte Cadbury Award • 568
Wyeth-Ayerst Laboratories Prize in Women's Health • 569

Museum/Preservation Work

Conservation Guest Scholars • 633
Davidson Family Fellowship Program • 139

Music

Anne Louise Barrett Fellowship • 995
Apha Delta Kappa Foundation Fine Arts Grants • 161
Nadeen Burkeholder Williams Music Scholarship • 922
Research Assistance Grants • 994

Music/Singing

American Orff-Schulwerk Association Research Grant • 347
AOSA-Training and Projects Fund • 348
Asian Cultural Council Fellowships • 91
Asian Cultural Council Residency Program in Asia • 140
Graduate Scholarship in Music Education • 367
Gunild Keetman Assistance Fund • 349
Kurt Weill Foundation for Music Grants Program • 843
National Vocal Competition for Young Opera Singers • 844
Shields-Gillespie Scholarship • 350
Sigma Alpha Iota Doctoral Grant • 368
Sigma Alpha Iota Graduate Performance Awards • 846
Sigma Alpha Iota Scholarship for Conductors • 847

Numismatics

American Numismatic Society/Frances M. Schwartz
    Fellowship • 905

Donald Groves Fund • 980

Photography/Photogrammetry/Filmmaking

Asian Cultural Council Residency Program in Asia • 140
Ta Liang Memorial Award • 34
William A. Fischer Memorial Scholarship • 35

Polish Language

Graduate and Postgraduate Studies and Research in Poland
    Program • 988
Kosciuszko Foundation Tuition Scholarship • 942

Writing

ChLA Beiter Scholarships for Graduate Students • 764
Harry S. Truman Book Award • 324
Institute of Current World Affairs/Crane Rogers
    Foundation Fellowship • 696
National Medical Association Slack Award for Medical
    Journalism • 565
Pratt-Severn Best Student Research Paper Award • 982
Stanley C. Hollander Best Retailing Paper Competition
    • 223

Notes

Notes

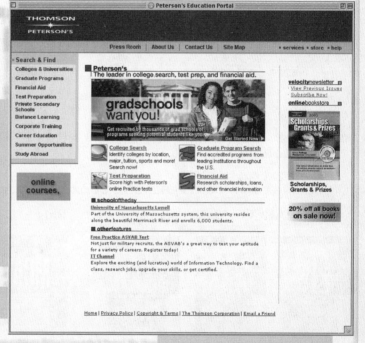